KU-662-715

THE
TOM HANKS
ENIGMA

THE BIOGRAPHY OF THE
WORLD'S MOST INTRIGUING
MOVIE STAR

DAVID GARDNER

JOHN BLAKE

NEWCASTLE UPON TYNE CITY LIBRARIES	
C288671100	
Bertrams	22.08.06
791.43028092	£17.99

Published by John Blake Publishing Ltd,
3 Bramber Court, 2 Bramber Road,
London W14 9PB, UK

www.blake.co.uk

This edition first published in hardback in 2006

ISBN 1 84454 243 2

All rights reserved. No part of this publication may be reproduced, stored in a retrieval system, or in any form or by any means, without the prior permission in writing of the publisher, nor be otherwise circulated in any form of binding or cover other than that in which it is published and without a similar condition including this condition being imposed on the subsequent publisher.

British Library Cataloguing-in-Publication Data:

A catalogue record for this book is available from the British Library.

Design by www.envydesign.co.uk

Printed and bound in Great Britain by William Clowes Ltd, Beccles, Suffolk

1 3 5 7 9 10 8 6 4 2

© Text copyright David Gardner

Papers used by John Blake Publishing are natural, recyclable products made from wood grown in sustainable forests. The manufacturing processes conform to the environmental regulations of the country of origin.

Pictures courtesy of Axis Entertainment, Kobal, Camerapress.

To Michelle

CONTENTS

ACKNOWLEDGEMENTS

MY HEARTFELT THANKS to the following people who helped make this book possible: John Blake, Rosie Ries, Betty Black Duval, Hilda Bauquier, Wayne Melton, Vincent Dowling, Winifred Martinez, Jon Finley, Melissa Marsh, Lawrence Hanks, Roderick Brown, Tim Miles, Wendy Henry, Jean Gardner, Richard Gardner, my wife Michelle, and children Mickey, Jazmin and Savannah.

In addition, two books, *The Films of Tom Hanks* by Lee Pfeiffer and Michael Lewis (Citadel Press, 1996) and *The Devil's Candy: The Bonfire of the Vanities Goes to Hollywood,* by Julie Salamon (Houghton Mifflin, 1991), provided some valuable information.

PROLOGUE

JUST A COBBLESTONE'S throw from the busy film set at historic Lincoln Cathedral, the angry nun was in no mood to back down as she disrupted shooting with an impassioned reminder that the Roman Catholic Church was in uproar over the religious sleuthing born out of the success of Dan Brown's controversial blockbuster *The Da Vinci Code*.

Sister Mary Michael called on God to combat the blasphemy committed by Tom Hanks in starring in the £90 million movie version of the Pope's least-liked potboiler, and she was confident it would be struck down by a lightning bolt of hostility at the box office.

The only problem was that this was Tom Hanks, and no one seems able to be angry with him for long.

So, after damning Lincoln Cathedral – used by Sony Pictures as a stand-in for the publicity-shy Westminster Abbey – for putting sanctity on sale by accepting £100,000 from director Ron Howard for permission to film in the 1000-year-old house of worship, and having roundly blasted the book's 'sinful' suggestion that Jesus sired a child with Mary Magdalene, Sister Mary turned her attention to Tom.

He was described in the local press as 'the first famous person to come to Lincoln since William the Conqueror' and was embraced by the city like a long-lost son. So Sister Mary decided she had to leave a peace offering. 'It was a rose plant,' she explained. 'On the card, I wrote: "No hard feelings. The protesting nun."'

It is a trifling story, but one which offers a clue to the appeal of the enigmatic actor who has navigated his way through the shark-infested, ego-inflating waters of Hollywood and still manages to be liked by a nun on the warpath over his pivotal role in a project which challenges the very pillar stones of her unbending faith.

Weeks later, he would invite ten-year-old Kerr Edwards on a private tour of medieval Rosslyn Chapel in Midlothian, Scotland, where the next leg of filming was under way, instantly disarming opponents of the film north of the border.

Throughout his latest filming trip to Britain to play cerebral sleuth Professor Robert Langdon and lead cinemagoers through the heart-stopping fictional labyrinth of *The Da Vinci Code*'s deeply buried papal secrets, Tom was every inch the laid-back, never-rattled Mr Nice Guy his legions of loyal fans would expect.

But Tom Hanks was hiding his own secret – his own life was in danger.

Ever since his thriller became an international phenomenon, selling more than 25 million copies around the world, author Dan Brown has lived with the possibility that he could be the target of an unhinged religious maniac intent on avenging perceived slights to some of the central tenets of Catholicism.

Now Tom found himself in the firing line and it was not a threat he took lightly. He appeared as friendly and approachable as ever, given the fact that his fame made for a very abnormal normality. But, during the UK filming, the actor was often surrounded by as many as five bodyguards to protect him from the mobs of well-wishers – and the possibility of a more sinister attack.

On his first night in Lincoln, Tom took tea with the Dean of Lincoln, the Very Reverend Alec Knight, and went out for a meal with his family at a local pub, the Wig and Mitre. Owner Toby Hope could not have been more delighted to welcome one of his film heroes, and set him up in the last free table before serving up smoked salmon and fillet steaks. But he couldn't help noticing the burly men dotted around the pub as if the Prime Minister had dropped in for a pint.

'It was funny,' he said to a newspaper reporter at the time. 'Because there were two bodyguards in the corner, two in the upstairs bar and one downstairs.'

The unease wasn't helped in Scotland when a 39-year-old intruder slipped past security and got into the grounds of Rosslyn Chapel before police intercepted him. It turned out that the man was merely a persistent fan who was obsessed with getting Tom's autograph. But the incident served to underline the ever-present threat.

Like everything else in his life – which he jokingly calls 'one damn thing after another' – Tom carried off any anxiety with a public panache that bears out comparisons with two movie stars from the past that he is most often identified with – James Stewart and Cary Grant. For all of his success, he has lost little of the restless energy and boyish charm that stole our hearts in his breakthrough films like *Splash* and *Big*. You won't be seeing this Tom jumping up and down on Oprah's couch, but he is quick to tell you how wife Rita is the love of his life and how important his four children are to him. He has a Rolodex full of Hollywood friends that would turn a Los Angeles plastic surgeon green with envy, two Oscars, three nominations, and he has totted up more than £3 billion in worldwide grosses since 1992.

Along with his unprecedented string of money-spinning

blockbusters are sprinkled exacting character studies in films like *The Terminal* and *The Ladykillers* and critically acclaimed TV mini-series like *Band of Brothers* and *From the Earth to the Moon*.

While some of his A-List contemporaries appear to have lost their way to the box office in recent years, Hanks has retained the sense of wonder in his stardom that left him breathless as a teenage fan at the prospect of starring with Paul Newman in 2002's *Road to Perdition*.

With *The Da Vinci Code*, his 41st film, Hanks truly has moved into a league of his own.

Through it all, he has managed to steer mercifully clear of the scandalous pitfalls that have buried many a more talented actor's career.

Perhaps his public could be forgiven for believing that Tom Hanks has always had it made. It is only natural that people would assume their American-as-apple-pie hero had an upbringing befitting his *The Right Stuff* persona.

But they would be very wrong. The reality was a childhood full of doubts, confusion and loneliness. By the time he was ten, Tom had had three mothers, gone to five different schools and lived in ten different homes. At one stage, he had so many siblings and stepbrothers and stepsisters that he was known simply as 'Number Eight'.

He would joke later: 'My parents pioneered the marriage dissolution laws for the state of California. I think a couple of clauses, in fact, are called The Hanks Family Clauses in the penal code... They were getting divorces way before divorces were hip.'

Tom's parents had a total of seven marriages between them, not really a recipe for laughter.

The complex emotions arising from such an unsettled start in life even spilled over into adulthood, with an unplanned pregnancy and a doomed marriage fitting the pattern of thwarted ambition set by Tom's father, an intelligent, determined man whose dreams were ultimately buried under the burden of responsibility.

Even after Tom's acting career took off, his path seemed to be heading down a burned-out cul-de-sac. With the collapse of his first marriage, and the guilt of failing his two young children just as his parents had failed him by separating when he was a boy, came an unseemly divorce battle and the obligatory Californian therapy sessions to attempt to lift his despair.

The reason Tom was able to turn his life around in such a huge way was thanks in part to luck and in part to the hold that family – or the lack of it – had on Tom's formative years.

The luck came in meeting just the right person at exactly the right time. Actress Rita Wilson is the wife he says 'saved' him. She gave him the kind of security he so desperately craved – the confidence to be himself.

Bubbly, extroverted and popular, Rita comes from a close-knit, conventional – if that is still the case in these dysfunctional times – family. She was always going to be an actress, growing up in Hollywood and even going to the same school where screen sirens such as Judy Garland, Lana Turner and Linda Evans were once pupils.

The second factor in the making of Tom Hanks was his own convoluted family. It is Tom's sense of family – both his alienation from it and his strong need for its embrace – that provides the central theme to this book.

From his father's unpublished memoirs, written shortly before his death in 1991, we get a unique perspective on the formative influences on the life of one of the most famous celebrities of our times. From stories about his relatives and ancestors – including the tragic murder of his grandfather and his ancestral links to Abraham Lincoln – we can better understand his roots and genealogical make-up.

And from this first, detailed look behind the curtains of a man who has lived much of his life in the spotlight, yet still hidden in plain sight, we are able to see just how many hurdles he has had to overcome in his personal life to achieve such unparalleled success, both on and off the screen.

Some of that private pain, Tom will openly admit, has helped him as an actor. Initially, acting offered a lost, mixed-up teenager an escape from the unhappiness of his home life and, later, it would benefit from a reservoir of loneliness in which he could occasionally immerse himself for inspiration.

It is interesting to note that many of Tom's lighter, fluffier roles came at a time he was going through tough periods at home, striding to get on in a business that is notoriously stressful on young families. When he had found fulfilment away from the set, many of the parts he chose took on a more dramatic, serious tone.

Of one thing we can be certain in a Tom Hanks film. Be it the physical comedy of *Big*, the emotional pathos of *Philadelphia*, the sentimental quirkiness of *Forrest Gump*, the shocking intensity of *Saving Private Ryan*, the gripping tour de force characters in *Cast Away* and *The Terminal*, or the sheer joyous fantasy in *The Polar Express*, they are all immensely enjoyable movies. Even the bad ones generally have a good performance by their star.

We read about Tom's Oscar triumphs. We have watched him grow up as an actor before our very eyes. He has repaid his primarily baby boomer audience by reflecting its interests in the choices he makes.

But he is still a most unlikely hero.

He has few of the physical attributes of his A-List rivals. There's the slightly bulbous nose, the tight, curly black hair that perches on top of his prominent forehead, and the pale blue, restless, almost Oriental, eyes. He tells directors that one profile is Richard Gere and the other is Richard Nixon, although a double chin is always threatening to unbalance the more attractive side of the equation.

He doesn't do blockbuster action movies, although he boasts he could play a James Bond 'baddie' in his sleep. Nor does he do sex scenes.

And he has been uniquely successful at keeping his private life largely a closed book to the public without anyone ever really realising it.

Tom would argue that his 'crack team of showbusiness experts' are amply rewarded for keeping him the most secretive of superstars. Yet this star, more than most, has much to be proud of in the way he has handled his immense fame.

To him, all the money, the adulation and the golden statuettes are secondary. His wife and children come first. 'I have no best friend,' he says. 'The family takes up the vast amount of time.'

And family leads us back to Tom's antecedents, particularly his great-grandparents, Selina and Amos, a couple to whom Tom owes a great deal more than he knows. From them, he has inherited many of the gestures and mannerisms that are now so familiar in his performances, particularly in his comedy roles.

Tom's aunt, Hilda Bauquier, now in her 80s, is his only relative who can still clearly remember the 'glint' in her grandfather's eye as he sat with his family around the kitchen table. She sees the same deprecating sense of humour in her famous nephew.

'The family always has had a great sense of humour,' she said. 'His great-grandfather had that same offhand way of putting himself down that Tom has.

'The movement at the back of Tom's head reminds me of his father and he moves like him. We all wave our arms around and we stand with our hands on our hips. I have a picture of a whole group of relatives standing in exactly that same way. Tom does it too.'

Over the years Tom has, ever so politely, distanced himself from the rest of his family. He gets an invitation every year to the reunions, and relatives have tried to send him details of the family tree. But, so far at least, he has shown little interest.

Perhaps that is because he no longer wants to look back. Approaching middle age, he has conquered the demons from his past and is comfortable with his role as our saint-next-door.

As he puts it: 'My dad was a guy who grew up on a farm during the Depression. I think there's a degree of communicative skills that my dad did not have. I knew he didn't have them, and for the longest time, I didn't have them either.

'But at my age I think I'm done with wrestling the ghosts of my dad, or my parents in general.

'Somebody once said to me that by the time you are 40, you'd better quit complaining and get on with your life. So now I'm in the "shut up, just do it" phase of my life and it feels right.'

Tom Hanks is larger-than-life proof that a nice guy really can finish first.

And therein lies the key to his success. He is not a comic-book hero with impossibly big muscles or telepathic powers of deduction. Up there on the screen, he is someone his audience can relate to; an ordinary man with all the hopes and fears and doubts that all of us carry around with us. If it seems unlikely that a man who describes himself as having 'a big ass, fat thighs, a goofy-looking nose, ears that hang down, eyes that make me look part-Chinese and a gut I've got to keep watching' can win the heart of a Meg Ryan or a Robin Wright Penn or a Catherine Zeta Jones then we are happy to suspend our cynicism for the space of 90 to 120 minutes or so. After all, we are all allowed to dream. And if Tom can do it, perhaps we can too.

Besides, extraordinary things do happen in life. It takes an extraordinary actor of the calibre of Tom Hanks to make them seem real in a place like Hollywood, where artifice so often takes precedence over accuracy.

Behind every successful person, be it in business, in

entertainment or any other field, there is another side to the story that will tell you how full their lives are. As much as Hollywood, with its controlling publicists and cash-hungry agents, may try to persuade people otherwise, the sum total of an actor cannot be counted on his work alone. The reason actors and actresses are paid countless millions while nurses and teachers toil twice as hard for a pittance is not just because they are easy on the eye or good at making pretend or, more often, both. It is because a huge number of people around the world identify with them as people. It is not just about the characters they play.

It is only fair then, that the audience that pays these vast salaries can hold the stars they worship to account.

There is no excuse for hounding anybody, but it is important to know where he or she has come from, to understand how they behave when the cameras stop rolling, to see how they are perceived by their friends and to gauge how they have coped with success and failure.

As much as these sentiments may irritate or even anger the artists, be sure that if a superstar did do something in his or her private life that upset or antagonised the public, their stock – and their fee – would quickly fall. Be sure, too, that the now-wealthy, high-living megastar was once a hungry actor, grateful for any morsel of publicity that came his or her way.

The impressive thing about Tom Hanks is that he has succeeded on both sides of the coin. We know much of his on screen successes. What many do not know is how hard he worked to hone his craft. He didn't hurtle into Hollywood on the back of a kids' TV show or an offbeat improvised cult comedy show. He spent years in the theatre, working his way up from the carpentry shop to centre stage, leading one senior director to call him the best comic Shakespearean actor he had ever seen. He did the rounds of forgettable bit parts in established television shows, where the proven stars jealously guarded all the best lines. And he worked his way through a kaleidoscope of movies before finally hitting his stride. To Tom, it is not all about being a movie star. It is all about being an actor.

In his life away from the spotlight, Tom is more of a mystery to his fans. He doesn't punch photographers or frequent trendy Hollywood showboating restaurants. His own experiences have taught him that he is happier caring for his own loved ones than carousing with someone else's. *Pretty Woman* director Garry Marshall says the actor is one of the Hat Pack – 'because the wildest thing he does is to occasionally put on a hat'.

If Tom commits to a project, you can be sure he will be out there on the promotional circuit in the weeks running up to its release. Having signed on to a (usually lucrative) deal, he feels obligated to do everything he reasonably can to make it a success.

If he sees a well-wisher or even a press camera in the crowd while shooting a film, he is more likely to offer a friendly wave than try to hide his face. While some stars go to the ridiculous lengths of covering their faces with umbrellas in between scenes on set, Tom will usually find the whole circus faintly amusing.

Early in his career, in particular, he spoke at some length about his childhood and his self-perceived shortcomings. While he quickly learned not to invite a magazine writer right into his home and thus avoid critiques on his carpets, furniture, colour schemes, etc., he nevertheless continued to give frank, sometimes quirky interviews.

Perhaps it is for these reasons that the entertainment press has largely given him a comfortable ride and has never pried too deeply into his private life, as with other stars of similar popularity.

To interviewers he is both courteous and understanding of their needs for an interesting angle. He understands the game and how to play it to his best advantage.

His determination to live as ordinary a life as possible under very abnormal circumstances has given him a more philosophical outlook on his fame, and an attitude many of his contemporaries would do well to heed. He told USA *Weekend*: 'I have been getting cuts in line at airports for quite some time, so it has its advantages. It is not so much the loss of privacy, it's how you protect what privacy you have. I made my peace with that a long time ago.

'I go to a restaurant and people take pictures. I go on a vacation and people come up and introduce themselves. Some things I just don't do any more, like go to the bank, because it's too much trouble. I try to go to the same restaurants and stores, so they are used to me. Every once in a while I will go to a new one and all hell will break loose. Sometimes it's funny and sometimes it's a hassle. But if the tragic loss of being a celebrity is that I don't get to go to baseball games as much as I would like to, that's a price I can pay without much difficulty.'

At an age many people are only just reaching their stride in their chosen careers, Tom has been dancing around the spotlight so long it is easy to overlook his early struggles, both as an actor and as a man.

For he has indeed come a long way. He successfully plotted a path through an emotional minefield to emerge a phenomenon. And he has pretty much found his own way through the maze with little help from anyone else.

It wasn't always an easy journey. In *The Da Vinci Code*, Tom leads the audience through the twists and turns from a murder at the Louvre to a sinister plot to uncover a secret that has been protected since the birth of Christianity. For the first time, this book unravels the secrets of the actor's own past to expose the real man behind the enigma that is Tom Hanks.

ONE

A FAMILY SECRET

CLUTCHING THE WOODEN deck rail on the rolling ship taking her from everything she knew in England to the perilous promise of the New World, Selina Scoble Ball was suddenly so overcome by a sickening dread that she could scarcely breathe. On the horizon halfway across the Atlantic, she had spied another ship steaming in the opposite direction, returning to the familiar bustle of 1881 London.

It wasn't homesickness. She hadn't been able to wait to start her North American adventure. Nor was she ill, although the cramped, dirty conditions on board made the long journey a gripping nightmare for many. The awful truth behind the wrenching heartache that had remained with her as she watched the other ship sail out of sight didn't dawn on Selina until she arrived with her newborn baby and three young children at their destination, more than 3,000 miles from home...

Selina had been in love with the dashing Amos Ball from the moment he tenderly replaced a little locket she was wearing around her neck with one of his own. The discarded locket had been given

1

to Selina by her fiancé in England, before she left to work as a maid for a wealthy family in St Helier, Jersey, in the Channel Islands. But as he clasped the new chain around her neck, Amos laughed: 'Now, I have taken his place.'

The adoring couple married and returned to Devon, where they quickly had three children. It was while Selina was expecting their fourth child that she and Amos decided to try their luck in the burgeoning Americas. He would go on ahead to Canada to find work while she had the baby and sold up their house and property. In time, she would follow Amos out with the rest of the family.

It was a sensible arrangement, the kind of route people follow to this day if they are considering emigrating to an exciting, if uncertain, new life.

But Amos was miserable in Canada on his own. He fretted about his children. He missed his wife. And eventually, he couldn't stand it any longer; he booked a passage back to England on the next ship.

Meanwhile, at home in Newton Abbot, Devon, Selina was finding life without Amos unbearable. There were no problems with the pregnancy and she gave birth to her second son, George. But she desperately missed her husband.

Unable to wait any longer to be with Amos, she ushered the children to London and caught the first ship across the Atlantic.

It was only when Selina arrived in Canada, exhausted from the trip and not knowing a single soul, that she discovered Amos had indeed been on that passing ship she had seen in the middle of the Atlantic Ocean. It would be several more months before he was able to get back to Canada to finally be reunited with his family.

Such a plot could easily come from a Tom Hanks film. A similar story about moonstruck lovers missing each other until the final frame is probably sitting in the actor's in-tray at this very moment, with Meg Ryan's name pencilled in as co-star.

It has everything: love, longing, a large slice of destiny and, of course, a happy ending.

What is so fascinating about this particular romantic farce is that not only is it all true, but it is also how Tom Hanks's family came to America.

The extraordinary addendum to the story is that this is probably the first time Tom has heard about it.

For an actor famed for his thorough and intelligent research into a part, that may seem unusual. But then Tom Hanks is an unusual man.

The first known members of the Hanks family lived in Buckland, England, in the mid-1400s. Little of the canvas of their lives can be coloured in, but the Hanks family tree, titled 'Bent But Unbroken', provides at least an outline, telling how John Hanks had a son, George, born in 1505, who moved to Malmesbury, Wiltshire. His son, Thomas, was born in 1536, and when he was 34 he had a boy, Thomas II, who moved on to neighbouring Stow.

Thomas, it seems, was a popular name in the Hanks family – a tradition Tom's father was determined to keep – and it was Thomas III, born in Stow sometime before 1630, who set sail in 1653 with his wife, Elizabeth, on the dangerous trip to the New World. Undertaken just 33 years after the *Mayflower* docked in America, the journey would have been painfully slow and uncomfortable. Travelling at a little over three miles an hour, the ship took nearly three months to make the crossing.

Thomas arrived in Virginia with a patent for 'one hundred acres of land situated in Gloucester County in woods upon the north side of a swamp on the east side of the Matapony River.' The Englishman prospered in his new home and became the owner of more than 2,000 acres. He is thought to have had four children, all born in America: William, George, Robert and Peter.

It was William, born in about 1650, who is the central link between Abraham Lincoln and Tom Hanks.

For he had three sons; Luke, William II and John, all born in Richmond, Virginia.

3

Tom's line in the family dates back to the youngest son, John, born in 1690, a genealogical journey which took eight generations to get to the movie star.

According to evidence compiled by Hanks historian Adin Baber, author of *Nancy Hanks, Destined Mother of a President* and *The Hanks Family Legacy*, John's elder brother, Luke, born 1685, was Abraham Lincoln's great-great-grandfather.

Luke's son, Joseph, born in Kentucky in about 1730, fathered a boy, Abraham, in Carolina when he was 29 years old.

It is said to have been this Abraham's daughter, Nancy Hanks, born in 1784, who was Lincoln's mother. After marrying Thomas Lincoln, she gave birth to the future President on 12 February 1809. 'All that I am, or hope to be, I owe to my Angel mother,' Lincoln is said to have told his law partner.

When Abraham Lincoln was seven, his father, Thomas, had moved the family from Kentucky to Indiana, where he built a one-room cabin. Then just two years later, his mother Nancy died, at the age of 36, from a fever called 'milk-sickness'. The boy carved the pegs for her coffin from green wood and helped bury her in the woods next to a deer run, without the benefit of a funeral.

Neither Nancy nor her husband could read or write and, for a while, the future 16th President of the United States and up to a dozen of his family lived together, crowded into a small, primitive cabin.

Curiously, one of America's most treasured Presidents and one of its most beloved film stars had some interesting parallels in their respective upbringings. Both were separated from their mothers at an early age – Lincoln by death and Tom by divorce – and both were brought up in cramped homes surrounded by step-siblings. The young Abraham Lincoln and his sister would be introduced to their new stepmother without any explanation other than: 'Children, this is your new ma.' Tom and his brothers and sister would have an identical experience when their father remarried. Furthermore, both men would go on to make the most of their meagre beginnings.

While today's politicians and film stars may feel that the scandal sheets are a modern-day invention, Lincoln faced question marks over both his legitimacy and that of his mother. So vicious were the rumours about his own birth that Lincoln sent a commission to Kentucky to find proof of the marriage of his parents. Unfortunately, they went looking in the wrong place and it wasn't until the turn of the century, in 1901, that proof was found that Nancy Hanks and Thomas Lincoln were indeed wed in 1806, three years before Abraham was born. Claims over Nancy's parentage were also rebuffed.

In a very different age, Tom Hanks now shares his time between a £2 million home in exclusive Pacific Pallisades, a luxurious, rambling ocean-front mansion in Malibu close to his friend Steven Spielberg, and a plush apartment in New York. He spares no expense to give his family everything they could possibly need. His four children have travelled first class around the globe with their father on fun-filled holidays and accompany him to exotic film locations.

For Tom's ancestors, however, it was a very different story.

The impish little boy looked close to tears as he walked purposely across the windswept cemetery, studying the names on the carefully tended headstones. It was his first visit to the family burial plot and the usually high-spirited six-year-old seemed particularly struck by the solemn serenity of the graveyard. Stopping at each stone bearing the name of his grandparents and generations of his ancestors, he dropped to one knee and elaborately crossed himself, looking for all the world like he would himself die of grief.

Only after finishing his grave task did the boy allow himself a glance at his watching family. And that proved his undoing. He couldn't help the big smile from destroying the dramatic moment he had created and his father, brother and sister were soon falling about laughing at his antics.

It was Tom Hanks's first performance and a lifelong lesson he would never forget – that he could ease people's pain by making them laugh. The sombre trip to the Hanks burial ground had been transformed into a precious family memory, particularly for Tom's father, Amos, who tried to hide the feelings of anger and resentment that were stirred every time he went back to the cemetery by Thomes Creek in the small northern California outpost of Paskenta.

To Tom, big brother Larry, then nine, and sister Sandra, 12, the trip brought to life a colourful family history that had always been something of a mystery to them. But Amos had his own reasons back then for keeping some of the family secrets from his young children.

The oldest headstone in the Hanks burial plot at Paskenta marks the grave of Tom's great-grandfather Daniel Boone Hanks, who was born in 1847 and joined the pioneer trail west from his home in Kentucky in 1873 with his wife, Mary Catherine. His granddaughter, Wanda Hanks Morning, submitted a letter written by her mother to the Hanks family history describing the gruelling journey to pre-Hollywood California.

It reads:

'In 1873 they came across the plains with oxen and six horses. They were six months on the way. They came across Dormer Pass and first settled in or near Bakersfield. Mary Catherine got malaria so they went to Modoc County. At that time there was just one small store the size of a small room in Cedarville and it sold everything. The building is still standing in a small park.

'Daniel and Mary decided to go back to Missouri and got as far as Flournoy, Tehama County. They were to travel with a group of people. Everything was arranged to leave a certain day and two of Daniel's horses got sick. They had sold the oxen. They were camped just west of the Flournoy bridge near the creek. They had to stay, so they went to live on small cabin on the sheep-shearing place and spent the winter there. They were sold about 160 acres with a one-room cabin on it and they moved there and filed papers to homestead. All they had to start house keeping were several large wooden boxes, barrels, bedding and their dishes and cooking utensils.

'Daniel made a table and benches out of some of the boxes. One of the barrels was used for the flour with a heavy board on top for a work table.

'At first they cooked outside on a campfire. The beds were small oak trees cut down and put in the corners of the room, then laced back and forth with buckskin for springs. Their big ticking bags were filled with wild straw for mattresses...

'They killed deer and quail and cotton tails for fresh meat and got fish in season from Stoney Creek. The first cow was just a calf when Mary got it and she worked for a lady who had a baby to pay for it. This is also the way they got their first two pigs...'

In spite of their tough times, Daniel and Catherine still found time to have 14 children. It was the fate of their eighth child, Tom's grandfather Ernest Beauel Hanks, that has caused so much anguish to the family that it lingers on even now.

Visiting Paskenta Cemetery that day in 1963 with his own three children, this was one particular story that Amos Hanks kept to himself. The painful memories had almost reduced him to tears before Tom's graveside performance broke the spell drawing him back to his childhood.

It would be years before Amos finally told his children that their grandfather had been murdered.

And, with a romantic yearning for the kind of rough justice lauded in books by his heroes Ernest Hemingway and Jack London, he went to his grave wishing he had been able to avenge his father's untimely death.

Members of the family had been slightly taken aback when Ernest Beauel, known as 'the fastest sack sewer in the Sacramento Valley', married elegant, well-educated librarian Gladys Hilda Ball in rural Willows, California, in 1915.

The schoolmarm with a rebellious streak had long had her eye on the handsome man who drove a horse to class, and who also happened to be the brother of her landlady. She had gone to the World's Fair in San Francisco early in 1915 and unbeknownst to her, Ernest had decided on a whim to go the same day. It was one of only two times he ever left the Willows area – the other time was a cattle drive to the neighbouring state of Nevada. Although they spent the day apart, the unlikely couple met up on train on the way home and Ernest plucked up the courage to ask for a date.

Her rather snooty siblings insisted Gladys was mistaken in agreeing to marry the local 'hillbilly' and the expectant bride was almost forced to agree on the day of her wedding. For the groom wasn't just minutes or hours late for the service – he was two whole days late!

Ernest had been hunting in the mountains with a friend, who had fallen and badly hurt himself. Knowing he couldn't leave the wounded man behind, even to get to his own wedding, he slowly carried the man down to safety. When he was finally able to get to a telephone, which he had never used before, he managed to get word through to Gladys. According to him, she fainted when she heard his voice. According to her, she told him: 'The wedding is just waiting for the groom!'

After tying the knot and celebrating at an aunt's house, the strapping farmer and his well-to-do, bespectacled bride settled happily into married life and had four children; Gladys Hilda, Ernest Beauel II, Amos Mefford and Mary Catherine.

Ernest struck up a friendship with Elisha Best, the former superintendent of the county hospital, and they worked together in the fields for almost 17 years. But their partnership came to a tragic end on the afternoon of 14 May 1935. According to a local newspaper report, the two men were working together digging hay on the Lester Killebrew Ranch in Willows when they got into a fiery argument over the horse team pulling their hay wagon.

The *Willows Daily Journal* recounted the fight, saying Hanks, who was on the wagon, jumped on Best's back and knocked him down. 'Best got up and warned Hanks not to get near him. He grabbed a pitchfork,' it reported. 'But Hanks made a rush for him and Best hit him with the pitchfork handle.

'Hanks sank to his knees and then got up and made another rush. Best hit him again. Hanks said: "You have drawn blood. I am going to have you arrested." Hanks got into the wagon and started for the house. Best climbed into the wagon and started driving. Hanks fell into the hay.'

When the wagon arrived back at the Hanks' house, Amos, then just eleven, was on his own with his sister Mary. Their father stumbled to the front door with blood gushing from his head wound as Best told the children: 'We just had a little scrap.'

By the time a Dr J.L. Rowhauser had arrived, Hanks had sunk into a coma, from which he never recovered, and died four hours later from loss of blood. He was just 45.

But the trauma of watching his father die in front of him was just the beginning of the ordeal for Amos. For what the Hanks family thought would be a straightforward murder trial turned out to be anything but. Best was tried in court three times and Amos was a witness in the first two trials. The jury couldn't reach a verdict in the first hearing and brought a manslaughter verdict in the second.

Finally, with Amos and his mother watching helplessly in the public gallery, Best was acquitted in the third trial.

The decision shocked and infuriated the young Amos. In his unpublished autobiography, he wrote: 'In the last days of his trial they seemed to be trying my father rather than his killer. They made much of the fact that he was not a man known for his piety or politeness.

'My father was misrepresented as some sort of monster by the defense attorney.'

The boy was so angered by the injustice he threatened to shoot Best, saying he would gladly swap his freedom to protect his dead father's good name, and his mother was worried enough to send Amos to stay with relations in another town at the end of the trial.

Best, he argued, was in his 60s, while his father was 'strong and agile.' Hanks had collapsed before being able to give his version and Amos remained convinced it could not have been a fair fight.

'It was a tough time for the family,' said Amos's elder sister, Hilda. 'I was 17 and it happened just before I graduated from high school, but my mother had to bring up myself and the three younger children by herself. My little sister was only eight when Dad died.

'Amos, or Bud as we always called him, had to testify at a trial at 11 years old. Now all the children in a school would get counselling if something terrible like that happened. It was bound to effect him.

'Tom's father had very strong feelings about Best not being convicted. Bud was a very intense person and couldn't forgive easily.'

Hanks's widow went on to be elected county tax collector in Willows, serving for three terms, and had a leg amputated before she died in 1966. She is buried alongside her husband in Paskenta Cemetery.

It was Gladys's parents, Amos and Selina Ball, who had left England towards the end of the 19th century on that farcical, sublimely romantic Atlantic ocean journey which opens this chapter. The roots of the Ball side of Tom's family warrant further investigation, both because they make fascinating reading and because of the obvious Legacy they bestowed upon Tom.

Amos Ball, Tom's great-grandfather, was born in Launceston, Cornwall on 13 May 1849, and left as a young boy to live in the relatively prosperous Channel Islands in Jersey. He grew up to become a local preacher in the Jersey Young Man's Christian Association and worked in a bakery. At the age of 14, he was thrown from the baker's cart he used to deliver bread to Elizabeth Castle and cut his face so badly that he wore a beard for most of his life to cover the scar. He later worked as a French translator.

When he was 25, he married a young maid whose heart he set out to win with long romantic walks along the beach – even though she was already engaged to a suitor back home in England. Her acceptance of his locket, as described already, signified her changed allegiance and the handsome couple was married in St Helier in 1874.

After the wedding, the Balls moved back to the mainland and settled in Kingsweek, Devon, where Amos worked for the Great Western Railway between 1874 and 1875. They moved on to Newton Abbott, Devon, the following year and Amos went back to working in a bakery.

By this time they already had three children: Amos II, Blanche and Elsie, and a fourth, George, was on his way. Still young, adventurous and madly in love, Amos and Selina decided to try their luck in the Americas, where they had been told they would be able to own their own land.

When they finally met up in Canada, in a small town along the coast, they were informed that there were better opportunities further south in America and given a contact to head for in Toledo, Iowa, where they hoped to open their own store. Unfortunately there was yet another mishap on the journey when they were misdirected and ended up in Toledo, *Ohio*, where once again they knew nobody, and so had to uproot and start off once more for Iowa.

Having opened a small feed store in the *right* Toledo, Amos and Selina settled down to have another three children: Evelyn, John Wesley and Gladys Hilda, Tom's great-grandmother. Another two girls, Lucy Emily and Violet Pinkham, died during childbirth

'I think that they had a very romantic life together,' said Tom's Aunt Hilda. 'I am the only one left who can remember my grandfather very clearly. He would tell stories about what happened in England and talk about grandmother.'

There was never very much money, but the family always had enough food and soon became a popular fixture in Toledo. Even then, Amos was opposed to the use of tobacco, but he sold it nevertheless as it was one of the most sought after products at his shop, which had become a popular meeting place for the local farm community.

The children, particularly Amos II, had hated working in the store, but they weren't given any choice. Eventually Amos left, going on to become Vice President of Standard Oil of Indiana. His son, George, would become an Under Secretary of State and work for the United Nations. Blanche, the eldest daughter, married the brother of the famous heavyweight boxer 'Gentleman' Jim Corbett.

When Selina fell ill there was little anyone could do for her in the small town and she went to Chicago, where she died in 1907. Heartbroken over his wife's death, Amos decided to move across to California where several sisters were by now settled, having themselves emigrated from England.

Closing down his feed and grocery store in 1914, he travelled west with several of his children for the tiny Northern California outpost of Willows, a day's ride from the state capital of Sacramento. Maria, his spinster sister from England, was to meet them there and help care for her widowed brother, who had made just enough money from the sale of his shop to retire in relative comfort.

Maria, once a dressmaker for Alfred Lord Tennyson's sisters, ruled the roost in her new-found home with an iron will, insisting that the children and grandchildren being raised as English gentlewomen. 'My mother was the next-to-youngest in the family and they would all have to drink their tea just right and hold their napkins the correct way. It was a very proper upbringing,' said Hilda.

Gladys had remained in Iowa where she had a teaching position, but she followed her father to California, where she got a job at the Flournoy School in Willows. After she was married, her father and Maria moved in with them, living there for more than a decade before moving to Long Beach, Southern California, to the home of his eldest daughter, where he lived out his final years, still with Maria at his side. He was buried alongside Selina in Toledo, Iowa.

With four adults – Amos, Maria, Ernest, Gladys – and four children – Hilda, Ernest, Amos, Mary – squeezed in, the house was very cramped. There was no hot water, no telephone, just one large room upstairs and two downstairs with the kitchen slotted into a section of the porch.

'My mother was always a rebel and grandfather loved that about her,' said Hilda. 'Nevertheless, we were all raised in a very proper way too. She was a responsible rebel. Dad was a very good looking, debonair man. My brothers were extremely fond of father, and so was my sister, but I didn't feel so close to him. I was closer to my mother. Tom's father and I were more Ball than Hanks.

'Mother was a wonderful Christian woman, but Dad didn't have any interest at all. It wasn't until I started going to high school that Dad started going to church.'

Hilda added: 'My brother Amos was different than the rest of us. He was a rebel from the church. He said he had been spoon-fed religion and blamed mother for forcing it on him.

'In those days, children did as they were told. But as soon as Bud was old enough to go his own way, he went his own way. 'Watching Tom now, it is very clear to me where he came from.'

Always a dreamer and an avid reader, Amos – or Bud as he was known to his friends and family for the rest of his life – tried his hand at a string of occupations, including logging, ranching, writing and an enforced spell in the US Navy during World War II, when he served in the New Hebrides Islands, near Australia. Returning to California, he went back to college, determined to graduate and become a writer. To help pay for his studies he would work in restaurants and bars in the California Bay area and planned to save enough money to go to Australia and write for a living.

But while working in a small restaurant in the college town of Berkeley, just across the bay from San Francisco, Amos met a pretty young waitress called Janet Frager, from nearby Livermore. Within a year they had eloped to Reno, Nevada, and married on 4 September 1950. Less than a year later, on 30 July 1951, their daughter, Sandra Lynn, was born.

His dreams of a new life in Australia dashed by the responsibility of providing for his young family, Amos threw himself into the catering business, working long hours to build a reputation as one of the best paid chefs in Northern California.

The couple's first son, Lawrence, was born in Livermore on 26 January 1953. Amos was a chef at the Sea Wolf in Oakland, turning over 200 tables at dinner each night, when three years later, on 9 July 1956, in Concord, California, they had a second boy, Thomas Jeffrey.

The family moved north to Bedding, where Amos got a job as chef-owner of the food operation in one of the town's larger hotels. To outsiders at least, everything seemed calm in the Hanks household, and Amos and Janet did their best to keep their arguments from the children. A snapshot taken at the Hanks family reunion in 1961, with little Tommy wearing a cowboy hat, offers no clue to the domestic turmoil between the parents.

The birth of a fourth child, Jimmy, later that year on 15 June did nothing to ease the strain.

But it was all about to change. After ten years of marriage, Amos and Janet had reached breaking point. And Tom Hanks was to discover that his first five years would be the most stable period of his extremely unconventional childhood.

HANKS PEDIGREE CHART

John Hanks
b. 1470 in Buckland, England

George Hanks
b. 1505 in Malmesbury, England

Thomas Hanks
b. 1536 in Malmesbury, England

Thomas Hanks II
b. 1570 in Stowe, England

Thomas Hanks III
b. bef. 1630 in Stowe, England

William I
b. about 1650 in Richmond Co., VA

SONS OF WILLIAM I

Luke Hanks
b. about 1685 in Richmond Co., VA.

William Hanks
b. 14 Feb 1679

John Hanks
b. 1690 in Richmond Co., VA.

Joseph Hanks
b. about 1730 in KY.

John Hanks II
b. 4 May 1728 in Richmond Co., VA.

Abraham Hanks
b. about 1759 in North Carolina

Abner Hank
b. 1763 in Richmond Co., VA.s

Nancy Hanks
b. 5 February 1784

Capt. Thomas Hanks
b. 11 March 1791 in KY

A FAMILY SECRET

Abraham Lincoln
b. 12 February 1809

Thomas Hanks
b. 5 May 1819

Daniel Boone Hanks
b. 10 September 1847 in KY.

Ernest Beauel Hanks I
b. 1890 in Flournoy, Tehama Co., CA

Amos Mefford Hanks
b. 4 March 1924 in Willows, Glenn Co., CA.

THOMAS JEFFREY 'TOM' HANKS
b. 9 July 1956 in Concord, CA.

TWO

A BROKEN FAMILY

ALL TOM HANKS can remember about the night his cozy world caved in was wanting to take all the toys in his closet when his father knocked on his bedroom door and told him to gather his belongings. He was told he could only take one or two, and to hurry into the pick-up truck his father had parked in the driveway outside the family's Bedding house.

Amos had left the home abruptly a month earlier without telling the children where he was going. In fact, he had gone to Reno, Nevada, to get a quickie divorce. His long working hours had taken their toll on the marriage, but relatives blamed Janet for the final split. Tom's uncle, Loyal Brummet, a 73-year-old retired San Francisco bus driver, recalled: 'Amos loved his first wife, but he couldn't forgive her for running around. He gave her three or four opportunities, but it didn't work.'

An apparently still bitter Amos wrote in his memoirs: 'Chronically dissatisfied and agog with the blandishments of one more in a series of attentive admirers, she decided, or was

19

persuaded, that she would prefer to be separated not only from me, but also, within a few weeks, from the children.'

Now Amos had returned for the kids, having found a new job at the Mapes Hotel in Reno, a celebrity hotspot at the time, and a small basement apartment. Still unaware of what was happening, first Sandra, then Larry and little Tommy threw what few belongings they could carry into the back of the truck and drove off into the night with their father. The youngest child, Jimmy, then just a few months old, was to stay with his mother.

'Separating the children was not what I wanted to do,' wrote Amos later, but needing some vestige of responsible parenthood to cling to, she would not have given Jimmy up easily.

'I had neither the time nor the money to fight with her for his custody even if I had a way to care for him. The older three were hampering her in her new life. Sandra was ten, Larry was eight and Tom was five.'

The Hanks children never were told their parents' marriage was over. But arriving in Reno in the early hours of the morning on 23 February 1962, they stopped outside a large corner house at 529 Mill Street, in a down-at-heel neighbourhood near an old brothel. Ushering them into the dusty basement flat, Amos told them: 'Welcome to your new home.'

The tiny, 600-square-foot apartment was owned by mother-of-eight Winifred Finley, who lived upstairs and had herself been left to bring five children up alone after her marriage failed. Her three older children had already married and left home and she desperately needed money to supplement her wages as a bookkeeper at the Guy Reade department store in Reno. So when she met Amos through her next-door neighbour, who worked at the same hotel as the cook, she offered him her basement to rent.

Both 38, with eight kids to care for between them, Winifred and Amos quickly became friends and then lovers. Shaken by the belated failures of their first attempts at marriage, they turned to each other for comfort at a particularly difficult time in their lives. Besides, Amos needed someone to take care of his kids.

Amos was again spending long hours at work as the Mapes expanded to become the world's first hotel/casino. As well as running the catering operation, he served personal meals to such big stars as Judy Garland, who performed there, and Marilyn Monroe and Clark Gable, who stayed at the hotel while filming *The Misfits*.

As the youngest, Tommy couldn't be left alone at home for long hours and was booked into the Holy Child Day Care Center, a nursery run by nuns on Reno Avenue, close to the neon lights and round-the-clock action of the casino district.

Wayne Melton, now a society and entertainment columnist for the *Reno Gazette Journal,* went to nursery school with Tom. 'It was run by Catholic Irish nuns and it was pretty strict. They used to slap me and Tom on the hand when we misbehaved.

'Tom and I were little buddies and we used to get into a little bit of trouble together. Tom used to spend the whole day there while his father was at work. We were both five years old – I am one month older than Tom – and he was always great fun and rather mischievous. We were always goofing around. He was very energetic and had a great sense of humour.

'His older brother also went to the school. I remember Tom was from a home where they didn't have very much. I know there was quite a number of children, but he moved away before I got to know him any better.'

Holy Child teacher Bonnie Miller, now in her seventies, remembers Tom being a very curious boy and 'a little devil.'

On 19 April 1962, a Judge Thomas Craven granted Amos a divorce from Janet on the grounds of 'extreme mental cruelty'. Divorce records in Reno show Amos gave all 'community property' to his ex-wife, claiming she treated him with 'a coldness and indifference' and starved him of love and affection.

Asked whether they quarreled, he answered: 'We did.'

Did she complain and criticise? 'She did,' he replied.

Was this continuous? 'It was.'

Was it difficult to do anything to please her? 'Impossible, I would say.'

Quizzed over the effect of the marred relationship on his health, Amos added: 'I have never experienced any sort of breakdown but it was detrimental.'

It made you extremely nervous? 'It did.'

On the same day, Winifred was granted her divorce from railway worker Theo Finley, the father of her eight children, and four days later, on 23 April 1962, she married Amos at the Reno Register Office with the kids all watching on, wondering how their lives had so quickly been turned upside down.

In the space of two short months, Tom, Larry and Sandra had a new home, a new mother and five new brothers and sisters. And still nobody had actually sat them down and explained how it came about. Tom said later that he felt 'lonely and in the dark' over the dramatic changes he was forced through.

But, at first at least, it all seemed to work out. Tom, in particular, got special treatment as the 'baby' of the brood. His stepbrothers and sisters, Melissa, Maureen, Norma, Debra and Jon helped take care of him and all eight children shared an 8 foot-by-18 foot bedroom in the basement, using curtains as dividers.

There were so many children running around that they were all given a number so their parents would know they hadn't left anyone behind. Tom was number eight.

'Suddenly, it was like, bang, zoom! – and there were kids all around,' recalled Tom in a 1989 *Playboy* interview. 'We were total strangers, all thrust together. I remember in school we had to draw a picture of our house and family and I ran out of places to put people. I put them on the roof. I drew Dad in bed, sleeping, since he worked so hard in the restaurant.'

He added later: 'There was a stepbrother and four stepsisters whom I would not recognise now if they walked into a room. Then there were three or more step siblings in another place. It seemed like there was always someone new coming or going. It was the odd, '60s dysfunctional version of the extended family.

'When he and she split up, I never saw those people again.'

At the time of the wedding, Melissa was 13, Maureen, 12, Norma, 11, Debra, ten and Jon was eight.

'It was just like the *Brady Bunch*,' said Jon, now a father-of-four who works for the fire department in Richland, Washington. 'When that programme came out, we were saying, "That was us!" It was chaotic – but it was fun too.'

Winifred, in her 70s and suffering from a serious heart condition, always had a soft spot for little Tommy. 'When we were first married, I remember Tom coming in and jumping on my lap and saying, "So you're my new mum, eh?"'

The house in Mill Street had the same shabby appearance as most homes in the working-class neighbourhood and the big basement bedroom, with its tatty, worn-out carpet, became the ideal stage for Tom to follow up his cemetery acting debut.

The other children's shining faces would collapse with laughter at his antics. So they happily encouraged the five-year-old to think up more sketches and plays. Suddenly, he had an audience.

Said Winifred: 'My kids would love to put on shows, but it was always Tom who was the star. He had something that was very special... and you could see it even then. The others would be captivated. Tom was a ham from the start. Even then, you could see where his future lay. It was definitely in his nature and he was wise enough to develop it when he got older.'

The oldest stepsister, Melissa, now a married mother-of-six living in Auburn, California, said: 'We all took care of Tommy. He was a sweet, friendly little kid.

'We used to do little plays and sketches and Tommy was right in there among us. It was only a small place. There were two bedrooms upstairs and the basement was filled up with kids. We used to pretend there was a 100-year-old man in the basement and Tom would get as scared as the rest of us. We all got along great as kids.' Winifred now lives in Carewood, Idaho, with her third husband, Grady Martinez, who used to work with Amos at the Reno hotel.

She said: 'When I met Tom's father he had just separated from his wife. We were both in a pinch at the time. I was single and raising five kids and I had gone to Reno to get a divorce. We met through the next-door-neighbour, a lady who worked with Mr. Hanks at the hotel. She said, "There is this man who I am working with and he needs a place to live. Why don't you rent him the basement?"

'I kept saying I didn't want anybody in the house. But when we met we hit it off right away and he moved in there and then. I think he needed me at the time. As soon as we realised we had something to work on, he brought the children up from Bedding to Reno. He brought the children to me because he needed a place for them. Tom was five.'

After a while, the new family left the cramped house in Reno for a more spacious home in Pleasant Hills, California.

'When we moved to Pleasant Hills there was a ton of kids in the neighbourhood,' recalled Jon. 'Larry was very quick and I was the scrapper. There was a lot of lads around and we'd all look after Tommy. I remember saving his bacon in the neighbourhood a few times.

'It was a small house with only three bedrooms. I remember Mum and Bud converted the garage into a room for us boys. I remember in pillow fights I used to pick on Tommy and pound on his chest – perhaps that's why he has never called!

'Their dad was a pretty good guy, but he always tried to keep us kind of separate.'

'Tommy would have Larry and I in stitches. He would really make us laugh. He had this way of getting what he wanted. Tommy was always theatrical. He was the little kid who knew how to push all the right buttons. He was just a natural '60s kid growing up.'

But as the honeymoon period wore off, the cracks in Amos and Winifred's rebound relationship began to show.

Winifred had become a Mormon while married to Amos and that soon became a source of conflict with her new husband, who was suspicious of religion in most forms. 'When we met his kids were Catholic and mine were Protestant and that had its difficulties,' said Winifred. 'Then I became enamoured of the Mormon Church and Mr Hanks didn't.

'It was funny because the kids enjoyed going to church. But after we had split up, Mr Hanks and I were at a friend's wedding and Tom ran up to me and said, "Mum, Mum, guess what? I'm not a Mormon any more. Now I am a darned old Catholic!"'

She went on: 'Tom got on very well with my children. But Sandy felt the loss of her mother. To her I was always an intruder.

'Larry was much quieter than Tom, but he would hold his own. I don't think anything was really difficult for Tom. He was one who could roll with the punches.'

The inevitable end, when it came, was just as dramatic and abrupt as Amos's first marriage collapse. He said only that he married 'hurriedly'. But, once again, the Hanks family saw Amos as the victim. 'The second marriage was like jumping from the frying pan into the fire,' said Amos's brother-in-law Loyal Brummet. 'It was never going to last. In the end, Bud got right out of that one.'

Winifred remembers things differently. A self-educated man and an avid reader, Amos was determined to give his own children the best education possible. He had no such aspirations for his stepchildren and remained distant and slightly aloof from them throughout the short-lived marriage.

Said Winifred: 'I loved Tom's father and he loved me. We needed each other very much. We had a wonderful time together. When I broke up with him it was heart-rending for everyone.

'It was very hard for Bud to be married to me because he couldn't see how he was going to send all eight children to college... and education was very important to him.

'I understand why my marriage to Tom's father didn't work out and there was never any bitterness over him leaving with his children. I had the greatest respect for him.

'I did worry about Tom and Larry and Sandy after they had gone, but I knew they were in good hands.

'Some reports I have read make it seem like Tom's father was some kind of itinerant cook. But that was not true. He was the best at what he did. He ran big hotels and banqueting halls. He was very highly regarded and a very intelligent man.'

The marriage had lasted less than two years when Amos once again instructed his three children to gather together their belongings and climb in the truck. Although the scenario was no longer novel to Tom, Larry or Sandra, it was no less unsettling. With the possible exception of Sandra, they had made friends, tried their best to put down some new roots and found solace in the topsy-turvy world of a big family. Tom felt strongly enough to call Winifred 'Mum', and she in turn felt very protective of the baby of her extended family.

Tom's stepbrother and stepsisters were deeply shocked at the sudden parting.

'We missed him when he went,' said Melissa. 'It was kind of abrupt. They went just like that and we didn't really see Tom again. My mother never told us why they left and I haven't talked to him since he was six years old.

'I liked Bud. He wasn't really warm, but he was always there to answer questions. He wasn't unpleasant as a stepfather.

'I hadn't really thought of Tommy for years and I was watching the TV show *Bosom Buddies* one night when I realised it was

Tommy on the screen. Now I have got most of his movies. I am proud of him. I guess he is our one claim to fame. I would like to talk to him about what it was like living in Reno back then and all of the things we used to do.'

Added Jon: 'I know Mum used to worry about the kids after she split up with Bud. I was told that Tom's favourite sandwich is still peanut butter, mayonnaise and lettuce. I don't know if he remembers, but that was my favourite sandwich and I used to make them for him too.

'I remember it being a good time for all of us. Our mum really was a good mum to Tommy, Larry and Sandra. She treated them exactly as if they were her own. The way he is acting now is a testament to how he was brought up. Growing up he has been able to maintain his perspective.'

Winifred would dearly love to speak to the former stepson she hasn't seen or heard from since shortly after the breakdown of her marriage to Amos in 1964. Until this interview, she had never spoken publicly of her days as Tom Hanks's 'Mum'.

Tom has never made any attempt to contact his 'secret' family and has been dismissive of them in interviews. Asked by the American entertainment magazine *US* in 1984 whether it was a *Brady Bunch* home, he replied: 'Oh, nooo. I wouldn't remember their names if they showed their faces today.'

In another interview, he said: 'My first stepmother was somewhat flaky. Her love of the Mormon Church was just one of the reasons I think Dad left her. Dad did kind of rebel against it. She's not a Mormon now. She's probably into astrology or something.'

Just in case she was in any doubt, Winifred was saddened by a more direct snub when she tried to get in touch with Tom. 'I wrote to Tom through his agent, but I didn't hear from him.

'Then I heard him say on TV that so many people tried to bother him and claim they were related. I didn't want to be thought a nuisance.'

With her ailing heart, Winifred is resigned to never seeing Tom again. But she follows his career closely from afar. 'We want him to understand that we don't want anything from him. We just want to tell him how proud we are of him. I suppose we are the missing link in his family. My current husband even knew Tom as a boy because he used to work with Mr Hanks.

'I would love to be able to see him and talk to him again after all these years. But I understand he must be very busy with his own life. I respect his privacy. I have always kept a very close eye on how Tom was doing. We are all very proud of what he has done with his life. He appears to be such a nice man. I'm very glad how things turned out for him. And he doesn't really look a lot different today to the way he looked all those years ago.

'Before he died, Amos phoned me and asked if I was surprised that Tom was doing so well as an actor.

'I told him, "I am not surprised at all. Tom was always the star of the family."'

THREE

HOME ALONE

'DID YOU HEAR what the little creep said?' Sandra shouted scornfully from the back of the car. 'Tommy heard a stupid bird and he said, "Hark, a mourning dove!"'

While his brother and sister made fun of this latest example of young Tom's thespian affectations, he was very pleased with himself. He amused himself for the rest of the 100-mile journey to his mother's home by working the line for all it was worth. 'After that, it was, "Hark, a big red truck. Hark, some cows in a field. Hark, I have to go to the bathroom,"' remembered his father, who titled his typed-out memoirs 'Hark, A White Mule.'

The children also had a portentous game they would like to play. 'We based it on Disneyland,' recalled Sandra, 'with the brothers playing paparazzi and Tom playing the obnoxious star. It was just another home movie, but it was fun.'

Throughout his childhood, Tom would spend most of the holidays and periodic weekends with his mother and younger brother at their modest house in Red Bluff, Northern California. If he was working, Amos would drop the three children off at the bus stop in Oakland and their mother would be waiting for them at the other end. Otherwise, he would drive them upstate, going on to stay with relatives in Paskenta while the children spent some time with their mother, who was still working as a waitress. Although Janet married three more times, she at least remained in the same area and this offered some small stability to her increasingly nomadic elder children. Pressed on his 'hometown', Tom will often say Red Bluff, recalling bike rides down to the Sacramento River and stops at the Foster Freeze ice cream shop on the way home. But, in truth, his relationship with his mother was never close and the visits to Red Bluff would, if anything, underline the fractures in the family that were magnified by the fact that Jimmy lived there all the time.

One visit ended in floods of tears when Sandra, nearing puberty, heard Jimmy giving his mother's surname at the time as his own, forsaking the Hanks name. As the baby of the family, Jim would often be the brunt of his sister and brothers ill humour. He complained later that Tom was an unlikely 'bruiser' as a boy, picking on him so much that when he locked Jimmy in the wardrobe, as was his wont, it came as a relief to the smaller child because it meant he couldn't hit him any more. Such dramas were not unusual.

Janet tried her best to make her wandering children feel at home on their visits. She would paint eggs with them at Easter and organise hunts in the garden and around the house, paying the eager egg seekers 50 cents a time for finding the hidden prizes. At Christmas, she would make sure there was turkey with all the trimmings. Tom had a Christmas stocking with his name on it hung over the fireplace.

'He was always entertaining,' she recalled. 'During his visits he would turn a sock into a puppet and put on a little show. When he said something cute and adults reacted to it with amusement, he'd repeat it endlessly, milking the line for all it was worth. Tom had a natural love of the limelight.'

Tom would never be close to his mother, but Janet did the best she could in difficult circumstances, ensuring the children all knew she loved them, even if she wasn't always there for them. In return, Tom held kinder memories of Janet than his father had of his first wife, saying later: 'Essentially, my dad could afford and wanted to have the kids and Mum couldn't. She could really only afford to have the baby at the time.'

Meanwhile, the Hanks children were back on the move with their father. Leaving behind their stepfamily for good, they were taken to live with Amos's strongly religious sister, the late Mary Brummet, and her husband, Loyal.

For Tom, used to the freedom and anonymity of a big, loose pseudo-family, it was a difficult period. Aunt Mary was a devout Nazarene and the children's antics were often at odds with her strict faith, an orthodox Wesleyan Christian church with a hard-line doctrine. 'That's a pretty hard-line religious thing,' Tom told *Première* magazine in 1989. 'We weren't allowed to watch the *Three Stooges*; there were an awful lot of rules... awfully long prayers.'

And there wasn't a lot of space. Tom's grandmother and his two nephews were already living in the four-bedroomed house in San Mateo, California, so Amos slept in a trailer in the back garden and the children shared a bed.

'They came to live with my wife and I for a while before Bud got an apartment,' said widower Loyal, who was married for 48 years. 'But it was rather crowded.

'Tom was very close to his dad. All the kids were. Bud worked very hard, but he always took care of his kids.'

The family moved after a couple of months to the first in a long succession of tatty flats in the Bay area. 'We moved about every six months,' said Tom. 'We must have moved a million times.' For a period of two-and-a-half years, the Hanks children pretty much raised themselves. There was little parental guidance or discipline, no one to ask for advice, no directions through the minefield of puberty.

For most of that time, they were home alone.

Like many single parents, Amos was caught in a dilemma. Determined to take good care of his children and obsessed with ensuring they had every chance of a good education, he had to work long hours to pay the bills. The price he paid was having barely enough time to spend with them once he was home, a Catch 22 he was painfully aware of when he decided to leave his second wife.

'Leaving was going to require new measures of self-sufficiency on the part of the kids. I would be working long hours. They would be alone,' he wrote. 'People expressed surprised disappointment that I didn't hire a housekeeper or a baby-sitter, but the kids didn't want to have any outsiders among us. I didn't either.

'They ate a lot of cold cereals, TV dinners and canned soup. The milkman had a key to the apartment and maintained the inventory at six quarts (years later I heard about milk-drinking competitions in our kitchen).'

While their father worked, Tom, Larry and Sandra took care of themselves, doing their own cooking, their own cleaning and laundry, their homework if and when they felt like it, watching whatever bad TV shows they chose and dealing with any crisis that may have arisen.

Inevitably, Tom was alone a lot of the time and suffered from a sense of loneliness that remains with him to this day. But it is the one part of his childhood he seems to remember fondly in interviews. Perhaps the funny sitcom-style stories of growing up without any parents around appeals more to his self-protective comic skills than the more serious, long-buried memories of deeply felt abandonment.

He told *Playboy:* 'We liked it because it was the first time we had lived alone with our dad. There were these TV shows like *Bachelor Father* that showed kids living with their father in this neat home. We used to think they were crazy. We lived in these ripped-up, stained apartments that we completely destroyed in the course of living there. And we had no Philippine house boy.'

But it was one of the many moves, this time to Oakland, that Tom recalled really growing up. He was nine at the time. 'Dad would work until 10 o'clock, so we were on our own,' he continued. 'We made our own dinners, which was more comical than anything else. I remember throwing away frozen peas and carrots and spinach so Dad would think we'd eaten them. We'd burn a steak and have some bread with it and make some instant mashed potatoes and that would be our dinner. I still can't eat tomato soup because of the constant smell of burned tomato soup that hovered over our electric stove.

'We gained something from our lack of nutrition. We learned a lot, we became really independent. We did our own laundry. We supposedly had to keep the house clean, though it never was. That house was a shambles, too, by the time we left. We were completely unsupervised, but we got into surprisingly little trouble.'

Tom had similar tales of kitchen chaos for *Première,* saying: 'Culinary experts we were not. We were always supposed to have the four basic food groups, of which we would have maybe one by the time we ate the meal. That meant frozen packages of peas that we would eat plain. We didn't know about sauces or butter or spices or things like that. And brussel sprouts – you know how they look like the brains of rats? Roll 'em over on their sides and they kinda look elongated, like you can almost see the skull encasing? I can't eat that stuff, just because for about two-and-a-half years, that was all there was.'

But, as he confessed, the premature freedom he enjoyed came at some emotional cost.

With his inquiring, understated intelligence, Larry was the inventor, collecting and squirreling away anything that set off his curiosity. At that time, Larry was also the comedian in the family. His famous brother would say years later: 'People used to say, "Tom's loud." And then they would say, "But Larry – Larry's funny." I used to steal the stuff Larry said at the dinner table and take it to school the next day and get a laugh out of it.' Sandra, bright and energetic, was just discovering the endless temptations of being a teenager in the late '60s. As the oldest, she was usually the sibling with the last word. Sandra was always the leader, devising games and ultimately ruling over who won or lost. As Tom would later attest, she was the sibling who held the boys' childhood together with her strength of character. As a result of Amos's long hours at work, it was Sandra who effectively brought up the two elder Hanks boys.

For Tom, there was always the television. It was switched on around the clock and, when he wasn't at school, Torn was a fixture in front of it, devouring everything from sappy comedies to cooking programmes to lengthy documentaries.

His long hours in front of the baby-sitting box gave him an encyclopaedic TV brain. The *Apollo* space programme became an obsession – an infatuation he was to put to good use in true *Boy's Own* fashion in the film *Apollo 13* and his self-produced television series *From the Earth to the Moon* – and he refused to miss a single moment of the extensive coverage. He coveted all 26 episodes of *The World at War.* Even now, he can describe the six-panel black-and-white logo for one of his early-60s favourites, *Biography,* which was illustrated with thumbnail pictures of Einstein, Gandhi, Greta Garbo, Winston Churchill, Franklin D. Roosevelt and baseball hero Babe Ruth. He watched *Fireball XL-5,* the *Batman* TV show, and Jacques Cousteau, and devoured the Charlton Heston and Burt Lancaster epics when they eventually reached the small screen.

He still remembers sitting absolutely still for three-and-a-half hours watching Kurosawa's *The Seven Samurai,* his eyes transfixed by the subtitles and the scope of the film classic.

Tom was part of probably the first generation to have its political and social views coloured by television. And there were some subjects that struck home more deeply than others. 'There was always a vicious imbalance between two prevailing images of

34

marriage,' he told *GQ* magazine in 1988. 'One was the fucking commercials, where marriage was waffle irons and "Love – American Style", and there was the reality of growing up in post-war America when my folks were divorced.

'I remember in grammar school and junior high, there were very few kids who came from multiple marriages, who had more than one mother and step siblings. No one at school knew about that stuff.

'I don't think you can have children at an early age and enjoy them the way they are enjoyed on fucking TV commercials. It was the same for my father – he turned around and he had all these kids and he said, "Jesus Christ holy cow..."'

In spite of everything, Tom continued to get As and Bs at a succession of schools where he became well used to being the new boy. One of his teachers became so attached to the mop-haired Tom that she wanted to take him on a holiday trip to Britain and Europe, but the idea fell through when her favourite pupil moved on to another school and yet another teacher.

Had his grades dropped alarmingly or had there been a domestic disaster more serious than burned soup, the law may have taken a dim view of Tom being left alone for such long periods of time. It is quite conceivable he could have been taken from the family home. Fortunately, there were no major mishaps. But there were a couple of occasions, both involving Tom, when Amos feared the worst.

'One afternoon,' he wrote in his memoirs, 'I got a panicking call from Sandra. 'The house door has slammed on Tom's fingers.'

Racing back from work, Amos was already preparing himself for the torrent of criticism he was likely to face for allowing such an accident to happen by leaving his young children on their own. He needn't have worried. 'I got back to find that Tom had a blood blister on the tip of his index finger... he was sitting there watching TV, eating a banana,' recalled Amos.

The second emergency call Amos received at work was much more serious. He wrote: 'I came home to find Sandra and Larry afraid and Tom in real distress. He was wheezing, struggling for breath. I had had experience with children with croup – using a humidifier in their bedroom and taking them into a closed bathroom with the shower running.

'This was more acute than anything I had seen. I bundled him up and ran red lights and exceeded speed limits all the way to the hospital. At the emergency room, both he and I were in such a state that they took us in ahead of other patients.'

There was no history of any breathing problems in the family and, for a while, Amos feared for Tom's life, so bad was his son gasping for air. But he said: 'The doctor administered a large shot with a needle into Tom's skinny little buttock. In seconds, as if by magic, his breathing became normal, his wheezing and struggling stopped. His expression of stricken terror changed back to his usual alert acuity.

'The doctor said this was probably the beginning of an ongoing problem. But there has been no recurrence.'

There was only one other time Amos could remember his son being in real peril. 'Tommy came in to go wee wee. He was just out of diapers and I saw the lid start to fall. I couldn't catch it. It was going to smash his little member like the flat of a cleaver does an *escalope de veau* on a meat block.

'But with masterful, unconcerned economy of effort, he thrust his little, round stomach forward to intercept it.'

On the rare occasions Amos could get time off work he was intent on teaching his sons some of the more manly pursuits he prided himself on as a young man. Tom was enrolled in judo classes and Little League baseball and the whole family was taken on camping trips to Grindstone Canyon, California.

When he got the chance, Amos would go hunting with a group of friends, but his children showed little interest in following suit.

Tom's only encounter with wildlife came on a camping trip when his father woke in the middle of the night to find Tom outside the tent screaming. 'Hey dad,' he shouted. 'There's a deer here. It's got horns. I could hit it with my BB gun.' By the time Amos had stumbled into the darkness the deer had disappeared. He recalled little Tom telling him in a baby voice: 'I was weally sca'wed.'

Another important ritual on these trips was learning to drive. The older two learned very quickly, chiefly because they were able to reach the pedals. For Tom, it was a bit more difficult. Wrote his father: 'Tom was too small to reach the pedals or see over the dashboard. I would sit him on my lap and steer while I did the necessary thing with the foot pedals and gear shift lever.'

It seemed the nine-year-old was a natural. 'He handled the wheel with authority and conviction,' his proud father boasted. 'I compared his skill with Sam Hanks, the famous driver of racing cars, a distant relative.'

Sandra recalled in an interview with *OK!* magazine: 'Our dad would throw a mattress in the back of a pick-up and on summer nights we'd sit in the back and go to a drive-in movie. Dad never even bothered to check what was playing – we'd just go.'

The snapshots of a regular family life were, however, few and far between. Although he dearly loved his father, Tom wrote a touching letter to his big sister 20 years later, in 1986, thanking her for 'holding it all together.' While all three were jokers, he said, they took their cue from Sandra. She was the one who made it fun.

In all, Sandra said she moved 31 times in 28 years. But she said: 'We never felt unloved or out in the cold. There were no foster homes, and we weren't shipped off somewhere or abandoned. I think we became flexible and closer to each other. Even if we weren't brothers and sisters we'd be friends – that's if we could find each other. We moved so many times.' Sandra remembers Tom as 'always a ham'. One of her abiding memories of Tom was his irritating, squeaky-voiced impressions of radio DJs.

Larry said they all made it up as they went along. 'We didn't really know what we were missing. That was just the way it was,' he said. 'We were almost feral children. We were probably the terrors of the neighbourhood. We certainly didn't have much in the way of parental control.

'We were quite young and there were the three of us and my father worked long hours in the restaurant business. So the three of us just took care of ourselves, basically.'

Larry remembers being very close to his brother and sister. 'We were siblings. There was just us. Nobody was famous at that time, with the complications that brings. Everybody was very equally loud when we were kids. There was no competition or anything like that.'

Although Larry did add: 'Tom has always been outgoing, always liked talking to people. And he could always talk to people better than I could.

'In high school, he used to borrow my tape recorder and do kind of his own radio news reports. They were pretty awful. I only discovered them later. For instance, he would announce urgently that an earthquake was coming, saying something like, "Leave the city immediately" and that type of thing.

'I have the tapes – it's great bribing material that might come in handy someday.'

Through adversity, the Hanks children became very close. But they couldn't always be right there for each other. At school, they were often on their own. 'It's not a great life for a kid to be the new kid in school all the time,' said Larry. 'And we did a lot of that.

'I don't think any of us particularly enjoyed that bit of it.'

'You could get lost in the shuffle,' said Tom, 'or you could be a loudmouth. I chose the latter route. My apprenticeship years, I called them.'

Tom told *US* magazine: 'The coolest place to be was at home because we were always cracking each other up. I was surrounded by goodness. No one was hitting me or telling me I was stupid or drinking themselves into oblivion. My dad was not a guy who had his fingers on the pulse of his own feelings, but he was a good guy. 'And my mum, even though she was far away, was always concerned about my well-being and always happy to see me. The skeletons in our closet were only a couple of femur bones.'

Reminiscing to *Première,* Tom went on: 'It wasn't that bad. We were wild, of course. I know I yelled a lot. But as I recall, it was two-and-a-half very pleasant years. Didn't get into any real trouble, and was very tight with my brother and sister throughout.'

But all that was about to change. If the gypsy years were the best of his childhood, the worst were those that followed. Amos had asked a Chinese waitress to become his third wife – and the freewheeling Hanks family would never be the same again.

FOUR

A FAMILY AT WAR

'TROUBLE WAS BREWING from the very start,' recalled Amos, who had met Frances Wong at the Jack London Square tourist spot in Oakland, where they both worked – Amos as a chef, Frances as a waitress. In the early throes of passion, he had dreamed of his children's lives being 'enriched by the blending of cultures.' At last, he thought, they would have a steady, secure home life with a house-proud stepmother more than happy to cook and clean for them. Being the youngest, Tom in particular would benefit from the belated stability.

He quickly discovered he could not have been more wrong. Within days of the wedding, Tom, Larry and Sandra had all assumed a sudden, intense dislike of Chinese food – and it went downhill from there.

Amos saw Frances as the 'romance of a lifetime'. To his children, at first she seemed the stepmother from hell.

Tom's father was now 40 and had got a job as a teacher in the Oakland school district – always a keen reader, he had taken correspondence courses to educate himself. It was Frances's second marriage and she had her own three second-generation American-Chinese daughters. The youngest, Debbie, aged five, stayed with her mother while the two older girls, Chris and Cheryl, went to live with their father in San Francisco.

From doing exactly as he pleased, ten-year-old Tom now found he had to ask to go out or stay up late. Cleaning his room was no longer an abstract concept. Mealtimes were held around a table rather than the television.

Frances, shocked at the wild ways of her new stepchildren, tried her best to tame them. She failed.

Up to now, despite all the moves, the new schools, the new brothers and sisters, the new friends, Tom had gone along, uncomplainingly, with his father's wanderlust. Any unhappiness or loneliness he felt he had largely kept to himself.

Now, older and unwilling to submit to the alien, new domestic regime, Tom, his brother and sister all rebelled. Sandra, by now 16, began getting in trouble for staying out late. After an explosive series of rows, Tom and Larry refused to speak to their embattled stepmum.

'The friction began then, in 1966. Everything started going crazy at that time,' Tom told *Playboy*. 'We had lived alone for two-and-a-half years. We had called our own shots. Now there was this woman telling us what to do. We weren't about to suddenly be told to make our beds when we hadn't made our beds for two-and-a-half years. Or to be told we couldn't go somewhere.

'This split the family right down the middle. My sister left and went to live with my mum. My brother and I lived by ourselves in the downstairs of the house. We talked to the rest of the family only at mealtimes, and barely even then.'

In a 1994 *US* interview, Tom called Frances the love of his father's life. But he said she most definitely did not raise him, even though he went to live with her when he was ten.

'I was already raised,' he said. 'You gotta understand, this union they had was very personal. For a few years, we tried to do family dinners. But it was a very ugly time. She had a daughter, and we're friends. But they were Asian – Frances is Chinese – and there were differences there.

'And this came on the heels of three of us kids being on our own for the better part of three years. You can't just change that.' Added Sandra: 'After spending so much time on our own, looking after each other, it came as a shock to us suddenly living with these Chinese stepsisters. On top of that, dad's Chinese wife was really traditional. We went from a steady diet of pizza to being served Chinese dishes at every meal.'

The situation came to a head when Tom let fly at his younger stepsister with an uncharacteristic attack. Realising the family feud was getting out of hand, Amos tried to make peace. 'I called a conference hoping to nip this thing in the bud. I failed. The conference became a shouting match,' he added.

Sandra went to live with her mother in Red Bluff. She hardly spoke to her father for the next five years.

After graduating from high school, Larry followed his sister to Red Bluff, leaving just Tom and Debbie at home in Alameda, a suburb of Oakland. An uneasy truce was called, but Tom, parted for the first time from his siblings, was earnestly looking for a way out.

At Bret Harte Junior School, he began taking his role as class clown seriously. Even then, his disarming sense of humour kept him out of any real trouble with the teachers. 'I was horribly, painfully, terribly shy,' he said. 'At the same time I was the guy who would yell out funny captions during the filmstrips.' But he was still learning to cover up his insecurities. And not everyone was fooled. 'Tom was appalled by the divorce. It hurt him, but he covered it up,' said his then best friend, Kent Mulkey. 'My mum always said that Tom was so funny because he was crying out for love. He survived by making jokes.'

Years later, Tom revealed what he really thought of his years at Bret Harte – it was 'pure hell.'

'It's just too painful a time to remember,' he said. 'A miasma of emotions, hormones and fears.

'It's like a way station, like waiting for a bus for three years. That's what I remember – pure, absolute hell. Three years of frustration, pain and loneliness.'

It was at Skyline High School that Tom found the escape he had been searching for and took the first unsteady steps on a path that would eventually lead to Hollywood: With a breathtaking, panoramic view of the Bay area, the busy school with its rich ethnic mix prides itself on the diversity of its studies.

To Tom, settled physically if not emotionally at home, the high school provided him with a source of friends and community he had never stayed anywhere long enough to find before.

Pouring over *The Catcher in the Rye* and immersing himself in the loneliness and isolation felt by J.D. Salinger's anti-hero Holden Caulfield, or glued to the faithful cathode tube, he was often sullen and uncommunicative with what remained of his family. Frances had given up trying to impress her will on the moody youngster, despairing of his obvious resentment towards her.

At school, a very different character began to emerge. The jokes were no longer necessary to make instant buddies and his confidence grew with his popularity. Most importantly, he saw himself as just another 'normal' student, earning mostly Cs but not having to prove himself to a fresh new set of faces every other term.

That doesn't mean he didn't still test his teachers with his quick wit. Recalling his schooldays in *Parade* magazine, he graded himself sternly: 'Math? Oooh – dead. Science? If they were talking about space I was interested.

'In the 6th grade we had to study South America. My question was always: Why? What does Simon Bolivar have to do with us? They said we studied American history in 5th grade. So like, we know everything there is to know about American history? Can't we go back and maybe just look at the Civil War once more?

44

'But I was not a troublemaker. I would only toy with authority up to the point that authority would get mad at me and then I would back off. If the teacher wasn't laughing, I'd shut up.'

While he was bombarded with the bohemian hippie urgings of the late 1960s and early 1970s, particularly where he lived in the Bay area, the home of the peace and love movement, Tom was looking in exactly the opposite direction.

He had had his share of freedom and he was too painfully shy in his early teens to even think about girls. Besides, he never much liked the music.

He tried playing soccer and running track, looking spindly and rather out of place among the high-school 'jocks'. Although his wacky humour would ensure acceptance, sport didn't provide the anchor he was searching for. Nor did the anti-authoritarian militancy sweeping the campus at that time. He had quite enough of that at home.

'It was big, urban public school. Two thousand kids. A big drug culture. Very well integrated,' Tom told *Playboy*. 'The rules were being completely redefined. As a matter of fact, I think everybody had given up by then. By the time I got there, the attitude was do whatever you want, just don't burn the place down, which, actually, some people still tried to do.

'I mostly just wanted to get out of the house; the house wasn't a good place to be.'

The path Tom took was to religion. A club at school led him to the First Covenant Church, just down the hill at Skyline, and a faith that would dominate his life for the next four years.

The church would provide friends, a girlfriend, structure, later even surrogate parents and a car. In return, the young recruit simply had to believe and to conform – two things born-again Tom was more than happy to do.

Sister Sandra remembers her brother as being 'self-righteous' around his Fundamentalist Christian period, 'as if he had seen the light and the rest of us were in the dark'.

His father was equally dismissive, saying Tom suffered 'an adolescent faith attack'.

But although he admits to being 'a geek, a spaz' as he entered his teens, the church answered a very real need in Tom at a time he was having trouble shrugging reality off with a ready quip.

He had already tried being a Catholic, a Mormon and a Nazarene. But those had always been forced on him by circumstance. Here was a religion that wanted him for himself, irrespective of who his mother happened to be.

'Because of all the people I lived with, I had a chequered religious upbringing. Then, when I was in high school, I had a serious born-again experience,' Tom explained in a *Los Angeles Times* interview. 'A great group of people ran a church near where I lived, and they provided a safe, nurturing atmosphere at a time there wasn't much else I could count on.

'The beliefs I embraced at that time don't mean the same thing to me now. When you're young and idealistic you tend to view things in absolute terms, and the absolutes didn't pan out, even within the confines of that place. You begin to see the contradictions without looking too closely.'

It was a while though, before Tom started looking back to the secular world. For now, he was enjoying his own, contradictory rebellion. While other kids his age were straining at the leash, growing long hair, pubescent moustaches, playing truant from church, and testing authority, Tom was joining the congregation youth group and choir and faithfully attending both the morning and afternoon Sunday services at the Oakland church that had become his second home. In time, he wasn't just joining Bible readings, he was leading them.

He says he was 'a Jesus freak', the sort of boy who would approach other students in the hallways at school and invite them to his house after class to discuss passages from the Bible.

But he couldn't grow his hair long if he tried. Emmy Perry, whose son D.J. also belonged to the church, clearly remembers Tom's odd Afro hairstyle. 'Tom had very curly hair,' she said. 'And it would never grow beyond his shoulders like the real Jesus freaks, no matter how much he plastered it down.'

The actor told *Vanity Fair* in 1994: 'It was not a Holy Roller place. They didn't speak in tongues. The only thing that was a little odd was that they really frowned on dancing...

'You did have to accept Jesus Christ as your saviour. You did have to pledge your life to Christ. You did need to accept Him into your heart. I was 14 and I needed something very badly – not just something to believe in, not just some sort of faith. I needed a brand of acceptance that would combat the loneliness I had felt all the way up to then. I wanted to belong to a group. I was young and scared and the world was fucked up.'

Apart from the church, the other main influence on Tom's life at the time was director Stanley Kubrick's classic *2001: A Space Odyssey*. Tom first saw it when he was 13 and he went on to see it an incredible 22 times at the cinema.

'It was probably the most influential film, movie, story, artistic package, whatever, that I ever saw. It was just bigger. It affected me much, much more than anything I had ever seen,' he said. 'There was just awe. Every time I saw it, I saw something new, something else that Kubrick had put in. He was able to suspend my disbelief. I just felt, "We are in space."'

As he was preparing to enter his senior year at high school in 1973, with his sister and brother long gone, Tom decided to make a break of his own. A family from the church, with a son in Tom's grade, offered to take him in. The house was much nearer to Skyline school than the houseboat Amos and Frances were living in at a marina in neighbouring Alameda. But the real reason was that relations between Tom and his stepmother had continued to deteriorate.

When his attempts to dissuade his 17-year-old son from leaving fell on deaf ears, Amos had little choice but to let him go. During this period, when he became involved with the Christian Fellowship drama section, he stayed with Bertie McColloch, a single mother with three children. Her little boy, Spike, suffered from Bell's palsy and it was Tom, remembers Bertie, who changed her son's life forever by encouraging him to overcome his handicap and go out and face the world.

'Tom would talk to the kids for hours,' she said. 'He would gently tease Spike and make him laugh at himself. Spike was so self-conscious that he didn't even want to go to school or out to play. But Tom convinced him through his sense of humour that there was nothing to be ashamed of.'

Sadly for Tom, he was still struggling to attract girls at school. 'I was death with women in high school – absolutely strikeout king,' he said. 'I was a little too geeky, a little too gangly, and much too manic.'

But, with time, his true personality began to shine through.

A more confident Tom had made many more friends, both inside and outside the church. Now he used his joker's mask to hide his unease with girls. But, with one girl in particular, Tom gradually found he was able to drop the comedy charade and share the kind of feelings he had kept locked inside for so long.

Carol Wiele was in the same year at Skyline as Tom and equally committed to the First Covenant Church. She was Tom's first love and his only real high-school girlfriend.

Now married and living near Sacramento, Carol remembers first meeting Tom in English class, when they had desks next to each other. 'Then we got to know each other better through the church. He wasn't a ladies man then at all. If he had been, I would never have dated him.

'He was a really nice guy. He was easy to be around and a lot of people liked him. But he was actually a very serious person underneath. He had a lot of things going on inside his head.'

Carol was Tom's date for the Skyline Senior Prom Night, the big party marking the end of school. 'We were the Class of '74 and Tom wasn't a turkey at all. He was delightful. We double-dated with some other friends and the guys worked very hard to make it a success. It was a trend at the time for guys to wear light blue tuxedos, but Tom chose a nice navy one.

'He was the perfect gentleman and we went out to a lovely dinner before going on to the prom.'

It was Carol's now brother-in-law who got Tom a job as a bellman at the Oakland Hilton hotel. The actor's hilarious tales of being a hotel gofer would later make him a big hit with chat show audiences in America. Late-night host David Letterman chose Tom for his final show with the NBC network because he wanted to hear more about his bellboy antics.

'That was the quintessential perfect job for somebody like me. I recommend it,' he said. 'It's a great job. Not much is expected of you, but you have to be smart. You can't be an idiot. Usually the bellman is unseen, the invisible employee. You can observe human behaviour as if you're looking through a keyhole.

'And you meet famous people. I met Cher when she was married to Greg Allman. I met Chris Evert. I told that story on some talk show Billie Jean King was on, because I had also carried Billie Jean's bags. It got back to Chrissy and she sent me a nice note asking if she had tipped me. There was a lot of stuff like that. I only worked three or four days a week because I was the late guy on weekends. But there was one time in the summer when I had to work regular business hours to fill in for a guy on vacation and I thought I was going to die!'

Other high points in Tom's bellman career included driving Sidney Poitier to the airport in the hotel limousine and carrying bags for Harry Belafonte and the Los Angeles Lakers basketball team.

There were few dull moments in that job, according to Tom, but the most bizarre occasion was when Elvis Presley and his entourage took 100 rooms for one night. 'Elvis's fans were absolutely crazy,' he said. 'There were entire families in 1942 DeSoto cars descending on the hotel to gawk at him.

'There must have been a thousand people jammed into the hotel lobby hoping for a glimpse of him. I only saw him for a few seconds in the lobby, as his bodyguards practically knocked me down to clear the way for him. The curtains in Elvis's suite were closed, but we fished at least ten stark naked women out of the swimming pool.'

'I don't know how much actual work they did, but they certainly seemed to have a good time there,' said Carol.

Although both Tom and Carol went on to the same college, they gradually drifted apart. 'We were friends for a long while, then we started dating. The truth is, it was probably better when we were friends. After he graduated, Tom was around for a couple of years and we would see each other around, but it wasn't the same. 'When he left to go to university, we kind of lost touch.'

The relationship broke up with Tom's virginity intact. 'It's this loneliness thing – it still kicks in,' he admitted in *Vanity Fair*. 'The confidence I had was in very few sides of my life. When the sex thing started happening, I was totally crippled when it came down to confidence with members of the opposite sex or... well... with... you know, people that I thought I was sexually attracted to or thought were neat.

'The sexual revolution didn't land on my shoulders quite so squarely. But I do think that a sense of humour gets you much farther in the movies than it does in real life. There was a long period of time where I swear to God being funny just didn't get you laid no matter how funny you were.'

For years, the only contact Carol had with her high-school sweetheart was through his films. 'He would have videos coming out and there would be pictures of Tom in the store,' she said. 'It would totally surprise me. I would think, "What's Tom doing up there?"'

While she was in San Francisco with her husband recently, Carol discovered she was staying at the same hotel as Tom and his wife, actress Rita Wilson. 'We got together over breakfast and talked about old times. It was really nice to see him and meet his wife and his two older children. They were all so charming,' she said.

Tom's split with Carol coincided with his cooling interest in the church. Although he had embraced religion to bring more focus to his jumbled life, he now found himself filled with more questions than answers. He decided to go back and live with his father.

'After about a year, Tom came home,' wrote Amos. 'Grateful as he was to the friends who had taken him in – they had even provided him with a car – they had expected commitment of which he was not capable. His adolescent religious zeal had run its course. He was no more receptive to fundamentalism than I had been.'

Tom is grateful to the church to this day. In 1994, he told the *Chicago Tribune:* 'It was an evangelical Christian youth group, and it was one of the best things I ever did. I made friends that I still have today. I had been a confused kid... Religion helped me.'

The church had played its part. But the impressionable teen had a new love, one he had been waiting his whole life for. Tom had discovered acting.

FIVE

THESPIAN TOM

TOM'S HIGH-SCHOOL yearbooks offer a clue to the teenager's growing interest in drama. As a member of the track team, where he ran the 440 metres in a respectable 61 seconds, and in the line-up for the soccer team, where he had struggled earnestly with the no handling rule, he was listed as Tom Hanks, or perhaps Thomas Jeffrey Hanks. The following year, as a budding member of the school's drama group, he had become Thom Hanks, the name better befitting his new thespian status.

'For a while,' he would later confess, 'I spelled my first name Thom, but decided that spelling my last name Hanx would be rather dumb.'

Skyline put on two plays a year, a musical in the spring and a play during the autumn term. While he was still trying to make his mark as a sportsman, Tom sat in the audience for a production of *Dracula,* starring one of his friends, Daniel Finnamore. 'I was into our high-school drama department before Tom was,' said Finnamore. 'I was Dracula and Tom wasn't really into acting, but he came to two performances and he was really excited about it.'

Tom remembers being 'utterly envious' of the actors on stage. He told *Interview* magazine in 1994: 'I sat in the audience and thought, 'How come I'm not up there doing that.' When they opened the curtain, it was all just so full of life; friends of mine were on the stage and running the lights, and I knew most of the people backstage.

'Up until then I'd had no clue that acting was ever an option. The next year I signed up for the drama class and tried out for all the plays, and got into them, and had more fun than I could possibly imagine. It was an incredible group of people, some of whom are still my friends.

'I got into this eclectic group that was kind of rootless and clique-less.'

For Tom, it was a group of people who, for a variety of different reasons, shared his sense of being apart. Like him, they were looking for a way to escape the mundane. They included a driven, flamboyant, bearded actor and designer called John Gilkerson, and Trudi Stillwell, who both formed close friendships with Tom. But the key to the dramatic new world of acting was Skyline's s drama teacher, Rawley Farnsworth.

Farnsworth, a Kansas farm boy who had done monologues and readings at community get-togethers in his youth, had taught drama in Wichita and in the Shawnee Mission district outside Kansas City before falling in love with San Francisco and moving to Skyline, the 'crown jewel' of the Oakland School District, in 1968. Coming from the conservative Mid-West, Farnsworth had good reason to enjoy the free-spirited bohemia of San Francisco. For he was gay and happy to live in a more liberal climate.

But across the bay in Oakland, the drama teacher chose to keep his homosexuality to himself. As we shall see later, the arrival of a 16-year-old Tom Hanks in his class in 1972 would one day have considerable consequences on the teacher's career-long decision to remain, as he puts it, a 'closet queen'.

Back then, Tom was left guessing along with the rest of his enthralled classmates over their charismatic teacher's sexuality.

'I had always been somewhat closeted. I never told my classmates that I was gay. My private life was not for discussion,' said Farnsworth. 'I was a different person when I walked into the school building in the morning than the person who left it at night.' He hid his homosexuality not because he feared losing his job, but because 'my biggest fear was the reaction of the kids. I thought they might blow things out of proportion, get carried away and write nasty things on my door. My discipline would have flown out of the window.'

Farnsworth's adoring pupils, however, had their suspicions. Tom later recalled studying his teacher in class and thinking he 'couldn't believe he was a "homo".'

Whatever his sexuality, Farnsworth brought the subject alive for his impressionable young student.

'Tom came along and took every course I offered,' said Farnsworth, who retired in 1985 after teaching for 14 years at the school. 'I do remember him clearly. He was always very open and happy-go-lucky. The yearbook voted him the class clown, but he was not a cut-up, just very witty. He was great fun to work with and a delightful teenager.'

While most of his best friends were happy to work off camera, Tom soon found that he was most comfortable in the footlights. The stage offered him a refuge from his problems at home, from the spectre of loneliness that haunted his quieter moments, from the trials and tribulations of being a teenager. More than that, it was fun.

'He had tremendous stage presence and wonderful timing. He needed very little direction. It all just came out naturally,' said Farnsworth.

He remembered quickly spotting Tom's comic ability. 'But I always preached to him that a good actor was a versatile actor – and Tom has been very smart in that respect.'

Even at school, Tom appeared to heed his mentor's advice, appearing first as Andrew Aguecheek, a self-infatuated fop in Shakespeare's *Twelfth Night,* then starring as a high-tempered, very intense stage director in *The Potboiler.* He was cast in *The Night of the Iguana* and, as a senior, he won the coveted role of Luther Billis in *South Pacific.* He was dressed in a grass skirt and had a tattoo of a battleship on his stomach – and he had a hoot. 'He won our own little Academy Awards for best actor,' said Farnsworth. 'Little did I dream that 20 years later, almost to the day, he would win the Academy Award. If I'd known, I would have passed out.'

Irrespective of his singing voice, Tom certainly made an impression in his one and only musical: 'I think it was probably after his third or fourth movie, his sister Sandra told *Première,* 'that my parents finally stopped referring to how good he was in *South Pacific.*'

Larry remembers being astonished at how impressive his kid brother was up on stage. 'It wasn't until we were in high school that I really had an inkling that he had any talent in that respect,' he said. 'It was when he was in *South Pacific* wearing an outfit with coconuts that it hit me. Before that I didn't even know he was interested in acting. His performance was so good that during the break everyone was talking about him. I remember thinking, "Well, there is something going on here." It really kind of blew me away. I knew he was dabbling in that sort of stuff, but I didn't know he was so serious about it.'

Did his first drama teacher know his lippy young pupil was bound for stardom? 'It crossed my mind,' said Farnsworth, 'but I had other students who I felt the same way about and they didn't do anything. I don't mean to put Tom down at all. He was just smart enough and did all the homework. And he must have had a terrific manager and agent. You have so many students that it is difficult to say who will make it and who won't. But Tom certainly went right to the top.

'And watching that ascent has been one of the biggest thrills of my life.'

Although Tom was the joker in the pack of students who hung around the drama department, it was his friend, John Gilkerson, who was widely thought to be the star-in-the-making. The talented, soft-spoken student was never in any doubt that his future lay in the stage.

'If I had to predict back then,' added Farnsworth, 'I would have expected John to have gone on to bigger acting roles than Tom. He was a tremendously gifted artist.'

It was Gilkerson who badgered Tom into joining Skyline's acting troupe and he kept cajoling his friend to keep involved in drama.

While drama had been fun and a good way to meet likeminded friends, it had never occurred to Tom that he might make a living from acting. Knowing the long hours his father had worked, he had no intention of following him into the catering trade. But, other than a life in the church, which he once considered and later rejected, he had no real clue what he was going to do with himself once his studies were over.

For now though, that wasn't a pressing problem. His bellman job gave him enough pocket money to keep him in petrol for his clapped-out VW and buy tickets to baseball games. And Amos's insistence that he continue his education gave him at least a couple of years reprieve from having to make any tough choices.

While his high school grades weren't bad, they weren't going to interest any Ivy League universities. So Tom signed on for two years at the Chabot Community College in nearby Hayward. Now back at home, although still generally at odds with his stepmother, Tom initially chose a smorgasbord of courses. As a treat to himself, he took one drama class a term.

Then one day he bumped into John Gilkerson, who was also going to Chabot. 'He asked me what I was doing with myself,' said Tom. 'I told him I was a bellman at a hotel and he said,

"Shame on you! You're not doing anything. You should try to do plays!"

'And that was really the beginning.'

The bug had already bitten. He had been going off to the theatre for months, seeing whatever production was being performed locally, from Shakespeare to Chekhov, at the American Conservatory Theater in San Francisco and the Berkeley Stage Company and the Berkeley Repertory Theater. Often, he would go alone, particularly when his friends were skiing or watching basketball games, two passions Tom never warmed to as a youngster. A devoted baseball fan – he loyally followed the Cleveland Indians team which became a national joke with its woeful record and even now makes a point of watching games at the nearest stadium when on location – he says he could never be bothered with a game where you can score 100 and still lose. And he was always more drawn to the beach than to the mountains.

He wouldn't take dates with him to the theatre. It became a ritual to drive there alone, buy his ticket, take his seat, read the programme from cover to cover and then immerse himself totally in the play. 'I spent a lot of time like that,' he recalled, 'seeing Brecht, Tennessee Williams, Ibsen and all that.'

At Chabot, it gradually dawned on Tom that this was something he wanted to do. Not only did it seem to fit his personality, he was really good at it. Early in 1975, he decided to audition for the school play, a production of Thornton Wilder's *Our Town*. He won the leading man role opposite fellow student Pamela Naibert, who played Emily Webb in the story of two turn-of-the-century New England families.

Apparently, Tom's chemistry with Pamela was a powerful portent of his celebrated partnership with the likes of Meg Ryan and Sally Field.

In Tom's first rave review in the college newspaper, the *Chabot Spectator,* stage critic Charles Sawyer wrote: 'Thom Hanks as

George Gibbs was convincing in a role that required him to be almost as decorous and virginal as Emily. Their best interaction together was undeniably the second act scene at the soda fountain. Talk about gentleness and warmth!'

That's not to say it went entirely without mishap. Sawyer went on: 'There were a few glaring foul-ups during the performance however, and they all seemed to be due to the confusion of the technical crew. Someone ought to take away their smocks for a week or until they promise to respond to the right cue with the right effect at the right time.

'But all-in-all, last Friday's performance of *Our Town* by the Chabot College Humanities Division was an enlightening and stunning treat. If you are the least bit sensitive to the human condition as interpreted by one of the foremost playwrights of all time, then DON'T MISS *OUR TOWN*.'

Thinking it was another acting class, Tom then signed up for lecturer Herb Kennedy's Drama in Performance class. He was surprised to discover the course was designed to encourage students to read play literature. In ten weeks, he saw five different types of theatre and found his calling.

He had already been to see Brecht's *The Good Person of Szechwan* and Albee's *Tiny Alice* when he was asked to read O'Neill's *The Iceman Cometh* in readiness for seeing the play. 'This,' he said later, 'was the big turning point.'

He told *Connoisseur* magazine in 1988: 'I literally couldn't wait to finish that play. I read the last page curled up on the front steps of my house. Then I went to see it at the Berkeley Repertory Theater – 150 seats, three-quarter staging. You were right on top of the stage, transported back to the Lower East Side of New York. 'This was the most magical thing that has ever happened to me. I came out of the theatre enthralled with what those people had done that night. Four hours of concentration. I had never seen that anywhere else.

'And I wanted to do something in the theatre, something as immediate and personal as that.'

'It was an epiphany moment for Tom,' said his old Chabot drama teacher Herb Kennedy, now retired and living in the Oakland area. 'When Tom came into the class, he really didn't know what it was about. But he stayed with it. He told me that after watching *The Iceman Cometh,* he knew that this was what he wanted to do.

'He was at Chabot for a relatively brief time. He did some backstage work and some acting. He's kept in touch over the years. The thing most of all about Tom, then and since, is that he is the original Mr Nice Guy. He is one of the few Hollywood big shots who you could say that about.

'A few years later, Tom got a job on a TV series called *Bosom Buddies*. But after the first season, the show was put on hold and I had the idea to bring Tom back to Chabot for a summer season to do *Charley's Aunt*. In the meantime, he had learned to juggle, so we worked that into *Charley's Aunt*. We had Tom up on stage juggling. 'He was great fun and a real professional.'

Now Tom was set on his path, he set out to graduate in drama at the Sacramento State University, about 60 miles from his home in Oakland, and the only higher-education institute he could get into where he could do plays. He never would get his degree, dropping out after one-and-a-half years – just six months from graduation – and has since turned down offers of an honorary degree. But he worked hard on the groundwork that would be so vital to his success as an accomplished, well-rounded actor.

Professor Larry Shumate taught two of Tom's classes. 'He was in my stagecraft group, which dealt with the building of sets, and theatre graphics, which involved things like set design and make-up.

'He was a typical student. In fact, he was a bit like the characters he played in his earlier roles. He was the class comic. He always had a quick comment or a joke. He had a buddy and the two of them used to play off each other all of the time. It's funny how things turn out. Tom made it – but his friend didn't.

'I know Tom was doing a lot of technical courses. He did lighting and acting classes. He has always remembered us very kindly and when I retired he sent me a very nice letter of thanks.'

For a while, Tom considered going into production and stage management rather than performing. After having worked backstage on several campus productions as a set builder, lighting technician and stage manager, however, he auditioned for and won a role in guest director Vincent Dowling's staging of Chekhov's *The Cherry Orchard*. Taken by the young actor's enthusiasm and intuitive understanding of his character, Dowling, then artistic director of the Great Lakes Shakespeare Festival in Cleveland, Ohio, recruited Tom in 1977 for the summer season.

'I think this is where he decided that this was his life's work,' said Bob Smart, another of Tom's old lecturers.

Tom is still remembered as the sound man who made all the stagehands laugh. The guy who hosted cast parties at his sparse midtown apartment on T Street, where he had a big sign reading 'Platypus Arms' hanging in the living room.

He was the theatre major who didn't particularly like school – a straight Bs student.

The only evidence that Tom ever acted in a university production is a photograph hanging in the hallway at the school's theatre arts department. Even then the picture of the 1976 cast of *Enrico Four* has a barely recognisable Hanks in the corner, with the brown hair and cap in blurry profile.

'Tom was a fresh-faced kid from Oakland and didn't want to act,' said his old friend Randy Fector. 'He wanted to teach dramatic art to kids – until he found out that it was possible to support himself acting.'

'I don't think Tom would have ever imagined he would become so successful,' said John Ickes, who runs his own PR firm and worked with Tom on the Civic Center's 1977 production of *The Cherry Orchard*.

'We used to talk about making it as an actor, about how hard it was going to be, and we talked a lot about money,' he added. 'Actors never have enough money.

'It couldn't have happened to a nicer guy. I will always remember Tom as a nice, funny guy who was always very professional. He did it because he loved the work.'

But as serious as he was about his chosen profession, Tom could still never resist a gag. Miriam Gray was auditioning with Tom for *The Cherry Orchard,* which was seen as a big deal at the time because an out-of-town director, Vincent Dowling, was in charge.

'Everybody was so serious,' said Miriam, who now owns an acting studio. 'Remember this was Chekhov, one of the big guys. We were all acting as if we were auditioning for the Royal Shakespeare Theatre, for God's sakes. We were so, so serious. Then Tom walks up the steps and pretends to trip. He hit himself and said, "Shake it off, don't get nervous." Everybody cracked up. He made fun of everybody being so serious. That was so Tom. He's a natural, a born stand-up comedian.'

Tom got the part of the manservant Yasha. In the opening night review, by *Sacramento Bee* critic William Glackin, he was described as making 'a valuable, clear-cut contribution'.

As well as performing, Tom also worked as an assistant stage manager, in charge of set design and construction. He once used a stapler to fix a broken strap on actress Phyllis Cupparo's platform shoes in the middle of *Death of a Salesman*. Moments before Cupparo was to head back on stage, Tom told her: 'If it breaks, that's OK. Play it.'

But Cupparo recalled: 'I was terrified. He could say that because he was a natural ad-libber, he was so quick. Anything could happen and he would go right along... I could not do that. Fortunately, the staple didn't come out.'

The TV culture Tom grew up with remained a major part of his life. Les Cockayne, a lighting and staff technician while Tom was at university, said: 'I remember he was running lights for a show and he was a Trekkie... You know, a *Star Trek* fan. Everything was, "Beam me up, Scotty," and that kind of stuff. It was funny when I saw his film, *Bachelor Party,* some years later. Tom was definitely *Bachelor Party.* He liked to have a good time.'

While the fledgling actor was putting in his groundwork, he also found a new social scene, which revolved around the drama department. Living away from home, he spent every spare moment in the student lounge nicknamed the Green Room, after the reception areas where actors and guests are entertained while they wait to go on TV shows.

Surrounded by 'luvvies' and drama queens, Tom was in his element. 'It was a place where everybody had an entrance, everybody was a star. It was a great mix of people,' he remembered.

There was one fellow student who especially caught Tom's eye. While he had settled quickly into his role as the Green Room joker, he found himself suddenly at a loss for words when theatre-studies student Susan Dillingham made her entrance.

Pretty and self-confident, Susan shared Tom's dreams of a life on the stage. It wouldn't be very long before they shared much more than that. College had been a happy playground where Tom was finally able to shed some of his loneliness and revel in the unconditional company of friends who asked nothing from him. After plucking up the courage to ask Susan out, Tom would soon discover that he must grow up very fast.

SIX

IN THE FAMILY WAY

SUSAN DILLINGHAM WAS the leading lady Tom had been searching for. For years he had been complaining to his friends that being funny never got him laid. With his bush of brillo-pad curls, his doughy face and tall, gangly frame, he was never going to be a stud. He would happily admit his sexual confidence was rated around rock bottom.

But at Sacramento, his personality all began to click into place with women. Suddenly, being funny was sexy. Then along came Susan, who was about to become the first of millions to discover Tom's talents as a leading man. What he lacked in rampant sex appeal, he more than made up for in a kind of trusting vulnerability – and, of course, in laughs.

In public, they were the perfect pair, hosting parties and living the student lifestyle to the max. In private, Susan offered Tom the stable relationship he had never before experienced with a woman. He had been taken away from his real mother and forced to live with two stepmothers. Now he chose to move in with Susan.

For a while it seemed that everything was going their way. Both were actors just starting out on their great adventure with dreams of Broadway, fame, fortune and, dare they admit it, Hollywood.

But halfway through their first year at university, the sky fell in. Susan realised as March turned into April in 1977 that her period was late. Her doctor soon confirmed her suspicions. She was pregnant with Tom's child. They were both 20 years old.

For Tom, it was as if he was reliving his parents' mistakes. Burdened by the toil of providing for his young family, Amos had forsaken his dreams to buckle down in the arduous catering trade. Just as he was certain what he wanted to do with his life, Tom feared he too would become too weighed down by responsibilities to succeed as an actor.

With Susan's profile swelling by the day, Tom took up director Vincent Dowling's offer to make some money that summer with the Great Lakes Shakespeare Festival in Cleveland, Ohio.

For the next three summers, Tom would return to Cleveland, paying his dues alongside other jobbing actors and actresses, winning his equity card and working as a paid, albeit poorly paid, performer.

After Tom's audition for *The Cherry Orchard* back in Sacramento, Dowling had been more impressed with Tom than he let on. 'When I came home that afternoon,' said the director, who now lives in Chester, Massachusetts, where he founded the Miniature Theater, 'I told my wife there was one kid there who had star quality.

'I said, "He's like a young Tony Curtis, but I think he has even more potential."'

'A friend of mine ran the Eaglet Theater in Sacramento and I had finished my second season as artistic and production director of the Great Lakes Shakespeare Festival and I was looking around America for promising young directors. He asked me to direct a play there and I agreed.

'To my horror, when I got there, he told me it was not a professional company but they were wonderful people from the university. I had a sinking feeling I can still remember now. But he was right. There was an extraordinary group of both faculty and students who had a lot of talent.

'Curiously enough, after I noticed the similarity with Tony Curtis, Tom went on to do *Bosom Buddies,* which was very much based around Tony Curtis's *Some Like it Hot.*

'Even before we started on the performance, I was very taken with Tom's presence and his understanding of the whole thing. It was that stance of his and his attitude.'

When he offered him an internship with his Cleveland-based company for the following summer, Dowling warned Tom there was little money in it for him.

'I told Tom, "In my view, it is the last form of legalised slavery. There is no money."'

'But Tom was not rich and he said he would need some money. I said there was housing and a stipend for food and the odd drink.'

Tom was not alone on his acting pilgrimage to Ohio. Six of his friends were also offered jobs as interns and they would all become quickly known in Cleveland as the 'Sacramento 7'.

'Tom was undoubtedly the leader of the whole group. Whatever he did would have to be the best,' said Dowling, who was himself an actor for 23 years with the Abbey Theatre in Dublin.

He also started a ritual at the opening party, where the whole company met together for the first time at a firehouse just outside Cleveland. 'Tom started the tradition of sliding down the fireman's pole, including doing it headfirst,' said Dowling. 'Tom kept everyone amused and kept morale up.

'At the end of the second season we did a benefit and we decided we would have an intern section. Tom came and he said he had an idea. It was for a court sketch all in rhyme. He put it all together himself, with a judge and jury and it was terrific – very funny, in rhyme and very fast.'

Tom played mostly small roles in a score of productions. Among the more showy parts were Grumio in *The Taming of the Shrew* and Proteus in *The Two Gentlemen of Verona,* for which he earned the Cleveland Critics Circle Award as best actor of the year in 1978. It was the last time Tom played anything remotely resembling a bad guy.

He also worked on the company's lighting and set crews.

Tom very quickly found himself a paid, professional actor. Dan Sullivan, who has directed some top Broadway shows, was directing *The Taming of the Shrew* for the company, but was having trouble finding anyone with the right comic skills to be cast as Grumio. As it would be necessary for the actor to tour with the show around Ohio after the summer season, whoever played the part would really need an Equity union card.

Said Dowling: 'Dan came to me and I said, "There is an intern here. I know he is something extraordinary and would be perfect for you. Will you at least audition him?"

'Well, he cast him and I knew that when the time came to tour I was going to have to either replace him or make him Equity. It was the only time in nine years I was there that I made an intern Equity.

'I knew he had star quality. I knew he was going to make it. He had that something special.'

Interns would help with the changeovers on stage and generally do odd jobs around the theatre which the professional actors would not do. On Tom's last night as an intern, the day before going on tour for the first time as a professional, he walked off stage at midnight and refused to help with his usual chores. 'He said, "I am an Equity actor now chaps, thank you very much,"' laughed Dowling. 'The next morning he was out there with his bags, waiting for the bus.'

Tom still has clear, fond memories of his time with the company.

'It was like learning to play the violin on a Stradivarius,' he said. 'This wasn't just singing and dancing. This was the Bard. It automatically gave me a professional attitude. You had to be disciplined. You had to do your homework.

'This was really my equivalent of being in the armed forces. A time when you just put your head down and did it until you said, "OK, now I'm done. I'm done here, thanks very much. I'm finished with this."'

After the first summer in 1977, Tom and Susan went back to university for the autumn term. But Tom, tiring of his studies and painfully aware of his looming financial responsibilities, dropped out to take an $800-a-month (£500) job as assistant stage manager at the Sacramento Civic Theater.

On 24 November 1977, Susan gave birth to a son, Colin.

With very little money, the couple managed to get by on Tom's meagre salary until the following summer, when the actor again headed for Cleveland.

Actor Holmes Osbourne, who was six years older than Tom, also starred in *The Two Gentleman of Verona,* and remembered sharing dingy motel rooms and cramped dressing quarters with his friend when they took the production on tour.

'Tom was so clean-living; he had no bad habits other than an addiction to peanut M&Ms. We were a pretty hard-drinking company, but Tom never drank, never even did tobacco.'

With a newborn baby at home in California, Tom could scarcely afford nights out on the town. But that didn't mean he had lost his sense of humour.

'Once I mentioned to Tom that I had played a role in a Navy recruiting film called *A Day in the Squadron*. So he snuck down to the Cleveland recruiting office and asked to see the film; then at a party he surprised me with this brilliant spoof of my entire performance. From that one viewing he had memorised my lines and my gestures.

'His sense of humour was what I enjoyed most,' added Osborne. 'It was always there – not in a frenetic Robin Williams way, but in a carefully calculated, mischievous way.'

Vincent Dowling remembered Tom and Osborne making a

dashing pair of young actors as they toured together on *The Two Gentlemen of Verona*. There would often be a crowd of young women waiting by the stage door, particularly after putting on shows for students.

There was one production at the Victory Theater in Dayton, Ohio, that still stands out in the director's mind. 'I shall never forget it,' he said, 'There were all these girls waiting outside after a student matinee and they were saying how wonderful Tom and Holmes were. Then one girl said to me, "We understood every word in the play today. But that's because you weren't doing it in Shakespeare, you were doing it in English." I thought that was a great tribute to the way they were able to bring it alive for young people.

'I have honestly never known a Shakespeare clown as brilliant as Tom.

'I have met few actors who have had the focus about their future that Tom had. It was not ruthless or damaging to anyone else. It was just his eyes set on the work to be done.

'My only complaint against him is that he has never come back to the theatre since his film stardom. The loss to Shakespeare is very considerable.'

There were still occasions, however, when the concentration slipped. The director recalled one time when an almost empty house at a theatre in America's Amish country led to the two leads 'messing around.'

'My wife was stage managing that season and she told me only recently that she went backstage and read the riot act to Tom and Holmes after the first act. They came out for the second act and were back to their normal, good performances. It was a lesson that Tom may well have remembered.'

The Cleveland company offered Tom the security of an acting 'family' where he could thrive. Once offstage, there were barbecues, parties, swimming in the lake, and the baseball games watching his beloved Cleveland Indians. Each year, the group would select a quiet pub and crowd it out for the whole summer season. The next year, another equally out-of-the-way hostelry would be chosen for an instant, but short-lived revival.

'I can still see Tom now, arranging a baseball game between the actors and the techies. It's as clear as if it was yesterday,' said Vincent Dowling.

After the 1978 summer season, Tom decided that another winter in Sacramento had little more to offer. Friends he had met in Cleveland suggested that he try New York, where he could get work with the Riverside Shakespeare Company. After a long talk with Susan, they decided to try their luck in the Big Apple, hoping that the greater opportunities would give Tom his big break. Their savings amounted at that time to a grand total of $35.

A more obvious starting point would have been Hollywood, but coming from Northern California he confessed to 'an inbred hatred' of Los Angeles. Tom thought he would disappear in LA and vowed never to move there unless he had a job waiting for him. 'We always said LA was like San Jose except 16 times as large, so there was no reason to go there unless you wanted to work in a bank or wait tables. Which I never had to do.'

So New York it was. Tom sold his beloved Volkswagen and hitched a ride east with fellow company member Michael John McGann in November 1978, just after Colin's first birthday, with the idea of finding a flat and sending for his wife and child. For a few weeks, he slept on the couch in McGann's large, busy apartment. 'He was heavenly,' recalled McGann, an actor who still lives in Brooklyn, New York: 'He was and still is the kindest man I have ever met.'

But life wasn't easy in New York for a young family without a job. They moved into a small, roach-infested walk-up tenement close to the railway in the notorious Hell's Kitchen neighbourhood – with no carpet or linoleum on the floor, just bare boards – and

Tom set out on his quest for work. It was only through the good graces of his bosses in Cleveland that he was able to survive at all through those first few months.

'The nicest thing they did was when I left,' he said. 'I had already been to New York and wanted to get back there because of some possibilities, but I needed to draw unemployment to live.

'But to get unemployment insurance, I couldn't quit. So I told them, "You have to fire me." They said, "You've done a lot for us. You're fired." It was a very nice thing they did for me.'

For months, Tom doggedly made the rounds of auditions for countless roles in theatre, television and films. Tom had his Equity union card, allowing him to work as an actor, but, having fallen pregnant, Susan didn't get the chance to win her card, which effectively barred her from getting any work.

Through 1979, they eked out a living, managing to pay their $285-a-month rent thanks mainly to unemployment cheques and the occasional cash-in-hand job. Things got so bad at one point that Tom's sister, Sandra, cashed in some coke bottles to get $20 to send to her beleaguered brother.

Said Tom: 'I got $25 once for doing a play at the City Court Building – after rehearsing for four weekends.'

'We were young and impetuous. It was a fervent time,' Tom told *Première* magazine. 'It was also real hairy. It was just the greatest thing that our son was healthy because if he had got sick – if we'd had to take him to a clinic – that just would have been hell. We didn't have the money.'

But he added: 'It made us have a certain amount of stick-to-itiveness. If I hadn't been married and had a family – well, then I could have done anything I wanted to. As it was, it was like, 'Okay, here it is: here's your living situation, here's the amount of time we're going to have to invest in it – and let's not complain!

'We have nowhere else to go and we couldn't if we wanted to.'

On the same theme, Tom told *Playboy*: 'It was a war of survival, really. I was a kid who had never been in such a big city before. I was on unemployment and trying to act. This went on for two years.'

Desperately needing work to pay the bills, the situation became so dire that Tom would take all of his money from the bank, about £60 ($100), and drive from city to city looking for work outside Manhattan, going for acting jobs that nobody else wanted. 'Sometimes I'd wake up at night,' he said, 'and I would go into the bathroom, look at myself in the mirror and think, "What's happened to me? My career is over before it's begun."'

By now, Susan was also looking for work using her stage name Samantha Lewes. Irish actress Bairbra Dowling had been in *The Cherry Orchard* back in Sacramento with Tom and had also been a member of the Cleveland company, where her father, Vincent, was the boss. Bairbra then went to live in the same area of Hell's Kitchen in New York to join the audition queues with Tom. 'We were all in the Clinton area. We were on 43rd and I think Tom and Samantha were on 45th. They were pretty awful apartments. All I can remember about Tom's was that it was pretty dark.

'There was a whole group of us and ours was kind of the most admired apartment. But our only furniture was a foam mattress: My sister and I would baby-sit for Tom and Samantha. We called ourselves the spinster aunts.

'We were all unemployed and looking for work. At that time, everyone had high hopes for the future. The world was ahead of us, even though money was short.

'Tom and Samantha were the only ones in the group who had a child, so it was tough for them. They weren't going out gallivanting like we were.

'But we would have Sunday brunches together and dinner parties and that kind of thing. After he got the part of *Bosom Buddies* he would come and visit, but we lost touch over the years, although strangely enough his daughter now goes to the same school as my daughter, so I see him there occasionally.

'He was so fun and great to be around, He was always so positive and lively.'

But even then, Tom would remain slightly apart, as if he cherished the sense of loneliness he had always carried with him as a form of protection. It was a shield that even his closest friends were aware of.

Bairbra, for instance, remembered: 'He was private. I don't think any of us really got to know him.'

After slogging around hundreds of auditions, Tom developed a defence mechanism – by appearing not to care too much whatever the outcome. He would appear so nonchalant and casual, and would try so hard *not* to be seen to be trying too hard that he would wreck his own chances. 'People hate you when you do that,' he said.

The pressures were beginning to get to Tom and, for a while at least, he couldn't see a way out of the depressing spiral he had become caught in. He would admit to *Evening Outlook* many years later: 'I have periods when the black dog follows me around and I can't shake him off, no matter how hard I try. I am a pessimist, pure and simple. I guess it is based on experience, on a certain amount of wisdom you acquire by the school of hard knocks. You always expect everything to stink to high heaven. That way you don't get disappointed.'

But just as his father had before him, Tom kept moving. He returned to Cleveland in the summer of 1979 to play a small role in *Othello* and portrayed the playwright Harold Pinter in another play. But he didn't feel he was being offered enough roles and went back to New York, where he finally landed a $800 (£500) part for three days work as a murderer in the independent slasher film *He Knows You're Alone*.

The breakthrough, small as it was, came while he was acting in a very off-Broadway comic stage production of Machiavelli's *The Mandrake*. 'One of the girls in the production knew a manager who was looking for someone,' said Tom. 'I went up and had a marathon meeting with him. He said, "I am going to send you out and get some feedback," which he did. I met a variety of agents and he called me up the next day and we solidified our business relationship. Then I finished my last season at the Great Lakes, which I had signed for previously. After I got back, there was this motion picture epic called *He Knows You're Alone*. It was one of those hack-and-slash movies they made out on Staten Island for about 40 bucks.'

Tom was eighth down the bill. 'It may have been bad, but it was the first job I had wearing regular pants, as opposed to sword belts, leather jerkins and sandals,' he said.

A poor relative of teen horror flicks like *Halloween* and *Friday the 13th*, the film included the obligatory multiple murders and a Psycho-style shower scene. The main storyline twist seemed to be that the killer had a penchant for killing pretty young girls as they were having sex.

Tom, as Elliot, bypassed all the gore and nudity, playing a student who escorts a couple of girls to a carnival and lectures them about the dangers of the human mind. He didn't hold his breath waiting for glowing reviews for his first movie. Kevin Thomas, in the *Los Angeles Times,* was fairly typical when he wrote: 'Standard, grisly rampaging killer fare... That people should pay money to see such films is ridiculous when you think about it.'

The manager who helped Tom get the small part was his new manager Simon Maslow, who did the rounds of agents and executives trying to get work for his keen young client.

But not everyone shared his belief in the Californian actor without the sunshine tan, muscles or looks. Johnnie Planco, then a rising agent at William Morris, remembers meeting Tom in the late seventies. He told *People:* 'Tom came in. He had long hair like an Afro and his skin wasn't in great shape. His teeth were not great. I was not impressed. When he came in, I couldn't get him to talk.'

At Maslow's urging, Planco gave Tom a second chance. 'And

Tom was more charming,' he recalled. 'But I still said, "I don't think so," since he's starting from ground zero.'

Although Planco would later represent Tom for William Morris, the first agency to sign him up was the J. Michael Bloom Agency in Los Angeles, which also helped launch the careers of Sigourney Weaver, Alec Baldwin, Macauley Culkin, Kathleen Turner and Wesley Snipes. Even then, the agency initially thought of Tom as a character actor, rather than a leading man.

On 4 January 1980, when Colin was two, Tom and Susan wed at the Church of the Holy Apostles.

While his part in the low-budget film marked a minor breakthrough in his career, the first sign that all was not well at home came when he started dabbling secretly in drugs.

There was no shortage of any kind of drug imaginable in Manhattan in the late '70s and early '80s, particularly in the entertainment world. Many clubs, and even some bars, would have people snorting openly on tables. Showbiz parties were awash with cocaine. It was the peak of the Studio 54 era where even out-of-work actors were expected to pep up their lives with some kind of stimulant.

Tom had been around drugs in the theatre since college days, but always said no. Even in New York, he showed no obvious interest, particularly as he was all too aware that smoking pot 'just made me the stupidest human being in the world'.

But unbeknownst even to his closest friends, Tom was dulling his unhappiness and frustration with the use of both marijuana and cocaine. It was, he admits, the most serious kind of drug taking.

'The nature of the drugs I did was a closet kind of thing,' he confessed in 1994. 'It was surreptitious.'

But the perils of his situation soon dawned on Tom. He continued: 'I realised rather early on that I couldn't do that. I thought, I can't be a responsible parent and do this. This has got to stop. This is not good... You can't hide behind the conviviality of it all. It put not just me, but all the people I loved in a degree of danger. So it became pretty easy to say, "No more."'

Then, just as it seemed the rounds of auditions were leading in an ever-decreasing circle of failure, a scout for the American ABC television network saw something he liked in the cocky young actor's everyman charm. In June 1980, he invited Tom to the dreaded Los Angeles to try out for roles in a number of new projects the station had in pre-production, including the pilot for the proposed series *Bosom Buddies,* a situation comedy about two philandering advertising copywriters who dress in drag in order to live in a low-rent hotel for women.

Tom caught the eye of Joyce Selznick, niece of legendary studio boss David Selznick, and the show's producers decided to take a chance on him, pairing him up with another young actor, Peter Scolari, and the first episode was screened in the United States in November 1980.

With his wife and child in tow, Tom switched coasts with the prospect of settling down for his first steady job.

At 23, he was suddenly earning close to $9,000 (£5,500) an episode. 'There was no reason to hire me,' said Tom, 'I made more money in two weeks than I had my whole career.'

But it was almost over before it began. For just as Tom arrived in Los Angeles, the Screen Actor's Guild and the American Federation of Television and Radio Artists called their members out on strike. As the dispute lingered on with the actor's unions holding firm on their pay demands, it seemed likely that the network would pull the plug on *Bosom Buddies.*

Tom was philosophical in public, joking that it allowed him more time to settle in with his young family. Privately, he was crestfallen that he had come so far, only to be knocked back once again by bad timing and the cruel hand of fate.

Fortunately, the two sides settled before *Bosom Buddies* was jeopardised and Tom went back to work.

The wacky premise for the show was explained by the spoken introduction that played over the opening credits. Tom was Kip and Scolari played his friend, Henry.

Henry: When we first moved to New York we had a great apartment that was dirt cheap.

Kip: And we found out why it was so cheap.

Henry: Our friend Amy said there was a great apartment in her building.

Kip: Dirt cheap – but it's a hotel for women. OK. We made one adjustment.

Henry: *Now* these other ladies know us as Buffy and Hildegarde.

Kip: But they also know us as Kip and Henry, Buffy and Hildy's brothers.

Henry: This experience is gonna make a great book.

Kip: See? It's all perfectly normal.

It wasn't exactly Shakespeare, but it was a regular, high-profile job at a very opportune time.

Working for the first time on TV was another valuable lesson for Tom. He said: '*Bosom Buddies* was great because it made us very fast. The whole thing was delivering the goods as best you could. If you couldn't deliver them good, you had to deliver them bad, as long as you delivered them. It's flying by the seat of your pants. You ask as many questions as you can, but eventually it's "Never mind, just do it." You can't be lazy. It became our whole life. We did so much of it in such a short time, it all blends. We were always working under some weird time frame. I can never remember now whether we were on that show for seven weeks or seven years. It was a dense, dense time.'

Scolari, who later went on to star in American TV hit shows such as *Newhart* and the small screen version of *Honey, I Shrunk the*

Kids, hit it off with Tom right away. 'Tom and I hooked up pretty quickly,' he said. 'We were very close in age and experience. We went out that first day and talked about our fathers and our lives. For the next two years we were virtually inseparable.

'We drove to work together every day because we lived within a half mile of each other and his wife needed his car. So I would pick Tom up and we would talk all the way to work and all the way home. And we became – we've often said this – closer friends than the characters we portrayed.'

As his fame grew, Tom's co-stars would often speak of his thoughtfulness and sensitivity in sometimes difficult situations. Scolari remembers a classic Hanks gesture.

He said: 'I went through one very difficult week of being asked to wear bikini briefs for this sequence where he would rip off this towel that I was wearing coming out of the shower, and then make fun of me. And Tom, bless his heart, knowing the kind of humiliation that was there for me, because it was kind of a beefcake effect they were playing with me, because at the time I still had an athletic build – Tommy, in front of the whole audience had gone and gotten a pair of the same briefs and came out in them in the next scene, doing some kind of hilarious Tarzan yell.

'At that moment I thought, Well this is a guy that I could live with on this series for the next ten years because he cares and he's willing to make me laugh when he knows how much that whole scene embarrassed me. Of course, for weeks after that he would insist on wearing bikini briefs in any scene that required it.'

Tom added: 'We were always having to do something that embarrassed us. Meanwhile the writers were sitting around laughing uproariously at our horrible predicaments. And we finally realised. This is going out to six million people. At least Peter looked good in his bikini then.'

Actress Donna Dixon, who also starred in the show and went

on to marry comedy star Dan Aykroyd, said: 'I was always in awe of Tom's comic timing and physicality. Working with him became play. He could do anything. He is always very positive and supportive, which makes a big difference. There are some great actors out there who have troubled personalities. Tom gives you everything.'

Although it got fairly good ratings, boosted by its position in the TV line-up right after the popular *Mork and Mindy,* which starred Robin Williams, the series was cancelled after just two seasons.

A *TV Guide* review summed up the reaction of the critics: 'Watching these two mince around in frocks is most of the fun in this little pastiche, but the boys are funny about it. Scolari in his Hildegarde disguise is a dithery dear who says "clappy as a ham", when she means "happy as a clam". Hanks in his Buffy getup is more like a female moose in distress and even more preposterous. The idea that anyone could be fooled by their female impersonations requires a prodigious suspension of disbelief, but I'll make the effort if you will.'

The last of 39 shows was aired in 1982, and, although ABC received 35,000 letters of protest, it never resurfaced. But *Bosom Buddies* effectively launched Tom into the big time and has a cult following in the US that still reveres the show today and still puts it among the actor's best comic work.

One of the guest stars, incidentally, was a young actress called Rita Wilson, of whom we will hear more of later.

Although Tom looks back on the series with affection, he is critical of his own behaviour at the time, admitting that his sudden success went to his head.

'When you're one of the guys in a show, something does happen to you; you do get an over inflated sense of your own importance,' he told *Première.*

With embarrassment, he remembers greeting the show's guest stars with jumped-up snobbery. 'It's like you are minister of architecture or something: "How nice to see you, please do as you are told, we hope you are funny, and please keep with us. And you'll be gone on Friday as soon as we are finished."

'You think you know all the answers,' he adds. 'You don't even know the fucking questions.'

It would be Tom's one and only TV sitcom. 'It was like going to an aeroplane factory every day,' he said. 'You go into a big hangar and build a plane and every Friday it has to fly. Unfortunately, sometimes the wings fell off.'

By now living in California's San Fernando Valley, Tom's short-lived TV fame, even if he was wearing a dress for most of it, had helped bring in more offers of work. The cancellation of *Bosom Buddies* coincided with the birth of Tom and Susan's second child, Elizabeth, on 17 May 1982. But there was no need to worry. The family would never again know the poverty of those early days in New York. As Tom had predicted, he would not have to wait tables or work in a bank in the world's movie mecca.

He found fairly steady employment as a supporting player in various episodes of the series *Taxi* (starring Danny DeVito and Marilu Henner), *The Love Boat* and *Family Ties*. He also starred in *Mazes and Monsters,* a made-for-television film about a fantasy game gone wrong that was first screened by the American CBS network on 28 December 1982.

The film centred on the pre-Nintendo game of Dungeons and Dragons, where the players would take on the identities of heroes and villains in a complicated board game adventure. In the early '80s, there were numerous news reports of participants getting carried away with the game, blurring fantasy with reality, sometimes with tragic consequences.

Playing Robbie Wheeling, a student who loses himself – and his mind – in the game, Tom used his own experiences playing Dungeons and Dragons, saying: 'I had a perception of the game that people who haven't played it wouldn't have. If you have a particularly vivid imagination, it can be quite scary. The deeper, darker demons we all have inside us can really come to the forefront.'

The role won Tom tempered praise and was a step up from the sitcom silliness of *Bosom Buddies*.

This *Entertainment Weekly* review was fairly typical: 'In this silly made-for-TV drama about fantasy role-playing adventures, Hanks plays a neurotic college kid who "flips into the game" and becomes convinced he really is "Pardieu, the Holy Man". He almost keeps a straight face too.'

But it was a one-off appearance on *Happy Days*, starring Henry Winkler and Ron Howard, which was to have the most fortuitous effect on his future. Tom played a youngster the Fonz had pushed out of a swing during childhood and who had returned as a judo black belt to claim his revenge. The episode had particularly tickled Howard, the show's Richie Cunningham, who found Tom's antics refreshing and hilarious.

It wasn't until two years later that Tom's agent got a call from Howard, then trying to make a break into directing major movies, and with two small pictures to his credit. Howard had remembered Tom from *Happy Days* and from the actor's extracurricular appearances on the show's softball team. He now wondered if Tom was interested in testing for a role in the upcoming film, *Splash*, which he was helming for Disney.

Initially, Tom auditioned for the part of the libidinous Freddie, which later went to the late John Candy. But Howard was captivated by the boy-next-door charm that would become Tom's trademark in a string of subsequent movies and he deemed it ideally suited for his leading man, Allen Bauer, the addled New York produce manager who falls in love with a mermaid.

That is not to say he was the first to be asked. A whole bevy of stars – including the big names of the day, Dudley Moore, Burt Reynolds, Chevy Chase and Michael Keaton – had already turned the part down. According to Howard's partner, Brian Grazer, they were 'looking for someone who had leading-man qualities – he could kiss the girl and drive a story. At the same time we wanted someone who was funny, but not quirky or eccentric in his comedy. And that was really hard to find.'

Grazer added: 'Tom came in wearing these 501 Levi's and construction boots and a T-shirt. He wasn't nervous at all – and here's a guy who had never had a major movie. I thought, 'Why is this guy so calm?' But we read him and we liked him and we hired him right away.'

The plot was pure Disney. As a boy, Allen Bauer had been rescued by a mermaid after falling off a Cape Cod ferry, but had persuaded himself over the years that he must have imagined it. Twenty years later, he is again saved from drowning by the same mermaid, who follows him to Manhattan, where, after dispensing with utensils to eat lobster, shell and all, in a restaurant, she is eventually captured and imprisoned in an oversized fish tank

There is, naturally, a happy ending with Tom and Daryl Hannah swimming off into the sunset together.

It may have been Tom's first major film. But the $80,000 pay cheque, although considerably more than anything he had ever seen before, was still a long way from the big leagues. At this point, Burt Reynolds was in the $5 million league, and Marion Brando was paid $2 million for a cameo.

And the initial buzz in Hollywood was not particularly hot for the film, a mermaid movie for Disney being directed by Ron 'Richie Cunningham' Howard. But on its release early in 1984, the romantic fantasy became one of the surprise hits of the year, grossing more than $69 million at the US box office and making another newcomer, mermaid Daryl Hannah, an instant superstar: It would also become a huge draw on video and ultimately grossed more than $120 million.

Although his understated role was somewhat overlooked by the critics, Tom was described in *New York* magazine as 'an expert comic' who was also able 'to command the emotional centre of his scenes'.

In *Newsweek,* critic David Ansen said Tom 'seemed disappointingly bland at first glance,' but he soon began to pick up 'sly comic edges' in the actor's performance that reminded him of 'all-American boys with mischief inside'.

Despite his outward cockiness, Hanks later confessed he began filming totally in awe of his co-stars John Candy and Eugene Levy 'because they're very, very funny guys. But my job in *Splash* was not to be particularly funny. That's what Ron kept drilling into me.' Howard also helped Tom learn another valuable lesson when the actor turned up on the set one day knowing neither the production schedule nor his part in a major scene.

'It took longer to shoot than it should have, and when we were done with the scene, Ron said, "You know, you should have been a little more prepared." He didn't yell at me. He probably knew that if he had yelled, I'd be paste for the rest of the day. He just let me know in no uncertain terms that I was starring in this movie and with that comes huge responsibilities, and one of them is to be ready to go. I've never forgotten that,' said Tom.

Although the critics may not have singled him out for adulation, the film industry certainly took note of his pivotal performance.

Tom emerged from *Splash* with a career momentum that, despite a number of false starts, would eventually carry him right to the top.

He was on his way. Hollywood was a long way from Cleveland – and certainly paid better than the Bard. Especially when you have just chalked up a bona fide blockbuster. 'Suddenly, here was this tidal wave of people saying very nice things about me and wanting me to be in their movies,' said Tom.

There was only one problem. While his acting career was all coming together, Tom's marriage was falling apart.

SEVEN

PLAYING THE BAD GUY

IT WAS PERHAPS Tom's most unlikely role. The Bad Guy. But this was no film part. It was real life. And the person doing the casting was his wife.

With the success of *Splash,* the actor took on a slew of projects, all offering good money and, invariably, bad scripts. As a result, Tom was spending less and less time at home with his wife and young family. The times he was not working were punctuated by angry rows that had grown in conjunction with his salary.

Susan, under her stage name of Samantha Lewes, was trying to get a foothold as an actress, but with two children to care for and a husband who was away for long stretches at a time on location, it was difficult to get work. While the pressures of the 'year-and-a-half of scary days' in New York had drawn the couple together, it was dawning on the one-time college sweethearts that all the money and success in the world wasn't going to make them any happier together.

'I was so young and determined to establish a beachhead in the entertainment world. I just wish I had been as good a father the first time as I am now,' Tom said in 1998. 'Fatherhood passed me in a blur because I was so busy working and trying to pay the rent.'

Ten years earlier, he had told *Gentleman's Quarterly*: 'I don't think you can have children at an early age and enjoy them the way they are enjoyed on fucking TV commercials. It was the same for my father.'

Still haunted by his own fractured childhood and his fear of following in his parent's much-married footsteps, Tom was determined to try and make the marriage work. After moving to California, Tom took a hiatus from his burgeoning film career to set up a one-woman showcase for Susan, building all the sets, doing the publicity and helping with rehearsals.

Splash was the number one movie in America, and friends fully expected Tom to bathe in his success and try and capitalise on his good fortune. But Hollywood's newest leading man could be found backstage at Los Angeles' Gene Dynarski Theater, manhandling scenery and sticking together the props. Susan was both producing and acting in *Passing Game* by writer Steve Tesich, and Tom was eager to help make the project a success.

He explained to *Drama-Logue* magazine in 1984: 'The reason I got involved was because of the impetus of my wife, Samantha [Susan's stage name]. We had always been desirous to get into the producing aspect of theatre, so this has been a learning by doing situation. We are already talking about two other projects we want to get evolving.

'Sam has a supporting role in this and she swears she will never produce anything and be in it again. She says the pressures are just too great on both sides.

'Listen, it's been an experience for both of us. I have been either driving a truck or pounding nails or sweeping up sawdust. I don't know if I can actually answer the question of why we are doing this. I don't know if I actually know. I think it goes back to the time that we were studying theatre and we all thought it would be great if we could have our own space and do the plays we wanted to do with our friends in them.'

For all their work together, the theatre partnership never really got off the ground. There were already too many holes in their marriage and by the beginning of 1985, they both realised the charade was over.

The couple's new £1 million home on Addison Street in North Hollywood was filled with angry voices. Like his father before him, Tom felt a strong urge to pack up and move on, to try again. He had an advantage over Amos that in acting he had chosen a career where escape from reality was a prerequisite for success. In throwing himself headlong into his work, he was able to either feed off his frustrations, or at least to hide from there for a little while. The cracks, however, continued to widen. It was an unhappy period for everyone in the family. There was never any question that both parents loved their children with all their hearts. Like so many young couples who commit to each other, for whatever reason, before they are truly ready, it was just too much, too soon. After a doomed attempt to patch up the marriage in the summer, Susan filed for divorce in October 1985.

And then things began to get ugly. It was a long, drawn-out, bitter divorce battle with both sides wrangling over money, custody of the children and even taking out restraining orders against each other at one point.

It is not a time in his life Tom likes to talk about to anybody, let alone in interviews, and he has long since made his peace with Susan and their two children. But the bulky divorce file, number D152300, lodged at Los Angeles Superior Court offers a fascinating insight into the other, more testy, side of America's favourite Mr Nice Guy.

It would be almost four years before the Hankses were officially divorced. The dispute became so bitter at one stage that Susan asked for a restraining order against Tom and told the court in written evidence: 'My husband has repeatedly verbally abused and humiliated me during the past 90 days in my home. This caused me to suffer great emotional distress.'

There was never any suggestion of physical violence, but feelings ran so high that an order was made barring both of them from molesting, attacking, striking, threatening or otherwise disturbing the peace of the other. It may have been legalese, but it illustrates just how much their relationship had deteriorated.

They couldn't even agree on the date of the split. A trial brief filed in February, 1987, by Tom's Los Angeles lawyers, describes both how the marriage finally ended and how the two parties differed over the date.

The divorce document tells how the couple split and lived apart after Susan asked Tom to leave and demanded that he told Colin that the marriage was over in February 1985. After living with a friend for a few days, Tom moved into the Sheraton Universal Premier Hotel in Studio City, Los Angeles.

They never resumed the marital relationship despite two attempts that summer to patch up their differences.

The first, explains the brief, was when Tom and Susan stayed together in a New York hotel room for five days. The second was when Tom moved back into the family home in Los Angeles for less than a week.

Any remaining thoughts of a reconciliation were dashed after Susan went to Chicago with the children and the couple had a 'bitter argument'.

The reason for the date dispute was that Tom had made two movies that year, a fact that would affect Susan's divorce pay-off. If the marriage was officially deemed over in February, it would mean the considerable fees Tom received for the two films wouldn't necessarily be involved in the final settlement.

Susan's lawyer hit back, claiming in a written declaration that the actor 'apparently is attempting to substitute over-cleverness and misinformation for the candour and professional disclosure properly required to remove surprise and encourage settlement.'

As the case dragged on, both sides fired broadsides at one another. In a court declaration, Susan complained that Tom 'refused to grant me any additional time to complete my trial preparation.' She continued:

'One of the things Tom now seeks is to take my deposition, in Los Angeles, for a second time in this proceeding, ostensibly for the limited purpose of inquiring about my recent return to the theatre, which Tom knows is the very reason why I am not now available for further deposition.

'As I expressly told Tom, I presently am living in Sacramento where I am in continuous rehearsal for a lead role in a series of theatrical productions of the Sacramento Theater Company.

'The shows now in rehearsal are essentially two person works with no understudies. My absence would, in effect, shut down rehearsals.

'Moreover, there is no need to depose me now. Tom knows as much as I do about my theatrical return. In addition, my counsel already has offered to provide to Tom under oath by written interrogatories whatever information he requires about my present employment and living arrangements.

'I reasonably believe that Tom's attempt now to depose me is designed to harass and upset me at a time when I should be focusing all of my energies on my job, in an effort to return to the theatrical world and, in addition, to divert my lawyer's time and energies from proper preparation for trial on my behalf.

'I respectfully request that the court grant a protection order to prevent Tom from moving forward with his eleventh discovery.'

Tom in turn claimed his wife was delaying the trial 'merely to harass me and try to squeeze an unfair settlement out of me'.

When Susan tried to put off the divorce hearing for four months, Tom complained in a declaration:

'I am a highly compensated actor. The entertainment industry requires actors at my level to make commitments for work in films and television far in the advance of the anticipated starting date.

'Petitioner and I were informed in early October that our trial would proceed on January 13, 1987. My present schedule is such that I am available for trial in January and February: I committed myself to begin a major film project in March. My involvement in this project is expected to last for two months. In addition, I have another work commitment that should end in May or June. Additional obligations past June are likely.

'If this court grants petitioner's motion for a continuance, then petitioner has effectively prevented me from earning money and making further work commitments. A trial after June will be at the expense of a work opportunity. Petitioner can then trade my unavailability for work against her seeking an unfair settlement. This is not just a theoretical concern. This dissolution has been a cloud on my career. I agreed to settle this case twice – each time mare favourably for the petitioner. Each time, petitioner's counsel argued that it was cheaper for me to pay petitioner more money rather than let this matter interfere with my work. Apparently, petitioner believes that this is such a good tactic that she is utilising the tactic once again.'

'Our lives must go on. Petitioner must be restrained from using court delays to harass me and to seek an economic advantage.

'Petitioner knows that any continuance will restrict my ability to pursue my career and earn a living. Nonetheless, after nearly two years of separation, over $80,000 worth of attorney's bills incurred by the petitioner's first attorney, depositions, document productions, answers to interrogatories and two settlements, petitioner now wants to continue the trial.'

Things really began to get ugly when it was time to try and divide Tom's by now considerable assets. Susan felt that her husband was trying to cut her out of some of his film fortune and bully her into accepting his demands.

In written evidence, Susan said:

'Respondent is a motion picture actor who has earned in excess of $2,000,000.00 during the current calendar year. There is at present in excess of $800,000 in cash and negotiable securities such as certificates of deposit in respondent's possession and in our corporation, Radioland Pictures Inc.

'My husband has stated to me during the past sixty days that if I did not accede to certain demands of his I would receive no community property or support.

'The above comprises a substantial portion of our community estate. If my husband is not restrained regarding the disposition of said assets and if I am not given possession of one-half thereof, it is my belief my interest herein will be dissipated and lost.

'I am informed and believe that respondent is planning to deposit or cause to be deposited approximately $150,000.00 of community property in a retirement plan for the benefit of respondent only. I have not been consulted in this regard. If said proceeds or any portion there are deposited immediate access to said funds at the time of trial herein will effectively be denied me and I may then be required to accept an interest in the said plan which would, in my opinion, be detrimental to my financial needs.'

The other major bane of contention was custody of the two children. By January 1987, the warring couple were communicating through their lawyers. A flurry of letters underlined the animosity.

The letters revolved around Susan's decision to move to Sacramento with the children, where she had found work with the Sacramento Theater Company. It was a move Tom claimed he only learned of after going to pick up the children from school in Los Angeles and discovering they weren't there.

Susan's decision to relocate to the other side of the state did not sit well with Tom, who instructed his lawyers to complain that he hadn't been consulted and to tell her he would be prepared to care for the children while their mother worked in Sacramento.

Susan said that at the beginning of 1987 Tom was already earning $1,750,000 'for a single motion picture appearance'. She insisted Tom should pay her enough support 'for a sufficient time to allow her to return and establish herself in the entertainment community which she left during the marriage to raise the parties' children and devote her energies to furthering Tom's career. Tom, of all people, knows that this is something which generally cannot be accomplished in a few months, or even a few years. Indeed, even Tom who is somewhat of an overnight success, struggled for many years before he was able to earn a reasonable living wage as an actor.'

The final paragraph underlines how bad relations between the couple had become.

'Permanent restraining orders prohibiting Tom from harassing or disturbing Susan's peace should here be issued, along with orders prohibiting each party from in any way disparaging the other in front of the minor children.'

Despite all Tom's fears that his marriage would follow the pattern set by his parents, the final settlement resulted inevitably in the children's time being divided between their parents, just as his own had been. He admitted to *Playboy:* 'We married young. We had a child. That was the last thing either of us needed, and yet there was the fact of the matter...

'It was a college relationship. I was going off to work in the theatre, but when my son was born, we decided to give it a shot and marry.

'Look, I was doing just a version of what my parents had done and what all of our parents had done. We tried. I was married for five years.'

Tom remained, however, fiercely protective of his children, particularly as his fame grew. 'You see these gossamer little creatures being born, and then you see them learn,' he told *GQ*. 'We all learn through disappointment. You think this guy at school is your best friend, and then he sticks a pencil in your neck one day and you can't figure out why, and you start to notice all the cruelty that goes down.

'I take my kids to Disneyland and we're standing in line, and some people come up to us, people from Oklahoma, "Hey, y'all, when yer in Oklahoma, come on and stay with us, we got a spare room, putcha up nice." And then they touch my kids. They touch my kids. Fuck it! That's beyond the realm: I'm waiting to see *Dumbo* and these people are touching my kids. What am I supposed to say, 'Don't touch my kids'? I have to protect them. Maybe I go overboard because I am not there all the time. They're innocent. I have to give them a fighting chance, have to make things as normal as possible.'

In the end, Tom and Susan settled things as best they could. It wasn't ideal, but Tom tried to see Colin and Elizabeth as much as possible.

He was granted the right to have the children on alternate weekends, between close of school on the Friday to 6.00pm on the Sunday evening, with the proviso they could stay until school on

Monday as long as he gave Susan enough notice. He was allowed to see them a number of weekdays a month after school and for five consecutive weeks in the summer holidays. In odd-numbered years, they spent Christmas with their father and on even-numbered years he had them for Easter. He also had them for his birthday, Father's Day and the Fourth of July celebrations.

When the court battle was finally over, Tom agreed to fork out about £8,000 a month to his wife plus more than £600 for each of the children. Tom took the two family Volkswagens, a 1986 Jetta and a 1983 Vanogon, while Susan drove off with the 1980 Volvo Turbo Sedan. Susan was to stay in the house on Addison with the children.

The settlement, when it came, ended one of the most painful chapters of Tom's life. In time, the deep rift driven between Tom and Susan would heal. Like divorced couples around the world, they learned to make their new relationship work for the good of their children.

Tom had little to draw on from his own upbringing in attempting to help his own children best deal with the break-up. His father, after all, had never discussed his divorces with his children and had never offered any explanations.

In 1994, Tom told *Vanity Fair*: 'I explained it to my son the best I knew how, but it was a hideous process. It was a nightmare. It was terrible... oh terrible.

'Their mother and I don't talk a lot any more, but we're very respectful of each other. I wouldn't say we're friends, or even friendly. But we are very respectful of each other's place and position. All that other stuff that can go along with it? It has not existed. I see my kids at my leisure and at their request and my request.

'There was certainly a period of discomfort and trouble. But once the legal stuff got worked out, it's been quite, well, I wouldn't say pleasant, but it's been easy. And their mother has been a wonderful parent.'

Although he was in the public eye as a famous actor, Tom refused to accept that his divorce was any worse than anyone else's.

'My work didn't ruin my marriage,' he said to the Los *Angeles Times*. 'You can't put all the blame on the film business. It's just as hard working at a bank and staying happily married as it is in the movies. For a long period of time you go through this period of swearing that you will never make the same mistakes as your parents. But then you realise that they didn't really make mistakes. They just did what had to be done. That's just the way it works out sometimes.'

In the same vein, Tom told *Cosmopolitan*: 'I had some personal problems. Big deal. Everybody has them. We are not talking about a nuclear holocaust. I was a little bit crazy. What I tried to do was turn it to my advantage for my work.

'In some ways I have been like a classic absentee father. My work has taken me away a lot – and certainly being separated, even more so. I think my marriage broke up for any of the reasons that any other marriage breaks up. Lack of communication plays a huge part, and the basic nature of the relationship.'

He added: 'In hindsight, I realise this was an absolutely hideous time for my parents, which is something I was not hip to until I started going through the same sort of things myself.

'My divorce really answered so many questions about how I grew up the way I did.'

Tom told the *Independent on Sunday* that going through the divorce was 'the worst period of time I had'. It was, he said: 'For all the reasons anybody has – a sense of complete failure and a sense of wasted time, a fear of what the future was going to be like. But mostly a sense that somehow, no matter what I would do to combat it, my offspring were going to feel abandoned. That's a bad thing. Because I remember feeling the same thing.'

'I have learned to accept personal failure without being completely demoralised by it for long periods of time,' he said to

Moviegoer, with just a hint of desperation. 'You can't let that bad dog follow you around for the rest of your life. And you can't believe the hype in either direction. Otherwise, it's peptic-ulcer time and you start to beat the kids.'

Despite all the legal trials and tribulations, Tom's career still seemed virtually unstoppable. And his shattered personal life was about to make a dramatic turn.

For even as he was fighting to save his first marriage, he had already met the great love of his life. She was beautiful, very grounded, and, like Susan, she was an actress.

Rita Wilson would become Mrs Hanks number two.

EIGHT

TOM MAKES IT BIG

WITH SWEAT POURING down his bristled face, the American passenger searched for the right answers as he was plied with searching questions by his Israeli captors. What was his business in Israel? How long was his stay? Did he have any links to Palestinian groups? What knowledge did he have about Britain's then Prime Minister Margaret Thatcher?

The gun-wielding airport police clearly suspected the suspicious-looking traveller could be a terrorist and decided not to take any chances. They detained him for more than two hours until Mrs Thatcher, who was flying in that afternoon on a state visit, had left the airport with her entourage.

Only then was the very relieved American allowed grudgingly on his way from Tel Aviv.

It could be yet another scene out of a Tom Hanks blockbuster, with everyone's favourite hero in a sticky situation. But this wasn't play-acting. It was very real.

Tom was in Israel in 1986 to shoot the low-budget drama *Every Time We Say Goodbye*, a lukewarm love story written and directed by Moshe Mizrahi. It was an attempt to give a dramatic new edge to Tom's hitherto zany image, in a role he accepted after *Splash* came out.

Tom plays David, a Protestant minister's son from Montana, who falls for a beautiful Sephardic Jew named Sarah in the treacly boy-meets-girl story. The lovebirds don't exactly thrill Sarah's very traditional family, who yell and carry on in true Romeo-and-Juliet fashion.

The script took David and Sarah to many of Israel's most historic sights as they wrestled manfully with their cultural differences and Tom was thrilled by what he saw. But it had not been an altogether happy trip. Far away from home and his children, he was visited for a fortnight on location by his father and stepmother and while they were watching a shoot one day, Frances's handbag, with hundreds of dollars in cash, travellers' cheques and credit cards, was stolen along with Tom's Levi jacket.

The problem was quickly rectified, but it threw a slight pall over the stay. That wasn't helped when Tom left for the airport after filming had wrapped on the drama, which co-starred Cristina Marsillach.

Mrs Thatcher's arrival coincided with the tired actor's departure and an over-zealous security guard became convinced Tom posed a security threat. Despite his protestations that he was a movie star appearing in an Israeli-made film, he was detained for two hours, powerless to do anything about it.

In his memoirs, Tom's father wrote: 'He was only released after Mrs Thatcher had left the airport... perhaps Tom did look rather like a terrorist.'

Some of the sights, however, literally took Tom's breath away. He remembered going out with the rest of the cast into the desert 'which was only a stone's thrown away and we lit a fire in the middle of nowhere. We lay back and we watched the satellites go over us, reflecting the sun off them, from horizon to horizon. And you can map out the Zodiac. There's Cancer. There's Leo. You can see them so clearly out there. Beautiful. Stunning.'

He added: 'I wouldn't want to rush through a place like Jerusalem. It's a city that you want to roam. And in Tel Aviv I wanted to see how people decorate their apartments, what their political views are, and since there wasn't as many camels as I had expected, what kind of cars do they drive. You don't have to be religious to understand the worldwide importance of Israel. This is essentially where all Western societies find their base. And the history here is the greatest ever told. As an American and a gentile, I envy the rich Jewish heritage.'

Though backed by the major studio Tri-Star, the film surprised nobody by bombing at the box office, although Tom still claims it was 'probably the most visually beautiful movie I've made,' and took the part 'without hesitation'.

While his personal life was still in tumult, Tom had also reached a crossroads in his career. With the unexpected success of *Splash,* Tom may not yet have been quite a household name, but he was certainly a very marketable star.

Unable to turn down a number of lucrative offers, he made a string of largely forgettable films to capitalise on his new standing in Hollywood. He said later, only half-joking, that he made the quick-fire films 'to get out of the house.'

But question marks were beginning to be raised in the fickle film capital over those choices. The films were rolling one after another, but the hits seemed to be drying up.

First there was *Bachelor Party,* released on the cusp of *Splash's* success in 1984, which, while doing little for his prestige, still brought in a healthy worldwide profit of more than $49 million (£30 million) and boosted Tom's profile among studio executives always on the lookout for a potential cash cow.

Naughty rather than sexy, he played Rick Gassko in the rowdy comedy from the *Police Academy* team of Pat Proft and Neal Israel. Tom was 28, still fresh from television and still at work on *Splash* when Proft approached him.

'It was an insane movie that needed somebody who had a sane centre, but was funnier than anyone around him. That's what Tom could bring to it,' Proft told the *Minneapolis Star Tribune*. 'Plus, he's one of those guys you like when you meet him.'

It took some convincing for the studio executives to agree to a leading man who, still prior to *Splash's* release, was a completely unproven quantity. 'They didn't know who he was,' said Proft.

Bachelor Party, in fact, began shooting with TV's *Mad About You* star Paul Reiser in the lead as a bridegroom reluctantly being dragged out by his pals for one final fling.

'He was hysterically funny, but the mix wasn't correct. So the studio said, "Why don't you get the guy you want?"'

Proft said Tom was an instant success on the set. 'He didn't have to think for a night and decide what the character would do. He was ready. We had a dumb party where we wanted him to dance, so he jumped up on a piano and did the Swim, the Pony and all these things. It was hilarious. The camera angles were atrocious because we were falling around helpless with laughter.'

It was never going to grab the attention of Academy Award judges, but Tom's performance swayed a few critics. *Variety* said the 'main reason to see the pic is for Hanks' performance... he's all over the place, practically spilling off the screen with an over-abundance of energy.'

Tom defended his decision to do the film to *Rolling Stone* magazine, saying: 'Doing *Bachelor Party* is not like doing *Richard III* or *Henry IV, Part II,* but that doesn't diminish the joy of scoring off something that somebody else has written. In fact, at times, it can be more difficult just walking down a hall and talking to somebody and making that interesting.

'That's what I find to be the big movies. Doing Shakespeare and

Bachelor Party is not that different actually. The cerebral processes are the same. The demands are certainly different. The overall appreciation is going to be different. Doing Shakespeare, doing classical theatre, is a luxury.

'This is what I do. I'm an actor. An actor has to act. What else am I supposed to do – sit around the house?'

Irrespective of its dramatic merits, *Batchelor Party* had one powerful effect on Tom's career. It proved that his audience-pulling power in *Splash* was not a fluke.

But then came *The Man With One Red Shoe,* in which Tom, as the movie bible, *Première,* put it, 'seemed to be under a court order not to be funny.' Even the film's star marks it down as his worst film. 'A dog,' is the way he describes it.

Tom plays a symphony violinist and eccentric composer mistaken for a spy in a failed Hollywood rehash of the French farce, *The Tall Blond Man With One Black Shoe.* The spoof, with the bemused Georgetown musician's mysterious rivals trailing him and the requisite bed scene with the beautiful spy, played by Lori Singer, struck a sour note with audiences, who stayed away in droves. The film couldn't even get a big-screen release outside the United States, relegated direct to video for the rest of the world's consumption.

What Tom did demonstrate, however, was his enthusiasm for preparing properly for a part. He spent months learning to play the violin to ensure he looked suitably authentic as a musician in the film. He also says he learned that violinists were invariably bad dressers, a discovery he tried to put over in his choice of wardrobe.

He was slightly less hard on himself in the looks department as he set out to publicise the film. 'I used to be a kind of geeky-looking guy,' he said. 'But I have outgrown my geekiness. Now I feel bad about the way I look only about every other day!'

The other film he made in 1985 was *Volunteers,* another box office flop memorable chiefly to Tom because it was the second time he worked with actress Rita Wilson, who was his girlfriend in the movie and would become his wife in real life.

He played snooty Lawrence Bourne III in the comedy about a self-centred young playboy who, unable to pay his gambling debts, flees to Thailand as a Peace Corps volunteer. The mixed reviews nevertheless noticed, for the first time, the star's stylish similarities to Cary Grant, a recurring comparison through the rest of his career.

In *Newsweek,* film critic David Ansen wrote: 'It's Hanks who gives the movie its seductively sardonic spirit. His character requires both the outsider smirk of a Bill Murray and the debonair inside moves of a Cary Grant, and Hanks has both. His brainy self-interest cuts through the cant.'

Tom worked on his role as a snobbish boor by going to master Hollywood dialogue coach Bob Easton. He would tape the sessions and play them repeatedly on his car stereo. Director Nicholas Meyer said directing Tom was 'like driving a Maserati – you touch it and the whole thing roars off.'

The film opened just one week after the première of *The Man With One Red Shoe,* and fared rather better, raking in $20.2 million in the US. But it didn't provide the jump-start to his career that Tom was hoping for.

Now working at a frantic rate, primarily to offset his domestic unrest, Tom had three films released in 1986. As well as *Every Time We Say Goodbye,* there was *The Money Pit* and *Nothing in Common,* none of which did particularly sterling business.

More Cary Grant comparisons inevitably followed *The Money Pit,* which was a remake of the 1948 comedy *Mr Blandings Builds His Dream House,* which starred Cary Grant and Myrna Loy. Shelley Long, from the TV series *Cheers,* was Tom's co-star in this story of an ill-fated couple who buy a mansion, only to watch it fall apart around them. The critics savaged the Hanks version as 'a miserable rip-off' but it still took more than $37 million in the US.

The Money Pit was a pet project for Steven Spielberg with his own production company, Amblin. He liked the slapstick idea and promoted it to his studio bosses at Universal as their major comedy release for Christmas 1985, although it actually came out in 1986. It was directed by Richard Benjamin, who had won critical acclaim for *My Favorite Year,* and the producers were Frank Marshall and Kathleen Kennedy, who worked with Spielberg on ET and the Indiana Jones adventures.

It was the first time Tom worked with Steven Spielberg. He had also reached another milestone in his career – he was commanding a fee of $1 million per film.

Tom confessed to the *Los Angeles Times* in 1993: 'I've made far too many movies. But when *Splash* came out and I started getting offered things, I didn't really know how you could say no, so I worked every chance I got. In retrospect, I can see that was a mistake because I ploughed through several mediocre movies: I don't regret making those choices because those were the only choices I had, but I did seem to get offered an awful lot of goofy, silly roles.'

Like many of Tom's early films, *Nothing in Common* boasted a worthy performance by its star – even if the movie itself came in for some criticism. But unlike the others, there was nothing goofy or silly about it. Through his portrayal of a selfish yuppie who is transformed into a sensitive, caring son when his father falls seriously ill, Tom attracted more attention to his all-round dramatic skills.

He may not have troubled the superstars of the day such as Sylvester Stallone or Mel Gibson. Yet, coming at that stage of his life, it was a very important film for Tom. Until then he had been, as he put it, 'purely a gun for hire', not involved at all in developing either a script or a character. When director Garry

Marshall came to him with the story of a young man's reconciliation with his dying father, Tom had a very personal reason for taking the part – and injecting his own ideas into the finished product.

'That really completely altered the way I approached making movies,' Tom told *Première*. 'As a result, that was the first movie where I thought I knew what I was doing, and it turned out that I pretty much did know what I was doing.

'I'm still ludicrously more proud of this movie than I should be, because it didn't do all that great, but still...'

Co-star Sela Ward, who played Tom's girlfriend, said Tom was a little shy during the love scenes. 'We were doing a montage shot were we're running by this lake and he was supposed to fail down and kiss me. The first time we did it, he bit my lip so hard that blood was pouring out. Oh, wow, it hurt. We were laughing hysterically. I said, "You're smooth, Tom."'

The reason for Tom's utter involvement in the film was that, in part at least, the storyline mirrored his own father's situation. Weeks before shooting started, Amos had almost died when his long-term kidney problems took a serious turn for the worse.

Tom's raw emotions were compounded by the fact that his father in the film was played by veteran TV star Jackie Gleason, who was himself very ill and died shortly afterwards. 'I think pretty much everybody knew he was not going to be with us much longer, although we were all surprised he went as soon as he did,' said Tom later.

And to add to the outside pressures, Tom's marriage was falling apart while he was making the film. Not that he let that harm his performance. Said director Garry Marshall: 'Tom is one of the few young actors who doesn't believe that the set should revolve around his private life.'

On the contrary, for the first time Tom really took the subject matter to heart, using the performance as a forum for his own feelings rather than an escape from them.

He invited his entire family to an early screening, telling his father: 'You're in this all over the place, Pop. Sorry about that.'

As the closing credits rolled, everyone was in tears. 'Oh yeah, the whole thing was pretty touching,' said Tom. 'I even joked about it. The father in the story had diabetes, so I said, "I pulled for the kidney thing, dad, but they just wouldn't go for it."'

His sister, Sandra, added: 'That was a really hard film for us to watch. Just because it hit real close to home, the illness aspect. We'd all just gone through that. We'd spent lots of time, Tom included, standing next to the bed with dad out like a light with us just yakking up a storm to him. God, we did that for weeks. I mean, they were saying he was going to die.'

The illness had come at a particularly bad time. Throughout his life, Amos had dreamed of being his own boss. Always a hard worker, he wanted to enjoy some of the fruits of his own labour but neither had the time nor the money to set up on his own while he was bringing up his children.

It was only after Tom had left home for good that he felt able to take the gamble and buy his own restaurant. With Frances, he went back to Hawaii, where he had first become interested in the catering trade while working at the Royal Hawaiian Hotel after World War II, and found the perfect site in Kona, the capital of the Big Island.

Amos and Frances put all their life savings into renovating the restaurant and planning the grand opening. Invites had gone out to all of their children and the menus were printed.

But just two weeks before the launch, Amos fell seriously ill from a kidney disease that would plague him for the rest of his life and ultimately cause his death. Toxic chemicals he had breathed in while painting a boat many years earlier had caused irreparable harm.

He had to sell up the restaurant and return to California after being told by worried doctors that the burden of running his own business would be too onerous.

He would have three kidney transplants – one donated by his sister, Mary, and two from cadavers – but all were unsuccessful and he remained on dialysis for the rest of his days.

Just before Tom filmed *Nothing in Common*, Amos sank into a coma and doctors gave him little chance of recovery. His children all spent long days by his bedside, hoping against hope.

In his father's memoirs, Larry describes the scene in the hospital room. 'Tom was washing his face with a warm washcloth, talking to him quietly,' he wrote.

Tom himself said his father's ailment 'wasn't diagnosed for an incredibly long amount of time.'

He recalled Amos's body rejecting the first transplanted kidney. 'And he almost died then, and then he received another transplant which didn't take, and that almost killed him,' Tom told *Première*. 'There was another time when they were doing this experimental thing of changing fluids just in one area of his abdomen, which kinda went sour on him as well.

'So over the course of seven or eight years, there were, like, four different times I thought I was driving to the hospital to see him for the last time – when I thought, 'Okay, look, we have to resign ourselves to the fact that dad's dead. So let's let him go and move on.''

As the start date for *Nothing in Common* loomed, there seemed to be nothing this time to save Tom's ailing father.

Amos's friend, Arlene Sukolsky, director of the Transpacific Renal Network, recalled: 'He was literally considered to be on his death bed. The doctors had given up. He was just about gone and his doctor said he simply didn't know what else to do.

'Then his Chinese wife asked if they would object to a herbalist coming in to help. They had some traditional Chinese medicine, which they put through a tube directly into his stomach.

'And he came back from the coma. It was incredible.'

The close brush with death had another very positive outcome. It finally healed the rift between Frances and her stepchildren. Together at Amos's bedside through long days and nights, they discovered a newfound respect and understanding of each other.

Amos wrote about Tom, Sandra and Larry's change of heart with a real sense of relief: 'Once feeling little but resentment towards her, they had come to understand something of what was between us, and to appreciate, love and respect her as they might never have done had I never been ill.

'She had once been vehemently disapproving of their ways: Now she could appreciate them and, with me, she was finding it hard to believe that everything had turned out so well.'

He continued: 'Childhood had been a mess for them. Much of the fault was mine, but how would I feel if they were involved in the sick, sordid things so common to their generation?

'Some of them could be in prison, addicted, afflicted, diseased – mentally and physically destroyed.'

After his father recovered, Tom had it written into all of his contracts that the studio concerned would pay for the provision of dialysis and ensure there were hospitals available nearby should his father want to see some new places and visit him on the set with Frances.

Said Tom at the time: 'His recovery really is miraculous. No lie about it. If you saw my dad now, you'd say, "He's a frail old man." And I'd say, "Well, dad's got no kidneys." He's on the dialysis machine three times a week for five hours, which is a major thing you have to make your peace with. He's got a little piece of cow vein in his forearm – you can see the blood flowing! It really is an amazing thing: "Hey, Pop, let's see your waterworks again." Talk about understanding how fragile the human body is...

'At the same time, it's really weird, because through the good use of various kidney foundations, he's travelled the world. When I go off on location, it's a thing I try to work out: well, can Dad come?'

Proud of all his children's accomplishments, Amos spent his remaining years helping fellow dialysis patients coping with the disability. Arlene Sukolsky hired him as a part-time patient advocate and he visited countless kidney patients assuring them that life could go on.

'He had been to the brink of death several times and he would visit dialysis units to offer patients help and support and encouragement. He was a very humorous and charming man,' said Sukolsky. 'After he had been doing this for a year or two, his wife Frances felt this was what Amos was destined to do. He was travelling and helping people right to the very end.

'He didn't talk about Tom as much as you would think. He kept that part of his life separate.'

In 1991, he was nationally honoured by *Nephrology News and Issues* magazine with its Quality of Life award and was named Patient of the Year for his work with kidney patients.

Amos Hanks died on 31 January 1992, aged 67, and was buried in the family plot in Paskenta, Northern California.

For Tom, his father's illness had helped bring his own life back into perspective. First marriage counselling and then intensive individual therapy also played their part.

'I'd been escaping into my work for months and had worked so much I was dead from the feet up,' he told the *LA Times*. 'I wound up in therapy three times a week for several months. I was sad, confused and emotionally crippled – I guess the house of cards has to fall in before you start to figure things out.

'I remember the guy I saw saying to me, "You have a lot to be sad about, but you're going to be all right," and though I didn't believe him for the longest time, I felt like a world of good had been done after several months had passed.'

With discontent over the divorce rumbling through the early part of the year, 1987 came and went with the spartan release of just one Hanks film, *Dragnet*, with Dan Aykroyd as no-nonsense Joe Friday and Tom as his new, freewheeling police partner in a spoof of the hit TV show.

His provisos to the studios were that he didn't want to end up with the girl at the end and he wanted to work with Aykroyd, since he liked the notion of working with another star in a knockabout comedy where he could have some fun after working on back-to-back dramas. The partnership didn't really gell and although it did reasonable business, the critics marked *Dragnet* down as a bit of a drag.

Vincent Canby in the *New York Times* said the laughs in *Dragnet* are 'as isolated as stoplights in the suburbs'.

But just as the death knell was growing louder for him among Hollywood's chattering classes, Tom really hit it Big in his tenth feature film.

The storyline seemed to be everything silly that he had been trying to avoid in films like *Every Time We Say Goodbye* and *Nothing in Common*. In *Big*, directed by Penny Marshall, Tom portrays a 12 year-old boy trapped in a 35-year-old man's body. That's what happens when young Josh Baskin makes a wish on a mechanical wizard at an amusement part. His request to be taller so he can date a girl in his class backfires when his age increases along with his height.

The predictable plot has Josh's parents wondering who the strange six-foot adult in the house is and why he is claiming to be their son; the man-boy becoming a huge success buying toys for a big store; a love scene with a pretty colleague beguiled by his childish innocence; and, of course, the magical transition back to being a schoolboy just in time for the end of the movie.

Like *Splash*, his other biggest film to date, the unlikely

ingredients all came together to make *Big* a huge hit, which took more than $114 million at the US box office alone.

And unlike *Splash,* which made a star out of Daryl Hannah, Tom carried the whole film. It even started a franchise, with *Big* drawing in hundreds of fans a night in a Broadway musical.

Most importantly for Tom, his virtuoso performance in the 1988 summer blockbuster won him a coveted Oscar nomination for Best Actor. He may not have won – Dustin Hoffman's *Rain Main* autistic beat out Tom, Gene Hackman, Edward James Olmos and Max Von Sydow. But while *Splash* established him as a Hollywood star, *Big* established him as a fine actor.

Two other much-vaunted actors, Harrison Ford and Robert De Niro, had already turned the part down before it came to Tom.

His success was all the more remarkable for the fact that *Big* was the fourth and last out of the gate of a spate of similarly themed movies. *Like Father, Like Son, 18 Again* and *Vice Versa* had all been roundly panned and the critics were sharpening their knives waiting for *Big's* release.

What they found was a delightfully funny, yet sweet and touching film, an almost Capra-esque parable of how much we lose as adults and how a childlike mentality can instruct the modern corporate world.

American TV celebrity Roger Ebert, film critic for the *Chicago Sun Times,* called *Big* 'potently funny, provocative and romantic.' He added: 'Tom Hanks brings sheer comic inspiration to his role as a 12-year-old boy trapped in a man's body. Okay, so there have been three so-so movies this year with the same child-man plot... *Big* is different.

'It is that rare film that can tickle the funny bone and touch the heart.'

Once again, Tom was able to draw from his own life to find inspiration for his part. He was all too painfully aware of the conflicting emotions of growing up too fast and leaving life as a kid behind before you are ready. He also studied his own two children to take his own leap back in time.

'If there's any age that I had gone back and analysed, even before preparing for the movie, it was those junior high years, when you can't figure anything out. You're cranky all the time; the chemicals in your body are out of whack.

'When I was 13,' he told *Playboy*, 'I was younger than my years. I could still play really well. I can remember things that I loved to do, the way you could have toy soldiers or a plane, and you could sit on the couch for hours and have incredible adventures. And I remember being clueless. I remember adults talking to me and just going, "Yeah, right," but not knowing what they were talking about.'

Explaining his approach to the film, he added: 'The issue was whether Josh wanted to skip all those years of pre-adolescence and jump right into the thick of things? And how he decides that he misses what is important to him, which is his family,' said Tom.

'I remember being 13 and being all elbows and knees,' he said at the lavish première party for the film. 'The girls had already grown up. I started the role with the point of view of a newborn giraffe. They have spindly heads that look geeky when they run.

'The expression on the faces of 13-year-old boys tells their whole story. If they try to act older, it's like a drunk trying to act sober. The key to his character was innocence.'

He told the *Chicago Tribune*: 'If we were to maintain our credibility with the movie, we had to tackle this issue of maturation very seriously. We had to confront head-on our own loss of innocence, of intimacy, that comes with adulthood and the competitive nature of the world.

'As adults, we can all probably pinpoint that single moment or month or year when we became adults, the last time of our youth. When it's gone, it's gone and you wish you could go back sometimes to when you were a kid and you could sleep in the back of the car while dad did the driving. None of us would really want to, unless maybe just for a day.

'But that, to me, is what the film is all about, and it's a tough line to walk, to do a comedy with a capital C, one you hope they laugh at, but find endearing and are enriched by as well.'

On the same theme, Tom told *Newsweek:* 'An image that I always carried around with me was that feeling you get when you're a kid and you're driving home from a vacation and you're snug in the back of the station wagon. You can curl up in a ball and fall asleep without a care in the world, and it's warm and the car is rocking and you hear the whoosh-whoosh of passing things... those kinds of memories and feelings you carry with you forever. Dredging them up was not all that unpleasant an experience.

'There were other things that were unpleasant – the loneliness of being a kid, the confusion, not being able to understand.'

The back-to-back filming, including another movie, *Punchline*, which was shot before *Big* but held back by the studio, had taken a toll on Tom's health and he ended up with a severe bout of pneumonia. For the first time since his enforced breaks between jobs in New York, Tom decided to take some time off.

But he didn't waste his five months of freedom.

By the time *Big* had wrapped in November 1987, Tom's divorce to Susan had been finalised. By the time the film opened the following summer, he not only had a new hit movie, he had a new wife.

NINE

THE PERFECT COUPLE

TOM WILL HAPPILY admit he has had sex with just seven women in his life. Sure, he had married young and his opportunities as a shy, slightly goofy teenager had been somewhat limited. But here he was, a fully-fledged 31-year-old Hollywood superstar with a very ex-wife, millions in the bank and his pick of beautiful women with stars in their eyes blinding them to bad haircuts and a thrown-together wardrobe.

Many men in his position would take advantage of their single status and international fame to push up their sex stats. With women literally throwing themselves at him, Tom certainly had plenty of chances to do just that. But there were no lurid headlines, no bimbos selling kiss-and-tell stories.

'Look,' he said to *Interview* magazine's Ingrid Sischy, 'I have bedded seven women in my life. That's a paltry sum. I have talked to guys who are into the high three digits, if not actually four digits. I'm not even off two hands.'

But he added: 'I think I have a degree of sexual confidence that is kept in its proper perspective and that is not flaunted. I know what that comes out of, because for years I had no sexual confidence. For years I was lonely. I don't feel a dope because of that. I don't feel as though I have missed out on anything.'

There was one very good reason why Tom kept such a low profile after the break-up of his first marriage. He had already fallen in love.

It didn't happen the first time they met, when the pretty young Californian actress appeared as a guest on *Bosom Buddies,* playing his partner Peter Scolari's girlfriend.

But when he saw Rita Wilson arrive on the Mexican set of *Volunteers* in 1984, Tom knew she was the one.

He was still very much married at the time and Rita was engaged. But he clearly recalled: 'I knew something was going on – Rita didn't, but I did. I knew it was powerfully strong and I knew it was going to have consequences.

'I think men can look at a woman for the first time and say, "Yes, she's the one. This is it." We can be made into drooling idiots much faster than women.'

The film, directed by Nicholas Meyer, was shot on location miles from anywhere by a river near the Mexican town of Tuxtepec, inland from the Gulf of Mexico. One night, the two stars started talking over coffee. They were still talking at two o'clock the next morning.

Although he didn't act on his feelings until much later, Tom was immediately smitten by the vivacious, bright actress who seemed so self-assured even though it was her first big film.

With fellow *Splash* graduate, the larger-than-life John Candy, also in the cast, the two months of shooting was the ideal antidote to the mounting difficulties in Tom's marriage.

The romantic setting and the lack of diversions soon made the emotional undercurrent between the co-stars palpable on the set. 'Rita glowed with niceness,' said actor Xander Berkely, who was in the cast. 'You could tell they were fond of each other.'

But when filming was over the couple went their own separate ways – Tom to his wife and Rita back to her fiancé in Los Angeles. It would be another eight months before they would go out on their first official date, to see director Jonathan Demme's concert film, *Stop Making Sense,* with the Talking Heads pop group, in October 1985, soon after Tom and Susan officially pronounced their marriage dead and buried.

Tom described the events that brought him together with Rita in an interview for *US* magazine.

'There was some magic definitely involved. When they were casting *Volunteers*, I remembered her from *Bosom Buddies* and thought maybe she would be good, but I couldn't remember her name. Then, when she was cast, I thought that was pretty wacky.

'I thought she was utterly stone-cold delightful when we met again. What a great gal! Then, when we made *Volunteers,* we became really good friends and made each other laugh.'

He continued: 'I was in a marriage that I don't think was good for anybody who was involved. I was in this treadmill of working. My 20s were rapidly coming to a conclusion and I was looking for something different than what I had. And Rita was there.

'It was very romantic. Yet it was fraught with all sorts of very uncomfortable things that really precluded anything that could honestly go on. I'd be lying to say that I just did not see something in Rita that was the greatest thing in the world. But when the movie finished, we went our ways.

'It was obvious we liked each other. But circumstances dictated that there had to be a degree of distance. We realised that there's a type of person who goes from one movie romance to another until they have been romantically linked with 1,800 different people. But she is not like that. Nor am I.

'That February to October everything went wrong! The first marriage was getting smashed on the rocks. We'd just bought a new home that I only lived in for two weeks, and I was off making a movie again. I had two kids I hadn't been home for. The worst aspect of separating was that I was going to be sentencing my own kids to the same sort of feeling I'd felt at the same age. I felt horribly guilty. Food didn't taste good, life wasn't nice. I didn't sleep. It was a time fraught with unhappiness.

'When we split up it was like moving back to Los Angeles again for the first time. I was living in a bad house with rented furniture. But then I could actually pick up with Rita. The magic was quite palpable before, but you gotta do the right thing.'

Tom and Rita were a match made in heaven. He told *Vanity Fair* that 'my notches fit her crooks.'

He went on, once again tracing his 20-something torment back to his childhood: 'When we met it was just bona fide friendship and delight, which rapidly became a kind of passion. I mean, there was a substantial amount of stuff I had to get through. I was married. I had two kids. I could not just... well, the thing that drove me to the couch was that all I was doing was repeating this kind of life that my parents had gone through, with an incredible amount of pain. Because my parents broke up when I was five, there began this kind of disconnectedness that hung in there until I was 30. But, I mean, everybody's got something that comes along and chews them up for a bit. My loneliness came out of that.

'There just didn't seem to be a table that I truly felt accepted at unconditionally. Coming across Rita, I found someone who could not understand that, and I got a glimpse of how life could be.

'Los Angeles, before I met Rita, was this hideous place where you ended up, not out of choice, but because they paid you to go there. It was a place where the holidays were always going on somewhere else.'

He believes, quite literally, that Rita rescued him from a lifetime of loneliness.

'You get these chances in America, sometimes, to kind of be saved by people. Rita saved me,' he told CNN talk-show host Larry

King. 'I'm going to embarrass her right now, but I have found a level of contentment and peace with my wife that I wish everybody could have. I was kind of a wandering and confused guy, and it took me a long time. We took it slowly as well, but as far as the work is concerned, you know, this is what we do for a living and my wife, it's going to sound hokey to say, "She supports me in everything I do," but I get the feeling that she just thinks I'm the greatest, smartest guy in he world, and maybe that's why she makes me so happy. It's never been a problem that we work in the same business, not for an instant.'

Tom had found the family he had been searching for his whole life. With Rita, the 'disconnectedness' was gone.

The daughter of immigrants – her father, Al, is Bulgarian and her mother, Dorothy, is Greek – Rita is the same age as Tom. But their backgrounds could not be more different. Her parents settled in Los Angeles, changing their name from Ibrahimoff to Wilson, the street where they lived, and they still live in the same house where Rita grew up.

Rita's father escaped from communist Bulgaria right after World War II. He managed to jump onto a train with a friend after it separated him and his fellow prisoners from their guards and made a daring bid for freedom that eventually led him to the United States.

Unlike most actresses who leave their small towns to come to Hollywood and then fight their way through the ranks to become stars, Rita was raised a few blocks from the studios and fell naturally into her career.

The second of three children – her older sister is a teacher and her younger brother is a chef – she earned quickly how to make people laugh by doing impressions of children in the neighbourhood.

At the age of 10, she appeared on a popular American TV show,

Art Linkletter's House Party, and won some luggage, a Parker pen, a lunch out and a limo ride. Coming from a secure, happy home, she never really had any doubt that she would one day be an actress.

Her school, Hollywood High, boasts a galaxy of stars as alumni, from Judy Garland and Mickey Rooney in the 1930s, to James Garner in the '40s, Ricky Nelson in the '50s, Linda Evans and Stefanie Powers, who both graduated in 1960, and Rita in the Class of 1974. Other famous pupils at the school one block south of Hollywood Boulevard included Lana Turner, Beatrice Potter, John Ritter, Carol Burnett and pop star Brandy.

A popular, pretty teenager, she was a cheerleader for the school's football team. As the daughter of immigrants, she developed an innate sense of how best to fit in. The pretty pom pom outfits were, to her eye, a much more preferable option to the 'black capes and floppy hats' worn by the would-be thespians in the drama group.

On her first day at Hollywood High, at 14, she was approached by a fashion scout, who persuaded her to send a portfolio of her pictures to the respected Nina Blanchard Model Agency in Los Angeles. Weeks after she was signed as a teen model, she was chosen for a bathing suit layout in the prestigious *Harper's Bazaar* magazine.

Nina Blanchard, who also helped launch the early modelling careers of such stars as Melanie Griffith and Rene Russo, said: 'Rita was still in school and I remember some pictures came through the mail. I get about 1,000 a week, but once in a while there is a face you are interested in. But I only signed about nine or ten people from mail-ins in all those years. And Rita was one.

'Then, after a very short time, she was modelling for *Harper's Bazaar.'*

Old schoolfriend Debbie Fuqua-Cuen said even then that her classmate had that special something. *'Teen* magazine came in and did make-overs and I remember Rita getting very involved. She had the look.'

Although the modelling was increasingly lucrative, Rita's first love was still acting and she again struck lucky when she went along with a friend to an audition for *The Brady Bunch* TV show in LA. She decided to try out and, to her amazement, won the role of Marcia Brady's cheerleading rival, a part she was well qualified to do.

As well as *Bosom Buddies,* the actress with the Jane Fonda looks played a beauty graduate in an episode of *Happy Days,* where she changed her hair colour and style in every scene. Her first, very forgettable, performance in a movie was the low-budget horror flick *The Day It Came to Earth,* complete with cornball script and tacky special effects.

To finance herself, she also kept up the fashion jobs, working in Milan and Paris after leaving school. 'I can remember at 16 years old saving up all my money to buy a Gucci handbag,' she said. But she soon tired of modelling. 'It was boring, ultimately. There wasn't a lot of room for personality.'

And the kind of acting work she was attracting also began to irritate her. Her roles in *Bosom Buddies, The Brady Bunch* and *Happy Days* were examples of the parts she was getting – the pretty girl brought in to spice up the plot without being too memorable or threatening to the sitcom regulars. The routine was to get passed around from show to show without rocking the boat.

'I've forgotten how many times I've played the girl,' she said, soon after completing her first starring role in *Volunteers.* 'Sometimes the girl is a bimbo, a dingbat or bitch whose purpose is to make the hero look heroic and the heroine look good... The girl is thrown into a script when there's not much going on with the permanent cast. But she's never a threat to the cast members or the formula of the show, whether it's *Hill Street Blues* or *Cheers.*

'I wanted to play less limited roles and the only way to do that was to break cleanly from the rut of playing the girl.'

Rita' s way of breaking free was to leave Hollywood completely and enrol in the London Academy of Music and Dramatic Arts.

Her modelling had allowed her to save enough money to pay for her digs and for her studies in the classics.

'At LAMDA they really are demanding and you soon discover if you are willing to pay the price. You either get better, change your priorities or drop out,' she said. Rita chose to stay for the full one-year course, appearing in *The Oresteia, A Midsummer Night's Dream* and *'Tis Pity She's a Whore,* all at London's MacOwan Theatre.

'They force you to strip away the fantasies you have about your talent and yourself. They take you down to zero so you can make a realistic appraisal of yourself and see what needs improvement. You attend classes from 9 to 5 every day, learning fencing, dancing, singing, elocution, dialects and, of course, rehearsing plays.

'I soaked up all I could at LAMDA and I have retained it. Now when I walk in front of the cameras I am able to create a character and not worry about anything else. Whatever else, I'm not the girl any more.'

After her year in London, Rita studied Greek tragedy in Paris to further hone her talents. Just to get in to Jacques Le Coq's prestigious school she needed at least five years acting experience to even be considered.

When she returned to Los Angeles in November 1985, Rita fired her old agents and signed up with a new manager, telling them she knew exactly what she wanted: the female lead in a major movie opposite a star in a foreign location. Within weeks, she was signed up to star opposite Tom Hanks in the jungles of Mexico. Again, luck played a part in snagging the prized part. She had auditioned as leading lady but was turned down by casting agents. Then the director spotted a photograph of her at a mutual friend's house and demanded to meet her. He cast her himself and soon she was in a first-class seat on her way to Mexico.

While Tom was instantly smitten with Rita almost as soon as they met up in Mexico, it took a little longer for Rita before the penny dropped. She had got engaged just before leaving to make the film and knew Tom had both a wife and two children.

'We started working on the movie and we became friends. He was really fun. I really liked him. But it was a long, long process before we fell in love.'

She added: 'If Tom and I had met in Los Angeles, our relationship might not have worked out. I can imagine some friend saying, "Rita, I want you to meet this guy. He's married, he has two kids and he's an actor." I would have said, "I don't think so."

'But that situation in Tuxtepec threw us together and we became friends first. There was nothing else to do.'

Rita told writer Candace Bushnell: 'It wasn't like, "Ohmigod. I have to have this man," and I didn't pursue him. The relationship just grew out of a friendship, which was shocking to me because I didn't think that was how love worked.

'When did I know? Probably the first time he kissed me. I was just like, wow-ooooow. Okay!'

The decision to break up with her fiancé was, she says, one of the big turning points in her life. It wasn't an easy choice at the time.

'He was a really sweet guy, a lovely person, but I wasn't completely convinced that I should be spending the rest of my life with him. And I broke up with him not knowing if I was making the hugest mistake of my life. That was terrifying.'

The break-up came after returning from Mexico, but while Tom was still struggling with the guilt and trauma of his first, failing marriage.

'I was very down and low about how I had gotten into this position and why I was with a person I wasn't really in love with. Because then you question your judgment. You think, What have I done? How did I get into this position? That leads to a lot of introspection. You look at that and hope you don't repeat those same mistakes... Then I met Tom.

'It was a bittersweet parting. You don't know if you are saying goodbye to the person you should be with. You just know you are unhappy in the relationship and you should do something about it.'

She added later: 'I didn't know what being in love was until I met Tom, because I had never experienced it.'

When they finally started dating in Los Angeles, Rita soon arranged for Tom to meet her parents. Although the normally cool actor was uncharacteristically nervous, the evening went well. Rita even noticed that some of her boyfriend's mannerisms, such as the way he stood or drove a car, mirrored those of her father.

But they were bemused by his appearance. Because he was so keen to create a good impression, he had worn two shirts, one over the other. 'My parents thought that was the strangest thing they had ever seen,' said Rita.

As the romance progressed over the ensuing two years, Tom felt reborn. After living in the San Fernando Valley for eight years, he moved in with Rita in the trendy Westwood suburb of LA. 'It's a new world,' he remarked soon after the move. 'It's the Los Angeles you see in movies and TV. It's beautiful girls driving convertibles and people jogging. It's like Starsky and Hutch will drive by at any time.'

Suddenly he was happy enough not to wonder too much about tomorrow. 'I don't know what is going to happen and I don't care,' he said in an interview with the *Orange County Register* about the same time. 'I have no goals. I think goals are something that are being forced on the American people by the powers that be.' More tellingly, he added: 'I've been off since November 1987, when we finished *Big*. I no longer miss working when I'm not working. Some people say when you're an actor if you are not working you are not living. I'm content to putter around and be interested in something else.

'Right now I am just enjoying a wonderful life.'

The cobalt-eyed actress brought out the gallantry in Tom. He took his then new girlfriend to the Oscar ball in 1986 only to find screen legend Bette Davis was sitting in her designated seat. Arlene Dahl, who was at the same table, urged Tom to go over and tell Davis to get out of the chair. Worried about upsetting the elderly icon, he finally went over and, in true Hanks style, said: 'Miss Davis, you're sitting in my girlfriend's seat, but if anyone can sit in her chair, you can.' The old lady stared at Tom blankly for several moments before saying loudly: 'I can't hear a word you're saying.'

For months, he drove around his determinedly unfashionable Dodge Caravan with a greetings card on the dashboard, which read: 'I love you always, Rita,' with a little hand-drawn heart.

With his divorce now official, Colin and Elizabeth had quickly taken to Rita. As with Tom, she integrated them into her close-knit family and at the same time helped Tom feel more comfortable with himself as a parent.

Tom had never stopped looking for a faith to embrace since his adolescent experiences at the First Covenant Church in Oakland, but the pressures of his career and fatherhood had left him little time for religion.

Now he started to go with Rita and her parents to St Sophia, the Greek Orthodox Cathedral in Los Angeles. The ritualistic side appealed to his sense of the dramatic; and the deeply ingrained sense of belief struck a strong chord with a man who had investigated and questioned the philosophies of religion at some length.

While the couple were holidaying on the Caribbean island of St Barts with *Robocop* star Peter Weller they met up with *The Graduate* director Mike Nichols and his wife, American TV news doyen Diane Sawyer. They all shared a table for a New Year's Eve party and Tom waited until the last few seconds of 1987 to do what he had known he would do almost from the moment he met Rita – he asked her to marry him. Ever the romantics, they would return to the same isle for their honeymoon five months later, this time without their celebrity friends.

The stag party was classic Hanks. There were no strippers, no lewd behaviour. But it did sound like a lot of fun. With six friends, Tom hired a boat to sail the 26-mile journey across from the California coast to the picture-postcard island of Catalina. He boasted proudly afterwards: 'We didn't shower or shave in 72 hours. It was a manly thing – we got very, very stanky.' The crew drank beer, smoked cigars and told a lot of old stories. Oh, and they played at being pirates.

His first marriage may have been due to unforeseen circumstances. But the second time around, Tom was not going to let anything go to chance.

When Tom and Rita emerged to wild applause from St Sophia's into the sunshine on the last Saturday in April, someone in the crowd shouted out: 'Now you are really and truly well-married at last!'

During the Greek Orthodox ceremony, the same golden crowns once used by Rita's parents were held over their heads. Tom's father was there, as were his children – Elizabeth was then five and Colin was ten.

'In the Greek Orthodox service,' Tom explained afterwards, 'you don't say anything. You don't sit there and say, "I, Edward G Schwartz, think you're the neatest thing since sliced cheese, and I swear to God from here on in I'm going to do exactly what you tell me." You walk around a table three times, and that's it. The first time you're not married, the second time you're not married, the third time – that's it, you're married.'

More than 150 people dined and danced at Rex's, the luxuriously expensive downtown art deco cafe. Among the glamorous guests were Peter Scolari and almost all of the old *Bosom Buddies* gang; Roger and Luisa Moore; actors John Lovitz, Jon Candy, Bob Sagett and actress Holland Taylor; Dan Aykroyd with his wife, Donna Dixon; director Penny Marshall and actress Kathleen Turner.

Just in case anyone failed to get their wedding picture snapped with the happy couple, a life-sized cardboard cut-out was on display for guests to pose alongside.

Still dancing at 1.00am, the newlyweds finally left for the Bel-Air

Hotel before flying back to St. Barts in the morning. 'It was the way it was supposed to be – romantic,' Tom said on his return timed to help promote the release of *Big*. 'On our honeymoon we ran around with almost nothing on and sometimes with nothing on.'

He saw the marriage as 'a cleansing separation between an old life and a new life,' and made absolutely no secret of which he preferred. Success had not made him happy, Rita had.

Tom told *US* magazine: 'You can have the nicest house in the world, but it can still be the shittiest place to live. There's no substitute for that great love that exists that says no matter what is wrong with you, you are welcome at this table.'

He later said that it was only after his second marriage that he conquered the rootlessness he felt and the need to move on every six months or whenever things got tough to deal with. With Rita, he finally became 'comfortable with the idea of home. Everything made sense for the first time, but that was a long time coming.'

Although Rita had not been married before, she had a very strong sense of 'what it should look like. We never go to bed mad and we never let things slide. It's always right out in the open.

'When we got married, we both knew we would be married forever. There's a great amount of serenity and peace in our relationship, so now if we hit rough spots it's not the end of the world,' she said.

Although determined to continue her acting career, Rita made the choice right from the start to put her family first, even if that had a detrimental effect on the roles she was offered. Every time her husband signs on to do a new movie, Rita packs up and goes with him on location, sometimes for as long as three months at a time. 'Everybody has their needs and requirements, and mine is that my family stays together,' she told *Redbook* women's magazine. 'Have you ever experienced what happens when you haven't been around someone for three or four weeks? It takes a long time to get back into a family rhythm. So why disrupt that?'

She didn't forsake her acting career altogether. She went on to appear in the 1996 Christmas film *Jingle All The Way*, opposite Arnold Schwarzenegger and Sinbad, and was part of an ensemble cast that included Melanie Griffiths, Demi Moore and Rosie O'Donnell in a girl's version of *Stand By Me*, called *Now and Then*.

In 1994, she starred with Steve Martin in *Mixed Nuts*, one of director Nora Ephron's less successful efforts, which also featured a young Adam Sandler, and she had a small but memorable role in Tom's *Sleepless in Seattle*.

Rita would also play the receptionist in the remake of Alfred Hitchcock's *Psycho* and had a substantial part in the 1999 summer hit *Runaway Bride* as Richard Gere's ex-wife in the reteaming of the greying star with *Pretty Woman* Julia Roberts.

There's little doubt that Rita – nicknamed 'Bobcat' by her friends – would have been busier had she concentrated on her once burgeoning acting career. But she has no regrets. And she insists her husband has played no part in holding her back. 'He supports me in everything I do,' she says. 'He is ego-less. People would say to me how hard it must be married to Tom, with all his success. I would look at them in total amazement. There was no guarantee that I would be any more successful if I weren't married to him. It's hard to get a job in this business. It's even harder to get a job in this business if you are a woman. Period.'

She said one of the reasons she married him was because he had stopped her in the street one night before they were married and said: 'You never have to change anything about who you are or what you do to be with me.'

'I started crying when he said it. I was standing on 57th Street and 5th Avenue in New York. This was before he proposed to me, and I thought, "Ohmigod, what a man. What a guy,"' she explained.

With Rita's bubbly, outgoing personality to rely on, Tom allowed his own more sociable side to surface. While he had always been superficially friendly, while still keeping most people at a safe distance, he started to lower his protective shield with an inner circle of pals.

So far had Tom come that every Sunday became Chinese food night, when the couple ordered in a vast array of dishes and friends and family dropped in unannounced to dip in their chopsticks. It was a far cry from the bad old days in Oakland when Tom would steadfastly refuse to eat his stepmother's Chinese fare. Once a week, there was Date Night USA, when the couple go out alone, for dinner or to the cinema.

Even the arrest in Los Angeles of Tom's former business manager Mick Schneider didn't throw a pall on the actor's newfound happiness. Schneider, accused of milking Tom of in the region of £150,000, was sentenced to one year's house arrest and ordered to pay back his ex-clients the money he embezzled.

The new family was complete when Tom and Rita had their own children, two boys – Chester, who was born in 1990, and Truman, who arrived on Boxing Day 1995.

In February 1996, they would be featured by *People* magazine in a special issue devoted to 'The Greatest Love Stories of the Century'. Tom would also, as we shall see, declare his love for his wife to a worldwide television audience of 81 million people.

Even after several years of marriage, Tom was still wooing his wife. Briefly parted from Rita while he was filming in Georgia, he arranged for her to fly down for her birthday. When she arrived, Rita discovered to her delight that her husband had rented Teddy Roosevelt's presidential yacht and he proceeded to lay on a lavish champagne-and-candlelight dinner for two on board.

While sometimes bored with the repetitive nature of interviews, Tom still becomes instantly animated when his wife's name comes up. 'I was really very immature and not very wise before I met Rita,' he says. 'I'm sure I was a difficult person to be in a relationship with. Thank God I had the good sense to woo and wed her.

'We had a lot of fights early on, but they were pretty fabulous fights that worked things out. She taught me an awful lot about being a better man, a better father and even a better actor. You know what? She taught me how to fight too!'

He tried to explain to *Interview* magazine just how much his second marriage meant to him. 'I felt lonely for a really long tune. That's why I say my wife saved me, because I didn't feel lonely any more. I did right up to the point where she crossed my path. The union of the two of you is better than the actual sum of the two of you. You don't just add two people; you multiply. That's what I think I have got. And it is not a purely romantic thought; it is just better.

'Rita and I have been through a lot just as a couple and certainly as a husband and wife. It takes a while to pound out a relationship, but I think that process ends up being the great hope. Somehow, it's the great hope that is reflected in a lot of the movies that I do.'

After all the excitement of the marriage and a big hit film, another fascinating project was in the pipeline. Tom was being touted for the much-sought after lead in Brian De Palma's screen version of Tom Wolfe's *The Bonfire of the Vanities*. What could possibly go wrong?

Every big name actor in Hollywood wanted the part. But this time, Tom was top of the list.

How was he to know that *Bonfire* was doomed to go up in smoke?

TEN

A VANITY PROJECT

IT WAS SUPPOSED to be the film that put him right up in Hollywood's A-list. His name had been above the title in a couple of hits, sure. He had even shown that he could act a bit. But Tom was still seen by the public – and the industry – chiefly as a funny guy. *The Bonfire of the Vanities* was the film that could focus his career in a serious way, away from the haphazard choices of such comedians as Chevy Chase and Bill Murray.

The novel by Tom Wolfe had been the must-read book of the late '80s, a morality tale charting the rise and fall of the decade of greed. In America alone, it sold 750,000 in hardback and more than two million paperbacks. The book seemed to cross over into real life in the United States at a time when the tabloid headlines in New York screamed out the unrest of an era of racial strife and corporate collapse.

Simply put, the lead character of *Bonfire's* Master of the Universe, junk-bond trader Sherman McCoy, had about as much in common with *Big's* Josh Baskin as Tolstoy has with Dr Seuss.

It is not a role many would have thought suitable for Tom, even though he had proved his name was more than sufficient to open a movie. It may not even have been a role he would have chosen to help make the transition.

But at the Academy Awards the previous year, having lost out for the Best Actor Oscar, producer-turned-studio head Peter Guber had searched out Tom at LA's Dorothy Chandler Pavilion to talk some business. He was going to be making *The Bonfire of the Vanities* and was interested in Tom as Sherman McCoy. Was Tom interested in the part? Rarely at a loss for words, Tom stuttered for a moment. 'Me?' he said, thinking Guber was joking. Quickly realising it was no joke, Tom gathered himself to impress upon Guber just how much he was interested. The part had been the talk of the industry for months, with all the top names of the time being linked with the project. The name of Tom Hanks hadn't featured in the gossip.

Tom heard nothing more after the awards show and assumed he had been passed over. Besides, there was no shortage of other projects. Another movie, *Punchline,* with double-Oscar winner Sally Field, was due to come out and Tom was getting a lot of advance buzz for his starring role as a hard-bitten stand-up comic in New York.

Although it was shot before *Big,* it came out after the family comedy and was expected to benefit from the other's success. Tom's Steven Gold, a failed medical student with a sulfurously burning ambition to make it as a comedian, was probably the actor's riskiest role to date and he remains one of his least redeemable characters.

The caustic comedian is no stand-up guy. His anger and mood swings are always just below the surface and they are on full display as he takes a New Jersey housewife with aspirations to be a comedian under his wing. To play Gold, Tom created a childhood for his fictional alter ego, growing up 'in a cold and lonely house, in this family that didn't get him in any way, shape or form.'

'I felt sorry for the guy,' said Tom. 'He's not a good human being, but he's an excellent stand-up comedian. I always viewed him as being trapped by this ability. It was never going to make him happy.'

It was almost as if Tom had drawn on the pleasant memories of his childhood for Big and the darker corners for *Punchline*. Steven Gold was the man Tom could have been had he not got such tight control over his inner demons.

Sally Field saw how much of himself her co-star was bringing to the screen. She told *Rolling Stone*: 'It would be one thing if he was just this great, goofy guy. But that lasts for about 30 seconds and then you want to meet somebody real. The reason he is a movie star and is going to stay one is that he's much more complicated than that.

'Yes, he's very entertaining and funny and easy to be around. But you know there is somebody else underneath, somebody dark. There's a sad side, a dark side. And that's what makes him so compelling on the screen.'

Punchline was a film Tom wanted badly to do. He asked writer-director David Seltzer back in 1986: 'Well, who do I have to sleep with to get the part?' At the time, he considered the film 'the greatest stakes of anything I've done'.

But when he first got the script, there was one major flaw that worried him – it wasn't very funny. A fan of legendary stand-up comedians Lenny Bruce and Richard Pryor, Tom brought in comedy writer Bary Sobel and an old friend from Sacramento State, Randy Fechter, who had been working in comedy in Off-Broadway productions, to write him some stand-up material.

Then he spent nearly two months trying out his act in some notoriously unforgiving comedy clubs. 'The first time I thought I had five minutes worth of material,' he said. 'I was gone in two. I was really terrible the first 15 times.

'But as time went by, we actually did assemble a pretty good act. It wasn't a bad set.'

He added: 'That kind of power corrupts... walking into a room of 400 people and taking them wherever you want for 20 minutes. Steven is god of his universe as long as he's got a microphone in his hand. You can't help taking that home with you.'

Seltzer recounts one incident on the film set that underlined his star's no-nonsense professionalism. He explained how Tom didn't want to be seen the morning he was due to shoot a very emotional scene where Gold notices his doctor father in the audience and erupts into a tearful monologue about why he quit medical school.

'He wanted to be called from his trailer when the cameras were literally rolling,' said Seltzer. 'Lord only knows what it was he dredged up, but he came out and just did it, and he did it all day long. I said to him at the end of the day, "Did you have any idea you were gonna walk up there and burst into tears?" And he said, "I had no idea I wouldn't be able to after three o'clock."'

Seltzer went on: 'I had to do some camera set-ups during that scene and Tom at that point was backstage and I was worried he was losing it. So I said, "How about we get the actors playing your father and brother up here? I'll just have them stare at you in the dark."

'And he said, "What is this, Acting 101? I don't need that crap. Go set the lights, I'm doing my work."'

Ever since that ticking off from Ron Howard on the *Splash* set, Tom had vowed never again to give cause for his professionalism to be questioned, a facet of his acting that made him popular with both cast and crew. If a director wanted to shoot a scene 322 times, he would be prepared to shoot it 323. 'That's my job,' he will say. At the same time, he is adamant about offering his own input into his character. 'I don't write scripts, I write on scripts,' he says.

His old friend Randy Fechter said: 'He's a regular dude who can't stand obsequious behaviour. If anything, he errs too much on not being a star. He could get more of what's coming to him, but he sees other people acting like stars and the last thing he wants is to abuse his position. He's a genuinely sweet person. He could get away with murder.'

The release of *Punchline* was delayed because of a changing of the guard at Columbia Pictures and when it finally came out, in September 1988, it was met with mixed reviews. Much of the criticism was aimed at Sally Field's housewife-turned-comedian and her character's relationship with Tom's corrosive comic. But, once again, Tom earned widespread praise for his portrayal.

Newsweek critic David Ansen glowed: 'You feel for Steven because Hanks understands him so completely and allows us to peer inside this brilliant s.o.b.'s stunted soul. You never catch him wallowing in the part. Steven may grandstand, but Hanks doesn't. His acting has wit, velocity, relaxation, and the extraordinary physical dexterity he demonstrated in *Big*. This guy may give you the creeps, but he holds you spellbound.'

The comparative commercial failure of the film was offset by the continuing critical praise poured on Tom, who was still just 32, and, although nothing came of it, the role garnered some support for an Oscar nomination.

Proud of the film, Tom told *Playboy* the year after its release that his only mistake may have been that he allowed himself to get too close to the part.

'The movie didn't do well, which was really disappointing,' he said. 'If I were going to figure out why, I would end up taking a bunch of cheap shots at an awful lot of people who tried real hard, and that's not fair. What can you say? But it's the best work I have ever done. We were talking some real naked truths about the characters and, in a lot of ways, about myself. I was too close.

'The guy in *Punchline* probably has the worst aspects of my worst aspects.

'He is extremely competitive, for one thing. Competitive to a fault. He is unable to balance his daily existence so that real life and what he does for a living have an equal weight. I've certainly had those problems; I think any actor has. The only time you feel alive is when you are working. I've gotten a little more mature since I was like that. But I think that is what really drives actors absolutely stark-raving mad and why they develop ulcers and drug problems.'

All in all, 1988 turned out to be a satisfying year for Tom, culminating in the Best Actor vote at the Los Angeles Film Critics Awards for his combined work in both *Big* and *Punchline*. And with the *Bonfire* project still hanging tantalisingly in the air, there was considerable promise that the next couple of years would add still further to Tom's box-office bankability.

But, although Tom's personal life had never been better with his marriage to Rita and his ever-improving relationship with his children, he was about to take a few steps backwards in his career.

He returned from a long break, refreshed and ready for three upcoming projects; *The Burbs,* with Carrie Fisher; *Turner and Hooch* with Mare Winningham; and *Joe Versus the Volcano*, with Meg Ryan.

All comedies with attractive leading ladies, they did nothing to improve Tom's Hollywood lustre. In *Turner and Hooch*, the only one of the three that didn't bomb, Tom shared top billing with a dog.

Having made 12 films in six years, Tom still hadn't learned the art of saying no. He confessed: 'Part of it is the insecurity factor – every time, you feel like you are never going to get another chance again. They're going to catch on, and that'll be it. Even when you're working a lot, you think, How many of these do I get? It's like they give you only so many dollars in your wallet and once those dollars are spent, you're broke.'

That would be fine but for the fact that even then, the actor was probably set for life. He was getting more than one million dollars for each movie and his fee was rising all the time. Even in January, 1988, he confided to *GQ*: 'Actually, I'm pretty well set. I could get by without working again.'

What was more surprising was that, after *Nothing in Common*,

Big and *Punchline,* the roles he took were not particularly challenging. He was, inevitably, the best thing about all three movies. But that didn't mean an awful lot.

It must have been all the more frustrating to Tom that two films he turned down, *Dead Poets Society* and *Field of Dreams,* went on to become massive commercial and critical hits, for Robin Williams and Kevin Costner respectively.

Tom was also lined up to star with Michelle Pfeiffer in the film *When a Man Loves a Woman,* about a female alcoholic and her relationship with her heavy-drinking husband. He even worked on the script with top Hollywood writer Ron Bass. But first Pfeiffer dropped out and then her replacement, Debra Winger, also found she couldn't commit to the film and Tom handed the project back to the studio.

When the film was finally released in 1994 starring Meg Ryan and Andy Garcia, it was hailed as one of the actress's best and most serious roles.

The Burbs, a black comedy of suburban paranoia was directed by Joe Dante. Tom liked his earlier films, *Gremlins* and *Innerspace,* because 'you see a world that is so completely pleasing on the surface yet deep down, something horrible's going on.' In *The Burbs,* filmed during a Hollywood writer's strike, Tom plays a hopelessly dull executive who spends his holiday investigating weird goings on with his nitwit neighbours. Based largely on *Big*'s success, the film opened to record weekend box office before sinking without trace when word got out that it was a stinker. *Time* magazine said: 'Hanks throws himself into this anti-audience movie with such suave energy that he seems determined to torpedo his hard-won rep as Hollywood's most comfortable new star.'

Turner and Hooch, released the same year, was a much bigger hit, even if its storyline was hardly original. Tom plays a small-town cop who teams up with a drooling junkyard dog that's the sole witness to a grisly murder. It was the first in a multi-film deal

Tom had signed with Disney, providing him with his own office and the chance to bring some of his own ideas to the screen.

It didn't start out well, with director Henry Winkler, formerly The Fonz, who Tom knew from his stints on *Happy Days*, leaving the set after 12 days complaining of 'creative differences' with his leading man. He was replaced by Roger Spottiswoode.

The differences between Tom and Winkler really showed as the actor had very definite views about his role – and was prepared to use his star power to ensure his vision of the movie wasn't disregarded.

Turner and Hooch wasn't exactly *Lassie Come Home*. It wasn't even *Beethoven* – any hopes of a sequel or a canine merchandising payday were killed off along with the dog at the end of the movie.

But a note sent from Tom to executive producer Daniel Petrie illustrates the kind of thought he puts into his craft. It read: 'My intention is to shape Hooch into a more unique character whom we have not seen before in a movie, who will constantly surprise the audience just when they think they have him pegged, and who is sexy and attractive in his own peculiar way. My story, from my point of view, is of a man who has developed a very particular mode of living, without realising he has closed himself off from a great deal of the joy that is found in everyday life. Hooch disrupts his life in the way some girlfriends do; he makes Turner crazy, costs him money, and gets him into trouble. But when he is gone, there is nothing Turner wouldn't do to get him back.'

How such an ugly dog can be described as 'sexy' is incomprehensible, but Tom gets to play a couple of scenes in his black briefs, which is about as much as you are going to see of his less-than-stellar body in a Hanks film. Mare Winingham is his love interest, a veterinarian who helps him to calm down.

If his next film, *Joe Versus the Volcano, is* memorable for anything it is for Tom's first screen romance with Meg Ryan. Although it wasn't a hit first time out, the chemistry between the two stars would go on to provide the basis for arguably the finest light-comedy pairing since Tracy and Hepburn.

Playing an office-bound hypochondriac who sets off on an unlikely adventure in the South Pacific after being given six months to live because of a rare disorder called a 'brain cloud', Tom was attracted to the offbeat story and the prospect of working with Ryan.

In one of her stranger films, Ryan gets to play three different women.

John Patrick Shanley, who got an Oscar for his screenplay for Cher's tour de force, *Moonstruck*, was given a big $49 million (£30 million) budget, and expectations for the film were high. But Warner Bros didn't get much return on their investment. Tom's father didn't even get to visit his son on location in the sunny South Pacific because, despite the production outlay, the island scenes were shot on the Hollywood sound stage where the Yellow Brick Road was once constructed for *The Wizard o f Oz*.

Both stars got reasonable reviews, but the film was generally felt to be too much of a mish-mash to work. While saying Tom gave a 'carefully thought-out performance,' the *New York Times* said: 'Not since *Howard the Duck* has there been a big budget comedy with feet as flat as this.' The Oscar drums that had been beating loudly over Tom's career a year or so back had now fallen silent.

In the meantime, however, Tom had finally been contacted over the role all of Hollywood was still coveting – Sherman McCoy.

Director Brian De Palma had called offering Tom the job, saying he saw him combining the comedic and dramatic aspects of the novel in a manner reminiscent of Peter Sellers in Stanley Kubrick's *Dr Strangelove*.

The choice of maverick genius director Brian de Palma for the *Bonfire of the Vanities* astonished Hollywood, as everybody from Steven Spielberg to Martin Scorsese to Mike Nichols had been considered at one time or another. De Palma was considered a stylish thriller maker in the Hitchcock mould rather than the man to take charge of a big budget comedy. But he was still hot from 1997's hit screen version of *The Untouchables* and was given free rein by Warner Bros.

The casting also astonished the movie capital, where William Hurt was considered the favourite and the names of Michael Douglas, Steve Martin and even Tom Cruise had been among those hotly tipped.

Tom admitted he was 'intimidated' by the project, but the challenge – and the $5 million (£3 million) salary – was irresistible. The problem, and even he would probably admit it now, is that the critics of the controversial casting were right – Tom was not Sherman McCoy.

The Ivy League, Park Avenue world of blue-blood McCoy was not something Tom could relate to. In all his best roles, Tom had found something of himself to bring to the screen, giving his performances a vulnerable credibility that audiences recognised. His gypsy childhood offered him nothing to draw on this time.

'All I could do,' he admitted, in preparation for his role, 'is to try to get a sense of the space that Sherman McCoy existed, which is as alien to me as Odessa, Texas, or the planet Mars.' The best he could do was to visit the most elite private schools in Manhattan. He went to Yale. He paced a Wall Street trading floor.

Tom was seen as too young, too middle-class, too goofy to play the WASPy bond trader. Tom's pug nose didn't have the definition of McCoy's Yale proboscis depicted by Wolfe in his seminal novel of the '80s. He was derided as looking like 'Dennis the Menace in worsted wool pinstripes.'

Before the film opened, Tom acknowledged he was never the obvious choice for the part. 'If there was any challenge in this, beyond the simple one that goes into doing what I do in the first place, it was that of the 2.4 million people who read the book,

Top left: Tom aged five, with his brother Larry and sister Sandra.

Top right: The dizzy heights of *South Pacific* at high school, aged seventeen.

Bottom: A prayerful moment for a cute Tom at the Holy Child Catholic Day Care Center, Reno.

Top: Rita Wilson, aged eighteen. She was to be Tom's second wife.

Bottom: Tom aged sixteen in the high-school soccer team line-up (middle row, centre).

Not *Richard III*, as Tom said – but good fun nonetheless. Tom plays a goofy bridegroom in the frantic comedy *Bachelor Party*.

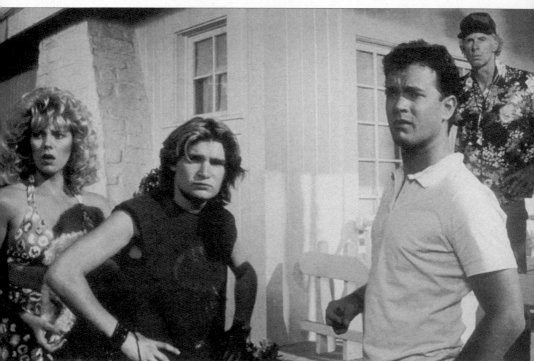

Top: Big – a massive success for Tom, leading to his first Academy Award nomination.

Bottom: The Burbs, with '80s heart-throb Corey Feldman, followed a year later.

Top: Tom stars as the scrupulously clean small-town cop, and Hooch is his slavering co-star in *Turner and Hooch*.

Bottom: Although Tom only plays a small part in it, this was his film – he wrote, produced and directed *That Thing You Do!*

Tom's brother Jim does some acting of his own – as a Forrest Gump-style character in soft-porn flick *Bufford's Beach Bunnies*.

thoughtful moment for Tom at the premiere of *Philadelphia*, his first Oscar-winning erformance.

Time out at a press conference, during the Venice Film Festival.

there were 2.4 million casting suggestions for Sherman McCoy – and I wasn't on any of those lists!' he said.

His research, incidentally, didn't include talking to Tom Wolfe. 'I didn't know what to say. "Here I am! Boy, you write really good books. Did you like *Punchline* at all?"'

The attraction of *Bonfire* was, essentially, its high profile. Few movies had been so eagerly awaited or so heavily hyped – or failed so miserably.

'It's not a matter of pressure that was put on me,' Tom told the *Orange County Register*. 'It's just that all the attention, the scrutiny on the choice of me and why I did what I do and why they put me in it in the first place. I don't have a Yale chin and da-duh-da-duh-da-duh. It is going to have that kind of focus on it. It's much different than if you were just making up a story that you were going to tell people for the first time.'

He put it even more succinctly: 'The idea of me playing Sherman McCoy is a huge, massive crapshoot.'

Tom was not the only questionable casting call, however. In *The Bonfire of the Vanities*, McCoy takes a terrible fall when he and his mistress are heading home to the posh Upper East Side of Manhattan one night and take a wrong turn into a run-down neighbourhood in the Bronx, which, to these denizens of a world of wealth and privilege, looks like hell itself. When they are approached by two black men, their racial paranoia sends them into a panic, resulting in a hit-and-run accident that leaves one of the strangers in a coma.

A drunken reporter latches onto the story in a bid to revive his fading career. And McCoy, who had once proclaimed himself Master of the Universe, sees his world fall around him like a pack of cards as he becomes a pawn in New York's political power games and a poster boy for the ills of society.

The character of drunken hack Peter Fallow was actually Australian in the book and the first actor in the running was Monty

Python's John Cleese. But De Palma thought an Englishman narrating the story would alienate an American audience, and decided that Bruce Willis would bring some big box-office starpower to the part.

This casting choice, and that of Melanie Griffith as McCoy's mistress, dumbfounded fans of the book as much as Tom's casting. It was actually Tom who was responsible for getting Griffith the job. According to writer Julie Salamon, whose book *The Devil's Candy* gives a fascinating insider's account of the making of the movie nicknamed 'The Bombfire of the Vanities', Tom had a lock on the role from the moment studio boss Peter Guber paid Wolfe £^{1}/$_2$ million for the rights for Warner Bros.

De Palma at first wanted Steve Martin. The studio wanted Tom Cruise: but Guber would call the director and the executives and chant: 'Tom Hanks, Tom Hanks, Tom Hanks, Tom Hanks...'

In his contract, Tom had it stipulated that he would have a say in his leading lady. Although Melanie Griffith was always in the running, De Palma was excited about Uma Thurman, particularly after she auditioned with Tom. But Salamon said Tom thought acting with Thurman would not work.

As nice a guy as he was, Tom certainly was not above pulling rank. And he preferred Griffith. Salamon said Thurman flew in for a screen test with Tom. 'She was marvellous, or maybe she just seemed to be because she was so very beautiful,' wrote Salamon. 'But there were dissenters, and in this case the only dissenter who mattered was Hanks. The studio had indeed asked for his opinion and he had given it.'

Ever the survivor, Tom came out of Salamon's book reasonably well, certainly compared with his co-stars, who are portrayed as insecure and professionally limited in comparison. Tom's icy wit was largely lost on both Griffith and Willis.

On one occasion, Griffith, who was married at the time to *Miami Vice* star Don Johnson, 'tottered' over to Tom, who that weekend had gone to his first Lamaze birthing class with Rita, who was expecting their first child that August, and sat on his lap. Salamon wrote: 'Griffith crawled onto his lap and asked him if he was nervous about their love scenes.

'"Not at all, no," he said, pulling his head back stiffly. "You know, Melanie," he said in a bantering tone, "I saw your husband on television. He was on a large boat looking very small." Griffith looked at him uncertainly.'

Halfway through shooting the film, Griffith shocked her colleagues by turning up with newly inserted breast implants. Fortunately, the sex scenes had not yet been shot so her breasts didn't seem to magically grow during the film.

Willis, fresh from his action man exploits in the first *Die Hard* film, was equally nonplussed by Tom's humour.

Wrote Salamon: 'In between takes, Willis and Hanks sat on their canvas chairs and watched themselves on playback on the video monitor. Hanks looked bored as Willis droned on about how much his work on *Moonlighting* improved his ability to play to the camera. Suddenly Hanks leaned forward until his face was just inches from the video monitor.

'He examined the close-up on Willis, whose image was wearing the wise-guy smirk that had become a subject of much mocking commentary among the *Bonfire* cast and crew over the past few weeks. "Big, shit-eating grin I see there on the monitor," said Hanks jovially. Willis showed no sign of registering the comment. Hanks peered at the monitor again. "Yup," he said. "There it is."

'Just then the Willis entourage converged around their boss. Hanks kept staring at the monitor.'

Willis's entourage, incidentally, included two bodyguards. Tom's only 'hanger-on' was his pregnant wife, who would pop onto the set periodically and made a fleeting appearance in the opening of the film, escorting an inebriated Willis to a society function.

Tom would later tell *Vogue* that Salamon 'did an amazing job. It was pretty fair and accurate. Of course, that doesn't mean I didn't want to throw myself off a bridge after I read it. Some people will assume that all that madness and indecision and overspending is how an unsuccessful movie gets made. But that's how every movie gets made. If *Bonfire* had been a stellar success, people would have looked at the book as some sort of blueprint of how chaotic making a great movie can be. The odds are always that you'll make an atrocious movie. The fact that you often don't is what makes you a hall-of-famer.'

The filming itself caused controversy with demonstrations in both the Bronx and New Jersey, where production was interrupted by real New Yorkers, who didn't see themselves as being on the edge of moral and political breakdown as depicted by Wolfe's book. There was also a considerable furore over the casting of the judge in the film. This began with De Palma auditioning a real-life Bronx judge, Burton Bennett Roberts. It was decided he wasn't likeable enough so the job trickled first to Walter Matthau, who agreed to do it but named his price too high at $1 million for a little over a week's work: then to Alan Arkin, before he, too, dropped out. In the end, the job of feisty Jewish judge Myron Kovitsky went to black actor Morgan Freeman, thus complicating the role the judge plays in the climactic, racially driven trial. The shoot was further distracted because Freeman was contracted to do a Shakespeare play *The Taming of the Shrew* immediately after *Bonfire*.

When shooting was over, Tom predicted the film would disappoint a lot of people 'because many will have a certain idea how the movie will look.' He was right. The film was a commercial and critical disaster.

Vincent Canby, in the *New York Times,* called it a 'gross, unfunny movie,' although he adds: 'Mr Hanks comes off best as the bewildered victim. He's nobody's idea of a prototypical Yale man, which is the way he's described in the novel, but he's a good comic actor...

'In one brief love scene, Miss Griffith's body appears to be so perfect as to be surgically reconstructed. Perhaps not, but *The Bonfire of the Vanities* is so wildly uneven that everything in it seems open to question.'

In its first 45 days of release in the US, the $50 million (£30 million) film took just over $15.7 million (£10 million) at the box office and was voted the worst film of the year in a poll of newspaper, magazine and TV film critics.

On 13 February 1991, the Oscar nominations were announced. *Bonfire* didn't get a mention.

Much later, Tom told *Time* magazine that ultimately, his Sherman McCoy was 'a pussy'.

'It comes down to that,' he said. 'In the nature of how Brian wanted to make that movie, McCoy couldn't be anything other than a pussy. Therefore, there was no mystery to it. He was a pussy from the beginning, and he was a pussy all the way through. He was just a big, fat pussy.'

He told the *Chicago Tribune:* 'The disappointment of a flop movie only stings for a few weeks, just like the Oscar euphoria only lasts a few weeks. I remember coming out of the shower, having forced myself not to think about *'Bonfire,'* having told myself all the usual stuff about everybody having a major flop, and feeling pretty much OK. But the television was on, and one of those morning shows came on, and the blistering review of *'Bonfire'* was the first thing on the show, and I went 'AAAUUUGGGHH!!'

'But by the time the movie came out, most of us knew *'Bonfire'* was not a good movie. When everyone looked at it, Brian De Palma said, "Hmmm. It might not be happening."

'Our mistake was that we made big changes in a novel that had entered the national consciousness and failed to pay attention to the minute details that made the novel so great on the page.' Nearly a decade after the film's critical and box-office nosedive, De Palma remained unrepentant about his spurned vision for the movie.

'Again it's an example of people not seeing what's on the screen,' he told the *Irish Times*. 'They bring these preconceptions of what they think the movie should be and then criticise it harshly because of that.

'In Europe, the film was better received because not so many people there had read the book. It was very much a book of its time. That happens. Some things tend to be very fashionable for a time, but they don't have the quality that makes them endure over the decades.'

What did the book's author, Tom Wolfe, have to say? In fact, he refused to join the throng criticising the film and the casting. 'I think it's bad manners in the Southern sense to harp and be critical of it,' he said. 'After all, I did cash the cheque.'

Tom's attempt to kick-start his roller-coaster career had failed, so he decided to take a longer break to recharge his batteries. Rita had given birth to their son and Tom was looking forward to playing dad for a while. Besides, he explained, Hollywood would wait. 'It's not like they stop kissing your ass right away. I think you really have to go a lot of years before you stop getting your ass kissed.'

ELEVEN

A SERIOUS STAR

IT SEEMED THE whole world was settling down to watch the 1994 Academy Awards on television. Tom was walking nervously into the Dorothy Chandler Pavilion, his wife on his arm, with a very real chance of winning a Best Actor Oscar.

If he was rightly considered an outsider when he won his first Academy Award nomination for his man-boy role in *Big*, Tom was the hot favourite this time for his memorable, bold performance as a lawyer dying of AIDS in the landmark film *Philadelphia*.

After one more flop, 1992's *Radio Flyer*, Tom was back on a winning streak. His next two films, A *League of Their Own* in 1992, with Geena Davis and Madonna, and *Sleepless in Seattle*, with Meg Ryan in 1993, had both been big hit comedies.

But *Philadelphia*, with its ground-breaking plot and serious message, was everything that *The Bonfire of the Vanities* was not. It was a thought-provoking, spellbinding drama with brave casting of actors who outgrew the shackles of their celluloid CVs to put in some magnificent performances.

More importantly, it was the darling of the critics and a big box-office success.

Even alongside such established serious actors as Denzel Washington and Jason Robards, as well as Latin heart-throb Antonio Banderas, Tom's star shone the brightest.

So it was no great surprise when Tom Hanks's name was read out ahead of fellow nominees Daniel Day-Lewis, Anthony Hopkins, Liam Neeson and Laurence Fishbourne as the winner of the Oscar for Best Actor.

* * *

The road to *Philadelphia* had begun more than three years earlier when Tom took a conscious decision to take a firmer hold on his career. After the *Bonfire* débâcle, where he even found himself being critiqued by a coffee shop waitress because he didn't have a 'Yale chin', Tom took his self-imposed sabbatical very seriously.

'It was the best thing for everybody,' he told *Vogue*. 'I needed a break from the industry. And the industry needed a little less of me for a while. How many times can you see somebody on yet another magazine cover? Plus with me it's always the same story. I'm an average guy, down-to-earth, kinda quirky, blah, blah, blah.'

He thought, simply, that he had been working too much. 'What had happened was, the kind of glamorous fun of making movies had just completely dissipated for me,' he told *Entertainment Weekly*. 'And I just felt as though I was no longer the hammer, but I was the anvil instead. I was very, very, very, very tired.'

Tom ended up staying away from Hollywood for 18 months, a risky recess for a star whose golden touch seemed to have deserted him of late.

He had now bought a beach house in Malibu, close to Steven Spielberg on the strip of beach hugging the Pacific Coast Highway that has become known as the stars' colony, and he fired his agent and allowed the scripts to build up as he played with his newly-born son.

The house had been owned by director John Frankenheimer and cost Tom and Rita more than $3 million (£1.8 million). Right on the sand, the two-storey 1928 home has two bedrooms downstairs and one upstairs in about 1,800 square feet. The master suite opens out onto a balcony overlooking the Pacific Ocean. There is also a separate maid's room and a two-bedroomed guest apartment with a kitchen.

The new oceanside home gave Tom the perfect excuse to take up a new hobby to mark up alongside 'hanging around the house, chatting on the phone and watching my stomach grow'. He bought a surfboard and found privacy and solace riding Malibu's famous rolling waves.

Only Tom's most fervent fans will remember his part in the ill-fated *Radio Flyer,* which nose-dived on its release in 1992. It was one of those movie projects that seem to crop up once or twice every few years in Hollywood: an idea that everyone gets very excited about and throws obscene amounts of money at – and then, just as quickly, loses interest in and condemns for its sky-high budget.

Director Richard Dormer's film tries to show how a boy escapes the daily misery of domestic beatings by building a fantastic flying machine from household odds and ends. But the mix of the child abuse theme underlying the plot and the whimsical fantasy of the story was an impossible sell.

It didn't help that the only famous name involved – Tom's – was unbilled and, although his narration runs through the film, he only appears briefly at the beginning and the end.

Sandwiched between the higher profile failure of *The Bonfire of the Vanities* and the start of his successful run of hit movies, *Radio Flyer* had virtually no effect on his career.

The same can certainly not be said of *A League of Their Own*. Tom's fully-fledged return to the screen in 1992 was as brave as it was unexpected. It was with Penny Marshall, the director he had made *Big* with a few years earlier.

But in *A League of Their Own*, Tom had little more than a supporting role. The film about women's baseball starred Madonna, Geena Davis, Lori Petty and Rosie O'Donnell in equally prominent parts. What's more, Tom piled on 30 pounds to play Jimmy Dugan, the broken-down, bloated, alcoholic ex-big-league baseball star who was reduced to coaching an all-girls professional team formed as a promotional gimmick during World War II.

Tom called it the start of the 'modern era' of Hanks movie making. What he couldn't have known at the time was that it was also the start of the most lucrative and consistently successful winning streaks in contemporary Hollywood history.

The actor was 36 at the time. The part he wanted to play in *A League of Their Own* was supposed to be fat, 50 and over the hill. It fitted right into Tom's new criteria, as long as he could barter down the age.

He had recently signed with Creative Artists, the most powerful talent agency in Hollywood. He told the *Observer*'s Lynn Barber that he instructed his new agent: 'I'm not going to play pussies any more.'

'What are pussies?' he continued. 'Those kind of guys that don't have a girlfriend, who can't commit, who run around trying to make sense of their lives and have some kind of Peter Pan syndrome.'

So he told his agent: 'If it's a story about a lawyer who loses his job and breaks up with his girlfriend, just throw it out. I'm looking to play men who are my age and are going through something bigger.'

'And that was actually a pretty big moment of clarity for me. Now I'll probably have to make some kind of decision like that again in another couple of years, but at that point, I decided that I was not going to take on a job unless it was a test of my range, and my abilities and my emotional horizon.'

At one point, he had asked Ron Howard how he could avoid the fate of Elliott Gould, whose poor choice in material eventually torpedoed his career. As a £3 million-a-film actor, he realised he had enough 'fuck-you' money to say no to studios dangling big fees for mediocre, type-casted comedies.

One of the first suggestions made by Tom's new, powerful CAA agent, Ron Meyer, was to go after the part of the coach in *A League of Their Own*. He had actually been offered the role several times already, but had rejected it as too small for a star of his stature. Now he went back and begged to be given the chance to take what was a supporting role.

Even though Tom was effectively taking a step back to do the baseball movie, Penny Marshall was not convinced at first that Tom would fit in. She told him: 'I don't want you to play cute. We don't need cute.' But cute was the last thing on Tom's mind. That wasn't part of his plan.

Another attraction was his love of baseball. While Madonna was moaning about the boredom of being on location in small-town Evansville, Indiana, Tom was enjoying every minute. When he wasn't on set, he was happy playing ball with the crew and Rita, as ever, had come to join him, renting a house in five acres of land for the whole family.

Tom's Jimmy Dugan, the big leaguer who overcomes his booze-tinged humiliation of coaching a girl's team to take pride in his players, was a delight, as was the 1992 film, which was a surprise hit, earning $107.5 million (£66,264,000) at the US box office.

Tom told *Entertainment Weekly*: '*A League of Their Own* did an awful lot for me, and this is strictly from the crass business point of view.

'I had any number of people saying, "What the hell are you doing? It's not even your movie, you're just a guy passing through.

Do you love Penny Marshall so much that you want to spend the summer and listen to her whine? Look what you could be doing!"'

But he had no idea what alternatives he had. 'I could have done *Popo Goes to the Big Town* and *Oops, I Tripped on a Lawn Chair.* Things like that. I was looking for something to do different and I think the message got out that he'll do anything. Which is a good thing. He'll get fat. He doesn't have to be the cute guy. He will cut his hair in an unattractive manner. He will be disgusting and sit there. He doesn't have to be the king of every scene that he is in. Well, that's a marvellous message to put out there.'

If his next film, the romantic comedy *Sleepless in Seattle,* wasn't exactly a stretch for Tom, then it certainly displayed the deft versatility that was to become his lasting trademark.

Sleepless not only called for his funny and his dramatic skills – Tom in fact turned it down originally, but changed his mind after a script rewrite. It also gave him the chance for the first time to play a role he had been practising for some time offscreen – that of a father and family man. He didn't have to dig through buried memories for motivation. It was right there at home.

Sleepless, which paired him up once more with Meg Ryan, scored with a public tiring of death and devastation on the big screen. Director Nora Ephron shamelessly romanced her audience.

Once upon a time, it provided the essential formula for every great Hollywood love story – the notion that each one of us has a perfect mate waiting for us out there in the tangle of humanity and that we know it the moment fate brings us together.

With *Sleepless in Seattle,* released opposite Steven Spielberg's *Jurassic Park* in 1993, romance came back into fashion. And while *Jurassic Park* broke box office records, its closest rival was the sleeping dinosaur weepie that eventually topped $126 million (£78 million) in the US.

The film made no attempt to disguise its debt to the golden days of Hollywood. From the opening moments using Jimmy Durante's rendition of *Casablanca's* 'As Time Goes By' to set the tone, to the closing scene at the top of the Empire State Building, it owed little to subtlety and everything to sentiment.

Star-crossed would-be lovers Tom and Meg don't meet until the closing minutes and even then they don't kiss. At that moment, when we would expect the music to rise and the cameras to close in for a lip-smacking close-up, we have to settle for a deep, mutually-longing stare and the slightest touch of hands.

The grand finale is consciously reminiscent of the sublimely soppy 1957 weepie *An Affair to Remember*. Throughout the film there are film clips and references to the Cary Grant and Deborah Kerr classic to underscore the romantic theme.

And, although her husband gets top billing, Rita – playing his sister – almost steals the show with a sobbing, three-minute monologue describing the maudlin 'chick movie' plot of the '50s tearjerker.

The *Sleepless* story is simple. Sam, played by Tom, is a widowed architect living with his son in Seattle who describes his feelings about perfect love over the phone to a national talk show psychiatrist. Annie – Meg Ryan – is a newspaper reporter listening on her car radio in Baltimore who becomes smitten by his sentiments.

That Sam and Annie are destined to meet and fall in love is never in doubt.

What writer and director Ephron, the ex-wife of Watergate journalist Carl Bernstein, succeeds in doing is to keep the audience's interest in the budding romance until their eventual dramatic meeting in the final frame.

After taking more than $18 million (£11 million) on its opening weekend, the film was credited with reviving the date movie in Hollywood.

Although it was a comedy, and a fairly soppy one at that, *Sleepless* was still a far cry from *Big*. Tom was very much an adult dealing with adult issues: the loss of a wife, bringing up a child alone, dealing with loneliness.

'He is one of the few actors around that can do tender and irritable and angry all at the same time,' said Ephron.

Tom identified strongly with the theme of finding love the second time around. After a miserable first marriage, his life with Rita was ample proof it wasn't a fantasy.

'That whole concept of the second chance is a powerful one to me,' he told *Vogue*. 'There's something wonderful about the notion that if you hang on long enough, it will all come around. If you just continue to breath in and out, eat and pay your rent, things will eventually get better.

'You know, I'm 36, and like us all, I've been through a bunch. It's petty pantywaist stuff, nothing terrible. The relative aspect of the human condition being what it is, I've gotten my ass kicked a number of times by life. I mean, I've had any number of reasons to have sleepless nights myself, so that helped make *Sleepless in Seattle* a pretty real story to me.'

At a time when many movies were focusing on how far they could push the special effects rather than push the acting envelope, Tom instinctively understood the attraction of the old-fashioned love story.

'It's a simple movie told within its confines and largely free of artifice,' he said. 'And I think audiences just responded to that. In order to enjoy most blockbuster hits these days, you've got to believe that dinosaurs can be genetically mutated, or that a guy in a bat-suit can drive through a city rounding up penguins.

'Here, the only thing you have to believe is that two people can still fall in love. When you look at Hollywood movies these days, that's a fairly original concept. And the strength of the whole thing is that you have a sense of these two people together until the end – well, what better way to end the movie?'

Sleepless made two hits in a row. Now *Philadelphia* was about to give him the critical respect – and the Oscar – that would elevate his career to an altogether new level.

Curiously, Tom had not always shared the general angst over the direction of his career. He always felt that the right roles were out there for him – and that in time they would land up on his desk. Now was that time.

He had met director Jonathan Demme in New York while doing publicity for *A League of Their Own*. The script for Philadelphia hadn't even been written then but Demme, whose previous film, *The Silence of the Lambs,* enraged members of the gay and lesbian community because of its depiction of a crazed transvestite serial killer, asked Tom if he was interested in being in the film.

'I probably would have run across the street just to watch him get into a car,' Tom told *Vogue*. 'We had one of those meetings where I just try not to sound like a dope. He told me about the idea for the movie and asked if would take a read of it when the script was done.

'And when I got it – well, all the adjectives won't do it justice. I want to say it's powerful, but it's more than just powerful. I thought it was a very real approach to what is going on. It's not one of those exploitative TV movie things that they always say is ripped right out of today's headlines – but the fact is, it is a story ripped right out of today's headlines.'

When Daniel Day Lewis, Demme's first choice for the role, turned it down because he was taking a six-month break, Tom jumped at the chance.

Although such prominent stars as Richard Gere, Al Pacino, William Hurt and Michael Caine have all played gay characters without jeopardising their careers – in some cases considerably enhancing them – the notion persists in conservative Hollywood that it can be a risky departure, leaving the question lingering, Is he really … ?

It wasn't a question that was ever really going to dog the twice-married father-of-four. But he was still asked all the time before the film came out. Why take the risk? What about your image? This time around there were no jokes, no Meg Ryan.

To Tom, that was never a factor. In fact, his cheerful, non-threatening image made him the perfect actor to dispel people's irrational fears about AIDS. Harking back again to his peripatetic childhood, he saw the constant moves and changes as a lesson that helped him early on to appreciate idiosyncrasy and diversity.

It also taught him that the easy path was not always the most satisfying. So when Demme offered him the choice of playing Andrew Beckett, the popular homosexual lawyer who gets fired when his bosses discover he has AIDS; or the cynical, ambitious Joe Miller, a family man who takes on Beckett's case without altogether losing his fear of gays, Tom was more intrigued by Beckett, even though he knew Miller was the more obvious choice.

He told CNN's Larry King: 'I felt from the very beginning that I had an awful lot in common with the character of Andrew Beckett. I thought that he was like me in so many aspects of my past and so many aspects of the way I look at life now. The fact that he was a gay man who was suffering from a terminal disease was, you know, in there, but I didn't see that as a massive obstacle.'

He added: 'I learned in making the film how much I have in common, how much we all have in common – but me specifically – with an awful lot of men out there who are supposed to be so different from us. We are so used to drawing the lines between the two poles, heterosexual and homosexual, and to find out that the men that I talked to had much the same sort of upbringing as I did, had the same sort of feelings of confusion when they were young. They had a lot of the same sort of adolescence. Came from a lot of the same sort of families, both for good and for bad.'

To learn how to emulate their lives, Tom interviewed AIDS patients who told him first-hand about growing up gay and living with the disease. Doctors taught him what happens to the body.

'To say the movie taught me a lot is really quite an understatement. I thought I was as hip and enlightened a man as you would find on average on the street. But this is the thing I think this movie and this script gave me when I read it was that I have never been very, very close to someone who has died of AIDS. I've known people, people in my family. I've lost a cousin. I wasn't very close and I haven't really witnessed it. What I thought this movie would give people who had never had it was the sense of a loss of someone that they loved and cared for to AIDS,' he said:

There was one particular encounter with an AIDS patient that made up Tom's mind to sign on for the project.

He explained: 'I went to see one man who was dying. We talked for hours and he was giving me tips on how I would look, act and feel at various stages of the illness. He told me that when he was first diagnosed, he went to the window and thought, "Clouds, this is the last time I am going to see you." I thought about that when I did one scene in the film and it brought tears to my eyes.

'When it was time to leave him I gave him a hug. His body was like it was on fire. AIDS was eating him up. As I hugged him, I knew I had to make the film.'

Tom didn't just have to prepare his mind for the part, he had to work on his body too, losing more than 30 pounds and having his hair thinned. He also read a lot of gay literature, including the memoirs of writer Paul Monette, author of *Borrowed Time*.

Co-star Denzel Washington would sneak sweets into Tom's pocket so he could 'smell the wrappers' and get a brief respite from his rice cake diet.

Inevitably, Beckett's character started to spill over into Tom's real life. 'You have to understand that I was always tired and hungry while I was making the movie,' he told the *San Francisco Chronicle*. 'We were also working with a lot of people who have AIDS. And every day I was coming out of the shower and seeing this emaciated body of mine. I was constantly bombarded with all these unsought images that you take home with you – about mortality and our society.

'I'm not a big Method actor. I don't immerse myself totally in a character. But I do end up being affected by all the stuff I do, and I found myself on this one crying over the most amazing and silly things.'

The intensity of the shoot meant Tom spent a lot of time thinking about the impact of the disease. He explained to the *Los Angeles Times*: 'Having thought about AIDS a good deal for quite a while now, I've come to think of it as a test of us as a civilisation, among other things. Is man more enlightened than he was during the Black Plague in Elizabethan England? I don't know. I do know there are still a lot of people who think this disease is about hedonism and is therefore deserved. All I can say is, that's not a very Christian response to suffering.'

But he wasn't always so politically correct with his interviewees. He told *Vanity Fair*: 'This woman reporter once asked me why there is this difference between the perception of gay men and gay women. I told her that I thought it is probably because most straight men think that gay men are forever lost, but that a gay woman can be cured with just one good big one right down the middle. She kind of looked at me like... I wanted to go, "Look, you asked me the question, sweetie."'

The film opened in December 1993 with some gay activist groups claiming Tom's lawyer wasn't intimate enough with his boyfriend, played by Antonio Banderas.

Larry Kramer, a leading light in the gay movement, lashed out at *Philadelphia* in the *Washington Post,* saying the film didn't portray gay life realistically, claiming it was unheard of for a family such as Beckett's to accept his homosexuality without prejudice. He also challenged the film's premise, since the passage of the Americans with Disabilities Act made it illegal to fire a person with AIDS, and he wondered why there were no gay love scenes, which would be standard in straight romantic movies.

Tom went on CNN's *Larry King Show* to promote – and defend – the film. He refuted Kramer's criticisms, but added: 'I think he has an awful lot of integrity and, out of the research I had done for the movie, I thought that if there was one bona fide hero from the beginning of the AIDS dilemma, it was Larry Kramer. At the same time, I signed autographs for a man downstairs who has an AIDS discrimination suit pending against his employers. I've received letters from the family members of men who died, who loved their sons or brothers just as much.

'There's one guy in the movie who plays my brother-in-law, who's pretty darned uncomfortable being in the same room with me there, but it's a very passive thing. How many times have we seen a door slammed in someone's face, especially in something like this? "No son of mine is going to bring this into my house!" We would have been dealing with some other brand of potboiler melodrama had we gone that way.'

Tom said a love scene between Beckett and his lover was discussed. 'There's a dancing scene, and we do kiss very briefly, and the fact that Antonio Banderas plays my lover, he's amazing. We're lovers who have been together for nine years. We're very secure in the relationship. But about the actual kissing scene, that we have both received heat for, there was a discussion – if it's the obligatory scene, or if we have that scene where everybody's saying, "OK, here's the two straight guys. They're going to kiss, and they are going to get credit for finally kissing."

'If we do that then the organic-ness of the moment is going to be lost somehow, because you are going to take it right away. There were other ways to show that these two gay men loved each other and would love each other for the rest of their lives, and that's what we found when they had the opportunity.'

In spite of the harping of some activists, the critics applauded the film – and raved about the performance of its star.

'Hanks makes it all hang together in a performance that

triumphantly mixes determination, humour, perseverance, grit, energy and remarkable clear headedness. Whatever else might nag about the film's treatment of a difficult subject, Hanks constantly connects on the most human level,' wrote Todd McCarthy in *Variety*.

People's Leah Rozen spoke for many when she said: 'Above all, credit for the movie's success belongs to Hanks, who makes sure he plays a character, not a saint. He is flat-out terrific, giving a deeply-felt, carefully nuanced performance that deserves an Oscar.'

The publicity plus the involvement of two trusted stars like Tom and Denzel Washington combined to shock the industry by pulling in a mainstream, as well as a gay, audience. The box office topped $77 million (£47 million) – not a blockbuster but more than anyone in the project had dared to hope for.

As the Oscar talk grew following the film's success, Tom declared: 'Let me tell you, I'll go to the Academy Awards to be a seat filler during the commercials. It's an honour to go. I'll park cars. I'll buff the plexiglass of that podium if they need somebody to do that. If I get nominated, I'll get to be able to go to my grave as a two-time Academy Award nominee, and that would make me very, very happy.' He wasn't to know he would soon become as close as the Oscars could get to a sure bet.

Tom had put 'the full force of my damned likeability behind the film' and it worked. He was even invited with Rita to spend the night at the White House after a special screening for President Clinton.

'What can I say? It was wild,' he told the *Los Angeles Times*. 'During the screening Clinton got up and walked out after a scene where Antonio Banderas and I are dancing together in military uniforms at a costume party, but I don't think he left because he objected to the scene. He said he thought the film was very nice and would be effective.'

Tom and Rita hardly slept they were so excited at staying in 'the most exclusive bed and breakfast in America': But in the morning, Tom bumped into the President in the kitchen. 'I was looking for breakfast and there was the President in his running shorts, carrying the *New York Times* and a mug of coffee. I said, "Good morning, Mr President," then we sat around for an hour and a half talking about everything under the sun.'

The success of *Philadelphia* meant he had finally left behind his zany image for good. He steeped himself in the part of a top corporate lawyer who is fired from a blue-chip firm when the partners discover he is dying from AIDS.

With a shaved head and make-up used to mask cancerous Kaposi's Sarcoma lesions on his face, there was no doubting his commitment both to the film and the cause.

* * *

So this, then, was the magic moment. The evening when all Tom had put into *Philadelphia* might be rewarded. The audience roared its approval as Tom was called to the stage. Clutching the golden statuette, a very emotional Tom went on to give one of the great, albeit rather rambling, acceptance speeches in Oscar history. Tears streaming down his face and sporting an AIDS red ribbon in his lapel, he paid a moving tribute to two gay men who had inspired his now Oscar-winning performance.

Following is the speech in full, with the first sentence alluding to Bruce Springsteen's 'Streets of Philadelphia' theme song, which also won an Oscar, and a nominated Neil Young tune.

'Here's what I know: I could not be standing here without the undying love that was just sung about by not Bruce, but Neil Young. And I have that in a lover that is so close to fine, we should all be able to experience such heaven right here on earth. I know also, that I should not be doing this... I should not be here. But I am because of the union of such film makers as Ed Saxon, Ron Nyswaner, Kristi Zea, Tak Fujimoto, Jonathan Demme – who seems to have these things attached to his limbs for every actor who works with him of late. And a cast that includes Antonio Banderas who, second to my lover, is the only person I would trade for. And a cast that includes many other people, but the actor who really put his film image at risk, and shone because of his integrity, Denzel Washington – whom I must really share this with.'

His voice shaking with emotion, Tom went on: 'I would not be here if it weren't for two very important men in my life. Two that I haven't spoken to in a while but I had the pleasure of the other night: Mr Rawley Farnsworth, who was my high school drama teacher, who taught me to act well the part, there all the glory lies; and one of my classmates under Mr Farnsworth, Mr John Gilkerson. I mention their names because they are two of the finest gay Americans, two wonderful men that I had the good fortune to be associated with, to fall under their inspiration at such a young age. I wish my babies could have the same sort of teacher, the same sort of friends. And there lies my dilemma here tonight. I know that my work in this case is magnified by the fact that the streets of heaven are too crowded with angels. We know their names. They number a thousand for each of the red ribbons we wear here tonight. They finally rest in the warm embrace of the gracious creator of us all. A healing embrace that cools their fevers, that clears their skin, and allows their eyes to see the simple, self-evident common sense truth that is made manifest by the benevolent creator of us all, and was written down on paper by wise men, tolerant men, in the city of Philadelphia two hundred years ago. God bless you all, God have mercy on us all, and God bless America.'

Speaking from her home on the outskirts of Oakland, where Tom and John had attended Skyline High School together in the early '70s, Mrs Gilkerson said they had once been very close friends.

'John was there for Tom during a very difficult time in his life when his parents were divorcing. John was never too busy to be a friend and was a great listener. When they were kids, John used to throw a lot of parties and Tom often came around to our house.

'He was the life and soul of the party – he showed the kind of wit that would later make him famous.

'But they drifted apart and did not stay in touch over the years. Maybe in his speech, Tom Hanks felt some regrets over the fact he was not there for John when he contracted AIDS.'

John Gilkerson died in 1989, aged 34, within a year of being diagnosed with the AIDS virus – never having heard again from Tom as the actor soared to fame and fortune in hit films such as *Splash* and *Big*.

A well-known ballet set and costume designer, John won an Emmy award for a TV puppet show. He collaborated on three ballets with eccentric rock star Frank Zappa and some of his stage designs are still used around the world.

Many of Tom's old friends, particularly actors he worked with in his early years, talk admiringly of his loyalty. Some even say he has helped them find work on his film projects. So his behaviour towards his old school friend – who helped him really belong for the first time in his life – is all the more curious.

Trudi Stillwell, a high school classmate of both men, said Tom had cold-shouldered his Skyline pals.

'I called Tom's publicist to get word to him immediately after John had died, but I never heard back. I had been in touch prior to that too when John was helping me to organise a reunion of our high-school drama class.

'I got the name of his publicist and I wrote several letters, but got no response. I got a number for Tom's agent and an old, old address. I called and wrote to his agent but I never heard from anybody. I suspect Tom probably would have known John had AIDS. But as far as I know he never wrote to him or called him. I know Tom had not been in touch with John since high school.

'John died a month before the reunion. It was very difficult for everybody. Some chose not to attend. We dedicated the reunion to John.

'Tom dropped out of sight from all of us right after high school. He didn't make any effort to stay in touch. I have a feeling that Tom mentioned John in his speech because he feels a bit guilty that he was not more in touch when John was dying.

'John lived life to the fullest right up until the end. He was a very fine, decent – and private – person.'

Added Trudi, a film projectionist: 'John had a strong influence on all of us. We all expected John to be in the famous position Tom is in today. I am just glad that Tom realised, after the fact, that John and Rawley Farnsworth had such an impression on his life.'

Ballet-company founder Ron Guidi, another of John's close friends who helped nurse him to the end, was also amazed at Tom's Oscar speech. 'I was so surprised when Tom Hanks mentioned John. I was very touched by his Oscar speech, but it sounded as though he thought John was still alive. I am sure someone must have kept him in contact with John's condition.

'It didn't take long for him to die. He was gone within a year. He refused to take medication. From the waist up he was like a skeleton – towards the end we had to carry him around. He got so thin that it hurt him to sit down.'

The other person from the past Tom saluted in his speech, high school drama teacher Rawley Farnsworth, was also effectively 'outed' by his old pupil. Farnsworth had never told any of his students during a long and distinguished career that he was gay and hadn't heard from Tom for nearly 18 years, following his career on the screen, along with everyone else.

Three days before Oscar night, he got a call at his San Francisco flat. 'I don't know if you remember me,' the caller said, 'but I'm an old student of yours. I've got a ticket to the Academy Awards and, if I win, I would like to use your name in regard to the content of *Philadelphia*.'

The student was, of course, Tom Hanks, and, although he didn't actually explain he was going to say his mentor was gay, Farnsworth said: 'I'd be thrilled.'

Farnsworth described sitting in front of the television on Oscar night. 'My friend and I had a couple of drinks and were planning to have dinner. It turned out that we never had dinner.'

Tom had told Farnsworth on the phone to 'just remember, when I'm looking into the camera, I'll be looking right at you.' After the speech, Farnsworth turned to his friend, dazed, and said: 'Did he say what I thought he said?'

The bemused teacher, now retired, said later: 'I would have had second thoughts about being outed as a gay if I had still been teaching. If I was still in professional life, I don't know how I would have reacted.

'Tom obviously feels strongly and wanted to get a message across. Now I am retired I don't really mind that my name was used. I actually thought Tom's speech was absolutely terrific. He had something he wanted to get off his chest and he did it in a very beautiful way that inspired people.

'When Tom Hanks phoned me three nights before the Oscars to ask permission to use my name, it was the first time I'd heard from him since 1977. I believe, like most straight men, Tom had stereotypical images of gay people and how they acted.

'But he said he had found inspiration in his association with John and I. Through us, he understood that not all gays are stereotypes.' Farnsworth, a teacher for 30 years, added: 'I was never aware that he knew I was gay. Evidently, he did. Ours was a teacher-student relationship and I didn't discuss it with him and I haven't discussed it since. I was very discreet with all of my students. My lifestyle is my own business, and not theirs.

'Tom seemed to know what had happened to John Gilkerson when we talked. I had stayed in touch with John and saw him for lunch six months before he died. It was very sad. He had lesions around his face which he used make-up to cover up, but I saw one behind his ear. He had a terrible cough and was going through physical deterioration.'

Although he admitted to being 'a little paranoid' after the speech, particularly when he was besieged with calls from the media, Farnsworth has used his 15 minutes of fame to help promote gay causes, even though he has never been an activist. The white-haired, slightly-deaf teacher became something of a celebrity. He was commended on the Congressional Record in Washington, constantly sought out as a spokesman for gay rights and was the recipient of a number of awards himself – one presented by Tom – recognising his role as a mentor and role model.

After the furore died down, he said: 'Tom wrote me a beautiful letter saying he hoped he hadn't brought the press down on my head. Some months later we had dinner together and I wondered if it was all to do with his ego, but after studying him, I saw no signs of it at all.'

In an ironic footnote to the story, Tom's 'outing' of his drama teacher was itself turned into a hit Hollywood film. Producer Scott Rudin watched the 1994 Oscars at home with theatre director friend Lori Steinberg and was struck by the drama of Tom praising his 'great gay teacher'. Rudin recalls Steinberg adding, 'whose job I just lost'. Thinking instantly that the story would make a great basis for a film, Rudin took the idea to Paramount Pictures, and the studio green-lighted a budget of more than £20 million.

Giving Farnsworth's alter ego a fiancé and a classroom was Hollywood's way of injecting drama into the movie, which vied for controversy by having Tom Selleck, as a gay TV reporter, kiss the teacher, played by Kevin Kline, full on the mouth.

The film, *In and Out*, also starred Matt Dillon as the old pupil who names his drama teacher as a big influence – and a homosexual – in his speech after collecting the Best Actor Oscar. On its opening weekend in 1997, the film took over $20 million

(£12 million), the second-highest September opening after *The First Wives Club*, which headlined Goldie Hawn, Bette Midler and Diane Keaton.

But Rawley Farnsworth, while stunned and awed by Tom's dramatic range in the powerful *Philadelphia,* was unimpressed with *In and Out*. He offered his services to Paramount, but was told, 'thanks but no thanks'.

He was especially critical of the film's climactic ending, where the townspeople revolt against a homophobic school board to announce, one by one, that, if Sir is gay, then so are they. Says Farnsworth: 'The ending is just stupid. People don't behave like that.'

Talking about his famous speech to the *New York Daily News* in 1998, Tom denied outing his teacher. 'I didn't out him. He was thrust into the public eye, which he kind of liked, which he deserved, which was kind of great. And I've gone back and been at some things where he has been honoured. He's a very sweet guy. I get a letter from him now and then.

'I hadn't seen him or spoken to him in many, many years. But Mr Farnsworth made acting in the theatre the most fun in the world for me. And I knew then that he was gay. So when I referred to him at the Oscars, the nature of the world had changed so much that he had no problem. I don't know what it would have been like in 1974 if a teacher were to say, "I'm gay." It could have been an ugly and much different circumstance. But one whole aspect of *Philadelphia* was: What's to be afraid of? And if I hadn't had this gay teacher in high school, I wouldn't have been up there getting an Academy Award, so think it was even more important to say I wished my kids had the same sort of influence that I'd had from a human being like I had from my gay drama teacher in high school.

'And then they made a movie out of it and I got the best reviews of my career for a movie I am not even in. And not a dime in residuals – but that's okay, I'm not making a fuss.'

Chief among critics of the now famous Academy Awards speech

was news review magazine *The New Republic,* which said one of the premier 'wince-making' moments of the Oscars was Tom's 'belaboured and incoherent attempt to immortalise those dead from AIDS'.

Tom's friend, Steven Spielberg, said he thought it was 'incredible'. The director, who won an Oscar the same year for *Schindler's List,* believed the speech 'in a sense communicated more about what *Philadelphia* was saying and reached more people than the movie itself will.'

Tom told *Vanity Fair*: 'I knew that I was going to have to say something to somebody, win or lose. So when the time came, I wanted to be armed somehow so that what I'd say would be germane to the work that I had done and the movie that I was connected with. I was also aware that there was going to be this big audience for what I was going to say.'

* * *

Unintentional furore aside, the Oscar-winning actor had come a long way. But the journey was far from over. He was about to become a box-office phenomenon... and an exceedingly rich man.

TWELVE

LIFE IS A BOX
OF CHOCOLATES

IT WAS EXACTLY one year later and Tom was back in the Dorothy Chandler Pavilion with Rita again by his side and his stomach full of the same butterflies. Surely he couldn't be the first actor since Spencer Tracy in 1937 and 1938 to win back-to-back Best Actor Oscars. John Travolta's thrilling comeback performance in Quentin Tarantino's *Pulp Fiction* was the sentimental favourite and the 1995 nominees included the venerable Paul Newman, Morgan Freeman and Nigel Hawthorne.

Tom's unique role in the offbeat *Forrest Gump* had helped the film become an unlikely triumph. Against all the odds, it was on its way to being one of the highest-grossing movies of all time. But the film breaks every mould of movie making. There's no quest, no bad guy. The hero is an idiot. And besides, Tom Hanks got his Oscar the previous year.

After his first nomination in 1988, Tom had spoken of his good fortune, telling the *Los Angeles Times*: 'I remember going through the phalanx of TV cameras at the 1988 Academy Awards and somebody said, "It is going to be hard to live this year down, isn't it?" I said there that I knew a year like I had comes once every 15 years if you are lucky, once every 10 years if you are amazingly lucky and once every five years if you are a phenomenon. And I am not laying any claim to being that.

'I just knew that it had been wild and it would probably fall apart somewhere down the line. I said that I would feel bad about it for a while when it happened, but that in the end I'd be okay.'

Well, even under his own classification, on that cool Californian evening in March, 1995, he became a phenomenon twice over.

For Tom would once again dumbfound the critics. A thunderous ovation greeted him as he accepted his second successive Best Actor Academy Award. This time, he didn't need anyone's permission for the tribute he planned to give from the podium. It was a love letter to his wife. It was also another memorable speech.

'Thank you. I'm standing here in lieu of my fellow nominees who are just as deserving, if not more so, of this moment. I'm standing here because of an army of people who, over the course of a backbreaking schedule that was set by Bob Zemeckis, worked mach harder than I did and had much more at risk if our efforts were not successful. I am empowered to stand here thanks to the ensemble of actors, men and women, who I shared the screen with, who, in ways they will never understand, made me a better actor.

'And I'm standing here because the woman I share my life with has taught me, and demonstrates for me every day, just what love is.

'Man, I feel as though I am standing on magic legs, in a special effects process shot that is too unbelievable to imagine and far too costly to make a reality. But here is my mark, and this is where I am supposed to look and believe me, the power and the pleasure and the emotion of this moment is a constant speed of light. It will never be diminished nor will my appreciation and the meaning between two simple words that I can only offer you here: Thank you. God bless you – in this room, and God bless you all around the world.'

The award, in such a contrasting role to that in *Philadelphia*, would cement his name in Hollywood lore forever and guarantee him just about any project he fancied in the future. It also earned him a fortune. For although it had a troubled history, Tom so believed in the project that he agreed to forego his upfront salary, which would have probably been in the region of £8-10 million. Instead, he was given a percentage of *Forrest* Gurnp's gross, meaning his financial benefits would live or die with the success or otherwise of the film.

At last count, Forrest Gump had taken close to $356.8 million (£219,934,000) in the United States alone and more than $600 million (£369,845,000) around the world. Tom's personal share was estimated at up to $60 million.

The great irony, however, was that Paramount was still claiming one year after its release that the fourth-highest grossing movie ever was $60 million (£36,984,000) in the red.

It was one of the most striking examples yet of creative Hollywood accounting – and a slap in the face to Gump writer Winston Groom, a former Washington journalist, who got a comparative pittance for allowing his novel to be put on the big screen. He was paid $300,000 (£184,922) for the book's rights and given a three per cent cut of the net profits.

The good news for Groom was that the movie turned out to be a great success and turned him from an obscure author into a household name. The bad news was that while some of the participants in the project – like Tom Hanks – were going to become incredibly rich incredibly fast, he was going to have to wait for any additional money to dribble in.

Groom's problem was that instead of signing a royalty deal

linked to gross profits, his deal depended on net proceeds and, as he found out to his cost, that is controlled by the vagaries of the studio money men.

By December of 1994, Paramount had collected about $191 million from domestic and international *Forrest Gump* ticket sales after cinema owners had already taken their 50 per cent cut, according to a Paramount accounting document quoted by the Associated Press news agency in a June 1995 article.

Paramount then took $50 million in production costs, added a distribution and marketing fee of about $74 million, $62 million in distribution expenses, payments to the film's star and director of close to $62 million and $6 million in interest.

The result: a loss of more than $60 million.

If there was a negative net profit, then Groom's percentage deal wasn't worth a bean, leaving cruel studio insiders to dabble with one of the film's stock aphorisms in reference to the unfortunate writer: 'Simple is as simple does.'

As you can see from the balance sheet above, Tom and director Bob Zemeckis were far wiser in the ways of filmtown. They did indeed take a gamble on the film being a success, but they stood to profit handsomely if their hunch about *Gump* was proved right. For they negotiated contracts which guaranteed each of them an estimated eight per cent of the film's gross receipts – that's *receipts, not profits*. The deal gave them a cut of the very first dollars that came in from cinemas, video stores and soundtrack sales.

There was little sympathy for the writer in Hollywood. Paramount advanced Groom another $250,000 against a projected net profit after he hired a lawyer to claim a fairer share. But the general feeling was that A-list guys like Tom and Zemeckis deserved the cash for making the project happen. As an untried writer who wasn't on any list before the movie, he should be happy for his success.

It certainly wasn't the first time Hollywood's 'net profits' *op:* The role of a degenerate baseball coach in *A League of Their Own* was another *f* Tom's great acting moments.

ottom: Sleepless in Seattle was a tear-jerker that broke box office records, and *stablished* a friendly partnership with co-star Meg Ryan.

Tom starred as the eponymous hero in *Forrest Gump*, the feel-good tale of an ordinary man in extraordinary circumstances.

Inset: Tom plays second fiddle to Dan Aykroyd in spoof cop-film *Dragnet*.

Top: Tom's sensitive portrayal of a twelve-year old boy endeared him to millions in *Big*.

Bottom: Never living up to the promise of the novel, *The Bonfire of the Vanities* starred Tom as a broker fallen on hard times.

Tom's childhood obsession with space finally found fulfilment with *Apollo 13*, the movie of the ill-fated space mission.

Top: Tom kept his band of 'soldiers' together during the boot-camp programme that director Steven Spielberg insisted they undergo.

Bottom: You've Got Mail was another successful partnership for Tom and Meg Ryan – a light, romantic comedy.

Tom found himself pitted alone against the elements and his own psyche (and a volleyball called Wilson) in his 2000 hit *Cast Away*.

Top: 2002's *Catch Me If You Can* – the film based on the true-life story of über-scammer Frank Abagnale Jr – included a subtle supporting performance from Tom. Here he is seen with co-star Leonardo DiCaprio and frequent collaborator, director Steven Spielberg.

Bottom: Tom catches 40 winks in his role as Viktor, an immigrant stuck in limbo at JFK Airport, in the ambivalently-received *The Terminal*.

Seen here in enigmatic style with co-star Audrey Tautou, Tom plays the lead role of symbologist Robert Langdon in the biggest blockbuster adaptation ever, *The Da Vinci Code*.

accounting has caused jaws to drop. In 1992, Warner Bros maintained that the hugely successful *Batman* movie lost more than $20 million.

One thing about *Forrest Gump* that pretty much everyone was in agreement about was that it was successful primarily because of its star.

'There is no one else like Tom working today,' said Gump co-producer Wendy Finerman. 'He has such a likeability. As an actor, and as a human being, he's a dream.'

What's more, while such popular stars as Julie Andrews and Dudley Moore once won the same kind of warm acclaim, their careers dipped after their hit films because of their limited range. Tom had shown he wasn't confined by any such handicap.

Finerman, who toiled for nine years to bring Groom's littleknown novel to the screen, found a great ally in Tom. He told her that if she could get together a good enough screenplay he would take the part. They had both been working on a project called *The Postman* which was later, much altered, a major box office flop for Kevin Costner. When that fell through, they persevered with *Gump*.

Warner Bros spent a considerable sum developing the project, commissioning first Groom and then two further writers to write screenplays. But because executives didn't think it was ever going to work, the studio wrote off the cash and passed on the project, allowing Paramount to resurrect it and put it on the fast track. Tom signed up immediately, as he had promised Finerman he would do.

It was another risky role and the tinseltown soothsayers were again predicting Tom was taking a wrong turn. The word was that the film about a low-IQ Southern simpleton would make the Academy-Award winner look stupid.

But Tom saw in the plot the same thing that his audience would. He was a baby-boomer. He had grown up with JFK, Elvis, The Beatles and Vietnam. With his slow-witted grace and honest to God truthfullness, Forrest was taking the audience back through 30 years of their own history, and making them laugh and cry along the way.

Said Finerman: 'The childlike innocence of *Forrest Gump* is what we all once had. It's an emotional journey. You laugh and cry. It does what movies are supposed to do – make you feel alive.'

Gump was an implausible hero, an opinion-free dimwit who naively fumbled his way to successive triumphs as football star, a Vietnam soldier and a shrimp-fishing mogul. But he tapped the sentiments and captured the hearts of filmgoers.

He always seems to turn up in the right place at the right time to become celebrated, wealthy or offer a pearl of wisdom – 'stupid is as stupid does' and the lasting 'life is like a box of chocolates – you never know what you are going to get', for instance.

Director Robert Zemeckis, who made *Back to the Future* and *Who Framed Roger Rabbit?*, used the latest technology to splice Gump into footage of the famous, from Kennedy to Elvis. His influence on events extends from helping to capture the Watergate burglars to collaborating with John Lennon.

The film is a celebration of innocence and Gump's invincible goodness found a resonance in a world where the weak and trusting are customarily abused by the strong and the crooked.

Nevertheless, the scale of its success remains a mystery even to its creators. 'You figure it out,' said Tom. 'There's no bad guys or suitcases full of money. Nobody is trying to solve a mystery or save the life of a cow.

'But you don't have any problem believing that he has met three presidents or that he played ping pong in China or won a medal in the army.'

The fact the unlikely character is so believable is primarily due to the actor who played him. Tom took six months researching his part, finding ways to make it real. He spent a lot of time at a school for the mentally retarded in Los Angeles, but, as he had done with all his most successful films, he also looked inside himself for inspiration.

The font of loneliness he had carried from his childhood right through to his early 30s was again the source he immersed himself in.

Tom told *Interview* magazine: 'It's about a guy with a limited IQ who operates at the speed of his own common sense. He lives an amazing life and sees amazing things, but the purity of how he sees the world was what I thought was amazing about the screenplay, and what he goes through to get to the point where we are all at. All the great stories are about our battle against loneliness: *Hamlet* is about that; so is *The Importance of Being Earnest*. That's what I always end up being drawn toward:'

Journeying through such uncharted territory, however, Tom still admitted he was 'scared every minute' of filming, never quite knowing how it was all going to turn out.

In fact, *Forrest Gump* was seen as anything but a sure thing before its release. The book was supposedly too wide-ranging, quirky and uncommercial, and Tom was perceived as making a major career blunder in taking the bizarre lead role.

The key to the character was when he found Gump's voice. Said Tom: 'We had none when we started. Then Jessica Drake, my voice coach, and I heard Michael Humphreys, who played the young Forrest Gump. He was from Mississippi up by Tennessee and he had this great vocal cadence with very particular characteristics, with hard "Gs" in the middle of things. Like he said, "sing-ging'. I listened to Michael a lot, she made linguistic templates and then I read the entire script to her. It took the better part of three weeks and by the end I was doing it without having to think about it.'

He needn't have worried what the public would make of the movie. When *Forrest Gump* opened on the Fourth of July weekend in 1994, it took more than $25 million in just three days. It was a considerable success for a non-action film with such a quirky plot and the phenomenon would only grow from there.

Having lost so much weight for *Philadelphia,* Tom, who has

always had to watch his waist, felt he was looking his very best for *Forrest Gump,* even if he had to put up with the bizarre haircuts. 'I was in incredibly good shape then,' he told the *Observer.* 'My God, I was my butt in that movie! When Forrest is running across the football field, I just say look at that, my legs! Actually, I hurt myself in the course of doing that, I pulled a muscle in my quadriceps and I had to get a massage therapy, because I had to keep running for the rest of the movie, so I was being worked on by a lady and she muttered, "My God, you have the legs of a 16-year-old!"'

Tom's reply was suitably Gumpian: 'Thank you ma'am.'

By now a regular on the annual Hollywood 'power lists', Tom followed such screen luminaries as Bette Davis and Cary Grant in November 1994 as a recipient of the Louella Parsons Award, granted by the Hollywood Women's Press Club for the star who 'represents the best image of the entertainment industry to the world.' The award also recognised 'the social consciousness of his films,' adding that Tom's work 'is proof that responsible film-makers can also win at the box office.'

And the acclaim kept coming. In 1995, the *Hollywood Reporter* named Tom one of the five most powerful stars in Hollywood together with Arnold Schwarzenegger, Mel Gibson, Harrison Ford and Tom Cruise. The following year, *Screen International* made him the top player, ahead of Cruise, Ford, Schwarzenegger and Brad Pitt. Harvard University even made him their Man of the Year. He dressed up in drag to accept the Ivy League college's Hasty Pudding Award, sashaying across the stage in high heels, a satin dress and a long auburn wig to tell the cheering tuxedo-clad crowd in his best *Bosom Buddies* voice: 'Not bad for a guy who didn't even make it through Sacramento State University.'

An interesting sidebar to the *Forrest Gump* success story involves Tom's youngest brother, Jim, who is also an actor.

Jim, four years Tom's junior, was drafted in as his famous brother's stand-in for the film. 'Tom had other doubles, but they couldn't do the run,' Jim told *People* magazine in 1995. 'That's a stupid Hanks thing.'

There has never been much doubt who has taken all the prizes in the unsaid sibling rivalry between the brothers, who grew up separately – Tom with his father and Jim, the 'baby' of the family, with his mother.

Despite various commercials and small movie roles, Jim has never broken through into the big time. But there is a connection between Tom's comic masterpiece in Gump and a character his lookalike brother played in a sex comedy film.

Hollywood producers who hired Jim in the soft-porn romp *Buford's Beach Bunnies* were stunned over the striking similarities. In the tacky B-movie, made three years before *Forrest Gump*, Jim plays lovable buffoon Jeeter Buford... with some of the same physical mannerisms that Tom used later to turn his character into a cult hero worldwide.

By astonishing coincidence, some of Jim's scenes are even similar to his brother's in *Forrest Gump*.

The largely forgotten *Buford's Beach Bunnies*, made in 1992, now gathers dust in the comedy section of some video shops. The low-budget film is hardly a classic. But it bears watching alongside one of the biggest movies in history.

As Jeeter Buford, the sexually repressed son of a burger bar king, Jim:

- Invents the now famous jerky run associated with Forrest Gump.
- Sits straight with his knees together and hands folded in his lap – the familiar Forrest Gump look which became a trademark of Tom's portrayal.
- Panics and freezes when a topless girl tries to seduce him –

as does Tom in a scene when he meets up with his old Vietnam war pal at a New Year's Eve party.

- Is dominated by his father who wants to help his dimwitted son get over his mental problems – in Gump's case, it is his mother, played by Sally Field, who is his mainstay in life.
- Demonstrates shy politeness to women, calling them 'ma'am' – as does Gump.
- Gets pushed around by bullies. At the start of *Forrest Gump*, Tom is shown as a crippled child in leg calipers being chased by stone-throwing little thugs.
- Keeps the flames of passion going for a girl he marries at the end. The main theme running through *Forrest Gump* is his love for his troubled childhood sweetheart Jenny – whom he eventually weds.
- In the Jim Hanks movie, the 'ghosts' of Humphrey Bogart, Marilyn Monroe and Clint Eastwood appear in front of Jeeter. Computer trickery in *Gump* allows Tom to be seen apparently meeting President Kennedy and John Lennon.

Director Mark Pirro, who went on to make a schlock horror movie called *Nudist Colony of the Dead*, said: 'When Jim first auditioned for the Buford role, he didn't tell me that he was Tom's brother.

'I kept saying he should get a job as a Tom Hanks lookalike. It was only afterwards that he told me he was his brother. I guess he didn't want me to know. He was pretty sensitive about it.

'We spent a couple of days filming at Venice Beach and a big crowd started gathering. Jim said to me, "They all think I'm Tom. I hate it when this happens."'

Michael Wojciechowski, who was director of photography on *Buford's Beach Bunnies*, commented: 'Jim's character and Forrest Gump are definitely very similar – the naïve, wide-eyed wanderer through life. Jim did the movie two years before *Forrest Gump*.

'I would have thought Tom saw his brother's film. Our movie

was shot in three weeks on a very low budget. It only cost around $300,000.'

Film distributor Edmund Fernando added: 'There are some similarities.'

Jim has never commented on the parallels, although he told the *Los Angeles Times*: 'The casting director said you should go in and not tell them your real name. So he took my headshot and cut my name off and I used my middle name. I went in as Jim Matthews.' Asked about his brother, Jim explained to *People*: 'Since I moved to Los Angeles, we have slowly built a relationship. It's strange. He sounds and looks a lot like me, but our backgrounds are very different.'

Unlike his sister and brothers, Jim grew up in the same area of Red Bluff, Northern California, attending the local Mercy High School and seeing his siblings only when they visited at weekends and during the holidays. The shy brother didn't share Tom's drive to be an actor as a young man and moved to Sacramento with his girlfriend Karen Praxel, where he found work waiting tables.

The couple married in 1986, with the whole family – including Rita – in attendance and Karen decided to try and give it a go as an actress in Hollywood. Soon after they moved, Karen found a job as a receptionist for an agent. The agent then managed to coax Jim into showbusiness.

He admitted his first auditions were 'horrific'. But he went on to make a modest living with advertising voice-overs and parts in small films. Jim and Karen moved into a home in trendy Venice Beach, Los Angeles and, in 1992, they had a son, Gage.

A commercial for the Volvo 960 in 1996 led to an outcry among Hanks fans who were incensed that their double-Oscar-winning hero was peddling cars on the small screen. The pitchman, of course, was Jim. Little brother also helped sell Jack in the Box fast food, Hyundai cars and fresh packaged salads.

The part in *Buford's Beach Bunnies* came after a few acting lessons and was followed by a role in a film called *Night Skies,* in which he was blown to smithereens, and a part in a pulp fiction sci-fi film *Xtro: Watch the Skies,* playing a wisecracking Marine. He also starred in an ill-fated series with original *Batman* TV actor Adam West called *The Clinic*. But reviews for the soap opera spoof were not very kind. The *Indianapolis Star* said: 'A curiosity here is Jim Hanks, Tom's brother, in a small, bizarre role. With the same high forehead and haircut, laugh and a very similar voice, Jim looks and sounds eerily like his sibling. But who got the family acting ability is evident from his performance – and his presence in a loser like *The Clinic*.'

He was supposed to team up with an actress with another famous name, Alison Eastwood, daughter of Clint, for another series called *High Hopes,* about staff working at the Universal Studios theme park in Los Angeles. Jim was going to play a father-figure entertainment director, but the show never got off the ground.

Comparisons with Tom have inevitably haunted his acting career. 'Some people are really great about it. Some aren't,' Jim told the *Los Angeles Times*. 'I auditioned for something recently and heard back later that because the casting director could not get over the fact that I looked so much like Tom, she didn't even hear me. She did not HEAR my audition.'

Novelist and director T.L. Lankford wasn't distracted by Jim's amazing similarity to his big brother. He cast him in *Dark Red,* a low-budget thriller, but even then he lost out on a bigger part because of one of Tom's hit films.

'At first, I wanted to cast him as one of the leads, a character who has suffered brain damage,' said Lankford. 'But when he read it, I realised it was far too close to *Forrest Gump*, and neither of us wanted to exploit Tom's name or that character.'

The director felt awkward asking Jim to play a policeman, a much more limited role. But Jim told him: 'At this point, a job's a job.'

However, Jim has turned down potentially lucrative projects because they were obviously aimed at cashing in on Tom's success. He was approached about doing a made-for-TV remake of *Splash*, and later a network wanted him to play the lead in a television series based on *Big*.

'I was contacted five different times,' he said in 1995. 'Then somebody from one of the studios called me at home on a Saturday morning pleading me to come in and read it. I said no.'

When he told Tom, his brother told him: 'You're right. You're absolutely right. It would be the most stupid thing you could possibly do.'

That didn't stop Jim from moving in on Tom's turf when Disney made a CD-ROM based on the hit *Toy Story* movie, which the actor made after winning his Oscars. Jim stepped in for Tom as the voice of the cowboy, Woody, on the computer disc.

He has since been featured as the voice of Spike the dog in a 1998 show called *Sunset Beach*.

Jim is the only other member of the Hanks family to try his hand at acting. Although Tom went on to greater fame and fortune, it was his big sister, Sandra, who was the first to hit it big in the entertainment world.

After being brought up by her father, she moved back to live with her mother as a teenager. Having finished her education, she moved to Sacramento and set up her own company supplying newsreel clips to television stations. The business was a huge success and, as she says, 'I actually had a fancy car and a huge house before Tom.'

Sandra – nicknamed 'Pandora' by Tom – has been married three times. She had two daughters, Jennifer and Jaren, with first husband, Stan Combes. After divorcing second husband, Scott Adamson, she met British bobby Mark Benoiton on holiday in the Seychelles. Sixteen years her junior, Benoiton joined the Dorset police after studying agriculture and working on pig farms.

He comes from the Seychelles and met Sandra there while on a visit home. The couple moved out to the paradise island to set up a restaurant after living in a comfortable flat in Bournemouth for a couple of years.

Sandra told *OK!* magazine: 'Mark grew up on a beach in a home with no electricity and no television. I've had to show him *Casablanca* and say "This is Ingrid Bergman and Humphrey Bogart," and he had never heard of them.

'But he knows about the sea and the jungle. He can fish for dinner and he can climb a coconut tree. Although our backgrounds are very different, our interests are the same. Jungles and wildlife are my passion, my obsession.

'I love to travel and I don't stay in fancy hotels. I backpack and eat and drink what the locals do. At the moment, I am writing a novel on environmental issues from home.'

Sandra's life in Bournemouth and then the Seychelles could not be more different than Tom's glamorous Hollywood lifestyle.

But, in the 1995 interview, Sandra said the family was still close. When Sandra and Mark got married, Tom couldn't make it to the wedding in the Seychelles because he was filming. But when he asked what gift he could buy, Sandra asked him for cash to help furnish their new Dorset home. The money he sent was 'great,' said Sandra. 'Tom doesn't throw his money around, but over the years his presents have got better. His wealth isn't a thing between us. He has never felt he has something to prove and he doesn't have a chip on his shoulder, which is why there aren't any horrible stories about him.'

Sandra is the only member of the family not living in the United States, but she said: 'As I'm the eldest and the only girl, I get to do all the organising of the family get-togethers. I'd describe the Hanks family together as really goofy – we play basketball in the living room and we're a noisy crowd.

'We're loud, funny and lively. We haven't had a row since we were kids but we love a good debate. Tom and I especially have strong political views.'

Sandra is probably the closest to Tom of the siblings. He credits her with holding the family together when they were children, and even for 'making it all fun'. The two boys always took her lead, he wrote in a touching letter he sent in 1986, which described how important she had been in moulding his personality. She told *OK!*: 'Despite the tearful speech he made when he won the Oscar for *Philadelphia,* Tom isn't one to walk around with his heart on his sleeve. He doesn't find it that easy to open up and talk. I know I can talk to him when I have a problem.

'We speak on the phone every few weeks, and when he was getting divorced from his first wife and having a tough time emotionally, we spent a lot of time talking. He was very supportive when my first marriage broke up.'

Sandra believes their California upbringing had a lot to do with keeping Tom so down to earth. She has met big names like Steven Spielberg, his wife Kate Capshaw, and Jamie Lee Curtis at Tom's Los Angeles mansion. 'Most of them are nice people,' she said.

But she added: 'Growing up in California teaches you not to be impressed by celebrities. For me, being Tom's sister isn't a factor on a daily basis. It doesn't really affect our lives. I'm impressed with Tom's work and I'm very proud of him. I'm still knocked out by the fact that he has won two Oscars.

'All my brothers have great taste in women and I get on great with Tom's wife, Rita. He introduced her to me when they were still dating.'

She sees all of Tom's films and makes a point of being honest about them. 'I was lukewarm about *Bonfire of the Vanities,* and I wasn't real hot on *Bachelor Party* either, although it made a ton of money. I thought *Splash, Big* and *Philadelphia* were great – especially *Philadelphia.*'

Sandra admitted there was one thing involving Tom that left her green with envy. 'I am stunningly jealous of the fact that Tom has stayed at the White House with the Clintons. To be able to sit down with the President of the United States and ask him what you want – that's what I call cool!

'I asked him, "Did you call the President Bill?"'

'But Tom said, "No, you can call anyone Bill. I called him Mr President."'

Their father had been insistent on giving all his children the best education available. But Larry was always the academic of the family, collecting and inventing things even as a young child.

Three years older than Tom, he became a doctor of entomology – that's an insect expert – and has gone on to become one of the leading researchers in his field in the world, first as an insect ecologist at the University of California in Riverside and then as a Professor at the University of Illinois at Urbana-Champaign, where he has specialised in wood-boring insects, in particular the Asian Longhorn Beetle, a 'major tree killer' which recently turned up in Britain.

Larry married girlfriend Jean Mahew in July 1996.

While very supportive of his younger brother, Larry has remained strictly out of the spotlight, hitting the headlines in *The New York Times* only when he was part of ground-breaking research into insect eating-patterns in 1994.

Although he is the academic of the family, Larry says Tom has followed their father's passion for reading and self-education. 'Tom started off at state college in California, but I don't think that traditional educational institutions really train you for that business. The only way to learn how to act is to actually act. I think that most reputable actors and actresses, like Tom, came through the school of hard knocks.

'But Tom's not uneducated. He reads a lot. He probably reads two entire newspapers a day. He really knows what is going on in the world. That may be why, rather than the fluff, he seems to be going for more important movie projects.'

Tom would always say that Larry was the comic in the family when they were young. But times have changed. 'He was the younger brother, but Tom eventually started telling his own jokes rather than taking mine. He has his own jokes now,' said Larry. 'I don't feel like I am the funny one in the family any more. Everybody seems to have developed their own sense of humour. I think I used to be the funny one because I was older.'

The siblings have always remained in touch, even as they went off in their own directions.

'With Sandra living in the Seychelles now we stay in touch mainly through E-mail as a phone call costs about $100. With Tom, he does a lot of travelling. Right now he's working on a movie in Fiji, an island movie he has to lose a lot of weight for. We also stay in touch through family occasions. Everyone would always converge on my mother's home at Thanksgiving and Christmas. The Hankses tend to marry a lot. My mother was married a number of times and my father was married a number of times and you tend to accumulate a number of people in your life that way. That's the positive side.

'We were young when we had our first stepmother. It's kind of strange but we lost touch with all of them. We still stay in touch with our second stepmother, my father's last wife. Any differences between us are all in the past now.

'We have all seemed to have turned out okay. Nobody has killed anyone.'

Larry has got used to some of the difficult experiences of his early years being replayed through Tom's interviews over the years. He said: 'Tom is pretty careful. Fortunately he doesn't go into any grisly details. He respects everyone's privacy.'

However, the professor has had to put up with fans visiting his office at the university asking for autographs or photographs of his famous brother, or just wanting to talk about him. 'It's just a big waste of time,' he added.

'Tom handles it all pretty well. He doesn't let it get to his head too much.'

Janet, Tom's mother, and his stepmother, Frances, stay in touch with Tom. Now retired from her job as a vice-president of a convalescent hospital chain, Janet still lives in the Red Bluff area with her third husband, Rudolph, who is retired from the construction industry. With Rita's parents, Janet was at the Oscar ceremony in 1995 to celebrate with her famous son.

The one-bedroomed bungalow she lives in is reported to have cost just £20,000. In the drive sits a new £18,000 car, which Tom reportedly bought for her.

Friends say she talks proudly of Tom's achievements and lives with husband 'Rudy' in the modest neighbourhood, a world away from the splendour of her middle son's luxurious Los Angeles mansions. She has no hired help and Rudolph likes to go hunting with his rifle for their dinner.

The night Tom won his first Oscar was, she says, 'one of the happiest moments of my life'.

The family had all gathered at Tom's house the night before the ceremony, one of the rare occasions they were able to get together at the same time, and taken snapshots of everyone.

'When he won the Oscar I cried,' Janet said. 'It was like, despite everything, we were a family again, all of us.'

In a 1998 interview with *New Yorker* magazine, Tom appeared to take a harsher line with his family than in previous interviews. Asked whether he was still in contact with Janet, he said: 'See, the thing is I never lived with my mum: So she's tighter with the other kids in the family. I was the only one who just never lived with her.

'Sometimes we talk really honestly about this. I say, "Mom, you didn't raise me!" There is a brand of peace that had to be made.'

He said his relationship with his sister and brothers was 'not the tightest. We're kind of terse.'

When it was suggested that the movie version would have been that the adversity they lived through would have brought them together, he replied: 'Well, life didn't quite work out that way.'

The article upset and angered Tom's close family and the actor quickly assured them that his comments had been taken out of context.

'It caused quite a stir,' said Larry. 'The story was very disconcerting to us. There was one quote saying that Tom doesn't have particularly good relationships with his siblings. But that's just not true. It said something about being terse, but I talked to Tom for about six hours the last time I was in California. That doesn't fit my idea of terse.

'Actually, I spoke to Tom about it. He was unhappy about the way it looked. My mother wasn't very happy about it either.'

The point is that as much as Tom has always liked to see himself as a free spirit, he has spent much of his life searching for the idealised family he had longed for as a child.

In one sense, he may hold his less than happy childhood memories against all those that shared them – his siblings – and those that crafted them – his parents and step-parents. But the fact that their actions did mean, and continue to mean, so much to him underline just how much family has always meant to Tom Hanks.

In truth, he has never been much of a free spirit. He had children, a wife and all the responsibilities they bring at a young age while he was still trying to make a place for himself in the world.

He is very aware that real life doesn't always end up like it does in the movies. The great tribute to him is that he has never let his family down and has learned enough to know how central that is to his own happiness.

In a business where egos are fed daily by sycophantic praise, Tom's sense of family is the key to his huge success. He has come to know what is important. And that is not sleek, fast sports cars, Gulfstream jets or Harry Winston jewels. To Tom, his wife and children are more important than all the money in the world.

THIRTEEN

REACHING FOR
THE STARS

SHOOTING THROUGH THE night skies, Tom kept blinking for fear that the most exhilarating feeling in his life was only a dream. Ever since the early *Apollo* missions, Kubrick's *2001: A Space Odyssey* and even *Fireball XL-5,* it had been his dream to fly in space.

As a little boy, he would sometimes fill his swimming trunks with rocks and sit on the bottom of the pool breathing through a garden hose to simulate weightlessness. With his science skills at schools extending little further than lighting the Bunsen Burner, he always knew that his abiding ambition would never realistically be achievable.

But now he was an actor, an extremely successful one at that, and in Hollywood anything is possible – even if it is only make believe.

After two successive Oscars, Tom could choose just about any project he cared to do. By simply attaching his name to a movie, he could ensure that a studio would automatically give it the green light and find however many millions were required to put it on the screen. The fee for the 'best actor' alone was now approaching £15 million per film.

The movie he had decided on was the story of the doomed *Apollo 13* mission, directed by his old friend Ron Howard.

Quite clearly, they wouldn't be shooting the film in space. Hollywood sound stages had been recreating stars of both kinds with varying degrees of success for many years.

But speeding through the pitch black skies over Texas, his hands clamped tightly on the controls of a small plane, this was about as close as he was ever going to get to experiencing what his boyhood heroes like Neil Armstrong, Buzz Aldrin and co. must have felt.

Previously, the closest he had come to copying them was in a comic routine he used to ease the tension, first at one of his very earliest auditions in New York and, many years later, as he walked into the press room at the Golden Globes. Tripping up a small step on purpose, he would regain his composure and say with a smile: 'One small trip for mankind...'

Now one of his heroes was in the plane seat behind him. Jim Lovell, veteran of two Gemini flights as well as *Apollo 8* and *Apollo 13* missions, wanted the actor who would portray him on celluloid to get an idea how it really felt to be lost in space.

Tom spent four days with Lovell at his home close to the Houston Space Center in Texas. Never one to take too much notice of 'the suits' as he called studio executives, Tom happily trusted his life to the former Navy pilot.

Lovell explained: 'Tom Hanks came down to my house in Horseshoe Bay to sort of get in the mould of the part. I don't think he's done much small plane flying. I wanted him to get the feeling of what it's like to be a test pilot and an aviator and an astronaut, so I let him fly the plane.

'That evening, I said, "Don't have anything to drink." We had dinner at home, then at 10.00pm I took him to the airfield at Horseshoe Bay.

'We took off and I told him, "Tom, the space capsule is in darkness all of the time. You see the sun, but there's no atmosphere to have nice blue skies. Essentially, you are going to be in the dark, except for stars occasionally."

'To recreate the constricted view from a spacecraft, I installed a triangular cardboard cut-out on his side of the cockpit.

'I took him out West where there are no lights. We flew around and I showed him the constellations and the stars that are used to navigate when we got on the backside of the moon and the sun wasn't there. I let him control the airplane, because it's a little bit like a spacecraft. He liked it a lot.'

In truth, Tom's initial emotion once up in the air was stark terror. He came out in a hot sweat and felt extremely nauseous. But he refused to admit his fears to Lovell and gradually relaxed. Soon, he was overwhelmed with the speed and the darkness and the feeling that this was something he had been waiting his whole life to experience, even if it was not quite the real thing.

With all his success, his love for his wife and his dedication to his children, he would still be among the first to volunteer if there was ever a chance for a civilian to fly into space. Tom told the *New York Daily News*: 'There's no way I'm going to be an astronaut because I don't have the math or anything. But if there was a lottery and they asked who wants to go, and I got picked, I'd be gone. Do it in a minute. Even if they said my job was to clean up the barf if anyone got sick. I'd do it.'

His friend Sally Field added one cautionary note however: 'Rita would kill him.'

As a baby boomer, Hanks reveres his space heroes as others worship film stars. 'They were princes among men,' he said. 'These guys in their gold flight suits with matching jackets – they were real stars. To be an astronaut in Houston in the 1960s. It was like being a Beatle.'

But studio bosses at Universal were less than happy about their own brightest star flying about in the middle of the night. They were terrified of a mishap and feared he was not properly insured.

'I told 'em not to worry,' said Lovell. 'His best insurance is sitting right next to him.'

To Tom and Ron Howard it was important to change the perception of the *Apollo 13* mission as the heroic failure that America wanted to forget.

For four heart-stopping days in April 1970, the world watched as Lovell and his crew struggled in total darkness and sub-zero temperatures to bring their crippled spaceship back to earth.

Despite their miraculous escape, the life-or-death saga 200,000 miles from home exposed the vulnerability of the US *Apollo* programme – and accelerated its nosedive. In a country where failures – however heroic – are poor substitutes for success, the episode was quickly relegated to the archives of space history.

Apollo 13, the Hollywood version, was finally going to give the men – and women – involved the recognition that had long been their due for probably the greatest rescue operation ever launched.

The script was based on Lovell's book, *Lost Moon*, and the former *Apollo 13* commander found a new job in retirement as the film's technical advisor. A quarter of a century after becoming the most famous astronaut NOT to walk on the moon, James Lovell would also finally become a household name, such is the power of Hollywood.

Lovell admits the mission had been neglected over the years 'because we like to forget our failures'. As if to prove his point, he talks about the study in his house, which is littered with awards and trophies from his first three space flights. The only recognition of *Apollo 13* was a letter from Charles Lindbergh.

The bittersweet irony is that it is now the familiar face of Tom Hanks the public will forever associate with the name Jim Lovell, a fact that is not lost on the ex-spaceman. While Tom was staying with him, the two men were drinking in a local bar when Lovell was asked to sign a framed picture hanging above the bar. Lovell said he pointed to Hanks. 'I told them, "Hey, that's the real Jim

Lovell, let him go over and sign it." Because after the movie's out, it's not going to be me any more. Tom Hanks is going to be Jim Lovell.' Lovell said he was delighted at the choice of Tom to play him and happily went out of his way to help the actor, who was playing a real person for the first time in his career.

Tom had been well aware of all the details of the *Apollo 13* story years before he contemplated recreating it, and had told his 'crack team of showbusiness experts' that he would definitely be interested if any of the studios came up with a script to bring the story to the big screen. When he learned Howard and his partner Brian Grazer had paid $600,000 to Lovell for the rights to his book, Tom joked that he held a broken bottle to Howard's neck in a Manhattan restaurant and told him: 'I've got to play Jim Lovell. I was born for that part. Give me the part or else!'

Both producers and star could have been taking a serious risk. Because of *The Right Stuff*'s failure at the box office, it was widely thought that *Apollo 13* would have the same crash landing on its release.

In fact, the film would help imprint the full details of the story onto the American consciousness.

It started with a normal launch from a mostly clear Cape Canaveral. Although it was supposed to be a routine flight, the omens were not good. *Apollo 13* was launched 13 minutes past the 13th hour. Scientists scoffed at such talk. But halfway to the moon, an oxygen tank exploded leaving the three astronauts – Lovell, Fred Halse and Jack Swigert – with little oxygen, almost no heat and a leaking spacecraft.

The explosion turned out to be the beginning of a four-day duel between the wonders of human engineering and the limits of technology.

Lovell recalls looking at Halse hoping the quaking sound he heard was the jolt from a lever his colleague had pulled in jest. The look Halse gave him told him otherwise. 'They were the eyes of someone who was truly frightened – truly, wholly, profoundly frightened,' he said.

At the time, *Newsweek* reported: 'The three astronauts faced a death no man had ever died before – death in space, cold and alone, outward bound into the blackness of the void.'

Battling the unknown, with a moon landing out of the question, the spacemen had just one aim – to avoid spinning out of control in a high-tech coffin.

As they orbited the moon in a cramped lunar module, with lights and heating turned off to conserve energy, they plotted a split-second manoeuvre to make it possible to re-enter the earth's atmosphere.

The cool strategies of the three men and their advisors at Houston mission control managed to guide the stricken craft to a successful splashdown in the Pacific on 17 April 1970.

Swigert, who was portrayed by Kevin Bacon in the film, successfully ran for office in the US Congress after leaving the space programme, but tragically died before taking office.

Halse, played by Bill Paxton, went on to pilot the shuttle prototype *Enterprise* five times and has survived five plane crashes. He went on to be chairman of Grumman Technical Services in Titusville, Florida – the same company that built the lunar module that saved his life.

'It is the ultimate human interest tale,' said Haise, who lives in Brevard County, Florida. 'It has a happy ending. That is definitely the most important thing – a Hollywood ending.'

Although the ensemble film would not add to Tom's Oscar collection ('If I won again there would be suicide jumpers from the roof of the Dorothy Chandler Pavilion'), its success – pulling in more than $30 million on its opening weekend and going on to make over $172 million – once again proved Tom's ability to take an unfashionable subject and turn it into a blockbuster. His track record was such that the public simply trusted his ability to lead a good film into the cinema.

Apollo 13 was also the first time he had the luxury of starring in a film he had a strong personal interest in, with the possible exception of *A League of Their Own,* which although about his beloved baseball, was still about women's baseball.

Tom's interest in space began early. He was at the heart of an era when ten-year-old boys were busy building Airfix kits of lunar modules and putting star charts on their walls alongside the pop posters and football rosettes. It is hard to believe now how quickly space flight sank in popularity. Trains, planes and football may have had their fluctuations in fascination among the young, but Man in Space fell into such a void that *Apollo 13* would reach a whole new generation that had probably thought at first that it was an offshoot from a *Rocky* movie.

He told *Daily News* writer Dennis Hamill: 'When I was a kid I paid a lot of attention to the space programme. The *Gemini* programme was done between 1965 and 1966, so I was aware of that because at school they would march us over from class to the auditorium to watch launches. But I distinctly remember *Apollo 7* going up in November 1968. Then in December we were on Christmas vacation from school, and in my mum's house and *Apollo 8* was all over the television. And here were these guys who were on their way to the moon. And that was a very big deal to me. I couldn't get enough of it. It was very glamorous, the nature of the adventure was, what's the word? It was romantic. Three guys in this little thing, going to the moon. Heroic.'

He continued: 'One of the biggest things I discovered in the course of doing *Apollo 13* and being able to meet all these guys, not just the astronauts, but also the flight directors at NASA, was the particulars of who they are and why they were doing it in the first place.

'The first real astronaut I got to know was Jim Lovell. Jim's a great guy, but he's the last guy you would pick to be that standard kind of Wheaties box vision of an astronaut. Astronauts are supposed to be these great, mythic figures. But they're all kind of short because you couldn't be too tall to be in one of those capsules. The tallest astronaut was like, six feet. They all have these backgrounds as engineers, physicists and rocket scientists. They're all very learned and almost bookish, and they all fly jets and stuff like that. Also, they're married, or divorced, with kids and houses.

'We went into Jim Lovell's house in Houston. And it's a small American house. And you connect to the idea that the kids were sleeping upstairs, and he'd get up at 5.30 in the morning, eat breakfast and drive off to Ellington Air Force field, get in a jet and in an hour-and-a-half he'd be at the Cape and he'd get into a simulator. Stuff like that, the real nuts and bolts of how they got there. It was a steady job: But they were utterly consumed by it. They just loved it. We've all done stuff in our lives where it's not even like working. You realise, gee, all this time has gone by and you didn't even think about it because you loved it so much. And that's how these astronauts lived their lives. They drank a lot of coffee and worked 16-18 hours a day.'

Tom said it was how he visualised it as a boy, sucking on his garden hose in the swimming pool. 'Back in Oakland, it was just the idea of three guys in a tin can, surrounded by the cosmos, drifting slowly into the history books. I dreamed about being one of them constantly.'

With *Apollo 13*, he realised that, although most people knew the outcome, very few knew the fascinating 'nuts and bolts'. People didn't know 'you could take a piece of gaffer tape, a plastic bag and a sock and you could make this thing that could clean the carbon dioxide in the craft.'

Even before signing on for the project, Tom had named his production company Clavius Base, after a crater in which the moon monolith is discovered in *2001: A Space Odyssey*. So strongly does he believe in the importance of the space programme that he even has a theory that the world can be divided into two periods of human history: before and after we landed on the moon.

Right after Neil Armstrong's *Apollo 11*, space travel dropped 'right off the face of consciousness.'

'And that's because,' Tom told Hamill, 'everyone born after World War II grew up thinking that eventually someone was going to land on the moon. And that was going to be a truly evolutionary moment in the history of our species. That once we did that, once we figured out how to put a man on the moon, we would have reached a technological level, after which, truly anything is possible. Now people say, "We figured out a way to put a man on the moon, but I can't get the paper out of my fax machine."

'But prior to the landing on the moon, there was still this great goal, that we were waiting to see become a reality. It was still like, "Man, how do you think they are gonna do it?" We knew there was this great enterprise that was afoot in 1961 which started the clock running. So for all those years, there was a question of who was going to do it first, who is going to win, which propelled things and made it happen much, much faster than it would have.

'But removed from all that, everyone in the world knew that all this technological stuff, both good and bad, from the atomic bomb to mechanical pencils to the telephone to thermos bottles and Saran wrap were all going to be used somehow or other to put a man on the moon. And what was he going to do? Claim it in the name of someone or the other, or stick a flag in it. Or he was going to maybe die getting there. But everyone was waiting for it to happen. And then it happened. Neil Armstrong, "One small step..." and all that stuff.

'How many times has the world literally stopped to watch something that was not a tragedy unfold on television? Precious few times. It wasn't a funeral. It wasn't cops chasing someone on the street. Instead it was all of us, as a planet, a species, sitting down and watching this truly extraordinary thing happen. Then, when that happened, it was all done.

'But the thing that's not fair about that, or the thing we're missing here, is that we explored the moon only for about three years. I think the last time was in December of 1972. And just getting there, and landing, and walking around was not nearly as important to me as all the stuff that has happened after that.

'All the things we've found out about the different places that we went. I mean, the moon is roughly five times the size of Africa. So what we explored would be equal to going to Paris, landing at the airport, getting in a cab, driving around Paris, and then going back to the airport and flying back home again. But what do we really know?'

None of this was something Tom had just thought of to help promote a film. The subject had consumed him for as long as he could remember. And he would put it to use again in another award-winning project, the 12 hour, £40 million TV series *From the Earth to the Moon*.

But first, Tom had some more down-to-earth things to worry about in the form of a specially designed training aircraft that simulated weightlessness for would-be astronauts and, in this case, for actors pretending to be astronauts. Howard spurned the expected use of computer graphics to send his actors on more than 600 trips on a unique jet plane they very quickly nicknamed the 'vomit comet'.

Tom and fellow 'astronauts' Bill Paxton and Kevin Bacon are shown weightless (or in ⅙th gravity, to be precise) for virtually half of the film.

And if Tom felt nauseous on his night flight with Jim Lovell, he was going to get used to the feeling when shooting began on NASA's KC-135, a stripped-down 707 used to introduce astronauts to the phenomenon before they get to space.

The plane achieves zero gravity the hard way. It flies steeply up to about 36,000 feet and then screams earthward in a prolonged dive. The aircraft's parabolic motion creates enough centrifugal force to counter gravity at the top of the arc, and as it reverses direction, everyone and everything inside is gently released from the earth's gravitational pull.

But it only lasts for 25 seconds. After that everything floating around is flung violently to the padded floor. So every bit of footage had to be shot piecemeal in a lunar capsule built into the plane's zero-gravity compartment.

Bacon didn't want to do it at first, but agreed, after Tom, who was thrilled at the idea, and Paxton voted to give it a try. 'I didn't want to be the weanie,' he joked.

For Tom, it was another playground and he proudly boasts that no one actually vomited. But after a few flights, he got confident enough to turn down the motion sickness pills they had all been advised to take. 'I wanted to see if I could handle it because the people who do this all the time don't use drugs. Well, my... it was bad. I'll tell you, I have never felt that sick.'

He said he came close to being sick when he moved his head too quickly. 'It took three hours for the nausea to die down.'

After that, he toned down the jokes aimed at his old *Forrest Gump* cast-mate Gary Sinise, playing Ken Mattingly, the astronaut who was grounded by flight surgeons the day before his scheduled ride on *Apollo 13*. Sinise had suffered so much with motion sickness that Tom said: 'I thought Gary looked nice in khaki, but not when the colour is his face.'

He added: 'The person I felt sorry for was the photographer Annie Leibowitz, who came up with us to shoot pictures for *Vanity Fair*. She was throwing up all the time. Yet she still took the pictures. She had the camera in one hand and a sick bag in the other. She's a real trouper.'

In the end, the actors spent more time in the 'vomit comet' even than astronauts going into space. Howard told *People* magazine:

'Saying something is better than sex rarely lives up to that claim. Weightlessness doesn't quite, either. But it came awfully close.'

Bob Williams, NASA's test director for the Zero-G Aircraft Programme, wasn't happy when he first learned that Hollywood's finest were about to descend on his operation. He said: 'All we knew about Hollywood folks is what we read and see on TV. We were expecting a bunch of prima donna Hollywood types.

'But I can't tell you how impressed we were with this group. There wasn't an ounce of prima donna in any of them.'

Back down on the ground, the actors likened shooting in the cramped *Apollo 13* capsule fabricated on the Universal back lot as like 'shooting a movie in a Volkswagen Beetle'.

During the last month of filming, Howard even had the temperature on the sound stage dropped to a near-freezing 34 degrees to simulate the frigid conditions when the crew turned off the heating to conserve energy.

To warm up, the actors huddled in Tom's trailer watching movies. One mini-film festival was devoted to comedian Buster Keaton, because they thought the silent films star looked like Tom.

Throughout the five-and-a-half months of filming, Tom gorged on every detail of the space mission. 'Oh, Hanks,' said Bacon, who watched his co-star devour NASA procedure manuals and physics lessons. 'You could just put him on the shuttle now and he would know how to fly it.'

Said Tom: 'I knew about 20 per cent of what was going on. But I was a pain in the ass.'

In his 21st film, Tom was as comfortable with himself as an actor as any star in Hollywood. He no longer had to wait until scripts were turned down by bigger stars to get the chance to shine. There were no bigger stars.

And while other so-called superstars may have been uncertain of their ground and blind to their limitations, Tom was very sure why he was a 'movie star'.

'I can't do what Gibson and Costner do. But they can't bring to their roles what I can bring. People relate to me as a regular guy. If Costner had played Jim Lovell (as was considered) it would have put a completely different focus on the story. It would have been about him. I am just one of the three guys in the pod. That's how it was.

Although the two became friends, Tom was also critical of Tom Cruise earlier in his career, perceiving his major A-list rival as losing himself in his stardom. 'Look at Tom Cruise,' he told *Cosmopolitan* in 1987. 'The way he walks, the way he talks. He's losing it as an actor. He's becoming a movie star. He's on the wrong track.'

The success of *Apollo 13* got its star thinking. There was still so much to learn about the space missions, about their effect and their standing in the cultural history of the 20th century. There were so many mind-boggling nuts and bolts an audience would, he was sure, find intriguing.

In dealing with one, specific *Apollo* mission, there was so much that had to be left out. It was a subject Tom had fervent opinions about, as exemplified by his theories about man reaching the moon. But he also had a more personal slant on the '60s that he was hankering to give vent to.

'I remember those as some of the worst years of my life. It was hell,' he told *The New York Times*.

'Our world was very, very polarised. If you had long hair, you were a good guy; if you had short hair, you were a bad guy. We mistrusted just about anything that had to do with the Government.'

To Tom, who was 13 when Neil Armstrong stepped foot on the moon, the space missions were among the few lasting, happy memories he had of the era. But for many, they were mistrusted along with everything else the government of the time was involved in. It was a historical viewpoint Tom had a vested interest in changing. In essence, he wanted to reclaim the '60s for his own generation by giving the space programme a context he felt it had been denied.

The ambitious idea of telling the entire space story, from President Kennedy's dare to beat the Russians right through to the last, half-forgotten flight of *Apollo 17*, was one that perhaps only a double-Oscar-winning star of Tom's magnitude could bring to television.

It took two years of his life and its £40 million budget made it the single most expensive project in television history, but *From the Earth to the Moon* showed just how far Tom had come. Not only did his involvement as a director, writer and star of the series guarantee it a budget, among the first to watch it was President Clinton, at another private White House screening.

Tom had read author Andrew Chaikin's 1994 book *A Man on the Moon: The Voyages of the Apollo Astronauts* while researching *Apollo 13* and had recommended it to his fellow actors. It was on this 584-page tome that he based and pitched his own series to America's Home Box Office cable channel.

Tired of the cops-and-robbers space mentality of *Star Trek* and *Star Wars,* he wanted to get it right.

HBO's director of original programming gave the series the go ahead after meeting Tom. He said: 'The amazing thing about first meeting with Tom was he knew exactly what he wanted to do. In that first meeting, he had a handful of index cards that contained an outline of every episode as he saw it. And we got lucky in that Tom wanted to take a break from being a movie star.'

Tom took a pay cut and enlisted the help of his *Apollo 13* cohorts Ron Howard and partner Brian Grazer to get the project off the ground. He was the executive producer, wrote one episode himself and co-wrote three more, directed one, and was in charge of choosing writers, directors and the cast. He only took a small acting part.

Using 500 actors and ten different directors, the series was not so much a series as a collection of filmed short stories, built around the belief that nearly every angle of the *Apollo* missions had its own inherent drama.

Author Chaikin, a space buff who looks upon Tom as a kindred spirit, was employed as a consultant on the series to ensure the details were accurate.

'I remember being on the set with him,' Chaikin said, 'and we walked by the *Gemini* spacecraft that they had created for the series. And I said to Tom, "This is the coolest thing I have seen all day!" And he said, "Yeah, I know. I think I am going to take it home and put it in the garage." He said, "Can you picture that? You know, like I'll put a TV in there. It's gonna be like, honey, I'm going to be in the spacecraft."'

The series, originally broadcast in the US in the April and May of 1998, went on to win an Emmy for best mini-series. And Tom repaid Chaikin by writing a new foreword for his book. In it, Tom wrote: 'The thing that still fuels me in my day-to-day life and what I want to convey to my children, and to the audience, is that if mankind can figure out a way to put 12 men on the moon, then, honestly, we can solve anything. That's why I believe the six *Apollo* landings are six of the seven best stories ever told.'

Like other projects Tom became involved in at this stage of his career, he made a point in using trusted friends to boost the show's cohesion and professionalism. As well as wife Rita, Tom used former co-stars Sally Field, who directed one episode, Peter Scolari, his old *Bosom Buddies* buddy, and Elizabeth Perkins, his leading lady in *Big,* as well as many others in smaller roles.

As much as he liked to consider himself a regular guy whose main hobby was watching his weight, Tom was no longer living an ordinary life, if indeed he ever did. He could count the President of the United States as a friend for goodness sake!

His close coterie now also numbered Hollywood's most powerful players. But, as we shall see, he hadn't forgotten all of his old friends.

FOURTEEN

FRIENDS TO DI FOR

JUST FOR ONCE, there were no autograph hunters, no over-earnest fans. There wasn't even any paparazzi. Tom stood with his best friend Steven Spielberg outside the doors of Westminster Abbey waiting for them to open.

Dressed in black, they chatted with fellow American Tom Cruise, wearing dark glasses, and his Australian actress wife, Nicole Kidman. At any other time, such a gathering would be a focus of considerable attention anywhere outside Hollywood.

But on this breezy September morning in 1997 the thoughts of the world were with someone else. Tom was among the grieving celebrities invited to Princess Diana's state funeral. From Luciano Pavarotti to Diana Ross to Elton John and George Michael, they joined the royals, politicians, charity representatives and close friends at the sombre celebration of Diana's memory.

A sensitive man, easily given to tears, Tom struggled during the service to hold his emotions in check. 'We all sang God Save the Queen, which was not something I do a lot, and then the first thing that happened was that the coffin came in,' he told the *Express*. 'It was electrifying and... well, you know,' he added, his voice trailing off as he tried to describe one of the most poignant moments of the 20th century.

Just two years earlier, Tom had spent the evening with Diana and was immediately struck both by her offbeat sense of humour and by her grace and intelligence. Their meeting came as Diana was asserting her independence from the Royal Family and beginning to organise her life around some of her pet charities.

The Princess and the movie star had spoken a number of times on the telephone after Diana phoned Tom to congratulate him on *Philadelphia,* a film she was particularly moved by as she had played such a large role in helping AIDS sufferers find acceptance in society. But this was the first time they had met in person.

The British première for *Apollo 13* had been held in Leicester Square the previous night on 6 September 1995, when Tom, Rita and most of the cast and crew left after the film for an informal party at Planet Hollywood.

Now Diana was holding her own, unprecedented mini-première to raise funds for Turning Point, a charity helping drug addicts to kick the habit. Forsaking the usual glitzy West End cinemas, she had taken over a cramped 46-seat theatre in an anonymous corner of Hammersmith, West London, and kept the event secret from all but a few, favoured press photographers.

An uncharacteristically nervous Tom, in dinner jacket and bow tie, with Rita and *Apollo* director Ron Howard, were greeted by a vivacious-looking Diana, wearing a tight black Versace dress, at the nearby United International Pictures office building and they were taken together to the cinema, where the Princess sat down beside the film's star.

When Steven Spielberg had been in a similar position during the Royal première of *Indiana Jones and the Temple of Doom,* he had apparently been told to cough loudly in Diana's ear the exact moment his wife-to-be, actress Kate Capshaw, starring in the film with Harrison Ford, shouted 'shit', so worried were her courtiers about offending royal protocol. But now Diana, unfettered by hangers-on, quickly put Tom at his ease.

When the film finished, with the Princess lavishing praise on Tom's stellar performance, she didn't quietly retire to Kensington Palace as she had been required to do in the past, to sit alone in her quarters while all the stars her own age high-tailed it to the première party. This time, Diana was the host – and she wasn't going to miss out on any of the fun.

The 46 guests were whisked in a fleet of limousines to the Green House restaurant in Mayfair, where another 50 guests in dinner dress were waiting. Once again, Diana took the seat next to Tom. She chatted gaily about films, asking him all about some of her favourites, which included *Forrest* Gump and *Philadelphia*.

After giving a brief speech describing the work of Turning Point, and making a thinly veiled request for support, Diana bade farewell to Tom, Rita, Ron and the *Apollo* executives. As a friend of President Clinton and some of the biggest names on the planet, it was not easy to impress Tom. But that was a night he would remember – and later treasure – as a very personal memory of a remarkable woman.

Tom had been asked by Spielberg to accompany him to the funeral as both were filming in London at the time. The director had known Diana ever since she had first appeared at the British première to his *ET* blockbuster. There was no problem getting an invitation to the funeral because Spielberg had lunched at Chequers with Tony Blair and his family just a few weeks before Diana's death. They had been mulling over the potential of turning the Hertfordshire location of the director's latest movie into a permanent British studio. Number 10 ensured Hollywood's grimfaced ambassadors would be able to pay their respects.

Tom was in England when the Princess was killed in the Paris car crash and had experienced at first hand the unforgettable outpouring of national grief that followed.

So involved did he feel that he later bristled at the feeling in the United States and elsewhere that the stiff upper-lipped Brits had suddenly become hysterical after losing their beloved Queen of Hearts.

He said: 'I saw all the crowds. I saw them every day. And these people were not hysterical. They were simply in mourning, showing their respect for the loss of someone very special.

'It really annoyed me the way it was made to look as if the people of Britain had lost their minds. What I saw was dignity and decency on a grand scale. It filled me with respect for the British.'

He told the *Mail on Sunday*: 'To be an American at the funeral was something else. But I have to tell you, no way in hell does America come to a standstill for any reason like that – I mean, the last time America came to a standstill was to watch the O.J. Simpson trial.

'And after the funeral, we had to listen to all of the incessant analysis of what was going on. 'Why is there such hysteria in the streets? What does it all mean?' And I thought the media are out of their minds. These people are just sad. 'Why are people piling up flowers outside Buckingham Palace?' Because they're sad you morons, that's why.'

When the Westminster Abbey service was over, the Duchess of York asked Tom and Spielberg if they were doing anything that evening. Apparently, they did have a dinner planned, but didn't want to be rude and so accepted an invitation to her home in Sunningdale that evening. Realising the Hollywood contingent were feeling low and slightly lost after leaving the Abbey, the Duchess also invited Tom Cruise and wife, Nicole Kidman, as well as Hong Kong businessman David Tang. It would be, she told them, 'a wake – a celebration of Diana's life'.

Spielberg's driver was so stunned when he phoned the number

the Duchess gave his boss to call for directions and Prince Andrew answered that he didn't write them down. According to the *Express*, the embarrassed driver phoned back only to be told by the amused Prince that it was not an unusual occurrence.

Fergie and her estranged husband met Tom and Spielberg at the door – their respective wives had returned to California with the children who were due back at school – and they found Sting, his wife Trudie, and singer Chris de Burgh were already there.

After dinner, de Burgh sang a lament dedicated to Diana and was persuaded to sing a medley of his hits, including one of the Princess's favourite songs, 'Lady in Red'. As he sang, Fergie stood close to tears by the fireplace in the living room, swaying in time to the music. Much of the talk, inevitably, revolved around memories of Diana, much as it did at dining tables around the world.

For Tom, it was a surreal end to a very emotional and unforgettable day.

Tom was in England shooting *Saving Private Ryan*, a World War II film being directed by Spielberg. It was an all-star collaboration both men had resisted up until then, fearing their friendship would in some way be harmed by a working relationship. They needn't have worried. The two men became, if anything, even closer and the film was a critical *tour de force*, of which more later.

Rita had, of course, spent a year in London as a teenage student, but Tom had always looked upon the city as just another stop on his jet-setting schedule. He'd been to Britain for film permières and publicity tours – the type of visit that often leaves Hollywood's visiting royalty thinking the UK is just a collection of TV studios and posh Park Lane hotels.

When he signed on to do the Spielberg movie, it went without saying that Rita and the kids would go too. The family moved into pop star Sting's Georgian house in Highgate, a short drive from the disused airfield in North London where most of the action would be filmed.

Cruise and Kidman were in town on their mammoth filming of *Eyes Wide Shut* with the capricious Stanley Kubrick, and fellow cast members included Americans Ed Burns, Tom Sizemore and Matt Damon. And Spielberg and his actress wife, Kate Capshaw, were regular visitors and welcome reminders of home.

But the Hanks family wasn't homesick at all. They fell madly in love with London. Said Tom after the trip: 'The Hanks family are big fans of Britain. We lived in Highgate for about two months and loved every minute of it. When I announced that we would be living in London for a while, we were all prepared for it to be hideous. I really don't mean to be rude, but in America there is a certain image of Britain which I now know is simply not true. So, as we were packing, we were all saying, "Oh no – we've got to go to shabby old London." But from the moment we arrived it was clear we were wrong and that the beautiful capital city is in great shape.

'It's going through a tremendous renaissance. It really is one of the world's great cities. Apart from the terrible traffic, every day was a true adventure for me and my family. We had this lovely house in Highgate and after a day at work I didn't want to go to the West End – so we would have a meal at the local Chinese restaurant and go to the pub across the street.

'It was fantastic. And Hampstead Health was like a treasure trove to us. Every spare moment, we were down there wandering about exploring. We all miss London terribly.'

Tom and his Hollywood friends would later take the brunt of criticism for 'snubbing' a charity ball arranged in Los Angeles to raise money for charities supported by the Princess. Tom and Rita, Spielberg, Tom Cruise and John Travolta, as well as Bruce Willis, Demi Moore and Kim Basinger had all been expected to attend the ball organised by Diana's butler, Paul Burrell.

When none of them turned up, patriotic rock star Rod Stewart blasted them as 'bastards'.

Stewart, who paid £1,200 for tickets for himself and his wife, Rachel Hunter, said: 'I think they are bastards for not coming.'

And, in a pointed reference to Tom, Spielberg, Cruise and Kidman, Rod's wife, Rachel Hunter added: 'They went to Diana's funeral because they knew they would get on television, but they can't be bothered to come here. It's disgusting.'

With the exception perhaps of this particular event, Tom appeared to have an almost Gump-like ability to be at the right place at the right time. And it wasn't just his professional life that seemed to dovetail into success. At Rita's urging, his private life was flourishing too. He had his family. Now he had his friends too.

One minute he is appearing on stage in New York as a favour to his friend, comedian Steve Martin. Then he is at Princess Diana's funeral. Back on America's East Coast, he is living it up as a guest at Spielberg's Quelle Barn estate in the fashionable Hamptons on Long Island. And in California again, Tom is one of the most prominent guests at the hush-hush 1998 wedding of Barbra Streisand to beau James Brolin, where, incidentally, he was spotted doing a limbo dance next to the swimming pool.

How many ordinary Joes have spent not one but three nights in the Queen's Bedroom at the White House; sent the most expensive caviar to showbusiness mogul David Geffen as a thank-you for allowing him to use his private jet; leased a luxury 12-seater suite at a cost of more than £160,000 a year to watch basketball and ice hockey games in Los Angeles; and can afford to spend more than £2 million on a house that 'needs a lot of fixing up'?

'I know, I know, I know,' Tom laughed, burying his head in his hands when *Vanity Fair* offered him evidence of his high-flying ways. 'Isn't it wild? Isn't it hilarious? What am I going to do?'

He went on: 'I can tell you exactly when it all began. We're friends with Peter Welter, and Peter Welter took us to St. Barts. We were on the American plan, for crying out loud! 'Oh, wow! This is great! The houses are so beautiful!' When we were there on that trip, we met Mike [director, Mike Nichols] and Diane [TV anchor, Diane Sawyer]. We were all at this table.

'I had just proposed to Rita during the last few seconds of 1987. I'd asked her to marry me, and she said, "You bet!"'

'So we've all ended up having this kind of history together. Between St. Barts and, say, Carrie Fisher's parties, you meet everybody who's on the creative axis of Western society... So, yes, there it is. I am actually a boulevardier. I am a member of café society. At the same time, I'm this kid from...

'Therein lies my charm.'

While Tom has the innate ability to turn on the charm at the push of a button, he can also switch off just as quickly if he is preoccupied. That privacy door he would slide down gave rise to the claim from even some of his closest friends over the years that they never really knew what was going on inside his head.

Tom is one of the very few people in Hollywood who would dare call Steven Spielberg 'chucklehead'. And their friendship has its professional boundaries. Tom wanted desperately to be cast as the camp commandant in Spielberg's *Schindler's List,* but the director went for Ralph Fiennes. Tom still argues he could have done the job well. 'I just know it,' he says. But their mutual respect and a recognition of aspects of themselves in each other provides the basis for their relationship.

In 1994, Spielberg told *Vanity Fair:* 'The nice thing about being with Tom is that when he feels comfortable around you he doesn't feel a responsibility to spearhead the conversation. There's no nervousness. And I think when you can get rid of the nervousness in a friendship between two guys, then it becomes a, well, older kind of relationship.

'Now we just take our kids to school and talk about the quality of the American teaching system.

'I think that the thing Tom and I have in common is that we were both loners and then we met two terrific women. A lot of our friendship can be traced to the fact that our wives are bestest friends. They get us out. I'd rather stay at home and watch television all night; Kate has to drag me out to a restaurant. Tom is the same way. So often, if we are dragged by our wives into a room together, we get along great.

'But, in a sense, I have never seen Tom as a lonely person. I think Tom is just really in touch with himself, and you can't be in touch with yourself if you are always serving others. I think he needs to spend time alone getting familiar with that part of him that he needs as an actor, as an artist.'

He added: 'Tom doesn't fit into the moulds of other American icons. It's too easy to find a couple of people that share the same all-Americanness that you can compare him to. But Tom Hanks will always be remembered as Tom Hanks. He is without peer.'

High praise indeed, but then the two friends do have more in common than just movie making. Like Tom, Spielberg met Kate Capshaw while still married to his first wife, actress Amy Irving. The director's passionate affair with Kate, who he had cast in the 1984 hit *Indiana Jones and the Temple of Doom,* effectively ended his marriage, although there were painful reconciliations between Spielberg and Irving before they divorced.

The Spielbergs' extended family includes his son with Irving and her daughter from an earlier marriage. Having put her career on the back burner to care for the family, Kate stepped up her acting again, much like Rita.

While Tom took up Rita's Greek orthodoxy, the Spielbergs did it the other way around, with Kate converting to Judaism.

Both families own houses on the oceanfront at Malibu and, after Tom and Rita bought the 'fixer-upper' on one acre in the upscale Pacific Pallisades neighbourhood of Los Angeles – his real life 'Money Pit' – in 1996, they are neighbours there too.

Families are at the heart of the friendship. Spielberg told *Time*: 'First, he's a wonderful daddy. In between raising his kids, he does pictures. We're friends because his interpretation of family life is so retro. It's car pools, barbecues, play weekends, talk about the PTA, take videos of the kids. The other thing is that he completely, unerringly loves his wife.'

Once a month, Rita's 'mummy group' – which includes Capshaw, Annette Bening, Goldie Hawn, Sally Field, Jamie Lee Curtis and Nancy Short, among others – meets up in one house while their husbands and partners meet in another. The wives call themselves 'Girls Night Out Productions'.

'We leave our dinners and we've had five million belly laughs, figured out someone's love life, and got two more kids sleeping through the night,' Capshaw told *Ladies Home Journal* magazine. 'The men come home from their dinners with three-picture deals.'

The superstar support group even takes night calls. When actress and talk-show host Rosie O'Donnell was having problems feeding her newly-adopted child, Rita and her mother rushed over to her home to help. Rita's mother proudly persuaded the baby to drink his first full bottle of milk.

Sally Field, who has worked with Tom on *Punchline, Forrest Gump* and *From the Earth to the Moon,* said her favourite co-star and his wife are a focus of Hollywood's most A-list inner circle.

She told *People*: 'They are both people who appreciate hard work and excellence. They are well read, they are aggressively curious, they drive each other. She is a mimic, really clever. More often than not, Tom's is the loudest laughter. He'll run over, pick her up and run out of the room. We go, "There they go again."' Tom told *Interview* magazine: 'I got lucky in love first, and now I finally got lucky in friends. I actually think I needed the foundation of a family before I got a group. I had to take that very, very slowly. It goes back to what we were saying about the imbalances of fame. I'm kind of ashamed of how many possibilities probably went by the wayside.

'Our group is the same kind of group that I was in at high school or in the Green Room at Sacramento. Everybody gets an entrance, you know, whether they are actors or not. Everybody has that kind of presence that emboldens the table, and we do stuff like old people do. We have cocktails and dinner parties and stuff like that.

'We go on vacations that are hanging on the edge of disaster all the time, because anything could happen during them! It's got the same bona fide *oomph* that is based partly on the fact that we laugh a bunch and that we have an awful lot in common, partly because we are parents.

'It's also an intellectually powerful kind of atmosphere to be in. Some of these people are famous or incredibly accomplished, and some of them aren't.'

Tom clearly feels more comfortable with these rarefied relationships. But that doesn't mean he has forgotten his old friends.

As an actor, Tom had always been credited for his subtle negotiating with directors to get his view of the movie across. Even on bad films, he usually took particular care of his own part and consequentially managed to avoid going down with the ship when the project sank without trace at the box office. It was only natural, particularly when you consider his close friendship with the likes of Spielberg, *Gump*'s Bob Zemeckis and *Philadelphia*'s Jonathan Demme, that he would one day want to try his hand at directing.

So while on what he called 'the trophy-run world tour of *Forrest Gump*' in 1995, he began seriously to write a script as an escape from 'too many airplanes and too many hotel rooms and too many journalists and too much free food'.

The script about a pop group of one-hit wonders in the 1960s would provide the basis for Tom's 'vanity project,' *That Thing You Do!*, the first Hanks-directed feature film, which opened in the autumn of 1996.

Although he only rated a few minutes of screen time in the film, he directed, wrote the script, handpicked the cast and even commandeered the soundtrack, writing four songs.

He also found time to give work to two old friends at times in their lives when it meant a great deal to them.

Peter Scolari, Tom's old *Bosom Buddy* had gone on to a solid, if not earth-shattering, TV career in popular American shows like *Newhart, Goodtime Girls* and *Baby Makes Five*. But in the mid-90s, he was having trouble finding the kind of work he wanted and was going through a costly divorce.

'I can tell you honestly that if it hadn't been for Tom Hanks, his friendship and his standing behind me in 1996, I would have had to declare bankruptcy,' Scolari told the *Pittsburgh Post-Gazette*. 'He put me to work in *That Thing You Do!* and *From the Earth to the Moon*. He said, "I've never done you a favour. I'm doing myself a favour by putting you in this movie." But he was my friend.'

Scolari was cast as the smarmy host of *The Hollywood Television Showcase*, the fictional show that helped launch the film's shortlived pop heroes. Tom said on an American TV interview afterwards that he enjoyed the perks of being the boss. 'You know, that's the best gig. The biggest plus about the job is that you really get to hire your pals. And you get to wrangle them on the phone a little bit. With Peter Scolari, I just said, "Look, I need you for a week. We have got to make up a bunch of stuff. So can you just come on down?" [Shooting for the film was on *The Price is Right* set] And I gave him a big trailer and he was able to take part.'

Another old friend Tom called up was his Cleveland Shakespearean cohort Holmes Osborne, the other half of *The Two Gentlemen of Verona*. Osborne had long given up his hopes of stardom, toiling for years making corporate workplace videos, commercials and doing regional theatre in his native Missouri.

At the age of 48, he was finally able to make his debut in a major motion picture – thanks to Tom. As the main character's curmudgeonly father, Osborne makes eight appearances in the film.

The role was the result of a pact the two men had made long ago – that if either of them became a director they would find the other a juicy part.

Osborne had watched from afar as Tom rose to fame and, although he couldn't help but envy his friend's career, they kept in touch with the occasional phone call or letter. On a trip to California in the early '90s, Osborne called Tom. 'I hadn't seen him for years, and I asked if he could help me find some work in films,' he told the *Kansas City Star*.

'Tom said, "No, no, no – I'm an actor. They don't ask an actor who should be in a movie. But if ever I get my own project, you're at the top of the list."

'I didn't doubt for a minute that he meant it. The public thinks of Tom Hanks as a great guy, and one of the reasons for that is that you can count on what he says. What I doubted was that he'd put all that pressure on himself. I mean, why should he direct? He was getting along great just acting.'

When Osborne read that Tom was writing a script about a '60s rock band he wrote and asked him to bear him in mind for a part. A few weeks later, he received the first draft of Tom's screenplay for *That Thing You Do!*

'Tom wanted any ideas I might have. Well, from 1963 to 1966, I played in a garage band called The Trends. I had lots of stories from that era. So I sent Tom a seven-page letter on my experiences. I didn't figure he'd pay much attention, but during the filming all these ideas I'd suggested started popping up.'

One souvenir Osborne later took away with him was a mock pop-concert poster used as a prop. The band being advertised was The Trends.

He was used to driving to auditions and finding his own motel room. But Tom sent a limo to pick him up from his home and take him to the airport for his first-class flight to the film set in Los Angeles.

'Tom was on the set telling everybody they had better look sharp because he's bringing in this guy from Bates City, Missouri.'

For his big scene in the film, Osborne was suddenly asked to improvise by Tom. 'So I did and Tom keeps the cameras going. I'm getting a round of applause from the crew. That's encouraging. Tom's feeding me ideas and laughing. When I get a laugh from Tom Hanks, I feel pretty secure. Truth is, he doesn't laugh much unless it really gets to him. So I'm having warm, bubbly feelings about the entire shoot.'

He added: 'I don't think of Tom as a huge star because he doesn't let me think of him that way. I mean, he drives a pick-up truck. A new pick-up truck, but it's still a pick-up truck.

'Inside, Tom hasn't changed much. In a one-on-one environment he's exactly the same as he was.

'The problem is that because of his fame he has to be guarded in public. During the filming he would always pose for pictures with people who came by the set to watch the movie being made. But he has to be careful. He can't just go anywhere whenever he feels like it.

'I wouldn't say that I've never envied Tom, but I'm not jealous. Yeah, I have some bitterness about struggling for so long. Why couldn't this have happened 20 years ago? But I didn't have the opportunity. As I told Tom in a letter, "If nothing else happens as a result of this, they can't take the experience away." At least this movie is finally giving me credibility with my kids. Shakespeare never did that.'

Following his screen role, Osborne was hoping it would be a springboard to more Hollywood roles. 'Tom Hanks gave me the opportunity to put my work before lots of people. The rest is up to me,' he said.

Tom made it perfectly clear that the hiring of a friend from his salad days in regional theatre was in no way meant to be charity. At the première of the film at the Toronto International Film

Festival in Canada, he said: 'For me, working with Holmes again was one of the added bonuses of making this movie. It wasn't a huge part, but I wanted a guy who could do the riffs. I've talked to Holmes periodically over the years and know him pretty well. I never doubted he could do it.'

Interestingly, Vincent Dowling, both men's mentor at the Great Lakes Shakespeare Festival, explained what separated the two actors. He said: 'Both Tom and Holmes are brilliantly talented. But there are a few actors who – when you first meet them – their charm, their humanness, the whole breadth of their personality comes bang over. They can walk into an interview or audition and it's all there from the first moment.

'Tom always had that. Holmes didn't.'

He said Tom has a 'quiet but absolute determination and need to win. While all actors have a need to act, certain actors have a need for fame and success. And that need is what puts a person continually in the right place at the right time.'

Tom couldn't leave out Rita, who had given birth to their second son, Truman (actually Truman Theodore, after two American Presidents), shortly before filming started. She plays a bargirl in a sexy, very revealing, outfit. 'It was Tom's idea of a cruel joke,' she laughed. 'Dressing me up like that just after I'd given birth.'

The roots of *That Thing You Do!*, like many of Tom's projects, has its beginnings in his childhood. Like most of young America in the mid-60s, Tom was caught up in the British pop invasion, but, ever the contrary child, he spurned the Beatles for a lesser-known London group, the Dave Clark Five.

He explained to the *St Louis Post-Dispatch*: 'I was always toying around with the notion of a band that, about the time they are ready for the biggest success of their careers, they flame out because of the various personalities involved.

'When I was a kid, eight years old, the youngest in a family of teenagers, the British invasion was it. It was a very evocative time for me, very glamorous, and you could see the Dave Clark Five every week, it seemed, on the *Ed Sullivan Show*.

'I was one of the kids convinced that the Dave Clark Five was way better than the Beatles. While we were working on *That Thing You Do!*, Dave Clark paid me a visit and it sent ripples of excitement through me.'

Tom's £20 million film tells the story of The Wonders, a fictional garage band from Erie, Pennsylvania, that reaches the top of the charts in 1964 with a tune called, surprise, surprise, 'That Thing You Do!' The four naïve musicians go on the road under the wing of their controlling, manipulative manager – played by Tom – and collapse without ever recording a second record.

Again, his personal experience came into play as a reference for the four young men who are totally blindsided by fame. 'It is like being hit by a freight train,' he has said.

Tom asked advice from his director friends. But he said two stood out as being particularly useful. Ron Howard told him: 'Look, the greatest movies are made by shooting wide, and then going in tighter, and then going in tighter.'

The aspiring director added: 'And Garry Marshall told me to change my shoes at lunchtime.'

The film, with its pretty much unknown cast – save Liv Tyler, best known at the time for being Aerosmith singer Stephen Tyler's daughter – did good, if not outstanding business and was well received by the critics.

It wasn't another in an ever-growing list of Tom Hanks blockbusters. But then, nobody really expected it to be.

It wasn't all fun either. Directing, as he discovered, could be downright hard work. 'I was working 18-hour days on *That Thing You Do!* and wasn't seeing my kids as much as I wanted,' he said. 'And I got into an elevator and this lady said, "Oh, Tom Hanks! What's it like living at the absolute top of the heap?" And I said, "Lady, life is just one damn thing after another, no matter where you are living."'

He told *Entertainment Weekly:* 'Any movie is going to be some sort of vanity project. There's no getting away from that. I did say, "Jeez, I'd really like to do this. Will you let me?" And they let me put my fat ass in the fire.'

It just shows how you can get by with a little help from your friends. And the critics were gentle with a film that, although without Tom's usual power, was still a pleasant, professionally made diversion. Said *Variety:* 'The best thing to be said about Hanks' feature debut as a director is that it bears all the elements that have made him into a movie star – boyish charm, natural ease, comic precision and, above all, generosity of spirit.'

If Tom spent little time on screen in *That Thing You Do!*, he hadn't even shown his face on the hit movie that preceded it – and he still helped it gross more than $191 million (£118 million).

He had taken most of the summer in 1995 off, meeting only with director Oliver Stone to discuss, and later reject, the lead role in the high-profile biopic, *Nixon.* The shamed president was eventually played by Anthony Hopkins. He took time out to nix any possibility of a *Forrest Gump II* on the grounds that 'it wouldn't be a good movie'.

More forthright, he added later: 'Stupid is as stupid does makes me sick. I'll be saying "life is like a box of chocolates" again about the same time as Sean Connery says, "I'm Bond, James Bond."'

Toy Story was released by Disney in November 1995 with very little fanfare or advance buzz. Tom had been attracted to the project through his long working relationship with Disney, which was making the film, and because he thought his own kids would like it.

He certainly didn't do it for the money, getting paid the union scale fee for the job, a fraction of his market value in Hollywood. Coming off back-to-back Oscars, he had also hoped to fade into the background for a little while, feeling that he was becoming too overexposed to a fickle public. In fact, his voice-over work as Woody, the toy cowboy, took a little over two years and he had to record most of it separated from co-star Tim Allen, the voice of the spaceman toy Buzz Lightyear, because they kept making each other laugh too much.

Neither Tom nor Disney could have expected the huge success of *Toy Story*, the first full-length feature film to be completely computer-animated.

The story centres around Andy, a six-year-old boy, whose toys come to life when humans are not around. Woody is the toy's leader and they all live in harmony in Andy's bedroom until the boy gets a new toy for his birthday – Buzz Lightyear, a technologically advanced astronaut that immediately gets all of Andy's attention.

The feud between the two toys provides the platform for a string of adventures that captured the heart of audiences around the world. Much to Tom's amazement, there was even talk of him being nominated again far a Best Actor Oscar, a first for an animated film.

Far from staying out of the spotlight, the film had thrust Tom back onto the entertainment pages with yet another hit movie, which topped many critics lists as the family film of the year.

It had been a fascinating – and challenging – diversion for Tom, and another remarkable string to his bow. But his next blockbuster was most definitely not one for his kids. In fact, he barred his two younger children from watching it.

Having finished his directing and all-round plate spinning act on *That Thing You Do!*, Tom was off to England to head the cast of a World War II movie called *Saving Private Ryan*. The film would unite him for the first time on a project with his friend Steven Spielberg. It would also shock cinema audiences as never before with its graphic scenes depicting the true horror of war.

Little did Tom know when he first discussed the movie with Spielberg, that his role as a wartime leader would cross over into real life for him to head off a threatened mutiny among his fellow actors.

FIFTEEN

HOLLYWOOD BOOT CAMP

HOLLYWOOD'S PAMPERED HEROES are used to California sunshine, first class travel, luxury hotels and fawning fans. The closest most of them have come to real inconvenience in years was when the battery ran out on their cell phones. Actors routinely prattle on about suffering for their art, of crawling inside the skin of a character to understand how to truly play a part. Few have suffered like those in *Saving Private Ryan*.

Tom Hanks, along with tough guy actor Tom Sizemore, who starred in *Heat* and *Natural Born Killers*, New York director/actor Ed Burns, and independent-film stalwarts Jeremy Davies, Barry Pepper, Giovanni Ribisi, Adam Goldberg and Vin Diesel all jumped at the chance of working with master film-maker Steven Spielberg. But none of them – not even Tom – had realised what the director had in store for them.

Spielbergs chief aim in making the film was to be as accurate as possible in recreating the nightmare of D-Day – 6 June 1944 – and the story of an American officer and his squad searching behind enemy lines for an elusive GI in the days after the Normandy Invasion. So he sent his actors to boot camp. The director remained at his Hamptons, Long Island, estate while his 'soldiers' went off to war in England, at an old British Aerospace site outside Hatfield, Hertfordshire.

The man whose job it was to test them to the limit, Captain Dale Dye, a 21-year veteran of the American Marine Corps, had already worked with the movie industry. Through his Warriors Inc. company, he had taught Tom how to throw a grenade in *Forrest Gump* and shown Tom Cruise how to search a Vietnamese hut for *Born on the Fourth of July.* He had also worked as a consultant on Oliver Stone's *Platoon* in 1985.

This time, his mission was simple: to erase any hint of Hollywood phoniness from the movie and the men starring in it. 'Most war movies are the biggest collection of rotten dog shit that I have ever seen,' he growls. He is not a man to mince words.

'This is not a high school play,' Dye barked at his troops. 'And if you think you are going to be actors who can fake your way through three months of shooting a movie about our fallen comrades, you are wrong.'

The men were forced to refer to each other only by their movie names, a dictum punishable with painful push-ups if forgotten. Anyone mentioning anything contemporary could expect similar excruciating penalties.

As well as the extreme demands of the daily routine – dawn exercise, mock battles, long hikes – there was the atrocious weather to add to the men's woes.

'It was utterly freezing,' Tom – or Turd Number One, as Captain Dye called him – told *The Times*. 'The only thing that we couldn't do was to go to the bathroom in the woods: The nature conservancy in Hatfield wouldn't allow us to do that, so we had to use an outhouse which was not a pleasant place.

'You have a brand of pitch blackness in England that I've never quite experienced.'

Given all they had to endure, something had to happen. And it did – there was the vote on them staying there to have more of it flung at them, or going home. It was the leader – Tom Hanks, playing Captain John Millar – who turned the situation round.

As we have seen, Tom was persuasive and to the point: 'Of course, we all felt like a bunch of idiots after that,' Adam Goldberg told *People*. 'Tom made a very strong case for sticking it out and turned us all around.'

Ed Burns added: 'The boot camp was, I think, the toughest thing any of us had ever done in our lives. You hated every second of the experience. But the minute it was over, you were just so happy that you got to be a part of it. You felt such a sense of accomplishment and you really felt like, "Hey, I did something here that a lot of people will never get the opportunity to do."'

To Tom, the arrested mutiny was a defining moment that helped bind the men into their roles. 'We got yelled at a lot and it was very physically gruelling and the food wasn't any good. We were very, very tired.'

But, quoting war historian Stephen Ambrose, consultant to the film, he said: 'There is nothing more terrified than a veteran going into combat.' And he went on: 'I wanted that to be a palpable thing that I could draw on as an actor, as opposed to some anonymous intellectual choice that I made.

'We were scared so much that we can still go back and remember the time we had to walk for an hour through the pitchblack darkness of the woods, only to be ambushed by Dye and his gang in a moment of absolute sheer terror. And not only did it scare us to death at the moment, but for 20 minutes we were walking with our hearts beating as though we were running a marathon.'

Tom told *The Times-Picayune* that the experience 'was only a cheesy microcosm of what really happened in World War II, but nonetheless as actors we had never been in that position before, and it was very important for us to go through it.

'It was five days of very little sleep at night. It was not even a fraction of what anybody in the service goes through. But for us, whose job it is to protect that – it was the most important thing we did.'

Over the campfire towards the end of the week, Dye opened up to his recruits, giving them some of his first hand knowledge of what it feels like to go to war. Asking them what they think it must feel like to watch a comrade die in front of you, the actors gave him the response he expected. They talked of sadness, rage and grief. 'Bullshit, bullshit, bullshit,' he stormed at them. 'You feel joy! You feel joy that the guy got it and you didn't. And shortly thereafter, you feel shame.'

Irrespective of his Oscars and his long, proven track record, Tom's officer rank gave him the right to remain aloof from his fellow actors, all of whom were both less experienced entertainers and under his command in the film. He was also best friends 'with the director, a fact not lost on the entire east and crew. But, true to form, when the cameras stopped rolling there was no star trip. He stayed close to the other actors, eating lunch with them and they spent off time chatting in each other's trailers.

Matt Damon, who by the time the film was in cinemas had won an Oscar himself for *Good Will Hunting,* said: 'What Hanks does is lead by example, whether by working long, hard hours or simply by eating off the catering cart like everybody else. He could have ordered cracked crab from Alaska every day, because this business really does indulge people. But he didn't want the special treatment.'

Added Ed Burns, known for directing and starring in his self-financed *The Brothers McMullen:* 'A lot of us hadn't been in such a big Hollywood film. Tom kind of took us under his wing. This is one of the biggest stars in the world, and he's not bossy or arrogant and is nice to everybody. Without being hokey, we all felt lucky to work with him and become his friends.'

Tom's leadership earned him a glowing recommendation from Captain Dye, who told *Time* magazine: 'The guy could be, should have been, a professional soldier. He has the mind, the motivation, the spirit and the body to make a good officer. He is inquisitive and highly intelligent. Strip away the Hollywood crap and he's like Captain Miller: a common man in uncommon circumstances who rises to uncommon levels.'

The idea of a Spielberg-Hanks collaboration came after both men read the *Saving Private Ryan* screenplay without the other's knowledge. 'Both of us just thought it was fantastic,' said Tom.

The result is a gripping two-and-a-half hour opus that showcases Hollywood's premium talents. The first half an hour of the movie – a raw, unvarnished bird's eye view of the stark horror of the Allied landing at the codenamed Omaha Beach – shocked even the most hardened cinema-goer with its blood-soaked carnage. Many veterans simply couldn't bear to watch, so realistic were the images conjured by the magic of Spielbergs cameras. Tom's understated performance held together the narrative with an equal intensity.

The concept of being an ordinary man caught up in extraordinary circumstances is one Tom had often used to explain his vaunted position as a millionaire movie star. It is no coincidence that his one spectacular failure in *The Bonfire of the Vanities* saw him struggling and failing to capture the elitist East-Coast attitude of Sherman McCoy, the WASP who watches his privileged life disintegrate. Now he was bringing his everyman hero to his part as Captain John Miller in *Saving Private Ryan*.

The dedicated but conflicted Miller is duty bound to put himself and seven of his men in harm's way in order to rescue a young soldier, played by Matt Damon, whose three brothers have all been killed in battle.

Although the return home of a surviving sibling is a US military tradition dating back to Abraham Lincoln's time, Miller's distaste at first losing two of his men, then facing an aborted mutiny from the others to find one man while others are dying all around them becomes a central theme of the film.

Miller, the consummate officer, finally reveals himself to his men as a schoolteacher with just one ambition – to return to the classroom: But duty is duty and orders have to be carried out if any sense was to be made of it all.

Critics hailed Tom's pivotal performance for reminding the shell-shocked audience that war is ultimately about people, many of them questioning what they are doing and why. Most of them terrified out of their lives.

'Heroes are cigar-chomping, leatherneck guys who against all the odds save the day,' Tom told *The Times*. 'I don't play anybody like that. I play guys who are scared, guys who've probably made some mistakes, guys who wonder how any of this stuff went wrong and guys who are just trying to do the right thing moment by moment. That's like 99 per cent of the people on the planet.'

Filming revealed another essential difference between Tom and many of Hollywood's most famous leading men. At one point, the script called for Tom's enigmatic captain to suddenly launch into a long speech revealing his innermost feelings to his stunned soldiers. It was, as Tom said, 'a monologue any actor would kill for' – the kind of breakout speech that attracts Academy Award judges. But Tom didn't want to drop the mantle of mystery that surrounded the captain's private life. On the spot, just as the cameras were about to roll, he cut the speech.

He told Spielberg he felt it would 'cheapen the character and compromise the integrity of who he is throughout the entire movie.'

Although a maddening perfectionist with definite views about his characters, Tom had developed over the years a way of changing directors minds in the nicest possible manner. He usually got his way.

Tom understandably had high hopes going into the film, but he was still unprepared for the emotional scope of the finished article.

He told *The Times-Picayune*: 'We were shooting for something, but I was shocked that the end result was what it was. I was amazed and broken up by it. I think we were hoping to have something that was going to be palpably emotional to the audience, but I think we did something that's much, much greater than we even could have imagined.

'When I saw the movie for the first time, I had the luxury of being in a room by myself, so I wept openly for a long time. I have never cried harder at a movie, or almost in real life, than at the end of this one – it was just so painful. I think an absolutely unbelievable thing has occurred here, and I am part of it, and I sort of can't believe it.'

Unlike other Oscar winners, like Nicholas Cage, a fine actor who turned to action movies for a new thrill – and a bigger fee – Tom says: 'I am sick of machine guns, cop chases and airplanes crashing into buildings. I'm sick of films where someone fires a gun along a crowded street, but you don't see innocent bystanders getting shot, only the bad guy.

'In *Saving Private Ryan,* all the violence has consequences. None of it is there just because it looks cool. Sure, it's grim. But it's brutally honest. It does not discount the fact that every time a trigger is pulled, someone's head may shatter into a million pieces.

'Kids who play Mortal Kombat computer games should see the film because it might just make them weep.'

The same Hatfield countryside where Hanks and co. fought their own private battles with Captain Dye was later transformed from scratch into a fictional French village, where the second wave of combat in the film was shot. A beach in Ireland's County Wexford doubled as Omaha Beach and 850 members of the Irish Army worked on the film.

Spielbergs attention to detail was such that his team discovered the American company which made the soldiers shoes during the war was still in business and still had a batch of the old dye it used at the time. The firm was immediately commissioned to make 2,000 pairs of shoes. Veterans told the director they remembered thousands of dead fish washing up as they tried to take the beach. One recalled seeing a Bible floating past him in the water. Both touches were added to the film.

A yard full of Nazi gear was found in London. Tanks were bought from the Czech Republic and Allied landing boats were discovered languishing in the desert site of a California dealer.

Said one technician: 'If someone had their legs blown off, Spielberg wanted a man without legs to do the scene. Plastic arms and legs were fitted to real life amputees and blown off.'

The production suffered its own casualties. On set on Ballynesker Beach, in County Wexford, 14 Irish reservist extras were taken to hospital with exposure after being in the sea too long. One extra strayed out of line and a dummy bomb blew him 10 feet into the air, breaking one of his legs.

Another was hurt when a dummy mine exploded under him as he crawled on the sand. And two more were reported to have broken legs when they were run over by a jeep. Tragically, one 17 year-old was killed in a car crash on his way home from the set. According to aides, the director was mortified and sent personal condolences 'and more' to the family of the young movie hopeful who had only just passed his driving test.

The army reservists had worked the previous year on Mel Gibson's *Braveheart* and were paid £44 a day for 14-hour shifts in hostile conditions. Spielberg worked even longer hours – albeit for better money – overseeing every scene himself.

While most of the cast and crew stayed in local inns, Tom and Spielberg took over half of one of Ireland's most exclusive small hotels, Marfield House, in Gorey, about 20 miles from the set, living in suites backing on to a private nature reserve.

Tom had Rita and all four of his children with him. Spielberg brought wife Kate Capshaw and several of their children.

After filming had finished, a pensive Tom walked alone along the French beaches recreated so chillingly in *Saving Private Ryan*.

Among the many small identifying plaques that litter the shoreline, he found one dedicated to the Second Battalion, C Company of the US Rangers, the company his character led in the movie. 'I looked up in disbelief at those bunkers, some of which are still there,' he told *Daily Variety*'s Army Archerd. 'I walked where they died, where some put on dry socks for the last time.' Overcome with emotion, lost in the silence where once there had been such a terrible cacophony of sound, Tom lay down and slept dreamlessly before walking back to his car and the present.

There is little dispute that the movie is the most authentic cinematic depiction of World War II in Hollywood history, towering above its closest rival, Darryl Zanuck's *The Longest Day*.

It's a remarkable compliment to Tom's career that the public that once delighted in him as an overgrown boy who ends up working for a toy company in *Big* would accept him ten years later as a war-weary captain close to collapse.

World War II veterans were strongly affected by *Saving Private Ryan*. Some old soldiers couldn't even bear to sit through the unrelenting drama of the D-Day landings portrayed in the first section of the movie. To others, it enabled their loved ones to understand fully for the first time the hell they survived.

Veteran groups in the US and Europe hailed the first 17 minutes of the film as the single most accurate depiction of field battle ever captured on film. And they found they were suddenly getting a new measure of respect from later generations. 'It's had a catalytic effect in terms of getting younger people interested in World War II,' said Leland Bellot, a history professor at California State University in Fullerton. 'This might have been something that would have happened without *Private Ryan*, but there are a lot of kids who really want to know about war right now who probably wouldn't have been interested if they hadn't seen it.

But there were some dissenting voices. Les Stapleton, who fought in World War II, came out from seeing the film, saying: 'Why does anybody need the detail? I've been though that, and I'll tell you it's not something that should be in a movie.' Travel agent Hal Ryder, a retired Lieutenant Colonel who fought in France in 1944, added: 'Why should I pay money to see something I've been trying my whole life to forget?' In addition, black, World War II veterans were also angry that the film denied African-American soldiers 'our rightful place in history'.

Nonetheless, the overall response to the project was remarkably enthusiastic. The film took $30 million on its opening weekend in America in July 1998, a record for a summer movie. That was even after Spielberg had warned that teenagers under 14 might find it too gruesome and Tom declared his younger kids would not be watching it. After 17 days, word of mouth and critical praise and pushed the box office up to $100 million and at Christmas of that year, it was over the $180 million mark – an incredible achievement for a three-hour epic with a R-Restricted rating, no romance and hideous violence. Feeling there was still an audience – and giving the movie an extra nudge towards the Oscars – *Saving Private Ryan* was also rereleased across cinemas in the US in February, 1999.

Further proof of the film's popularity came on the Internet, where by the Monday after the opening, America Online's message boards were receiving 25 messages a minute praising it, totalling over 10,000 by the end of the day – a figure only beaten once, the occasion of Princess Diana's death.

On Tuesday 9 February 1999, Tom got word that he had been nominated for his fourth Best Actor Oscar for his portrayal of Captain Miller. He was on his way to a film shoot in Fiji when the nominations were announced, reserving him yet another prime seat at the Dorothy Chandler Pavilion the following month, and the chance of a historic first ever hat-trick of golden Best Actor statuettes. Tom made one of his traditional short, but sweet, thank you pronouncements, saying: 'Making *Saving Private Ryan* was a life experience for all of us. To be nominated is a very great honour, to be nominated for *Saving Private Ryan* all the more. I am delighted and proud.'

Despite already winning two Academy Awards for *Philadelphia* and *Forrest Gump* and being pipped at the post for *Big*, Tom was still hot favourite among his fellow 71st academy nominees Ian McKellen, Roberto Benigni, Nick Nolte and Edward Norton. A third win would put him on a plateau no other actor had ever reached. Previously, actor Walter Brennan won three Best Supporting Actor awards and Jack Nicholson has won two Best Actor Oscars and one for Best Supporting Actor.

The first call Tom received was from an equally jubilant Steven Spielberg, who told him their film had won an astonishing 11 Oscar nominations, including one for Spielberg in the Best Director category.

Spielberg was in Berlin to attend the Golden Camera awards and was so nervous he had asked his assistant to watch the nominations being read out on live television from Hollywood. She knocked on his door shortly after 5.30pm and breathlessly read out the list to her boss. 'I was flabbergasted; I just leaned against the wall,' said Spielberg, who has been nominated for five Best Director Oscars, including an emotional win for *Schindler's List*.

'I never, ever get blasé about this. This day is always indelibly tattooed on the frontal lobe of my brain. I'm usually never nervous about these kinds of things but this always makes me so nervous. I was very anxious this year. In fact, I think I set a new record for anxiety this year.'

Spielberg said the success of *Saving Private Ryan* was far from a foregone conclusion, even with Hollywood's most bankable star on board. 'Actually, just the opposite was true,' he added. 'Two weeks into the shooting of the Omaha Beach scenes which open the film, I turned to the entire cast and crew and told them, "At this point in the movie, every single Tom Hanks fan is going to stand up, leave the theatre and never come back. This film is going to cost Tom a lot of fans."

'The fact that the film has done so well is thrilling to me. The people have spoken. They said they were ready to go back a half-century to a blasphemous time and have the courage to experience *Saving Private Ryan*. I think their courage was remarkable.'

The nominations, along with two for the animated feature *The Prince of Egypt,* were the first for the DreamWorks movie studio owned by Spielberg, David Geffen and Jeffrey Katzenberg and a major boost to the fledgling company.

For Tom, seven hits out of seven meant he no longer agonised over his film choices. As he headed out on a wearying promotional tour for the film, he said: 'I don't fight with myself over which movie to do next. I don't try to top myself with every new movie I make. If I specifically set out to do that, I would be making terrible, artificial films. What am I supposed to do? Die of another horrible disease?

'All the audience cares about is watching a decent movie. They don't care how good your last movie was. They want to see a good movie NOW.

'Being an actor can be fun. The people around you are funny, and you get sandwiches whenever you want some. Still, at the end of the day, you have to tell yourself that, well, it's the end of the day. So, you drive home to your family, have a nice dinner and watch a dart competition on TV Some actors flog themselves to death. Me, I do not treat my job as if it is a circus act. You do not have to perform around the clock.'

With the movie completed, an unreserved triumph, with the reputations of both Tom and Spielberg further enhanced, there was an added bonus. The friendship between the two men had not only survived, it had flourished in the work environment.

Spielberg had this to say about Tom: 'It was wonderful working with my friend, and even better that we stayed friends after the experience. I've always had tremendous respect for Tom, and this project enhanced my respect for him, both as an actor and a human being. He offered great suggestions that benefited the film and was completely open to my ideas about his character.

'Tom Hanks represents to me what is best about idealised America. Tom is Gary Cooper and Jimmy Stewart. He is what I think is America.'

And Tom repaid the compliment: 'Making this movie was like walking into Thomas Edison's laboratory. You're in the presence of this genius who in real life is this badly dressed, nebbishy kinda guy who talks in tangents and only vaguely answers a question. But seeing him on the set, he's a dynamo, a source of incredible vision and information that's hard to keep up with.

'Steven is even more of a mystery to me now than he was before we had this experience. I think he probably gets about four hours sleep because he is always up thinking about stuff. I think he lives his regular life at the same pace that he lives his movies, except that when he's making a movie he's actually got something to occupy his time, whereas when he's not, he's just got to foment stuff. I mean, who is Albert Einstein's good friend? That's the way I look at it.'

To keep their friendship free of cash concerns – and shave about £30 million from the budget – the two men sacrificed their usual salaries in return for a share of the grosses. Although it was never going to touch the phenomenal box office of *Forrest Gump*, Tom would still recoup his requisite £15 million fee, with some quite considerable change.

There was only one disappointment in all this. Despite being a hot favourite to win his third Best Actor Oscar, Tom lost out to Italy's maverick comedian Roberto Begnini, who climbed on chairs and talked on stage in broken English how thrilled he was to win for his film tragi-comedy about the Holocaust, *Life is Beautiful*.

Tom, sporting a fuzzy beard, grown for a forthcoming project, kept a low profile with wife Rita as *Shakespeare in Love* beat out his *Saving Private Ryan* for the lion's share of the Oscars. Tom's only public comment on the day was that he prepared by taking his kids out to a toy shop and an In-and-Out fast food burger restaurant. The Miramax comedy took Best Picture, Best Actress for Gwyneth Paltrow and Best Supporting Actress for Judi Dench among its seven Oscars.

Out of its 11 nominations, *Saving Private Ryan* culled five statuettes, including Best Director for Steven Spielberg. The four other Oscars were for Cinematography, Editing, Sound and Sound Effects Editing. In spite of his denials, Spielberg looked put out at the tally and there was a heated row in the press over whether *Shakespeare in Love* studio Miramax had bamboozled voters by spending a fortune on publicity to promote its film heavily.

Apart from industry awards, however, there were other aspects of *Saving Private Ryan*'s success. Amid the publicity hoopla, Tom also found time to lend a cash-raising hand in aid of the World War II Memorial, a £70 million project to built a lasting tribute in Washington DC to those who lost their lives. After pitching the memorial while picking up a gong at the national televised People's Choice Awards in America, more than 30,000 calls were logged in less than 24 hours, raising £200,000. The plea 'hit a responsive chord,' said memorial spokesman Mike Conley.

Tom and Steven Spielberg have also quietly helped finance a D-Day museum in New Orleans. Founder Stephen Ambrose, the historian who worked with both men as a consultant on *Saving Private Ryan*, said they jointly donated hundreds of thousands of pounds to save the project. The museum was opened on 6 June 2000, the 56th anniversary of the Normandy invasion.

With all its success, *Saving Private Ryan* had been a wearing project with a lot on the line, not least of those his friendship with Steven Spielberg and the unspoken need to further earn his respect.

Even many of the wisecracks traditional to most Hollywood war films had been swept from the original script, mainly at the insistence of Tom, who asserted there was little to laugh about when you were terrified out of your wits.

Through Tom and Steven's friendship with war historian Ambrose, another battle plan to work together began to emerge. As fulfilling as *Saving Private Ryan* had been, neither man felt ready to leave the subject. The minds of the men who went into conflict had proved a fertile creative field they felt deserved further examination and Ambrose had just the project to do it.

His *Band of Brothers* followed E Company of the 506th Regiment, 101st Airborne, through the Second World War, and Tom, in particular, became obsessed with the soldiers' dramatic journey.

While the germs of *Band of Brothers* wouldn't bear fruit until the finished series was screened in 2001, it was time to have some fun in the meantime after the intense *Saving Private Ryan* shoot with Steven Spielberg. And who better to have some fun on screen with than another of his close friends, Meg Ryan?

SIXTEEN

TOM AND MEG

IT WAS A private moment that best defined the deeply-rooted connection that has made two stars of considerable individual accomplishment a partnership to match any of the great pairings of Hollywood's golden past.

Meg Ryan and her then husband, actor Dennis Quaid, were guests at a Fourth of July barbecue being thrown by Tom and Rita at their Los Angeles home. As Tom heated up the coals, his 'bohemian' neighbours were celebrating rather more rowdily a few feet away. 'Those were the people who intimidated me in high school,' said Ryan, with the characteristic mixture of bemusement and insight that have preserved her place in movie stardom since that famously faked orgasm in *When Harry Met Sally.*

Tom, a friend of Ryan's since their first film together, 1990's *Joe Versus the Volcano,* told *People* magazine he was charmed by the Proustian realisation. 'It's not everybody,' he said, 'who can remember exactly how disconnected she felt in those primal stages of adulthood.'

It was meant as a throwaway comment for a magazine cover story on one of his closest friends. But the point was that Tom had recognised something in Ryan that he knew existed in himself. Tom could certainly remember how disconnected he felt for most of his life until he met Rita.

Like him, Ryan had a troubled family life growing up, which had extended into adulthood.

Like him, her parents split when she was a child, leaving her lonely and confused – and being brought up by her father.

And like him, she found a partner she felt had 'saved' her, and built up her own family around that new nucleus.

That connection, consciously or not, has cemented a chemistry between them that radiates onto the screen.

Spencer Tracey and Katherine Hepburn had it. So did Fred Astaire and Ginger Rogers. And James Stewart and June Allyson. Call it on-screen romantic chemistry. Or a mystical blending of two distinctive personalities into something unique and memorable. But in the Hollywood of the 1990s, Tom Hanks and Meg Ryan had it too.

Both come across on screen as ordinary people, the boy and girl next door. In this sense, they are classic movie stars, perfect for pictures patterned on earlier Hollywood romances. Two of their three films together were indeed based on old favourites: *Sleepless In Seattle* is a revision of Cary Grant and Deborah Kerr's *An Affair to Remember* and *You've Got Mail is* a loose reworking of *The Shop Around the Corner,* which starred James Stewart and Margaret Sullavan.

We know how Tom came to this point. To better grasp the genesis of the Hanks-Ryan partnership it is necessary to examine Ryan's background and the upbringing that provides the shared foundation for their understanding.

To her adoring fans, she has that girl-next-door image and sweet smile that women want to copy and men can't resist. But Margaret Hyra, or Peggy, as she was known in the little town of Bethel, population 15,000, where she grew up in Connecticut, 60 miles north of New York, certainly hasn't had a conventional life.

Her parents split up when she was 16 and still at school, a traumatic parting that continues to have ramifications today. Her father, Harry, was a mathematics teacher and sports coach at the nearby Danbury High School. Her mother, Susan, was an actress who settled down as a housewife and mother to their four children, of which Margaret was the second oldest.

When the marriage unravelled it was Susan who left the family home, leaving Harry with the children until she could find a job and take them to live with her. As she packed her bags into the back of her old Ford Pinto car, a sobbing Ryan begged her to stay. Although she remained living in Connecticut while she commuted into Manhattan to try and find acting work, Susan says her daughter never forgave her for leaving.

Like Tom, Ryan ended up being cared for by a father who was not really fully equipped to handle the job. Friends say she found the new chapter in her life painful and upsetting. Her father, trying his best to be both mother and father to four children, says now he had trouble giving them enough time and attention. 'Maybe Meg felt out on her own,' he confessed.

By the time Susan had found a steady teaching job and was ready to take her children back three years later, Ryan had left home to go to the University of Connecticut, doing TV commercials to help pay her fees.

Echoing stories from Tom's youth, Ryan's old school friend Tracy Parsons told *People* magazine that her classmate didn't even tell her about her parents' break-up until a year had passed. 'She didn't want to let other people in on her pain,' said Parsons. 'She had to take care of herself. Her father tried, but it was overwhelming for him.

'It was hard for her not to have her mother at home, in terms of proms and first dates and first kisses. She was very unhappy. Susan never left the family, just the house. Still, Meg got the idea that her mother abandoned her.'

After university, relations between mother and daughter improved, with Susan helping the then Margaret Hyra to get her acting union card and giving her daughter her maiden name – Ryan – which she took as her own in tandem with the more cosmopolitan Meg.

The relationship again became tense when Susan married writer Pat Jordan, whose strong personality conflicted with his headstrong stepdaughter.

Shortly after Ryan met roguish actor Dennis Quaid on the set of the 1988 thriller *D.O.A.*, the slender bond was broken for good. Susan, angry at continually being cast as the bad mother by an unforgiving daughter, said Ryan refused to talk to her after she tried to warn her about Quaid's drug-taking. The star of *The Big Easy* and the Jerry Lee Lewis biopic *Great Balls of Fire* later went into rehab to beat his cocaine use when Ryan gave him an ultimatum that he must give up drugs before she would marry him.

Ryan denied the drug confrontation with her mother was the reason for the impasse. She told *Vanity Fair* in 1995: 'It's a very long story. It's 32 years of stuff with this woman.'

The two women have not seen each other since 1990 – Susan has never seen grandson, Jack – and Ryan has rebuffed all attempts at a reconciliation. 'All I have of my grandson is a photograph,' said Susan. 'It is like looking at a total stranger. It breaks my heart.'

After a two-year stint in New York on the daytime soap *As the World Turns,* Ryan had a small role as Anthony Edwards' wife in Tom Cruise's *Top Gun* and then her big breakthrough in *When Harry Met Sally* opposite Billy Crystal.

She first met Tom by chance in a hotel lift in New York in 1987. 'He was with his wife Rita and I had just seen him in *Punchline* and blurted out that I thought it was one of the best things he'd done,' said Ryan. 'He was so gracious and humble and that's exactly how he turned out to be when I worked with him.'

Ryan teamed up with Tom for the first time in 1990's poorly received *Joe Versus the Volcano* and the two hit it off at once. The chemistry was a bit confused as although Ryan was playing Tom's leading lady, she was also playing two other women in the film as well.

It was really *Sleepless in Seattle,* released three years later, that established the romantic comedy partnership.

Tom and *Sleepless* director Nora Ephron immediately thought of Ryan when they began looking for an actress for the part of Annie Reed, a reporter who falls in love with the voice of Tom's character, Sam Baldwin, on the radio. Tom felt they had clicked in *Joe Versus the Volcano,* even if the film hadn't quite come together. Ryan felt the same.

Perhaps the most unusual thing about the love story is that the two principals do not actually meet until the very final moments of the film. They only actually spent one week filming together because their characters spend the entire movie just searching for one another. Ryan would later describe the whole film as 'foreplay'.

The couple would pass each other on the set and ask how the other's half of the movie was going. 'I got to thinking how nice it would be to work with Tom,' Ryan said.

Director Nora Ephron raved about both of her favourite stars, saying they were 'without vanity. They will do anything that is required.'

She added: 'When you do a romantic comedy, any romantic comedy, Tom and Meg are the ideals. They're intelligent and they have incredible instincts for comedy. I know Tom's wife and Meg's husband, but when I'm making these movies, I get to the point where I actually think Tom and Meg should be together. They are from the same food group.'

Rita even gave the onscreen romance her blessing, saying: 'Meg is one of the all time great people I know. It is a lot nicer when you know that it's your good friend kissing your husband.'

When Meg's marriage to Quaid eventually collapsed, it's sad to note that her career also took a dive. By submerging herself into darker movies like *In the Cut* and *On the Ropes*, she buried the girl-next-door quality that made her famous. Her short-lived but explosive romance with co-star Russell Crowe didn't help, and neither did her excruciating guest appearance on Michael Parkinson.

Who knows what would happen if Tom's marriage to Rita hits the rocks? *You've Got* Hate *Mail* just doesn't have the same appeal!

In spite of his Tom 'Hankies' reputation in the aftermath of his emotional Oscar speeches, Tom wouldn't claim to be romantic either. He says he never sends flowers and resists Rita's attempts to get him to watch old weepie movies. 'My favourite movie couple is R2D2 and C3P0,' he joked.

But he does advertise his love for his wife in interviews and speeches that reach millions – a hard feat for most romantics to beat. And he knows how to put a smile on his wife's face in the morning.

'Well, I do make breakfast for Rita,' he says. 'I guess that's romantic. I'm the morning guy. I can make a morning the most delightful thing that you could experience. How do I do it? There's a way to wake people up. There's s a way to make French toast with just the right amount of powdered sugar. Listen, I can't make lunch or dinner to save my life but breakfast, man, I got that covered.'

When Tom had wrapped *Saving Private Ryan,* he was looking forward to a change of pace. Romantic comedies were, in effect, the only remnants of his previous, pre-Oscar, career and when Nora Ephron showed him her *You've Got Mail* script, he knew there was only one person who could play New York bookstore owner Kathleen Kelly. He called up Ryan and she agreed on the spot to do the film. To get an instant decision from the notoriously picky Ryan, that was a feat in itself and a testament to Tom's pulling power.

In the old days of the all-powerful Hollywood mogul, even the biggest stars could be virtually forced into continuing partnerships because most of them were contractually tied into studios.

With the greater freedoms of the century's last three or four decades it was much more difficult first to find a durable star pairing and then to keep them together. Studios largely found it easier to flog solo action star vehicles such as *Rocky, Rambo* or *Die Hard,* or team up male buddy partnerships such as *Lethal Weapon*'s Mel Gibson and Danny Glover for big money productions.

The producer of *You've Got Mail,* Lauren Shiner-Dormer – married to *Lethal Weapon* director Richard Dormer – said the Hanks-Ryan team is the only one filling a major public demand for old-fashioned romantic comedies. 'I don't think you can quite put your finger on the chemistry,' she said. 'They are both very intelligent and they have a remarkable gift for comedy. They are both unafraid on screen. They're willing to be clowns, and that leads to a certain vulnerability. But beyond that...'

Ephron, who wrote the *You've Got Mail* script with sister Delia – the sisters also co-wrote *Sleepless* – defines the chemistry as 'two brains falling in love'.

Tom cannot rule out the sexual connection. He told the *Ottawa Citizen*: 'I think a bona fide amount of attraction is there. When you're into the dynamics of man-woman stuff, I don't really think you can fake it.

'Obviously, Meg is very attractive. She's easy on the eyes. She's also inspiring, so there's this intellectual thing there at the same time. I don't think there is a man in America who doesn't have a crush on Meg Ryan, but on top of that for me she's a really tight kind of friend and there's something very attractive in that as well.

'I don't want to go into the cheesy analogy mode, but it's like if you are going to play tennis with someone who's really good, you know it's going to be a good tennis game.'

He continued: 'Meg is very smart. She is a friend. It's getting together with a competitor, yet there's no competition to it whatsoever. What's truly good about it is that I don't think we can get stale because we don't really do it unless we love it. We don't do it unless it's going to be fun. It's not some forced union. It's almost a crime that we get paid for doing it because it is not like working.'

Ryan adds: 'This is a strange genre because it's not ha-ha-hilariously funny and it's not like real drama. There's this weird little tightrope you walk on.'

She is not much better at putting a finger on what makes the partnership work so well. 'I feel it's not really for me to say,' she says. 'I have such an incredibly easy time. I just love being around him. I feel it's like stealing money from the studio. It's just a great time. I liked going to work in the morning and I was sad when the movie was over.'

'All I know,' she says, 'is that it was easy from the first moment of the first day. One of the great things about Tom is that he could, by all rights, be on an Elvis trip. He could come to the set with all these things and people, but he's just this guy that you feel like you know, and you probably do. Even after all this stuff that has happened to him, he's gracious enough to feel lucky. I love the way he is in the world. He's a great example for all of us.'

She told *Entertainment Weekly:* 'Chemistry is a really weird thing. Sometimes you feel like you don't have it, but it ends up on the screen anyway. Other times you feel a really strong connection, and it ends up looking flat and dead. So the thing with Tom – I don't think it behooves me to examine it too closely. If I started trying to dissect it, it might go away.'

In *You've Got Mail,* Ryan's character runs a cosy, family

bookshop on New York's West Side driven out of business by the dreaded Fox Books, a chain store offering a huge range and discount prices, that bulldozes its way into the neighbourhood. Tom plays Joe Fox, the ruthless chain store boss with, you guessed it, a heart of gold.

The rivals meet and fall out, becoming enemies as Ryan tries in vain to fight back at the big-brother book chain. But at the same time as they are bickering in person, they are unwittingly falling in love over the Internet, E-mailing each other anonymously after meeting in an America Online chat room. His sign-on, if you are interested, was NY152. Hers was Shopgirl.

The final scene, to the surprise of no one, has the couple sharing a big, juicy kiss having belatedly discovered what their mutual cursors looked like in the flesh.

Once again, the stars spend much of the time on screen avoiding one another, just missing each other or corresponding to each other on the Internet. 'I'm dying to do a movie with Tom where we are in every scene together. This is getting ridiculous,' Ryan laughed after wrapping their third film.

But she added: 'I don't think this is the last time we'll work together.' That's quite likely because as well as being a lot of fun, Tom and Ryan are handsomely rewarded for their services, to the tune of £15 million for him and £7.5 million for her.

The bonhomie of good friends working together was clearly evident on location in New York, where Tom happily waved at gawkers who stopped to watch some of the street scenes being shot: The crew, many of them well used to working with spoiled prima donnas, spoke of 'a nice reunion' feeling about the shoot.

While taking a break at Starbucks coffee shop, Tom went behind the counter to learn about making the drinks while his costar quietly sipped her skim-milk mochaccino.

On another time-out, during a long night scene, the couple dropped into the gourmet food store Zabar's, where Tom had Ryan doubling up with laughter. The shop's general manager, Scott Goldshine said: 'We have a loud PA system in the store and Tom Hanks would pick up the microphone and yell, "Meg Ryan to cheese! Meg Ryan to coffee!" He had her in hysterics.'

Not that it was all fun and games. 'It's movies like *Mail* that wear you down,' Tom told *Entertainment Weekly*. 'Going into a dark soundstage every day, stepping over cables and ladders, getting your hair done for three hours, shooting the same shot from so many different angles. And having to be so aggressively fresh for every scene.

'That's when it almost feels like you're working for the post office.'

In real life, Tom surfs the waves, but rarely surfs the net. 'I do occasionally search for those nude pictures I did 20 years ago,' he laughed. 'Thank God, I have yet to find them.' He does, however, have a passion for typewriters. In *You've Got Mail*, Ryan's Luddite boyfriend, played by Greg Kinnear, gets a gentle ribbing for going on about his collection of old typewriters. Tom actually has up to 20 old portable typewriters, some of them worth several thousand pounds, and most of them in working condition. He first found an old Hermes 2000 in a Cleveland junk shop, loved its Swiss-made preciseness, and became hooked.

You've Got Mail lived up to expectations and opening as America's number one film just before Christmas 1998. The pairing had worked its magic again, making eight hits out of the last eight films Tom starred in.

It generally got good reviews, but there was a feeling that some critics may be tiring of the Hanks-Ryan formula. 'This romance is pleasant but not extraordinary. Even Ryan is reportedly tired of these silly soufflés which force critics to invoke the word "twinkly",' said the *Pittsburgh Post-Gazette*. However, such opinions were not the norm. *Patch Adams*, the Robin Williams comedy about an offbeat doctor, was released on the same day as *You've Got Mail*, and eventually grossed $20 million more than the E-mail romance, but even so, this Hanks-Ryan project delivered exactly what most cinema-goers had wanted.

Nonetheless, as Tom tests his range with future projects, it is a comfort that movie-making with Meg Ryan, Nora Ephron, etc. can still be fun.

And there will always be an audience waiting for the next Hanks-Ryan romantic comedy.

SEVENTEEN

PRESIDENT HANKS?

THE TALK OF the party was the similarity in hue of Hillary Clinton's Pamela Dennis gown and the Ronit Zilkha ensemble worn by Britain's first lady, Cherie Blair. Among the 240 guests invited to the White House reception for Prime Minister Tony Blair – a high-wattage mix of Hollywood celebrities and Beltway bigwigs – the M-word was strictly forbidden.

It was just days after the Monica Lewinsky scandal had exploded onto the world's front pages and the humiliation of Bill Clinton's prime-time confession and the ensuing impeachment was still many months away.

A few brave souls dared to joke under their breaths that Elton John, who was providing the entertainment, should serenade his host with 'Scandal in the Wind', but otherwise the theme was very much business as usual.

Dining in the East Room on an eclectic menu of honey mango chicken, grilled salmon and chocolate replicas of Big Ben, Tom and Rita were in their element. They had, of course, stayed in the White House as guests of the Clintons three times in the past five years and were among the President's most fervent supporters. Blair and his wife mingled happily among guests like Secretary of State Madeleine Albright, who was with Jackie Onassis's longtime beau Maurice Tempelsman, John F Kennedy Jnr and senior Democrats. The starstruck Blairs were introduced to actor Harrison Ford – who played a save-the-day president in *Air Force One* – by Clinton with the quip: 'This guy's got a better plane than I do.'

But every eye was on a select Hollywood group that had aligned itself at Clinton's side from the beginning. 'This is a night to have a good time,' said Rita, setting the agenda. 'We sent the Clintons our message of support a week-and-a-half ago.' Her husband, with his Gump-like ability to be in the heart of the action, enthused: 'This is an exciting place to be.' Steven Spielberg, with wife Kate Capshaw, noted quietly that the President's through-the-roof approval ratings 'are exactly as I feel about him'. And Barbra Streisand, whose name had been closely linked to the President in the past, insisted: 'Whatever he does behind doors is his business. We did elect him President, not Pope.'

Clinton, happily unaware of the knife-turning twists the Lewinsky affair had in store for him, danced with Hillary until 1.00am. To the President, with the eyes of the world watching his reaction to the latest sex allegations against him, the mere presence of such vaunted guests at such a difficult time spoke volumes. 'This has been a great night,' he said. 'Hillary and I are very grateful.'

Before the year was out, Hollywood's strict party line in full-blooded favour of the bad-boy President would be broken by one of this select group. Who would have dreamed back then that it would be Tom Hanks?

But then Tom has always been able to see the bigger picture. He turned down the chance of playing America's most disgraced

President in one film and passed on the chance to portray the nation's most debased President in another.

But does the actor who, as we saw, named his youngest son Truman Theodore after two other former Presidents have a more serious role in mind? Having tried the White House guest bedroom out for size on three occasions, does Tom have aspirations of moving into the master suite? As President Hanks?

Like a good politician-in-waiting, he didn't rule it out. And then he did. But along the way, perhaps just as he had intended, the suggestion was out there that Tom Hanks just possibly, some way down the line, could be tempted to forsake his position as the most powerful actor in Hollywood to try his hand at being the most powerful man in the world.

Hadn't Ronald Reagan managed the same feat and served his country with aplomb? And he wasn't even a very good actor.

Tom Hanks may not have much of a history in politics, but his campaigns had earned his fair share of votes from the Academy Award judges over the years. If it had been Tom's intention to test the water by talking openly of running for presidential office, it certainly succeeded. Newspapers and TV stations around the world picked up on his comments in an interview with *New Yorker* magazine – and no one was laughing.

Even an alleged about-face comment to the same publication that he regretted giving financial support to help the cash-strapped President Clinton to fight his way out of the mire of sexual allegations involving Paula Jones and Monica Lewinsky was perceived as a strategic and politically astute move to distance himself from a fatally damaged leader.

Surprised at the furore his comments caused, Tom immediately denied ever having any intention of running for office and made the expected jokes about movie star as president and how anybody in their right minds could think he was serious about it.

Nevertheless, he is certainly not a stupid or naïve man and he is extremely well-versed in the ways of the media. Rarely does anything pass his lips that wasn't carefully thought out beforehand, even if it does all appear to be off the cuff.

Tom has always had very forthright political views even if, as he says, they are largely kept around the kitchen table. He remains, either by luck or design, the most trusted star of his times. And despite all he has achieved, he is still driven by ambition and new challenges. What better way for a child once tagged Number Eight to show that he really could become Number One? Friends of the actor say privately that they believe Tom would make an excellent President, perhaps even following Reagan's route by first serving as governor in his native California.

One clue to Hollywood's aspirations for Tom came when he strode on stage to make a presentation at the 2004 Academy Awards and the orchestra struck up the President's theme tune, 'Hail to the Chief'.

An avowed Democrat, he nevertheless keeps his views on George W. Bush for dinner-table conversation and resists the kind of outbursts preferred by colleagues like Warren Beatty and Susan Sarandon. He appeared with the President at the World War Two Memorial dedication in Washington, the creation of which he played a notable part in, and resisted joining the chorus of protest over the Iraqi quagmire.

But he insists he will not follow his old friend Terminator-turned-California Governor Arnold Schwarzenegger into politics. 'I know Arnold. He's a driven man,' he told *Entertainment Weekly*. 'He loves to mix it up politically. And he's got a very clear-cut vision of what he thinks needs to be done. But I've never had any type of political aspiration. I don't think I'd do a better job in politics of educating anybody – and certainly not of entertaining anybody. I just don't think it's my forte... I'm the observer. I'm the artist.'

But his disclaimers didn't stop the speculation.

Ronald Reagan was not just President of the United States, he was one of the country's most beloved Presidents. Peggy Noonan, the writer who scripted some of Reagan's best speeches, said in 1994 that there was one Hollywood actor who shared a lot of her old boss's characteristics. His name was Tom Hanks.

It is interesting to examine exactly what Tom said to his *New Yorker* profiler Kurt Andersen, an experienced American writer and editor who himself moves in influential media circles.

The article appeared in the prestigious magazine just before Christmas in 1998, when President Clinton was at the height of his 'Sexgate' troubles. His claim that he did not have sex 'with that woman' had come back to haunt Clinton, who was accused of lying under oath about his affair with White House intern Monica Lewinsky. Facing certain impeachment and fighting a rearguard action to save his political skin, the last thing the President needed was another attack by a high-profile 'supporter', particularly one that the American public identified with.

On Tom, Andersen wrote: 'The man who still believes in heroes and the old-fashioned virtues also maintains a faith in politics, and what he unselfconsciously calls "the good fight".

'His own politics are almost oxymoronic: He's a moderately conservative Hollywood Democrat. He's a death penalty proponent who said "God bless America" at the end of an Oscar speech but finds the "religious right that controls the Republican Party kind of scary".

'He's an actor-director-producer who decries the "despicable, shallow" run of Hollywood entertainment and "pornography delivered to the home" on cable TV. Yet he believes in "this concept that the government can do work that is really good. And it's not just building roads and bridges. I think that the government can do things that truly do better society and give people a hand up and still let them do what they want to do."'

At first, Tom seems to be merely playing down his relationship with Clinton, who had played host at Tom's three overnight stays at the White House saying: 'I'm friendly with him. But I don't think I've ever had a true connective conversation with him. I just can't. I'm still too much in the "Jeepers, creepers, he's talking to me" kind of thing.'

Andersen mentions the widespread rumours that had been circulating in both Washington and Hollywood circles for some time, namely, that a house Tom had bought recently in Los Angeles was being reserved for his friend the President's retirement. A parallel rumour – that Tom and Clinton's mutual friends Steven Spielberg, David Geffen and Jeffrey Katzenberg also had a job ready for the President with their DreamWorks studio as well as a possible position at Tom's Playtone production company when he left office – was also given a wider airing.

Tom says the new house was bought for his growing family. But he goes on to court further controversy. Saying he wrote a cheque for Clinton's legal defence fund, he said he regretted making the donation.

Andersen reported Tom as saying: 'We gave ten thousand bucks. Very early on. In all honesty in the light of events since, it would be awfully hard to say now, "Oh, here, let me help you out with this problem." Or buy him a house.

'But – well, the other side has plenty of figures that pony up an awful lot of dough, too. So you try to fight fire with fire, or something.

'But he ain't getting that house. I'll tell you that, right now. Forget it. And he ain't working at the Playtone Company [Tom's production company], either.'

Andersen said he quizzed Tom over a potential career in politics, only half-seriously suggesting a spell in the US Senate followed by a run for the presidency. Said the writer: 'I expected a snort, a roll of the eyes, an emphatic disavowal. But instead he said, vaguely, "I'd have to know more about law or economics."' Andersen said Tom later sent him an E-mail that was a 'squishy non-denial of political ambition'. It actually reads like a campaign statement: 'My image is a really good one,' he wrote. 'I made a nice acceptance speech on TV a couple of times: I handle myself pretty well in the glare of the entertainment media: The actual ideology that anyone can glean as projected by my appearances on TV is that America is good because we are all so different and respecting each other is not so hard a thing to do. 'Not a bad platform, I suppose, to run for some office.'

The comments – particularly those about his friend the President – put Tom on the front page of the *New York Post* the morning after the *New Yorker's* publication, and the story was followed in Britain and around the world.

His comments were all the more surprising in the light of a previous interview in which he had criticised celebrities who turned to politics. 'When I saw Sonny Bono at the Republican National Convention with Gerald Ford in 1976 all I could think of was, What the hell is he doing there?' he said in the *New York Times*. 'I was 18 years old and thought that was the stupidest, dumbest thing I had ever seen. I don't feel that anybody is influenced in any way by the fact that a public figure on the show business level embraces any sort of political cause. The images just balance out after a while. For every Warren Beatty, there's a Charlton Heston.'

Nevertheless, the story was mushrooming around the world. The *Guardian* headlined its report 'Wholesome Hanks turns his back on the Clintons' and started the story: 'Tom Hanks, one of Hollywood's biggest stars, tore apart the curtain of celebrity shielding President Clinton yesterday when he said that he regretted giving financial support to the former governor of Arkansas.'

The *Daily Mail* asked: 'Hanks hints at lofty ambition – is Forrest Gump in line for President?'

The *New York Post* put it more prosaically: 'Gump dumps on his buddy Bill – Tom Hanks is first Hollywood defection.'

Maureen Dowd, a much-respected former White House correspondent for *The New York Times,* devoted a whole column to Tom's apparent political aspirations, saying: 'A slap from Tom Hanks must sting the President more than a slap from Congress.'

She wrote: 'Tom Hanks will have some explaining to do before we elect him President. We'll want to know if he enjoyed wearing that dress in *Bosom Buddies.* We'll want to know exactly what happened under the blanket with that stewardess in *Nothing in Common.* We'll want to know what possessed the man who went to the moon to moon in the December *Vogue.** We'll want to know if he is truly contrite about making *Turner and Hooch.*

'But on the other hand, he would have definite assets as a candidate. He served in World War II, Vietnam and the Peace Corps. He brought *Apollo 13* back safely. He learned about suffering in *Philadelphia.* He got that magic handshake from J.F.K. in *Forrest Gump.* And he has a catchy campaign slogan "Life is a box of chocolates".'

'Jeepers, creepers, as Mr Hanks likes to say, why not? In Washington, we've had no-one to root for in a very long time. A faux hero would be better than no hero. We have a groupie for President. Why not have a star.'

She said the campaign donation controversy was 'a striking reversal. It used to be that Hollywood was drawn to Washington's issues, and Washington to Hollywood's sex appeal.'

Dowd goes on: 'Hollywood will soon realise: Why give millions to prop up Democratic candidates when it can field its own? With President Hanks, at least the stars sleeping in the Lincoln bedroom would be real friends.

'President Clinton has increased our appetite for entertainment to the point where we may not even be satisfied with Tom Hanks

* The December 1998 edition of *Vogue,* with Hillary Clinton on the cover, has a photo inside, taken by famed photographer Herb Ritts, of Hanks mooning to readers with a 'not particularly trim' bottom.

the person. We may need to go all the way and elect Tom Hanks the character.'

Carefully thought out, or carelessly ad-libbed, Tom's debut into the political arena had caught fire.

The very next day, however, Tom was rapidly backtracking, realising perhaps that his comments put him at odds with his Hollywood cabal of close friends. Spielberg, his wife, Kate Capshaw, Barbra Streisand, Michael Douglas and Ron Howard had all, like Tom, contributed $10,000 to the Clinton fund. Streisand, in particular, had been vociferous in her public support for the beleagured President. Tom's $10,000 was the maximum allowed under the rules of Clinton's second legal defence fund – the first fund allowed only $1,000 and was shut down because it didn't rake in nearly enough money to help pay the mountain of lawyer's bills that were growing daily.

Clinton, who was spending most late nights alone in his office flicking through the TV channels to gauge his standing in the polls – his main hope for survival – was said to be deeply upset and hurt by Tom's outburst, which came at a crunch time days before a vote in the House of Representatives' judiciary committee on whether to impeach or censure the President. Tom may have played more heroes than anyone since John Wayne, but a fourth invitation to the world's most exclusive bed and breakfast now looked unlikely.

Rather than moan about the magazine taking what he said out of context and deflecting any criticism the way of the media, the usual path of attack for embarrassed politicians and film stars, Tom took the upbeat approach. He still said his comments had been taken out of context, but said he 'loved' the interview and enjoyed the novelty of creating a stir. 'I love being controversial... I've never been controversial before,' he told a local cable TV station in New York as he was about to be honoured at an AIDS benefit.

He went on to enthusiastically reaffirm his support for Clinton, saying: 'You couldn't get a bigger supporter of the President than I am. He is doing a great job.'

Having told Andersen he wished he hadn't given cash to the President, he was doing a complete volte face and telling TV reporter Eleanor Mondale, a close friend of Clinton: 'Well, I tell ya, as a person, as an American, as a voter, who has supported the President, still continues to support our President, there's been a couple of times over the last year or so where sitting, reading the morning paper, I slapped myself upside the head and said, "What the heck is this?" You know, I ponied up 10 grand for our President's legal defence fund, and if I had never done that and he asked me today, I'd probably give twice as much.'

But he did add: 'For a moment or so I might have questioned my original intentions in donating to the defence fund. I do regret the country is still going through the entire affair.' Tom carried on yanking his foot out of his mouth in a *Time* magazine interview several weeks later. He supposedly went 'all stammery' as he tried to explain: 'Look, if I hadn't given it then, I would have given it now. As a guy who supports the President of the United States, I think he's doing a fabulous job and I'm glad I gave him the money.

'In the vast, surrealistic expanse of the Story of the Year, who didn't at one point or another slap themselves upside the head and say, "Holy smoke! Holeee smoke! Can you believe this?" And you can't believe it, but it's the reality. But you know what? He's my guy.

On the question of becoming the new Ronald Reagan, he insisted: 'I'm not running for the President of the United States. I'm an actor who makes movies, and that's how I was answering the questions.

'Good Lord Almighty! This is how trivial the times we are living in are. I don't even want to talk about it! Argggghhhh!'

Tom's big brother, Larry, was equally disbelieving, saying: 'The

President? Oh boy! That's not going to happen. That was a real media thing.'

Tom's attempt to defuse the controversy once more showed his deft touch with the media.

Everyone knows what an uncontroversial image Tom has, so by claiming to enjoy the sudden notoriety brings a smile rather than a grimace to the faces of the assembled media hordes and to the audience they represent.

He didn't appear rattled or aggrieved at the attention even though he completely changed his stance while laughing about the speculation launched by his original claims.

The outcome was exactly as he had intended. He was seen as an unconcerned fisherman casting about ideas, rather than as a worm wriggling on the hook of public opinion. A born politician?

The controversy was all the more surprising because the friendship between Clinton and Tom was widely thought to be the at the root of Hollywood's unswerving support of the former President.

Even before the Lewinsky scandal, Tom had turned down the plum role of the randy, slick-talking Southern governor based on Clinton in the movie *Primary Colors*. The book by Joe Klein had caused a sensation as a thinly veiled, fictionalised account of Clinton's 1992 White House election campaigning. The book depicts the central character, Jack Stanton, as a habitual and remorseless philanderer.

President Clinton, knowing the film was being made with director Mike Nichols at the helm, made it clear who he wanted to play Stanton. He even said Tom would be his choice as an actor if they did a movie version of the William Jefferson Clinton story. 'If I had to cast it today just in an instant, I'd like Tom Hanks to play me. I mean, we don't look alike, and we're not the same size or shape or anything, but I know him and respect him as a person and an actor, very much,' Clinton said in an interview with CBS in America. 'And I think he has shown a range of capacity that's quite remarkable, and if someone were trying to play me and actually go through this job, in the kind of roller coaster way that life takes you, I would want a person with a lot of range and a lot of feeling.'

Tom was also thanked profusely from the stage by Clinton for his support after the actor, with all his usual charm and savoir faire, emceed a star-studded 1996 Hollywood benefit for the President at Green Acres in Los Angeles that raised an estimated £2 million. In spite of the glowing references, Tom still passed on *Primary Colors* and the role went to his friend John Travolta.

Tom strenuously denied his decision was because of his close ties with the President. 'It's a hilarious amount of ink for a story that's not true,' he said. 'I've met the President – that's a big difference between being friends with him.'

He claimed the real reason he turned tail on the film was that he was simply too busy. 'I went to Mike and said, "You know, I can no longer do this thing because life has caught up with me. You're going to have to cast someone else,"' he said.

But he still insisted that being in the film, which co-starred Emma Thompson as the Hillary-like wife, would not have offended Clinton. 'I was at an event with him recently,' he said. 'He joked, "It's okay with me if you do *Primary Colors*." I laughed harder than anybody else did.'

Muddying the waters slightly, he also told *The Times*: 'I was interested in doing *Primary Colors*, but I never saw the script. In all honesty, I'm a supporter of the President and I wouldn't have gone off and attempted to obviously slag off the President of the United States. It probably would have been a very different movie had I been involved.'

Tom had also rejected Oliver Stone's overtures for him to play Richard Nixon, a subject and an era that would normally have interested the baby-boomer star. The 1995 film, in which Sir Anthony Hopkins played the villain of Watergate as a foul-mouthed and manipulative drunkard, courted controversy, sparking protests from Nixon's daughters and supporters.

Whether or not Tom will now admit to any ambition for high office, the *New Yorker* episode has shown that the public – and the media – will take him at his word. They will also take him seriously, no mean feat for an actor once shrugged off as lightweight and goofy.

As strange as it may seem, for a restless man with an incisive, inquiring mind it may no longer be enough to be regarded as the best film actor of his generation. It may not even be enough to have a loving, intelligent, beautiful wife and a settled, satisfied family.

His comments on the presidency may have unwittingly allowed us a glimpse into a game plan that looks long beyond the next two or three movies.

He calls himself 'the luckiest man in the world', but maybe Tom's most important role will not be left to chance. The world of politics is beckoning even now. Tom may never get to play a President in the movies.

Perhaps it is his destiny to play one in real life. Whether he likes it or not, his comments have already started the ball rolling – fans at the 1999 Academy Awards held aloft signs and placards reading 'Tom Hanks For President'.

EIGHTEEN

CASTING AROUND

THE LITTLE BOY sat on his grandfather's lap, just as his father had done, trying desperately to stretch out his legs far enough to reach the accelerator pedal. The old man fretted that perhaps the family ritual would be lost on his grandson, who had probably seen more of the world in his few years than all of his ancestors combined. This was a boy, after all, who had taken the pilot's seat on a supersonic flight from New York to London on Concorde as a special birthday treat.

It was the first time Amos Hanks had taken grandson Colin – Tom's eldest child – to visit the family burial plot at Paskenta Cemetery in Northern California. But he needn't have worried. Amos had the boy in his thrall as he showed him how to drive the car, and talked about his love for hunting and his admiration for the books and lifestyles of his heroes, Hemingway and London, authors who wrote of the wild side of life, a far cry from the razzamatazz of Hollywood.

And, just as he had with Tom and his sister and brothers, Amos led Colin around the graves where his ancestors were buried. The

263

poignancy of the moment was not lost on the misty-eyed grandfather, remembering Tom's dramatic graveside performance many years before.

How could he have guessed back then at the heady heights his second son would rise to?

For Colin, the path would be clearer, but the expectations much more daunting. Growing up with both parents and a stepmother as actors and with the likes of Spielberg, Steve Martin, Martin Short, Barbra Streisand and John Travolta popping in for dinner or sharing the car pool, Hollywood was fluttering her eyelids right from the earliest age.

Tom, Rita and Susan have gone to great lengths to protect their children from the constant spotlight that comes with being associated with a star of Tom's magnitude in this instant-access era. But they have never pretended it isn't fun to be famous. So, when Colin told his parents he wanted to leave school to become an actor, they could hardly complain. In fact, both older children appeared in *That Thing You Do!* and Elizabeth had a small part in *Forrest Gump*.

A fiercely protective father, Tom said his children were rarely starstruck. 'My work doesn't make much of a blip at the house,' he told *Time*. 'There is always a hubbub of activity because we are going somewhere, but they don't say, "Hey, Dad, you're on TV!"'

'All my kids can look and see what I do for a living and see that it's really fun. It produces a vast amount of joy. It's hard work if you can get it, but it's great work too.'

Sometimes, even for the most grounded children, the line between Hollywood and reality can become a little blurred. When Chester was four, he was sitting at home watching his father in *Turner and Hooch* on cable television and at the end of the film he went over and stood by the door, waiting for Tom. 'Isn't that sweet?' said his proud dad. 'I was done in the movie – so I must be coming home.'

Tom praises his children for helping to keep life in perspective. 'If you haven't sorted it out by the time you have your fourth kid, if you are actually going to be undone by the fact that they're not sleeping through the night or down with the measles, you should never have had number two,' he said.

'It also helps to keep you grounded. You come home and you've got an eight-year-old who wants to wrestle on the floor and a teenager who's having trouble at school – they don't care if you couldn't pull off a tracking shot. They just want you to be a dad. It keeps life real, and the attention where it should be.'

Tom made no secret of the guilt over his older children's upbringing. Of Colin, he told *Time*: 'Throughout the vast majority of his youth and adolescence I did not have a clue as to how to be a father or a parent. I was at that point in my career when it was all about getting work.'

With equal candour, a Hanks family trait, Colin admitted: 'I hated him when I was a kid, just like every kid [hates their father]. But he's my dad. He changed my diapers, yelled at me when I was in trouble, and wanted me to get good grades. But I respect what he's done. Who wouldn't?'

He said Tom never pressured him to be an actor – and didn't lift a hand to help once his son had decided to follow him into the business. 'He never made any calls for me, not a single one, not even to help me find an agent. I never asked him for a single thing. I did everything on my own.'

So the moment was all the more sweet when the proud dad turned up at the LA premiere of Colin's first starring role in the hit teen comedy *Orange County*, which co-starred comic Jack Black.

'It was like being stoned,' Tom said in an interview. 'I was laughing and crying through the entire thing. Understand that when he was five or six-years-old I was doing *Bosom Buddies* and he'd come to the Paramount Studios and we'd have lunch and hang out. Now I'm driving back to Paramount and my son's picture is on the side of the soundstage bigger than life and I'm watching him come down the press line… I was both giddy and sobbing with emotion at the same time.'

Having been hanging around film sets his whole life, Colin knew enough to initially begin work at his father's production company, a big enough leg-up in itself. At 20, he was cast in Fox TV show *Roswell High* as one of six teenagers – three of which were aliens – who briefly caught the imagination of a youthful television audience.

Orange County, not dissimilar in style to some of his dad's early movies, provided an ideal vehicle to move up to the big screen and have a stab at stringing out the Hanks family celluloid legacy.

When he won a part in director Peter Jackson's highly touted *King Kong* remake and spent several months filming in New Zealand, his father called to joke he was jealous of his son's role. Asked whether Tom was heading out to see him halfway across the world, Colin noted, his dad was something of a busy man himself and was far from ready for retirement.

But, while he may not have been ready to rest on his laurels, Tom was looking for a change of pace. There was the potential to play a bad guy for the first time and a pairing with America's favourite horror writer, both projects that would offer a new challenge other than simply rolling out multi-million-pound smashes one after the other.

Tom signed up to star in Stephen King's *The Green Mile* after a deal to play super-cool Dean Martin opposite his old pal Travolta – who was to portray Sinatra – in a Rat Pack movie fell through.

In the screen version of King's 1996 serialised horror novel, Tom doesn't look cool at all. He looks fat. He packed on more than 30lbs for his role as prison guard Paul Edgecombe in the death-row thriller set in a grim prison in America's Deep South in 1935.

The film tells Edgecombe's flashback recollections of magical goings-on during his stint as a death row guard at the Louisiana State Penitentiary, Cold Mountain. The head cell-block guard develops an unusual relationship with a gentle giant of a man who is convicted of raping and killing two little girls and sentenced to death in the electric chair. The 'green mile' refers to the line of green linoleum on the floor of death row.

Edgecombe relates his strange tour-of-duty watching over a quartet of convicted killers awaiting execution. Michael Clarke Duncan, who was in the Bruce Willis action flick *Armageddon* and Warren Beatty's *Bulworth,* also stars as John Coffey, the seven-foot-tall inmate convicted of murder whose caring, naïve nature and weird powers raise questions in Edgecombe's mind about his guilt.

The film marks Frank Darabont's return to the director's chair for the first time in five years. He wrote and directed *The Shawshank Redemption,* which received seven Oscar nominations, including one for Best Picture.

In a far from glamorous role, Tom doesn't look any better in the opening and closing sequences of the film, when his character is supposed to be 90 years old. Tom spent most of the second half of 1998 shooting the film, travelling between Tennessee and Stage 3 at Warner Bros studios. It didn't help that the film fell well behind schedule and Tom spent much of it with a painful ear infection.

The delays did not wear too well with the film's star and, even before its release, it was gaining a reputation as what the sinister Hollywood Lexicon calls 'a troubled project'.

Tom told the *San Diego Union-Tribune* in December, 1998: 'It is still going on. It's just one of those movies that is taking this much time. Some movies you can just crank out – this isn't one of them.

'*Green Mile is* a death row movie. We're on death row for a long time, and you've got to have that look a little different every time. It was never going to be easy to make, and it's not – that's just the way it is.'

He added later: 'We're a month over shooting schedule, but it seems like three months. It's a death row movie that seems like eternity.'

But there was one major advantage. 'The great thing is I get to eat a few more cheeseburgers, which is fine with me,' he said. 'I get to be fat because I'm playing a prison guard in 1935. You don't want to look like you have buns of steel.'

Right up to the film's US release date in December 1999, there was a mystery over whether it would be completed in time. Several months before it was due to hit cinema screens the film's beginning and ending still hadn't been shot, special effects were being created and the musical score wasn't ready. Bad weather had prevented the opening and closing sequences of Tom's character looking back over his life from being shot the previous autumn and were further delayed because the star was committed to another project early in 1999.

To make matters worse, Tom's make-up test was a disaster. He simply did not look old enough. At the end of the film, his character is supposed to be 90 years old. But Darabont told *Entertainment Weekly*: 'When the angle was just right, old Tom looked completely credible. Then he'd turn three inches and suddenly he'd look like Condom Head. When we saw him in sunlight, he looked like the Elephant Man.'

In the end, Darabont chose to cast veteran actor Dabbs Greer as the ancient Hanks.

Whispers of a jinx were further fuelled by author Stephen King's near-fatal accident, when he was knocked down by a minivan while walking near his summer house in North Lovell, Maine, in June 1999. King landed in a ditch 14 feet away and suffered multiple broken bones in his right leg, a collapsed lung, cracked ribs, a fractured hip, and cuts to his head. Five life-saving operations later he was allowed out of hospital to begin a long rehabilitation.

Shortly before the accident, King was pondering publicly over whether *The Green Mile* director Darabont, who he hand-picked to helm the movie, should consider cutting it by 15 minutes or so after he saw a working print.

'I think it's maybe 15 minutes too long,' King said to *Entertainment Weekly*. 'Frank's very adamant about not cutting it.

He won't cut the film on the basis of what I say. But if he thinks about it for a while, I think he might.'

Darabont, putting the final touches to one of the most highly-charged electric chair scenes ever shown on the big screen, insisted: 'Everything's under control.'

The critics may have sensed a *Bonfire of the Vanities*-type fall from grace for the actor who seemed unable to put a foot wrong. But they would have to wait a few more movies before raising a sliver of a doubt about Tom's prowess at the box office. Once again, the take was well over $100 million in the US alone and, once again, he was being tipped as an Oscar contender.

The end of the century came with Tom comfortably at the top of his game. During one week in December 1999, *Green Mile* was beaten out for the top spot only by Tom's reprise of his role as Woody in the hugely profitable *Toy Story 2*, which ended up with a worldwide box office approaching £300 million.

Tom's next project had one of the most unusual filming schedules in film history – and ensured the star who admits to an obsession with his rollercoaster waistline worked off all the flab he so happily gained for *The Green Mile*.

The actor had no one to blame but himself. He came up with the idea for the script after watching a TV interview with a man who was shipwrecked during the Second World War. 'He had to cling to some coral atoll for a few days and he thought he was going to die,' Tom told CNN.

'He was on television, being interviewed, and the interviewer couldn't get past the idea that this must have been an adventure somehow.

'The person said: "No, it was not an adventure, it was a harrowing experience, and I thought I was going to die." And she asked: "Do you ever want to go back and visit the place?" "No, I never want to see that place again."

'So here was this dichotomy of what it should be and what it really was in real life and I thought, Well, now that's interesting. I've never seen that. The idea of Swiss Family Robinson always makes it seem as if humankind, on an island like this, can do a few simple things and survive and even flourish and enjoy it.

'What would it do to a human being to have all the connection to all humanity removed? What is going to happen to the human psyche? And then, what's going to happen when it's suddenly all over, gone in the wink of an eye? It turned out to be something more complex and sophisticated than I thought it was going to be.'

It also turned out to be a lot more expensive to make.

The film united Tom with *Forrest Gump* director Bob Zemeckis – and the price tag was already up to about $80 million before half the film was shot!

The reason is the lengths Tom and the film-makers were prepared to go to make his performance look realistic.

In *Cast Away,* Tom plays a courier for an international company similar to Federal Express. *En route* home with an agonising toothache, his plane crashes onto a deserted island. Tom's character is the only survivor and manages painfully to extract his infected tooth. But as he does so, he blacks out and the picture fades to black with him.

When the audience sees Tom again, it is supposed to be months and months later, and he is looking emaciated, a shadow of his former self.

Rather than use camera trickery or make-up to create the effect of losing weight, Tom and Zemeckis decided the star would lose weight the old-fashioned way – through dieting and exercise. So they spent eight weeks through January and February of 1999 filming and then packed away the cameras while Tom went on a crash (*sic*) diet. Tom took an enforced sabbatical from *Cast Away* to shed 50lbs and Zemeckis scheduled another movie, *What Lies Beneath*, a supernatural thriller with Harrison Ford and Michelle

Pfeiffer. To save some cash, Zemeckis used much of the same crew to shoot both films.

Tom grew the beard he was sporting at the 1999 Oscars ceremony for this film. At an American Museum of the Moving Image fête for Hanks at the beginning of May, he was looking beefier than usual, and admitted he needed to lose 40lb by the autumn. He said he wasn't dieting. 'Not yet,' he added, 'as I have just eaten everything on my plate – I start again tomorrow.'

When he lost enough weight, an extremely thin Tom Hanks flew back out to Fiji in 2000 with the director and crew to restart filming. 'It's insanity,' he said at the time. 'I mean, what if someone dies? Whoops, I shouldn't say that.'

The multi-million-pound gamble relied on Tom staying out of harm's way during the hiatus, as most of the crew had to be kept on salary the whole time.

The gamble didn't start out too well when Tom almost had to cancel his visit to the 1999 Oscars after his right knee became infected by a bacteria he picked up in Fiji on the *Cast Away* shoot which, if left untreated, could have ultimately led to amputation.

At first, physicians at St John's Hospital in Santa Monica, California, couldn't work out what was wrong with the star, who was in excrutiating pain. But they diagnosed the ailment as cellulitis, a bacterial infection that had caused his knee to become painfully swollen.

Filming long hours in the warm water in Fiji, where he was unable to keep a blister properly dressed in the tropical climate, he returned to Los Angeles and was given antibiotics by his doctor. But he had to be admitted to hospital under a false name when the infection spread.

Because of his illness, the actor missed the pre-Oscar luncheon with his fellow nominees. But he made it to the big night and the condition soon cleared up under treatment.

Zemeckis told the *New York Times*: 'The Tom Hanks character has to emotionally and physically survive many years of loneliness. He doesn't have anything to eat but fish and coconuts. Tom had to transform his body.

'We have to do things this way. There's no way to hide the different looks of his body. When Tom read this, he said, "This is a great story, but how do you do it? How do you show a modern guy in a movie becoming emaciated?" This is what we came up with. It will end up believable because it's so real.'

The director was worried that Tom's dramatic weight loss midstream would dominate publicity – but he needn't have worried. The last time the actor slimmed down for *Philadelphia*, he took home an Oscar for his troubles.

Tom admitted the weight issue 'was frustrating for a while because it was the only thing anyone cared about. Losing weight was just time and discipline; it wasn't as if I was living on bacon and grapefruit for eight months. I was just watching what I ate, and working out with a very specific task at hand, which couldn't be avoided no matter how much I wanted to rest.'

And there wasn't much sympathy from his brother, Larry. 'It has got to be good for him to lose all that weight. He had too many fat roles in a row. He had to put the weight on for the parts he was playing. But I am sure he enjoyed the eating.

'If someone would give me $1 million [£650,000] to lose a few pounds, I would do it too. There is some kind of inspiration in that. It is certainly one way to lose weight.'

Losing weight proved to be the least of Tom's worries. He had to keep the audience's attention for most of the film – about one and a half hours of screen time – alone on a desert island with his best lines directed at a volleyball he famously named Wilson. Actual lines of dialogue were even written out for the ball to improve the odd couple's interaction. 'Hey, you want to hear something funny?' Tom's Chuck said to his ball'd pal. 'My dentist's name is James Spalding.'

An early draft had Chuck's duelling personalities – good and bad

– talking to each other, but Wilson turned out to be such a star one of the three volleyballs used by the filmmakers was later sold at auction for £12,500.

Tom's offbeat humour spices the details of the film: Chuck's licence plate reads KAZ 2AY, and using the initial for his character's first name makes C Noland or 'see no land'.

One shot where Tom squats on the ground to examine some debris washed up on shore is clearly a homage to the actor's favourite film, *2001: A Space Odyssey*.

Cast Away co-stars former *Mad About You* TV star Helen Hunt, who later won an Oscar for *As Good As It Gets*, but it is an absolute tour de force for Tom and earned him yet another Oscar nomination for best actor. Had he not already won two, there is a very good chance he would have followed up a Golden Globe trophy with an Academy Award triumph. But he ended up with something he prized almost as much – a flat stomach.

With yet another successful film under his belt, Tom turned back to a favourite theme with another favourite collaborator on the medium that helped mould his childhood.

Following the success of the Hanks–Spielberg allies in their first sortie, the *Saving Private Ryan* veterans launched another war project, this time for TV. They returned to the Second World War battlefield to produce a critically acclaimed 13-hour multi-million-pound mini-series based on the bestselling 1993 combat tome *Band of Brothers*, written by historian Stephen Ambrose, who was special consultant on *Ryan*.

Much of the filming for the series was done in Europe and, although he didn't pull back on his military uniform, Tom co-wrote the series and produced one episode. Both he and Spielberg were executive producers for the show, which was a huge hit on both sides of the Atlantic.

Band of Brothers tells the story of 'Easy Company', an elite group of paratroopers formally known as the 506th regiment of the 101st Airborne Division. The drama followed the unit's gritty journey through the Second World War, from their torturous training in Georgia to their landing in France on D-Day, and through the Battle of the Bulge. It went on to show how the paras liberated the Dachau concentration camp and took Adolf Hitler's Eagle's Nest compound at Berchtesgaden, in the Alps.

As a history buff, Tom was fascinated by the human story behind the battles, and the hold of *Saving Private Ryan* was so strong that it pulled him back to the subject.

'I can tell you that everybody on *Saving Private Ryan*, particularly the cast, went through an emotional and psychological thing with that movie. It wasn't just like showing up and knocking it out. It changed our lives, and our perceptions of ourselves as men and as actors. So, when it was done, I didn't want to leave it. There was still so much I wanted to talk about, and to bring to light, and dramatise in some other fashion.'

He became engrossed by Ambrose's book and its companion *Citizen Soldier* and devoted more than a year to bringing it to the small screen. Just as he had with his *Apollo* movie, Tom looked to TV to give him the wider canvas to follow through with his ideas and, once again, he looked to HBO to help bring the vision to the small screen.

Tom used his experience and commitment to draw superb performances from his largely unknown cast. The show was a commercial and critical success and proved once again that Tom had an uncanny ability to plug into his own mindset and subsequently reach a vast audience of fellow baby-boomers who share his interests.

But a real-life declaration of war almost made him take it off the air days after its world premiere.

The first episode was screened just two days before September 11, and Tom and Steven considered putting their show on the shelf.

'We thought we should take it off the air and not even bother because no one's going to be in the mood to see this stuff now,' Tom told *Men's Journal*. 'But it turned out to be a tonic in some ways. Which was very surprising.'

NINETEEN

HIT MAN HANKS

AS WITH ALL the biggest movie stars, after no small number of false starts, Tom has an unwritten pact with his fans. He is the ordinary man dealing with extraordinary circumstances. His characters don't climb buildings or save the world single-handed. They do their best. Usually, in films like *Sleepless*, *You've Got Mail*, *Forrest Gump* and *The Terminal*, things work out. Sometimes, as in *Saving Private Ryan*, they don't. But we can always see the better parts of ourselves in a Tom Hanks character – and he usually provides the moral core to the subject central to the movie.

It is a reflection of his character. He doesn't profess to be the perfect dad; indeed, he openly admits he wasn't there enough for his older children, and, with one failed marriage behind him, he doesn't lay claim to being the greatest husband. But you know darned well he is trying his best to succeed on both counts.

So what was the world to make of Tom's next role as a cold-blooded hit man for the mob? For the first time in his career, Tom was playing a bona fide bad guy in the Depression-era drama *Road to Perdition*.

277

By taking on the role, he was all too aware of the risk. The droves that turn up at any movie starring Tom Hanks don't necessarily demand a happy ending, nor do they insist on a clean-cut hero bleached of any flaws. But they don't want to see their everyman reflection get distorted by a character without any redeeming virtue.

To Tom, the matter was much less black and white. 'There are no bad guys,' he told *Men's Journal*. 'And this is the one thing I've said over and over again. Talk to any of my team. I make this big deal about, "Let's not turn anybody into bad guys. Everybody has motivations that make sense. They're just wrong. That's it."'

Tom's character, Michael Sullivan, is a pretty bad man, whichever way you look at it. He is the morally ambivalent loyal enforcer to a mafia boss who rules with an iron fist. At the same time, he is a loving family man who cares for his wife and children with an equal intensity.

It is this latter trait that Tom prefers to focus on – and the father-and-son dynamics that provide the underlying theme to the film provided an attraction that any reader of this book will quickly understand.

In an interview with the BBC, he insisted the role was not such a radical departure from his previous films. 'It's just that the extent that he goes to in order to provide for his family is a very, very different one.'

Interestingly, Tom Cruise played a modern-day hit man in *Collateral* several years later in an effective performance that nevertheless lacked any kind of redemption. It may be coincidence that his popularity dipped soon after that movie. Although his couch-jumping performance on Oprah Winfrey's chat show, his over-the-top wooing of actress Katie Holmes and Scientology rants against psychiatric medicine may have played their parts, the fact that their *Top Gun* hero played such a chilling, cold-blooded character certainly could have turned off some of his loyal audience.

For Tom, there was an added incentive in taking the part in *Road to Perdition*, in addition to the fact that it was British director Sam Mendes's follow up to his Oscar triumph *American Beauty*. It was the chance to share the screen with his hero Paul Newman.

For an actor little taken by the trappings of Hollywood, there was a breathlessness in his voice as he swooned to *Time* magazine: 'For me, the first day, the first time, the first take – forgive me, Paul – but I had an out-of-body experience. I hadn't felt that since the first time I went on *The Johnny Carson Show*. From now on, the world's a different place for me because I'm on film with Paul Newman. Paul can do anything he wants. If he wants to call me "kid" and never learn my name, fine. If he wants to do one take and walk away, fine. If he wants to come in with two little lapdogs and talk to them all day long, he could have done that too. Because he's Paul. But here's a guy who's just part of the ensemble and trying not to feel as uncomfortable as we all do. I thought our work together was seamless.'

Newman, whose wife, Joanne Woodward, played Tom's mother in *Philadelphia*, hardly knew his younger co-star, but their admiration proved mutual. He was particularly impressed during one 19-hour shoot when Tom's character was supposed to be sitting in the same room but off camera. 'Tom's character was sitting on a chair over there in a corner watching,' he said. 'Every time they said actors on stage, he was over there, off camera. He only had one line to say in the entire scene, and he stayed there for 19 hours.'

Newman plays Tom's surrogate father in the film, a relationship that bends and ultimately breaks when things begin to go awry. But the key dynamic is between Tom's hit man and one of his sons, who is forced to deal with the reality of his dad's profession when he sees him killing another man.

Much of the film shows Sullivan and his son trying to avoid a menacing assassin played with grim relish by Jude Law, but – and this is where Tom would argue that his character redeems himself – the dad tries everything he can to steer his son away from a life of violence.

The subject of a father's relationship with his son hit a nerve with Tom, enabling him to draw from his own complicated upbringing and the dynamics of his two sets of children from his past and present marriages.

While the stylised violence and film noir shadows were not to every critic's taste, the film still broke the $100 million barrier at the US box office, testifying to Tom's enduring appeal. It was one of the most lucrative runs in Hollywood history, unparalleled in terms of money and duration.

But it wasn't going to last.

After a prison epiphany, fights for personal survival on a desert island and saving the world from Adolf Hitler, not to mention the misery of prohibition gangsters, Tom was looking for a good old-fashioned script with a fast-moving story where he could relax and leave the worries to the director. And who better to trust than Steven Spielberg?

The close personal friendship between the two men would suggest Tom is always at the top of Spielberg's list for leading men. In 2002's *Catch Me If You Can*, Tom was clearly too old to play audacious conman Frank Abagnale Jr., a part that went to Leonardo DiCaprio, who came to the set fresh from director Martin Scorsese's intense *Gangs of New York* shoot. The role of FBI agent Carl Hanratty, who chases and ultimately tracks down his prey in the cat-and-mouse plot, was supposed to go to James Gandolfini, better known as the TV mob boss in *The Sopranos*. But a scheduling conflict meant he had to step down and Tom readily signed on.

The film is based on the real-life story of Abagnale, an expert forger and scam merchant who lied and cheated his way around the US in the swinging Sixties, always keeping one step ahead of the

FBI. He was finally caught and the real Abagnale now teaches agents how to identify and catch a new generation of conmen.

It is entertaining and fun, notwithstanding the questionable morality of a hero who makes millions scamming innocent victims with scarcely a backward glance.

There were some good reviews, a hefty chunk of change in Tom's pocket and another £100 million-plus movie (US box office of $164,615,353). The Tom Hanks juggernaut was hurtling along nicely.

But it was all about to come to a screeching halt.

TWENTY

IN TERMINAL DECLINE?

THE FIRST CLUE that something could go wrong was the fact that *The Ladykillers* was Tom's third remake – and the first two, *The Man With One Red Shoe* and *Dragnet*, came before his box-office domination began and were poorly received. He has always insisted there was no master plan to his success, no route map to fame and fortune. Well, this was where he took a little detour.

The premise was promising enough. *The Ladykillers* is a remake of the old 1955 Ealing comedy that starred Sir Alec Guinness as the boss of a gang of crooks who are foiled by a frail old lady. Incidentally, the original featured both Peter Sellers and Herbert Lom, who would later play off each other so hilariously in the *Pink Panther* movies. The new directors were Joel and Ethan Coen – oddball outcasts turned Hollywood's favourite family tag team after their chiller thriller *Fargo* won a Best Actress Oscar for Frances McDormand. Tom is a big fan of the Coen brothers and had been looking for a chance to work with them for years. He had to turn down one of their previous scripts when it clashed with his drawn-out *Cast Away* sojourn, but this time around he could see himself as Professor Goldthwait Higginson Dorr III, PhD, a verbosely pretentious Southern academic who rounds up a bunch of hoods to carry out the ultimate heist on a casino.

The white-suited Colonel Sanders lookalike and his moronic henchmen are defeated in their attempts to burrow underneath a riverboat casino because of the innocent efforts of their landlady, played by Irma P. Hall.

The low-rent *Ocean's Eleven* spiced up – or bogged down, depending on your view – the original script with Coen trademarks like a gaseous character suffering from irritable bowel syndrome, a dog that suffocates to death and a prolonged racial joke.

'What happens with a lot of screenplays is there is a massive amount of change,' Tom told the *Saint Pioneer Press* in a junket for the film. 'You know, it's, "Let's get this straight. I signed on to play a shortstop who plays for the Cubs, and now I'm playing a cook on a submarine?"... I'm being facetious, but you knew that wasn't going to happen here. The script was finished and I liked it.'

He added: 'I read it and I got him. I have affection for any knucklehead with delusions of grandeur. He really is this Southern gentleman who was a professor at the University of Mississippi at Hattiesburg, although his sabbatical has probably lasted 11 years. Everything he says is an embellishment, but it's not a lie. That's different from the usual caper/gang movie, where he would turn out to be some regular guy from Detroit.'

For the Coens, it was important that Tom wasn't too big for his boots. 'He is a really good actor who can work in an ensemble situation. Some movie stars can't be part of a group like that, and he's done character roles before and comedies.'

So he liked the Coens and they liked him. Unfortunately, according to one reviewer, Tom ended up giving 'probably the worst and most ill-conceived performances of his career'. Another critic called his portrayal 'profoundly tiresome'.

Cinema audiences agreed. The film took a little over $39 million, ending Tom's reign of invincibility at the box office.

If it shook the actor, he didn't let it show, telling *Entertainment Weekly* magazine, 'I think the Coens are like John Cassavetes was in the Sixties and Woody Allen was in the Seventies. They go off and make these movies that interest them. And, in all honesty, box office has very little to do with their motivations. Certainly, you want everything to do business. But not everything you do can be that frigging important. How often can you enter into the national consciousness? *The Ladykillers* is already in profit. It's going to make a nice, substantial chunk of change. But if that were the criterion beyond all other things, well, good Lord... I would've made *Forrest Gump 4* by now. And what would have been the excitement or the art or the newness of that?'

If Tom could be forgiven for his belated foray into the comparative artistic freedom of indie-style Hollywood renegades like the Coens, it would be harder to explain away a dud involving a well-tried partnership with the most successful director in history. But *The Terminal* was another movie dreamed up by Hanks and Spielberg. Their past projects made hundreds of millions and won almost universal acclaim. What could go wrong this time?

The Terminal has much in common with *Cast Away* in that Tom's character is caught on a form of island from which he cannot escape and the lens is levelled almost exclusively on our hero and his attempts to free himself from the enforced captivity. The difference was that, instead of a deserted island, Tom's character was cast adrift in an airport terminal teeming with thousands of people.

Following in the vein of their last collaboration, *Catch Me If You Can*, *The Terminal* reflects Tom and Steven's desire to return to a simpler form of storytelling. It doesn't add anything new to the art, doesn't break new ground; it is a simple, feel-good film about the unexpected ways people have the ability to touch each other.

Tom plays Victor Navorski, an immigrant from a fictional

Eastern European country who finds himself stranded at JFK Airport in New York, barred from entry into the US and unable to return to his homeland, which was swallowed up in a political coup.

A plot that has a man living for months in diplomatic limbo in a busy international airport seems far-fetched. But the film is, in fact, inspired by the bizarre story of Merhan Nasseri, an Iranian refugee who washed up at Charles de Gaulle Airport in Paris in 1988 and has lived there ever since.

Nasseri, known as 'Sir Alfred' to airport workers, calls home a red plastic bench at Terminal One and washes up in the public toilets. Ironically, he finally got papers to pass through customs and into France and pocketed almost £100,000 from the filmmakers to finance the transition, but Nasseri preferred to remain the airport's only full-time resident, his life punctuated by the arrival and departure of flights.

Admittedly, Hanks had the bonus of a romantic interest with Catherine Zeta Jones as a flight stewardess, which, however unlikely, added a little romance to his character's terminal confinement. In truth, Tom had to draw on memory for some of the hardships of flying because his fame means he flies mainly by private jet, in part because it avoids having to deal with all the fuss and partly because he can.

It's not in Tom's nature to choose parts based on their Oscar-worthiness. After all, he had two already. The problem was that his audience was never quite convinced that Tom would hold their interest in the film. Perhaps too many had been stranded for too long themselves in an airport to pay their hard-earned cash to see someone else suffer, however famous.

It wasn't the roaring success that was expected. For the second successive time, a Tom Hanks movie failed to hit the $100 million mark in America. It wasn't as dire as *The Ladykillers*, but the $77,872,883 box office take was low enough in comparison to the actor's other films to set tongues wagging. It didn't help that *The*

Terminal's $18.7 million opening weekend in America left it in second place behind the crude Ben Stiller comedy *Dodgeball: A True Underdog Story*, which grossed $30 million.

Suddenly, Tom was no longer untouchable. *The Village Voice* in New York dared to suggest *The Terminal* was too trite and melodramatic. British critic Toby Young went further, calling the film 'a damp squib' and writing: 'Is it time Tom Hanks was put out to grass?'

Young expresses some bemusement over why Tom's Viktor elects not to leave the airport, adding: 'After a year or so has passed, he does leave – but only to visit a New York jazz club for ten minutes, after which he returns to the airport and flies home. It's one of the most bizarrely pointless big-budget films I've ever seen.'

He concludes: 'He's been ranked among the 10 biggest box office stars for 20 years when he had his first hit with *Splash*, which isn't a bad run by any measure. Perhaps it's time he wheeled himself into the engine shed for a well-earned retirement.'

Although retirement was never really an option, Tom no doubt decided the time was ripe to drop back behind the cameras for a while.

His golden touch had already helped turn the small-budget *My Big Fat Greek Wedding* into a Hollywood phenomenon. When wife Rita saw Nia Vardalos's autobiographical play, she convinced her husband to produce a big-screen version. The premise was pretty formulaic, with the bookish ugly duckling heroine transforming herself into a swan and trying to convince her Greek family to accept her American fiancé, but it touched a nerve with cinema audiences around the world. When Tom originally called Vardalos to tell her about his interest in becoming involved under the umbrella of his production company, Playtone, she hung up on him because she didn't believe it was really him. He took on the role of main producer; the couple plunged some of their own money into the project – which only cost a total of £3 million to make – and the 2002 film went on to become the highest-earning independent film in history, taking more than £100 million.

The success of the film may explain Tom's next, very brief appearance before the cameras in a cameo as 'mailbox Elvis' in 2004's *Elvis Has Left the Building*, which was helmed by *My Big Fat Greek Wedding* director Joel Zwick. The odd film, which starred Kim Basinger and *Greek Wedding*'s John Corbett, went straight to DVD, so at least it wasn't another black mark on Tom's box-office slate.

Although Tom wouldn't actually be appearing in the flesh in his next big film, an adaptation of the classic Christmas book *The Polar Express*, there were big expectations, especially when you consider the £100 million-plus budget for a new brand of filmmaking. He was reuniting with Robert Zemeckis, the director behind *Forrest Gump* and *Cast Away*, and, as in their earlier projects, the film represented a considerable risk for both men, who were putting their reputations on the line for uncharted technology that turned actors' faces and bodies into digital data offering the audience a unique blend of acting and animation they had never seen before.

Tom played five separate cyber roles, including the train conductor, Santa Claus and the eight-year-old boy at the centre of the favourite fable by Chris Van Allsburg. Wearing special suits with electronic markers on each joint, Tom and the rest of the cast acted out their scenes on a special stage, with their every movement recorded through infrared receptors on to a computer. Faces were applied with 180 reflective pellets, which generated up to 80 per cent of expressions into the digital realm. Up until now, even the most sophisticated animation techniques translated 3-D characters back into the 2-D world of traditional filmmaking in movies that tried to combine the two, such as the *Lord of the Rings* trilogy. In *The Polar Express*, Zemeckis and co maintained the three-dimensional picture on the computer and, ultimately, through to the final product.

The technique allowed for a certain flexibility in even the most difficult scenarios. For instance, when Oliver Reed died during the filming of Russell Crowe's *The Gladiator*, it was a huge challenge to complete the shoot. When actor Michael Jeeter, who plays two characters in *The Polar Express*, passed away in the middle of production, Zemeckis was able to use other actors to fill in the gaps in his performance.

As surreal as the filming process was and as interested as he was in breaking new ground, Tom had a more prosaic reason for being interested in the book. It brought back happier memories of his own childhood, the magic of youth outliving the harshness of growing up in a broken home.

'In *The Polar Express*, when the little boy is on the train heading to the North Pole, that's not far from me getting on the Greyhound bus every year,' he told *Life* magazine. 'Sometimes I'd be riding with my brother and sister. Sometimes I'd be by myself on this confusing but magical journey. It would be dark outside. I might see some lights going by now and again. There would be muted conversation inside the bus. After a while I'd read not just the comic books I'd brought but all the ads in the comic books as well. Eventually, I'd just be looking out the window and dreaming.

'By and large, it was like a road trip, in the great way road trips can be, but without your mom and dad in the front seat. I had a certain amount of money in my pocket and a certain distance I had to go. It was like travelling along in a peaceful cocoon. It fuelled the imagination.'

There may have been a link between Tom identifying himself with *The Polar Express* and the eventual draw at the cinema. His baby-boomer instincts had been proven long ago. In any case, Tom was back on track. The film took a whopping $172,796,043 at the US box office and set him up for the kind of challenge he had not faced since the debacle surrounding *The Bonfire of the Vanities*.

He had signed up with a big director to make a movie out of an

THE TOM HANKS ENIGMA

incredibly popular and successful book. The novel was a cultural touchstone of controversy, just as *Bonfire* had been, and, once again, expectations were incredibly high.

The film was *The Da Vinci Code* – and Tom was heading to England with the world watching to see whether it would crown his incredible career with a solid gold triumph… or shatter it into a million pieces.

TWENTY-ONE

MONA LISA TOM

CRITICS AND FANS alike have as much trouble explaining Tom Hanks's ascension to the very peak of Hollywood's pecking order as they do the allure of *Mona Lisa*'s smile.

Tom is an enigma – and he was about to try and break the code!

To his friend, Ron Howard, there was never any doubt of his number-one choice to play the redoubtable Professor Robert Langdon in *The Da Vinci Code* and, as much as he tried to temper his enthusiasm, Tom knew from the moment the director optioned the book that the role was his if he wanted it.

The book actually describes the central character as 'Harrison Ford in Harris tweed' but the choice of Tom was unanimous and the actor made little attempt at driving a hard bargain, agreeing to a 25 per cent cut of the film's profits rather than the 40 per cent that stars of his calibre could have expected in the past. The agreement was in part a nod to the changing economics of a movie business under assault from the encroaching internet and plasma home theatres and in part an admission that he wanted himself, and not Ford or Russell Crowe or Hugh Jackman, to play Langdon.

Written by American author Dan Brown and first published in 2003, *The Da Vinci Code* has become a publishing sensation, selling more than 25 million copies and spawning myriad books theorising how to 'crack the code' and examining the controversy the novel caused within the Catholic Church. As the biggest-selling adult fiction book ever, it was bound to attract Hollywood's undivided attention.

The breathless page-turner's unlikely hero is Harvard symbologist Robert Langdon, who is initially called in to help decipher a baffling clue left by the body of an elderly curator who is mysteriously murdered after-hours at the Louvre in Paris. With French cryptologist Sophie Neveu, played in the film by Audrey Tautou, Langdon discovers a trail of clues hidden in the works of Leonardo Da Vinci he believes will lead him to religion's Holy Grail.

Brown's clever mixture of fact and fiction, particularly involving secret societies affiliated to the Vatican, threads into the story of a desperate race through the cathedrals and castles of Europe as Langdon tries to uncover an explosive historical secret – a conspiracy to hide the 'truth' that Jesus Christ was married to Mary Magdalene and had a child with her.

The genesis of Ron Howard's interest in directing the movie version came, as it often does, through his producing partner, Brain Grazer, who first got wind of the book from the creator of his company's real-time TV hit *24*. Joel Surnow read the book soon after it was published and thought it provided an ideal plotline for his hero, played by Kiefer Sutherland. He asked Grazer to check into the possibility of acquiring the rights, but the uber-producer told *Newsweek*: 'It quickly became clear that we had no chance.'

Months later, Sony paid Brown £4 million for the film rights and brought Grazer and Howard on board to ensure the biggest film adaptation since the *Harry Potter* movies lived up to all its multi-million-pound promise.

It was an unusual chain of events for the hugely successful team, whose Imagine company made films like *Apollo 13*, *The Grinch*, *Cinderella Man* and *A Beautiful Mind*. They usually prefer to mine and develop their own projects, but this time they were brought in by Sony bosses as hired guns.

They quickly got to work – and their next move was to tempt Tom. Howard told *Newsweek* that the casting for the cerebral Langdon was perfect. 'Tom is an exciting actor to watch thinking,' he said. We probably don't need his status from a box-office standpoint by now, *The Da Vinci Code* sells itself, but he gives Langdon instant legitimacy.'

Screenwriter Akiva Goldman agreed, adding, 'Tom is wildly intelligent and you can't fake intelligence. A good actor can act anything – except the sense that he's thinking deeply if he really isn't.'

Pre-production didn't start too well when Howard and Grazer fell foul of bureaucracy in London when, after three months of filling in forms and meeting anyone who could help smooth their path, their request to film in London's Westminster Abbey was rejected. They feared a similar fate at the Louvre until French President Jacques Chirac became involved, notwithstanding his reported suggestion that his daughter's best friend should play the female lead!

With a budget of more than £80 million, the film brings together an international cast, including Ian McKellen, Paul Bettany, Jean Reno and Alfred Molina.

Howard says he looked to horror classics like *The Exorcist* and *Rosemary's Baby* to up the ante on the spiritual tension and to loquacious films like *All the President's Men* to push the dialogue along.

Brown was a believer from the start. 'The novelist is always the adaptation's most sceptical audience,' he said. 'But I think this movie will blow people away. I truly believe moviegoers will come out of the theatre feeling like they've just watched the novel.'

For one magical week, Tom had the world's most incredible walk to work from his trailer parked outside the Louvre through the treasure-filled galleries to the areas cordoned off for the seven nights' shoot inside the hushed museum.

Filming was very controlled, nevertheless. 'We had to be very specific about every single shot we were going to do, for both security and preservation reasons,' the director told *Newsweek*. 'There were all kinds of things we couldn't do. Blood on the floor – that's in the script and we couldn't do that. We couldn't take paintings off the wall, obviously. We couldn't write coded messages on the *Mona Lisa*, obviously.'

Mona Lisa was actually off limits totally to the cast and crew, because of worries that the lights could damage the masterpiece. 'You turn a corner,' said Tom, 'and you see this room holding all the stuff you make movies with – boxes, tools, camera stands, disassembled cranes... and the *Mona Lisa*.'

From Paris, the shoot moved on to some of the book's other religious centrepieces at London's Temple Church and Rosslyn Chapel in Scotland.

By the time the last shot had been captured to Howard's satisfaction, the hype was already projecting it as the big film of the year – even the decade – months before the May 2006 première.

The movie was booked to open with great fanfare at the Cannes Film Festival and go on general release two days later.

Tom took it all in his stride. He'd seen it before, after all, and is only too aware of the fickle nature of Hollywood. That's why he leaves the Mr Nice Guy quips in the trailer when he goes to work. Directors quickly learn that he is a perfectionist and a stickler for accuracy. He not only turns up on time to hit the mark himself, he expects others around him to do the same. And because he is a decent reasonable man with an unparalleled track record, they usually do. He doesn't rant and shout and show off, but that doesn't mean he can't be insistent with a steely resolve that few would argue with.

Producer Brian Grazer, Ron Howard's partner and a longtime friend of Tom, said the actor is strong-willed and competitive. He told *The Sunday Times:* 'If you think he is easygoing, you should see him make a movie. He's like the truth police. He's intense, precise and judgemental. He judges everyone around him. If he thinks something in the movie isn't right, he says, "This is bullshit."'

Even Spielberg once remarked: 'For an Everyman, he's pretty damned opinionated.'

Yet directors line up to work with him again. The reason is simple. In a town where money rather than quality is often the dominating factor, Tom can deliver both. He will make a film better. He will treat both fellow cast members and the lowliest gofer on the set with respect. And he will return the trust the public has conferred upon him.

'He's so versatile and has such range,' said Frank Darabont, director of *The Green Mile,* 'that you don't have to take the character to him. He brings the character to the screen.'

Occasionally, he allows a small insight into his competitiveness, such as with his very rare public comments about fellow stars like Cruise, Gibson and Costner being movie stars rather than actors. Tom's heroes are the old professionals, such men as Jason Robards and Robert Duvall.

He spoke glowingly about Duvall to *Screen Actor* magazine, saying: 'Though he is not particularly a chameleon, it took me a long time to recognise him from one movie to another. He is not unique looking – doesn't put a hump in his back or do much more than walk a little different. Yet this man keeps entire movies together, as in *The Godfather* pictures. As Boo Radley in *To Kill a Mockingbird,* he stood behind a door and committed something worse than your worse nightmare. He made you feel sorry for him too. To me, this is a film actor: a man who conveys so much without saying anything.'

It is interesting to note that Tom made those comments in 1989, when he was still thought of as a more physical actor. Ten years later his acting was far more understated. In both *Saving Private Ryan* and even *You've Got Mail,* he was able to convey so much simply by sitting in a bomb shelter reading with a shaky hand, or pondering over a computer as he typed out an E-mail love letter. He had clearly been watching and learning from actors like Duvall, even as he conquered the movie industry.

Perhaps the most pertinent comparison would not be with the megastars of his day, but the icons from the golden days of Hollywood, an era which, in some ways, Tom has recreated for his fans.

Like the celluloid heroes of a bygone time, Tom has an unwritten pact with an audience.

There is no sex in a Tom Hanks movie, you can take that as a given. You may have seen him in his Y-fronts once or twice, or reading the paper in bed, but that's about as revealing as it gets. Even when he gets the girl at the end, the kiss looks like one of those black-and-white smooches when the lips lock without ever moving and the couple seems more engrossed in moving so the camera angle zooms in on the back of their heads. Asked why he doesn't do sexy scenes, Tom is happy to quote James Garner, an actor who has straddled old and new Hollywood and who says: 'I don't do horror movies!'

He is most definitely a leading man, but not on the modern sense of the word. Tom Cruise, Brad Pitt, Mel Gibson, Sly Stallone, Bruce Willis, Kevin Costner, John Travolta, Harrison Ford and even Jim Carrey have the brands of good looks – pretty, rugged, chiselled, or downright sexy – expected in a screen hero. With the exception of perhaps Robin Williams, Tom is the only superstar of his day who has none of those things.

He has been compared with Jimmy Stewart and Cary Grant throughout his career. And for good reason. There is a similarity in style between the three actors. His diffident humour has echoes of Grant and the basic decency of the characters he often plays is reminiscent of Stewart. And, although he tries to play down the comparisons, he has, after all, starred in loose remakes of films made famous by both legendary stars.

But as his career moves into the new millennium, it is another American icon who comes most to mind. For four decades, John Wayne was the American hero, embraced for the true grit strength and patriotism he epitomised as his country blossomed into a superpower.

With the passing of the sixties, a confident young audience was looking for surprises in Hollywood and if the end results were sometimes erratic and the stars unreliable, then it was still worth the ride. Or at least the price of admission: Sitting on top of the world, America could stand a little retrospection, even a little criticism, as long as Hollywood remembered the boundaries.

But with the dawning of the nineties and the uncertain future of a new century, who better to look to than a man who ended two successive Oscar acceptance speeches with the sincere, if not very trendy 'God bless America.'

If the world recognised a great actor in those two films, *Philadelphia* and *Forrest Gump*, America recognised a hero who was truly one of their own in those emotional speeches. Tom Hanks may have been a gifted, intelligent, well-travelled star. But first and foremost, he was an American.

Unashamedly patriotic, he once said he was told by an astronaut there are just six flags on the moon, all of them American. 'I must say I feel proud about that,' he added. 'Pure and simple.'

And Tom has not let anyone down. He has lived the American dream, coming all the way from a dank basement in Reno to being courted by Princesses and Presidents. He has a loving wife, a happy family and, as he puts it: 'I don't F a lot of starlets.'

As a result, the tabloids have never made him a target. 'There is nothing particularly glamorous about me,' he adds. 'I don't go to clubs. I'm not that much of a jet-setter. So the best they can do is take pictures of me when I'm on vacation with my family and talk about how fat I've gotten. That's as bad as it gets, and that's not too bad.'

He has also starred in quality film after quality film, all of them making a mint of money.

Saving Private Ryan, in particular, established Tom as a heavyweight of the grandeur of John Wayne, rather than simply another leading Hollywood star, at a time his country was again questioning its place in the world. With his added weight and muscle, he even looked like Wayne during some of the formidable action sequences. His friend, producer Walter Parks, affectionately dubbed Tom 'John Wayne Gump'.

You can be sure that Tom has never seen himself as another John Wayne, but he hasn't been able to ignore comparisons with the likes of Grant and Stewart, comparisons that have been made by such illustrious friends as Spielberg and Nora Ephron, among many others. If he has to choose, Tom sees himself more in the James Stewart category. 'Jack Lemmon I can understand. Jimmy Stewart I would love to be compared to. Another Cary Grant? I can't see it. Cary Grant was Cary Grant,' he said to *Connoisseur* magazine.

'Sure, I'd like to have the class of a Cary Grant. I would like to have the enthusiasm of a Jack Lemmon. But above all, I would like to be like Jimmy Stewart. He's not the most handsome man in the world, and he has a kind of geeky voice, but it doesn't matter – there are women out there who are rabidly in love with him, and men who admire him. Mostly, without a drastic altering of look or personality, you believed him in everything he did. If he is playing the sweetheart at the Savings and Loan, if he is playing the tough guy who has to shoot someone, if he's playing the funny guy who thinks he sees a rabbit six feet tall – no matter what, you believe him.'

Once again, the way Tom described James Stewart back in 1986 could easily be the way a critic or a fan would describe the Tom Hanks of today.

While he is happy to recreate the good old days of Hollywood in his comedies, it is his unerring ability to choose the right subjects for his more contemporary movies that have made him so unique.

The ability to plug into the baby-boomer psyche is not lost on Tom, who told an interviewer at the Venice Film Festival: 'I think I represent the sensibilities of my generation.'

And what is the perspective of the leading film critics on this rather unlikely superstar?

Alexander Walker, film critic for the London *Evening Standard,* noticed something darker behind Tom's Mr Nice Guy image. He wrote: 'There's something a bit creepy about Tom Hanks. Yes, he's direct and decent; but also, you feel, somehow devious and even dangerous – as if some emotional injury in childhood has mended well on the outside but left the inner man remote and watchful.'

Yet Walker perceives the way Hollywood, and Tom Hanks in particular, have tapped into the public consciousness in America. 'The movies form opinions, set attitudes and provide a self-image for people who find their elected leaders less vivid and immediate than their box-office icons,' he wrote. 'Tom Hanks hardly seems a name made for such elevation. Yet this cheerful, likeable son of a broken home and a father who was an itinerant cook, has achieved a Hollywood ascension that puts him closer to the mood of America than even the man in the White House.'

Walker goes on: 'Hanks is living proof that what matters most in movie-making is timeliness. Talent counts but other people have that – more, perhaps, than he has. A rare asset for an actor is making the right choice at the right time.

'His ascension to being his country's unlikely spokesman

coincided with the decline of one-time American icons like Stallone and Schwarzenegger. The muscle-flexing grandiloquence of S & S now seemed hollow and impotent in a country dazed by internal violence, confused about its external role.

'Ordinary people achieving extraordinary things: the stoicism of an AIDS victim; the faith of a Gump; the ingenuity of a space-missionary. It's fallen to the unlikely talent of Hanks to incarnate this trilogy – and provide his country with the fictions it needs these days to face reality. But that's what stars are for.'

The *New Yorker's* inimitable Pauline Kael, in a compilation titled *Hooked,* says of Tom's starring role in *Big*: 'Hanks gets by with his little-boy act: he doesn't hit any wrong notes, and he doesn't make you want to hide your face. You feel his essential boyishness all the time. Of course, you feel the kid in just about all of Hanks's roles, though generally it's a wise-guy adolescent. I prefer him that way. As a child, he's too predictably "spontaneous".'

Many of Tom's closest friends and admirers, a crowd of more than 800 people, gathered at the New York Waldorf-Astoria in April 1999, for the American Museum of the Moving Image's tribute to the star, the youngest ever to be thus honoured.

Speakers tried to put their finger on Tom's elusive, yet undeniable appeal. Spielberg called his friend 'the most moral man I have ever known' and spoke with great affection about the special friendship the two men share.

But it was another old friend, Sally Field, who perhaps captured best the unconventional blend of talents that have so beguiled the public over the years. She told the crowded Grand Ballroom audience: 'I first met Tom Hanks in 1986. We had lunch and he talked about his wife, his kids, his girlfriend, Rita, and his world: Every once in a while he'd break away from his crabcakes... I thought he was half Goofy, half Nureyev. And then when he got up to leave, I realised his fly was open and his shirt was hanging out.'

Intriguingly, the *New Yorker* tried to build up a case against the world's most likeable star in an article, 'The Tom Hanks Phenomenon – How Did He Pull It Off?' In fact, it didn't amount to a lot. After much research and questioning of Tom's closest friends and the actor himself, the magazine presented the dark side of the saint next door:

1) He tried cocaine while starring in the sitcom *Bosom Buddies*.
2) During one six-year period he starred in *Bachelor Party, Volunteers, The Money Pit, Dragnet, The Burbs, Turner and Hooch, Joe Versus the Volcano* and *The Bonfire of the Vanities*.
3) He was rude and unco-operative with a magazine reporter in 1986; his publicist gave the excuse that his marriage was falling apart.
4) His first marriage fell apart.
5) He gets 'a little peevish' about comparisons with James Stewart, despite the fact that his recent movie *You've Got Mail* was a remake of Stewart's *Shop Around the Corner.*
6) At the Venice Film Festival, when his *Saving Private Ryan* co-star Tom Sizemore thanked him for sharing some press attention, he replied, his mouth full of pasta, 'Yes, I'm throwing you the bones – and I had a boner as I was throwing them.'
7) He made a large donation to Bill Clinton's legal defence fund.
8) He thinks the comedy *Friends* is 'hilarious'.

The article goes on: 'That is the extent of the case against Tom Hanks. In other words, he is, as billed, the most disarming and successful of American movie stars.'

He has an advantage over his Hollywood rivals in that neither he, nor his audience, are particularly concerned about his leading man looks. Brad Pitt's directors may feel duty bound to linger the camera lovingly on his blond hair and blue eyes and Tom Cruise has to be sure to look, well, like Tom Cruise. But an extra few pounds or a naff haircut aren't going to turn off Hanks fans. Don't they themselves sometimes feel a little overweight or regret a trip to the barber's?

It is interesting to note that, like another thinking woman's favourite, Harrison Ford, Tom rarely acts with women who have a strong presence. His romantic comedies with Meg Ryan follow a by-now familiar pattern, with neither of them spending more than the odd climactic scene on screen with the other. Robin Wright had very much a supporting role in Gump, as indeed did Antonio Banderas, his partner in *Philadelphia*. Daryl Hannah, while a fine actress, wasn't exactly required to act her tail off in *Splash*. The only time he shared serious screen time with a leading lady was with Sally Field in *Punchline,* and the relationship proved to be the chief hiccup in an otherwise impressive film.

But while he may veer away from sharing the screen with the likes of Sharon Stone, Tom has no fear of working with the industry's best directors. As well as his friend Steven Spielberg, Tom has worked with a 'Who's Who' of top directors, including Robert Zemeckis, Jonathan Demme, Ron Howard, Sam Mendes, the Coen Brothers, Richard Donner, Nora Ephron, Joe Dante, Penny Marshall and Brian De Palma.

Indeed, the quality of direction may have done as much as anything to elevate him into the film industry's acting elite. With the notable exception of *That Thing You Do!,* it also helped eliminate costly vanity projects from his resumé. He is shrewd enough to know good directors produce good films – and at the same time offer him a serious challenge to impress his peers.

* * *

So what drives Tom Hanks? He doesn't need the money. Although he has more in the bank than he will ever need, friends believe him when he says that has never been motivated by his monster paydays. There was a time when he was tempted by £3 million fees, even when he knew the scripts were excruciating. But those days are long gone. When his contemporaries were driving around in Ferraris and Rolls Royces, Tom was tooling around LA in a VW Jetta. He's never bothered with boats and planes. On friend John Travolta's state-of-the-art Airstream trailer, Tom says simply: 'If I had one like that, I would never want to leave it to go to work.'

Although he could afford to hire a regiment of household staff, Tom and Rita prefer to care for their children themselves, taking them and picking them up from school and helping them with their homework. He certainly doesn't spend his money on clothes. At one point, he would only buy shirts that didn't have designer labels, not an easy task in many of LA's finer retailers.

Neither is Tom being driven by the need to be recognised by his peers. Back-to-back Oscars put paid to any such worries long ago and the wide variety of his roles means no one could ever accuse him of being a one-trick pony.

Interestingly, Tom shows little sign of taking cameo parts in art-house or *auteur* movies. Perhaps he feels he doesn't need to impress anyone with his acting prowess. He may have felt burned by his unbilled role in 1992's *Radio Flyer,* which he narrated and appeared briefly in at the beginning and the end. The film bombed, making a huge loss.

Asked in a *New Yorker* interview if he would ever star in a $9 million independent film. He said: 'I'm open to any sort of suggestions. The problem is I read those things and say, "Look, I don't get it. This is just the same scene over and over and over again. You don't get any credit from me because it's only a $9 million movie."'

He adds, in a mock *artiste* voice: 'What do you mean? Don't you want to be a renegade?

'If someone had come to me and said, "Do you want to make *Fargo*?" I'd have said, "Well, yeah." But I didn't get to read that. I can tell in seven pages of reading a screenplay if I'm interested in doing it. More often than not, you read stuff that just doesn't work. It has no surprises in it. The character to me always has to have some logic to him that I understand.'

No, the reason Tom Hanks is still making such an impact on Hollywood is simply that he finds the job fun.

He told the *Mail on Sunday* in 1998: 'No one believes me when I say it, but this is still just as fun and challenging as it was when I was in the high school play. And I still feel like I did when I saw my name on the cast list for *Night of the Iguana* in 1971 at Skyline High School in Oakland, California.

'Every time I take a job it's the most exciting thing in the world, because this is the greatest job in the world.

'I don't do it for the money or the power or anything else. I do it because it is fun.'

He added that he doesn't have any goals. 'I just try to make it through the next job. I mean, the communists had goals, you know, the five-year plans. Look where it got them.'

As a child, forever glued to the television, Tom dreamed of being an astronaut, of being a soldier, of getting the beautiful girl. He would never have dared dream of doing all of those things, particularly as he was not overly bright at school, not especially brave or tough and rather plain-looking with a perpetually bad haircut.

Through acting, all his dreams came true, and more besides. There wasn't just one beautiful girl. There were lots of leading ladies – one being his wife.

His success hasn't come without a price. The collapse of his first marriage, he blames chiefly on spending so much time away from his family on location, making his way in a business that doubles as a marital graveyard. He has known failure too. *The Bonfire of the Vanities* débâcle was far more of a setback at the time than it now seems in the wake of his ensuing triumphs.

He wasn't swayed by the comparative failures of *The Ladykillers* and *The Terminal*. In fact, they may have spurred him on to work on a big film like *The Da Vinci Code* and reposition himself as Hollywood's number-one draw.

And it wasn't really until he was into his 30s – and had met Rita Wilson – that he could truly put his itinerant childhood to rest. Like many children who grow up too soon, he couldn't help but carry over his misgivings into adulthood.

Even now, close friends like Steven Spielberg and Meg Ryan admit they don't truly know Tom. The only residue of the lonely, confused boy from Northern California remains in the silent reveries he can fall into even in a crowded room.

It is like a switch being flicked in his head, taking him away from the present to somewhere no one – not even Rita – can reach.

In those moments, Tom Hanks the movie star is gone. He's little Tommy reaching for the pedals in his father's car.

Trying to see how far he can go.

FILMOGRAPHY

He Knows You're Alone (1980) Director: Armand Mastroianni. Producer: George Manasse. Executive producers: Edgar Lansbury and Joseph Beruh. Screenplay: Scott Parker. Director of Photography: Gerald Fell. Editor: George T. Norris. Art Director: Susan Kaufman. Music: Alexander and Mark Peskanov. Released by: Metro Goldwyn Mayer. Running time: 94 minutes. Cast: Don Scardino (Marvin), Caitlin O'Heaney (Amy), Elizabeth Kemp (Nancy), Tom Rolfing (Killer), Lewis Arlt (Gamble), Patsy Pease (Joyce), James Rebhorn (Professor), *Tom Hanks (Elliot)*.
Fee: *$800*
US Box Office: N/A
Plot: A reluctant wife-to-be is stalked by a serial killer who only targets brides and the people around them. While her friends get knocked off one by one, a renegade cop whose own bride was killed years before tries to hunt down the murderer before it is too late. Cliché-ridden slasher movie with Tom in small part as a smarmy psychology student. The role is so tiny he doesn't even get a gruesome death scene, which put him in the minority in this film.

Rona Jaffe's Mazes and Monsters (1982) Director: Steven H. Stern. Producers: Tom McDermott and Richard A. Briggs. Teleplay: Tom Lazarus. Director of Photography: Laszlo George. Art Director: Trevor Williams. Editor: Bill Parker. Music: Hagood Hardy. From the novel by Rona Jaffe. Released by: CBS-Lorimar (for television). Running time: 103 minutes. Cast: *Tom Hanks (Bobbie Wheeling),* Chris Makepeace (J.J. Brockaway), Wendy Crewson (Kate), David Wallace (Daniel), Susan Strasberg (Meg), Vera Miles (Cat), Anne Francis (Elle), Lloyd Bochner (Mr Wheeling).

Fee: N/A

US Box Office: TV only

Plot: In Tom's first starring role in a film, he plays a student hooked on the fantasy game Dungeons and Dragons. The made-for-TV movie was based on a real life case, when police searching for a missing student found a maze of tunnels and caves beneath a college campus. Tom's character 'flips into the game' and becomes convinced he is 'Pardieu the Holy Man'.

Splash (1984) Director: Ron Howard. Producer: Brian Grazer. Executive producer: John Thomas Lenox. Screenplay: Lowell Ganz, Babaloo Mandel, Bruce Jay Friedman. Screen story: Bruce Jay Friedman based on an idea by Brian Grazer. Director of Photography: Don Peterman. Underwater Director of Photography: Jordan Klein. Production designer: Jack T. Collis. Editors: Daniel P. Hanley, Michael Hill. Costume Designer: Mary Routh. Special Visual Effects Supervisor: Mitch Suskin. Mermaid Design and Construction: Robert Short. Music: Lee Holdridge. Released by: Touchstone. Running time: 111 minutes. Cast: *Tom Hanks (Allen Bauer),* Daryl Hannah (Madison), John Candy (Freddie Bauer), Eugene Levy (Walter Kornbluth), Dody Goodman (Mrs Stimler), Shecky Greene (Mr Buyrite), Richard B. Shuli (Dr Ross), Bobby DiCicco (Jerry), Howard Morris (Dr Zidell), Tony Di Benedetto (Tim the doorman).

Fee: $80,000

US Box Office: $69.8 million

Plot: Tom gets the chance to show his value as a comic actor in this fantasy co-starring Daryl Hannah as a beautiful fish out of water. Hannah's landlocked mermaid falls in love with Tom and gets a taste of Manhattan as she dines on lobster – shells and all – while her hero tries to keep her out of hot water. The film that made Tom and Daryl Hannah stars.

Bachelor Party (1984) Director: Neal Israel. Producers: Ron Moler, Bob Israel. Executive Producer: Joe Roth. Screenplay: Neal Israel, Pat Proft. Story: Bob Israel. Director of Photography: Hal Trussel. Art Directors: Kevin Conlin, Martin Price. Editor: Tom Walls. Music: Robert Folk. Released by: 20th Century Fox. Running Time: 106 minutes. Cast: *Tom Hanks (Rick Gassko),* Tawny Kitaen (Debbie Thompson), Adrian Zmed (Jay O'Neill), George Grizzard (Mr Thompson), Robert Prescott (Cole Whittier), William Tepper (Dr Stan Gassko), Wendie Jo Sperber (Dr Tina Gassko), Barry Diamond (Rudy), Gary Grossuran (Gary), Michael Dudikoff (Ryko), Brad Bancroft (Brad), Martina Finch (Phoebe), Deborah Harmon (Ilene), Tracy Smith (Bobbi).

Fee: $60,000

US Box Office: $38.6 million

Plot: As Tom says, it's not *Richard III,* but this distinctly low-brow comedy keeps the dumb and dumber laughs going with an *Animal House/Police Academy*-style slapstick frenzy. Amidst it all, Tom, as the goofy groom-to-be who promises to behave himself at his bachelor party, stays slightly above the grossness and comes out smiling.

The Man With One Red Shoe (1985) Director: Stan Dragoti. Producer: Victor Drai. Screenplay: Robert Klane. Director of Photography: Richard H. Kline. Production Designer: Dean E. Mitzner. Editors: Bud Molin, O. Nicholas Brown. Music: Thomas Newman.

Based on the French farce *The Tall Blond Man With One Black Shoe*, written by Francis Veber, Yves Robert. Released by: 20th Century Fox. Running time: 92 minutes. Cast: *Tom Hanks (Richard Drew)*, Dabney Coleman (Cooper), Lori Singer (Maddy), Charles burning (Ross), Carrie Fisher (Paula), Edward Herrmann (Brown), Jim Belushi (Morris), Tom Noonan (Reese), Gerrit Graham (Carson), David L. Lander (Stemple).

Fee: N/A

US Box Office: $8.7 million

Plot: Tom is a symphony violinist and eccentric composer mistaken for a spy in this so-so comedy. The Georgetown musician is unwittingly caught up in a game of CIA one-upmanship, with one spy, Lori Singer, luring him into bed, and Carrie Fisher turning up as a bedmate with a weakness for Tarzan-and-Jane games. The shoe doesn't really fit casting Tom in this comedy of errors.

Volunteers (1985) Director: Nicholas Meyer. Producers: Richard Shepherd, Walter F. Parkes. Screenplay: Ken Levine, David Isaacs. Story: Keith Critchlow. Director of Photography: Ric Waite. Production Designer: James Schoppe. Editors: Ronald Roose, Steven Polivka. Music: James Horner. Released by: Tri-Star. Running time: 106 minutes. Cast: *Tom Hanks (Lawrence Bourne III)*, Rita Wilson (Beth Wexler), John Candy (Tom Tuttle), Tim Thomerson (John Reynolds), Gedde Watanabe (At Toon), George Plimpton (Lawrence Bourne Jnr), Ernest Harada (Chung Mee), Allan Arbus (Albert Bordonaro).

Fee: N/A

US Box Office: $20.2 million.

Plot: When his rich, stuffy dad won't give him any cash to pay his gambling debt, Tom's Lawrence Bourne III switches places with a roommate and heads to Thailand with the Peace Corps. In the jungle, he finds love and himself and, naturally, saves the day. Most memorable for Tom as the film where he met future wife Rita Wilson.

The Money Pit (1986) Director: Richard Benjamin. Producers: Frank Marshall, Kathleen Kennedy, Art Levinson. Executive Producers: Steven Spielberg, David Giler. Screenplay: David Giler. Director of Photography: Gordon Willis. Production Designer: Patrizia von Brandenstein. Editor: Jacqueline Cambas. Special Effects Supervisor: Michael Wood. Music: Michael Colombier. Released by: Universal. Running time: 91 minutes. Cast: *Tom Hanks (Walter Fielding)*, Shelley Long (Anna Crowley), Alexander Godunov (Max Beissart), Maureen Stapleton (Estelle), Joe Mantegna (Art Shirk), Philip Bosco (Curly), Josh Mostel (Jack Schnitturan), Yakov Smirnoff (Shatov), Carmine Caridi (Brad Shirk), Jake Steinfeld (Duke).

Fee: $750,000

US Box Office: $37.5 million

Plot: Hapless homeowners Tom and Shelley Long buy a £1 million house for a fraction of the cost and regret it for the rest of the film as everything possible goes wrong in the house from hell. A lessthan-successful attempt to update the Cart' Grant classic *Mr Blandings Builds His Dream House.*

Every Time We Say Goodbye (1986) Director: Moshe Mizrahi. Producers: Jacob Kotzky, Sharon Harel. Screenplay: Moshe Mizrahi, Rachel Fabien, Leah Appet. Story: Moshe Mizrahi. Director of Photography: Giuseppe Lanci. Editor: Mark Burns. Music: Philippe Sarde. Released by: Tri-Star. Running time: 97 minutes: Cast: *Tom Hanks (David)*, Cristina Marsillach (Sarah), Benedict Taylor (Peter), Anat Atzmon (Victoria), Gila Almagor (Lea), Monny Mashanov (Nessim), Avner Hiskyahu (Raphael), Caroline Goodall (Sally), Esther Parnass (Rosa), Daphne Armony (Clam), Orit Weisman (Mathilda).

Fee: N/A

US Box Office: $300,000

Plot: Tom's first real break-out straight drama role as a World War

II pilot who falls in love with a beautiful Jewish girl, much to the chagrin of her devout family. A beautifully filmed love story shot on location in Israel.

Nothing in Common (1986) Director Garry Marshall. Producer: Alexandra Rose. Executive Producer: Roger M. Rothstein. Screenplay: Rick Podell, Michael Preminger. Director of photography: John A. Alonzo. Production Designer: Charles Rosen. Editor: Glenn Farr. Music: Patrick Leonard. Released by: Tri-Star. Running time: 118 minutes. Cast: *Tom Hanks (David Basner),* Jackie Gleason (Max Basner), Eva Marie Saint (Lorraine Basner), Hector Elizondo (Charlie Gargas), Barry Corbin (Andrew Woolridge), Bess Armstrong (Donna Mildred Martin), Sela Ward (Cheryl Ann Wayne), Cindy Harrell (Stewardess), John Kapelos (Commercial Director), Carol Messing (David's Secretary). Fee: $1 million
US Box Office: $32.5 million
Plot: Tom is a cocky advertising executive whose life turns upside down when his parents break up and his father falls seriously ill. The father-son bonding between Tom's character and his dying dad is the central, touching theme. It was American TV legend Jackie Gleason's last film.

Dragnet (1987) Director: Tom Mankiewicz. Producers: David Peanut and Robert K. Weiss. Executive Producer: Bernie Brillstein. Screenplay: Dan Aykroyd, Alan Zweibel, Tom Mankiewicz. Director of Photography: Matthew F. Leonetti. Production Designer: Robert F: Boyle. Editors: Richard Halsey, William D. Gordean. Music: Ira Newborn. Released by: Universal. Running time: 110 minutes. Cast: Dan Aykroyd (Joe Friday), *Tom Hanks (Pep Streebek),* Christopher Plummer (Reverend Whirley), Dabney Coleman (Jerry Caesar), Alexandra Paul (Convie Swail), Harry Morgan (Captain Bill Gannon), Elizabeth Ashley

(Commissioner Kirkpatrick), Jack O'Halloran (Emit Muzzy, Kathleen Freeman (Enid Borden), Bruce Gray (Mayor Parvin), Lenka Peterson (Granny Mundy).

Fee: $1.2 million.

US Box Office: $57.4 million

Plot: Tom plays second banana to Aykroyd's no-nonsense Joe Friday in a spoof of the Los Angeles-based cops and robbers show that ran for more than a decade in the '50s and '60s. The odd couple's chief mission is to tame the PAGANS (People Against Goodness and Normalcy). But they don't manage to scare up too many laughs.

Big (1988) Director: Penny Marshall. Producers: James L. Brooks, Robert Greenhut. Co-producers and Screenplay: Gary Ross, Anne Spielberg. Director of Photography: Barry Sonnenfield. Production Designer: Santo Loquasto. Art Directors: Tom Warren, Speed Hopkins. Editor: Barry Malkin. Music: Howard Shore. Released by: 20th Century Fox. Running time: 104 minutes. Cast: *Tom Hanks (Josh Baskin)*, Elizabeth Perlons (Susan Lawrence), John Heard (Paul Davenport), Jared Rushton (Billy Kopeche), Robert Loggia ('Mac' MacMillan), David Moscow (Young Josh), Jon Lovitz (Scotty Brennen), Mercedes Ruehl (Mrs Baskin), Josh Clark (Mr Baskin), Kimberlee M. Davis (Cynthia Benson), Oliver Block (Freddie Benson).

Fee: $1.75 million

US Box Office: $114.9 million

Plot: Tom plays a 12-year-old boy in a 35-year-old man's body and spends much of his time, hilariously and sensitively, trying to get back to his childhood. Whether he is astonishing the other grown-ups with his childlike sincerity or beguiling toy company colleague Elizabeth Perkins with his innocent charm, it is a big, big leap for Tom, who was rewarded with his first Academy Award nomination.

Punchline (1988) Director: David Seltzer. Producers: David Melnick, Michael Rachmil. Screenplay: David Seltzer. Director of

Photography: Reynaldo Villalobos. Production Designer: Jack DeGovia. Editor: Bruce Green. Music: Charles Gross. Released by: Columbia. Running time: 128 minutes. Cast: Sally Field (Lilah Krytsick), *Tom Hanks (Steven Gold),* John Goodman (John Krytsick), Mark Rydell (Romeo), Kim Greist (Madeline Urie), Paul Mazursky (Arnold).

Fee: $1.5 million

US Box Office: $21 million

Plot: Tom called it the closest had had come to playing 'an unredeemable character'. Playing a stand-up comedian, he takes Field, as a New Jersey housewife, under his wing as they both try and break into the tough New York comedy circuit. Tom moves from comic glibness to manic intensity with an understated ease that makes it a powerful performance, even if Oscar-winner Field is miscast.

The Burbs (1989) Director: Joe Dante. Producers: Michael Finnell, Larry Brezner. Screenplay: Dana Olsen. Director of Photography: Robert Stevens. Production Designer: James Spencer. Editor: Marshall Harvey. Music: Jerry Goldsmith. Released by: Universal. Running time: 103 minutes. Cast: *Tom Hanks (Ray Peterson),* Bruce Dern (Mark Runsfield), Carrie Fisher (Carol Peterson), Rick Ducommun (Art Weingartner), Corey Feldman (Ricky Butler), Wendy Schaal (Bonnie Rumsfield), Henry Gibson (Dr Warner Klopek), Brother Theodore (Uncle Reuben Klopek), Courtney Gains (Hans Klopek), Gale Gordon (Walter), Dick Miller, Robert Picardo (Binmen).

Fee: $3.5 million

US Box Office: $36 million

Plot: Dull suburbanite executive takes a holiday to get a little excitement into his life and goes to war with his loony neighbours against the new family on the block. With lots of lame jokes, explosions and screaming, the haunted-house spoof has too much going on for such a thin script and wastes its leading man.

Turner and Hooch (1989) Director: Rodger Spottiswoode. Producer: Raymond Wagner. Executive Producer: Daniel Petrie Jnr. Screenplay: Dennis Shryack, Michael Blodgett, Daniel Petrie Jnr, Jim Cash, Jack Epps Jnr. Story: Dennis Shryack, Michael Blodgett. Director of Photography: Adam Greenberg. Production Designer: John DeCuir Jnr. Editor: Garth Craven. Music: Charles Gross. Released by: Touchstone. Running time: 98 minutes. Cast: Tom *Hanks (Scott Turner),* Mare Winningham (Emily Carson), Beasley (Hooch), Craig T. Nelson (Chief Hyde), Reginald VelJohnson (David Sutton), Scott Paulin (Zack Gregory), J. C. Quinn (Walter Boyett), John McIntire (Amos Reed), David Knell (Ernie).

Fee: $3.5 million

US Box Office: $71.1 million

Plot: Hooch, Tom's big, drooling canine co-star, witnesses his owner's murder and leads our hero, a compulsively clean smalltown cop, to solve the crime. Includes a couple of scenes with Tom in black briefs. But don't expect a sequel – the dog gets it in the end.

Joe Versus the Volcano (1990) Director: John Patrick Stanley. Producer: Teri Schwartz. Executive Producers: Steven Spielberg, Kathleen Kennedy, Frank Marshall. Writer: John Patrick Shanley. Director of Photography: Stephen Goldblatt. Production designer: Bo Welch: Editor: Richard Halsey. Music: Georges Delerue: Released by: Warner Bros. Running time: 102 minutes. Cast: *Tom Hanks (Joe),* Meg Ryan (De De/Angelica/Patricia), Lloyd Bridges (Graynamore), Robert Stack (Dr Ellison), Abe Vigoda (Chief of the Waponis), Dan Hedaya (Mr Waturi), Amanda Plummer (Dagmar), Ossie Davis (Marshall), Carol Kane (Hairdresser).

Fee: $3.5 million

US Box Office: $39.4 million

Plot: Tom's hypochondriac character throws in his boring job for a South Seas adventure after being diagnosed with a fatal disease. In the course of his hi-jinks he meets and falls in love with Ryan for the first of many times – even though she is playing three parts in the one movie – and discovers, surprise, surprise, that he is not going to die after all.

The Bonfire of the Vanities (1990) Director and Producer: Brian DePalma. Executive Producers: Peter Guber, Jon Peters. Co-producer: Fred Caruso. Screenplay: Michael Cristofer. Director of Photography: Vilmos Zsigmond. Production Designer: Richard Sylbert. Editors: David Ray, Bill Pankow. Music: Dave Grusin. Based on the novel by: Tom Wolfe. Released by: Warner Bros. Running time: 125 minutes. Cast: *Tom Hanks (Sherman McCoy)*, Bruce Willis (Peter Fallow), Melanie Griffith (Maria Buskin), Kim Cattrall (Judy McCoy}, Saul Rubinek (Jed Kramer), Morgan Freeman (Judge White), John Hancock (Reverend Bacon), Kevin Dunn (Tom Killian), F. Murray Abraham (D.A. Weiss), Donald Moffat (Mr McCoy), Robert Stephens (Sir Gerald Moore), Alan King (Arthur Buskin), Beth Broderick (Caroline Heftshank), Mary Alice (Annie Lamb), Rita Wilson (PR Woman).
Fee: $5 million
US Box Office: $15.7 million
Plot: Tom simply doesn't fit the William Hurt-type role as the WASPy broker whose millionaire lifestyle goes down the pan after he becomes involved in an accident with his mistress on the wrong side of town. Never lives up to the promise of Wolfe's best-selling novel.

Radio Flyer (1992) Director: Richard Donner. Producer: Lauren Shuler-Donner. Executive producers: Michael Douglas, Rich Beieber, David Mickey Evans. Screenplay: David Mickey Evans. Director of Photography: Laszlo Kovacs. Production Designer: J. Michael Riva. Art Director: David Frederick Klassen. Editor: Stuart Baird. Music: Hans Zimmer. Released by: Columbia. Running time: 114 minutes. Cast: Lorraine Bracco (Mary),

John Heard (Daugherty), Adam Baldwin (The King), Elijah Wood (Mike), Joseph Mazzello (Bobby), Ben Johnson (Geronimo Bill), *Tom Hanks (Unbilled, Mike as adult).*
Fee: $2 million
US Box Office: NlA
Plot: Tom serves as the narrator of an unsettling story about two boys who dream of flying away from their drunken, abusive stepfather.

A League of Their Own (1992) Director: Penny Marshall. Producers: Robert Greenhut, Elliot Abbott. Co-producers: William Pace, Ronnie Clemmer, Joseph Hartwick. Executive Producer: Penny Marshall. Screenplay: Lowed Ganz, Babaloo Mandel. Director of Photography: Miroslav Ondricek. Production Designer: Bill Groom. Editor: George Bowers. Music Hans Zimmer. Based on a story by Kim Wilson, Kelly Candaele. Released by: Columbia. Running time: 128 minutes. Cast: *Tom Hanks (Jimmy Dugan),* Geena Davis (Dottie Hanson), Madonna (Mae Mordabito), Lori Petty (Kit Keller), Jon Lovitz (Ernie Capadino), David Strathairn (Ira Lowenstein), Garry Marshall (Walter Harvey), Megan Cavanaugh (Maria Hooch), Rosie O'Donnell (Doris Murphy), Bill Pullman (Bob Hanson).
Fee: $5 million
US Box Office: $107.5 million
Plot: Tom changes gear completely to play baseball coach Jimmy Dugan, an overweight alcoholic given the job of coaching a wartime women's baseball team because of his past glories. The dedication of his team – Madonna, Geena Davis, Rosie O'Donnell, etc. – finally sobers him up enough to care again and strike up a meaningful, if platonic, relationship with his star catcher, Davis.

Sleepless in Seattle (1993) Director: Nora Ephron. Producer: Gary Foster. Executive Producers: Lynda Obst, Patrick Crowley.

Screenplay: Nora Ephron, David S. Ward, Jeff Arch. Director of Photography: Sven Nykvist. Production Designer: Jeffrey Townsend. Editor: Robert Reitano. Music: Marc Shaiman. From a story by: Jeff Arch. Released by: Tri-Star. Running time: 104 minutes. Cast: *Tom Hanks (Sam Baldwin),* Meg Ryan (Annie Reed), Bill Pullman (Walter), Ross Malinger (Jonah Baldwin), Rosie O'Donnell (Becky), Gaby Hoffman (Jessica), Rita Wilson (Suzy), Rob Reiner (Jay), Victor Garber (Greg), David Hyde-Pierce (Dennis Reed).
Fee: $7.5 million
US Box Office: $126.5 million
Plot: Get your hankies out. He's sleepless in Seattle, grieving over his lost wife. She's baffled in Baltimore, obsessed by the widower she knew only through his voice on a late night radio talk show. It takes them the whole movie to get together on top of the Empire State Building, but it's worth the wait.

Philadelphia (1993) Director: Jonathan Demme. Producer: Edward Saxon, Jonathan Demme. Executive Producers: Gary Goetzman, Kenneth Utt, Ron Bozman. Screenplay: Ron Nyswaner. Director of Photography: Tak Fujimoto. Production Designer: Kristi Zea. Art Director: Tim Gavin. Editor: Craig McKay. Music: Howard Shore. Released by: Tri-Star. Running time: 126 minutes. Cast: *Tom Hanks (Andrew Beckett),* Denzel Washington (Joe Miller), Jason Robards (Charles Wheeler), Mary Steenburgen (Belinda Confine), Antonio Banderas (Miguel), Joanne Woodward (Sarah Beckett), Anna Deavere Smith (Anthea Burton), Lisa Summerour (Lisa Miller), Ron Vawter (Bob Seidman), Charles Napier (Judge Garnett).
Fee: $8 million
US Box Office: $77.3 million
Plot: The story of a bright, up-and-coming young lawyer whose life and career is blighted by AIDS was a watershed in Hollywood's handling of the disease. Tom's brave character takes his homophobic bosses to court and wins, but he cannot beat the AIDS

virus that ravages his body in front of our eyes. Tom lost up to 30 pounds in weight for his Oscar-winning performance.

Forrest Gump (1994) Director: Robert Zemeckis. Producers: Wendy Finerman, Steve Tisch, Steve Starkey. Screenplay: Eric Roth. Diector of Photography: Don Burgess. Production Designer: Rick Carter. Special Visual Effects Supervisor: Ken Ralston. Editor: Arthur Schmidt. Music: Alan Silvestri. Based on the novel by: Winston Groom. Released by: Paramount. Running time: 142 minutes. Cast: *Tom Hanks (Forrest Gump)*, Robin Wright (Jenny Curran), Gary Sinise (Lt Dan), Mykelti Williamson (Bubba), Sally Field (Mama Gump), Michael Humphreys (Young Forrest), Hanna Hall (Young Jenny).

Fee: Eight per cent of gross. Estimated at up to $60 million US Box Office: $356.8 million

Plot: Life is a box of chocolates for Tom's Forrest Gump, a naive simpleton whose remarkable journey through contemporary American history touched a nerve around the world. Like the man who plays him – Tom got his second Oscar here – Gump is always at the right place at the right time, making you laugh and cry and, always, care.

Apollo 13 (1995) Director: Ron Howard. Producer: Brian Grazer. Executive Producer: Todd Hallowell. Screenplay: William Broyles Jnr, Al Reiner. Director of Photography: Dean Cundey. Production Designer: Michael Corenblith. Visual Effects Supervisor: Rob Legato. Editors: Mike Hill, Dan Hanley. Music: James Horner. Based on the book *Lost Moon* by James Lovell and Jeffrey Kluger. Released by: Universal. Running time: 136 minutes. Cast: *Tom Hanks (Jim Lovell)*, Kevin Bacon (Jack Swigert), Bill Paxton (Fred Haise), Gary Sinise (Ken Mattingly), Ed Harris (Gene Kranz), Kathleen Quinlan (Marilyn Lovell), Mary Kate Schellhardt (Barbara Lovell), Emily Ann Lloyd (Susan Lovell), Jean Speegle Howard (Blanch Lovell), Clint Howard (Eecom White), Joe Spano (NASA

Director), David Andrews (Pete Conrad), Chris Ellis (Deke Slayton).
Fee: $15 million
US Box Office: $172 million
Plot: The crew of *Apollo 13* may have never landed on the moon, but the story of the ill-fated mission and the incredible rescue of a spacecraft literally almost lost in space makes a spellbinding story – and Tom, a lifelong space nut, knew he was born to play Lovell, the cool-hand veteran who helps bring his crew home safe.

Toy Story (1995) Director: John Lasseter. Producers: Ralph Guggenheim, Bonnie Arnold. Executive Producers: Edwin Catmull, Steven Jobs. Screenplay: Joss Whedon, Andrew Stanton, Joel Cohen, Alec Sokolow. Supervising Animator: Pet Docter. Editors: Robert Gordon, Lee Unkrich. Music and songs: Randy Newman. Based on an original story by: John Lasseter, Pete Docter, John Ranft, Andrew Stanton. Released by: Disney. Running time: 80 minutes. Voices: *Tom Hanks (Woody),* Tim Allen (Buzz Lightyear), Annie Potts (Bo Peep), Don Rickles (Mr Potato Head), Jim Varney (Slinky the Dog), John Ratzenberger (Hammy), Wallace Shawn (Rex), John Morris (Andy), Erik Von Detten (Sid), Laurie Metcalf (Mrs Davis), R. Lee Ermey (Sergeant).
Fee: $200,000
US Box Office: $191.7 million
Plot: Andy's toys are happy with Woody the cowboy as their leader until the little boy gets a flashy new toy for his birthday. Buzz Lightyear's arrival in the bedroom sets the toy caste system out of sinc and jealous Woody tries unsuccessfully to dispose of his rival, turning the other toys against himself in the process. But, hey, it's a Disney movie, so it all turns out all right in the end.

That Thing You Do! (1996) Director: *Tom Hanks.* Producers: *Tom Hanks,* Jonathan Demme, Gary Goetzman, Edward Saxon. Associate Producer: Terry Odem. Screenplay: *Tom Hanks.*

Cinematography: Taki Fujimoto. Production Designer: Victor Kempster. Art Director: Dan Webster. Visual Effects Supervisor: Steve Rundell. Original Music: Adam Schlesinger (title song), Howard Shore. Released by: 20th Century Fox. Running time: 110 minutes. Cast: Tom Everett Scott (Guy Patterson), Liv Tyler (Faye Dolan), Jonathan Schaech (James 'Jimmy' Matingly II), Steve Zahn (Lenny Haise), *Tom Hanks (Mr White)*, Ethan Embry (The Bass Player), Charlize Theron (Tina), Giovanni Ribisi (Chad), Peter Scolari (Troy Chesterfield), Rita Wilson (Marguerite), Chris Isaak (Uncle Bob), Holmes Osborne (Mr Patterson).

Fee: N/A

US Box Office: $46 million

Plot: Tom only makes a brief appearance as the manipulative manager of a pop group that hits the top of the charts with 'That Thing You Do!', a catchy pop ditty that has the girls screaming. But not for long. The group goes into the annals of one-hit-wonder bands when the honeymoon ends and they break up. Tom may not do much acting, but he wrote, directed and produced this charming '60s period piece.

Saving Private Ryan (1998) Director: Steven Spielberg. Producers: Steven Spielberg, Ian Bryce, Mark Gordon, Gary Levinsohn. Co-Producers: Bonnie Curtis, Allison Lyon Segan. Screenplay: Robert Rodat. Director of Photography: Janusz Kaminski. Editor: Michael Kahn. Costume Designer: Joanna Johnston. Production Designer: Tom Sanders. Music: John Williams. Released by: DreamWorks Pictures/Paramount. Running time: 170 minutes. Cast: Tom *Hanks (Capt Miller)*, Tom Sizemore (Sgnt Horvath), Edward Burns (Private Reiben), Barry Pepper (Private Jackson), Adam Goldberg (Private Mellish), Vin Diesel (Private Caparzo), Giovanni Ribisi (Medic Wade), Jeremy Davies (Corporal Upham), Matt Damon (Private Ryan), Ted Danson (Capt Hamill), Paul Giametti (Sgnt Hill), Dennis Farina (Lt Col Anderson), Joerg Stadler (Steamboat Willie).

Fee: Percentage of gross. Estimated at $20 million US Box Office: $190 million

Plot: When you have recovered from the intensity of the first half hour, which shows the slaughter on World War II's Omaha Beach in the most realistic and shocking detail ever seen on the big screen, you regroup to discover Tom's Captain Miller leading his men on a dangerous mission behind enemy lines to find the only surviving one left of four brothers who went to war for their country. A powerful film and a powerful, understated performance from its star.

You've Got Mail (1999) Director: Nora Ephron. Producers: Nora Ephron, Lauren Shiner Dormer. Executive Producers: Delia Ephron, Julie Durk, G. Mac Brown. Screenplay: Nora Ephron, Delia Ephron. Cinematography: John Lindley. Music: George Fenton. Released by: Warner Bros. Running time: 119 minutes. Cast: *Tom Hanks (Joe Fox)*, Meg Ryan (Kathleen Kelly), Parker Posey (Patricia Eden), Greg Kinnear (Frank Navasky), Jean Stapleton (Birdie), Steve Zahn (George Pappas), David Chappelle (Kevin Scanlon), Dabney Coleman (Nelson Foz), John Randolph (Schuyler Fox), Heather Burns (Christina).
Fee: $20 million
US Box Office: $111.1 million
Plot: Hard to believe it, but Tom and Meg hate each other when they meet. His character is a take-no-prisoners bookstore-chain boss. Hers is a caring owner of a small, family children's bookshop being driven out by the newcomer on the block with its vast range and big discounts. Unbeknownst to both, they are falling in love via the Internet, chatting anonymously by E-mail. By the end of the film (just) all is revealed and everyone goes home happy.

The Green Mile (1999) Director: Frank Darabont. Producer: David Valdes. Based on a novel by Stephen King. Released by: Castle Rock. Running time: 187 minutes. Cast: *Tom Hanks (Paul*

Edgecombe), Patricia Clarkson (Melinda Moores), James Cromwell (Hal Moores), Michael Clark Duncan (John Coffey), Graham Greene (Arien Bitterbuck), Bonnic Hunt (Janice Edgecombe), Barry Pepper (Dean Stauton), Sam Rockwell (William 'Wild Bill' Wharton), Gary Sinise (Burt Hammersmith), Harry Dean Stauton (Old Toot Toot).
Fee: $20 million
US Box Office: $136.8 million
Plot: Tom's grisly prison guard reflects on his bizarre tour-of-duty on death row in the 1930s and his relationship with a convicted rapist and killer whose gentle, healing nature leaves his captor wondering about his guilt and worrying whether he deserves to go to the electric chair.

Toy Story 2 (1999) Directors: John Lasseter, Ash Brannon, Lee Unkrich. Producers: Karen Robert Jackson, Sarah McArthur, Helene Plotkin. Writers: John Lasseter, Peter Docter, Ash Brannon, Andrew Stanton, Risa Hsiao, Doug Chamberlain, Chris Webb. Music: Randy Newman. Cinematography: Sharon Calahan. Released by: Disney. Running time: 92 minutes. Voices: Tom Hanks (Woody), Tim Allen (Buzz Lightyear), Don Rickles (Mr Potato Head), Joan Cusack (Jessie), Kelsey Grammer (Stinky Pete), Jim Varney (Slinky Dog), Wallace Shawn (Rex), Annie Potts (Bo Peep), John Ratzenberger (Hamm), John Morris (Andy).
Fee: $5 million
US Box Office: $245.8 million
Plot: Tom has no trouble keeping his box-office bankability on track with this can't-miss sequel to the hugely successful *Toy Story*. With Andy off to summer camp, his animated toys are left alone to cause havoc and the resulting storyline that has Buzz and his pals rescuing Woody from an obsessive toy collector makes sense to children and their parents alike.

Cast Away (2000) Director: Robert Zemeckis. Producer: Tom Hanks, Jack Rapke, Steve Starkey, Robert Zemeckis. Executive Producer: Joan Bradshaw. Associate Producer: Stephen J. Boyd. Screenplay: William Broyles Jr. Cinematographer: Don Burgess. Music: Alan Silvestri. Editing: Arthur Schmidt. Released by: 20th Century Fox/DreamWorks. Running time: 143 minutes. Cast: *Tom Hanks (Chuck Noland)*, Helen Hunt (Kelly Frears), Nick Searcy (Stan), Christopher Noth (Jerry Lovett), Lari White (Bettina Peterson), Paul Sanchez (Ramon), Leonid Citer (Fyodor), David Allen Brooks (Dick Peterson), Wilson (Itself).

Fee: $20 million

US Box Office: $233.6 million

Plot: In a stunning tour de force, Tom shares most of his best lines with a volleyball he names Wilson as he is pushed to the very edge of his physical and emotional limits trying to survive on a desert island after his character, a Fedex executive named Chuck, crash lands on the way to deliver a package over the Christmas holidays. Santa would be proud.

Road to Perdition (2002) Director: Sam Mendes. Producers: Walter F. Parkes, Joan Bradshaw, Richard D. Zanuck. Writers: David Self, Max Allan Collins II, Richard Rayner. Director of Photography: Conrad L. Hall. Casting: Debra Zane, Judith Bouley. Released by: DreamWorks. Running time: 117 minutes. Cast: *Tom Hanks (Michael Sullivan)*, Paul Newman (John Rooney), Jude Law (Maguire), Jennifer Jason Leigh (Annie Sullivan), Daniel Craig (Connor Rooney), Stanley Tucci (Frank Nitti), Tyler Hoechlin (Michael Sullivan Jr.), Liam Aiken (Peter Sullivan), Ciaran Hinds (Finn McGovern).

Fee: $20 million

US Box Office: $104 million

Plot: The dream team of Hanks and Newman do not disappoint in this gritty mob drama significant for being Tom's first bad-guy role.

His success in playing a hit man with a heart, albeit only when his own family is placed in harm's way, underlines his range and just how far he has come from the knockabout humour of *Bachelor Party* and *Big*. Jude Law plays a mean turn as an irredeemable killer with rotten teeth.

Catch Me If You Can (2002) Director: Steven Spielberg. Executive Producers: Barry Kemp, Michael Shane, Laurie MacDonald, Anthony Romano. Producers: Steven Spielberg, Walter F. Parkes. Screenplay: Jeff Nathanson. Based on book by Frank W. Abagnale. Director of Photography: Janusz Kaminski. Editor: Michael Kahn. Music: John Williams. Released by: DreamWorks. Running time: 141 minutes. Cast: Leonardo DiCaprio (Frank W. Abagnale), *Tom Hanks (FBI agent Carl Hanratty)*, Christopher Walken (Frank W. Abagnale Sr.), Martin Sheen (Roger Strong), Nathalie Baye (Paula Abagnale), Amy Adams (Brenda Strong), James Brolin (Jack Barnes).
Fee: $20 million
US Box Office: $164.6 million
Plot: It could be argued that Tom plays second fiddle here to both his pal Spielberg and DiCaprio. But he clearly enjoys the fun of the chase as a relentless FBI agent on the trail of a flamboyant young conman in the morally ambiguous piece of movie fluff when compared to the intensity of his previous collaboration with Spielberg in *Saving Private Ryan*. The film is based on the life of a real-life con artist and, although never one to cheat an audience, Tom could play this role with his eyes closed.

The Ladykillers (2004) Directors: Ethan and Joel Coen. Producers: Ethan and Joel Cohen, Barry Josephson, Tom Jacobson, Barry Sonnenfeld. Co-producer: John Cameron. Associate Producer: David Diliberto. Writers: Ethan and Joel Coen, William Rose, Max Adams. Director of Photography: Roger Deakins. Editor: Roderick Jaynes II. Casting: Rachel Tenner, Ellen Chenoweth. Music: T-Bone

Burnett, Carter Burwell. Released by: Buena Vista. Running time: 104 minutes. Cast: *Tom Hanks (Prof Goldthwait Higginson Dorr)*, Marlon Wayans (Gawain MacSam), Irma P. Hall (Marva Munson), Ryan Hurst (Lump), George Wallace (Sheriff Wyner).
Fee: $12 million
US Box Office: $39.8 million
Plot: The Coen brothers' remake of this madcap 1955 Ealing Studios drama that starred Peter Sellers and Alec Guinness didn't do too well at the box office. Tom took some flak for his over-the-top portrayal of a Southern professor-cum-criminal mastermind, but fans will celebrate the finer subtleties of his underrated performance.

The Terminal (2004) Director: Steven Spielberg. Producers: Steven Spielberg, Walter F. Parkes, Laurie MacDonald. Executive Producers: Jason Hoffs, Patty Whitcher. Writers: Dacha Gervasi, Jeff Nathanson. Director of Photography: Janusz Kaminski. Editor: Michael Kahn. Casting: Christiana Celeste, Debra Zane. Music: John Williams. Released by: DreamWorks. Running time: 128 minutes. Cast: *Tom Hanks (Viktor Navorski)*, Catherine Zeta-Jones (Amelia Warren), Stanley Tucci (Frank Dixon), Diego Luna (Enrique Cruz), Chi McBride (Mulroy), Zoe Saldana (Torres), Barry Shabaka Henley (Thurman).
Fee: $20 million
US Box Office: $77.8 million
Plot: Another Spielberg/Hanks film based roughly on a true story. Viktor comes from a country no one's ever heard of, speaks with an Eastern European accent, sings in gibberish and spends the whole movie in an airport. It sounds like *Cast Away* without the palm trees and beautiful sunsets, but Tom somehow pulls it off. It's easy to see how he charms the audience, although less believable that he woos the gorgeous Zeta-Jones.

Elvis Has Left the Building (2004) Director: Joel Zwick. Producers: Sharon Harel, Tova Laiter. Writers: Mitchell Ganem, Adam Michael Garber. Cinematography: Paul Elliot. Music: David Kitay. Released by: Straight to DVD. Running time: 90 minutes. Cast: Kim Basinger (Harmony Jones), John Corbett (Miles Taylor), Annie Potts (Shirl), Sean Astin (Aaron), Denise Richards (Belinda), Billy Ray Cyrus (Hank), *Tom Hanks (Mailbox Elvis)*.

Fee: Very little.

US Box Office: $0 (straight to DVD)

Plot: Blink and you'll miss Tom in his two brief appearances as mailbox Elvis in a flimsy story about a serial Elvis killer on the run. One can only assume Tom was paying director Zwick back by appearing in his follow-up to his *My Big Fat Greek Wedding*, which was the surprise hit of the year and earned Tom another stack of cash as producer and financier.

The Polar Express (2004) Director: Robert Zemeckis. Executive Producers: *Tom Hanks*, Jack Rapke, Chris Van Allsburg. Producers: Steve Starkey, Robert Zemeckis, Gary Goetzman, William Teitler. Co-producer: Steven J. Boyd. Directors of Photography: Don Burgess, Robert Pressley. Editors: R. Orlando Duenas, Jeremiah O'Driscoll. Screenplay: Robert Zemeckis, William Broyles Jr, Malia Scotch. From the book *The Polar Express* by Chris Van Allsburg. Music: Alan Silvestri, Glen Ballard. Released by: Warner Bros. Running Time 99 minutes. Cast: *Tom Hanks (The Conductor/Hero Boy/Father/Scrooge/Santa Claus/Hobo)*, Michael Jeter (Smokey/Steamer), Chris Coppola (Toothless Boy), Peter Scolari (Lonely Boy), Nona Gaye (Hero Girl), Jimmy Pinchak (Know-it-all Boy), Charles Fleischer (Elf General), Steven Tyler (Elf Lieutenant/Elf singer).

Fee: $20 million

US Box Office: $172.8 million

Plot: Using revolutionary animation techniques to bring the characters of this children's Christmas classic to life, Tom plays a smorgasbord of the leading characters, young and old, to find the true spirit of the season with the help of a magic steam train and a bucketload of money spent on creating a winter wonderland in an imaginary North Pole. But the faith of *Cast Away* buddies Hanks and Zemeckis was repaid at the cinema and in years of DVD sales every yuletide.

The Da Vinci Code (2006) Director: Ron Howard. Producers: Brian Grazer, John Calley. Executive Producers: Dan Brown, Tod Hallowell. Co-producers: Louisa Velis, Kathleen McGill. Cinematography: Salvatore Totino. Writers: Dan Brown (book), Akiva Goldman (screenplay). Music: Hans Zimmer. Released by: Columbia Tristar. Cast: Tom Hanks (Robert Langdon), Audrey Tautou (Sophie Neveu), Ian McKellen (Sir Leigh Teabing), Paul Bettany (Silas), Jean Reno (Bezu Fache), Etienne Chicot (Lt. Collet), Alfred Molina (Bishop Aringarosa).
Fee: 25 per cent of gross
US Box Office: N/A
Plot: What starts out with a mysterious murder of an elderly curator at the Louvre in Paris becomes a breathless race around the castles and churches of Europe as Professor Robert Langdon and his beautiful French symbologist sidekick try and crack an ancient code that has guarded an explosive secret for centuries that threatens the foundations of the Catholic faith.

DIRECTOR
FILMOGRAPHY

From the Earth to the Moon – TV mini-series – 1998
That Thing You Do! – Feature film – 1996
Fallen Angels – TV – 1993
A League of Their Own – TV series – 1993

Writer Filmography
From the Earth to the Moon – TV mini-series – 1998
That Thing You Do! – Feature film – 1996

Producer Filmography
From the Earth to the Moon – TV mini-series – 1998
Band of Brothers – TV series – 2001

Television Credits
I Am Your Child – Host – 1997
Bosom Buddies – Kip 'Buffy' Wilson – 1980-82
Saturday Night Live – Guest Host – 1985-96
The Naked Truth – Himself – 1995
Family Ties – Uncle Ned – 1982
Taxi – Gordon – 1978
The Love Boat – Rick Martin – 1977
Happy Days – The Fonz's old 'friend' – 1974

KU-113-331

The Complete Encyclopedia of Cooking
Supercook

The Complete Encyclopedia of Cooking

Supercook

Marshall Cavendish
London Sydney New York

Introduction

Everything you will ever need to know about food – what to buy, how to cook it, how to serve it and – most important of all – how to enjoy it. You'll never need another cookbook.

'Supercook' is an important and valuable collection which makes every other cookbook seem incomplete – or even obsolete. As well as including thousands of recipes, 'Supercook' explains about raw ingredients, weights and measurements and kitchen utensils, and details oven temperatures and cooking times, basic cooking terms and cooking and baking techniques. It shows you how to plan a well-balanced menu and how to serve attractive and delicious food from around the world.

Starting with 'A' and progressing through every letter of the alphabet to 'Z', 'Supercook' builds into a complete encyclopedia of international cooking. Each volume contains about 200 recipes, as well as basic techniques and instructions. Every volume includes starters, main courses and desserts, so you have a wide choice of dishes from which to create thousands of interesting meals. In addition, there are recipes for snacks, cakes, pastries, preserves and delicious home-made sweets, as well as new ideas for picnic food and informal indoor get-togethers. By arranging the volumes in alphabetical order we have made it easier to find what you need – especially in a hurry.

The 'Supercook' staff have combed the world to bring you interesting recipes, so that you will never get bored with cooking, and your family and friends will find an even greater enjoyment in the meals you prepare. Each recipe includes information on how the dish is served in its native country and its traditional accompaniments.

The recipes also suggest suitable dishes to complete the menu and offer guidance about wines or other beverages to serve. The more you know about food, the more you will enjoy cooking and eating.

All the recipes have been tested, tasted and – if it met with the approval of our panel of experts and home economists – passed on to you with clear, easy-to-follow instructions.

Every recipe in 'Supercook' is coded with coloured symbols that quickly indicate everything necessary for planning a meal: how long it will take to prepare, whether it is easy or complicated, and the relative cost of the main ingredients in season. Certain recipes are marked *Low-cal*, to guide you if you are watching your calorie intake. (See pages 8-9 for a full explanation to using the low-calorie recipes.)

Practical help for those who are learning to cook
'Supercook' recipes are easy to follow. They are written clearly with nothing left to chance and never include vague directions, like 'throw in a handful of flour' or 'add a little grated cheese'. Every stage of the preperation of a dish is explained in easy-to-follow detail. Many of the recipes are beautifully illustrated in full colour, and the more complicated ones have step-by-step pictures to guide you.

With 'Supercook' as a guide, you really can't go wrong. Even the least experienced of cooks will be impressed by the ease with which they learn to produce perfect results every time.

Exciting ideas for the more experienced cook
Each volume of this unique encyclopedia includes hundreds of ideas for breakfast, lunch and dinner . . . ideas for simple family meals, or elaborate and impressive dinners . . . ideas for starters, main courses and desserts – and even fourth and fifth courses if you're really going to town! With 'Supercook' in the kitchen you will never again be at a loss for an answer to the eternal question, 'What on earth am I going to feed them?'.

The World of International Cooking

A whole new world of culinary delights will open up and family mealtimes will acquire an international dimension when you use this illustrated A-Z encyclopedia of step-by-step recipes, cooking terms and techniques.

The aim of compiling this encyclopedia with more than 5,000 recipes from around the world has been to give all readers – from beginners to gourmet cooks – the knowledge, enthusiasm and understanding to help them become creative and exciting cooks. Foreign recipes and unusual ingredients are clearly explained. 'Agneau aux Tomates' may sound like a complicated dish from French cuisine, but don't be intimidated – the clear explanation and instructions in the recipe for this simple lamb casserole will turn it into a family favourite.

As your collection of *'Supercook'* volumes grows, so will your cooking repertoire – to include such diverse

international specialities as stir-fried Oriental dishes, Italian pastas and sauces, Irish fruit breads, spicy Eastern curries, sharp Mediterranean fish dishes, delicate French pastries and new versions of American favourites. Many of the recipes are accompanied by colour photographs, and the more complicated techniques are illustrated in step-by-step photographs. Every recipe includes an indication of how many average-sized portions it will make, and our home economists have included lots of suggestions for dishes to serve with many of the recipes to turn an informal meal into a dinner party with an international flavour.

Learn how to turn an ordinary meal into a special one – and a special meal into a sensational one! Enjoy adding to your repertoire dishes you know you can cook with confidence, which will please your family and impress your friends and enhance your reputation as a cook and a host or hostess.

Every volume that follows includes interesting new tastes and additional helpful hints. Nothing could be more enjoyable than cooking your way through the alphabet until you reach the classic Italian dessert, Zabaglione.

'Bon appetit!'

Symbols in Supercook

'Low-Calorie' Recipes

The description 'low-calorie' has been given to recipes in *'Supercook'* which contain fewer calories than other comparable recipes in the book. For instance, the pudding recipes marked 'Low-cal' have the fewest calories when compared to other pudding recipes in *'Supercook'*. Some – but not all – of the recipes labelled

'Low-cal' would be suitable for people who are following strict slimming or low-calorie diets. Each recipe should be examined carefully to ascertain whether the ingredients are permitted for a particular special diet.

The labelling 'Low-cal' will be more helpful for those aiming to lose weight slowly by reducing their calorie intake slightly or those who frequently experiment with new recipes but wish to avoid a very high consumption of calories. These recipes can also guide the person entertaining for weight-conscious friends. However,

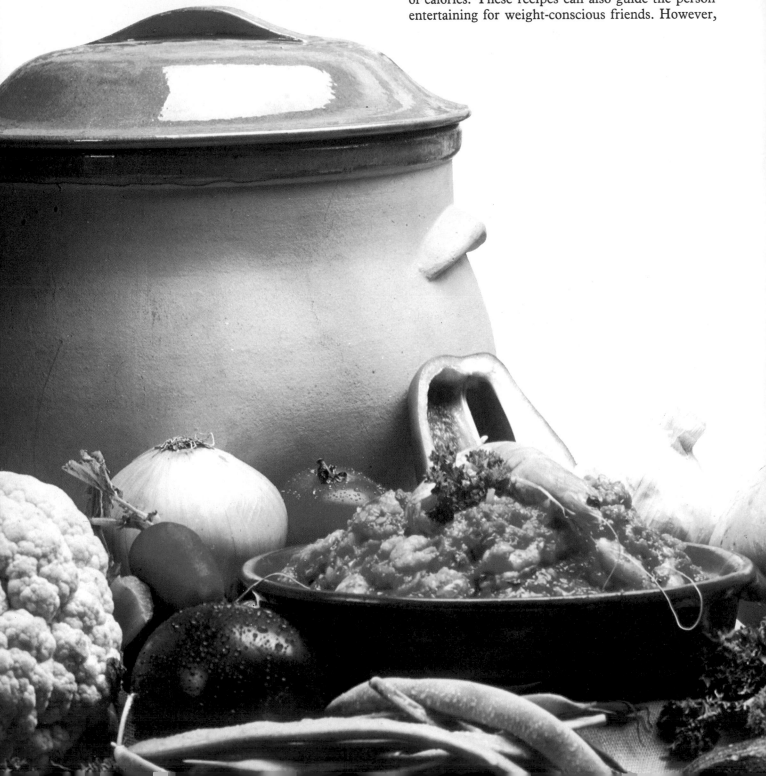

thought should also be given to what is to be served *with* the 'low-calorie' recipe. An over-enthusiastic combination of these recipes will not guarantee a low-calorie meal!

In deciding which recipes to consider in the 'low-calorie' category, each ingredient needs to be considered for its calorific contribution. Low-calorie ingredients such as vegetables, fruits, white fish and eggs may be combined with a moderate amount of fat or fat-containing foods and still be relatively 'low-calorie'. A generous combination of fats and fat-containing foods will produce a high-calorie recipe. Similarly, recipes which rely heavily on sugar, alcohol, flour or a combination of these foods with or without fat will be excluded from the 'low-calorie' rating.

In some recipes it may be possible to make further reductions in the amount of fats and sugars used, such as substituting low-fat yogurt for cream, or to grill [broil] food and drain off fat rather than frying, although the end results will differ slightly.

The calorie chart under the alphabetical heading CALORIES (p. 302) may be used to work out the approximate calorific value of individual recipes.

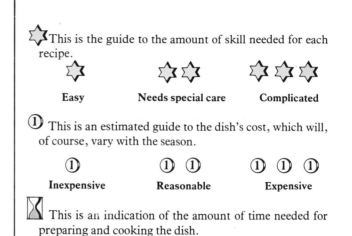

This is the guide to the amount of skill needed for each recipe.

Easy   **Needs special care**   **Complicated**

This is an estimated guide to the dish's cost, which will, of course, vary with the season.

Inexpensive   **Reasonable**   **Expensive**

This is an indication of the amount of time needed for preparing and cooking the dish.

Less than 1 hour   **1 hour to 2½ hours**   **Over 2½ hours**

Front Cover: Crown Roast of Pork, p. 511

**Published by Marshall Cavendish House
58 Old Compton Street
London W1V 5PA**

This Edition Published 1985

©*Marshall Cavendish Ltd 1985, 1979, 1978, 1977, 1976, 1975, 1974, 1973, 1972,
58 Old Compton Street, London W1V 5PA*

All rights reserved. No part of this publication may be reproduced, stored in any retrieval system, or transmitted in any form or by any means, electronic, mechanical, photocopying, recording or otherwise, without the prior permission in writing of the Publishers.

*Printed and bound by
New Interlitho Spa, Italy*

Cataloguing in Publication Data

*Supercook
1. Cookery
1. Cameron-Smith, Marye
641.5   TX717   79-52319*

*ISBN (for set) 0 85685 5340
ISBN (this volume) 0 85685 5359
Library of Congress catalog card number 78-52319.*

Cooking measures & terms

MEASUREMENT CONVERSIONS

Solid measures

(1 ounce = 28.352 metric grams, but for convenience it is usually calculated, as in this chart, 1 ounce = 30 grams)

½ ounce = 15 grams	3½ ounces = 100 grams
1 ounce = 30 grams	1 pound 1½ ounces = 500 grams
2 ounces = 60 grams	2 pounds 2 ounces = 1,000 grams
2½ ounces = 75 grams	(1 kilogram)

Liquid measures

20 fluid ounces = 1 pint (UK)
16 fluid ounces = 1 pint (US) or 2 cups (US)
 8 fluid ounces = 1 cup (US)

fluid ounces	Imperial	Metric	American
1	2 tablespoons	¼ deciliter	2 tablespoons
2	4 tablespoons	½ deciliter	¼ cup
4		1 deciliter	½ cup
5	¼ pint	1½ deciliter	⅔ cup
6		1¾ deciliter	¾ cup
8		2¼ deciliter	1 cup (½ pint)
10	½ pint	2¾ deciliter	1¼ cups
16		4½ deciliter	2 cups (1 pint)
20	1 pint	5½ deciliter	2½ cups
32		9 deciliter	4 cups (1 quart)
36	1⅓ pint, plus 1 ounce	1 liter	4½ cups

Frequently-used measurements

	Imperial	Metric	American
butter or margarine	½ ounce	15 grams	1 tablespoon
	4 ounces	120 grams	¼ cup
	½ pound	250 grams	1 cup
plain flour	1 ounce	30 grams	¼ cup
	2 ounces	60 grams	½ cup
	4 ounces	120 grams	1 cup
self-raising flour	1 ounce	30 grams	¼ cup
	2 ounces	60 grams	½ cup
	4 ounces	120 grams	1 cup
raisins	6 ounces	180 grams	1 cup
rice	8 ounces	240 grams	1 cup
brown sugar	⅓ ounce	10 grams	1 tablespoon
	3 ounces	90 grams	½ cup
	6 ounces	180 grams	1 cup
castor sugar	½ ounce	15 grams	1 tablespoon
	4 ounces	120 grams	½ cup
	8 ounces	240 grams	1 cup

The weights and measures equivalents are approximate only.

USEFUL KITCHEN TERMS

British equipment & terms	American equivalents
cake tin	cake pan
entree	main course
frying pan	skillet
heatproof baking dish	flameproof casserole
greaseproof paper	waxed paper
to grill	to broil
kitchen paper	paper towels
pudding	dessert
sieve	strainer
starter	appetizer
tea towel	dish towel
to whisk	to beat

British ingredients	American equivalents
aubergine	eggplant
bacon rashers	bacon slices
bicarbonate of soda	baking soda
biscuit	cookie
castor sugar	superfine sugar
cornflour	cornstarch
chutney	relish
cos lettuce	romaine lettuce
courgettes	zucchini
demerara sugar	pale brown granulated sugar

digestive biscuits	graham crackers
double cream	heavy or whipping cream
fillet steak	filet mignon
gammon slice	ham steak
haricot beans	dried navy beans
icing	frosting
icing sugar	confectioners' sugar
marrow	large zucchini or squash
Martini	vermouth
minced meat	ground meat
pancake	crêpe
pastry case	pie crust
plain flour	all-purpose flour
potato chips	French fries
potato crisps	potato chips
prawns	shrimp
salad cream	creamy salad dressing
salt beef	corned beef
scone	baking powder biscuit
self-raising flour	self-rising flour
single cream	light cream
sorbet	sherbet
sprats	smelts
spring onion	scallion
treacle	molasses
veal escalopes	veal scallops
wholemeal flour	whole-grain flour

Recipes in Volume 1

Abaisse

There is no English equivalent for *abaisse* (AH-bays), a French pastry-making term generally used to describe a sheet or piece of pastry which, depending on the use for which it is intended, has been rolled out to a certain thickness. The word *abaisse* is also used to describe a layer of sponge cake or the undercrust of pastry.

Abalone

A mollusc native to the waters of the Pacific Ocean, the shell of the abalone yields mother-of-pearl which is used in button-making and inlaying. Abalone meat has long been a popular food in China, Japan and in California.

Fresh abalone meat has a subtle flavour, but it is tough and must be tenderized. Most of the fresh abalone meat sold in California, for example, is ready to use. If, however, the meat has not been filleted and tenderized it can easily be softened by pounding thin slices with a wooden mallet. Today, tenderized canned abalone is exported all over the world and is readily available in speciality and Chinese provision shops.

Overcooking abalone will make it tough and disappointing. Fresh abalone, sliced thin, can be sautéed in melted butter for 45 to 55 seconds, turning once. Fresh abalone can also be cut into thin strips, dipped into batter and quickly deep fried.

This is the meat of small abalone which has been tenderized and canned. The shells of the mollusc, found in the waters of the Pacific Ocean, yield high-grade mother-of-pearl.

Abalone Chinese Style

Canned abalone is an ingredient of many Chinese dishes which are easy to prepare and quickly cooked. 4 SERVINGS

5 large Chinese dried, black mushrooms or ¼ lb. fresh mushrooms, washed and sliced
1 chicken stock cube dissolved in 15 fl. oz. [2 cups] boiling water
1 small can water chestnuts
2 tablespoons cornflour [cornstarch]
2 tablespoons cold water
1 lb. can abalone, drained and cut into very thin slices
4 spring onions [scallions], split in half and cut into 1-inch lengths
1 tablespoon soy sauce

If you are using Chinese mushrooms put them in a small bowl, cover with cool water and soak for 2 hours. Drain. Cut them in strips.

In a large, heavy frying-pan heat the chicken stock to boiling, add the water chestnuts, drained and sliced, and the mushrooms. Reduce heat and simmer for 5 minutes.

Dissolve the cornflour in the cold water and set aside.

Add the abalone, spring onions and soy sauce to the ingredients in the frying-pan and continue to simmer for 1 minute.

Slowly stir in the cornflour and cold water mixture. Lower the heat and stir continuously until the sauce thickens. Serve immediately in a warm serving dish accompanied by hot, boiled rice.

Abbacchio Brodettato
ITALIAN BRAISED LAMB

This Roman entrée (ahb-BAHK-ee-oe broh-det-TA-toe) is robust and delectable and is neither expensive nor difficult to prepare. It cannot be made quickly, however, for quite a bit of preparation is required and the meat must be cooked in the oven for about 1½ hours. It makes a delicious main dish for an informal dinner accompanied by lots of crusty Italian bread, a green salad and dry white wine.

6 SERVINGS

4 tablespoons diced fatty bacon
2 tablespoons oil
2 lb. lean shoulder of lamb, boned and cut into cubes
1 garlic clove, crushed
1 small onion, finely chopped
4 oz. [½ cup] canned, drained tomatoes
4 fl. oz. [½ cup] dry white wine
2 pints [5 cups] beef stock, fresh, canned or made with beef stock cubes
3 tablespoons flour
1 teaspoon salt
freshly ground black pepper
1 bay leaf
½ teaspoon of dried oregano
½ teaspoon of dried basil
3 egg yolks
2 tablespoons lemon juice
3 tablespoons chopped fresh parsley

Preheat oven to moderate 350°F (Gas Mark 4, 180°C).

In a large, heavy frying-pan over high heat, fry the bacon, until crisp and brown. Stir frequently to prevent it from sticking. With a slotted spoon, remove the bacon and discard it.

Add the oil to the remaining fat and when it is hot lower the heat to moderate, add the lamb, a few cubes at a time and fry them until golden brown. As they brown, transfer them to a medium-sized, flameproof casserole.

In the remaining fat fry the garlic and onion for 8 minutes or until the onion is transparent. Stir in the tomatoes and add the wine and boil for about 10 minutes or until it is reduced by half. Pour in the stock, and with a wooden spoon stir well to mix. Bring to the boil again.

Sprinkle the flour, salt and 4 grindings of black pepper over the meat in the casserole. Place the casserole over moderate heat and, stirring all the time, cook until the meat and flour are blended.

Pour the wine and stock mixture over the meat in the casserole. Add the bay leaf, the oregano and basil. Bring to the boil over moderate heat, stirring occasionally.

Cover the casserole and transfer it to the oven. Braise for 1½ to 2 hours, or until the meat is tender.

With a slotted spoon, transfer the meat to a heated, deep, serving dish, cover with a lid or piece of aluminium foil and keep hot.

Strain the stock in the casserole into a medium-sized saucepan. Leave it to rest for a minute or two, then skim any fat from the surface.

In a small bowl beat the egg yolks and lemon juice together with a whisk or rotary beater and slowly stir in 4 tablespoons of the stock.

Whisk the egg mixture back into the remaining stock. Place the pan over low heat, and cook gently for a few seconds, until the mixture thickens enough to coat the back of a wooden spoon. Be careful not to let the sauce boil or it will curdle.

Taste the sauce and add more salt and pepper if necessary. Pour the sauce over the meat and sprinkle with parsley.

Aberdeen, or Arbroath, Smokies

A Scottish speciality, these small haddocks are split, gutted, closed again and smoked whole. Golden brown and headless, they need no further cooking and can be eaten cold, with buttered toast or cut up in a salad. They may also be buttered outside and inside and lightly grilled or warmed in the oven. For a tasty first course, smokies can be filleted and served in a light cheese sauce.

A Scottish speciality, Aberdeen, or Arbroath, Smokies are small haddocks which are gutted and smoked whole.

Abbacchio Brodettato is a classic Roman entrée of braised lamb with a delicate egg and lemon sauce.

Adam and Eve Pudding is a dessert of apples baked with a sponge topping.

Absinthe

Distilled from wormwood, anise and aromatic plants, this pale green liqueur with a very high alcoholic content was invented at the end of the eighteenth century and immediately gained great popularity in France. The oils from wormwood, however, can cause delirium, blindness and insanity. Consequently, the sale of absinthe has been prohibited in France, Switzerland and the United States.

Acetic acid

This acid, which forms the basis of vinegar, is produced by the fermentation of ciders and wines and is used in very small quantities in the making of some sweets. A dilute synthetic solution is sometimes used as an inexpensive substitute for white wine vinegar or for pickling.

Acidify

To add acid, such as lemon juice or vinegar, to a culinary preparation.

Acidity

An acid taste which exists naturally in certain vegetables and fruit and can be eliminated or diminished by BLANCHING.

Acidulate

To make a preparation slightly sour, acid or piquant by the addition of such acids as lemon juice or vinegar. Acidulated water, cold water to which vinegar, lemon or lime juice is added, is used to prevent peeled and cut fruit and vegetables from discolouring when they are exposed to the air.

Adam and Eve Pudding
APPLE AND SPONGE PUDDING

A traditional, inexpensive English pudding, this is an appealing dessert for an informal family lunch or dinner. It should be served hot and can be accompanied by cream or custard sauce. It is easy to make, but care must be taken when preparing the sponge topping.

4 SERVINGS

1 lb. cooking apples
5 oz. [⅝ cup] sugar
½ teaspoon cinnamon
2 tablespoons cold water
4 oz. [½ cup] butter or margarine, softened
4 oz. [1 cup] self-raising flour
2 medium-sized eggs, lightly beaten

Preheat the oven to moderate 350°F (Gas Mark 4, 180°C).

Peel and core the apples. Cut into thin slices and put them into a medium-sized oval pie dish.

Sprinkle the apple slices with the cinnamon, water and 1 ounce [2 tablespoons] of sugar.

To prepare the sponge mixture, put the butter and the remaining 4 ounces [½ cup] of sugar into a mixing bowl and beat with a wooden spoon until light and creamy. Add the beaten eggs, a little at a time, to the sugar and butter mixture, beating well between each addition. Sift the flour into the bowl and stir it into the mixture.

Pour the sponge mixture over the apples and spread it evenly with a palette knife. Bake in the middle of the oven for 30 minutes or until the sponge mixture has risen and has begun to turn a pale golden brown. Reduce the oven heat to cool 300°F (Gas Mark 2, 150°C) for another 30 minutes. Serve immediately.

Adrak Chutney
GINGER CHUTNEY

An ideal accompaniment for curry, this Indian recipe for Adrak (AH-druk) Chutney is quick and easy to make. If you have a blender the whole operation takes no more than 10 minutes. This chutney must be eaten immediately or, if stored in a closed jar in the refrigerator, within two days.

6 SERVINGS

juice of 2 lemons
4 teaspoons sugar
4 oz. fresh ginger, peeled and chopped
3 oz. sultanas [½ cup golden raisins]
1 clove garlic, crushed
1½ teaspoons salt

Put the juice of 1½ lemons, 2 teaspoons sugar and all the other ingredients into an electric blender. Blend until the mixture is smooth. Taste and if necessary add the juice of the other half lemon and the rest of the sugar. If you are using a hand chopper be sure to chop the ginger thoroughly as it tends to be fibrous. Serve in a small glass bowl.

Advocaat

A yellow, Dutch liqueur made with brandy, thickened with egg yolks and flavoured with vanilla.

Agar-agar

The gelatine-like product of a red seaweed which has strong setting properties, agar-agar is chiefly produced in Japan, China, the Soviet Union and the United States. Sold in sheet or strip form, it is used commercially in canning, in the production of jellies, creams and emulsions, and as a medium for the laboratory culture of bacteria.

Agneau

A young sheep before the age of one year, which is called lamb in England and spring lamb in the United States, is in France known as *agneau* (AHN-yoh). The French *agneau de lait* is milk-fed lamb, a yearling or a baby lamb which has never been weaned or put out to graze.

Agneau à la Bonne Femme
RAGOÛT OF LAMB

A simple and inexpensive brown stew, Agneau à la Bonne Femme (AHN-yoh ah la bon fahm) is a French ragoût of spring lamb which is cooked on the top of the stove. It can be made early in the day and reheated immediately before serving. It is traditionally served with rice.

4 SERVINGS

2 lb. shoulder of lamb, boned
3 tablespoons rendered fresh pork fat or cooking oil
2 tablespoons [¼ cup] flour
1 teaspoon salt
½ teaspoon black pepper
1¼ pints [3 cups] water
1 small clove garlic, crushed
1 bouquet garni, consisting of 2 parsley sprigs, 1 bay leaf and ⅛ teaspoon of dried thyme tied in a piece of cheesecloth
8 small potatoes, peeled
12 small onions
12 small carrots
2 oz. sultanas [⅓ cup golden raisins], washed

Cut the lamb into 2-inch cubes and dry them well on kitchen towels. Heat the fat, or cooking oil, in a large, heavy saucepan. Add the meat, a few pieces at a time, and brown on all sides. As the cubes are done, lift them out of the pan with a slotted spoon, place in a dish and keep warm.

When all the pieces have been browned, return them to the pan and sprinkle with the flour, salt and pepper. Toss the pieces of meat with a spoon to coat them with the other ingredients. Cook over a moderate heat, mixing occasionally, until the flour is lightly browned.

Add the water, the garlic and the bouquet garni. Cover the saucepan, bring to the boil. Lower the heat and simmer for 40 minutes.

Add the potatoes, onions, carrots and sultanas. Replace the lid and simmer for another 45 minutes or until the meat is tender when pierced with a table fork and the vegetables are cooked. Taste the stock and add more seasoning if necessary.

To serve, remove the bouquet garni, put the meat and vegetables into a warmed serving dish and pour the stock over.

Agneau en Brochette
LAMB ON SKEWERS

Agneau en Brochette (AHN-yoh on broh-shet), cubes of lamb marinated for 3 hours in olive oil and white wine and grilled [broiled] with vegetables on skewers, makes a splendid main course for a dinner party. On grand occasions the lamb can be doused with warmed brandy, set alight and served on a metal platter.

4 SERVINGS

1½ lb. boned leg of lamb
3 tablespoons olive oil
3 tablespoons white wine
1 clove of garlic, crushed
1 teaspoon dried rosemary
1 teaspoon salt
16 small tomatoes, washed
16 small [pearl] onions, skinned
2 large green peppers, washed, seeded and cut into large pieces
freshly ground black pepper

Low Cal

Trim the excess fat from the lamb and cut into 1½-inch cubes. In a bowl mix the oil, wine, garlic, rosemary, 8 grindings of pepper and the salt. Add the cubes of lamb and turn well with a spoon so that all the pieces are coated. Leave to marinate for 3 hours. Mix occasionally.

Line grilling pan with aluminium foil. Thread the lamb pieces on 8 skewers alternating with tomatoes, onions and green pepper. After placing the skewers on the pan, brush with the remaining marinade. Turn the grill to high and, when red hot, grill the kebabs approximately 2 inches away from the heat for 8 to 10 minutes. Serve with rice, a green salad and garlic bread.

A French ragoût of lamb, Agneau à la Bonne Femme is traditionally made with spring vegetables.

An unusual main dish, Agneau à la Hongroise is cooked on top of the stove and flavoured with herbs, paprika, mushrooms and white wine.

Agneau à la Hongroise
LAMB STEW WITH PAPRIKA

An unusual lamb stew, Agneau à la Hongroise (AHN-yoh ah la ON-grwahz) is flavoured with paprika and mushrooms. A good main dish at lunch or dinner, it may be served with buttered noodles and a fresh, green salad.

6 SERVINGS

3 lb. lower ribs or shoulder of lamb, boned
5 oz. [⅝ cup] butter
2 medium-sized onions, peeled and chopped
½ teaspoon salt
1 level tablespoon paprika
2 tablespoons [¼ cup] flour
6 fl. oz. [¾ cup] white wine
10 fl. oz. [1¼ cups] veal stock, or stock made with a veal or chicken stock cube
2 tablespoons tomato purée
1 bouquet garni, consisting of 1 heaped teaspoon of equal quantities of crushed, dried parsley, thyme and bay leaf, tied in a piece of cheesecloth
8 oz. [1 cup] mushrooms, washed, stalks trimmed and sliced
10 fl. oz. [1¼ cups heavy] double cream
2 tablespoons chopped fresh parsley

Cut the lamb into small cubes, dry them on kitchen paper towels and brown them in 4 ounces [½ cup] of butter in a deep, heavy saucepan. When the lamb cubes are well coloured, add the onions, the salt and the paprika and mix thoroughly. Sprinkle with the flour and stir it in. Pour on the white wine, bring to the boil and continue to boil briskly for 5 minutes. Stir in the veal or chicken stock, the tomato purée and add the bouquet garni. Cover and simmer for 30 minutes.

Put the remaining 1 ounce of butter into a frying-pan and lightly sauté the mushrooms. Remove the lamb cubes from the saucepan with a slotted spoon and add to the mushrooms. Remove frying-pan from the heat. Set aside.

Increase heat under saucepan to high and boil briskly until the sauce is reduced by half. Add the lamb and mushrooms and mix together. Reduce heat to low. Cover and simmer for 20 minutes. Remove the bouquet garni. Stir in the cream.

To serve, put the lamb, mushrooms and sauce on a warmed serving dish and sprinkle with fresh, chopped parsley.

Agneau aux Tomates
LAMB STEW WITH TOMATOES

A simple lamb dish, Agneau aux Tomates (AHN-yoh oh toh-MAHT), is easy to prepare and is a suitable main dish for an informal lunch or dinner. Serve with a green vegetable and creamed potatoes.

4 SERVINGS

2 lb. boned shoulder of lamb, trimmed of excess fat
3 tablespoons vegetable oil
1 garlic clove, crushed
4 fl. oz. [½ cup] white wine
8 fl. oz. [1 cup] veal or chicken stock
½ teaspoon salt
¼ teaspoon black pepper
1 lb. small tomatoes, blanched, peeled and seeded
1 tablespoon flour, dissolved in 2 tablespoons wine
2 tablespoons finely chopped parsley

With a sharp knife, cut the lamb into 1½-inch cubes, dry them well on a kitchen towel.

In a large, heavy saucepan, heat 2 tablespoons of the oil, over moderate heat. Add the lamb cubes and fry them, stirring frequently for 6 to 8 minutes or until they are browned all over.

Add the garlic, wine, stock, salt and pepper and stir well. Bring the liquid to the boil. Reduce the heat to low and simmer for 30 minutes or until the lamb is tender when pierced with the point of a sharp knife.

Meanwhile, in a small frying-pan heat the remaining amount of oil over moderate heat. When the foam subsides, add the tomatoes and cook them gently, stirring frequently, for 5 minutes. Remove the pan from the heat. Set aside and keep warm.

Stir the dissolved flour into the lamb mixture in the saucepan. Cook, stirring constantly, for 3 minutes or until the liquid has thickened slightly. Stir in the tomatoes. Remove pan from heat and transfer the stew to a warmed serving dish. Sprinkle over the parsley and serve.

Agurkai su Rukcscia Grietne
CUCUMBER AND SOURED CREAM SALAD

Refreshing, tasty and attractive, this cucumber and soured cream salad (ah-GOOR-ki soo rook-schee-a gree-et-ney) originated in the Baltic States. It is easy to make, does not take very long and could accompany almost any plainly cooked fish or meat dish. If fresh dill is not available parsley can be substituted. It will be equally decorative, but it will not give the same flavour.

4 SERVINGS

3 medium-sized cucumbers, peeled
5 teaspoons salt
3 tablespoons white wine vinegar
1 teaspoon French mustard
6 tablespoons soured cream
½ teaspoon sugar
⅛ teaspoon white pepper
3 eggs, hard-boiled
1 tablespoon finely-chopped, fresh dill or 2 tablespoons chopped parsley

Aïgo Bouïdo
FRENCH PROVENÇAL GARLIC SOUP

Quick and easy to make, Aïgo Bouïdo (ai-go BWEE-doe), a French Provençal soup, is inexpensive and unusual. It has the added advantage that most of it can be prepared early in the day on which it is to be served. Because the garlic is boiled, its flavour becomes delicious, aromatic and almost indefinable. Served as a prelude to steak, salad and an elegant chocolate dessert, Aïgo Bouïdo will be a unique beginning to a delightful dinner.

4 SERVINGS

16 garlic cloves, unpeeled and
   coarsely chopped
1 bay leaf
½ teaspoon dried thyme
1 tablespoon dried sage
1 teaspoon salt
3 cloves
3 parsley sprigs
2 pints [5 cups] water
3 egg yolks
4 tablespoons [¼ cup] olive oil
2 tablespoons chopped fresh
   parsley

Place the garlic, bay leaf, thyme, sage, salt, cloves and parsley sprigs in a large saucepan. Pour the water into the saucepan and bring to the boil. Reduce the heat and simmer the soup, uncovered, for 30 minutes.

Pour the soup through a strainer into a large bowl, and press all the juice from the garlic with a wooden spoon. Wash the saucepan and return the soup to the clean pan.

Place the egg yolks in a bowl and with a wire whisk, or rotary beater, beat them until they are thick and creamy. Add the oil drop by drop, beating continuously, until all the oil is incorporated and the mixture is smooth.

Just before serving, bring the soup back to the boil. Spoon the egg and oil mixture into a warm soup tureen and with a wire whisk beat in about one-quarter of the hot soup. Pour in the rest of the soup and stir.

Sprinkle the chopped parsley over the soup.

The soup may be served with French bread, bread sticks or toast and a bowl of grated Parmesan Cheese which is sprinkled on the soup when it is served.

Cut the cucumbers into ½ inch thick slices. Place the salt and 2 tablespoons of the vinegar into a large mixing bowl and stir until the salt is dissolved. Add the cucumber slices to the salt and vinegar and, using a large spoon, toss them gently until thoroughly mixed.

With a slotted spoon, remove the cucumber slices from the bowl and place them on kitchen paper towels to drain.

In a small mixing bowl mix together the mustard, the remaining 1 tablespoon of vinegar, the soured cream, sugar and white pepper.

Halve the eggs, remove the yolks and put aside. Cut the egg whites into thin strips. Using the back of a wooden spoon, press the egg yolks through a fine sieve, or strainer, on to a plate.

With a wire whisk beat the sieved egg yolks into the soured cream mixture. Continue to beat until the dressing is smooth and creamy. Add the strips of egg white and mix well.

Place the drained cucumber slices in a shallow serving bowl. Pour the dressing over the cucumber and with a wooden spoon toss gently until they are well-coated. Sprinkle with chopped dill or parlsey. Place in the refrigerator to chill for at least 1 hour before serving.

Agurkesalat
DANISH PICKLED CUCUMBER SALAD

In Denmark, Agurkesalat (ah-GOOR-keh-sa-LAHT) is often used to garnish smørre-brød, the famous Danish open sandwiches of thin slices of rye bread topped with a *huge variety of appetizingly arranged meats, seafood, eggs and cheese. Agurkesalat can also be served as an accompaniment to meat or poultry dishes. It is inexpensive and simply prepared, but it must be made early in the day on which it is to be used because it takes a total of at least 5 hours for the cucumbers to pickle.*

4 SALAD SERVINGS

3 cucumbers, washed
1 tablespoon plus 1 teaspoon salt
1 tablespoon sugar
¼ teaspoon white pepper
4 fl. oz. [½ cup] white vinegar
1 tablespoon lemon juice
3 tablespoons chopped fresh
   dill or 1 tablespoon dried dill

With a table fork score down the skin of the cucumbers to make ridges. Cut the cucumbers into very thin slices. Place the cucumber slices in a shallow dish and sprinkle with 1 tablespoon of the salt. Cover and set aside for 2 hours. (This removes the excess water from the cucumbers.)

Meanwhile, mix the remaining 1 teaspoon of salt with the sugar, pepper, vinegar and lemon juice. With a fork beat lightly until the sugar is dissolved.

With a slotted spoon remove the cucumber slices and place them on a double piece of kitchen paper towel. Place another piece of paper on top and press to remove the liquid.

Arrange the cucumber slices attractively in a serving dish. Pour the vinegar dressing over the cucumber slices and sprinkle the dill over the top. Place in the refrigerator and leave for at least 3 hours before serving.

Aïgo-Sau

MEDITERRANEAN FISH STEW

A traditional dish in the South of France, Aïgo-Sau (ai-go-saw) is easy to prepare. It can be made with one or more types of fish and is an excellent lunch or informal dinner party dish.

4 SERVINGS

1½ lb. fresh fish, boned
6 medium potatoes, peeled and sliced
1 bay leaf
1 onion, peeled and finely chopped
1 celery stalk, chopped

2 cloves of garlic, peeled and crushed plus 1 whole, peeled garlic clove
1 teaspoon salt
½ teaspoon black pepper
1 teaspoon each of fennel, chopped parsley and grated orange rind
3 fl. oz. [⅜ cup] olive oil
boiling water
8 fl. oz. [1 cup] alioli
4 slices of dry, toasted, French bread

Cut the fish into serving-size pieces and arrange in the bottom of a large saucepan. Cover with the potatoes. Add the bay leaf, onion, celery and crushed garlic.

Sprinkle with salt, pepper, fennel, parsley and grated orange rind. Pour on the olive oil and add boiling water to cover. Boil rapidly for 20 minutes or until the potatoes are tender.

Strain the broth into another saucepan and put the fish and potatoes on a warmed serving dish. Just before serving the broth, remove the saucepan from the heat and, stirring constantly, very slowly add the alioli.

Place rounds of toast, well rubbed with the peeled garlic clove, in individual soup bowls and pour the broth over them. Serve the fish and potatoes separately on a warmed serving dish.

Left: A simple Mediterranean fish stew and broth, Aïgo-Sau can be made with one or more types of fish.

Aiguillette de boeuf

Aiguillette de boeuf (ai-GWEE-yet deh berf) is the French cookery term for the top part or rump of beef which is usually braised or poached.

Aillade

A term which is used in the South of France, aillade (AYE-yahd) is applied to different preparations which are all predominantly flavoured with garlic. Among these are aillade sauce, an oil, vinegar and garlic dressing, which is served with cold meat and fish as well as with potatoes, and bread *à l'aillade*, slices of toasted bread which are well rubbed with garlic and sprinkled with olive oil.

Ajja

SPICY SCRAMBLED EGGS WITH SAUSAGE AND GREEN PEPPERS

A Tunisian dish, Ajja (AJ-ja) is easy to prepare and can be served at lunch or an informal dinner. Although the Tunisians use a great deal of cayenne pepper in this dish, the first time you make it, unless your palate is accustomed to very hot food, it might be wise to use only a few grains.

4 SERVINGS

4 medium-sized, sweet, green
   peppers
$\frac{1}{2}$ teaspoon ground cayenne pepper
$\frac{1}{4}$ teaspoon ground cumin
$\frac{1}{8}$ teaspoon salt
2 tablespoons olive oil
1 lb. spicy sausage such as hot
   Italian sausage or Spanish
   chorizos, cut into 1-inch rounds
1 garlic clove, finely chopped
14 oz. canned Italian, peeled plum
   tomatoes; or 3 large, ripe firm
   tomatoes, peeled and quartered
4 tablespoons [$\frac{1}{4}$ cup] cold water
   freshly ground black pepper
6 eggs, lightly beaten

Cut the peppers into quarters, remove the seeds and trim off the white pith. Cut lengthways into $\frac{1}{2}$-inch wide strips. Set aside.

In a small dish mix the cayenne, cumin and salt together. Set aside.

Right: Scrambled eggs with sausage and green pepper, Ajja is an unusual and spicy Tunisian dish.

Pour the oil into a large heavy frying-pan and place over high heat until the oil is hot. Add the sliced sausage and fry, turning frequently, until the sausage is brown.

Stir in the garlic, the cayenne, cumin and salt mixture, the tomatoes and water and 6 grindings of black pepper. Cook over moderate heat until the mixture is thick. Stir occasionally to prevent the tomatoes sticking to the pan. Add the strips of pepper, cover the pan and cook for another 5 minutes.

Pour the beaten eggs over the sausage mixture. Cook over low heat, stirring constantly until the eggs are just cooked. Do not over cook as the eggs will be too hard and will not blend with the other ingredients.

Albacore

A large, deep-sea, game fish, albacore, a species of tuna fish, has white meat and is used for the best canned tuna fish and for the most delicate dishes.

Albóndigas

MEAT BALLS IN TOMATO SAUCE

A traditional Mexican dish, Albóndigas (al-BON-dee-gas) probably has its origins in Spain. It is also made in Brazil and in Scotland where it is known as Almundigoes. An inexpensive, filling, lunch or dinner dish, it is usually served with plain boiled rice.

4 SERVINGS

1 lb. minced [ground] beef
$\frac{1}{2}$ lb. minced [ground] pork
1 thick slice white bread
   cold water
1 medium-sized egg
1 teaspoon salt
$\frac{1}{2}$ teaspoon dried sage
$\frac{1}{2}$ teaspoon dried mint
$\frac{1}{2}$ teaspoon black pepper
2 tablespoons cooking oil
2 medium-sized onions, chopped
$1\frac{1}{2}$ lb. tomatoes, peeled and chopped
1 clove garlic, crushed
$\frac{1}{2}$ teaspoon dried coriander

In a large bowl mix together the beef and pork. Soak the slice of bread in the cold water and squeeze dry. Crumble the bread and mix into the meat. Stir in the egg and the salt, sage, mint and pepper. Mix well.

With your hands, shape the meat into balls the size of walnuts.

Put the cooking oil into a deep, heavy saucepan and fry the meat balls until they are brown. Remove with a slotted spoon and set aside.

Put the onions into the saucepan and fry them until they are golden brown. Add the tomatoes, garlic and coriander. Cover and simmer for 30 minutes.

Add the meat balls and continue to simmer, covered, for another 30 minutes. Taste and add salt and pepper if necessary.

To serve, place the meat balls in the centre of a deep, warmed serving dish, pour the sauce over them and surround with rice.

Albóndigas Soup

Albóndigas is also the name given to a spicy, Mexican tomato soup which includes a few small balls of the albóndigas meat mixture.

6 SERVINGS

1 oz. [2 tablespoons] butter
2 onions, chopped
¼ teaspoon chilli powder
½ teaspoon dried oregano
2 lb. tomatoes, peeled and sieved
water
1 teaspoon salt
MEAT BALLS
½ lb. minced [ground] beef
1 slice white bread, grated into breadcrumbs
1 small egg
1 small clove garlic, crushed
a large pinch of dried sage, mint and coriander
freshly ground black pepper
½ teaspoon salt

In a large saucepan melt the butter over moderate heat. Add the onions and cook gently until they are soft, but not brown. Add the chilli powder and oregano. Stir and cook for 30 seconds before adding the sieved tomatoes which have been made up to 4 pints [2½ quarts] with water. Add the salt and cook uncovered, over moderate heat, for 1 hour, or until the liquid is reduced by half.

Put all the ingredients for the meat balls in a medium-sized mixing bowl and mix well with your hands. Roll the mixture into small balls the size of walnuts. Add these to the soup. Cover and simmer over low heat for 40 minutes.

Albumen

This is the name sometimes used for the whites of eggs. It is frequently confused with ALBUMIN which is the protein part of egg white.

Albumin

A protein which forms part of blood, milk and egg white. Soluble in water and dilute salt solutions, albumin coagulates when heated.

Albumin powder can be substituted for egg whites when making meringues and some cake icings.

Alcohol

Alcohol, a word of Arabic origin, is as old as man. There are a large number of alcohols, a whole chemical series with varying characteristics, each composed of carbon, hydrogen and oxygen combined in a similar pattern.

The alcohol which is the principal active ingredient of wines, spirits and beers is known as ethyl alcohol. It is a colourless liquid with a faint odour.

Alcohol is easily made by yeast fermentation of fruits, grains and vegetables and, as a consequence, was known to early man in the form of mead, ale and wine.

Al Dente

An Italian cooking term, *al dente* (ahl-DEN-tay) literally translated means 'to the tooth'. It is used to describe the point at which food, particularly pasta and rice, is properly cooked, that is, it is firm to the bite, but not soft.

Ale

A word originally used to describe an alcoholic beverage which was brewed from barley malt, ale was the common drink in northern countries where there were few or no vineyards and, therefore, little or no wine.

After the introduction of hops into England from Flanders in the sixteenth century, ale was increasingly flavoured with hops and today the term ale is almost synonymous with beer although it is never applied to black beers or lager.

Alebele

COCONUT FILLED DESSERT PANCAKES

Alebele (al-a-beel) *originates in Goa on the west coast of India where Portuguese influence is evident in the cooking. The original recipe calls for fresh coconut and*

jaggery, a crude, dark, palm sugar. This recipe is an adaptation using desiccated coconut, brown sugar and treacle [molasses].

4 SERVINGS

PANCAKES
4 oz. [1 cup] flour
2 teaspoons castor sugar
1 egg plus 1 egg yolk
6 fl. oz. [¾ cup] milk mixed with 2 fl. oz. [¼ cup] water
2 tablespoons melted butter
FILLING
4 teaspoons brown sugar
2 teaspoons treacle [molasses]
2 oz. fine desiccated coconut soaked in 7 tablespoons milk for 1 hour
1 teaspoon fresh ginger, finely grated
½ teaspoon aniseeds

For the pancakes, sift the flour and sugar into a medium-sized mixing bowl. Make a well in the centre of the flour and break the eggs into it. Add a tablespoon of the milk and water to the eggs and stir with a wooden spoon, mixing well. Slowly incorporate the flour and sugar.

Add the milk and water a little at a time. Continue mixing until all the flour and half the milk mixture is blended to make a thick batter. Add 1 tablespoon cooled, melted butter and whisk briskly. Whisk in the rest of the milk and water. Cover and keep in a cool place for 30 minutes.

Meanwhile mix together all the ingredients for the filling in a small bowl and set aside.

Heat a medium-sized frying-pan. Grease lightly with melted butter. Pour one tablespoon of the batter into the pan and tip the pan quickly to spread the batter evenly. Cook over a high heat until the pancake is brown on the underside. Turn over with a palette knife and cook for 30 seconds or until brown. Turn on to a plate and keep warm.

Spread one spoonful of the coconut filling across the lower third of each pancake and roll neatly. Arrange the pancakes on a plate and serve.

Ale Berry

This drink is traditionally drunk in the North of England at bedtime to prevent a cold.

2 PINTS

2 pints [5 cups] brown ale
2 tablespoons rolled oats
1 small piece fresh ginger, grated, or ½ teaspoon ground ginger
½ teaspoon grated nutmeg
2 tablespoons brown sugar
juice of half a lemon

Roll out each half of the pastry between two pieces of floured greaseproof or waxed paper to prevent it sticking.

Fold the edges to make a neat rectangle of pastry and role out again between the sheets of paper.

Remove the top sheet and lift the pastry by the lower sheet onto the buttered baking tray.

Spread the raspberry purée evenly over one half of the baked pastry leaving about ¼ inch around the edges.

Carefully slide the other piece of baked pastry off the baking tray onto the raspberry covered piece.

When the torte is iced leave it to cool for at least 4 hours before cutting it into 2 inch by 3 inch pieces.

Put the ale into a large saucepan over moderate heat and stir in the oats, ginger and nutmeg. Bring to the boil and simmer for 15 to 20 minutes. Strain the liquid into a warmed jug through a fine sieve. Stir in the sugar and lemon juice and taste. Add more sugar if necessary.

Serve very hot in glass or pottery mugs.

Ale Posset

An old-fashioned English drink, this is made of equal quantities of hot ale and hot milk mixed together. It is sweetened with sugar, flavoured with grated ginger or nutmeg and drunk very hot.

Alewife

An important food fish, the alewife is a member of the shad family. It is caught off the Atlantic coast of North America and in some lakes and rivers. It exists in great abundance in Lake Ontario.

The alewife grows to about a foot long and resembles the herring. In the St. Lawrence Bay area this fish is known as Gaspereu or Sawbelly and is called Round Pompano in Bermuda.

Fresh alewife is cooked in the same ways as shad or herring. Alewife is generally salt-packed, but it is also sometimes smoked.

Alexander Torte

ICED RASPBERRY-FILLED PASTRY CAKES

 ①

Delicately flavoured, crisp and cut into cakes, Alexander Torte was traditionally eaten as a lunch or dinner dessert in Latvia, but it can also be served at tea. It should be made early on the day you plan to serve it, or even the night before, because the icing must be hard before the torte is cut.

ABOUT 24 CAKES

12 oz. [3 cups] flour
¼ teaspoon salt
4 oz. [½ cup] unsalted butter, cut into pieces
4 oz. [½ cup] margarine, diced
3 tablespoons sugar
1 egg lightly beaten
12 oz. [1½ cups] raspberry jam
2 oz. [¼ cup] butter, softened
8 oz. icing [1¾ cups confectioners'] sugar, sifted
3 tablespoons cold water
2 tablespoons lemon juice

Sift the flour and salt into a large mixing bowl. Add the butter and margarine. With your fingertips, rub the butter and margarine into the flour until the mixture resembles fine breadcrumbs. Add the sugar and the egg and mix well. With a knife stir the pastry until it begins to form a ball, then with your hands, gently knead the pastry until it is smooth.

Wrap the pastry in aluminium foil and chill in the refrigerator for 1 hour.

To make purée of the jam, hold a strainer over a small saucepan and, with a wooden spoon, press the jam through. Place the saucepan over low heat, and cook, stirring all the time, until the purée thickens. Set aside to cool.

Preheat the oven to cool 300°F (Gas Mark 2, 150°C).

Halve the pastry. Cut out 4 pieces of greaseproof paper 9 × 16 inches. Dust the paper with flour. Place half of the pastry on a piece of the floured paper and place another on top, flour side down. Roll out the pastry to the shape of the paper, fold over uneven edges and roll again. Repeat with other half.

Grease two baking sheets with the softened butter. Remove the top pieces of paper from the pastry, and lift the other pieces of paper and pastry and place them, paper side up, on to the baking sheets. Remove the paper. Place the baking sheets in the oven and bake the pastry for 45 to 50 minutes, or until it is crisp.

Allow the pastry to cool on the trays for 5 minutes. Spread the raspberry purée over one piece of the pastry and carefully slide the other piece on top.

Mix the icing sugar in a bowl with cold water and lemon juice. Spread the icing evenly over the top of the torte. Leave the icing to set for at least 4 hours.

Algérienne, à l'

Algérienne, (al-JAIR-yen) is the name of a garnish, usually for meat, which consists of small, whole tomatoes braised in oil, and sweet potatoes cooked in butter.

Alicante Wine

A sweet, red, table wine, very popular in Spain, Alicante wine comes, as its name suggests, from the surrounding areas of Alicante. Rarely stocked in Britain today it was quite popular in Victorian England.

Alioli

The name literally means garlic oil and this sauce has been known in many parts of Spain and in Provence for hundreds of years. It was also known and appreciated by the Romans 2,000 years ago.

The basic recipe is garlic pounded in a mortar and mixed with olive oil, salt and lemon juice. There are many variations which include the addition of cream cheese, walnuts, almonds or eggs.

The Spanish claim that alioli was the original recipe from which mayonnaise was developed in France. According to one story, the Duc de Richelieu, while on a visit to Mahon in Minorca in 1756, so enjoyed the alioli and egg sauce that he took the recipe back to France. The French changed it by excluding the garlic and increasing the lemon juice and the result was called *Mahonaise*.

In France the sauce is called aïoli (i-oh-lee) and is usually served with boiled fish, but it also sometimes accompanies cold meat. A popular Provençal dish is aïoli garni, a combination of boiled cod, octopus, fennel, onions, carrots, French beans, artichokes, baked potatoes, hard-boiled eggs, little snails and chick peas, arranged on a platter and served with aïoli sauce.

Alioli Sauce

GARLIC MAYONNAISE

Alioli (A-lee-o-lee) *is a garlic flavoured sauce which is the traditional accompaniment to boiled and grilled [broiled] meat and fish in Spain.*

4 SERVINGS

4 garlic cloves, peeled
$\frac{1}{2}$ teaspoon salt
2 tablespoons lemon juice
2 egg yolks
10 fl. oz. [1$\frac{1}{4}$ cups] olive oil

Crush the garlic in a garlic press, with a pestle in a mortar or with the flat side of a table knife. In a small mixing bowl

add the salt and lemon juice to the crushed garlic and mix thoroughly.

Using a table fork beat in the egg yolks one at a time until the mixture thickens. Beating constantly, add the oil a few drops at a time. When about a third of the oil has been absorbed by the egg-yolk mixture the oil can be added in a slow stream, still beating continually.

If the mixture becomes too stiff to beat easily add a teaspoon of cold water. The finished mayonnaise should be the consistency of thick cream.

Alivenci
CHEESE AND SOURED CREAM SOUFFLÉ

Adapted from an old Romanian recipe, Alivenci (ah-lee-VEEN-che) *can be served with a salad as an unusual lunch or light supper dish. Sprinkled lightly with icing [confectioner's] sugar and accompanied by a hot fruit sauce it is a delicious dessert.*

4 SERVINGS

$\frac{1}{2}$ oz. [1 tablespoon] butter, softened
3 teaspoons flour
8 oz. [1 cup] cream cheese
6 tablespoons [$\frac{3}{4}$ cup] soured cream
3 egg yolks
6 tablespoons [$\frac{3}{4}$ cup] milk
$\frac{1}{2}$ teaspoon salt
3 egg whites

Preheat the oven to moderate 350°F (Gas Mark 4, 180°C).

Using your fingertips or a piece of paper, spread the softened butter over the bottom and sides of a 7-inch soufflé dish. Sprinkle 1 teaspoon of flour into the soufflé dish and shake it so the flour evenly coats the bottom and sides. Leave aside until ready to use.

With a wooden spoon beat the cream cheese into a deep bowl until it is soft and creamy. Using a wire whisk beat in the soured cream, a spoonful at a time. Continue to beat until the mixture is smooth.

Add the egg yolks one at a time, beating well after each one is added. Mix in the milk, salt and the remaining 2 teaspoons of flour. Beat well until the mixture is smooth.

In a medium-sized bowl, beat the egg whites with a wire whisk until they form soft peaks when you lift the whisk out. Fold the whites into the egg-yolk and soured-cream mixture.

Pour the mixture into the prepared soufflé dish. Bake in the centre of the oven for about 35 minutes or until the top has risen and is light golden brown.

Serve immediately.

Allemande, à l'

A term which is applied to dishes garnished or accompanied by such German specialities as smoked sausage, sauerkraut, potato dumplings or pickled pork. The term also refers to dishes served with ALLEMANDE SAUCE.

Allemande Sauce

This classic, French, white sauce is also known as Sauce Blonde or Sauce Parisienne. One of the richest and smoothest of sauces it is served with poultry, veal and eggs.

1 PINT

1$\frac{1}{2}$ oz. [3 tablespoons] butter
1$\frac{1}{2}$ oz. [3 tablespoons] flour
15 fl. oz. [2 cups] hot, strong chicken or veal stock, free of fat
$\frac{1}{2}$ teaspoon salt
$\frac{1}{8}$ teaspoon white pepper
2 egg yolks
5 fl. oz. [$\frac{5}{8}$ cup] single [light] cream

Melt the butter in a medium-sized saucepan over moderate heat. Add the flour and stir with a wooden spoon to blend. Lower the heat and cook for a minute or two. The mixture must not change colour.

Remove from the heat and add the hot stock a little at a time, stirring briskly. When all the stock has been added return the pan to the heat and, stirring all the time, bring the sauce to the boil. Boil for 1 minute.

Remove from the heat and add salt and pepper. The sauce should be quite smooth with no lumps. If, however, it does have lumps push the sauce through a fine sieve.

In a medium-sized mixing bowl blend the egg yolks and cream with a wooden spoon or wire whisk. Slowly add the hot sauce, whisking all the time. When all the sauce has been added and well blended return it to the saucepan. Place it over low heat and, stirring all the time with a wooden spoon, cook the sauce gently for 1 minute. Do not allow it to boil or it will curdle.

Taste the sauce and add more salt and pepper if necessary.

Remove the pan from the heat and pour the sauce into a warmed sauceboat.

Serve at once.

Alligator Pear

A name used in some areas of the United States for the AVOCADO.

Alivenci is an unusual soufflé made with cream cheese and soured cream.

All

Allspice

This spice comes from a tropical tree that is cultivated in the West Indies and Jamaica and is native to Central America. Sometimes called Jamaica pepper or pimento, the small, sun-dried berries are known as allspice because their taste, as well as their aroma, seem to be a combination of nutmeg, cinnamon and cloves.

Ground allspice is used as a flavouring for cakes, soups, meat dishes and vegetables. Tied in a muslin bag, the allspice berries are often used in the preparation of preserves and pickles.

Allspice Veal Roll

This veal roll is an easily prepared main dish that looks very attractive, particularly if it is garnished with sprigs of watercress or parsley and thin orange slices.

4 SERVINGS

2 lb. breast of veal, boned and trimmed of excess fat
2 oz. [1 cup] fresh white breadcrumbs
1 tablespoon raisins or sultanas
    grated rind of 1 orange
1 tablespoon finely chopped parsley
$\frac{1}{4}$ teaspoon dried sage
$\frac{1}{4}$ teaspoon dried thyme
1 tablespoon finely chopped onion
$\frac{1}{4}$ teaspoon salt
    freshly ground black pepper
$1\frac{1}{2}$ oz. butter [3 tablespoons], cut into pieces
1 tablespoon ground allspice creamed with 1 oz. [2 tablespoons] softened butter
2 oz. [$\frac{1}{4}$ cup] butter, melted
3 tablespoons orange juice

The juice and grated rind of orange flavour this Allspice Veal Roll.

1. Lay the boned breast of veal, fat side down, on your work surface. Spread the prepared breadcrumb mixture evenly over the meat, keeping it away from the edges. Sprinkle on the salt and 4 grindings of pepper.

2. Put the small pieces of butter on the breadcrumb mixture and, pressing down, tightly roll up the veal. Just before the roll is complete, tuck in any of the breadcrumb mixture which has been squeezed out.

3. With white cotton string, tie up the veal roll at 1-inch intervals. To do this, cut the string into short lengths. Make a loop at the end of each piece. Put a length round the meat, thread one end through the loop, pull it tight and knot it. Continue with the remaining string.

Preheat oven to moderate 350°F (Gas Mark 4, 180°C).

Mix together the breadcrumbs, raisins, or sultanas, orange rind, parsley, sage, thyme and the onion.

Put the veal flat on your work surface fat side down. Spread the breadcrumb mixture evenly on the meat. Sprinkle with salt and 4 grindings of pepper. Dot with small pieces of butter. Roll the meat up tightly and tie round with string at 1-inch intervals.

Rub the outer surface of the veal roll with the butter and allspice mixture. Put in a baking dish with melted butter. Pour the orange juice over the meat.

Bake in the centre of the oven, basting occasionally, adding more orange juice if the liquid in the pan reduces too much. Allow 25 minutes to the pound and 25 minutes over.

Put the veal roll on a heated serving plate. Remove the string before serving.

Allumettes

The word *allumettes* (AH-loo-met) literally means matchsticks and is a term used to describe a type of hors d'oeuvre. These are usually strips of pastry stuffed with various fillings, such as a purée of chicken livers, anchovies, sausage meat, breast of chicken with truffles or Parmesan cheese.

Allumettes is also used to describe potatoes which have been cut fine to resemble matchsticks, and then deep fried.

Of Swiss origin is a sweet cake called allumettes which consists of puff pastry cut into strips, spread with a royal icing and baked.

Allumettes

MATCHSTICK POTATOES

Tiny, crisp matchsticks, Allumettes (AH-loo met) *are a variety of French deep-fried potatoes. For the best results you need a deep, heavy pan, a wire frying-basket and a cooking thermometer.*

4 SERVINGS

2 lb. potatoes
    vegetable oil
    salt

Peel the potatoes and trim them into neat rectangles about 2½-inches long. Drop them into a bowl of cold water to prevent them from discolouring.

With a sharp knife, slice the rectangles lengthways into sticks about ⅛-inch wide and ⅛-inch deep. Soak them in a bowl of cold water for 30 minutes.

Drain the water off the potatoes and dry them thoroughly with a tea towel or kitchen paper. Put at least 3 inches of oil in the pan and heat to 350°F (180°C). Place a handful of allumettes into a wire frying-basket and lower into the hot fat. Fry for 3 minutes, shaking the basket occasionally to ensure even cooking. Lift the basket to drain the oil from the potatoes and empty them on to kitchen paper.

When all the potatoes are fried, raise the temperature of the oil to about 375°F (190°C). Place the allumettes in the basket and fry again, shaking the basket frequently, for 1 or 2 minutes, or until the

potatoes are golden brown. Drain on kitchen paper, sprinkle lightly with salt and serve, very hot, in a warm serving dish.

Almejas a la Marinera

CLAMS IN TOMATO AND GARLIC SAUCE

A Spanish dish, Almejas a la Marinera (ahl-MAY-has a la MAR-in-aira) *is clams steamed in white wine and covered with a sauce of tomatoes, onions and garlic. If clams are not available small oysters or cockles can be substituted. This dish may be served as a main course with buttered rice, cooked with a bay leaf, and a salad of lettuce and spring onions [scallions]. For a first course halve the quantities and serve with crusty rolls or French bread.*

4 SERVINGS

1½ lb. tomatoes
2 hard-boiled eggs
3 tablespoons olive oil
1 large onion, chopped
2 cloves garlic, crushed
1½ oz. [¾ cup] fresh, coarse, white
    breadcrumbs
½ teaspoon salt
    coarsely ground black pepper
4 dozen fresh, small clams in shells
15 fl. oz. [2 cups] inexpensive, dry,
    white wine
2 tablespoons finely chopped
    parsley
2 lemons, cut in wedges

Put the tomatoes into a bowl. Cover with boiling water. Leave for two minutes.

Thin, crisp Allumettes are a variety of French, deep-fried potatoes.

Remove the tomatoes from the water with a slotted spoon. When they are cool enough to be handled nick the skin with a knife and peel. Chop into small pieces and set aside.

Separate the egg whites from the yolks. Chop the whites into small pieces. Press the yolks through a strainer or if you have a garlic crusher use it instead to sieve the yolks. Set aside.

Heat the oil in a medium-sized frying-pan. Add the onion and fry for 3 minutes. Lower heat, add the garlic and sauté until the onions are soft and transparent but not brown. Add the breadcrumbs, tomatoes, egg yolks, salt and 6 grindings of pepper. Stir and mash with a wooden spoon until the mixture becomes a smooth, thick purée. Set aside.

Place the clams in a heavy pot. Pour the wine over them and bring to the boil. Cover, reduce the heat and simmer for 10 minutes or until the clams open. Throw away any clams that have remained closed.

Place the clams in a deep, heated serving dish. Strain the liquid from the pan and add to the purée. Taste and adjust seasoning by adding more salt and pepper if necessary. Pour the sauce over the clams. Sprinkle with parsley and the egg whites and serve immediately. The lemon wedges should be served on a separate dish.

Almond

The kernel of the fruit of the almond tree of which there are sweet and bitter varieties. The trees are widely grown in Jordan, Spain, North Africa, France and the United States. Sweet almonds are used in making cakes, biscuits, sweets and in savoury dishes. They are also roasted, salted, sugared and ground.

Bitter almonds contain a small amount of poisonous prussic acid. When this is removed the almond oil can be used as a flavouring agent.

Almonds contain protein, fat and minerals, but no starch. More than half their weight is oil which is extracted and used in perfumery or the manufacture of soothing emulsions.

Blanched Almonds

Blanched almonds are those from which the skins have been removed. Although almonds which have been commercially blanched are readily available, almonds are very easy to blanch yourself.

Put the almonds in a small bowl. Boil water in a kettle and pour the boiling water over the almonds until they are completely covered. Leave for about 3 minutes. Remove the almonds one at a time with a spoon and press between the thumb and forefinger. The skin should slip off easily. Dry the almonds on a cloth.

If the blanched almonds are not to be used immediately, put them on a rack in a very cool oven, 225°F (Gas Mark ¼, 110°C), for 2 hours to dry. Store the nuts in an airtight container.

Chopped Almonds

Blanch the almonds. Using a sharp knife, chop the almonds into pieces before they are dry. The fineness of the pieces depends on the recipe for which they are required.

Devilled Almonds

Blanch the almonds. Heat a very little butter in a small frying-pan. Add the almonds and toss them in the butter. Dust liberally with salt and a pinch of cayenne pepper. Sprinkle lightly with paprika. Serve with cocktails.

Flaked Almonds

Flaked almonds are mainly used for decorating puddings and cakes. They are available in shops already flaked, but are more tasty done at home immediately before using.

With a sharp knife slit the blanched almonds flatways along the grain so that you make a flat, broad flake. Each almond should make a minimum of four flakes.

Ground Almonds

Used in the making of pastries, biscuits and desserts, commercially ground almonds are widely available. They are, however, easily prepared at home and you will find that they taste better.

Blanch the almonds. Mix them with a few drops of water and a little castor sugar and put them through a fine mincer. They can also be pounded in a mortar with a little castor sugar. If you have a liquidizer, put 4 ounces at a time in the machine and grind at top speed.

Ground almonds should be stored in an airtight container, but if they are not used as soon as possible after grinding they will quickly lose their flavour.

Roasted Almonds

Salted and served as an accompaniment to cocktails or an unsalted, crunchy addition to salads and other dishes, roasted almonds are easy to make at home.

Spread whole, blanched almonds in one layer on a baking tin. Place in a pre-heated, moderate oven 350°F (Gas Mark 4, 180°C), for 10 to 15 minutes. Shake the tin or stir the almonds frequently. Watch carefully to see that they do not burn. Remove from the oven when the almonds are an even, golden brown.

Salted Almonds

An excellent accompaniment to cocktails, salted almonds are widely available in jars and cans, but they are easy to make at home.

4 oz. [½ cup] butter
4 tablespoons [¼ cup] cooking oil
8 oz. [1⅓ cup] whole almonds, blanched
salt

Melt the butter with the oil in a large frying-pan. Put in the almonds and sauté them over a moderate heat, turning them frequently with a slotted spoon. When the almonds are golden brown, remove them with the spoon and spread them out on kitchen paper towels. Sprinkle them with salt while they are still warm, making sure they are well coated.

Salted almonds can be stored in an airtight container for several weeks.

Shredded or Slivered Almonds

Shredded or slivered almonds are used frequently in pastry making and also in confectionery. Blanch the almonds and while they are still damp cut them lengthways into about 15 pieces. If the recipe requires roasted slivers, brown the almonds in the oven after they have been shredded.

Sugared Almonds

Almonds with a sugar or honey coating have been known from earliest times and were recorded as having been served in Ancient Rome at family celebrations. Home-made sugared almonds may not look as beautiful as the commercially made variety, but they surpass them in flavour and texture. They can be stored, for about a week, in an airtight jar.

1 lb. [2 cups] granulated sugar
4 fl. oz. [½ cup] water
1 teaspoon cinnamon
1 lb. [2⅔ cups] unbleached almonds

In a saucepan over low heat dissolve the sugar in the water stirring constantly.

Add the cinnamon, stir, raise the heat and briskly boil the syrup until it falls from the spoon in thick drops. Add the almonds and stir until they are well coated.

Remove the pan from the heat and continue stirring until the syrup dries into sugar.

Put the almonds in a sieve and shake to dislodge the excess sugar. Put the excess sugar back in the pan, add a little water and dissolve again over a low heat. Raise heat and boil until the syrup clears. Add the almonds, stir again until the almonds are coated. Leave to cool and dry.

Almonds

Ground ▶
Chopped ▶
Roasted ▶
Flaked ▶
Sugared ▶
Shelled ▶
Blanched ▶
Unshelled ▶

Almond Apples

This is an inexpensive and attractive dessert. The apples should be very tart for the best results.

4 SERVINGS

8 oz. [1 cup] granulated sugar
12 fl. oz. [1½ cups] water
4 large, well-shaped, cooking apples, peeled and cored
¼ teaspoon powdered cloves
½ teaspoon powdered cinnamon
½ oz. [1 tablespoon] butter
2 oz. [⅓ cup] almonds, blanched and slivered

In a medium-sized saucepan, over low heat, dissolve the sugar in the water. When the sugar is completely dissolved raise the heat to high and boil the syrup for 5 minutes. Add the apples, lower the heat and simmer covered until the apples are tender.

Preheat the oven to moderate 350°F (Gas Mark 4, 180°C). Remove the apples from the saucepan, place them in an ovenproof dish and set aside. Blend the cloves, cinnamon and butter into the syrup in the saucepan and return it to the heat. Boil the syrup rapidly until it becomes thick.

Pour the syrup into the centres of the apples. Spike the apples all round with the slivered almonds. Bake in the oven for about 15 minutes or until the almonds become brown. Serve very cold with cream.

Almond and Black Cherry Aspic Salad

In the United States sweet aspic salads are often served as an accompaniment to meat and poultry, in the place of the more con-

Almond and Black Cherry Aspic Salad is served with meat or poultry.

ventional green or mixed salad. This aspic salad could be served with roast chicken or a roast leg of lamb.

6 SERVINGS

1 tablespoon powdered gelatine
4 fl. oz. [½ cup] cold water
8 fl. oz. [1 cup] orange juice
4 tablespoons sugar
⅛ teaspoon salt
2 fl. oz. [¼ cup] lemon juice
10 oz. [1¼ cups] stoned black cherries, fresh or canned and drained
3 oz. [½ cup] blanched almonds
lettuce

Low Cal

Soak the gelatine in the cold water. Bring the orange juice to the boil. Dissolve the gelatine in it. Add the sugar, salt and lemon juice. Allow to cool to room temperature.

When the mixture begins to set add the cherries and almonds and mix gently. Pour the aspic into a 1½-pint [3¾ cups], wet mould. Chill in the refrigerator until it is firm.

Before serving, dip the mould quickly into a pan of hot water. Unmould the salad on a bed of lettuce leaves.

Almond Cherry Cake

A moist cake which is simple to make, it keeps well and retains its freshness for at least 10 days if it is stored in a tightly-covered cake tin. With this cake, as with all cherry cakes, there is always the problem that the cherries tend to sink to the bottom of the cake. Some cooks recommend rolling the cherries lightly in flour before adding them to the cake batter. This method,

however, is not always effective. But whether the cherries are well-distributed or sink to the bottom, this cake is delicious.

4 oz. [½ cup] plus 1 teaspoon softened butter
5 oz. [¾ cup] castor sugar
3 large eggs
3½ oz. [⅔ cup] almonds, blanched and ground
1½ oz. plus 2 teaspoons [½ cup] self-raising flour
4 oz. [½ cup] glacé cherries, cut in half
1 teaspoon vanilla essence

Preheat oven to moderate 350°F (Gas Mark 4, 180°C).

Evenly smear 1 teaspoon of butter on the bottom and the sides of a 6¾ × 3¼-inch round cake tin. Sprinkle with 2 teaspoons of flour. Shake the cake tin from side to side to coat the inside surface with a fine film of flour. Tip out excess flour.

In a medium-sized mixing bowl, beat the butter with a wooden spoon until it is very creamy. Add the sugar and beat well until the mixture is light and creamy. Beating continuously, add the eggs one at a time alternating with spoonfuls of ground almonds.

Fold in the flour, cherries and vanilla essence. Turn into the prepared cake tin, gently tapping the tin on the table so that the mixture settles evenly. Bake in the oven for 50 minutes or until a warm, dry skewer comes out clean when inserted in the centre of the cake.

Almond Chicken

An excellent dish for lunch or dinner parties. Almond Chicken can be prepared in advance, reheated in the oven and put under the grill [broiler] just before serving. Serve with buttered broccoli, a tomato salad, crusty rolls and cold, white wine.

4 SERVINGS

1½ oz. [3 tablespoons] butter, plus 1 tablespoon cooking oil
2 chickens each about 2 lb., cut into 6 pieces each
1 small onion, chopped
1 clove garlic, crushed
2 tablespoons flour
12 fl. oz. [1½ cups] chicken stock or a chicken stock cube dissolved in 12 fl. oz. [1½ cups] boiling water
2 tablespoons sherry
2 oz. [⅓ cup] almonds, blanched and shredded
½ teaspoon salt
freshly ground black pepper
1 teaspoon dried tarragon
4 tablespoons [¼ cup heavy] double cream
1 tablespoon Parmesan cheese, grated

In a large, heavy frying-pan heat the butter and oil until the butter is melted and the mixture is hot but not burning. Put in the chicken pieces a few at a time and brown all over. Remove with a slotted spoon or kitchen tongs and set aside on a plate.

Add the onion and garlic to the pan and sauté for 5 minutes, stirring constantly with a wooden spoon. Sprinkle the flour on the onion mixture and stir well. Add the chicken stock and sherry a little at a time stirring constantly until the sauce is smooth. Raise the heat and bring the mixture to the boil. Add the almonds, salt, 4 grindings of pepper and the tarragon. Return the chicken pieces to the pan and cover. Lower the heat and simmer very gently for 35 to 40 minutes, or until the chicken is tender when pierced with a table fork.

Remove the chicken pieces and arrange in a heated, shallow, fireproof serving dish. Stir the cream into the sauce and heat but do not boil. Pour the sauce over the chicken pieces and sprinkle with grated Parmesan cheese.

Place the dish under the grill [broiler] and brown at high heat, but be careful not to let the cheese burn.

If the dish has been prepared in advance, reheat by covering the serving dish tightly with aluminium foil and placing in a warm oven, 325°F (Gas Mark 3, 170°C) for 45 minutes. Remove and place under the grill and brown.

Almond Cookies

This American cookie recipe is unusual in that no flour is used. Crisp on the outside but chewy inside these cookies are very easy to make.

24 COOKIES

8 oz. [2 cups] almonds, blanched and ground
8 oz. [1⅓ cups] soft brown sugar
1 large egg white
1½ teaspoons butter, melted
cornflour [cornstarch]

Preheat the oven to warm 325°F (Gas Mark 3, 170°C). Prepare a baking sheet by lining it with non-stick silicone paper.

Combine all the ingredients, except the cornflour, in a large mixing bowl and stir until blended. With your hands, mix the ingredients together to form a smooth paste. Shape first into small balls, then flatten into circles. If the mixture is too sticky to handle, first dip your fingers into cornflour and then shape the balls.

Place the circles on the baking sheet and bake for 20 to 25 minutes, or until the cookies are golden brown. Cool the cookies on the baking sheet.

Almond Crunchies

  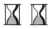

These crunchy biscuits are easy to make and can be served with ice cream, fruit desserts, and with tea.

ABOUT 50 SMALL BISCUITS

6 oz. [¾ cup] sugar
8 oz. [1 cup] softened butter
1 egg yolk
8 oz. [2 cups] flour, sifted
8 oz. [1⅓ cup] almonds, blanched and chopped
¼ teaspoon almond essence

Preheat the oven to moderate 350°F (Gas Mark 4, 180°C).

Line baking sheets with greaseproof paper. In a medium-sized mixing bowl, beat the sugar and butter with a wooden spoon until they are light and creamy. Beat in the egg yolk. Mix in the flour, chopped almonds and almond essence.

Put flour on your hands and pat the dough into a ball. Cover it and chill in the refrigerator for one hour.

Shape the chilled dough into small balls and flatten into rounds. Place on baking sheets and bake for 15 to 20 minutes.

Almond Cherry Cake, which is made with a large proportion of ground almonds and little flour, will keep moist for several days.

Almond and Cucumber Salad Dressing

This is an unusual and delicate dressing for a salad which includes fruit or even for a plain lettuce salad. This recipe makes about 16 fluid ounces [2 cups] of dressing, enough for a salad which serves 8 people. It will keep for several days in the refrigerator in a tightly covered container.

16 FLUID OUNCES

2 egg yolks
2 teaspoons sugar
1 tablespoon melted butter
5 fl. oz. [⅝ cup] milk
2 fl. oz. [¼ cup] vinegar
2 teaspoons salt
  a few grains cayenne pepper
1 teaspoon dry mustard
2 teaspoons cornflour [cornstarch]
2 egg whites
4 oz. [½ cup] cucumber, peeled and sliced
2 oz. [⅓ cup] almonds, blanched and shredded

In the top of a double boiler, or in a bowl over hot water, beat together the egg yolks, sugar, melted butter, 3½ fluid ounces [½ cup] of the milk, vinegar, salt, cayenne and dry mustard. Dissolve the cornflour in 1½ fluid ounces [3 table-spoons] of milk and add it to the other ingredients.

Cook and stir the dressing over boiling water until it is thick. Remove from the heat and set aside. In a mixing bowl beat the egg whites until they form stiff peaks when the whisk is raised. When the dressing is at room temperature fold it into the egg whites. Add the cucumber and almonds and mix lightly. Chill in the refrigerator until ready to serve.

Almond Curry Sauce

A spicy sauce to serve with pot-roasted chicken and browned rice. The recipe calls for a green chilli, but if you are not accustomed to eating pungent food remove the seeds before mincing the chilli. Garam

masala is a prepared, ground spice mixture of cinnamon, cardamom, cloves, cumin seeds, coriander seeds and black pepper. All the ingredients in this recipe are widely available at grocery stores or at Indian, Bangladeshi or Pakistani grocers.

4 SERVINGS

2 tablespoons cooking oil
2 medium-sized onions, minced
¾-inch piece of fresh ginger, peeled and minced or grated
1 green chilli [chili], minced
1 oz. [¼ cup] almonds, blanched and ground
2 teaspoons ground turmeric
1 teaspoon ground coriander
1 teaspoon garam masala
1 x 8 oz. can, Italian tomatoes, sieved
1 oz. [2 tablespoons] creamed coconut
  juice of ½ lemon
1 teaspoon sugar
½ teaspoon salt

Heat the oil in a medium-sized saucepan, add the onions and stir well. Lower the heat to moderate and fry for 8 minutes or until the onions are golden. Add the

22

Left: Almondine Sauce is a classic almond and butter sauce for fish.
Centre left: Almond Custard Sauce is served with puddings, pies and fruit.
Above: This Almond and Cucumber Salad Dressing is rich and unusual.
Right: Almond Curry Sauce is served with pot-roasted chicken and rice.

ginger and chilli and fry for another minute. Add the almonds, turmeric, coriander and garam masala. Fry for 7 minutes, stirring continuously. If the mixture gets too dry or sticks to the bottom of the pan add a spoonful or two of water.

Add the sieved tomatoes and creamed coconut. Stir until the coconut has dissolved. Add lemon juice, sugar and salt. Stir, raise the heat and bring to the boil. As soon as the sauce is bubbling reduce the heat as low as possible, cover and simmer for 30 minutes. If the sauce is too thick add a little water. Taste and add more salt, sugar or lemon juice if necessary. Serve hot in a separate bowl.

Almond Custard Sauce

The addition of almonds and brandy to a boiled custard makes a delicious sauce for sponge puddings, pies and stewed fruit.

4 SERVINGS

2 egg yolks
1 tablespoon castor sugar
a pinch of salt
10 fl. oz. [1¼ cups] milk
1 oz. [¼ cup] almonds, blanched and ground
2 teaspoons brandy or 1 teaspoon vanilla essence

In a mixing bowl beat the egg yolks lightly. Beat in the sugar and salt. Put the milk into a saucepan and bring slowly to the boil. Remove from the heat, wait for the milk to go off the boil and pour on to the eggs slowly, stirring all the time.

Return the custard to the pan and cook over a low heat or, preferably, over simmering water until it begins to thicken. Do not let it boil. Stir in the almonds.

Strain the custard. Add the brandy a few drops at a time. Serve warm.

Almond Essence

This flavouring comes from bitter almonds after the oil has been extracted. Today, however, the almond essence used to flavour cakes, puddings and biscuits is generally synthetic.

Almondine Sauce

Simple to make and with a delicate flavour, this classic almond sauce for fish transforms grilled [broiled] or poached fish into a special dish.

4 SERVINGS

2 oz. [¼ cup] unsalted butter
3 oz. [½ cup] almonds, blanched and shredded
½ teaspoon salt

Melt the butter in a small saucepan or frying-pan. Add the almonds and sauté, stirring continuously, until they just begin to brown. Add the salt. Pour over the hot, cooked fish and serve immediately.

Alouettes sans Têtes
STUFFED BEEF ROLLS

An interesting and unusual way to serve inexpensive steak, Alouettes sans Têtes (AH-loo-wet sawn tet) makes a good dish for a dinner party. It can be prepared early in the day and warmed in a low oven before serving. Good accompaniments are creamed or sautéed potatoes and a purée of fresh French beans.

4 SERVINGS

- 8 slices of lean beef, each about 5-inches square and ¼-inch thick
- 2 tablespoons cooking oil
- 2 onions, diced
- 2 carrots, diced
- 10 fl. oz. [1¼ cups] beef stock, fresh or made with a stock cube
- ½ lb. tomatoes, peeled, seeded and sliced
- 1 clove garlic, crushed
- 1 bay leaf
- 2 tablespoons chopped parsley

STUFFING
- 6 oz. [¾ cup ground] minced pork or veal
- 1 small onion, finely chopped
- 1 oz. [2 tablespoons] butter softened
- 1 oz. [½ cup] fresh, white breadcrumbs
- 1 tablespoon finely chopped parsley
- 1 teaspoon rubbed sage
- grated rind of 1 lemon
- 1 egg, lightly beaten
- 6 green olives, stoned and coarsely chopped
- ½ teaspoon salt
- black pepper, freshly ground

Preheat the oven to moderate 350°F (Gas Mark 4, 180°C).

To prepare the stuffing, mix the minced pork or veal, the onion, butter, breadcrumbs, parsley, sage, lemon rind and olives together in a bowl. Stir in the egg. Season with the salt and 3 grindings of black pepper. Spread an eighth of stuffing on each piece of steak, roll up carefully and tie with fine thread.

To braise the beef rolls, heat the oil in a large saucepan and brown them a few at a time. Remove them with a slotted spoon and keep them warm.

Add the onions and carrots and, stirring occasionally, cook until brown. Add the stock, tomatoes, garlic and the bay leaf and bring to the boil.

Pour the contents of the saucepan into a casserole dish. Place the beef rolls on top. Cover with a well-fitting lid and cook in the oven for 1½ hours.

Remove the beef rolls from the casserole with a slotted spoon. Carefully unwind the thread and place the rolls on a serving dish and keep hot. Holding a sieve over a small saucepan, press the stock and vegetables from the casserole through the sieve with the back of a wooden spoon.

Taste the gravy, add salt and pepper if necessary. Pour over the beef rolls. Sprinkle with chopped parsley just before serving.

Alouettes sans Têtes is a traditional French dish of stuffed beef rolls in a seasoned tomato sauce.

Alsacienne, à l'

A great number of preparations are called *à l'alsacienne* (ah-lahl-SAH-see-en). The predominant ingredients in these dishes are sauerkraut, ham and Strasbourg sausage. Certain dishes which are based on *foie gras* are also described by this name.

Alsatian Wines

Alsace, a northeastern province of France, bordering on Germany, is one of the principal wine-producing regions of the country. Alsatian wines are distinguishable by their fruity flavour and fine bouquet. As such, they differ greatly from those of the rest of France, being far closer to wines of German origin.

Among the best-known wines of the Alsace regions are the Riesling, a fresh white wine with a particularly fragrant bouquet; Sylvaner, a lighter wine than the Riesling with a less sweet fragrance; Gewurztraminer, a dry white wine with a German name and a spicy taste; Muscat, with its characteristic muskiness; Traminer, smooth, fragrant and white, with a sweet flavour; Gentil, white, but remarkably like a rich, red Burgundy in taste.

Aluminium Foil

A wide variety of foods cooked in aluminium foil retain more flavour and food value and remain more moist than when cooked in other ways. Aluminium foil keeps ovens, meat tins and grill [broiler] pans cleaner. It can also be used to shape and mould cake tins and other utensils and to replace lost or broken pan and casserole lids.

When food is cooked in foil, it should always be wrapped loosely to enclose as much air as possible. The enclosed air, when heated, helps to cook the food. Consequently, such foods as vegetables, fish, chops and chicken portions should be wrapped in a large sheet of foil and the edges sealed with double folds or by gathering the edges together to make a bag shape.

For roasting, the foil should not be sealed because a constant supply of the oxygen in the air is needed to brown the meat. To prepare the food for roasting, tear off a piece of foil about three times the length of the meat or poultry. Place the meat in the centre of the foil, lift the two long edges up at right angles, bring the other ends over the top and press firmly together to prevent the parcel from opening during cooking. The foil will contain the fat and juices and prevent the oven from being splashed. It will also allow the meat to brown. If the meat is not as brown or crisp as desired at the end of cooking, open the foil, pour off the fat and juices and return the meat in the open foil to the oven for 10 to 15 minutes.

Individual portions of chicken, chops and steaks are prepared by frying the meat until browned and then wrapping them in a loose foil parcel with sealed edges. Herbs, chopped vegetables and sauces can be added to give extra flavour. Cook at 350°F (Gas Mark 4, 180°C) for 45 minutes to 1½ hours according to thickness.

Vegetables wrapped in loose foil parcels can be cooked in the oven with the meat, or boiled. Add seasonings,

Roasting in Aluminium Foil			
Times given can only be an approximate guide because the shape of the roast and the proportion of bone affects the required cooking time.		Minutes per lb. At 400°F Gas Mark 6, 200°C	Minutes per lb. At 325°F Gas Mark 3, 170°C
Boneless beef:	Rare	20	27
	Medium	25	33
	Well-done	30	40
Beef with bone		Allow 5 minutes less per lb.	
Mutton and lamb		25	33
Pork, veal and stuffed meat		30	40
Gammon and ham		25 to 30	33 to 40
Chicken		15 to 20	20 to 27
Turkey		12 to 15	16 to 20
		At 375°F Gas Mark 5, 190°C	
Fillets and steaks of fish		20 to 30 minutes	according to
Whole fish		30 to 40 minutes	thickness

butter and, if baked, 1 to 2 tablespoons stock or water. If the vegetables are sliced or cut into small pieces, they will cook more quickly than if they are left whole. Allow 1½ to 2 times the normal boiling time.

Ambrosia
ORANGE DESSERT

A favourite dessert in the Southern States of America, in its simplest form Ambrosia consists of thinly sliced oranges sprinkled with shredded coconut and sugar. The

A favourite dessert in the Southern States of America, Ambrosia is made of oranges, pineapple and coconut.

following recipe includes pineapple, but other fruits can be substituted.

4 SERVINGS

3 large oranges
1 small pineapple
1 oz. [⅛ cup superfine] castor sugar
3 oz. [⅜ cup] fresh coconut, coarsely grated, or coarse, desiccated coconut soaked in 4 fl. oz. [½ cup] of water for 30 minutes and then drained

Peel the oranges, carefully removing all the white pith, and cut into thin slices. Peel, slice and core the pineapple and cut each slice into 8 pieces. Combine the sugar and coconut.

In a serving bowl or individual glasses, arrange the orange slices in alternate layers with the pineapple. Sprinkle each layer with a little of the coconut and sugar mixture, keeping enough aside to sprinkle on the top. Chill in the refrigerator for at least 2 hours before serving.

Américaine, à l'

À l'Américaine (ah-lah-MAY-ree-cane) is the name given to various methods of preparing meat, fish, eggs and vegetables. The most famous of these preparations is HOMARD À L'AMÉRICAINE. According to the renowned nineteenth-century chef, Escoffier, this dish originated in Le Restaurant Français in Nice. Made from crayfish and prepared with tomatoes and white wine, it was originally called Langouste de la Méditerranée. Its present name was given it by a Provençal chef who emigrated to the United States in the nineteenth century. Using lobsters instead of crayfish, he first served Homard à l'Américaine in New York in 1860. Since then it has been famous and the classic recipe is given in Escoffier's book, *Ma Cuisine.*

American Apple Pie

Traditional American Apple Pie differs from other apple pies in several ways. First, the pastry is made with a greater proportion of fat to flour than are other pie crusts. In the filling, the apples are cut in rather thick slices. The filling is spiced with cinnamon, allspice and nutmeg and thickened with cornflour [cornstarch]. In the United States, apple pie is frequently served warm with a dollop of vanilla ice cream atop each wedge.

6 TO 8 SERVINGS

PASTRY
12 oz. [3 cups] flour
¼ teaspoon salt
6 oz. [¾ cup] white vegetable fat [shortening]
5-6 tablespoons ice water
1 tablespoon milk or thin cream for glazing
castor [superfine] sugar for dusting

FILLING
2¼ lb. large tart cooking apples
1 tablespoon lemon juice
6 oz. [¾ cup] sugar
1 oz. [2 tablespoons] cornflour [cornstrach]
1 teaspoon finely grated lemon rind
1 teaspoon ground cinnamon
½ teaspoon ground allspice
½ teaspoon freshly grated nutmeg
1 oz. [2 tablespoons] butter, in small pieces plus extra

For the pastry, sift the flour and salt into a large bowl. Cut the fat into the flour until the mixture resembles coarse breadcrumbs. Sprinkle with water, 1 tablespoon at a time, tossing lightly with a fork until the mixture begins to cling together and forms a soft dough.

Gather the mixture into a ball with your fingers. Divide into 2 pieces, making 1 piece larger than the other. Wrap separately in cling film and chill in the refrigerator.

Preheat the oven to 425°F (Gas Mark 7, 220°C).

For the filling, peel, quarter, core and thickly slice the apples, then sprinkle with lemon juice to prevent discoloration.

A traditional American Apple Pie has a double crust and spiced filling.

For the American Apple Pie, line the dish with half the pastry and trim off the excess with a knife.

Put the apple filling in the lined dish and, lifting the pastry on the rolling pin, lay it over the top.

Trim the pastry to within ¼-inch of the dish. Tuck the overhanging pastry under the edge of the bottom crust.

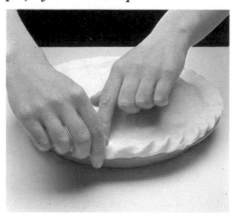

Press the two edges of the pastry together to seal them and to make a crimped pattern on the crust.

Mix the sugar with the cornflour [cornstarch], lemon rind and spice; sprinkle over the apples and toss.

Roll out the larger piece of pastry 1½ inches larger all round than the top of a 2¼-pint pie dish. Lift the pastry on a rolling pin and unroll over the dish. Press gently in place with your fingers.

Spoon the apples into the dish, mounding them. Dot with butter. Brush the pastry edge lightly with water.

Roll out the remaining pastry ½ inch larger all round than the top of the dish. Lift the pastry on the rolling pin and unroll over the filling. Trim the pastry to within ½ inch of the dish. Tuck the overhang under to build up the edge, pressing the edge and crimp.

Brush the top crust with milk or cream and sprinkle with castor sugar. Cut 3 or 4 small slits in the top or prick in several places with a fork, to make small vents, to allow the steam to escape during cooking.

To prevent overbrowning, cover the pastry edges with foil before baking.

These cocktail snacks, Amuse-Gueules au Fromage, are made with blue cheese.

Remove the foil for the last 10-15 minutes.

Place the dish on a baking sheet and bake for 15 minutes. Lower the heat to 375°F (Gas Mark 5, 190°C) and bake for 30-35 minutes more, until the pastry is crisp. This pie can be served warm or cold.

If you intend to freeze it, set aside to cool completely then freeze in a rigid container for up to 8 months. Defrost for 30 minutes then reheat at 350°F (Gas Mark 4, 180°C).

Amuse-Gueules au Fromage
CHEESE COCKTAIL SNACKS

Amuse-Gueules au Fromage (AH-moozgerl oh froh-MAJ) *are good cold hors d'oeuvre to serve with pre-dinner drinks or at a cocktail party. They are best served on cocktail sticks. Very simple and quick to make, the cheese balls look elegant and can be prepared well before the time you will need them. Although traditionally prepared with Roquefort cheese they can more economically be made with any blue cheese.*

3 oz. [⅜ cup] butter, softened
½ lb. Roquefort or other blue cheese
1 tablespoon finely chopped onion
1 tablespoon finely chopped celery
¼ teaspoon freshly ground black pepper
½ teaspoon Worcestershire sauce
1 teaspoon brandy
2 tablespoons chopped parsley
½ teaspoon paprika
5 tablespoons fine white breadcrumbs

Place the butter in a mixing bowl. Cut the cheese into pieces and add to the butter. Using a wooden spoon, cream the butter and cheese until they are blended. Beat in the onion, celery, black pepper, Worcestershire sauce and brandy.

If the mixture is very firm, beat in more butter, a little at a time. Divide into small pieces and roll into small balls.

Mix the parsley, paprika and breadcrumbs together in a bowl.

Dip the cheese balls into the breadcrumb mixture and press them gently so the cheese balls are well coated.

Arrange on a serving dish and put into the refrigerator for at least 45 minutes.

Anchovy

A small member of the same family as the herring, which it resembles in colour and shape, the anchovy is usually not more than 3 inches long. The fresh anchovy has a very delicate flavour but, as the flesh quickly deteriorates, it is eaten fresh only on the Mediterranean coasts and the Atlantic coasts of Portugal and Spain where it is caught.

Anchovies are preserved in salt and this develops their special flavour and colour. They are widely available canned or bottled in oil, or preserved in brine. Because of their very strong, distinctive flavour, preserved anchovies are used only in small quantities as an ingredient of sauces for cold meat and poultry, and for flavouring meat and fish dishes. Fillets of anchovies are often included in French hors d'oeuvre and Italian antipasto, and are a garnish for many dishes.

Dry, salted anchovies should be soaked in cold water for several hours before use to remove some of the salt. The skins can be removed by rubbing on a cloth or by gentle scraping with a knife. The tails should be cut off and the bone removed after splitting the fish open with the index finger and thumb.

Salted anchovies will keep well if they are covered by the brine. Those preserved in oil will also keep well, after the can or bottle is opened, if they are covered by oil.

Anchovy Butter

This quickly prepared savoury spread may be used for hors d'oeuvre, canapes, or as an unusual topping for grilled fish.

4 OUNCES

4 oz. [½ cup] butter
8 anchovy fillets, finely chopped
2 teaspoons lemon juice
2 teaspoons chopped parsley

Cream the butter until it is soft. Add the anchovy fillets and, with a wooden spoon, beat until smooth. Mix in the lemon juice and chopped parsley. Chill.

Anchovy Essence

Commercially made for flavouring sauces and stuffings, anchovy essence is a mixture of anchovies, cayenne pepper, capers and various herbs.

Anchovy fillets, which have a strong distinctive flavour, are used as a garnish and are the main ingredient of many savoury dishes.

Anchovy Rolls

These small savoury rolls can be served as canapés at cocktail parties or as an accompaniment to drinks before a dinner party.

thinly sliced, 1-day-old, white
bread
butter for spreading
prepared mustard
salt and pepper
hard cheese, grated
anchovy fillets
melted butter

Preheat oven to hot 425°F (Gas Mark 7, 220°C).

Remove the crusts from the bread. Spread each slice with butter and mustard. Sprinkle with salt, pepper and cheese. Put an anchovy fillet on each slice and roll up, securing with a wooden cocktail stick.

Prepare as many rolls as you require. Place them on a baking sheet, brush with melted butter and bake in the oven until the rolls are golden brown, about 7 to 8 minutes.

Cut each roll in half, so that they are easy to handle. Serve immediately.

Anchoyade
ANCHOVY HORS D'OEUVRE

In Provence, from where this recipe comes, Anchoyade (on-show-yahd), is served with a glass of wine or with drinks. There are many variations of Anchoyade. Minced, raw onion and chopped, hard-boiled egg can be sprinkled on the top. A few drops of

brandy can be added to the paste, and after spreading the toast, it can be browned in the oven. This is a simple recipe.

4 SERVINGS

2 oz. canned anchovies
1 clove garlic
1 tablespoon olive oil
½ teaspoon vinegar
  several grindings of black pepper
4 slices brown bread

Put the anchovies and garlic in a mortar and, with a pestle, pound to a coarse paste. Add the olive oil, vinegar and pepper and mix well. Meanwhile, toast the bread on one side only. Cut each slice into 4 pieces. Spread the anchovy paste on to the un-toasted side. Serve with drinks.

Anchoyade à la Niçoise

Another variation of Anchoyade, Anchoyade à la Niçoise (on-show-yahd ah lah nee-SWAHZ) may be made with fried bread instead of toast.

2 SERVINGS

2 oz. canned anchovies
1 tablespoon plus one teaspoon
  olive oil
½ teaspoon vinegar
  black pepper
8 shallots, or small onions, chopped
5 sprigs parsley, chopped
4 slices brown bread, toasted
  on one side only
2 tomatoes, sliced
2 tablespoons breadcrumbs
1 clove garlic, crushed

Pound the anchovies in a mortar to a paste. Add 1 tablespoon of oil, vinegar and pepper and mix well. Add the shallots and parsley, less 1 teaspoon, and spread on the toast. Place the sliced tomatoes on top. Mix the breadcrumbs, crushed garlic, 1 teaspoon of parsley and 1 tea-spoon of olive oil together and sprinkle on top. Brown under a hot grill for a few minutes.

Ancienne, à l'

A l'Ancienne (ah l'on-SEE-en) literally means 'in the old style'. It is usually applied to preparations with a mixed garnish. It is most commonly used to describe braised dishes, ragoûts in pastry shells and for some veal and chicken BLANQUETTES *and* FRICASSEES.

Andalouse, à l'

A l'Andalouse (ah l'ON-dah-looze) is the name given to preparations which are characterized mainly by tomatoes, sweet pimientoes, rice and, sometimes, small sausages.

Andalousian Beefsteaks

This Spanish recipe for minced steak is enlivened by the addition of sherry to the gravy. Served with a simple pilaff and sautéed tomatoes, it is a delicious variation of the inexpensive and ordinary hamburger.

Andalousian Beefsteaks are a variation of the inexpensive hamburger.

4 SERVINGS

PILAFF
8 oz. [1 cup] long-grain rice
19 fl. oz. [2⅜ cups] water
2 bay leaves
1 teaspoon salt
1 onion, chopped
2 tablespoons butter
4 cloves
STEAKS
2 oz. [¼ cup] butter
1½ lb. minced [ground] steak
1 medium-sized onion, chopped
1 small clove garlic, crushed
1 teaspoon salt
  freshly ground pepper
4 tablespoons flour
3 tablespoons cooking oil
4 tomatoes, cut in halves
3 fl. oz. [⅜ cup] sherry

Wash and soak the rice in cold water for 30 minutes. Drain the rice and put in a medium-sized saucepan with the water, the bay leaves and salt. Bring it to the boil over high heat. When the water is boiling vigorously, cover the pan and turn the heat to very low. After 10 minutes, the rice should be cooked and the water completely absorbed. If the rice is still damp, leave covered for another 5 minutes.

In a small frying-pan over moderate heat, sauté the onion and cloves in the butter until the onion is soft. Discard the cloves and mix the onion into the boiled rice. Set aside and keep hot.

To prepare the steaks, melt half the butter in a small frying-pan over moderate heat and lightly fry the onion and garlic. Put the minced beef in a mixing bowl. Add the cooked onion and garlic, salt and 7 grindings of pepper. Mix well, using your hands, and shape into 8 flat, round patties. Dip each patty into the flour and fry in oil in a large frying-pan. While the meat is cooking, melt remaining butter in a small frying-pan and sauté the tomato halves.

When the steaks are cooked, about 15 minutes, pile the pilaff in the centre of a serving dish and place the patties around it. Place a half tomato on each steak. Raise the heat under the large frying-pan and add the sherry to the meat juices. Boil quickly for 2 minutes. Pour over the steaks and serve.

Andalousian Chicken

Chicken stuffed with ham and rice and colourfully garnished, this adaptation of a Spanish dish is inexpensive and impressive, but it does take time to prepare.

4 SERVINGS

1 chicken, about 4 lb.
2 oz. [¼ cup] butter
1 tablespoon olive oil
1 large onion
1 bouquet garni (consisting of 3
    sprigs of parsley, 1 small bay leaf
    and 1 spray of thyme tied together)
    or ½ teaspoon dried bouquet garni
1 teaspoon salt
    freshly ground pepper
1 scant tablespoon flour
2 tablespoons tomato purée
4 fl. oz. [½ cup] white wine
STUFFING
4 oz. [2 cups] cooked rice
4 oz. [½ cup] cooked ham, diced
2 teaspoons paprika
1 teaspoon salt
GARNISH
2 tablespoons oil
1 large onion, sliced in rings
2 large sweet peppers, sliced in
    rings, seeded and with the white
    pith removed

Stuffed with ham and rice, Andalousian Chicken is a delicious and attractive way to serve pot-roasted chicken.

---

1 lb. tomatoes, peeled and chopped
1 teaspoon salt
    freshly ground pepper

Wash the chicken inside and out and dry it using kitchen paper towels. Mix the rice, ham, paprika and salt together and stuff the chicken with the mixture. Pin the neck flap neatly over the back with a small skewer.

Heat the butter and oil in a heavy stewing pan. Lightly brown the chicken on all sides. Add the onion and the bouquet garni. Lower the heat, cover and cook for about 1 hour, or until the chicken is tender.

While the chicken is cooking, make the garnish. Heat the oil in a frying-pan over moderate heat. Sauté the onions for 2 to 3 minutes. Add the peppers, tomatoes,

salt and 5 grindings of pepper and cook gently until the vegetables are soft. Set aside and keep hot.

Remove the chicken from the pan. Place on a heated serving dish. Remove the skewer. Surround with the garnish.

Discard the onion and bouquet garni from the stew pan. Place the pan on a high heat. Sprinkle in the flour, stirring constantly with a wooden spoon. Stir in the tomato purée and the wine. Still stirring, bring to the boil. Pour over the chicken. Serve immediately.

Andouille

A very large pork sausage, which is popular in Normandy in France, Andouille (ON-dwee) is made from the large intestines and stomach of the pig. It is usually eaten cold, cut in thin slices, as an hors d'oeuvre. Also sold uncooked, Andouille may be served hot, after being poached and grilled, with a garnish of mashed potatoes.

Andouillettes

Similar to ANDOUILLE, Andouillettes (ON-dwee-yet) are made from the small intestines of the pig. In France, Andouillettes are usually sold already poached. They are then grilled and served with mashed potatoes.

Angelica

This herb, which grows wild in the Alps, in the Pyrenees and in northern Europe, has always been highly valued because every part of the plant has some use. Oil distilled from the seeds and roots is used in flavouring liqueurs and wines. The leaves are used for flavouring stewed fruit. The fresh stalks and leaf stems, candied in sugar, are used to garnish desserts and as a flavouring.

Angelica Tart

This pleasant dessert is a rich, shortcrust pastry filled with a bland cream cheese filling and flavoured with candied angelica.
ONE 8-INCH TART

PASTRY
4 oz. [1 cup] flour
⅛ teaspoon salt
2 oz. [¼ cup] butter
2 teaspoons sugar
1 egg yolk
2 to 3 tablespoons cold water
FILLING
8 oz. cream cheese
3 oz. [⅜ cup] sugar
2 tablespoons double [heavy] cream
2 eggs, lightly beaten
2 oz. [⅓ cup] crystallized angelica, chopped into very small pieces

Sift the flour and salt into a large mixing bowl. Add the butter and using your fingertips rub it into the flour until the mixture resembles fine breadcrumbs. Stir in the sugar.

Beat the egg yolk with 2 tablespoons of the water. Stir this into the flour-and-butter mixture. Add the extra water if necessary to make a firm dough. Lightly knead the pastry and chill in the refrigerator for 15 minutes. Preheat the oven to moderate 350°F (Gas Mark 4, 180°C).

For the filling, press the cream cheese through a strainer into a bowl. Add the sugar and beat until well blended. Stir in the cream and eggs. Beat well to mix, then fold in the angelica.

On a floured board, roll out the pastry and line an 8-inch pie dish. Ease the pastry into the dish and trim the edges with a knife. Prick the bottom of the pastry with a fork. Spoon in the filling and bake for about 45 minutes until the filling is firm. Cool before serving.

Angélique Confite

CANDIED ANGELICA

If you grow your own angelica or can buy it fresh, it is worthwhile making your own Angélique Confite (on-JAY-leek con-feet). Although it takes over a week to prepare —most of which time it is drying on a rack—it is easy to do. Once made it must be kept in a well-stoppered jar. Use it for cakes, trifles and tarts.

12 x 4-inch lengths of tender, young angelica stems
1 pint [2½ cups] boiling water
1 lb. [2 cups] granulated sugar
1 pint [2½ cups] water
extra sugar

Place the angelica in a mixing bowl. Pour the boiling water over it and leave to soak for 24 hours.

Remove the angelica. Peel and wash in cold, running water. Put remaining water and the sugar in a saucepan.

Over a low heat, dissolve the sugar. When it is completely dissolved raise the heat and bring to the boil. Boil for 10 minutes. Add the angelica and continue to boil for 20 minutes.

Remove the angelica from the pan and place on a rack. Cover the syrup and set aside. Leave the angelica to dry for 3 days.

After 3 days, bring the syrup to the boil, add the angelica and boil for 20 minutes. Remove the angelica and leave on a rack for 4 days. Sprinkle with sugar and store in an airtight bottle.

Angel Cake

A truly North American cake, Angel Cake has an incredibly light and airy texture.
8 SERVINGS

7 oz. [⅞ cup] castor sugar
3 oz. [¾ cup] flour
1 oz. [2 tablespoons] cornflour [cornstarch]
¼ teaspoon salt
10 egg whites
1 tablespoon lemon juice
1 tablespoon hot water
1 teaspoon cream of tartar
1 teaspoon vanilla essence

Low Cal

Preheat oven to moderate 350°F (Gas Mark 4, 180°C), with a shelf placed just below centre of oven. Select a 9-inch American angel cake pan or spring-form cake tin with a tube centre (ungreased).

Sift the flours with the salt, add one third of the sugar and sift together 3 times.

Put the egg whites into a bowl with the lemon juice and hot water, whisk until foamy. Add the cream of tartar and 1 tablespoon of sugar and whisk until soft peaks form. Gradually whisk in the remaining sugar, 1 tablespoon at a time.

Add the vanilla. Sift ¼ flour mixture over the egg whites and fold in until incorporated. Repeat with the remaining flour.

Turn the mixture into the tin and level the surface, then cut through the mixture with a palette knife to burst air pockets.

Bake the cake for 45 minutes or until dry and firm.

Invert the tin over the neck of a bottle and leave until cold.

Run a palette knife around the sides, then turn out.

Angels on Horseback

An English savoury, this unusual hot hors d'oeuvre may be served as an accompaniment to before-dinner drinks or as a first course.
4 SERVINGS

8 oysters without shells
8 strips of bacon
8 wooden cocktail sticks
8 buttered slices of toast
salt
pepper
parsley, chopped

Preheat grill [broiler] to high.
Roll each oyster in a strip of bacon, sprinkle with salt and pepper, fasten with

An American favourite, Angel Cake is a very light, impressive dessert.

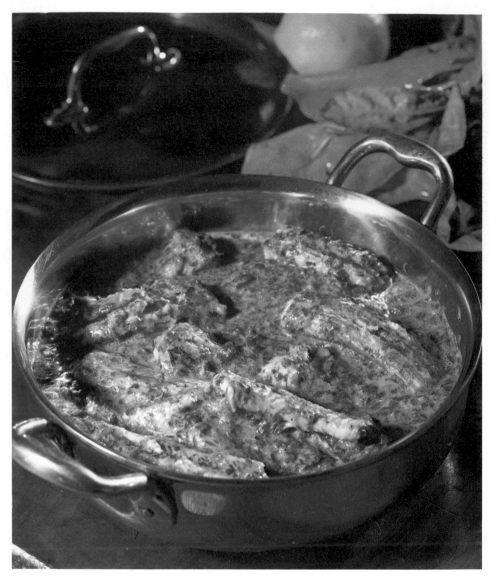

Eels simmered in wine and green herbs, Anguilles au Vert is a Flemish dish which is usually served cold.

Anguilla Marinate
MARINATED EEL

A favourite Venetian dish, Anguilla Marinate (ahn-GWEE-lah mah-ree-NAH-tay) can be prepared a day in advance and kept covered in the refrigerator. The flavour of the eels improves with several hours of marinating.

6 SERVINGS

6 tablespoons oil
1 lb. onions, finely sliced
2 cloves garlic, finely chopped
2 bay leaves
1 teaspoon dried rosemary
8 peppercorns
6 fl. oz. [¾ cup] wine vinegar
6 fl. oz. [¾ cup] water
2½ lb. eels, skinned and cleaned
4 oz. [1 cup] flour
½ teaspoon salt
½ teaspoon pepper

In a saucepan, heat half the oil and sauté the onions and garlic for 5 minutes over moderate heat. Add the bay leaves, rosemary and peppercorns and continue cooking for another 4 minutes. Pour in the vinegar and water. Season with the salt and pepper and simmer uncovered over a low heat for 15 minutes.

Meanwhile, cut the eels into 3-inch pieces. Season the flour with salt and pepper and roll the pieces of eel in the mixture. Fry the eel in remaining oil in a large frying-pan for about 10 minutes. Place the fried eels in a deep dish and pour the hot marinade over them. Cool, then refrigerate. Leave for several hours before serving.

To serve, arrange the eel pieces on a serving dish and spoon a little of the marinade over them.

Anguilles au Vert
EELS IN GREEN SAUCE

A Flemish dish, Anguilles au Vert (on-GWEE-yeh oh vair) are eels simmered with wine, butter and green herbs. Occasionally eaten hot, it is preferable to serve this dish when it is cold. Fresh herbs should be used whenever possible, but if they are not available, half quantities of dried herbs can be substituted. Such herbs as sorrel and chervil can be included when available. Tender nettles can be substituted for the spinach. Anguilles au Vert can be served as

---

a cocktail stick and grill, turning frequently, until the bacon is cooked. Remove cocktail sticks and place on hot, buttered slices of toast. Garnish with parsley and serve very hot.

Anglaise, à l'
A l'Anglaise (ah LON-glaze) is the name given to preparations which are most often cooked in water or in white stock. The term also applies to fish poached in court bouillon, fish rolled in breadcrumbs and then grilled or fried, and potatoes which are steamed or boiled in water.

Angler Fish
Also known as Frogfish and Sea Devil, this large and ugly fish has a flat, spiky head with an enormous mouth. Three filaments grow out of its forward dorsal fin, the longest one acting as a bait to attract prey. Angler fish is a bottom-living fish and is found on the Atlantic seaboard of Europe and North America. It has no scales and is flabby and sticky to

touch. Gastronomically, it is rather tasteless and is used mainly as an ingredient of fish soups.

Angostura
The bark of a small South American tree, angostura is aromatic and bitter and is used in medicines and beverages. It is also the patent name of a brand of bitters which has a basis of rum and is flavoured with aromatic herbs. Although originally intended to be used for medicinal purposes, angostura is now used in the preparation of pink gin and other cocktails and as a flavouring for some fruit dishes.

Animelle
A culinary term for the testicles of animals, in particular those of rams. In the past, *animelle* (a-nee-mehl) were eaten in France, Italy and Spain, but they are less popular today. They can, however, still be found in meat markets in many Middle Eastern countries.

a main dish or, if the quantities are halved, as a first course.

4 SERVINGS

3 oz. [⅜ cup] butter
½ lb. spinach, washed and chopped
1 teaspoon chopped, fresh tarragon
3 tablespoons chopped, parsley
1 teaspoon chopped, fresh sage
2 eels, about 1 lb. each, skinned, cleaned and cut into 3-inch pieces
  freshly ground pepper
1 teaspoon salt
10 fl. oz. [1¼ cups] white wine
3 egg yolks
1 tablespoon lemon juice

In a large, heavy frying-pan, melt the butter and lightly sauté the spinach, tarragon, parsley and sage. Add the eel pieces and stir with a wooden spoon to mix all the ingredients. Season with the salt and 8 grindings of pepper. Add the wine and bring to the boil. Lower the heat, cover and simmer for 10 to 15 minutes or until the eel pieces are tender. Remove from the heat.

In a bowl, lightly beat the egg yolks until mixed. Stir in, a spoonful at a time, 4 tablespoons of the hot liquid from the pan in which the eels cooked. Pour the egg mixture very slowly into the pan, stirring continuously. Add the lemon juice, taste and add more salt and pepper if necessary. Pour into a serving dish and refrigerate. Serve very cold.

Anise

Anise, which is also known as sweet cumin, is one of the sweetest smelling of

herbs. It produces aniseed which are small, light brown and have a liquorice flavour. The plant is a member of the carrot family and has feathery leaves. Found mainly in Egypt, Greece and Asia Minor, anise is a popular flavouring throughout Europe.

Anise has certain medicinal uses, although its main use is in the manufacture of liquors. It is also used as a flavouring in many culinary preparations.

Anise Fork Biscuits [Cookies]

Aniseed makes a change of flavouring for fork biscuits which are traditionally flavoured with lemon or chocolate.

ABOUT 28 BISCUITS

4 oz. [½ cup] butter, softened
2 oz. castor [¼ cup fine] sugar
1 heaped teaspoon aniseed
1 large egg
5 oz. [1¼ cups] self-raising flour
  a pinch of salt

Preheat the oven to moderate 350°F (Gas Mark 4, 180°C). Line a baking sheet with non-stick silicone paper.

Beat the butter with a wooden spoon until it is soft. Add the sugar and continue beating until the mixture is light. Mix in the aniseed. Add the egg and beat until it is well mixed. Add the flour gradually with the salt and stir in well.

Shape the dough into small balls. Place them on the baking sheet leaving space between them. Using a fork dipped in water, flatten out each ball. Bake in a moderate oven for 15 minutes.

Aniseed-flavoured carrots make an unusual and interesting vegetable dish.

Aniseed Carrots

This is an unusual combination of flavours and makes a most interesting vegetable dish to serve with roasted or grilled meat, chicken or fish.

4 SERVINGS

1½ lb. carrots
1 tablespoon soft brown sugar
2 oz. [¼ cup] butter
1 heaped teaspoon aniseed
1 teaspoon salt
¼ teaspoon pepper

Wash and scrape the carrots and cut off the tops. If you are using small carrots leave them whole. Large carrots should be cut in quarters lengthways.

Put the sugar, butter, aniseed, salt and pepper into a saucepan. When the mixture begins to bubble add the carrots. Stir well, cover, lower the heat and simmer for about 15 minutes or until the carrots are tender when pierced with a table fork. Serve hot.

Aniseed Sugar

Aniseed sugar is used for flavouring cakes, sponges, biscuits [cookies] and creams. The proportion of aniseed to sugar varies according to the strength of flavour required. For instance, for a cake, 2 tablespoons aniseed are added to 1 pound of castor sugar. For creams and custards, however, the proportion can go

Ani

up to 4 ounces [½ cup] of aniseed to 1 pound of castor sugar.

To make aniseed sugar, clean the aniseed by rubbing the seeds on a sieve to remove the stalks. Dry them in a very cool oven for about 6 hours and then pound in a mortar with the sugar until it is very fine. Push through a fine sieve and use.

Anisette

A liqueur the flavour of which is obtained principally from aniseed. The best French Anisette is made at Bordeaux.

Antipasto

In Italy, dinner begins with antipasto, the appetizer. There are no rules about the combinations of food included in an antipasto but the preparation of an attractive antipasto plate requires ingenuity. Its taste and colour appeal depend on the variety of foods as well as on their arrangement.

Lettuce and sliced fennel, for example, used as a green and white border will improve the appearance of even a simple selection of celery, radishes, small pickled beets, salami and anchovies. To this platter a few large green and/or black olives and strips of brilliant pimiento can be added.

Another typical Italian antipasto would include pickled mushrooms, halved or sliced hard-boiled eggs, tuna fish roe, lettuce, and very thin slices of prosciutto, Italian ham.

Small pickled green peppers, artichoke hearts, pimiento strips, slices of fennel, sliced dry pork sausage and anchovy fillets would be another delicious combination.

When the choice of foods has been made and the serving plate arranged, it is customary to pour a little olive oil and a very small quantity of wine vinegar over the food.

Apéritif

Apéritif (ah-PAY-ree-teef) is the French name for a drink which is taken before meals and considered an appetite stimulant. *Apéritifs* differ in alcoholic content and flavour and are often bitter. They are drunk alone or diluted with water. One of the most popular *apéritifs* is VERMOUTH.

Antipasto, the colourful Italian first course of meat, eggs, fish and raw and cooked vegetables, arranged for two, four and six servings.

Apfelbettelmann
GERMAN APPLE PUDDING

An apple pudding which comes from the south of Germany, Apfelbettelman (AHP-fehl-bet-tel-mun) is very easy to make.

6 SERVINGS

3 oz. [½ cup] raisins
3 fl. oz. [⅜ cup] orange juice
   grated rind of 1 small lemon
2 oz. [¼ cup] butter, softened
8 oz. [2½ cups] breadcrumbs, made
   from pumpernickel bread
6 oz. [¾ cup] brown sugar
4 oz. [⅔ cup] almonds, chopped
1 teaspoon ground mixed spice
4 tablespoons melted butter
1½ lb. cooking apples

Soak the raisins in a mixing bowl with the orange juice and lemon rind for at least 30 minutes.

Preheat the oven to moderate 350°F (Gas Mark 4, 180°C). Grease a 3-pint ovenproof dish with 1 tablespoon butter.

Add the breadcrumbs, sugar, almonds, mixed spice and melted butter to the raisins.

Peel, core and thinly slice the apples. Put one-third of the breadcrumb mixture into the dish and place half the apple slices on top. Add another third of the breadcrumbs and then the remaining apples. Finish with the remaining breadcrumbs. Dot with the rest of the softened butter and bake for 35 minutes.

Apfelkuchen
GERMAN APPLE AND CUSTARD TART

An unusual apple tart from Bavaria, Apfelkuchen (AHP-fehl-KOO-khen) is a combination of apples, rum, eggs and cream.

6 SERVINGS

PASTRY
6 oz. [1½ cups] flour
3 oz. [⅜ cup] unsalted butter
1 tablespoon castor sugar
   grated rind of 1 lemon
2 egg yolks
FILLING
1 oz. [⅓ cup] breadcrumbs mixed
   with 2 tablespoons melted butter
1 lb. cooking apples, peeled, cored
   and sliced thinly
2 tablespoons currants soaked in
   2 tablespoons rum
CUSTARD
1 whole egg plus 1 yolk
2 tablespoons castor [fine] sugar
10 fl. oz. double cream [1¼ cups heavy
   cream]
1 tablespoon sugar

Preheat the oven to moderate 350°F (Gas Mark 4, 180°C).

For the pastry, sift the flour into a mixing bowl. With a knife, cut in the chilled butter until it forms small pieces. Using your fingertips, rub the butter into the flour until the mixture looks like fine breadcrumbs. Add the sugar and lemon rind. With a spoon, mix in the egg yolks one at a time. Then, using your hands, work the pastry until it is smooth.

Line a cake tin which is about 7½-inches in diameter, 2-inches deep and has a removable bottom, with the pastry, using your fingers to press it evenly into the bottom and sides.

To fill the tart crust, first spread the breadcrumb and melted butter mixture on the bottom. Place the apples on top. Remove the currants from the rum and put the rum aside. Sprinkle the currants over the apples. Bake in the oven for 25 minutes.

Reset the oven to warm 300°F (Gas Mark 1, 150°C).

To make the custard, beat the eggs and sugar with a whisk until thick. Beat in the rum and cream. Pour half the mixture evenly over the apples. Return to the oven and bake for 20 minutes or until the custard is set. Pour the remaining custard over the top and bake for 30 minutes more.

Remove the tart from the oven and reset to moderate 350°F (Gas Mark 4, 180°C). Sprinkle the top of the tart with the sugar. Place the tart on the topmost rack of the oven and brown lightly for about 10 minutes. Let the tart cool. Carefully remove from the cake tin before serving.

Apfelstrudel

Apfelstrudel (AHP-fehl-SHTROO-d'l) is delicious, inexpensive and time-consuming. If you have never made it before, give yourself plenty of time—possibly a whole afternoon. It requires a great deal of practise to make a perfect strudel and the more often you make it, the better it will be. The quantity given in this recipe should make enough dough for a 6-foot strudel. But beginners may wish to start by making a 3- or 4-foot strudel. Because the dough must be very smooth and thin it is important that it is kneaded very thoroughly. Otherwise the texture will be heavy instead of light and flaky and as it is important to use a large surface, you may have to use your dining room table.

Serve Apfelstrudel as a hot or cold dessert with cream.

PASTRY
10 oz. [2½ cups] flour
½ teaspoon salt
1 egg, lightly beaten
7 fl. oz. [⅞ cup] tepid water
2 tablespoons melted butter
FILLING
3 lb. cooking apples, peeled, cored
   and cut into thin slices
4 oz. [½ cup] sugar
1 teaspoon ground cinnamon
3 oz. [½ cup] raisins
3 oz. [½ cup] almonds or walnuts,
   chopped
   grated rind of 1 lemon
4 oz. [½ cup] melted butter
2 oz. [⅔ cup] white breadcrumbs

Sift the flour and salt into a large mixing bowl. In a small bowl mix together the egg, water and butter. With a wooden spoon, stir the egg-and-water mixture into the flour and mix well. Then knead until a firm dough is formed.

Place the dough on a floured board and continue kneading until it is smooth and elastic. This will take about 10 minutes. Place the dough in a warm, large mixing bowl. Cover the bowl with a cloth and set it aside in a warm draught-free place for 30 minutes.

Meanwhile prepare the filling. In a medium-sized mixing bowl mix together the apples, sugar, cinnamon, raisins, almonds or walnuts and lemon rind.

Spread out a large, clean cloth (a sheet is ideal) on a table. Sprinkle the cloth with flour. Place the dough on the cloth and, with a floured rolling pin, roll the dough out as thinly as possible.

With the back of your hands, lift and stretch the dough, pulling the dough until it is wafer thin. This should be done as carefully as possible. Do not worry if a few small holes appear in the dough. With scissors, trim the outer edges of the dough so that the sides are straight.

Preheat the oven to very hot 450°F (Gas Mark 8, 230°C). Grease two baking sheets with 1 tablespoon melted butter.

Brush the dough with half of the melted butter and sprinkle it with nearly all of the breadcrumbs. Spoon the apple mixture in a long strip on to the dough, 3 inches away from the edges of the pastry nearest to you, and within 2 inches of each end.

Using the cloth, lift the dough over the filling and roll it up like a Swiss [jelly] roll. Tuck in the ends. Brush the top of the dough with the remaining melted butter and cover with the rest of the breadcrumbs.

With a sharp knife, divide the strudel into pieces long enough to fit the baking sheets. Place the strudel on the baking

For the Apfelstrudel, on a large clean cloth sprinkled with flour, roll out the dough as thinly as possible.

With the backs of your hands pull the dough until it stretches over the table and is wafer thin.

Brush the stretched dough with the melted butter and then cover it with almost all of the breadcrumbs.

Place the apple filling on the edge nearest to you 3 inches from the edge and to within 2 inches of the ends.

Lift the cloth and use it to roll the dough over the filling. Continue rolling until all the pastry is rolled.

Brush the top of the roll with melted butter and sprinkle it with breadcrumbs before cutting.

Bacon, apples and onions are fried to make Äppel-Fläsk, a Swedish dish.

Preheat the oven to moderate 350°F (Gas Mark 4, 180°C). Grease 12 patty tins with a little butter.

In a medium-sized mixing bowl, cream the butter with the sugar using a wooden spoon, or electric mixer, until the mixture is light and fluffy. Beat in the egg and then fold in the flour. With your hands, lightly knead the dough until it is smooth. Chill it in the refrigerator for 15 minutes.

For the filling, melt the butter in a small saucepan over low heat. Add the apples to the pan and cook them gently for about 15 minutes or until they are beginning to soften. Stir in the sugar.

Set aside one-third of the dough. Divide the remaining two-thirds into 12 and roll each piece into a ball. Flatten each ball with the heel of your hand and press it into a patty tin.

Spoon the apple filling into the pastry cases and put a teaspoonful of apricot jam on top. Sprinkle each one with a few slivered almonds.

Roll out the reserved dough and, using a pastry cutter a little larger than the patty tins, cut out 12 rounds. Dampen the edges of each pastry case and press the pastry rounds on top. Press the edges together with a fork to seal.

Bake the pies in the centre of the oven for 35 to 45 minutes or until firm and golden brown. Allow to cool slightly, then remove from the tins. Sprinkle with icing [confectioners'] sugar.

sheets with the seams underneath.

Bake the strudels in the centre of the oven for 10 minutes, then reduce the oven temperature to fairly hot 400°F (Gas Mark 6, 200°C), and continue to bake for a further 20 minutes or until the apfelstrudel is crisp and golden brown.

Appareil

Appareil (ah-PAH-ray) is a french cooking term which is synonymous with the word 'mixture'. It is used to describe the preparations necessary for the making of a dish.

Äppel-Fläsk
BACON COOKED WITH APPLES AND ONIONS

A very simple and tasty dish from Sweden, Äppel-Fläsk (EHP-pel flesk) is inexpensive and easy for a busy housewife to make for lunch or supper.

4 SERVINGS

2 tablespoons oil
1 lb. onions, sliced
1 lb. cooking apples, cored and sliced
　freshly ground black pepper
½ teaspoon dried dill (optional)
¾ lb. bacon slices
1 tablespoon chopped parsley

In a large frying-pan, heat the oil over moderate heat. Add the onions to the pan and fry them until they are transparent.

Stir in the apples. Cover the pan and cook for about 10 to 15 minutes or until the apples are soft. Stir occasionally. Add pepper to taste and the dill, if you are using it. Transfer the apple mixture to a warmed serving dish and keep warm.

With a sharp knife remove the rind from the bacon and discard it. Wash out the frying-pan and in it fry the bacon until it is crisp. Remove the bacon from the pan and drain it on kitchen paper towels.

Mix the bacon into the apple mixture and sprinkle with the parsley.

Äppelformar
SMALL APPLE PIES

Small pies filled with apple, apricot jam and slivered almonds, Äppelformar (EHP-pel-FOR-mar) is a Scandinavian recipe. Usually served with coffee they are equally delicious for tea or a picnic.

12 SMALL PIES

PASTRY
3 oz. [⅜ cup] butter
4 oz. [½ cup] sugar
1 large egg
6 oz. [1½ cups] self-raising flour
FILLING
2 tablespoons butter
2 large cooking apples, peeled, cored and thinly sliced
2 oz. [¼ cup] sugar
4 tablespoons apricot jam
1 oz. [¼ cup] almonds, slivered
icing [confectioners'] sugar

Appenzell
This full fat cheese derives its name from the eastern Swiss canton of Appenzell. It has a delicate flavour and is similar in appearance to the Swiss cheeses Emmenthal and Gruyère.

Apple
The most important and widely grown fruit in the temperate climates of the world, the apple has been cultivated for over 3,000 years. Apples were always particularly valued for their keeping qualities and, until refrigeration, gas and other storage methods were introduced in the twentieth century, they were almost the only fresh fruit available during the winter.

Apples were probably introduced into Britain from Europe. From there they were taken by settlers to America and Australia and, later, seedlings of new varieties were sent back to Britain.

During the nineteenth century, amateur and professional growers developed many new varieties of apples. The most famous English dessert apple is probably Cox's Orange Pippin. In about 1850, a Mr. Cox, a retired brewer, raised a seedling from Ribston, another popular variety. The resulting fruit was of exceptional quality with a sweet, crisp flesh and a strong, aromatic skin. From this apple many other dessert varieties have been developed.

Apples have a low vitamin C content and, do not have great food value, but they are one of the most popular and versatile fruits. In addition to their decorative value in a fruit bowl and, served raw, as an enjoyable sweet, apples can be cooked in many different ways to produce a huge variety of desserts. They can be prepared to accompany certain meat and cheese dishes and they can be baked, stewed, fried, puréed, cooked in pastry or used as a garnish. They can be preserved as jelly, jam, pickles, chutney and dried apple rings. Certain varieties are used to make CIDER and apple wine.

Cooking apples are rich in pectin and are useful in making jam because they can be combined with fruits that have little pectin.

Apple Amber

A delicious and good-looking dessert, Apple Amber can be served hot or cold.

4 SERVINGS

SHORTCRUST PASTRY
4 oz. [1 cup] flour
¼ teaspoon salt
2 oz. [¼ cup] vegetable shortening
cold water, to mix
FILLING
1 lb. cooking apples
2 oz. [¼ cup] butter
sugar
grated rind of 1 lemon
juice of 1 lemon
2 egg yolks, lightly beaten
MERINGUE
2 egg whites
3 oz. castor [⅜ cup fine] sugar

To make the pastry, sift together the flour and salt. With your fingertips, rub the fat very lightly into the flour mixture until it resembles fine breadcrumbs. Mix to a stiff paste with very little cold water.

An apple-filled pastry shell, Apple Amber is topped with meringue.

The dough should bind together into a ball, leaving the sides of the bowl clean.

Turn out on to a floured board and knead very lightly. Roll out, handling the dough as little as possible. Line an 8-inch pie dish with the pastry.

Preheat oven to very hot 450°F (Gas Mark 8, 230°C).

For the filling, peel, core and slice the apples. Put 2 tablespoons of cold water into a saucepan, add the apples and the butter and cook until tender, about 10 minutes. Add sugar to taste.

Rub the mixture through a sieve or beat until smooth. Add the lemon rind, the lemon juice and the egg yolks to the apple mixture. Mix together and pour into the pie dish. Bake for about 30 minutes or until the pastry is browned and the filling is set.

For the meringue, whisk the egg whites until they are very stiff. Fold in 2 ounces [¼ cup] of sugar.

When the pastry and apple filling are done, reset the oven temperature to very cool 250°F (Gas Mark ½, 130°C). Pile the meringue lightly on top of the apple filling. Dredge with the remaining sugar. Bake for 30 to 40 minutes or until the meringue is crisp and lightly golden brown on top.

Apples, Baked

This recipe for Baked Apples, is inexpensive, easy to cook and a pleasant dessert. It can be varied by adding cinnamon, nutmeg, ground cloves or mace to the sugar. Dried fruit may be substituted for the sugar or the apples may be basted with dry sherry during the baking and served with sherry-flavoured custard sauce.

4 SERVINGS

4 cooking apples
2 oz. [¼ cup] light brown sugar
water
1 oz. [2 tablespoons] butter

Preheat the oven to moderate 350°F (Gas Mark 4, 180°C).

Wash the apples and with an apple corer remove the cores. Peel off about 1 inch of skin from the tops of the apples.

Arrange the apples in a baking dish and fill the centres with sugar. Top each apple with a little butter and pour enough water into the baking dish to a depth of ½-inch.

Bake the apples for about 30 minutes or until they are soft, basting frequently with the syrup in the baking dish. Serve hot or cold.

Apple Brandy

A colourless spirit distilled from cider, apple brandy is widely made in the apple-growing regions of France and in some parts of North America. CALVADOS, the famous apple brandy, is made in Normandy.

A simple dish, Baked Apples may be flavoured with spices or sherry.

Apple Bread Pudding

A pleasant dessert for Sunday lunch, Apple Bread Pudding can be prepared in advance and served cold with a hot sauce or baked at the last minute and served with cream.

4 TO 6 SERVINGS

8 fl. oz. [1 cup] milk
5 oz. [2½ cups] fresh breadcrumbs
2 egg yolks
1 oz. [2 tablespoons] butter
2 tablespoons brandy or 1 teaspoon vanilla essence
2 oz. [⅓ cup] almonds, slivered
2 oz. [⅓ cup] raisins
2 oz. [⅓ cup] currants
4 oz. [½ cup] sugar
½ teaspoon ground cinnamon
½ teaspoon ground cloves
1½ lb. apples, peeled, cored and thinly sliced
2 egg whites

Preheat the oven to moderately hot 375°F (Gas Mark 5, 190°C).

In a small saucepan, heat the milk over moderate heat. Add the breadcrumbs and cook for 2 minutes. Cool slightly before beating in the egg yolks, butter, brandy or vanilla essence, almonds, raisins, currants, 6 tablespoons sugar, cinnamon and cloves. Add the sliced apples and mix well.

With a whisk or rotary beater, beat the egg whites until they are stiff and form peaks. Gradually add the remaining sugar and continue beating until the egg whites and sugar are well mixed. Fold into the apple mixture.

Grease a medium-sized baking dish and fill it with the pudding mixture. Bake for 40 minutes.

Apples Bristol

An unusual apple and orange dessert, Apples Bristol are best made with Cox's Orange Pippin apples, but other dessert apples can be used. This dish should be served very cold and can be accompanied by whipped cream.

4 SERVINGS

15 fl. oz. [1⅞ cups] water
4 oz. [½ cup] sugar
6 dessert apples
2 large oranges
CARAMEL
3 oz. [⅜ cup fine] castor sugar
4 fl. oz. [½ cup] water

Put the water and granulated sugar in a medium-sized saucepan over a low heat.

An apple and orange dessert, Apples Bristol is sprinkled with caramel.

Stir until the sugar has dissolved and then boil rapidly for 5 minutes.

Peel and core the apples and cut them into quarters. Add all the apples to the syrup in the saucepan, cover and simmer gently for 10 minutes, or until the apples are tender when pierced with a table fork. Remove from the heat, replace the lid and leave to cool.

With a sharp knife, score around the centre of one orange and pull off one-half of the rind. Cut the rind into fine strips. To remove the bitter taste, put the strips into a small pan of boiling water and simmer for 5 minutes. Drain the orange strips, rinse them in cold water and drain again. Set aside.

With a very sharp knife, cut the peel and white pith from the oranges. Slice the oranges into thin rounds and set aside.

To make the caramel, put the water and sugar in a small saucepan over moderate heat and stir until the sugar has dissolved. Bring to the boil and continue boiling until the syrup turns a dark golden brown. Pour on to a lightly greased baking sheet and leave to harden.

To serve, remove the apples from the saucepan with a slotted spoon and put them into a serving bowl. Arrange the orange slices on top of the apples and add 4 tablespoons of syrup from the saucepan. Scatter the orange strips over the orange slices. Crush the caramel into small pieces and sprinkle over the top.

Put the serving bowl into the refrigerator for at least 2 hours before serving.

Apple Brown Betty

This dessert is a form of charlotte. It can also be made with other fruits, such as apricots, gooseberries or a mixture of apples and blackberries.

4 SERVINGS
2 oz. [¼ cup] plus 1 teaspoon butter
6 oz. [3 cups] fresh breadcrumbs
2 lb. apples, cored, peeled and thinly sliced
4 oz. [⅔ cup] brown sugar
¼ teaspoon grated nutmeg
grated rind of ½ lemon
2 tablespoons lemon juice
4 oz. [⅔ cup] raisins
3 fl. oz. [⅜ cup] sherry

Preheat the oven to fairly hot 375°F (Gas Mark 5, 190°C). Grease a medium-sized, ovenproof dish with 1 teaspoon butter.

Place a layer of one third of breadcrumbs on the bottom of the ovenproof dish. Dot with some butter. Place half the apples next, sprinkled with half the sugar, nutmeg, grated lemon rind and raisins. Sprinkle with 1 tablespoon of lemon juice. Lay another third of breadcrumbs on top. Dot with butter and place the rest of the apples on top, sprinkled with the remainder of the sugar, nutmeg, lemon rind, raisins and lemon juice. Cover with the remaining breadcrumbs, dot with butter and bake in the oven for about 40 minutes or until the apples are tender and the top is golden brown.

Pour the sherry over the pudding and bake for 5 minutes more. Serve hot with cream or custard sauce.

Apple Butter

Apple butter, or apple marmalade as it is sometimes called, is a useful and tasty addition to your store cupboard. Not only can apple butter be used as a spread, but it is also an excellent base for a mousse or as a filling for tarts and cakes.

ABOUT 5½ PINTS
4 lb. well-flavoured apples
16 fl. oz. [2 cups] cider
granulated sugar
2 teaspoons powdered cinnamon
1 teaspoon ground cloves
½ teaspoon ground allspice
juice and grated rind of 1 lemon

Wash and quarter the apples, but do not peel them or remove the seeds. Put the apple quarters and the cider in a large preserving pan or saucepan. Bring to the boil over high heat. Lower the heat and simmer uncovered until the apples are very soft.

Rub the fruit and cider mixture through a fine sieve. To every 8 fluid ounces, add 4 ounces [½ cup] of sugar. Return the apple and sugar mixture to the saucepan and add the cinnamon, cloves, allspice, lemon juice and rind. Stir constantly, over low heat, until the sugar is dissolved.

Raise the heat and boil rapidly until the apple butter thickens. To test, place a spoonful of the butter on a cold plate. When no rim of liquid separates around the edge, the apple butter is ready.

Pour the butter into hot, clean, dry jars and seal with waxed paper and cellophane covers.

Apple Charlotte

This delicious hot pudding is said to have been named after the heroine in Goethe's novel Werther.

4 TO 6 SERVINGS

FILLING

2 lb. cooking apples, peeled, cored and cut into quarters

4 oz. [½ cup] sugar
the rind of 1 lemon

2 oz. [¼ cup] plus 1 teaspoon butter

1 loaf of white bread a day or two old, crusts removed and cut into as many thin slices as required

4 tablespoons melted butter
castor sugar

SAUCE

5 tablespoons apricot jam

3 tablespoons water

2 tablespoons sherry

Preheat the oven to moderate 350°F (Gas Mark 4, 180°C). Grease a charlotte mould or ovenproof dish with 1 teaspoon butter.

Put the apples, sugar, lemon rind and butter in a medium-sized saucepan and, stirring occasionally with a wooden spoon, simmer gently until the apples are very soft. They should neither be completely whole nor completely mashed. Discard the lemon rind.

Cut the bread slices in halves. Dip the halved slices in the melted butter and line the bottom and sides of the mould or pudding bowl, overlapping the slices slightly. Fill with the apple mixture and cover with a layer of bread slices dipped in melted butter. Sprinkle the pudding with castor sugar and bake in the oven for 40 minutes, or until the top is golden brown.

While the charlotte is baking, put the jam and water in a small saucepan. Stir and bring to the boil. Lower the heat and simmer for 3 minutes. Remove from the heat and stir in the sherry.

After taking the apple charlotte from the oven, let it stand for a minute or two before turning it out on to a warmed serving dish. Pour the warm, but not hot, jam sauce over it and serve immediately.

Apple Corer

This useful tool for removing complete apple cores neatly is sometimes combined with apple peelers or with gadgets which simultaneously cut an apple into quarters. Apple corers can also be used to take a neat plug out of some fruits and vegetables before stuffing them.

An Apple Dumpling is a whole, cored apple wrapped in pastry and baked.

Apple and Cucumber Salad

A simple, fresh salad, this is a good accompaniment to cold fowl, fish or meat.

4 SERVINGS

1 lb. crisp dessert apples
  juice of 1 lemon
1 small cucumber
½ teaspoon salt
2 grindings black pepper
2 fl. oz. double cream [¼ cup heavy
  cream], whipped
  lettuce leaves, washed and dried

Peel, core and cut the apples into thin slices. Put the apple slices in a dish and sprinkle with the lemon juice to prevent them from discolouring.

Wash the cucumber and cut it into thin slices. Add the slices to the apple in the bowl. Sprinkle with salt and pepper. With a spoon, gently toss the apple and cucumber slices so they are evenly mixed. Stir in the whipped cream.

To serve, line a salad bowl with lettuce leaves. Pile the apple and cucumber mixture in the centre.

Apple Dumplings

This is an attractive, traditional English pudding which is usually eaten in the winter.

6 SERVINGS

PASTRY
11 oz. [2¾ cups] flour
½ teaspoon salt
3 oz. [6 tablespoons] butter, diced
3 oz. [⅜ cup] white vegetable fat
  [shortening], diced
3 tablespoons cold water
FILLING
6 large dessert apples, cored
4 oz. [½ cup] soft brown sugar
  grated rind of 1 lemon
½ teaspoon cinnamon
2 oz. sultanas [⅓ cup golden raisins]
6 cloves
  milk, to glaze
  castor sugar

Preheat the oven to hot 400°F (Gas Mark 6, 200°C).

For the pastry, sift the flour and salt into a large mixing bowl. Add the diced fats and cut them into the flour with a pastry cutter or a knife. With your fingertips, rub the fats into the flour until the mixture resembles fine breadcrumbs.

Make a well in the centre of the flour mixture and add the water. With your hands, mix and knead until smooth. If the pastry is too dry add more water, a little at a time. Chill for 30 minutes.

Roll out the pastry fairly thinly and trim to a rectangle 21 × 14 inches, reserving the trimmings. Cut into 6 squares. Centre an apple on each square.

Mix together the brown sugar, lemon rind, cinnamon and sultanas [golden raisins] and use to fill the centre of each apple, inserting 1 clove in the middle.

Lift the edges of the pastry squares to enclose each apple completely. Moisten the edges with water and seal.

Place the dumplings on a greased baking sheet. Cut 24 leaves from the reserved pastry. Moisten and attach 4 leaves to each apple. Brush the dumpling with milk and dust with castor sugar.

Bake for 30 minutes then reduce the oven temperature to 275°F (Gas Mark 1, 140°C) and bake for a further 10 minutes, cover with foil to stop overbrowning. Serve hot or cold with ice cream.

Apple-Filled Pancakes

This unusual and inexpensive dessert is known in Germany, where it originated, as Apfelfannkuchen (AHP-fehl-fahn-KOO-khen). The pancakes could also be served for tea or at a late Sunday breakfast.

4 SERVINGS

PANCAKES
4 oz. [1 cup] flour
2 teaspoons sugar
1 egg plus 1 egg yolk
10 fl. oz. [1¼ cups] milk
1 tablespoon melted butter
FILLING
2 oz. [¼ cup] butter
2 lb. cooking apples, peeled, cored
  and cut into thin slices
2 tablespoons brown sugar
1 teaspoon ground cinnamon
  a little castor sugar and cinnamon

Sift the flour and sugar into a large mixing bowl. Make a well in the centre of the flour mixture and put the eggs into it. Add a tablespoon of milk to the eggs. Stir the eggs and milk with a wooden spoon until they are mixed. Slowly incorporate the flour and sugar, adding the milk a little at a time.

Continue mixing until all the flour and half the milk are blended to make a thick batter. Change to a whisk or rotary beater and briskly whisk the batter, adding the remaining milk. Cover and keep in a cool place for 30 minutes.

For the filling, melt all the butter in a frying-pan over moderate heat. Put in the apples, sugar and cinammon. Sauté gently, stirring occasionally, until the apples are soft. Set aside, but keep hot.

Heat a medium-sized frying-pan. Grease lightly with melted butter. Pour two tablespoons of the batter into the pan and tip the pan quickly to spread the batter evenly. Cook over a high heat until the pancake is brown on the underside. Turn over with a palette knife and cook for 30 seconds or until brown. Turn on to a plate and keep warm. Make all the pancakes.

Spread a large spoonful of the apple filling on the lower half of each pancake and roll neatly. Arrange the pancakes on a plate, sprinkle with castor sugar and cinnamon and serve.

For Apple-Filled Pancakes, put a spoonful of apple mixture on each pancake.

Starting from the side with the apple mixture, neatly roll up each pancake.

Arrange the pancakes on a plate and sprinkle with sugar and cinnamon.

Apple Florentine

  ①

A classic recipe, this English single-crust apple pie is traditionally made with flaky pastry. It should be served very hot with plenty of thick cream.

6 SERVINGS

FILLING

2 lb. cooking apples
2 oz. [¼ cup] butter
4 oz. [⅔ cup] brown sugar
¼ teaspoon ground cinnamon
½ teaspoon grated lemon rind
5 fl. oz. [⅝ cup] sweet cider
¼ teaspoon grated nutmeg
¼ teaspoon lemon juice
½ teaspoon ground cinnamon
2 teaspoons sugar
   icing [confectioners'] sugar

PASTRY

6 oz. [1½ cups] flour
½ teaspoon salt
2 oz. [¼ cup] butter
2 oz. [¼ cup] lard
3 to 4 tablespoons cold water

Peel and core the apples and cut them into quarters. Melt the butter in a medium-sized frying-pan over a moderate heat and add the apples. Sauté gently, stirring occasionally until the apples are soft and light brown. Drain off any remaining butter.

Sprinkle the apples with the brown sugar, ¼ teaspoon of the cinnamon and the grated lemon rind and mix thoroughly. Put into a shallow 8-inch earthenware or glass pie dish. Set aside.

Preheat the oven to hot 425°F (Gas Mark 7, 220°C).

To make the pastry, sift the flour into a mixing bowl and add the salt. Divide the butter into two pieces and add one piece to the flour. With your fingertips, rub the fat into the flour until it resembles fine breadcrumbs. With a knife, mix in the water to form a firm dough.

Put the dough on a floured board and with your hands shape it into a square. Roll out the dough into an oblong and dot two-thirds of it with small pieces of half the lard. Fold over one-third of the pastry and then the other third to make a neat, square parcel. Press the edges with the rolling-pin to seal.

Turn the pastry round so that the

A classic recipe, Apple Florentine is flavoured with spiced cider.

---

sealed ends are facing you and roll out again into an oblong. Dot with pieces of the remaining lard, fold in three, seal the edges, turn the pastry and roll out again. Repeat this process with the remaining butter. Wrap dough in waxed paper and chill in the refrigerator for 10 minutes.

Roll out the pastry, fold again in three, and, with your hands, shape quickly into a round. Roll out into a circle slightly larger than the pie dish and, using the rolling pin, lay the pastry on the pie dish. Trim the excess pastry with a sharp knife. Crimp the edge of the pastry with your thumb and forefinger to make a pattern.

From the surplus pastry make a rose to decorate the centre of the pie. Bake this separately. Bake the pie in the oven for 30 minutes, or until the pastry is golden brown.

While the pie is baking, prepare the spiced cider. Put the cider into a small saucepan over low heat with the nutmeg, lemon juice and remaining cinnamon. Heat gently, add the sugar and stir until it is dissolved. Taste the cider, adding more sugar if necessary.

When the pie is baked, remove it from the oven. Cut a small hole in the centre of the pie and pour in the spiced cider. Fill the hole with the pastry rose. Dust the pastry with icing sugar and serve very hot.

Apple Flambé

Apple Flambé (flom-bay) is an elegant and more expensive version of the simple baked apple. The slow method of cooking ensures that the apples stay white and whole. The amount of sugar needed may vary according to the tartness of the apples used. This is an ideal hot dessert for a winter lunch or dinner party and is delicious served with whipped cream or hot custard sauce.

4 SERVINGS

4 large, juicy, crisp, dessert apples
4 oz. [⅔ cup] raisins and candied peel, mixed
4 oz. [⅔ cup] hazelnuts, chopped, or almonds, blanched and chopped
a pinch of grated nutmeg
2 tablespoons castor [fine] sugar
2 fl. oz. [¼ cup] water
1 tablespoon butter
4 tablespoons brandy or Grand Marnier

Apple rings dipped in batter and fried, Apple Fritters make a good dessert.

Preheat the oven to 300°F (Gas Mark 2, 150°C).

Wash, core and peel the apples. Put them in an ovenproof serving dish.

Put the raisins, candied peel, chopped nuts, nutmeg and sugar in a bowl and mix well. Stuff the centres of the apples with the mixture. Put the water and the butter in the bottom of the dish and place in the centre of the oven. Cook for 2 hours or until the apples are tender. Baste the apples with the liquid every half hour.

When the apples are cooked, remove them from the oven. Just before serving, pour a tablespoon of warmed brandy or Grand Marnier over each apple and ignite it. Bring to the table flaming.

Apple Fritters

This is a simple and inexpensive dessert. Make the batter and prepare the fruit ahead of your meal, then dip the fritters in batter and cook just before serving.

4 SERVINGS

4 oz. [1 cup] flour
¼ teaspoon salt
1 egg
1 tablespoon vegetable oil
5 fl. oz. [⅝ cup] milk
1 lb. firm dessert apples
2 tablespoons lemon juice
castor sugar for dredging
oil for frying

Sift the flour and salt into a medium-sized mixing bowl. Make a well in the centre of the flour, break in the egg and add the oil.

With a wooden spoon, mix the egg and oil, slowly incorporating the flour and gradually adding the milk. Mix to a smooth batter, then beat well. Cover and keep in a cool place for 30 minutes.

Peel and core the apples and slice into rings ¼ inch thick. Lay the apple rings on a plate sprinkle with lemon juice and sugar.

Heat the oil in a deep-fat fryer with the basket in place to 350°F (Gas Mark 4, 180°C). Cook the apple rings in two batches. Using a skewer dip them into the batter then place in the basket and lower into the hot oil. Cook the rings on both sides until they are golden.

Drain well on absorbent paper. Arrange on a plate, dredge with sugar and serve.

Apple Hat

Apple Hat is a traditional, steamed, English pudding. Very filling and satisfying, it is good served as the dessert for a winter luncheon.

4 SERVINGS

butter for greasing
5 oz. [1¼ cups] self-raising flour
½ teaspoon salt
3 oz. [⅜ cup] coarsely shredded beef suet
about 4 fl. oz. [½ cup] milk
3 cooking apples, peeled, cored and sliced
2 oz. [¼ cup] soft brown sugar
grated rind of 1 lemon
1 oz. [2 tablespoons] raisins
1 oz. [2 tablespoons] currants
1 tablespoon water

Generously grease a 1½-pint pudding basin.

Sift the flour and salt into a mixing bowl and stir in the suet. Add enough milk to make a soft dough. Knead until smooth.

Roll out the pastry on a lightly floured surface to a 10-inch circle. Cut out a quarter wedge from the circle and set aside. Use the remaining pastry to line the basin.

Fill with layers of apples, sugar, lemon rind, raisins and currants. Sprinkle with water.

Roll out the reserved pastry to a circle large enough to fit the top of the basin. Brush the edges with water and place on top of the filling. Press the edges down firmly to seal.

Grease a large circle of greaseproof [waxed] paper and make a pleat in the centre. Cover the pudding basin with the paper, greased side down and secure with string.

Place the basin in a saucepan and pour in boiling water to come two-thirds of the way up the side. Cover and steam over low heat for 3 hours, adding more boiling water if necessary.

Turn the pudding out on to a serving plate and serve with hot custard sauce or cream.

Apple Mousse à la Chantilly

The basis of this dessert, Apple Mousse à la Chantilly (ah lah SHON-tee-yee), is apple 'marmalade' or 'butter' flavoured with vanilla essence rather than with the usual cinnamon, cloves and lemon. The apples should be of a well-flavoured dessert variety.

4 SERVINGS

2 lb. apples
16 fl. oz. [2 cups] cider
granulated sugar
1 teaspoon vanilla essence
10 fl. oz. double cream [1¼ cups heavy cream]

Wash the apples, cut them in quarters, but do not core them. Place the apples in a medium-sized saucepan with the cider and simmer over low heat until soft.

With the back of a wooden spoon, push the apple and cider mixture through a sieve. Measure the pulp in a jug and add 4 ounces [½ cup] of granulated sugar to every 8 fluid ounces [1 cup].

Return the apple pulp to the pan. Over low heat, stirring all the time with a wooden spoon, dissolve the sugar. When the sugar is dissolved raise the heat to high and boil the mixture rapidly until it is very thick and a small drop will not fall from the spoon.

Put the apple mixture in a bowl. When it is cool place the bowl in a basin with ice in it and whisk the apple mixture.

In a small mixing bowl, beat half the cream until it is thick but not stiff. Fold it into the apple mixture with the vanilla essence. Pile the mixture into individual glass dishes. Top with the rest of the cream, stiffly whipped.

Apple Pie

This single-crust, English apple pie is traditionally served with custard sauce.

4 SERVINGS

PASTRY
6 oz. [1½ cups] plain flour
2 teaspoons castor sugar
a pinch of salt
1½ oz. [3 tablespoons] butter
1½ oz. [3 tablespoons] vegetable fat
1 to 2 tablespoons iced water
castor sugar
FILLING
1½ lb. apples
¼ teaspoon freshly grated nutmeg
or ½ teaspoon ground nutmeg
6 oz. [¾ cup] brown sugar
2 cloves
1 tablespoon butter

Preheat the oven to hot 400°F (Gas Mark 6, 200°C).

Sift the flour, sugar and salt into a medium-sized mixing bowl. Put in the butter and vegetable fat and cut them into small pieces with a table knife. With your fingertips, rub the fat into the flour until the mixture looks like fine breadcrumbs.

Add 1 tablespoon of iced water and, using the knife, mix it into the flour mixture. With your hands, mix and knead the dough until it is smooth. Add more water if the dough is too dry. Chill the dough in the refrigerator for 10 minutes.

Peel, core and cut the apples into thin slices. Arrange the apple slices in a medium-sized pie dish, sprinkle with nutmeg and with all of the sugar if the apples are very tart, less if they are not. Add the cloves and dot the top with butter. Cover with foil and bake for 20 minutes. Remove from the oven and cool.

Roll out the pastry ¼-inch thick. Lift the pastry on your rolling pin and lay it over the pie. Press down the edge and trim the pastry with a sharp knife. Mark the edge with the knife or the back of a fork. Brush the top of the pie with water and dredge with castor sugar. Return the pie to the oven and bake for 30 minutes. Serve hot.

Apple and Pork Casserole

A simple pork dish, served in the casserole in which it is cooked, this is a good family lunch or informal dinner-party dish which can be made with inexpensive cuts of pork. It can be served with a green or root vegetable.

4 SERVINGS

2 lb. lean pork, boned
1 oz. [2 tablespoons] butter, softened
2 medium-sized onions, chopped
½ teaspoon dried sage
½ teaspoon salt
2 grindings black pepper
2 medium-sized cooking apples, peeled, cored and thinly sliced
3 tablespoons water
1½ lb. potatoes, peeled
2 tablespoons hot milk
1 tablespoon butter, cut into pieces

Preheat the oven to warm 325°F (Gas Mark 3, 170°C).

Remove any excess fat from the pork, then cut it into cubes. Grease a large oven-proof casserole with teaspoon of butter.

Put the onions, sage, salt and pepper in a mixing bowl and stir to mix.

Into the casserole place about one-third of the pork cubes. Cover them with one-half of the onion mixture and then with half of the sliced apples. Continue to fill the casserole with the remaining pork, onions and apples finishing with a layer of pork. Add the water.

Cover the casserole with a lid or piece of aluminium foil. Cook in the oven for 2 to 2½ hours or until the pork is tender.

About 30 minutes before the pork is

cooked, boil the potatoes in lightly salted water in a covered saucepan. When tender, drain thoroughly, return to the saucepan and shake over a low heat to dry them. Press the potatoes through a coarse sieve or mash them thoroughly. Return them to the pan and beat in the hot milk and softened butter until the potato is light and fluffy.

When the pork is cooked, spread the potato over it. Using a fork, roughen the surface of the potato layer into small peaks. Dot with small pieces of butter and return the casserole to the oven for 15 minutes, or until the potato topping is golden brown. Serve immediately.

Apple and Potato Stuffing

This is an excellent stuffing for goose. It should be well seasoned, so taste it before using and add more salt and pepper if necessary. This quantity is sufficient for one goose.

1 oz. [2 tablespoons] butter
1 lb. onions, peeled and sliced
1 lb. apples, peeled, cored and finely sliced
juice of 1 orange
3 parsley sprigs
6 leaves fresh sage or 1½ teaspoons dried sage
1 teaspoon salt
freshly ground black pepper
1 lb. potatoes, boiled and mashed
grated rind of 1 orange

Melt the butter in a medium-sized saucepan over moderate heat. Add the onions and sauté until they are soft but not brown. Add the apples, orange juice, parsley, sage, salt and 7 grindings of pepper. Cook until the apples are soft.

Press the apple and onion mixture through a sieve and mix well with the

Flavoured with sage and onions and topped with mashed potatoes, Apple and Pork Casserole is easy to make.

mashed potatoes and grated orange rind to make a fairly firm stuffing. Taste and correct seasoning if necessary.

Apple and Rice Pudding

An inexpensive dessert, Apple and Rice Pudding looks attractive and has a pleasant sour-sweet taste. The quantity of sugar needed depends very much on the tartness of the apples.

6 SERVINGS

4 oz [⅔ cup] long-grain rice
10 fl. oz. [1¼ cups] milk or milk mixed with single [light] cream
grated rind of 1 lemon
4 oz. [½ cup] plus 2 tablespoons sugar
a pinch of salt
2 egg yolks, plus 2 egg whites
1½ lb. apples, peeled and thinly sliced
2 oz. sultanas [⅓ cup golden raisins]
1 oz. [2 tablespoons] butter
4 fl. oz. [½ cup] cider or apple juice

Preheat the oven to moderate 350°F (Gas Mark 4, 180°C).

Wash the rice thoroughly, soak for 30 minutes in cold water and drain. Put the milk, lemon rind, 2 ounces [¼ cup] of sugar and the salt in a medium-sized saucepan. Bring to the boil over moderate heat. Add the rice and, when the mixture comes to the boil again, reduce the heat to very low. Cover and simmer for 10 minutes, until the rice is cooked and the milk absorbed. Remove from the heat. With a fork, thoroughly mix in the egg yolks.

Put half the rice mixture in a deep baking dish, then half the apples and sultanas. Sprinkle with 2 tablespoons of sugar and dot with half the butter. Put the remaining rice on the apples and top with the remaining apples, sultanas and 2 tablespoons of sugar. Dot with the remaining butter. Pour the cider or apple juice over the apples and bake for 45 minutes. Reset the oven to cool 300°F (Gas Mark 2, 150°C).

In a small bowl beat the whites of the eggs until stiff. Fold in the 2 tablespoons of sugar. Spread the meringue over the apples. Return the pudding to the oven and bake for about 20 minutes or until the meringue is golden. Serve immediately.

Apple Sauce

Tart Apple Sauce is a delicate accompaniment to goose, duck or pork dishes. Apple Sauce and horseradish is excellent served with pork dishes. Just add horseradish to taste and blend into the Apple Sauce. A somewhat sweeter Apple Sauce, served with cream, is a simple and tasty dessert.

ABOUT 9 FLUID OUNCES

1 lb. cooking apples, peeled, cored and sliced
    finely grated rind of 1 lemon
2 tablespoons lemon juice
2 tablespoons sugar, or to taste
2 tablespoons water
1 oz. [2 tablespoons] butter, cut into small pieces

Place the apples in a large saucepan with the lemon rind and juice, sugar and water.

Place the pan over high heat and bring to the boil. Reduce the heat to low, cover and simmer for 20 minutes or until the apples are soft.

Either rub the apples through a sieve or purée in a blender or food processor. Beat in the butter. Serve hot as an accompaniment to roast pork, or cold as a dessert with custard or whipped cream.

Spoon the apple sauce into a rigid container or polythene bag or yoghurt carton and freeze for up to 9 months. Defrost at room temperature for 4 hours.

Apple Sauce Cake

This moist, spicy cake has a pleasant cinnamon flavour. It can be served plain or covered with a caramel icing.

6 SERVINGS

7 oz. [1¾ cups] self-raising flour
¼ teaspoon salt
1 teaspoon baking powder
1 teaspoon cinnamon
½ teaspoon ground cloves
4 oz. [½ cup] butter, softened
5 oz. [⅝ cup] soft brown sugar
3 eggs
4 oz. [⅔ cup] raisins
4 oz. [1 cup] walnuts, chopped
9 fl. oz. [1⅛ cups] apple sauce
    sifted icing [confectioners'] sugar

Preheat the oven to moderate 350°F (Gas Mark 4, 180°C). Grease an 8-inch cake tin, line the base with greaseproof [waxed] paper and grease the paper.

Sift the flour, salt, baking powder, cinnamon and cloves into a bowl.

Cream the butter and sugar in another bowl. Beat in the eggs, one at a time, adding a little flour with each one.

Fold in the remaining flour. Stir in the raisins, walnuts and apple sauce.

Pour into the cake tin. Bake in the centre of the oven for 50 minutes or until a fine warmed skewer inserted into the centre comes out clean.

Leave for 5 minutes before turning out on to a wire rack to cool completely.

Dust with the icing [confectioners'] sugar before serving.

Apple Snow

Apple Snow is a light, frothy dessert which can be served with sponge fingers or biscuits. It is inexpensive and easy to make.

4 SERVINGS

1 lb. cooking apples
    rind of ½ lemon
2 tablespoons water
4 oz. castor [½ cup fine] sugar
2 egg whites

Preheat the oven to fairly hot 375°F (Gas Mark 5, 190°C).

Core the apples and, with a sharp knife, slit the skin round the centre. Place the apples in a fireproof dish with the lemon rind and 2 tablespoons of

water. Bake until the apples are soft. This will take about 1 hour.

Discard the lemon peel. Allow the apples to cool, remove the skins and rub through a sieve.

Whisk the egg whites until they are frothy. Add the sugar a little at a time and beat until the mixture stands up in peaks when the whisk is removed. Gradually add the apple pulp, beating until it is thoroughly mixed with the egg white. Taste and add more sugar if necessary. Serve cold.

Apple Sonning

This delicious dessert can be eaten hot served with a hot sabayon sauce, or cold with the same sauce chilled and made with an additional egg yolk.

6 SERVINGS

4 oz. [½ cup] butter
1½ lb. apples peeled, cored and sliced
½ teaspoon powdered cinnamon
1 oz. cornflour [¼ cup cornstarch]
6 oz. [¾ cup] sugar
2 eggs plus 1 egg yolk
SABAYON SAUCE
3 egg yolks
3 oz. castor [⅜ cup fine] sugar
½ teaspoon arrowroot
4 fl. oz. [½ cup] sherry

Preheat the oven to warm 325°F (Gas Mark 3, 170°C). Grease a soufflé dish or pudding basin with a little butter and dust lightly with flour.

Melt the butter in a medium-sized saucepan over moderate heat. Add the apples and cinnamon. Cover and simmer until the apples are soft.

Rub the apples through a sieve. Put the pulp back in the saucepan and add the cornflour and sugar. Stir with a wooden spoon over low heat until the mixture thickens. Remove from the heat and turn into a mixing bowl to cool.

In a large bowl, using a whisk or a rotary beater, whisk the eggs and yolk until they are very pale. Fold the beaten eggs into the apple mixture and mix well. Pour into the soufflé dish and bake for 1 hour.

Just before the dessert is ready, make the sauce. In a medium-sized bowl, whisk the egg yolks with the sugar and arrowroot until they are almost white. Stand the bowl in a pan of hot water over a low heat and whisk until the sauce becomes thick. Add the sherry and raise the heat until the water boils. Whisk for a minute or two more. Pour the sauce into a sauce boat or bowl and, if serving the dessert hot, serve immediately.

Apple Turnovers

These apple-filled pastry triangles make a delicious and decorative luncheon dessert. They are also suitable to serve with tea.

12 TURNOVERS

PASTRY

½ oz. [1 tablespoon] **butter or margarine**

3 large **cooking apples, cored and sliced**

2 oz. **sultanas** [⅓ cup golden raisins]

2 oz. [⅓ cup] **currants**
grated rind of 1 lemon

2 oz. [¼ cup] **soft light brown sugar**

7 oz. **made-weight puff pastry, defrosted if frozen**

GLAZE

1 large **egg white, lightly beaten**
castor sugar

Preheat the oven to fairly hot 400°F (Gas Mark 6, 200°C).

Melt the butter or margarine in a heavy-based saucepan. Add the cooking apples, sultanas, currants, lemon rind and

Crisp apple-filled triangles of puff pastry, Apple Turnovers are delicious hot or cold.

soft brown sugar, simmer for about 10 minutes, stirring occasionally, until the apples are soft.

Roll out the pastry on a lightly floured board to a 16- × 12-inch rectangle. Cut into 12 squares.

Place a little of the apple mixture on each square. Brush the edges with water and fold over to make triangles. Press the edges together to seal, knock up by tapping the edges horizontally with a knife blade.

Place the triangles on a baking sheet and pierce each one with a skewer or the top of a knife, to allow the steam to escape and prevent the filling from boiling over. Lightly brush the top of each turnover with the beaten egg white and generously sprinkle with sugar.

Bake for 10 minutes. Reduce the oven temperature to moderate 350°F (Gas Mark 4, 180°C) and bake for a further 20

minutes.

Sprinkle with extra castor sugar, if wished. A mixture of castor sugar and ground cinnamon adds extra flavour. Serve hot for dessert with custard sauce or whipped cream, or cold for picnics or packed lunches.

Apricot

The fruit of a tree which is native to North China, the apricot was brought from Armenia to Italy, where it was cultivated over 2,000 years ago. Apricots are now widely grown in the warmer temperate countries. They are exported in fresh, canned and dried form from Spain, South Africa, the United States and Australia.

Like the peach, the apricot must be really ripe to be sweet and juicy. It is popular as a dessert fruit, in fruit dishes and in salads. It is one of the fruits most used in pastry making and confectionery. Apricots have a low sugar content and, when dried, are rich in iron.

To peel apricots easily, put them in boiling water for a minute or two.

Apricot Bourdaloue Tart

A pretty apricot tart which has an orange-flavoured crème filling. The sharp taste of the apricots contrasts pleasantly with the sweet crème. This classic French dessert is guaranteed to impress your guests.

6 SERVINGS

6 oz. made-weight shortcrust [pie crust] pastry, defrosted if frozen
FILLING
4 oz. [½ cup] sugar
9 fl. oz. [1⅛ cups] water
1 tablespoon lemon juice
1 lb. large apricots, halved and stoned or 16 oz. [1 lb.] apricot halves canned in natural syrup, drained
2 egg yolks
2 oz. [¼ cup] castor [superfine] sugar
grated rind of 1 orange
1½ oz. [3 tablespoons] flour
1½ oz. [3 tablespoons] cornflour [cornstarch]
9 fl. oz. [1¼ cups] milk
1 egg white
1 oz. [2 tablespoons] flaked toasted almonds

Preheat the oven to hot 425°F (Gas Mark 7, 220°C). Carefully roll out the pastry on a lightly floured surface and use to line an 8-inch loose-bottomed fluted flan tin or pie dish.

Line the pastry with foil and baking beans and bake for 15 minutes. Remove the foil and beans, reduce the oven temperature to 375°F (Gas Mark 5,

A flan filled with orange-flavoured cream, Apricot Bourdaloue may be made with fresh or canned apricots.

190°C) and bake for a further 10 minutes until the pastry is crisp, then set aside and leave until cold.

Meanwhile, to make the filling, dissolve the sugar in the water and lemon juice in a saucepan over moderate heat. Bring the mixture to the boil. Add the apricots and simmer for 10 minutes, without stirring, or until the apricots are just tender but still firm to the touch.

Drain the apricots. Boil the syrup until reduced and thick; then set aside until completely cold.

Whisk the egg yolks with half the castor sugar in a bowl. Add the orange rind, flour and cornflour [cornstarch] and beat until the mixture becomes smooth and glossy.

Bring the milk just to boiling point in a small saucepan over moderate heat. Slowly pour it into the egg mixture, stirring until smooth.

Return the mixture to the saucepan and cook over moderate heat, stirring occasionally, until thick and smooth. Set aside until cold.

When everything is cold, place the pastry case on a serving plate. Whisk the egg white with the remaining castor sugar and fold into the cream with a large metal spoon or spatula. Spoon the chilled custard into the case and smooth the surface.

Decoratively arrange the poached apricots on top of the custard filling.

Lightly brush with the reduced syrup and sprinkle the top with the flaked almonds.
Serve immediately.

Apricot Brandy

This alcoholic liqueur has a sweetened spirit or brandy base flavoured with dried apricots. Made in Britain, Holland and France, it is usually sold as a liqueur. In Southern Hungary, where apricots are very plentiful, a superb apricot brandy is distilled from fresh, crushed apricots and apricot kernels.

Apricots in Brandy

Elegant and expensive, this dessert is easily made and can be prepared a week or even two weeks in advance of a special dinner party. Apricots in Brandy can be served alone or as a sauce for ice cream.

6 SERVINGS

1 lb. dried apricots
4 oz. [½ cup] sugar
brandy

Place the apricots and sugar in a mixing bowl. Pour over enough brandy to completely cover the fruit. Cover and leave in a cool place for at least 36 hours. The longer the apricots are soaked the more the flavour improves. Serve chilled.

Apricot Condé

A classic French dessert, Apricot Condé is easy to prepare and makes an elegant end to a special dinner.

6 SERVINGS

1 teaspoon vegetable oil
4 oz. [⅔ cup] round-grain rice
1½ pints [3¾ cups] milk
12 oz. [1½ cups] sugar
1 oz. [2 tablespoons] butter
⅛ teaspoon salt
1 teaspoon vanilla essence
6 egg yolks, lightly beaten
2 lb. apricots, peeled, halved and stoned
8 fl. oz. [1 cup] water
2 tablespoons kirsch
1 oz. [¼ cup] flaked almonds

Preheat the oven to cool 300°F (Gas Mark 2, 150°C). Lightly grease an 8-inch soufflé dish with the oil. Set aside.

Apricot Condé, a classic French dessert of apricots, rice and eggs, is ideal for a dinner party.

In a large flameproof casserole, bring the rice, milk, 4 ounces [½ cup] of the sugar, the butter, salt and vanilla essence to the boil over moderate heat, stirring constantly.

Cover the casserole and transfer it to the oven. Bake for 1 hour, or until all the liquid has been absorbed.

Remove the casserole from the oven. Stir in the egg yolks and place the casserole over low heat. Cook, stirring constantly, for 3 minutes. Remove the casserole from the heat and set it aside to cool.

Slice half a pound of the apricots. Set aside.

When the rice mixture is cool, spoon one-third of it into the soufflé dish. Place half the apricot slices on top. Continue making layers, ending with the rice mixture. Cover the dish and place it in the refrigerator to chill for 2 hours or until the rice mixture is firm.

Meanwhile, to make the sauce, in a medium-sized saucepan, dissolve the remaining sugar in the water over moderate heat, stirring constantly. Add the remaining apricot halves. Reduce the heat to low and simmer for 10 minutes or until the apricots are tender but still firm. Remove the pan from the heat.

With a slotted spoon, remove 12 apricot halves from the pan and set them aside.

Purée the remaining apricot halves with the syrup in a strainer or blender and return the purée to the saucepan. Return the pan to high heat. Boil for 3 minutes. Remove the pan from the heat.

Stir in the kirsch and almonds. Pour the sauce into a bowl and set it aside to cool.

Then place it in the refrigerator to chill.

Unmould the pudding on to a serving dish. Arrange the reserved apricot halves on the top and around the sides. Spoon over the sauce and serve immediately.

Apricot Glaze

Jam glazes are used to give a glossy surface to fruit flans and tarts. In classic recipes, apricot jam forms the basis of the glaze for yellow fruits.

4 FLUID OUNCES

4 tablespoons apricot jam
3 fl. oz. [⅜ cup] water
1 teaspoon lemon juice

Combine the jam and water in a small saucepan. Stirring, cook over moderate heat for 5 minutes. Add the lemon juice and stir well. Remove from the heat and strain.

Apricots Granville

The brandy in this recipe may be omitted but it does make a dish of poached apricots into a more delicious dessert.

4 SERVINGS

1½ lb. firm apricots
2½ pints [6¼ cups] water
1 lb. [2 cups] granulated sugar
½ vanilla pod
4 fl. oz. [½ cup] brandy

Blanch and peel the apricots and cut them in halves. Crack the stones with a hammer or nutcracker and remove the kernels.

Put the water, sugar and the vanilla pod in a medium-sized saucepan over moderate heat. Stir to dissolve the sugar, raise the heat and bring the syrup to a boil. Add the apricots and kernels to the syrup. Lower the heat and simmer for 5 minutes.

Remove the pan from the heat and allow the apricots to cool in the syrup for about 20 minutes. Remove the fruit and the kernels with a slotted spoon and place in a bowl.

Take out the vanilla pod. Return the pan to the stove and boil rapidly until the syrup is thick. Remove from the heat. Add the brandy. Pour this sauce over the apricots. Chill in the refrigerator and serve with cream.

Apricot Jam

This jam, which is excellent for making apricot sauce and apricot glaze, is made with fresh apricots. Only firm, flavourful fruit should be used. Over-ripe fruit will prevent the jam from setting.

MAKES ABOUT 5 POUNDS

3 lb. fresh apricots, halved and
    stoned
1 large lemon, quartered
9 fl. oz. [1⅛ cups] water
3 lb. [6 cups] sugar
1 tablespoon orange-flower water

Put the apricots, lemon quarters and the water in a large, heavy-based saucepan. Bring to the boil, then simmer for 15 minutes or until the fruit is tender and the water reduced slightly.

Meanwhile heat the oven to 225°F (Gas mark ¼, 110°C). Spread the sugar on a baking tray and warm it in the oven. Warm the clean jars.

Apricot Jam may be made with fresh fruit, or dried fruit and almonds.

Add the orange-flower water and sugar to the fruit and stir until dissolved. Boil rapidly for about 15 minutes, or until the jam has reached setting point. To test for setting, place a spoonful of jam on a cold plate; if set, the surface of the jam will wrinkle when pushed with a finger. If it has not reached this point; boil for a few minutes more, then repeat the test.

Skim the surface of the jam with a slotted spoon to remove any scum, remove the lemon quarters and allow jam to cool slightly.

Pour the jam into warm jars, cover immediately and allow to cool, then label and store.

To give a lovely almondy flavour to the jam, crack open a few of the apricot stones, soak the kernels in boiling water, then remove the skins and put the kernels in a muslin bag. Place the bag in the preserving pan with the apricots; remove it before bottling.

Apricot Jam with Almonds

Made with dried apricots, this jam can be prepared at any time of the year.

ABOUT 5 POUNDS

1 lb. dried apricots
3 pints [7½ cups] water
  juice of 1 lemon
3 lb. sugar
2 oz. [⅓ cup] almonds, blanched

Wash the apricots and put them in a large bowl with the water, making sure that they are completely covered. Leave them to soak for 24 hours.

Transfer the apricots and the water to a preserving-pan or a very large saucepan. Over moderate heat, stirring occasionally with a wooden spoon, simmer for 30 minutes, or until the fruit is very tender.

Add the lemon juice and sugar. Stir until the sugar is dissolved. Put in the almonds, bring the jam to the boil and continue to boil rapidly for 15 minutes.

To test the jam for setting, remove pan from the heat and put a spoonful of jam on a cold plate or saucer and allow it to cool. Setting point has been reached when the surface of the jam sets and wrinkles when you push it with your finger. If the setting point has not been reached, return the pan to the heat and continue boiling, testing every few minutes.

When the setting point is reached, skim the scum off the surface of the jam with a slotted spoon.

Using a jug or ladle, fill clean, warm, dry jars to within ½-inch of the tops.

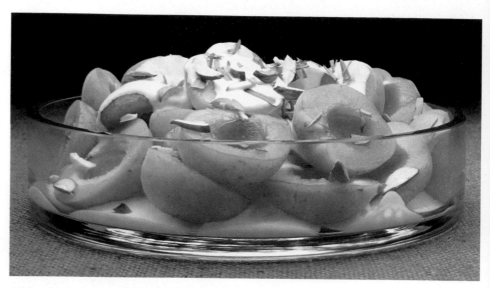

This Apricot Salad has a dressing of soured cream with fresh tarragon.

Wipe the outside and the inside rim of the jars with a warm, damp cloth to remove any drops of jam.

While the jam is still hot, put a small round of wax paper in each jar. Then put on a vegetable parchment or cellophane cover and fasten with string or an elastic band. Label the jars and, when cold, store them in a cool, dry cupboard.

Apricot Pudding

This delicious pudding, made with dried apricots, is firm on top but soft and creamy underneath. It is inexpensive and very easy to make.

6 SERVINGS

6 oz. [1 cup] dried apricots
10 fl. oz. [1¼ cups] water
4 eggs
  grated rind and juice of 1 lemon
5 tablespoons flour
2 tablespoons melted butter
6 oz. [¾ cup] sugar
  a pinch of salt
10 fl. oz. [1¼ cups] milk

Preheat the oven to moderate 350°F (Gas Mark 4, 180°C). Lightly grease an oven-proof soufflé dish.

Put the apricots in a medium-sized saucepan with the water. Bring to the boil, lower the heat and then simmer for 10 minutes, or until the apricots are tender. Put the apricots and the liquid into an electric blender and blend, or push through a sieve to make a purée.

Separate the whites of the eggs from the yolks. Set the egg whites aside. In a medium-sized mixing bowl, beat the yolks thoroughly with a whisk or a rotary beater, adding the grated lemon rind and the juice, the flour, melted butter, sugar, salt, milk and the apricot purée. Beat until well mixed.

Whisk the egg whites until they stand up in peaks when the whisk is removed. Fold the egg whites into the apricot mixture. Pour into the soufflé dish.

Put 1 inch of water into a baking pan and place the soufflé dish in it. Place in the centre of the oven and bake for 40 minutes or until the top of the pudding is firm to the touch. Eat warm or cold.

Apricot Salad

This salad, made with fresh apricots and served with a tarragon cream dressing, is a good accompaniment to hot or cold ham.

4 SERVINGS

2 lb. ripe apricots
DRESSING
4 tablespoons thick sour
  cream
3 tablespoons tarragon vinegar
1 tablespoon sugar
½ teaspoon salt
4 grindings black pepper
  a few tarragon leaves,
  chopped

Blanch and peel the apricots. Cut each apricot in half and remove the stone. Arrange the apricot halves in a glass serving bowl. Crack the stones with a nutcracker or hammer. Take out the kernels, chop them and set aside.

To make the dressing, put the sour cream into a bowl and stir in the vinegar, sugar, salt and pepper. When it is thoroughly mixed taste the dressing and adjust the seasoning if necessary.

Just before serving, pour the dressing over the apricots. Sprinkle with the tarragon leaves and chopped kernels.

Apricots and Gammon or Ham

An easy-to-make and satisfying hot supper dish, this can be served with mashed potatoes and a green vegetable. If fresh apricots are not available, drained, canned apricots may be substituted. They should be put on the gammon slices without additional cooking and the syrup in which they are packed can be used in the baking.

4 SERVINGS

6 oz. [¾ cup] sugar
10 fl. oz. [1¼ cups] water
1 lb. fresh apricots, blanched, peeled, halved and stoned
4 thick slices gammon or ham, 6 to 8 oz. each
8 cloves
4 teaspoons soft brown sugar
1 oz. [2 tablespoons] butter

Preheat the oven to fairly hot 375°F (Gas Mark 5, 190°C).

In a medium-sized saucepan, dissolve the sugar in the water over moderate heat. Bring to the boil. Add the apricot halves, lower the heat and simmer for about 10 minutes or until the apricots are tender but still firm. Remove from the heat.

Place the gammon or ham in a large baking dish. Insert the cloves into the fat and sprinkle the slices with the brown sugar.

Drain the apricots and arrange them on top of the gammon, adding a tablespoon of the syrup around each slice. Dot with butter and bake uncovered for 40 minutes, basting occasionally.

Apricot Tart

Inexpensive and easy to prepare, this is a summer dessert to be made when apricots are in season. Use half bananas and half apricots as a variation.

4 SERVINGS

PASTRY
5 oz. [1¼ cups] flour
1 tablespoon sugar
1 oz. [2 tablespoons] butter
1½ oz. [3 tablespoons] vegetable fat
1 egg yolk, lightly beaten
1 to 2 tablespoons iced water
GLAZE
3 large tablespoons apricot jam
1 tablespoon water
a squeeze of lemon juice
FILLING
1 lb. apricots, blanched, peeled, halved and stoned
4 oz. [½ cup] sugar
1 oz. [2 tablespoons] butter
1 oz. [¼ cup] almonds, blanched and shredded

Sift the flour and sugar into a medium-sized mixing bowl. Add the butter and vegetable fat and cut them into small pieces with a table knife. With your fingertips, rub the fat into the flour until the mixture resembles very fine breadcrumbs.

Add the egg yolk and ½ tablespoon of iced water and, using the knife, mix it into the flour mixture. With your hands, mix and knead the dough until it is smooth. Add more water if the pastry is dry. Make a ball of the pastry. Cover it with greaseproof paper and chill in the refrigerator for 20 minutes.

Preheat oven to fairly hot 375°F (Gas Mark 5, 190°C).

Roll out the pastry and with it line an 8-inch or 9-inch flan tin with a removable bottom. Cover the pastry with aluminium foil. Weigh it down with dried beans or peas and bake for 10 minutes. Remove the beans and the foil, prick the bottom of the pastry with a fork and return it to the oven for 5 minutes.

To prepare the glaze, boil the jam and water in a small saucepan for 5 minutes. Sieve the mixture and add the lemon juice.

Brush a little of the glaze on the bottom of the pastry. Place the apricots, cut sides down, in the pastry case. Sprinkle with the sugar and dot with the butter. Place the tart in the oven and

---

Fresh or canned apricots and ham or gammon baked together is an easy-to-prepare lunch or dinner dish.

bake for 35 minutes, or until the fruit has coloured slightly.

Remove the tart from the tin and place on a rack. Sprinkle with the shredded almonds and brush over with the glaze. Serve warm or cold with cream.

Aquavit

A Scandinavian liquor distilled from potatoes or grain and flavoured with caraway seeds, there are many varieties of aquavit. They range from colourless to light orange, and some are flavoured with other herbs and spices. In Scandinavia, aquavit is usually served before or at the beginning of a meal and is tossed down in one gulp.

Arabian Stewed Lamb

This recipe is an adaptation of a classic Arabian dish. The lamb is stewed with prunes and flavoured with cinnamon and turmeric. It is inexpensive, easy to make and unusual.

4 SERVINGS

2 tablespoons cooking oil
2 lb. lamb leg or shoulder, boned and cut into 1½-inch cubes
1 large onion, sliced
1 clove garlic, crushed
1 teaspoon powdered turmeric
2-inch cinnamon stick
1 teaspoon salt
    freshly ground black pepper
1 tablespoon flour
12 fl. oz. [1½ cups] beef stock
1 tablespoon brown sugar
16 prunes, stoned and soaked in water for 2 hours

Heat the oil in a large saucepan over moderate heat. Add the lamb cubes and sauté, stirring occasionally, until the cubes are brown on all sides. Using a slotted spoon, remove the pieces of lamb and set aside on a plate.

Add the onion to the pan and fry until it is golden brown, stirring occasionally. Add the garlic, turmeric, cinnamon, salt and 7 grindings of pepper. Stir and sauté for 5 minutes. Add the flour, stir and cook for a few seconds before gradually adding the stock.

Raise the heat and continue stirring until the mixture comes to the boil. Return the meat to the pan, lower the heat and simmer for 40 minutes or until

Left. Arabian Stewed Lamb, flavoured with prunes, cinnamon and turmeric, is an adaptation of an Eastern recipe.

the lamb is tender. Ten minutes before the lamb is cooked, add the sugar and the prunes. Serve hot with rice which has been boiled with a bay leaf.

Aragosta Fra Diavolo

LOBSTER WITH DEVILLED SAUCE

Aragosta Fra Diavolo (ah-rah-GO-stah frah dee-AH-voh-loh) is a spicy, Italian lobster dish. Serve it as a main course with a green salad and crusty bread.

4 SERVINGS

2 large lobsters, cooked
1 oz. [2 tablespoons] butter
1 tablespoon oil
4 shallots, finely chopped
2 cloves garlic, crushed
14 oz. canned tomatoes, drained
½ teaspoon dried thyme
½ teaspoon powdered bay leaf
1 tablespoon chopped parsley
1 teaspoon Tabasco sauce
2 teaspoons vinegar
1 teaspoon salt
¼ teaspoon black pepper
1 teaspoon sugar
5 fl. oz. [⅝ cup] red wine

Halve the lobsters and crack the large claws. Place the lobsters in a casserole.

Melt the butter in a saucepan over moderate heat. Add the oil. When hot, add the shallots and garlic and fry until they are soft. Add the tomatoes, thyme, bay leaf, parsley, Tabasco sauce, vinegar, salt, pepper and sugar. Stir, cover the pan and cook over low heat for 5 minutes.

Preheat the oven to moderate 350°F (Gas Mark 4, 180°C).

Light buns topped with brown sugar, almonds and raisins, Aranygaluska are traditionally eaten hot in Hungary.

Add the wine to the sauce, raise the heat and cook briskly, stirring occasionally, until the sauce is fairly thick.

Pour the sauce over the lobsters. Cover the casserole and bake in the oven for 20 minutes.

Aranygaluska

HUNGARIAN BUNS

Light, golden buns with a sugary filling and topping, Aranygaluska (AH-rahn-y'-GAH-loosh-kah) are traditionally served with morning or afternoon coffee. They are best eaten fresh from the oven, but they can be reheated.

ABOUT 14 BUNS

5 fl. oz. [⅝ cup] milk
1 tablespoon butter
3 tablespoons sugar
1 large egg, lightly beaten
2 fl. oz. [¼ cup] tepid water
1 tablespoon dried yeast
14 oz. [3½ cups] sifted flour
    pinch of salt
4 tablespoons melted butter
FILLING
2 oz. [⅓ cup] soft brown sugar
3 oz. [½ cup] raisins
2 oz. [⅓ cup] blanched almonds, finely chopped
¼ teaspoon ground cinnamon

Put milk, 2 tablespoons sugar, and 1 tablespoon butter in a small saucepan over low heat, stir until the butter has melted and the sugar dissolved. Remove from the heat. When the mixture has cooled, beat in the egg.

Pour the tepid water into a bowl, stir in the remaining amount of sugar and sprinkle the yeast over the top. Set aside and leave for 20 minutes or until the mixture is frothy. Stir the yeast mixture into the milk, butter and egg liquid.

Put the flour and salt into a mixing bowl and make a well in the centre. Pour in the mixture from the saucepan, and, with a wooden spoon, mix it into the flour to form a stiff dough. Cover the bowl with a clean cloth and put it in a warm place until the dough has doubled in size.

For the filling, mix together the sugar, almonds, raisins and cinnamon.

When the dough has risen, put it on a floured surface. Knead it thoroughly with your hands for about 10 minutes, or until the dough is elastic and smooth. Then divide the dough into small pieces the size of a walnut and roll into balls.

Grease a 10-inch loose based cake tin with a little of the melted butter. Coat half of the dough balls in butter and place together in the bottom of the cake tin. Sprinkle half of the filling on top. Coat the remaining dough balls in butter and place on top of the filling. Spoon the remaining filling over the top.

Preheat the oven to cool 300°F (Gas Mark 2, 150°C).

Cover the cake tin with a piece of oiled plastic wrap and leave in a warm place

Sweet pepper salad with black olives and cheese, Ardei cu Untdelemn is an adaptation of a Romanian recipe.

for 30 to 40 minutes until the buns have risen.

Bake in the oven, on the middle shelf, for 30 minutes. Then raise the heat to fairly hot 400°F (Gas Mark 6, 200°C) and cook for 15 to 20 minutes, or until the buns are brown and firm.

Allow to cool in the tin for 5 minutes then turn the cake tin onto a wire rack and press the base of the tin to loosen the buns. Remove the base and reverse the buns back onto the wire rack. Leave to cool. Separate the buns.

Archbishop

A hot sherry or wine punch, this is an excellent drink for cold evenings or for a winter party.

4 TO 6 SERVINGS

1 Seville orange
20 cloves
1 tablespoon brown sugar
1 bottle medium-dry sherry, dry Bordeaux or dry, white wine

Preheat the oven to moderate 350°F (Gas Mark 4, 180°C).

Press the cloves into the skin of the orange. Place the orange on the middle shelf of the oven and cook for about 30 minutes, or until the orange is brown.

Cut the orange in half and sprinkle

the flesh with the sugar. Put the halves in the bottom of a punch bowl, or a large glass or china bowl.

Pour the sherry, or wine, into a stainless-steel or enamelled saucepan and heat until it is hot but not boiling. If you are using a glass bowl, put a metal spoon in it to prevent the bowl from cracking and pour in the wine. Serve immediately in punch cups or warmed wine glasses, putting a spoon in each glass.

Archiduc, à l'

A French cooking term, *à l'archiduc* (ah LAHR-chee-dook) is applied to a large number of dishes and usually indicates preparations seasoned with paprika and blended with cream.

Ardei cu Untdelemn
MARINATED PEPPER SALAD

A Romanian sweet pepper salad, Ardei cu Untdelemn (ahr-DAY koo oon-deh-LEM) can be served as an hors d'oeuvre, as a salad course or as an accompaniment to a meat dish. The peppers in the marinade, without the cheese and olives, can be kept in a jar with a tight fitting lid and stored in the refrigerator for a few days.

4 SERVINGS

4 green peppers
4 red peppers
6 tablespoons white vinegar
2 tablespoons medium dry sherry
1 tablespoon Worcestershire sauce
6 tablespoons olive oil
1 teaspoon salt
    freshly ground black pepper
2 teaspoons sugar
1 teaspoon paprika
12 black olives, stoned
8 oz. cream cheese cut into cubes

Wash and dry the peppers. Halve and remove the seeds and white pith. Cut the peppers into quarters. Half fill a saucepan with water and bring to the boil. Add the peppers and blanch for 3 minutes. Drain and dry on kitchen paper towels. Cool.

In a large mixing bowl, put the vinegar, sherry, Worcestershire sauce, oil, salt, 8 grindings of pepper, sugar and paprika. Stir well to mix. Taste and add more seasoning if necessary.

Put the peppers into the marinade and turn and mix until they are coated with the dressing. Cover and marinate for 24 hours in the refrigerator.

To serve, place the peppers in a shallow bowl or dish. Spoon a little of the marinade over them. Place the olives and cheese over the top and serve.

Ardei Umplutzi cu Orez

STUFFED GREEN PEPPERS AND TOMATO SAUCE

An unusual way of cooking peppers which comes from Romania, Ardei Umplutzi cu Orez (ar-DAY- oom-plootz koo oh-rayz) makes an excellent accompaniment to any braised meat.

4 SERVINGS

4 large green peppers
5 fl. oz. [⅝ cup] yoghurt
   chopped parsley
FILLING
1 tablespoon oil
2 onions, finely chopped
2 stalks celery, finely chopped
6 oz. [3 cups] cooked long-grain
   rice
2 tablespoons chopped parsley
¼ teaspoon mixed herbs
1 teaspoon salt
   freshly ground black pepper
1 egg
SAUCE
1 oz. [2 tablespoons] butter
1 onion, finely chopped
1 tablespoon flour
8 fl. oz. [1 cup] chicken stock
¾ lb. tomatoes, peeled and chopped
½ teaspoon salt
½ teaspoon sugar
2 teaspoons tomato purée

Cut the tops off the peppers and scoop out the seeds and white pith.

For the filling, heat the oil in a saucepan over medium heat. Add the onions and celery and stirring occasionally, fry for 3 to 4 minutes until soft but not brown. Stir in the rice, parsley, mixed herbs, salt, 6 grindings of pepper. Remove the pan from the heat and leave to cool slightly. Stir in the egg and mix well. Stuff the peppers pressing the filling down with the back of a spoon.

Preheat the oven to moderate 350°F (Gas Mark 4, 180°C).

For the sauce, place the butter in a flameproof casserole and melt over moderate heat. Add the onion and fry gently for 2 to 3 minutes until they are soft but not brown. Stir in the flour and cook for 1 minute. Pour the chicken stock slowly into the onion mixture stirring all the time with a wooden spoon. Continue stirring and cook until the sauce is thick and boiling. Add the tomatoes, salt, sugar and tomato purée.

Remove the casserole from the heat. Place the green peppers in the sauce, cover the casserole and cook in the oven for 35 to 40 minutes until the peppers are cooked. Remove the lid and spoon the yogurt over each pepper, sprinkle with parsley and serve immediately.

A Romanian dish, Ardei Umplutzi cu Orez is stuffed peppers in a tomato sauce topped with yogurt.

Areca Nut

The areca nut, or betel nut, is the fruit of the areca palm tree, which is indigenous to Malaysia but is also grown in Sri Lanka, India, Thailand and the Phillipines. The betel nut has a red or orange outer skin and the actual nut is a light brown colour with white flesh. The people of South Asia chew this nut which is considered to aid the digestion and is a mild narcotic. The nut is often chopped into small pieces, wrapped in a betel leaf with lime and aromatic flavouring and chewed. Chewing the betel nut produces a flow of red saliva which temporarily stains the mouth and teeth.

Arlésienne, à l'

A French cooking term, à l'Arlésienne (ah lahr-LAYZ-yen) is used to indicate dishes garnished in three different ways. One consists of sautéed aubergines, [eggplants] tomatoes, onion rings, and another is applied to a garnish of small, whole tomatoes fried in butter, and pickled chicory hearts sautéed in oil. Small tomatoes filled with a rice mixture, olives stuffed with a chicken and anchovy mixture, and new potatoes form the third garnish.

Armagnac

Famous brandies distilled in the Gers Department of France, armagnacs are considered to be equal to the best cognacs. The sandy soil of the vineyards produces a special wine from which the brandies are distilled in one operation. The resulting liquid is aged in barrels made of black Gascony oak which imparts a distinctive flavour to the armagnacs.

Armoricaine

Armorica is the Latin name for the region in northwestern France which includes the Gaul coast between the Seine and the Loire Rivers. The name derives from two Celtic words: *ar* which means on and *mor* which means sea. This region is more commonly known as Brittany. The culinary term *à l'Armoricaine* (ah lahr-MOH-ree-ken) applies to the many French dishes originating from this region and should not be confused with the term *à l'Americaine*.

Armoricaine also refers to a particularly delicious variety of Brittany oyster.

Arnavut Cigeri

LAMB'S LIVER WITH PEPPERS

A Turkish dish, Arnavut Cigeri (ahr-na-VOOT gee-ayr-ay) is spicy sautéed liver accompanied by an onion and pepper salad. It is quickly and simply prepared and is served as a first course. Larger quantities may be served as a main course.

4 SERVINGS

1 lb. lamb's liver, cut into cubes
3 fl. oz. [⅜ cup] anisette
3 onions, sliced
2 tablespoons chopped parsley
2 red peppers, seeds and white pith removed and sliced
½ teaspoon salt
freshly ground black pepper
1 teaspoon garlic salt
1 teaspoon sugar
2 teaspoons lemon juice
3 tablespoons flour
5 fl. oz. [⅝ cup] vegetable oil

Put the lamb cubes and anisette into a mixing bowl. Mix well and set aside. Blanch the onion rings in boiling water for 4 minutes. Drain and place in a bowl with the parsley, pepper slices, ½ teaspoon salt, 7 grindings of black pepper, ½ teaspoon garlic salt, sugar, and lemon juice. Toss well together and set aside.

On a large plate mix the flour and the remaining ½ teaspoon of garlic salt. With a slotted spoon, remove the liver cubes from the anisette and coat in the flour mixture.

Heat the oil in a frying-pan until it is very hot. Shake off the excess flour from the liver and fry for 2 to 3 minutes or until the cubes are lightly brown. Drain the fried liver on kitchen paper towels.

Place the liver on a heated serving dish and arrange the onion and red pepper salad around the dish.

If liked the salad may be served separately in a bowl.

Arni Psito

ROAST LEG OF LAMB

Arni Psito (ahr-nee psee-toh) is considered a great delicacy in Greece and is traditionally eaten at Easter.

6 SERVINGS

5 lb. leg of lamb
1 garlic clove, crushed
1 teaspoon grated lemon rind
1 teaspoon salt
freshly ground black pepper
1 oz. [2 tablespoons] butter
2 tablespoons oil
2 tablespoons lemon juice
4 fl. oz. [½ cup] stock or water
2 onions, chopped
2 tablespoons chopped parsley
6 oz. mushrooms, sliced

Preheat the oven to very hot 475°F (Gas Mark 9, 240°C).

In a mixing bowl, put the garlic, lemon rind, salt and 6 grindings of black pepper. Mix well. Spread the garlic mixture over the lamb. Place the lamb, skin side up into a roasting tin.

Place the butter and oil in a small saucepan and melt over low heat. Add the lemon juice and the stock, or water. Bring to the boil and pour into the roasting tin. Cook in the oven for 20 minutes.

Reduce the heat to moderate 350°F (Gas Mark 4, 180°C). Add the onions, parsley and mushrooms and continue cooking for about 2 hours.

Place the meat on a serving dish and arrange the onion mixture around it with cooked rice sautéed in butter.

Aroma

This word, when applied to a food or a wine, indicates its characteristic smell. Aroma is an important aspect of all foods as it contributes greatly to the appetizing quality of a dish. It can tell the cook much about the food being prepared, its freshness and the balance of seasoning. A particular method of cooking brings out an aroma or may impart one.

Aromatic

The term aromatic is used to describe the many fragrant herbs, spices, fruits, flowers and vegetables which are used to add aroma in cooking, pastry-making and confectionery.

A delicious Greek way of roasting leg of lamb, Arni Psito is served with a savoury mushroom and onion sauce and rice.

Aromatic Bitters

Aromatic bitters are alcoholic drinks flavoured with roots, barks, herbs or fruits. They are drunk either as aperitifs to whet the appetite, as liqueurs after a meal, or are used in small quantities in mixed drinks.

Some aromatic bitters, for example Orange Bitters, are sold under the name which gives them their predominant flavour. But, more commonly, they have commercial brand names. The best known are Abbots Aged Bitters, which are made in the United States, Amer Picon in France, Angostura in Trinidad, Boonekamp in Holland, Campari in Italy and Underberg in Germany.

The preparation of aromatic liqueurs originated in France in the sixteenth century, although early Hebrew literature records that sweet or bitter herbs were sometimes added to wine to improve its flavour.

Some bitters are said to be digestive aids. In the United States during prohibition in the 1920s, Dr. Seigert's Angostura Bitters were considered to have medicinal properties and so were exempt from prohibition.

Arrack

Derived from the Arabic *araq*, meaning sweat and juice, arrack is the name for a wide range of strong, rough spirits which are distilled from whatever ingredients are widely and cheaply available. In Asia these ingredients include fermented rice, dates, palm sap, molasses, grapes or grain.

In the Middle East and the Balkans, arrack is known under many names—*raki* in Turkey, *ouzo* in Greece, *mastika* in Bulgaria, *zibib* in Egypt and *arrack* in the Lebanon, Syria, Iran, Iraq and Jordan. In these regions the drink is flavoured with aniseed and is superior to the fiery brews of the Far East.

Arrosto Perugina
ITALIAN ROAST PORK

This roast loin of pork, flavoured with fennel, cloves and garlic and basted with dry white wine, can be served hot or cold. An Italian dish, Arrosto Perugina (ah-ROH-sto per-roo-JEE-neh) is roasted in a slow oven so that the meat remains moist and juicy. Serve it with a green salad and white wine.

4 TO 6 SERVINGS

3½ to 4 lb. pork loin, boned and rolled
4 garlic cloves
4 cloves
½ tablespoon finely chopped fennel leaves or ½ teaspoon dried fennel
1½ teaspoons salt
freshly ground black pepper
10 fl. oz. [1¼ cups] dry white wine
10 fl. oz. [1¼ cups] water

Preheat the oven to cool 300°F (Gas Mark 2, 150°C).

Peel the garlic cloves and slit them into four lengthways. Moisten the garlic slivers with water and roll them in the fennel. With a sharp, pointed kitchen knife, make incisions in the pork large enough to insert 1 sliver of garlic and 1 whole clove. Insert all the garlic, fennel and cloves and rub the meat with the salt and 5 grindings of pepper.

Lay the meat in a deep baking dish and pour in the wine and water. Place the baking dish in the middle of the oven. Basting occasionally, allow 45 minutes cooking time per pound of meat. When cooked, the meat should be quite moist.

If the pork is to be served hot, remove it from the baking dish and place on a warmed serving dish. If the pork is to be served cold, allow it to cool in the juices in the baking dish before removing it.

Arrowroot

Arrowroot is a pure starch which is obtained from the root of a tropical plant. Dried in the sun, the root is ground to a fine, white powder. Very nutritious, arrowroot is easily digested and was once a popular ingredient in foods for children and invalids.

Used for thickening sauces, soups and puddings in place of flour or cornflour, only half as much arrowroot is required to produce the same result as with flour. For making milk puddings, arrowroot is used in the same way and in the same

A chicken and rice casserole with peas, Arroz con Pollo is flavoured with parsley, saffron and garlic.

proportions as cornflour. As a thickening agent for clear liquids, arrowroot is particularly good because it does not cause clouding.

The name arrowroot is said to come from its American Indian name, *aranuta*, which means 'flour-root'. Most arrowroot is imported from the West Indies.

Arroz con Pollo
CHICKEN WITH RICE

A chicken and rice dish from Spain, Arroz con Pollo (ah-ROHS kohn poh-loh) is flavoured with garlic and spices. Cooked in a casserole it makes a delicious main course.

4 SERVINGS

3 tablespoons vegetable oil
6 slices streaky bacon, chopped
1 x 5lb. chicken, cut into serving pieces.
2 tablespoons seasoned flour
2 onions, chopped
1 garlic clove, crushed
14 oz. canned tomatoes, drained
3 oz. [½ cup] canned pimientos, drained
2 teaspoons paprika
¼ teaspoon saffron
8 oz. [1⅓ cup] long grain rice
1 teaspoon salt
1 pint [2½ cups] water
6 oz. frozen peas
2 tablespoons chopped parsley

Heat the oil in a flameproof casserole over medium heat. Add the bacon and fry for about 5 minutes until crisp. Remove the bacon with a slotted spoon and drain on kitchen paper towels. Set aside.

Coat the chicken pieces in the seasoned flour, and add to the fat in the casserole. Place over moderate heat and fry the chicken on all sides until a light golden brown. Remove the chicken pieces from the casserole and set aside.

Preheat the oven to moderate 350°F (Gas Mark 4, 180°C).

Drain off most of the oil from the casserole. Put the onions and garlic in to the casserole and fry over moderate heat, stirring occasionally for 2 to 3 minutes until the onions are soft.

Place the chicken on top of the onions and add the tomatoes, pimientos, paprika, saffron, salt and water. Raise the heat and bring to the boil. Add the rice and bacon and stir well to mix the ingredients.

Cover the casserole with a lid or piece of aluminium foil and place in the oven, cook for about 30 minutes.

Add the peas and cook for a further 10 minutes or until the chicken is tender. Sprinkle with the chopped parsley.

To prepare an artichoke, cut off the stalk with a sharp knife and pull off any tough or bruised outer leaves.

Lay it on its side and slice off the top third. Rub all the cut edges and the base with a piece of lemon.

With kitchen scissors, trim ¼-inch off the points of the remaining leaves and rub the cut edges with lemon.

Artichoke

This is the name given to three quite different vegetables, the globe artichoke, the JERUSALEM ARTICHOKE, and the JAPANESE, or Chinese ARTICHOKE.

The globe, or leafy artichoke, which looks like a large thistle, is indigenous to Europe and North Africa, but is now grown in almost every part of the world. There are many varieties which are cultivated for the bud of the flower. The part of the artichoke where the bud joins the stem is called the heart, or *fond*, and has a delicate flavour. Growing from this are the fleshy leaves. At the base of each leaf is a small edible section. Inside the leaves is the inedible choke, a fine, hair-like growth which develops into the flower.

Globe artichokes are rich in iron, mineral salts and iodine and contain some vitamin C. They can be boiled whole, fried, baked stuffed, used to make soup, or the hearts served in a salad. Very small, young artichokes can be eaten whole, raw or fried in batter. In Italy these are bottled in olive oil and are served as an hors d'oeuvre.

Artichokes should never be cooked in aluminium or iron saucepans, as the flesh will turn grey. The best tasting artichokes are heavy, with compact, fleshy, green or purple-green leaves and firm, green stems.

To eat an artichoke, pull off a leaf with your fingers and dip the bottom part of it in melted butter or sauce. Now scrape off this tender flesh between your teeth. Only the tender flesh at the bottom of the leaf is edible. When you have removed all the leaves, you will come to the heart. Scrape off and discard the hairy choke surrounding it. The heart is eaten with a knife and fork.

Artichokes, Boiled

Boiled artichokes may be served hot with melted butter, Hollandaise sauce, or various

Artichokes are cooked in boiling, salted water until the bases are tender.

---

cream sauces. They may also be chilled and served with vinaigrette sauce or mayonnaise. They make a delicious first course, but they can also be served instead of a salad or as the vegetable accompaniment to a meat dish. The dechoking of the artichokes may be done before or after cooking.

6 SERVINGS

6 medium-sized artichokes
1 lemon, cut in quarters
8 pints water
3 tablespoons salt

With a sharp knife, cut the stalks off the artichokes. Pull off any bruised or tough outer leaves. Lay each artichoke on its side and slice off the top third of it. With kitchen scissors, trim ¼-inch off the points of the rest of the leaves. Wash the artichoke under cold running water. Rub the cut edges with a piece of the lemon to prevent them discolouring.

If you wish to remove the chokes before cooking, spread the top leaves apart and pull out the prickly leaves surrounding the hairy choke. With a teaspoon, scrape out the choke. Squeeze a little lemon juice into the centre and press the leaves back together again.

Put the water into a large saucepan and bring to a boil over medium heat. Add the salt. Drop in the artichokes, base down, and bring the water to a boil again. Boil briskly, uncovered, turning the artichokes occasionally. If you have removed the chokes, cook for about 15 minutes. If the chokes have not been removed, cook for about 30 minutes. The artichokes are cooked when their bases are tender when pierced with a sharp knife and the leaves pull out easily.

With a slotted spoon, remove the artichokes from the saucepan and drain them upside down in a colander.

To remove the choke, spread the top leaves apart and pull out the prickly leaves surrounding the hairy choke.

With a teaspoon, scrape out the choke. Squeeze lemon juice into the centre and press the leaves back together.

Rub all the cut edges with lemon to prevent the artichoke from discolouring. It is now ready to cook.

To prepare artichoke hearts, bend back the lower leaves of each artichoke until they snap off.

Remove all outer leaves until you reach those bending inwards. With a sharp knife, slice off the stalk.

Place the artichoke on its side and cut off the remaining leaves just above the white heart.

Rotating the base of the artichoke against the knife blade, trim off all the green leaf bases.

Artichoke Hearts

Artichoke hearts are the tender, fleshy bases of artichokes. They make a delicious but rather expensive hors d'oeuvre. They may be stuffed with mushrooms, spinach, pâté or sausage meat mixed with chopped onions. As a vegetable course for a dinner or lunch party, they may be braised with butter or served with a Mornay or Hollandaise sauce.

To prevent discolouring, drop each trimmed heart into a bowl of acidulated water in a proportion of 1 tablespoon of lemon juice or vinegar to 1½ pints of water.

4 SERVINGS

12 large artichokes
2 pints [5 cups] water containing
  3 tablespoons lemon juice
½ lemon
2 oz. [½ cup] flour
3 pints [7½ cups] cold water
4 tablespoons lemon juice
2 teaspoons salt

Hold each artichoke and bend the leaves back until they snap off. Continue until you reach the inside leaves which have begun to fold inwards.

With a sharp knife, cut off the stalks of the artichokes.

Place each artichoke on its side and slice off the remaining leaves just above the heart. Rub the cut parts of the artichoke well with lemon juice. Rotating the base of the artichoke against the knife blade, trim the base of all pieces of green to expose the whitish surface of the heart. As each heart is trimmed, drop it into the bowl of acidulated water.

Put the flour in a medium-sized saucepan and stir in 2 tablespoons of water to make a smooth paste. Stir in the rest of the water, the lemon juice and the salt. Bring it to a boil and simmer for 5 minutes.

Add the artichoke hearts. Bring the liquid to the boil, then simmer for 30 to 40 minutes, or until the hearts are tender when pierced with a knife. Make sure that the liquid covers the artichoke hearts all the time they are cooking, adding water if necessary.

Drain the hearts and serve with melted butter, or use any of the following recipes for artichoke hearts.

Artichoke Heart Soufflé

Serve this unusual soufflé as a first course or as the main course for lunch or supper. It may be accompanied by allumette potatoes and a salad of cold, cooked French

beans with a vinaigrette sauce, or a tossed green salad. A well-chilled, light, dry, white Italian or French wine would go well with this soufflé.

Unusual and delicately flavoured, Artichoke Heart Soufflé may be served as a first course or as a light main course for lunch or supper.

4 SERVINGS

2 oz. [¼ cup] plus 1 teaspoon butter
2 oz. [½ cup] flour, sifted
¼ teaspoon salt
5 grindings black pepper
¼ teaspoon grated nutmeg
10 fl. oz. [1¼ cups] milk
2 tablespoons single [light] cream
2 oz. [½ cup] Gruyère cheese, grated
6 artichoke hearts, cooked fresh, or canned
4 egg yolks
5 egg whites

Preheat the oven to 400°F (Gas Mark 6, 200°C). Grease a 3-pint soufflé dish with 1 teaspoon butter. Tie a strip of greaseproof paper around the rim of the soufflé dish so it projects 2 inches above the top.

Melt the remaining amount of butter in a large, heavy saucepan over low heat. Remove from the heat and, with a wooden spoon, stir in the flour. Replace the saucepan on the heat and, stirring constantly, cook for 2 minutes. Add the salt, pepper and nutmeg. Mix well. Add the milk, a little at a time, and, stirring continously, bring to the boil. Boil for 2 minutes, still stirring, until the sauce thickens. Remove from the heat and stir in the cream and the grated cheese.

Place the artichoke hearts in a bowl and, with a table fork, mash them well. Add to the cheese mixture. Add the egg yolks to the mixture and stir well.

Beat the egg whites in a medium-sized mixing bowl with a whisk until they form stiff peaks. Be careful not to over-beat the whites or they will begin to collapse.

Fold a large tablespoon of beaten egg white into the sauce. With a rubber spatula, scoop the rest of the egg whites on top of the mixture and fold in very gently. Pour the mixture into the soufflé dish. It should fill two-thirds of the dish.

Place the dish on the middle shelf of the oven and reduce the heat to 375°F (Gas Mark 5, 190°C). Bake for 35 minutes. When the soufflé is ready, the top should be brown and it should have risen 2 or 3 inches above the top of the dish. To be sure the soufflé is cooked, plunge a thin knife into the centre. If the soufflé is ready the knife will come out clean.

Serve immediately.

Artichokes Braised with Mixed Vegetables

This tasty artichoke casserole with the addition of other vegetables makes a nourishing and tasty dish. For a complete meal, sausages or bacon may be added to this vegetable and artichoke casserole. It can be prepared in advance and reheated just before serving.

4 SERVINGS

4 large artichokes
4 pints [5 pints] water
1 tablespoon plus 1 teaspoon salt
4 oz. [½ cup] butter
4 onions, sliced
1 large garlic clove, chopped
6 stalks celery, sliced
2 large potatoes cut into quarters
4 carrots scraped and sliced
2 turnips, peeled and cubed
   freshly ground black pepper
3 fl. oz. [⅜ cup] white wine
15 fl. oz. [1⅞ cups] beef stock
1 bouquet garni, consisting of 4
   sprigs of parsley, 1 spray of
   thyme and 1 small bay
   leaf, tied together
2 oz. mushrooms, washed
   and sliced
2 tablespoons chopped parsley

Low Cal

Prepare the artichokes for cooking. Cut off the tops of the leaves so that the artichokes are about 2½ inches high. Slice them lengthways into quarters and cut out the chokes.

In a large saucepan, bring the water to a boil and add 1 tablespoon of salt. Drop the artichoke quarters into the boiling water. Boil for 10 minutes and drain well on kitchen paper towels.

Preheat the oven to moderate 350°F (Gas Mark 4, 180°C).

In a large casserole, which is big enough to hold the artichokes in one layer, melt most of the butter. Fry the onions over low heat for 5 minutes, or until they are golden, but not brown. Stir in the garlic.

Place the artichoke hearts in the casserole. Add the celery, potatoes, carrots, turnips, 4 grindings of pepper and remaining salt. Cook over low heat for 10 minutes.

Pour the wine into the casserole and bring to the boil over high heat. Add the beef stock and the bouquet garni.

Cover the casserole, transfer it to the oven and cook gently for 1 to 1¼ hours, or until the liquid has almost evaporated and the vegetables are tender.

Ten minutes before the vegetables have finished cooking, put the remaining butter in a small saucepan and sauté the mushrooms for 5 minutes. Add them to the casserole.

Before serving, discard the bouquet garni and sprinkle the vegetables with chopped parlsey.

Artichokes with Dill Sauce

Artichokes with Dill Sauce is a way artichokes are served as a first course in Greece. The dill sauce gives the artichokes an unusual flavour.

6 SERVINGS

6 tablespoons lemon juice
4 tablespoons flour
8 fl. oz. [1 cup] water
6 medium-sized artichokes
8 fl. oz. [1 cup] olive oil
1 medium-sized onion, chopped
3 tablespoons finely chopped fresh
   dill or 2½ teaspoons dried dill
1½ teaspoons salt

Pour the lemon juice into a large mixing bowl. Add the flour and, using a whisk, beat the mixture until it is smooth. Add the water and continue beating until the liquid is a thin, smooth paste.

Prepare and trim the artichokes, removing the chokes. Put them into the lemon-and-flour mixture and turn them until they are evenly coated. Leave them to soak.

Heat the olive oil, over moderate heat, in a large casserole. Add the onions, reduce the heat and sauté them gently for 5 minutes. Do not allow them to brown.

With a slotted spoon, remove the artichokes from the lemon-and-flour mixture and set aside. Drain the lemon-and-flour mixture into the casserole. Add the dill and salt. Stirring continuously with a wooden spoon, bring the liquid to the boil.

Place the artichokes side by side in the casserole and baste them thoroughly with the liquid. Reduce the heat to low. Cover the casserole and simmer gently for 20 minutes. Turn the artichokes over and simmer for another 25 minutes. The artichokes are cooked when their bases are tender when pierced with the point of a sharp knife.

Arrange the artichokes on a serving dish and pour the sauce over them.

Artichokes à la Grecque

Pickled baby artichokes make a piquant hors d'oeuvre or may be served as part of an antipasto. The artichokes must be very small, tender and completely edible.

4 SERVINGS

20 baby artichokes, outer leaves removed and the remaining leaves cut short
4 pints [5 pints] water
juice of 3½ lemons
5 fl. oz. [⅝ cup] olive oil
½ teaspoon coriander seeds
6 peppercorns
1 bay leaf
1 sprig of thyme
1 teaspoon salt

Put 3 pints of water and 1½ tablespoons of lemon juice into a large pan. Add the artichokes and bring to the boil over moderate heat. Boil for 10 minutes. Drain the artichokes in a colander and cool in running cold water. Drain again.

Put all the remaining ingredients in a large pan and bring to the boil over high heat. Add the artichokes. When the liquid comes to the boil again, lower the heat, cover and simmer for 20 minutes.

With a slotted spoon, remove the artichokes from the pan and place in a serving dish. Pour 6 tablespoons of the liquid from the pan over them. Chill thoroughly before serving.

Artichokes à la Provençale
ARTICHOKES WITH GARLIC AND TOMATOES

This is a classic French method of cooking artichokes. Served on its own it makes an attractive and unusual hors d'oeuvre. It is also an excellent vegetable accompaniment to grilled [broiled] chicken.

4 SERVINGS

4 artichokes
2 pints [5 cups] water
2½ teaspoons salt
2 tablespoons olive oil
4 slices bacon, rinds removed and cut into pieces
2 onions, finely chopped
2 garlic cloves, crushed
freshly ground black pepper
½ teaspoon dried basil
12 oz. canned tomatoes
1 tablespoon tomato purée
2 tablespoons brandy (optional)
4 fl. oz. [½ cup] white wine
8 fl. oz. [1 cup] chicken stock or water and 1 chicken stock cube
1 bouquet garni, consisting of 3 parsley sprigs, 1 spray of thyme and 1 bay leaf, tied together

Cut off the stems of the artichokes, remove the small leaves at the bases and cut off the tops of the leaves, leaving the artichokes about 3 inches high.

Slice the artichokes into quarters, and, with a spoon, scrape out the chokes. Put the water and 2 teaspoons of the salt into a large saucepan and bring to the boil. Add the artichokes and boil for 5 minutes. Drain the artichokes on kitchen paper towels and set aside.

Heat the oil in a large heavy saucepan or flameproof casserole over moderate heat. Add the bacon and fry until crisp. Stir in the onions and garlic and fry for 5 minutes or until the onions are soft.

Place the artichoke quarters into the casserole and spoon the bacon mixture over them. Stir in the remaining ½ teaspoon of salt and 6 grindings of black pepper. Add the basil, tomatoes, tomato purée and brandy, if used. Bring to the boil over high heat then reduce heat to low and simmer for 5 minutes.

Pour the wine and stock over the artichokes, add the bouquet garni. Cover and cook over low heat for ¾ hour.

If there is too much liquid raise the heat and boil quickly until the liquid has reduced slightly. Remove the bouquet garni before serving. Serve immediately.

Artichokes Stuffed with Pork and Almonds make a delicious, although expensive, main course.

Artichokes Stuffed with Pork and Almonds

This is an unusual and rather expensive way to serve artichokes. They may, however, be served as a main course for lunch or supper. Serve some melted butter mixed with a few drops of lemon juice into which the artichoke leaves and hearts can be dipped.

4 SERVINGS

4 large artichokes
1 lemon quartered
2 fl. oz. [¼ cup] lemon juice
enough boiling water to cover the artichokes
1 tablespoon salt
STUFFING
2 oz. [¼ cup] vegetable fat

½ lb. minced [ground] pork

1 medium-sized onion, chopped

2 oz. [1 cup] fresh breadcrumbs

2 tablespoons chopped parsley

½ teaspoon salt

freshly ground black pepper

½ teaspoon celery salt

2 oz. [¼ cup] blanched almonds, finely chopped

1 egg, lightly beaten

1 tablespoon vegetable oil

Wash and prepare the artichokes for boiling. Squeeze lemon juice over the cut areas to prevent them discolouring. Using a sharp knife, cut off the top third of each artichoke. Pull open the centre leaves carefully and pull out the yellow and purple leaves from the centres. Using a teaspoon, scrape and pull off all the fuzzy chokes to expose the heart. Squeeze a little lemon juice into the hollows. Push the leaves back together again.

Stand the artichokes in a large saucepan. If they do not fit snugly into the saucepan, tie a piece of string around each one so they will keep their shape while boiling.

Pour the boiling water and the remaining lemon juice over the artichokes so that they are completely covered. Add the salt. Cover the saucepan and simmer the artichokes, over medium heat, for 25 minutes, or until the bases are tender when pierced with a sharp knife. When the artichokes are cooked, remove them from the water with a slotted spoon and turn them upside down in a colander to drain.

While the artichokes are boiling, preheat the oven to moderate 350°F (Gas Mark 4, 180°C) and make the stuffing.

In a large, heavy frying-pan, melt the fat. Add the pork and the onions and sauté them until they are lightly browned. Remove the frying-pan from the heat and add the breadcrumbs, parsley, salt, 4 grindings of pepper, celery salt, almonds and beaten egg.

Stir the mixture well.

Place the artichokes in a baking dish and fill the centres with the stuffing.

Pour a little water around the artichokes. Brush the artichokes generously with oil. Cover the dish with aluminium foil and bake on the centre shelf of the oven for 30 to 40 minutes until the artichokes are tender.

Serve hot.

Artichokes Stuffed with Prawns and Spicy Mayonnaise

Cold artichokes filled with prawns and herbs and anchovy flavoured mayonnaise makes an attractive first course for a dinner party or a tasty and appetizing main dish for a summer lunch. This recipe uses a home-made mayonnaise but a bought one may be substituted if time is short.

6 SERVINGS

6 artichokes
   juice of 1 lemon
4 pints [5 pints] water
2 tablespoons salt
MAYONNAISE
6 egg yolks
½ teaspoon salt
   freshly ground pepper
¼ teaspoon French mustard
1 teaspoon sugar
1 pint [2½ cups] olive oil
4 tablespoons wine vinegar
1 tablespoon lemon juice

2 tablespoons finely chopped chives
1 teaspoon chopped capers
1 garlic clove, crushed
1 tablespoon chopped fresh or 1½ teaspoons dried tarragon
6 canned anchovies, drained and finely chopped
2 tablespoons chopped parsley
⅛ teaspoon cayenne pepper
2 lb. peeled prawns or shrimps (if frozen allow to thaw)
2 lemons, sliced

To make the mayonnaise, place the egg yolks in a medium-sized mixing bowl. Beat with a fork, rotary whisk or electric blender. Add the salt, 4 grindings of pepper, mustard and the sugar. Continue beating until the yolks are thick and creamy.

Still beating continuously, add 4 tablespoons of oil very slowly by dripping it from a spoon. If you are using an electric blender, set the speed to slow when adding the oil. If the sauce becomes too thick to beat easily, dilute it with a few drops of vinegar. Beating constantly, add the remaining oil a little at a time, until it is incorporated into the egg yolks. Add the vinegar and lightly beat to mix.

Add the lemon juice, chives, capers, garlic, tarragon, anchovies, parsley and cayenne pepper to the mayonnaise and beat well with a wooden spoon.

Taste and add more salt and pepper if necessary.

Put 1½ lbs. prawns into a large bowl and stir in half of the dressing. Mix well and place in the refrigerator to chill.

Wash and prepare the artichokes for cooking. Dip the trimmed tops into the lemon juice. This prevents them from going brown.

Pour the water into a large saucepan, add the salt and bring to the boil. Place the artichokes in the water and boil for about 30 minutes or until they are cooked. Remove the artichokes with a slotted spoon and place upside down on kitchen paper towels and leave to drain and cool.

Gently pull the leaves of each artichoke apart and remove the yellow inner core. With a fork or spoon, scrape out the choke and discard it.

When the artichokes are really cold, fill the centre of each one with the prawn filling. Garnish each one with the remaining prawns or shrimps.

Serve on individual plates and place lemon slices around the edge. Serve the remaining filling separately.

Artichokes Stuffed with Prawns is a very attractive cold dish.

Artichokes with Veal and Peppers

This is a decorative supper dish which is worth the time and effort required to prepare it. Serve a sauce with it of melted butter mixed with a few drops of lemon juice for the artichoke leaves and heart.

4 SERVINGS

4 artichokes
1 lemon, halved
2 fl. oz. [¼ cup] lemon juice
   enough boiling water to cover the artichokes
1 tablespoon salt
STUFFING
3 tablespoons olive oil
1 onion, finely chopped
1 lb. minced [ground] veal
1 green pepper, halved, seeded and finely sliced
1 garlic clove, crushed

1 teaspoon salt
freshly ground black pepper
½ teaspoon ground nutmeg
4 tomatoes, blanched, peeled and
chopped
2 oz. [½ cup] grated Cheddar cheese

Wash and prepare the artichokes for boiling. Squeeze lemon juice over the cut areas to prevent them discolouring. Using a sharp knife, cut off the top one-third of the artichoke. Pull open the centre leaves carefully and pull out the yellow and purple leaves from the centre. Using a teaspoon, scrape and pull off all the fuzzy choke to expose the heart. Squeeze a little lemon juice into the hollow. Push the leaves back together again.

Stand the artichokes in a large saucepan. They must fit snugly into the saucepan so they keep their shape while boiling or tie a piece of string around each one.

Pour the boiling water and lemon juice over the artichokes so that they are completely covered. Add the salt. Cover and simmer the artichokes over medium heat for 25 minutes, or until the bases are tender when pierced with a sharp knife.

Meanwhile, heat the oil in a large saucepan. Add the onions to the oil and cook over medium heat, stirring, for 3 minutes. Add the veal and continue cooking until the meat is brown. Add the green pepper, garlic, salt, 4 grindings of pepper and the nutmeg and mix well.

Stir in the tomatoes and cheese. Reduce the heat to low and cover the saucepan. Simmer gently for 20 to 25 minutes, stirring occasionally.

While the veal mixture is cooking, remove the cooked artichokes from the water with a slotted spoon. Turn them upside down in a colander to drain. Keep the artichokes warm.

When the veal mixture is ready, fill the artichokes with it and serve hot.

Artichoke Hearts à l'Allemande

An elegant vegetable dish for lunch or dinner parties, Artichoke Hearts à l'Allemande may be served as an accompaniment to veal, cold meats or sautéed chicken.

4 SERVINGS

12 artichoke hearts
1½ pints [4 cups] cold water
2 tablespoons lemon juice
1 teaspoon salt
1½ oz. [3 tablespoons] butter
10 fl. oz. [1¼ cups] Allemande Sauce

Bring the water to a boil in a medium-sized saucepan. Add the lemon juice and salt. Drop the artichoke hearts into the water and simmer on a low heat for 10 minutes. Remove the saucepan from the heat and drain the artichoke hearts.

Artichoke Hearts in Butter are baked in the oven and flavoured with spring onions [scallions] or shallots.

Melt the butter in a medium-sized frying-pan. Add the artichoke hearts and sauté gently until they are tender. With a slotted spoon, transfer them to a heated serving dish. Pour the hot Allemande Sauce over them and serve immediately.

Artichoke Hearts in Butter

This is a simple, well-flavoured dish which can be served as a first course or as a vegetable accompaniment to chicken, veal or egg dishes.

4 SERVINGS

12 artichoke hearts, cooked and cut
into quarters
4 oz. [½ cup] butter
4 tablespoons chopped shallots or
spring onions [scallions]
½ teaspoon salt
freshly ground pepper
4 tablespoons chopped parsley

Preheat the oven to warm 325°F (Gas Mark 3, 170°C).

Melt the butter in a medium-sized, flameproof casserole. Put in the shallots, or spring onions, and the artichoke hearts

1. To prepare the asparagus, peel or scrape the stalks with a knife, thickly at the butt end and very thinly towards the tip.
2. Wash the stalks and tie them with string in neat bundles of not more than 10. Cut off the ends of the stalks evenly.
3. Stand the asparagus in a jar of boiling water and cover it with pierced aluminium foil. Place the jar in a pan of boiling water.
4. When the asparagus is cooked, take the bundles out of the jar, drain, remove the string and put the stalks on a serving plate.

and stir, making sure the hearts are well coated with the butter. Sprinkle on the salt and 4 grindings of pepper and mix well.

Cover the casserole and bake in the centre of the oven for 20 minutes. Sprinkle with parsley, and serve immediately.

Artichoke Hearts with Herbs

An unusual vegetable dish for a lunch or dinner party, this may accompany veal, roast or sautéed chicken and egg dishes.

4 SERVINGS

12 fresh artichoke hearts
1½ pints [4 cups] cold water
2 tablespoons lemon juice
1 teaspoon salt
1½ oz. [3 tablespoons] butter
½ teaspoon dried chervil
½ teaspoon chopped parsley

Bring the water to the boil in a medium-sized saucepan. Add the lemon juice and salt. Drop the artichoke hearts into the water and simmer for 10 minutes. Drain and slice the artichoke hearts.

Melt the butter in a heavy frying-pan

and very gently sauté the sliced artichoke hearts. Put them in a heated vegetable dish and sprinkle with the chervil and parsley.

Asafoetida

Asafoetida is a gum resin usually obtained from the plant ferula foetida which is native to Iran and Afghanistan. The resin is dried and in India and Iran it is used as a condiment. Asafoetida has an acrid taste and a strong garlic-like odour.

Asbestos Mat

Mats made of asbestos, a grey fibrous mineral, are noncombustible, reflect heat and are good insulators. For these reasons, the mats can be placed under a saucepan when an extremely low heat is required, or to prevent burning. They can also be used on the stove under a utensil which is not fireproof, to prevent it cracking.

Ashberry

This bright red berry is the fruit of the mountain ash. More commonly known as ROWAN BERRY, it is used to make jelly and to flavour preserves.

Ashe Reshte

NOODLE SOUP

Ashe Reshte (ah-sh RESH-teh), *a Persian recipe, is a tasty, unusual and filling soup. It is ideal to serve on cold winter evenings.*

4 SERVINGS

½ lb. minced [ground] beef
1 medium-sized onion, chopped finely
½ teaspoon ground cinnamon
grated rind of ½ lemon
freshly ground black pepper
1½ teaspoons salt
2 pints [5 cups] water
2 oz. [¼ cup] dried peas
2 oz. [¼ cup] lentils
4 oz. fine egg noodles
2 tablespoons chopped parsley
1 tablespoon dried mint

Put the minced beef, onion, ¼ teaspoon cinnamon, grated lemon rind, 4 grindings of black pepper and ½ teaspoon salt into a medium-sized mixing bowl. Using your hands, mix the ingredients well and shape into small balls the size of walnuts.

Put the water in a large pan with the dried peas and lentils and the remaining

1 teaspoon of salt. Bring to the boil and simmer for 15 minutes. Add the meatballs, noodles, 3 grindings of pepper and the parsley. Simmer for 40 minutes. Add more boiling water if the soup is too thick.

Crush the dried mint with your fingers and add to the soup with the remaining cinnamon. Serve immediately.

Asparagus

Asparagus is a member of the lily family of which there are more than a hundred species. The best known species is garden asparagus, which is now grown in most temperate and subtropical regions of the world.

Wild asparagus was known to the early Greeks and to this day it grows on the Mediterranean coast. As a cultivated plant, asparagus was known in the second century B.C. and was highly prized as a vegetable by the Romans. But in the West extensive cultivation of the plant did not begin until the sixteenth century.

Although there are a number of varieties of asparagus, the best known for culinary purposes are French asparagus, especially the white Argentcuil asparagus and Lauris, grown in the Vaucluse

district in the South of France, English asparagus, which is a thin, green variety, Italian or Genoa asparagus, which is purplish in colour, and white Belgian asparagus.

To prepare asparagus, peel or scrape the stalks with a sharp knife. At the butt end, the asparagus may be peeled as much as $\frac{1}{16}$ of an inch. But the peeling should gradually become very thin towards the tip. Wash them carefully. Make bundles of no more than 10 stalks, tie the bundles in 2 places and cut the ends off the stalks evenly.

To cook asparagus, bring about 4 inches of salted water to the boil in a deep pan. Stand the bundle of asparagus in the pan so that the stalks are in the water and the tips are out of it. Cover partially, leaving space for the steam to escape, and cook for 15 to 20 minutes.

There are special asparagus pans on the market which are deep and narrow and have holes in the lid. If you do not have a special asparagus pan, you can use a glass jar. Fill the jar with boiling water and stand the asparagus in it. Place the jar in a pan with boiling water and cook for 30 minutes. When the asparagus is cooked, take out the bundle carefully, drain and cut the strings.

To serve asparagus, pile the hot, cooked stalks on a plate lined with a folded napkin. Estimate 6 stalks per person. Serve with melted butter or with a Hollandaise sauce. Cold asparagus is delicious served with a vinaigrette sauce.

Asparagus may be served alone as a first course. It also makes an excellent vegetable accompaniment to meat, fish and chicken dishes. It may also be served cold in place of a salad.

Asparagus au Beurre

As well as making a simple but elegant hors d'oeuvre, asparagus is a delicious vegetable accompaniment to meat and fish dishes. The season for fresh asparagus is a short one so frozen asparagus may be used in any other asparagus recipe.

4 SERVINGS

1 lb. frozen asparagus
2 pints [5 cups] water
1 tablespoon plus $\frac{1}{4}$ teaspoon salt
6 tablespoons hot, melted butter
 freshly ground pepper

Boil the water in a large saucepan and add 1 tablespoon of salt. Drop the aspara-

75

gus into the water. When the water returns to the boil, boil rapidly for 4 minutes, or until the asparagus is almost tender.

If the asparagus is not to be served immediately, put in a colander and run cold water through it to prevent it from cooking further and to retain the colour and texture.

Just before serving, put the asparagus in a warmed serving dish and pour the butter over it. Taking care not to break the asparagus, gently toss it in the hot butter to finish the cooking and to coat it with butter. Sprinkle with ¼ teaspoon of salt and 4 grindings of pepper and serve.

Asparagus Cream Soup

This delicious soup is made with fresh asparagus, cream and eggs. The base is a home-made vegetable stock which should cook for at least 2 hours.

4 SERVINGS

2 lb. asparagus
1 small onion, finely sliced
10 fl. oz. [1¼ cups] water
1 teaspoon salt
4 grindings fresh black pepper
4 tablespoons flour
2 tablespoons butter
2 egg yolks
5 fl. oz. single [light] cream
STOCK
1 tablespoon butter
1 lb. carrots, sliced in large pieces
1 lb. onions, peeled and sliced
½ head celery, sliced
1 small turnip, sliced in large pieces
6 peppercorns
  a bouquet garni, consisting of 4
  sprigs of parsley, a sprig of
  thyme and 1 bay leaf tied
  together
1 teaspoon salt
5 pints [6¼ pints] hot water

For the stock, melt the butter in a large pan. Add the slices of carrot, onions, celery and turnip to the pan. Cook over low heat, stirring occasionally, until the vegetables are brown. Add the peppercorns, bouquet garni, salt and hot water. Bring to the boil, half cover the pan and simmer for 2 hours, or until the stock has a good flavour and has reduced to 1½ pints [2 pints]. Strain before using.

For the soup, wash and trim the asparagus. Cut off 2 inches from the tips of the asparagus and put them aside. Peel stalks and cut into 1-inch lengths.

Put the sliced onion and asparagus stalks in a medium-sized saucepan. Add the strained stock and simmer over low heat for 30 minutes.

Meanwhile, put the water and ½ teaspoon of salt into another medium-sized saucepan and bring to a boil. Drop in the asparagus tips and boil for 5 minutes, or until they are tender. Drain.

Pour the asparagus stock through a fine sieve into a medium-sized bowl. With the back of a wooden spoon, rub the asparagus stalks and the onion through the sieve. Rinse the saucepan and pour back the sieved stock. Reheat the stock, adding the remaining ½ teaspoon of salt and the pepper.

Put the flour and the butter in a small bowl and work them together into a soft paste. Roll it into small pellets. Remove the stock from the heat and add the butter-and-flour pellets one at a time, stirring continuously with a wooden spoon. When the stock is thoroughly blended and smooth, replace it on moderate heat and continue to stir until it comes to a boil. Remove the stock from the heat.

In a medium-sized bowl, beat the egg yolks and stir in the cream. Stirring constantly, add ½ pint of hot stock, a spoonful at a time, to the egg-and-cream mixture. Still stirring continuously, pour this mixture into the stock. Over a very low heat, whisk the soup for 2 minutes. Do not allow it to boil or it will curdle. Add the asparagus tips and serve.

Asparagus au Gratin
ASPARAGUS WITH CHEESE SAUCE

Asparagus au Gratin (oh GRAH-tan) *may be served as a first course or as a vegetable dish with the main course for lunch or dinner. It goes well served with chicken breasts, veal escalopes, brains, sweetbreads and egg dishes.*

4 SERVINGS

3 lb. fresh asparagus
1 blade of mace or ¼ teaspoon
  ground mace
1 bay leaf
1 shallot, sliced
5 peppercorns
10 fl. oz. [1¼ cups] milk
1 tablespoon butter
2 tablespoons flour
1½ oz. [½ cup] Gruyère cheese, grated
2 tablespoons single [light] cream
½ teaspoon prepared mustard
¼ teaspoon salt
3 grindings fresh pepper
2 tablespoons grated Parmesan
  cheese

Put the mace, bay leaf, peppercorns,

shallot and the milk in a medium-sized saucepan. Place on low heat and allow to simmer very gently for 8 minutes.

Prepare the asparagus and cook until tender.

In a heavy, medium-sized saucepan, melt the butter over low heat. Remove from the heat and with a wooden spoon, stir in the flour. Return the saucepan to the heat and cook for 2 minutes, stirring continuously.

Pour the milk through a strainer, a little at a time, into the butter-and-flour mixture and continue stirring over moderate heat. When all the milk has been stirred in, bring the mixture to a boil. Reduce the heat and simmer gently for 3 minutes. Remove the saucepan from the heat and stir in the Gruyère cheese, cream, mustard, salt and pepper.

Arrange the cooked asparagus in a fireproof serving dish. Pour the hot sauce over the asparagus. Sprinkle the Parmesan over the top and brown under a moderate grill [broiler], or until the top is golden brown.

Serve immediately.

Asparagus aux Oeufs
ASPARAGUS WITH EGGS

A delicately-flavoured dish, Asparagus aux oeufs (oz-erf) *is an elegant way to serve this vegetable. It makes a good first course or a light lunch or supper dish. This sauce is quick and easily prepared.*

6 SERVINGS

3 lb. fresh asparagus
3 hard-boiled eggs,
  shells removed and chopped
2 tablespoons finely chopped parsley
½ teaspoon salt
4 grindings fresh black pepper
6 oz. [¾ cup] butter, melted and
  cooled
2 tablespoons lemon juice

Prepare the asparagus and boil until it is tender.

Meanwhile with a fork, blend the eggs, parsley, ½ teaspoon of salt and pepper in a medium-sized mixing bowl. Stirring constantly, add the melted butter. Continue stirring until the sauce is smooth, and add the lemon juice.

Drain and transfer the asparagus to a large, heated serving dish. Pour on the sauce and serve immediately.

Asparagus Cream Soup is made with fresh asparagus stalks, stock and cream and is thickened with eggs. It is garnished with the asparagus tips.

Asparagus Polonaise

Vegetables Polonaise are sprinkled with buttered breadcrumbs and sieved eggs. Asparagus is most delicious served with this classic garnish.

4 SERVINGS

3 oz. [⅜ cup] butter
1 oz. [⅓ cup] fine breadcrumbs, made from stale bread
2 lb. asparagus, cooked and drained
1 hard-boiled egg, sieved
2 tablespoons chopped parsley

Melt the butter in a small saucepan. Add the breadcrumbs and sauté until they are lightly browned.

Sprinkle the crumbs and butter over hot, freshly cooked asparagus and then sprinkle with the sieved egg and chopped parsley.

Serve immediately.

Asparagus with Sour Cream

Served with grilled meat, chicken or fish, this casserole, which is very easy to prepare, will make the most simple meal quite elegant.

1 tablespoon margarine
3 lb. asparagus, cooked and drained
½ teaspoon garlic salt
freshly ground black pepper
12 fl. oz. [1½ cups] sour cream
6 oz. [2 cups] dry breadcrumbs
3 tablespoons melted butter
1 tablespoon chopped parsley

Preheat oven to moderate 350°F (Gas Mark 4, 180°C).

Grease an ovenproof casserole with the margarine. Place the asparagus in the casserole. Sprinkle with garlic salt and 2 to 3 grindings of pepper and stir in the sour cream.

Mix the breadcrumbs with the melted butter and spread over the asparagus.

Bake for about 40 minutes or until the crumbs are golden brown. Sprinkle with the parsley before serving.

Asparagus Timbale

This savoury asparagus custard, accompanied by Hollandaise sauce, makes an excellent light lunch or supper dish, or may be served as an accompaniment to grilled chicken or fish. The sauce should be served while it is still warm.

Asparagus Polonaise is a simple dish of fresh, boiled asparagus with an egg and sautéed breadcrumb garnish.

4 SERVINGS

3 lb. fresh, boiled asparagus, or 1 lb. frozen asparagus
4 eggs
¾ teaspoon salt
1 teaspoon grated nutmeg
4 fl. oz. single [light] cream
8 fl. oz. [1 cup] chicken stock or milk
SAUCE
5 tablespoons wine vinegar
6 peppercorns
1 bay leaf
6 oz. [¾ cup] butter
3 egg yolks
pinch of salt

Preheat the oven to warm 325°F (Gas Mark 3, 170°C). Lightly butter a 2½-pint ring mould or soufflé dish.

If you are using fresh asparagus, cut off tough part of the stalks and discard.

Cut the asparagus into ½-inch pieces and set aside. In a medium-sized mixing bowl, using a whisk or rotary beater, whisk the eggs with the salt and grated nutmeg. Gradually add the cream and the stock, or milk, beating all the time. Fold in the asparagus pieces.

Pour the mixture into the greased mould or soufflé dish. Place the mould or soufflé dish in a baking pan of boiling water and bake for 35 minutes, or until the custard is set. Test by plunging a warm, dry knife into the centre of the custard. If it comes out clean, the custard is set. If you use a ring mould, test the custard after 20 minutes of cooking.

Remove the custard from the oven and let it stand for 5 minutes. Run a knife round the edge of the custard and un-mould it on to a heated serving dish.

While the custard is cooking, make the sauce. Put the vinegar, peppercorns and bay leaf in a small saucepan and cook, over moderate heat, until the vinegar is reduced to 1¼ tablespoons. Strain and set aside.

In a small bowl, beat the butter until it is soft. In another bowl, beat the egg yolks with a wire whisk or wooden spoon. Add a heaped teaspoon of softened butter and a pinch of salt to the egg yolks. Cream well. Stir in the strained vinegar.

Put the bowl in a saucepan containing warm water and place over low heat. The water should heat gradually, but never come to boiling point. Stir the mixture until it begins to thicken. Add the remaining butter, cut in small pieces, stirring continually. When all the butter has been added, taste the sauce. Add a little more salt if necessary. If the sauce is too sharp, add a little more butter. If the sauce is too thick, add a tablespoon or two of cream to dilute it. Serve the sauce separately.

Asparagus Pea

Also called Winged Pea and Goa Bean, the asparagus pea is the seed of a vine of which one variety is native to India and one to Southern Europe. The green-winged pods are eaten when they are between 1 and 3 inches in length. Although this vegetable is not related to the asparagus, it does have a similar flavour. Asparagus peas should be boiled in salted water for 10 to 15 minutes, drained and served with melted butter.

Aspic

Aspic is a jelly (the French term is *gelée*) made from strong chicken, veal, beef or fish stock. This stock is so strong in gelatinous matter that it is not necessary to add any gelatine. There are occasions, however, when to save time or money it is advisable to use gelatine. The quantity of gelatine used for the firmest aspic is usually ½ ounce to 1 pint

of liquid. For decorative aspics, the proportion is ½ ounce to 1½ pints of liquid and for jellied soups, ½ ounce to 2 pints of liquid.

Aspic jelly is transparent and light coloured and is used as an ingredient or an accompaniment to many cold dishes. Because it is used mainly for decorative purposes, the consistency and clarity of the aspic are important. The stock is made clear by simmering with egg whites and straining before it is allowed to set.

Before using, the jelly must be tested for consistency. Pour ½ inch of jelly into a small, chilled bowl or saucer and place it in the refrigerator for 10 to 15 minutes. Then cut it into pieces and leave it at room temperature for 10 minutes. The jelly should then be fairly stiff if it is going to be used to line a mould, less stiff, but able to hold its shape, if it is to be used as an aspic to coat various dishes, and softly holding its shape if it is required for a jellied soup. Time is required when working with jelly, for if the decoration is complicated, several coats of jelly may be required and this may take several hours.

Chopped aspic makes an attractive border or bed for many cold dishes. To make chopped aspic, put a ½-inch of jelly in a tin. When it is set, cut it into small cubes with a knife. In the same way, decorative cutouts in the shape of diamonds or triangles can be made.

Sprays of tarragon and fennel leaves are often used for decoration in aspic, as are pimentoes, carrots, the yolks and whites of hard-boiled eggs, olives and truffles. A layer of jelly is spooned over the chilled food, the decoration is then dipped into the almost set jelly, placed in position, chilled to setting point and then covered with a final layer or two of jelly.

Aspic—I

This is an elaborate recipe for making aspic. The setting depends upon the gelatinous matter in the ingredients. Both the preparation and the cooking take a long time.

ABOUT 3½-4 PINTS

1 calf's foot, skinned and cleaned
5 lb. veal or beef bones and meat, chopped into 3-inch pieces, poultry carcasses and giblets
4 oz. pork rind
2 carrots, scraped
2 onions, peeled
2 celery stalks
2 leeks

1 bouquet garni, consisting of ½ teaspoon thyme, ½ teaspoon tarragon, 1 bay leaf, 6 sprigs of parsley, 2 garlic cloves, and 2 cloves, tied in a piece of cheese cloth
2 teaspoons salt
2 egg whites and shells
2 oz. minced [ground] beef
1½ teaspoons dried tarragon
4 fl. oz. [½ cup] Madeira

Wash and scrub the calf's foot. Soak it in cold water for 8 hours, changing the water several times. Put it in a medium-sized pan, cover it with water and boil for 5 minutes. Rinse in cold water and set aside.

Put the bones and meat in a large pan with enough cold water to cover by 2 inches. Slowly bring to the boil. Remove the scum with a large spoon. When the scum stops forming, add the calf's foot, the pork rind, vegetables and seasonings. Add more water, if necessary, to cover all the ingredients by 1 inch. Bring to the simmer and remove the scum.

Cover with a lid, leaving space for the steam to escape. Cook for 5 hours, simmering very gently. Occasionally, remove the scum and fat and, by adding boiling water, keep the level of the liquid above that of the ingredients.

Strain the stock into a bowl and leave to cool. Remove the fat which has hardened on top when the stock is cool. The stock is now ready for clarification.

Scald a large enamel or glass saucepan and a wire whisk with boiling water. Pour 4½ pints [5½ pints] of the stock into the saucepan. Place the pan over moderate heat and bring the stock to the boil.

Meanwhile, in a small mixing bowl, lightly beat the egg whites with a fork.

When the stock is boiling, add the egg whites and shells. Using the whisk, whisk vigorously in an anti-clockwise movement. As soon as the stock begins to boil again, stop whisking and allow it to rise to the top of the pan.

Remove the pan from the heat and allow the stock to settle.

Repeat the boiling process twice more, being careful not to break the egg white crust that will form. After the third boiling, remove the pan from the heat and leave it for 5 minutes.

Line a large strainer or colander with a scalded clean flannel cloth and place it over a large mixing bowl. Slowly strain the stock through the strainer or colander without squeezing the cloth (this will make the aspic cloudy). Do not break the egg white crust.

If the stock is not perfectly clear, strain it again through the cloth and egg white

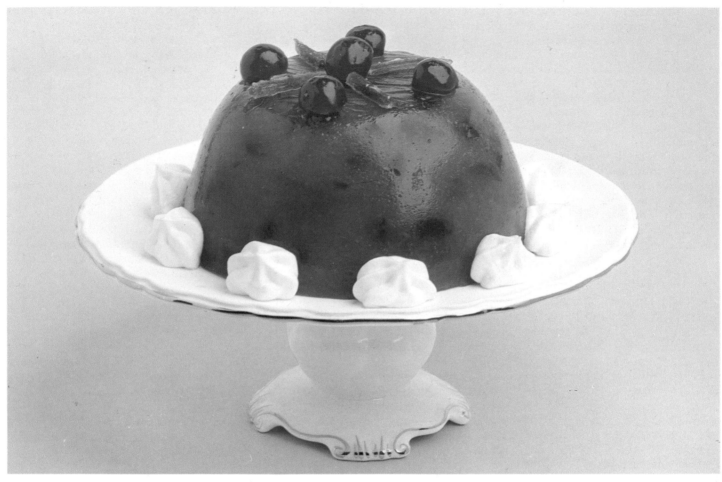

crust into another bowl.

Remove the strainer or colander and stir in the Madeira.

When the aspic cools, keep it in the refrigerator, covered, until you are ready to use it.

Aspic—II

This is a recipe for a very quick, easy and inexpensive aspic jelly. Although the result lacks the flavour of aspic made from bone stock, it is quite acceptable.

APPROXIMATELY ¾ PINT

1 chicken stock cube
½ pint [1¼ cups] boiling water
½ oz. [2 tablespoons] gelatine
3 fl. oz. [⅜ cup] dry white wine

Put the stock cube in a mixing bowl. Add the boiling water and stir to dissolve the cube.

Put the gelatine in a cup and pour a little of the hot stock into it. Stir until all the gelatine has dissolved and add it to the rest of the stock. Taste the stock and add salt if necessary.

Mix in the wine and leave the aspic to cool. When it is cool, cover the bowl and refrigerate. The aspic is now ready for use.

Aspic de Pommes
APPLE ASPIC

A dessert with a pleasing texture, Aspic de Pommes (as-peek d'pohm) requires no gelatine to make it set. The pectin in the apples makes a firm jelly which can be unmoulded before serving.

6 SERVINGS

1 teaspoon vegetable oil
4 oz. [⅔ cup] mixed glacé fruit, cherries, angelica, pineapple or orange
4 fl. oz. [½ cup] water
1 lb. [2 cups] sugar
2 tablespoons lemon juice
3 lb. firm cooking apples
1 teaspoon grated lemon rind
2 fl. oz. [¼ cup] sweet sherry
8 fl. oz. double cream [1 cup heavy cream] beaten

Grease a 1½-pint mould with 1 teaspoon oil.

Reserving a few cherries and some angelica for decoration, chop the rest together and set aside.

Put the water, sugar and lemon juice into a large pan and, over moderate heat, stir to dissolve the sugar. When the sugar is completely dissolved, remove the pan from the heat.

A mould of apple purée flavoured with sherry, Aspic de Pommes is decorated with glacé cherries and angelica.

Peel, core and quarter the apples and cut the quarters into thin slices. Drop the apple slices into the syrup as you cut them to prevent them from discolouring.

Put the pan back on the stove, raise the heat to high and, stirring continuously to prevent the apples from sticking and burning, boil rapidly for 20 minutes.

Press the apple pulp through a sieve. Stir in the sherry, and the chopped mixed fruit and the grated lemon rind.

Pour the mixture into the mould and chill in the refrigerator for at least 5 hours.

Before serving, run a knife round the edge of the mould. Place a serving plate on top of the mould and turn it upside-down to unmould the aspic. Decorate the aspic with the remaining cherries and angelica and serve with lightly whipped cream.

Assiette Anglaise
The French culinary term for an assortment of cold meats served on one plate, *Assiette Anglaise* (AH-see-YET on-glaze)

always includes a slice of York ham, a slice of beef tongue, a slice of roast beef and, sometimes, slices of galantine and brawn. It is garnished with chopped aspic and cress and is usually served at lunch.

Asti Spumante

One of Italy's best known sparkling white wines, Asti Spumante (ah-stee spoo-MAHN-teh) is made from Muscat grapes, which are grown in the vineyards of Asti and other Piedmontese vineyards. Always sweet and sometimes very sweet, it is preferable to drink this wine well chilled with the dessert or fruit course at the end of a meal.

Asynpoeding
VINEGAR PUDDING

A South African pudding, Asynpoeding (ah-sane-poo-ding) is an unusual ginger flavoured dessert baked with a vinegar flavoured syrup. Serve hot with custard.

8 SERVINGS

6 oz. [¾ cup] butter
6 oz. [¾ cup] sugar
3 eggs
¼ teaspoon salt
14 oz. [3½ cups] sifted flour
2 teaspoons ground ginger
2 teaspoons bicarbonate of soda
    [baking soda]
    a little milk
6 oz. [½ cup] pineapple jam
SYRUP
1 pint [2½ cups] cold water
4 fl. oz. [½ cup] white vinegar
12 oz. [1½ cups] sugar

Preheat the oven to fairly hot 400°F (Gas Mark 6, 200°C).

In a medium-sized mixing bowl, using a wooden spoon, cream the butter well and gradually add the sugar. Beat in the eggs, one at a time, beating thoroughly. Sift in salt, flour, ginger and mix.

In a small bowl, blend the bicarbonate of soda with a little milk and add to the egg-and-flour mixture.

Blend the ingredients into a dough. On a floured surface, roll out the dough into a rectangular shape, about 5 inches wide and 12 inches long. Spread the dough evenly with the pineapple jam and roll up as for a jam roll. Cut into 2-inch slices and place on the bottom of an ovenproof casserole dish.

Mix the cold water, vinegar and sugar together. Pour over the pudding in the casserole. Cover and bake in the centre of the oven for 1½ hours. Serve immediately.

Athenian Walnut Cake

Crunchy with walnuts and steeped in brandy and syrup, this Greek cake may be served with coffee, or as a dessert.

6 TO 8 SERVINGS

2 oz. [¼ cup] butter
5 oz. [⅝ cup] sugar
4 eggs
1 teaspoon ground cinnamon
8 oz. [1½ cups] walnuts, chopped
8 oz. [2 cups] sifted flour
SYRUP
6 oz. [¾ cup] sugar
10 fl. oz. [1¼ cups] water
4 fl. oz. [½ cup] brandy

Preheat the oven to moderate 350°F (Gas Mark 4, 180°C). Grease a medium-sized loaf or cake tin with a little butter and dust with flour.

In a medium-sized mixing bowl, beat the butter and sugar together with a wooden spoon until they are well creamed. Separate the egg yolks from the whites and set the whites aside. Add the yolks, one at a time, to the creamed butter and sugar and mix thoroughly.

Using a whisk or rotary beater, beat the egg whites until they are stiff. Add half of the egg whites and the cinnamon to the creamed mixture and mix well.

Set aside 2 tablespoons of chopped walnuts. Mix the rest of the walnuts and flour together and add gradually to the creamed mixture, mixing thoroughly. Fold in the remaining egg whites.

Put the mixture in the cake tin and sprinkle the top with the remaining 2 tablespoons of chopped walnuts. Bake for 1¼ hours or until the cake is cooked. Test by inserting a thin warmed skewer into

---

An adaptation of a Greek recipe, Athenian Walnut Cake is steeped in sugar syrup and brandy.

the centre of the cake. If it is clean and dry when removed, the cake is ready.

To make the syrup, dissolve the sugar in the water in a small saucepan over a low heat. When the sugar is completely dissolved, raise the heat and boil rapidly until the syrup thickens. Remove from the heat and mix in the brandy.

When the cake is cooked, remove it from the tin and place it upside down in a deep dish.

With a skewer, pierce the bottom of the cake in many places. Pour the hot syrup slowly over the cake while it is still hot. Set the cake aside to cool and to absorb the syrup. Turn right side up and serve cold.

Athénienne, à l'

À l'Athénienne (ah LAH-tay-nee-YEN) is a French term which is used to describe dishes which are flavoured with onions, aubergine [eggplant], tomatoes and sweet peppers cooked in olive oil.

Atholl Brose

A Scottish drink of oatmeal steeped in boiling water, strained and added to whisky, cream and honey, Atholl Brose is traditionally considered a good cure for a cold.

Aubergine [Eggplant]

The fruit of a plant native to Southern Asia, the aubergine is now widely grown in tropical, subtropical and warm temperate regions of the world. A member of the potato family, it is also known as eggplant, brinjal, melanzana, garden egg and patlican. There are many varieties of aubergines, which range from dark purple to pale mauve, and from yellow to white. They vary in shape from long and thin to pear shaped and quite round. The long, purple variety of aubergine is the one most commonly eaten.

Aubergines may be cooked whole in the skins or sliced and fried, baked, grilled or stuffed. They may also be stewed with mutton or lamb. The aubergine is one of the most popular vegetables in the world. It is eaten in the Far East, South Asia, Eastern Europe and America.

In the West, aubergines are usually sliced or chopped, sprinkled with salt and left to drain. The slices are then dried before cooking. Salting and draining removes some of the bitterness as well as the excess moisture, therefore requiring less fat for frying.

Only firm, smooth, shiny aubergines of uniform colour should be selected for cooking.

Aubergines Farcies Duxelles
BAKED AUBERGINES STUFFED WITH MUSHROOMS

Aubergines Farcies Duxelles (oh-bair-jeen FAHR-see doo-sell) *may be served as a first course or as an accompaniment to roast lamb or grilled, sautéed or roast chicken. This dish may be prepared the day before it is baked.*

It is also an ideal dish for freezing. When the aubergines are stuffed, allow them to cool. Place in the freezer and leave until hard, then wrap in aluminium foil. Return to the freezer to store. To serve them, place in a casserole and sprinkle with the cheese and breadcrumbs. Cook in the oven until hot throughout.

6 SERVINGS

3	large aubergines [eggplants]
1¼	tablespoons salt
3½	tablespoons olive oil
1	onion, finely chopped
1	garlic clove, crushed
1½	oz. [3 tablespoons] butter
1	lb. mushrooms, chopped
	freshly ground black pepper
6	oz. [¾ cup] cottage cheese
3	tablespoons chopped parsley
¼	teaspoon dried thyme
2	tablespoons grated Parmesan cheese
4	tablespoons white breadcrumbs

Remove the green stems from the aubergines and cut them in half lengthwise. With a sharp knife, make cuts in the pulp to within ¼ inch of the skin. Sprinkle with 1 tablespoon of salt and lay the aubergines, cut-sides down, on kitchen paper towels for 30 minutes to drain.

Squeeze the aubergines to remove as much liquid as possible and dry on kitchen paper towels. Put the aubergines, skin side down, in a flameproof dish. Pour a little olive oil over each one. Pour a little water into the dish to just cover the bottom.

Place under the grill [broiler] and cook for about 10 minutes until they are soft. Remove from the dish.

Using a spoon, scoop the flesh out into a bowl, leaving the skins intact. Roughly chop the flesh.

Preheat the oven to fairly hot 400°F (Gas Mark 6, 200°C).

Put the remaining olive oil in a large frying-pan. Fry the onion and garlic slowly over low heat for about 5 minutes or until it is tender but not browned.

Add all of the butter to the frying-pan and add the mushrooms. Sauté the mixture gently for another 5 minutes. Season with the remaining salt and 3 grindings of

pepper. Remove from the heat and stir the aubergine flesh into the mushroom-and-onion mixture.

In a small bowl, mash the cottage cheese with a fork. Stir into the aubergine mixture. Add the parsley and thyme. Add more salt and pepper if necessary.

Fill the aubergine shells with the mushroom mixture. Sprinkle with the grated cheese and breadcrumbs. Grease a clean flameproof dish with a little butter. Put the filled aubergines into the dish and cover with aluminium foil. Cook in the oven for 20 minutes, remove the foil and cook for a further 10 minutes or until the crumbs are crisp, golden and brown.

Aubergines Farcies Provençale

A tasty vegetarian luncheon dish, Aubergines Farcies Provençale (oh-bair-jeen fahr-see proh-von-sahl) *is easy to make and inexpensive when aubergines are in season.*

4 SERVINGS

4	aubergines [eggplants]
	water
2	tablespoons olive oil
2	small onions, chopped
2	cloves garlic, crushed
4	large tomatoes, blanched, peeled and chopped
12	green olives, stoned
½	teaspoon salt
	freshly ground black pepper
2	oz. [½ cup] grated cheese
1	oz. [⅓ cup] dry breadcrumbs
1	oz. [2 tablespoons] butter

Preheat the oven to moderate 350°F (Gas Mark 4, 180°C).

Put the aubergines in a large saucepan. Cover them with water and bring to the boil. Cover and cook over low heat for 15 minutes. Drain the aubergines and cut them in halves lengthways. Scoop out the pulp carefully, leaving shells ¼-inch thick. Set aside.

Heat the oil in a large frying-pan over moderate heat. Add the onions and cook slowly until they are soft but not brown. Add the garlic, tomatoes, olives, aubergine pulp, salt and 4 grindings of pepper. Simmer for 10 minutes, stirring occasionally.

Fill the aubergine shells with the mixture, sprinkle with the cheese and breadcrumbs, dot with the butter and place in an ovenproof dish. Bake for 30 minutes or until brown. Serve hot.

Filled with mushrooms and onions, Aubergines Farcies Duxelles are sprinkled with cheese and baked.

Aubergine Fritters—I

These fritters are a crisp and tasty accompaniment to serve with chicken, fish and rice dishes.

6 SERVINGS

3 aubergines [eggplants]
salt
BATTER
4 oz. [1 cup] flour
¼ teaspoon salt
a pinch of turmeric
2 egg yolks
1 tablespoon oil
5 fl. oz. [⅝ cup] milk
1 egg white
1 pint [2½ cups] cooking oil

Cut the aubergines into thin slices, sprinkle with salt and place in a colander to drain for 30 minutes.

Prepare the batter by sifting the flour, salt and turmeric into a medium-sized bowl. Make a well in the centre of the flour mixture and pour in the egg yolks and oil. With a wooden spoon, or wire whisk, beat the egg yolks and oil until they are mixed, slowly incorporating the flour. Add the milk a little at a time and continue beating until the batter is smooth. Cover and set aside in a cool place for 30 minutes.

Put the egg white in a small bowl and whisk until stiff. Fold into the batter.

Dry the aubergine slices with kitchen paper towels. Heat the oil in a deep frying-pan until it is very hot. Dip the aubergine slices in the batter and fry them in the oil until they are crisp and light golden in colour. When the fritters are cooked, drain them on kitchen paper towels, arrange on a warmed vegetable dish and serve hot.

Aubergine Fritters—II

This is another way to make aubergine fritters. They should be well seasoned and spicy and may accompany a rice and chicken dish.

4 SERVINGS

1 large aubergine [eggplant]
4 fl. oz. [½ cup] water
1 onion, grated or chopped very finely
¼ teaspoon cayenne pepper
¼ teaspoon ground turmeric
½ teaspoon salt
1 egg, lightly beaten
1½ oz. [⅓ cup] flour
1 teaspoon baking powder
milk
5 tablespoons oil

Peel the aubergine and cut into cubes.

Put the cubes in a small saucepan with the water and cook, covered, for 15 minutes, or until tender. Drain and put the cubes in a mixing bowl. With a fork mash the aubergine well. Mix in the onion, cayenne pepper, turmeric, salt and egg. Add the flour and baking powder and stir in enough milk to make a thick batter.

Heat the oil in a large frying-pan. When the oil is very hot drop in the aubergine batter a tablespoonful at a time and fry the fritters on each side until they are brown. Remove the fritters with tongs or a slotted spoon and drain on kitchen paper towels. Serve immediately.

Aubergines Gratinées

An excellent vegetarian dish, Aubergines Gratinées (oh-bair-jeen GRAH-tee-nay) *can be served either as a main course on its own or as an accompaniment to meat or chicken. The tomato sauce can be prepared well in advance and the dish put together an hour before it is required.*

4 SERVINGS

4 aubergines [eggplant]
1 tablespoon salt
  flour
3 fl. oz. [⅜ cup] vegetable oil
5 oz. [1¼ cups] cheese, grated
1 oz. [⅓ cup] white breadcrumbs
1 oz. [2 tablespoons] butter
SAUCE
1½ oz. [3 tablespoons] butter
1 small onion, finely chopped

3 tablespoons flour
12 oz. canned tomatoes
2 teaspoons tomatoe purée
½ teaspoon dried basil
  freshly ground black pepper
½ teaspoon salt

Slice the aubergines into rounds ¼-inch thick. Sprinkle the slices with salt and leave on a plate to drain for 30 minutes.

For the sauce, melt the butter in a saucepan, add the onions and fry over moderate heat, stirring occasionally, until the onions are soft. Add the flour and cook for 1 minute.

Strain the liquid from the tomatoes and stir into the onion mixture. Add the tomatoes, tomatoe purée, basil, 4 grindings of pepper and the salt. Bring to the boil stirring all the time. Lower the heat, cover the pan and simmer the sauce for 15-20 minutes.

Preheat the oven to moderate 350°F (Gas Mark 4, 180°C).

Dry the aubergine slices with kitchen paper towels. Dip the slices into the flour to coat well. Heat the vegetable oil in a large frying-pan over high heat. When the oil is very hot put in the slices of aubergine, a few at a time. Turn them over with kitchen tongs after a few seconds. When well fried, remove, drain on kitchen paper towels and keep hot until all the slices are fried. Add more oil to the frying-pan if necessary.

Put a layer of sauce in the bottom of a medium-sized ovenproof casserole. Sprinkle with some of the cheese and then put in a layer of aubergine slices.

Aubergines Gratinées is a tasty casserole of aubergines with tomato sauce topped with cheese and breadcrumbs.

Continue with these layers until the ingredients are used. Finish with a layer of tomato sauce. Sprinkle with cheese and breadcrumbs. Dot with a little butter. Bake in the oven for 25 minutes or until golden brown.

Aubergines Grillées

GRILLED AUBERGINES [EGGPLANT]

Grilled aubergines may be served as a vegetable or can be used as a foundation for escalopes, noisettes, tournedos or other small pieces of meat.

4 SERVINGS

2 aubergines [eggplant]
salt
5 fl. oz. [⅝ cup] olive oil
1 tablespoon chopped parsley

Peel the aubergines. Cut them into thick slices. Sprinkle both sides of each slice with salt and leave to drain in a colander for 30 minutes. When drained, rinse the slices in cold, running water and pat dry in a clean cloth, or kitchen paper towels.

Coat the slices of aubergine with olive oil and place in a shallow flameproof dish. Place under a heated grill [broiler] and cook for 3 minutes. Turn the slices, add more oil if too dry, and cook until the slices are soft. Sprinkle with parsley.

Aubergine and Lamb Casserole

This is a tasty way of using leftover lamb and makes an interesting supper dish. You can substitute beef stock for the chicken stock. Serve with boiled potatoes and a green salad.

4 SERVINGS

2 aubergines [eggplant]
1 tablespoon plus ½ teaspoon salt
1 lb. mushrooms
2 oz. [¼ cup] butter
1 medium-sized onion, chopped
1 garlic clove, crushed
4 tablespoons flour
1 pint [2½ cups] chicken stock
1 green pepper, seeded and chopped
1 lb. cooked lamb, diced
1 teaspoon dried oregano
½ teaspoon dried rosemary
4 tablespoons fresh breadcrumbs
½ teaspoon freshly ground black pepper

Cut the aubergines into 1-inch cubes. Place the cubes in a colander, sprinkle with 1 tablespoon of salt and leave to drain for 30 minutes. Rinse under cold running water and dry on kitchen paper towels.

Preheat the oven to fairly hot 400°F (Gas Mark 6, 200°C).

Chop the mushrooms into thick slices. Melt 1 tablespoon of butter in a medium-sized frying-pan and fry the mushrooms for 10 minutes. Set aside.

Melt 2 tablespoons butter in a medium-sized saucepan and fry the onion and garlic until they are golden. Add the flour and stir with a wooden spoon until it is well blended. Stirring constantly, gradually add the chicken stock to the pan. Continue cooking until the sauce is thick and smooth.

Place the aubergine cubes, mushrooms, green pepper, lamb, oregano, rosemary, ½ teaspoon of salt and the pepper into an ovenproof casserole.

Pour the sauce into the casserole and stir gently to mix.

Cover the top with the breadcrumbs, dot with the remaining butter and bake in the oven for 30 minutes or until the top is golden.

Aubergine and Lamb Stew

Aubergines and lamb are an excellent combination. In this stew, the addition of coriander seed, mint and garlic enhances their flavour. A bowl of chilled yogurt, to which

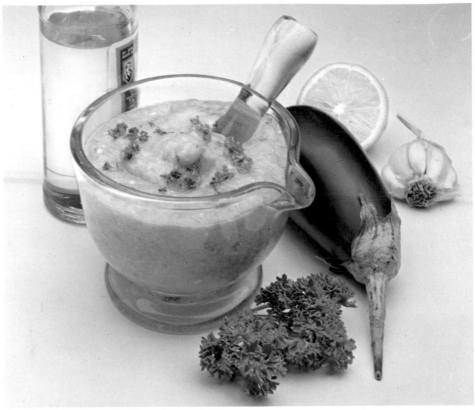

half a diced cucumber has been added, makes an excellent accompanying salad.

4 SERVINGS

2 aubergines [eggplant]
1 tablespoon plus ½ teaspoon salt
5 tablespoons olive oil
2 lb. lean, boned leg or shoulder of lamb, cut into 1-inch cubes
2 teaspoons coriander seeds, coarsely crushed
1 large onion, sliced
1 garlic clove, crushed
2 tablespoons chopped fresh mint
1 lb. tomatoes, blanched, peeled and chopped or 14 oz. canned peeled tomatoes, drained
freshly ground black pepper

Cut the aubergines into 1-inch cubes. Place the cubes in a colander, sprinkle with 1 tablespoon of salt, put a plate with a weight on it on top of the aubergines and leave to drain for 30 minutes. Pat the cubes dry with kitchen paper towels before cooking.

Heat the oil in a large frying-pan. Add the lamb cubes, a few at a time, and the crushed coriander seeds. When all the lamb has been browned, remove the cubes with a slotted spoon, put on a plate and set aside. Add the onion to the pan and fry until golden. Add the garlic and all the mint and cook for 1 minute. Add the aubergine cubes and fry, stirring frequently, for 10 minutes.

Return the lamb to the pan with the tomatoes, ½ teaspoon of salt and 6 grindings of black pepper. Cover, lower

Aubergines, garlic, parsley and olive oil combine to make this unusual and attractive Aubergine Salad.

the heat and cook for 1 hour. If the stew seems too liquid, simmer without a cover for the last 20 minutes.

Aubergine Salad

This Greek dish is usually served as a meze, or appetizer, as an accompaniment to an aperitif. Traditionally, flat Greek bread is dipped into the aubergine purée. It can also be served as a salad. If you find the natural greyish colour of the purée unattractive, add 2 or 3 drops of red food colouring.

4 TO 6 SERVINGS

2 large aubergines [eggplant]
1 large garlic clove, crushed
2 fl. oz. [¼ cup] olive oil
juice of 1 lemon
1 teaspoon salt
4 parsley sprigs, chopped

Preheat the oven to moderate 350°F (Gas Mark 4, 180°C).

Place the whole, unpeeled aubergines on a baking sheet and bake for about 40 minutes, or until they are soft. When the aubergines are cool enough to handle, cut them in half lengthways and scoop out the pulp. Mash the pulp to a purée in a mortar or by pushing through a sieve.

Put the purée in a medium-sized mixing bowl. Mix in the crushed garlic. Beat in the oil a little at a time. Add half the lemon juice, the salt and parsley. Mix well and taste. Add the rest of the lemon juice if necessary.

Aubergines Sautéed

This is a quick and easy way to serve this vegetable. Sautéed aubergines go well with light meat or fish dishes.

4 SERVINGS

- 3 aubergines [eggplant]
- 2 tablespoons salt
- 4 tablespoons flour
- 6 tablespoons cooking oil
- 2 tablespoons chopped parsley

With a sharp knife, peel the aubergines. Cut them into ¾-inch cubes.

Put the cubes into a colander, sprinkle them with salt and leave them to drain for 30 minutes.

Dry the aubergines on kitchen paper towels and sprinkle them with the flour.

Heat the oil in a heavy, medium-sized frying-pan over moderate heat. Put in the aubergine cubes and fry them briskly for 10 minutes, or until they are tender.

Remove the aubergine cubes with a slotted spoon. Put them in a warmed vegetable dish and sprinkle on the parsley.

Aubergine Soufflés

An elegant and tasty first course, these individual Aubergine Soufflés can also be served as an accompaniment to a main dish of meat, chicken or fish. The aubergine shells are not for eating in this dish because they may not be completely cooked by the time the soufflés are ready.

4 SERVINGS

- 2 aubergines [eggplant]
- 1 pint [2½ cups] boiling water
- ½ tablespoon vinegar
- 1½ oz. [¾ cup] fresh breadcrumbs
- 2 egg yolks, beaten
- 1 tablespoon melted butter
- 2 oz. [½ cup] grated cheese
- ½ teaspoon salt
  freshly ground black pepper
- ½ teaspoon dried basil
- 2 egg whites
- 2 tablespoons dried breadcrumbs
- 1 tablespoon butter, cut into pieces

Low Cal

Preheat the oven to fairly hot 375°F (Gas Mark 5, 190°C).

Cut the aubergines in halves lengthways with a sharp knife. Scoop out the pulp, leaving a shell ¼-inch thick. Set the shells aside.

Put the pulp into a medium-sized saucepan and cover with 1 pint of boiling water. Add the vinegar and simmer for 15 minutes or until the pulp is tender.

Drain the pulp and put it in a large bowl. With a fork mash it to a purée. Add the fresh breadcrumbs, egg yolks, melted butter, grated cheese, salt, 4 grindings of black pepper and the dried basil. Mix well. If the mixture is too stiff add a spoonful of the cooking liquid.

Beat the egg whites in a small bowl with a whisk until they are stiff. Fold them into the aubergine mixture.

Fill the aubergine shells with the mixture. Sprinkle the dried breadcrumbs over the top, dot with small pieces of butter and place in an ovenproof dish. Put the dish in a large baking pan which has a little water in it and bake for 30 minutes. Serve immediately.

Aubergines à la Tunisienne

This dish is equally delicious served either hot or cold. Aubergines à la Tunisienne (oh-bair-jeen ah lah too-NEEZ-yen) goes well with lamb dishes and is especially good with lamb kebabs.

4 SERVINGS

3 aubergines [eggplant]
1 tablespoon plus ½ teaspoon salt
4 tablespoons olive oil
2 onions, sliced
1 garlic clove, chopped
¼ teaspoon cayenne pepper
¼ teaspoon ground cloves
½ teaspoon ground cumin
1 lb. tomatoes, peeled and chopped
1 teaspoon ground coriander
1 tablespoon fresh chopped mint
2 tablespoons raisins
½ teaspoon black pepper
2 tablespoons chopped parsley

Cut the aubergines into cubes. Sprinkle with 1 tablespoon salt and put in a colander to drain for 30 minutes. Dry the cubes on kitchen paper towels.

Heat the oil in a large frying-pan over moderate heat. Add the onions and fry until soft. Add the garlic, the cayenne pepper, cloves and cumin and cook for 2 minutes. Add the aubergine cubes. Stir well and brown the cubes lightly on all sides. Add the tomatoes, coriander, mint, raisins, remaining salt and the pepper. Cook gently, stirring occasionally, until almost all the liquid has evaporated. Stir in the parsley.

Serve hot or cold.

Aubergines à la Tunisienne is an exotic and spicy accompaniment to any lamb dish.

Aubergines à la Turque

Stuffed with a spicy mixture of meat and rice and served with a thick tomato sauce, Aubergines à la Turque (oh-bair-jeen ah lah toork) is an easy-to-make supper dish.

4 SERVINGS

4 aubergines [eggplant]
2 teaspoons salt
5 tablespoons olive oil
1 onion, chopped
1 garlic clove, crushed
1 lb. minced [ground] lamb
1 tablespoon chopped parsley
¼ teaspoon cayenne pepper
grated rind of 1 lemon
1 teaspoon salt
½ teaspoon black pepper
4 oz. [2 cups] cooked rice
juice of 1 lemon
SAUCE
1 tablespoon olive oil
1 onion, minced
1 garlic clove, crushed
½ teaspoon dried basil
14 oz. canned peeled Italian tomatoes
½ teaspoon salt

First make the sauce. In a small saucepan, over moderate heat, fry the onion in the oil until golden brown. Add the garlic and basil and fry for 1 minute. Add the tomatoes and salt. Stir well and bring to the boil. Cover, lower the heat and simmer for 1 hour, or until the sauce has thickened. Stir occasionally with a wooden spoon, mashing the tomatoes with the back of the spoon.

Wash the aubergines and, with a sharp knife, cut them in half lengthways right through the stalk. Scoop out the pulp, but be careful not to damage the shells. Sprinkle the inside of the shells with a little salt. Place them upside down on a plate and set aside. Put the pulp in a bowl and set aside.

Heat 4 tablespoons of olive oil in a large frying-pan over high heat. Add the onion, lower the heat and fry until golden brown. Add the garlic and fry for 1 minute. Add the meat and brown it thoroughly. Add the aubergine pulp, parsley, cayenne pepper, grated lemon rind, salt and pepper. Stir to mix, lower the heat, cover and simmer for 25 minutes. Stir in the boiled rice and mix well.

Preheat the oven to fairly hot 375°F (Gas Mark 5, 190°C). Wipe the aubergine shells with kitchen paper towels. Brush them liberally all over with the remaining olive oil and place them in a large baking dish. Fill them with the meat-and-rice mixture. Sprinkle a little lemon juice over the top and bake for 40 minutes, or

until the shells are cooked and the top brown.

Serve with the tomato sauce.

Au Beurre

Au beurre (oh burr) is the French term for any dish cooked in butter or served with butter.

Au Beurre Noir

Au beurre noir (oh burr nwahr) is the French description of a dish served with black or nut-brown butter. Black butter is made by cooking butter in a pan until it becomes dark brown. Vinegar, salt and pepper are added and the sauce is then cooked until it is reduced by half. *Beurre noir* is used as a sauce for eggs, fish and some vegetables.

Au Blanc

Au blanc (oh blonk) is to keep white while cooking by using a *blanc*, the French name for a solution of salted water, lemon juice and flour, which is used for the preliminary cooking of any food which discolours. The term *au blanc* also applies to food cooked or served in a white sauce.

Au Brun

Au brun (oh broon) is the French term for a dish cooked in or served with a brown sauce. This sauce is sometimes called ESPAGNOLE and accompanies steak, cutlets, game, some vegetables and eggs.

Au Four

Au four (oh foor) is a French cookery term which means 'baked in the oven'.

Aufschnitt

Aufschnitt (owf-schnit) is a German term which refers to a variety of cold meats and sausages sold in German delicatessen shops.

Au Gras

A dish cooked in a rich meat gravy or meat stock is referred to by the French term *au gras* (oh grah).

Au Gratin

Au gratin (oh grah-tan) is the French cookery term for a dish which has been browned on top. Such a dish is usually covered with a sauce, sprinkled with bread-crumbs or grated cheese and baked in an oven or browned under a grill.

Au Jus

Au jus (oh joo) is the French term for meat served with its natural juices or gravy.

Au Lait

A dish or drink, such as coffee, which is served or cooked with milk is referred to by the French term *au lait* (oh lay).

Au Maigre

Au maigre (oh MAY-gr') is the French cookery term for a dish cooked without meat or meat stock and is, therefore, suitable for serving during Lent.

Au Naturel

Plainly cooked or simply cooked food is known by the French term, *au naturel* (oh nah-too-RELL).

Augolemono Soup
EGG AND LEMON SOUP

Augolemono (ahv-GOH-le-MOH-noh) *is a traditional Greek soup with an unusual*

lemon flavour. The alternative spelling is Avgolemono.

6 SERVINGS

3 oz. [$\frac{3}{8}$ cup] long-grain rice
3 pints [$7\frac{1}{2}$ cups] chicken stock
4 eggs
  juice of 2 lemons
$\frac{1}{4}$ teaspoon black pepper
2 parsley sprigs, chopped

Low Cal

Wash the rice thoroughly. Soak it in cold water for 30 minutes and drain it.

Put the stock in a large saucepan and bring it to a boil. Add the rice and simmer over low heat for 15 minutes, or until the rice is tender. Remove the pan from the heat.

Break the eggs into a medium-sized mixing bowl and beat with a wire whisk until they are well beaten.

Gradually add the lemon juice, beating continuously. Add a few spoonfuls of stock, a little at a time, beating constantly until it is well mixed. Stir this mixture into the saucepan containing the rest of the stock.

Over moderate heat, cook the soup for two or three minutes. Do not let it boil or it will curdle. Add the pepper, sprinkle with chopped parsley and serve immediately.

A traditional first course in Greece, lemon-flavoured Augolemono Soup tastes as delicious as it looks.

Aurore Sauce

This sauce, which can be served with fish, meat, eggs or vegetables, is based on a velouté sauce.

1 PINT

1$\frac{1}{2}$ tablespoons butter
3 tablespoons flour
10 fl. oz. [1$\frac{1}{4}$ cups] chicken or veal stock
$\frac{1}{2}$ teaspoon salt
5 fl. oz. [$\frac{5}{8}$ cup] tomato purée
5 fl. oz. single [$\frac{5}{8}$ cup light] cream
3 egg yolks

Melt the butter in a small saucepan over moderate heat. When the butter is melted, remove the pan from the heat and stir in the flour. Return to the heat and cook for 4 minutes, stirring continuously. Gradually add the stock and the salt, stirring all the time. When the mixture is blended, bring to the boil and simmer for 5 minutes. Add the tomato purée.

In a small bowl, mix the cream and

egg yolks thoroughly. Add half of the hot sauce, a spoonful at a time, stirring continuously. When it is well mixed, pour the egg mixture slowly into the pan with the remaining sauce. Stir to blend and cook over low heat until the sauce is smooth and thick. Do not allow the sauce to boil.

Au Rouge

A French culinary term, *au rouge* (oh rooj) is applied to a dish served with or finished in a red sauce.

Australian Wines

Australia is a comparative newcomer to the world of wine. The first vine was planted in 1788, but not until the early nineteenth century was there any success in wine production. Now Australia exports wines in bulk, chiefly to Britain. These consist mainly of light table wines and dessert-type wines which are fortified with spirits. The southeast of Australia falls within the temperate zone and so is naturally endowed with good vineyard conditions. Australian wines are generally robust and full in flavour. The Hunter River area, in New South Wales, has the vineyards which provide the best Australian table wines, while the Murray River area, extending through New South Wales, Victoria and South Australia, is where the grapes for the finer fortified wines are grown. The Barossa Valley, where the annual wine festival is held, is one of the most famous growing areas.

Austrian Boiled Beef

This is a good Sunday lunch dish. Serve it with a hot horseradish sauce, red cabbage cooked with onions and apples, and boiled potatoes. The potatoes can be added to the pot and boiled with the meat. The stock, makes an excellent soup.

6 SERVINGS

4 pints [5 pints] water
1 teaspoon salt
1 carrot, scraped and cut in half
3 parsley sprigs
1 celery stalk
1 leek, wash and trim
1 bay leaf
6 peppercorns
3 to 4 lb. boneless top beef rump
2 oz. ox liver

(Low Cal)

Put the water, salt, carrot, parsley, celery, leek, bay leaf and peppercorns in a large pot and bring to the boil. Add the

beef and the liver. The meat must be covered with water so add more if necessary. Bring to the boil again and skim off the scum.

Lower the heat, half cover the pot and simmer very gently for 2 to 2½ hours, or until the meat is tender. Add more boiling water whenever necessary during cooking to keep the beef covered at all times. For the last hour of cooking, cover the pot completely.

Remove the beef from the pan and serve on a heated dish.

Austrian Cabbage

This is an interesting and unusual way to cook dark green winter cabbage. Serve with roast pork or beefburgers.

4 SERVINGS

1 oz. [2 tablespoons] butter
1 onion, sliced
1 garlic clove, crushed
1 cabbage, shredded
10 fl. oz. [1¼ cups] sour cream
1 teaspoon paprika

Preheat the oven to moderate 350°F (Gas Mark 4, 180°C).

Melt the butter in a large saucepan over moderate heat. Add the onion and garlic and sauté until the onion is nearly soft. Add the cabbage. Stir to mix well and cook for 4 minutes.

Put the cabbage mixture into a baking dish. Mix the sour cream and paprika together and pour over the cabbage. Bake for 20 minutes. Serve hot.

Austrian Coffee Cake

This decorative and delicious dessert is very easy to make. Soaked in a mixture of coffee and brandy, the cake is decorated with whipped cream and walnuts.

4 SERVINGS

4 oz. [½ cup] butter
4 oz. [½ cup] plus 2 teaspoons sugar
2 eggs
4 oz. [1 cup] self-raising flour
2 oz. [¼ cup] crushed walnuts plus a few halves for decoration
6 fl. oz. [¾ cup] strong black coffee
2 fl. oz. [¼ cup] brandy
10 fl. oz. double cream [1¼ cups heavy cream]
½ teaspoon vanilla essence

Preheat the oven to moderate 350°F (Gas Mark 4, 180°C). Prepare a 7-inch cake tin by greasing the inside with a little butter and dusting with a little flour.

In a medium-sized bowl, beat the butter with a wooden spoon until it is soft. Add 4 ounces [½ cup] sugar and beat until the mixture is creamy. Add the eggs, 1 at a time, with 1 tablespoon of flour. Beat to mix and then fold in the remaining flour and the crushed walnuts. Turn the batter into the prepared cake tin. Bake for 50 minutes, or until a thin skewer inserted in the centre of the cake comes out clean.

Remove the cake from the tin and place on a rack to cool. Mix the brandy and coffee. Put the cake back in the cake tin and slowly pour the coffee and brandy over it. When all the liquid has been absorbed, turn out on to a dish.

Whip the cream with the remaining 2 teaspoons of the sugar and the vanilla essence. Using a spatula, spread the cream in whirls over the cake to cover it completely. Decorate with walnut halves.

Austrian Jam Doughnuts

Traditionally served during Fasching, a spring carnival in Austria and Germany, these jam doughnuts are light and delicious and may be served with morning coffee or afternoon tea.

ABOUT 24 DOUGHNTUS

½ oz. fresh yeast
3 tablespoons plus 1 teaspoon sugar
1 tablespoon warm water
1 lb. [4 cups] sifted flour, warmed
¼ teaspoon salt
6 egg yolks, well beaten
5 fl. oz. single [⅝ cup light] cream
1 tablespoon rum
1 teaspoon vanilla essence
1 teaspoon grated orange rind
1 teaspoon butter
12 oz. [1 cup] apricot jam
vegetable oil for deep frying
icing [confectioners'] sugar

Crumble the yeast into a small bowl and mash in 1 teaspoon of sugar with a kitchen fork. Add 1 tablespoon of water and cream the water and yeast together to form a smooth paste. Set the bowl aside in a warm, draught-free place for 15 to 20 minutes, or until the yeast has risen and is puffed up and frothy.

Sift the flour, the remaining sugar and the salt into a warmed, large mixing bowl. Make a well in the centre of the flour mixture and pour in the yeast and the egg yolks, cream, rum, vanilla essence and grated orange rind. Using your fingers or a spatula draw the flour into the liquid. Continue mixing until the mixture forms a firm dough.

For the Austrian Jam Doughnuts, cut 40 circles of dough and drop a teaspoon of apricot jam on to 20 of the circles.

Place a circle of dough on top of each one with jam on it and press the edges of the circles together.

Using a slightly smaller pastry cutter, trim the edges off the doughnuts to seal the circles together.

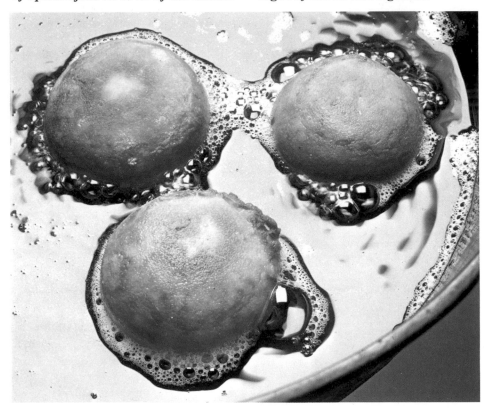

Grease a large bowl with the butter. Shape the dough into a ball and put it into the bowl. Cover it with a clean, damp cloth. Set the bowl in a warm place and leave it for 1 to 1½ hours, or until the dough has nearly doubled in size.

Punch the dough down in the bowl to deflate it and turn it out on to a lightly floured board.

With a rolling pin, roll the dough into a circle, ¼-inch thick. Using a lightly floured 3-inch pastry cutter, cut circles of dough. Collect up the remaining dough and shape into a ball. Roll it out ¼-inch thick and cut out more circles of dough.

Put 1 heaped teaspoon of the jam on to the centres of half the circles of dough. Place another circle on top of each one

Fry the doughnuts until they are golden brown, crisp and puffy. Then turn them and fry on the other side.

and press the outer edges of the two circles together.

With a slightly smaller pastry cutter, trim the edges off the doughnuts. Place waxed paper on baking sheets and dust them lightly with flour. Put the doughnuts on them about 1 inch apart. Place the doughnuts in a warm place for 30 minutes, or until they have risen and become slightly puffy.

Put the vegetable oil in a heavy frying-pan over moderate heat.

When the oil becomes hot ease the

doughnuts into the pan a few at a time. Do not crowd the pan.

The doughuts will puff up and after about 1 minute they should be golden brown on the underside. Turn the doughnuts over and fry them for a minute longer until they are golden all over.

Drain the doughnuts on several layers of kitchen paper towels on a plate, as they are cooked. Continue until all the doughnuts are fried, adding more fat to the frying-pan if necessary.

Arrange the doughnuts on a warmed plate, dust with the icing [confectioners'] sugar and serve hot.

Austrian Pudding

This is a delicious dessert and a good way to use leftover cake.

4 TO 6 SERVINGS

1 tablespoon plus 1 teaspoon butter, softened
1 lb. raspberries
6 oz. [¾ cup] sugar
4 egg yolks
4 oz. [1 cup] cake crumbs
2 oz. [½ cup] almonds, ground
1 tablespoon single [light] cream
4 egg whites
2 oz. [¼ cup] glacé cherries, halved

Preheat the oven to moderate 350°F (Gas Mark 4, 180°C). Grease a medium-sized soufflé dish with 1 teaspoon of butter.

Mix the raspberries with 3 ounces of sugar. Put them in the soufflé dish and set aside.

Place the egg yolks in a medium-sized mixing bowl with the remaining 3 ounces of sugar and beat with a wire whisk until the mixture is thick and creamy. Mix in the cake crumbs, ground almonds, cream and the remaining butter.

In another mixing bowl, whisk the egg whites until they are stiff. Fold the eggs whites into the pudding mixture and pour over the raspberries. Decorate the top with the glacé cherries and bake for 50 minutes, or until the pudding is firm and golden brown. Serve hot.

Austrian Wines

Austria produces mostly light white wines, many of which are exported to Germany. Austria's greatest wine, however, is considered to be Ruster Ausbruch, a golden dessert wine with a sweet and spicy aroma. The Heuriger, a fresh young wine, is the best-known product of Austrian vineyards.

Many of the Austrian wines are drunk when they are quite new. From the Wachau, one of the most beautiful wine areas in the world, come wines made from the Riesling grapes of the Rhine, which are similar in character to the German Rhine wines. The pleasant white wine of Gumpoldskirchen is one of the internationally better-known Austrian exports.

Au Vert

A French culinary term, *au vert* (oh vair) refers to any dish which is served with a green sauce.

Aviyal

VEGETABLE CURRY

An Indian dish of mixed vegetables cooked with coconut and spices, Aviyal (ah-VEE-yahl) should be served with boiled rice. You may use a combination of any vegetables, carrots, beans, aubergines [eggplant], turnips, cauliflower, green peppers, potatoes, spring onions [scallions] and okra.

4 SERVINGS

4 tablespoons cooking oil
1 teaspoon mustard seeds
1 onion, minced
1 green chilli, minced
2-inch piece of fresh ginger, peeled and minced
2 garlic cloves, peeled and cut into quarters lengthways
1½ teaspoons ground turmeric
1 tablespoon ground coriander
1½ lb. mixed vegetables, sliced
1 teaspoon salt
8 oz. [1 cup] fresh coconut puréed in an electric blender with
6 fl. oz. [¾ cup] water, or 1-inch slice creamed coconut
2 tablespoons coriander leaves, chopped (optional)

Heat the oil in a large saucepan over high heat. Add the mustard seeds, ginger and garlic and fry for 30 seconds. Add the onion and green chilli, reduce the heat and, stirring occasionally, fry gently for 10 minutes, or until the onion is golden.

Add the turmeric and ground coriander and cook for 1 minute. Add the vegetables and stir to mix well with the fried spices. Add the salt and the coconut purée and stir to mix. If the mixture is too dry, add 1 or 2 spoonfuls of water. Cover and simmer for 30 minutes or until the vegetables are tender. Sprinkle with the chopped coriander leaves and serve.

A spicy combination of flavours, Aviyal is a tasty and attractive Indian vegetable curry.

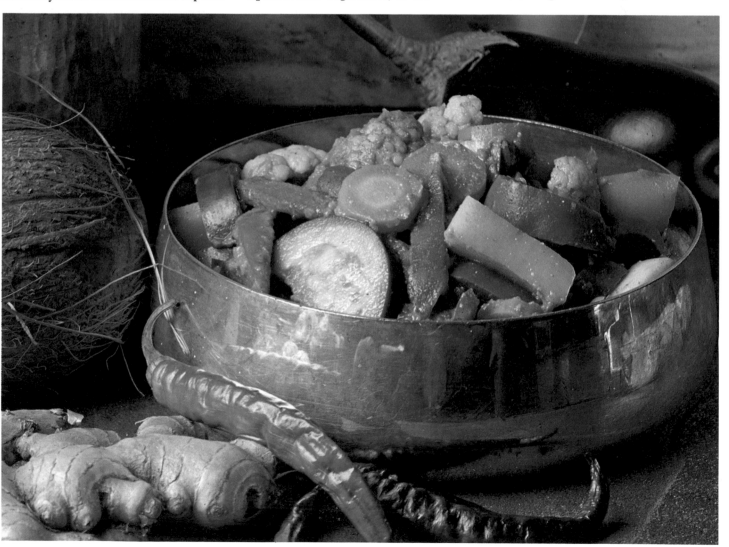

Avocado

The avocado is a delicately-flavoured, subtropical fruit that is best eaten when the flesh has ripened to the consistency of soft butter and is light yellow-green in colour. The large, brown-skinned stone and the thick green or black skin are never used. However, if you place the base of the stone in water until it sprouts roots and shoots, and then plant it in soil, it will grow into a small, decorative tree.

The fruit of a small to medium-sized tree native to Central America, avocados are now widely grown in tropical and subtropical areas such as the southern states of America, Mexico, Israel, South Africa and Australia.

Avocados are exceptionally rich in protein, Vitamin A and Vitamin B. Although high in calories, they have almost no carbohydrate content. They also contain a rare, highly digestible oil which is not found in other fruits.

The flesh of the avocado can be used in salads, sauces, soups and desserts. Diced or sliced, avocados are an attractive garnish for clear soups and hot dishes.

To halve an avocado, cut in half lengthways round the stone. Holding the two halves, gently twist them apart. Then remove the stone with the point of a knife. To prevent the flesh from darkening, rub it with a little lemon juice. Half an unpeeled avocado filled with a chicken or seafood salad, or with curried meat or chicken, tastes as good as it looks.

The most simple avocado recipe is the fruit eaten by itself with an oil and vinegar dressing.

Avocado Aspic

Serve this decorative aspic as part of a buffet supper or as a salad course at dinner.

6 TO 8 SERVINGS

1 oz. gelatine
4 fl. oz. [½ cup] cold water
1¼ pints [3 cups] chicken stock
2 avocados
  lemon juice
2 teaspoons finely chopped onion
2 celery stalks, diced
2 tablespoons diced cucumber
2 tablespoons canned diced
  pineapple

In a medium-sized saucepan, soften the gelatine in the cold water. Heat, stirring until the gelatine is dissolved. Add the chicken stock and cool the mixture.

Cut the avocados in half, peel and remove the stones. Slice the avocado

halves into thin even slices. Sprinkle with lemon juice.

Cover the bottom of a ring mould with a layer of gelatine and chill until it is set. Keep the remaining gelatine in a warm place so it will not set.

Arrange the avocado slices on top and cover with a layer of the gelatine. Chill until it is set.

Arrange more slices around the sides and add a thin layer of gelatine to hold them in position.

Chop any remaining avocado and mix it with all remaining ingredients and the remaining gelatine. Turn into the decorated mould and chill until firm.

Before serving, dip the mould quickly into hot water. Unmould on a bed of lettuce leaves on a serving plate.

Avocado Chicken Soup

A delicious and delicately flavoured soup, this can be served as the start to an otherwise heavy meal. Do not place the soup over direct heat after the avocado mixture is added.

4 SERVINGS

1½ pints [3 cups] chicken stock, fresh or made from a stock cube
1 small onion, finely minced
2 avocados, peeled and stoned
1 tablespoon butter, softened
1 teaspoon salt
4 grindings of black pepper
2 teaspoons lemon juice

Simmer the chicken stock and onion in a covered saucepan for 30 minutes.

Purée the avocados by pushing them through a sieve. Combine the purée with the butter, salt, pepper and lemon juice.

Remove the stock from the heat and fold in the avocado mixture.

Serve immediately in heated bowls.

Avocado Chicken Supreme

A good way to use leftover chicken or turkey, this dish could be served as a first course or as a light lunch or supper entrée.

4 SERVINGS

2 oz. [¼ cup] butter
2 tablespoons flour
10 fl. oz. [1¼ cups] milk
½ teaspoon salt
¼ teaspoon white pepper
½ teaspoon dried tarragon
12 oz. [1½ cups] chicken, cooked and diced
3 tablespoons chopped mushrooms
1 tablespoon chopped green pepper

2 large avocados
  juice of ½ lemon
2 tablespoons dry breadcrumbs

Preheat the oven to moderate 350°F (Gas Mark 4, 180°C).

In a medium-sized saucepan, melt 2 tablespoons of the butter over low heat. Stir in the flour to make a smooth paste. Gradually add the milk, stirring constantly until the sauce thickens. When the sauce boils add the salt, pepper, tarragon, chicken, mushrooms and green pepper. Simmer for 4 minutes.

Cut the unpeeled avocados in half lengthways. Remove the stones and rub the cut surfaces with the lemon juice.

Fill the cavities with the chicken mixture. Sprinkle the top with the breadcrumbs and dot with the remaining butter. Put the avocados in a baking dish with ½ inch boiling water. Bake in the oven for 10 minutes.

Avocado and Courgette [Zucchini] Salad

An unusual and decorative salad which could be served with any veal or beef dish, the courgettes can be cooked the day before you are going to use them.

4 SERVINGS

1 lb. courgettes [zucchini]
1 pint [2½ cups] water
2 teaspoons salt
1 garlic clove, crushed
¼ teaspoon dried tarragon
¼ teaspoon black pepper
½ teaspoon sugar
2 tablespoons white wine vinegar
6 tablespoons olive oil
1 avocado
12 stuffed green olives
  lettuce leaves
4 sprigs watercress

Wash the courgettes. Cut off the ends. Cut into slices ½-inch thick. In a saucepan, bring the water to the boil. Add 1 teaspoon of salt and the courgettes. Cover and cook for about 6 minutes. Drain the courgettes, put them in a bowl and allow to cool.

In a cup, mix the remaining salt, garlic, tarragon, pepper, sugar, vinegar and oil. Pour over the courgettes and toss well. Leave the courgettes to marinate in the refrigerator for 6 hours or overnight.

Peel and stone the avocado and cut it

A striking combination of greens, this Avocado and Courgette Salad goes well with any main dish.

into slices. Drain the courgettes and reserve the marinade. Cut the olives in half. Put the lettuce leaves on individual plates and arrange the courgettes, avocado and olives on top.

Garnish with watercress. Serve with the marinade separately.

Avocado Dip—I

This inexpensive, quickly made dip or spread can be served at cocktail parties or with pre-dinner drinks, accompanied by potato crisps, biscuits, toast slices, celery or other vegetable sticks.

ABOUT 32 OUNCES

4 medium-sized avocados
2 tablespoons lemon juice
2 tablespoons grated onion
⅛ teaspoon Tabasco sauce
¼ teaspoon salt
⅛ teaspoon black pepper

Peel and stone the avocados. Using a wooden spoon, push the avocado flesh through a sieve into a bowl. Mix in the lemon juice, grated onion, Tabasco sauce, salt and pepper. Cover the bowl and refrigerate until well chilled.

Avocado Dip—II

Spicy and delicious, this dip is quickly made. It can be prepared early in the day and covered and refrigerated until it is to be served.

ABOUT 24 OUNCES

3 medium-sized avocados
3 tablespoons mayonnaise
¼ teaspoon salt
¼ teaspoon pepper
¼ teaspoon chilli sauce
1 garlic clove, crushed
1 teaspoon prepared mustard
2 teaspoons lemon juice

Peel and stone the avocados. Using a wooden spoon, push the avocado flesh through a sieve into a bowl. Mix in the mayonnaise, salt, pepper, chilli sauce, garlic, mustard and lemon juice. Cover the bowl and refrigerate.

Avocado Herb Salad Dressing

A good way to use a soft, slightly over-ripe avocado, this dressing can be used for a simple lettuce and tomato salad.

ABOUT 8 OUNCES

1 teaspoon salt
4 grindings black pepper
½ teaspoon dried basil
½ teaspoon dried oregano
2 fl. oz. vinegar
6 fl. oz. [¾ cup] olive oil
1 medium-sized avocado, peeled, stone and puréed

In a small bowl, mix the salt, pepper, basil, oregano, vinegar and oil.

Gradually add the mashed avocado to the dressing until well blended.

Avocado with Jellied Consommé

An unusual first course for a summer lunch or dinner, jellied tomato consommé piled into avocado halves and garnished with watercress is elegant but inexpensive.

6 SERVINGS

14 oz. canned, peeled tomatoes
1 onion, sliced
½ teaspoon dried basil
4 allspice berries
1 bay leaf
½ oz. gelatine
12 fl. oz. [1½ cups] condensed consommé
½ teaspoon salt
½ teaspoon black pepper
3 avocados
juice of ½ lemon

Put the tomatoes, onion, basil, allspice and bay leaf in a medium-sized pan and bring to the boil. Lower the heat and simmer uncovered for 40 minutes. Strain through a sieve into a bowl.

In a cup, mix the gelatine with 4 table-spoons of the hot tomato liquid. When it has dissolved add it to the bowl.

Warm the consommé and add it with the salt and pepper to the tomato liquid. Mix well and pour the mixture into a shallow dish. Chill in the refrigerator until it sets.

Cut the avocados in half lengthways and remove the stones. Sprinkle the cut surfaces with the lemon juice.

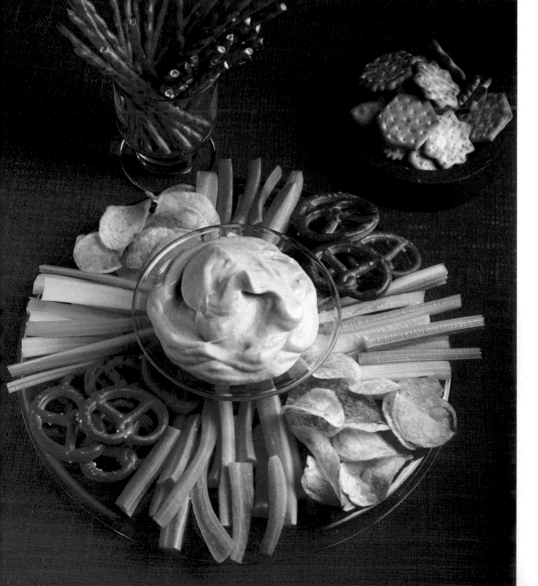

This inexpensive Avocado Dip takes only a few minutes to prepare and is ideal to serve with drinks.

Chop the jellied consommé and pile it into the avocado halves. Garnish with watercress.

Avocado Soup

An easy-to-make, inexpensive, cold soup, this may be served at the start of a summer lunch or dinner. It may be garnished with chives, dill or parsley.

6 SERVINGS

1 large avocado
1½ pints [3¾ cups] chicken stock, fresh or made from a stock cube
1 teaspoon grated onion
⅛ teaspoon cayenne pepper
5 fl. oz. single [⅝ cup light] cream
1 tablespoon chopped dill

Peel and stone the avocado. Using a wooden spoon, push the avocado through a sieve into a bowl.

Add the stock, onion and cayenne pepper. Beat well with a whisk until the mixture is smooth. Alternatively, blend the ingredients in an electric blender. Mix in the cream.

Pour the soup into individual soup bowls. Put the bowls in the refrigerator and chill thoroughly. Garnish with the dill and serve.

Azerbaijan Pilaff

This pilaff from Azerbaijan is delicately flavoured with sesame seeds and a little ginger. It makes an excellent accompaniment to roast chicken, roast lamb or a curry.

4 SERVINGS

2 oz. [¼ cup] butter
10 oz. [1½ cups] long-grain rice, washed, soaked for 30 minutes in water and drained
½ teaspoon ground ginger
1½ teaspoons sesame seeds
1 pint [2½ cups] chicken stock
½ teaspoon salt
½ teaspoon black pepper
2 oz. [½ cup] slivered, toasted almonds

Preheat the oven to moderate 350°F (Gas Mark 4, 180°C).

Melt the butter in a flameproof

Avocado halves filled with jellied tomato consommé is an elegant, yet easy and inexpensive first course.

casserole dish over moderate heat. Add the rice and cook for 10 minutes, stirring all the time. Add the ginger and sesame seeds and cook for 3 minutes. Pour in the stock, salt and pepper and bring to the boil, stirring constantly.

Put the casserole in the oven uncovered for 35 minutes or until all the liquid is absorbed and the rice is cooked. Toss the rice with a fork after 10 minutes and again after 20 minutes. Taste and add more salt if necessary. Sprinkle with the almonds and serve immediately.

Azarole

A member of the hawthorn family, the azarole tree grows in France, Italy, Algeria and Spain, where its fruit is used to make preserves and flavour liqueurs. The fruit resembles that of the hawthorn, but it is slightly larger. Its haws are usually orange-yellow or reddish in colour and have an apple-like flavour.

B

Baba

A rich, light-textured cake, a baba is made with flour, yeast, butter and eggs, and baked in the oven. It is said that the baba was invented by Stanislaus Leszczynski, King of Poland in 1704, when he poured rum over a dry yeast cake, naming it Ali Baba after the hero of his favourite story from *The Thousand and One Nights*. Introduced to Paris at the beginning of the nineteenth century, it became very popular and was known as a baba.

Baked in small or large round moulds, babas are soaked with syrup which is flavoured with rum or kirsch. They can be glazed with apricot jam, decorated with glacé fruit and served with Crème Chantilly.

Baba au Rhum

The best-known baba, Baba au Rhum (bah-bah oh rum) makes a delicious dessert for a lunch or dinner party. Babas can be baked a day or two in advance of serving, but should be reheated in a cool oven for 5 minutes so that they are warm when they are soaked in syrup.

MAKES 12 SMALL BABAS

BABA DOUGH
2 oz. [¼ cup] butter
7 oz. [1¾ cups] flour
¼ teaspoon salt
1 sachet easy-blend dried yeast
2 eggs, beaten
1 tablespoon milk
   butter for greasing
SAUCE
11 fl. oz. [1⅜ cups] water
5 oz. [⅝ cup] sugar
5 fl. oz. [⅝ cup] dark rum (light rum can also be used)
APRICOT GLAZE
4 tablespoons apricot jam
5 tablespoons water
DECORATION
1 teaspoon lemon juice
   glacé cherries, to decorate

toasted almond slivers,
   to decorate

To make the babas, melt the butter in a small heavy-based saucepan over a very low heat. Be careful not to brown the butter.

Set aside to cool.

Sift the flour, salt and dried yeast into a large mixing bowl. Make a well in the centre of the flour mixture and gradually pour in the beaten eggs, cooled melted butter and milk.

Blend all these ingredients thoroughly together with a wooden spoon, then beat and knead the dough with your hands, lifting it and slapping it. To begin with the dough will be quite sticky. If it is too sticky add a spoonful of flour. If it is too dry add a spoonful of milk.

When the dough begins to lose its stickiness, turn on to a lightly floured board and continue to knead. When it is completely elastic and can be stretched and twisted without breaking, roll it into a ball.

Butter a large mixing bowl and carefully place the ball of dough in it. With a sharp knife cut a cross on the surface of the dough and lightly sprinkle it with 1 teaspoon flour.

Cover the bowl with a clean cloth and leave in a warm draught-free place for 1½-2 hours, or until the dough has almost doubled in bulk. Press the dough with your fingers, if the impression remains the dough has risen sufficiently and is now ready for the second kneading. If the dough has not risen sufficiently, leave it for another 10 minutes and check again.

When the dough has risen enough, deflate it by kneading it gently for 2 more minutes.

Butter the insides of 12 individual baba moulds. Divide the dough into 12 portions and gently press each portion into a mould. The mould should only be two-thirds full.

Place the uncovered moulds in a warm, draught-free place and leave to rise for about 35-45 minutes, or until the dough

Rich and light-textured, Babas au Rhum are soaked in a rum-flavoured syrup and glazed with apricot jam.

has risen to just over the top of the baba moulds.

Preheat the oven to moderate 375°F (Gas Mark 5, 190°C).

Bake the risen dough in the middle of

the oven for 15 minutes, or until the babas are cooked, when the tops are brown and an inserted skewer comes out clean. Unmould them carefully on to a cake rack and set aside to allow them to cool slightly.

While the babas are cooling prepare the sauce; put the sugar and water in a heavy-based saucepan and gradually bring to the boil to completely dissolve the sugar.

Simmer for 5 minutes and remove from the heat.

Allow the syrup to cool completely and gradually stir in 4 fluid ounces [½ cup] of the rum.

Place the babas in a shallow dish large enough to hold them all comfortably and prick them all over with a fork. Pour the warm syrup over them and, basting with the syrup every few minutes, leave to soak

for 30-40 minutes or until the babas have absorbed enough syrup to be well moistened. Carefully transfer the babas to a rack and leave to drain.

To prepare the apricot glaze, put the jam and water in a small heavy-based saucepan and cook over medium heat for about 5 minutes, stirring constantly with a wooden spoon. Add the lemon juice and stir well, then strain through a fine nylon

Baba aux Fraises, accompanied by Crème Chantilly, is an interesting way to serve a baba with strawberries.

sieve.

When the babas have drained, arrange them on a serving dish and sprinkle with the remaining rum. With a pastry brush, paint the babas with the apricot glaze. Decorate the outside of the babas with the glacé cherries and the toasted almond slivers, sprinkling the almonds in the centre and on top of the rings. Serve cold, with cream if liked.

If the babas are made in dariole moulds, decorate the tops with cherries and the sides with almonds.

Baba aux Fraises

Baba aux Fraises (bah-bah oh fraze) *is a delicious way to serve a rum baba when strawberries are in season, but other soft fruits, or a mixture of fruits, can be used. It is usually served with Crème Chantilly.*

12 SERVINGS

1 lb. fresh strawberries
   leftover baba syrup
1 large rum baba
CREME CHANTILLY
15 fl. oz. double cream [2 cups
   heavy cream]
1 teaspoon vanilla essence
   icing [confectioners'] sugar

Put the strawberries in a bowl and pour over the syrup. Leave for 20 minutes.

Put the rum baba on a serving dish. Fill the centre with the strawberries, putting a few around the baba.

To make the Crème Chantilly, place the cream and essence in a chilled bowl and, using a cold whisk, whip lightly, adding the icing sugar to taste. Serve the Crème Chantilly in a separate dish.

Bacalhau

SALT COD CASSEROLE

A traditional Portuguese dish, Bacalhau (bah-kah-loah) makes an unusual, tasty family lunch or dinner dish and may be served with a green salad. The salt cod should be bought the day before you wish to cook it, so that it can be soaked in cold water for 12 hours to remove some of the salt.

4 SERVINGS

2 lb. salt cod
6 fl. oz. [¾ cup] olive oil
1½ lb. potatoes, peeled
1 lb. onions, cut in slices and
   separated into rings
1 lb. tomatoes, coarsley sliced
2 garlic cloves, finely chopped
½ teaspoon coarsley ground black
   pepper
10 black olives, stones removed
4 hard-boiled eggs, sliced
2 tablespoons finely chopped
   parsley

Put the cod in a medium-sized mixing bowl and cover with cold water. Leave covered for at least 12 hours to soak. Change the water every 3 or 4 hours, or whenever convenient.

Drain the cod and rinse it well to wash off the salt. Put the fish in a medium-sized saucepan, cover with water and bring to the boil over high heat. Lower the heat, cover the pan and simmer the cod for 15 minutes or until it is cooked.

Pour away the water and drain the cod

well. Skin and bone the fish. Flake it and set aside.

Preheat the oven to fairly hot 375°F (Gas Mark 5, 190°C).

Half fill a large saucepan with salted water and bring it to the boil. Add the potatoes and boil them for 15 to 20 minutes, or until they are just cooked. Drain and cut the potatoes into slices and set aside.

In a large frying-pan heat 4 tablespoons of the olive oil over moderate heat. When it is hot add the onions and fry for 5 minutes, stirring occasionally until they are soft but not brown. Add the tomatoes, garlic and pepper and cook stirring carefully for 4 minutes. Draw the pan off the heat.

Arrange the potato slices, the cod, onions and tomatoes in layers in the casserole until it is full. Pour the remaining oil over the top. Put the casserole in the centre of the oven and cook for 30 minutes or until all the ingredients are thoroughly heated and the top is brown.

Garnish the dish with the black olives, egg slices and chopped parsley. Serve hot.

Bacardi Rum

A light, white rum which was first produced in Cuba in 1862, Bacardi rum developed international popularity in the twentieth century. Bacardi is the main ingredient of the DAIQUIRI and many other cocktails. The chief producers of Bacardi today are the Bahamas and Puerto Rico.

Bacon

The word bacon usually refers to the cured meat from a specially bred pig. Most British bacon is cured in the Wiltshire style. The two sides of the pig are immersed for about five days in a tank of brine which is composed of salt, sodium nitrate, saltpetre and, sometimes, sugar. The bacon is then drained and matured for a further seven days. Many other cures, however, such as sweetcure and tendercure, have been developed in recent years. For the distinctive smoked flavour, cured bacon is hung over smouldering oak sawdust or chips for 12 hours.

Unsmoked bacon, commonly called green bacon, or white bacon, has a white rind and a milder flavour than smoked bacon, which has a brown rind. Country-smoked bacon is more heavily smoked than the commercial variety.

In Britain, a side of bacon is usually

A traditional Portuguese casserole made with salt cod, Bacalhau is a colourful main dish.

divided into the following cuts. From the fore end of the bacon, the cuts are called forehock and collar. Those from the middle of the bacon are called prime streaky, thin streaky, flank, top back, prime back, oyster back and long back. From the gammon, which is the hind quarter of a side of bacon, the cuts are called slipper, corner, prime middle and knuckle.

In America, there are only two types of bacon available. Smoked or hickory, smoked strips of bacon without rind, are very much like English rindless thin streaky bacon. Canadian bacon is cut from the eye of a pork loin and is more like ham.

The choicest bacon slices, or rashers, for frying or grilling are those from the back, which are called prime, long and top back. The fat and lean in these rashers are not intermixed, unlike streaky bacon which alternates streaks of lean and fat, but which can be fried or grilled.

Collar rashers are wider and leaner than streaky bacon. Often too coarse for grilling and frying, they are suitable for pies. Gammon rashers and steaks are cut thick and can be fried and grilled. Oyster or flank rashers are quite fatty and are used for larding poultry and meat.

The most suitable cuts of bacon for boiling or baking are the gammon cuts. A whole gammon usually weighs about 15 pounds and is divided into many cuts. The most popular are middle and corner gammon which are lean and boneless. The smaller, cheaper cuts, gammon slipper and gammon hock, include some bone.

Collar cuts of bacon, which can also be boiled or baked, are less expensive than gammon and include a good proportion of lean meat. The best collar cut, prime collar, is boneless and meaty. A cut called forehock has some bone and knuckle, is less tender than gammon, but is ideal for soups or stocks. It is also sold boned and rolled for boiling.

Bacon stored in a cool place should keep for 10 days in winter and up to four days in summer. Bacon fat can be kept in a covered jar in a cool place or in the refrigerator and used for frying eggs, liver, tomatoes or bread.

In many parts of the world, particularly

Bac

in England and America, bacon is traditionally served at breakfast with eggs, either fried or scrambled.

To fry bacon, cut off the rind with kitchen scissors, make little snips in the fat to prevent the rasher from excessive shrinking and arrange the rashers in a cold frying-pan in one layer, with the slices barely touching each other. No fat needs to be added unless you are cooking gammon or collar rashers. The bacon should be cooked over moderate heat until it is crisp. The rashers should be turned frequently to ensure even cooking. Bacon is not properly cooked until the fat has entirely lost its transparency. Drain the bacon on paper towels for 1 minute before serving.

To grill [broil] bacon, put it under a hot grill and cook, turning frequently, until the fat loses its transparency. Another method of cooking bacon, which is easy and ensures crispness, is to cook the bacon in a moderate oven on a rack set in a baking tin.

Fried or grilled bacon is delicious in a sandwich with lettuce and sliced tomatoes or served with calves' liver.

Cuts of bacon are frequently very salty and should be soaked in tepid water for at least two hours before boiling. The saltiness can also be removed by putting the cut of bacon in a saucepan of cold water and bringing it slowly to the boil. When it reaches boiling point, remove the saucepan from the heat and pour off the water. Refill the saucepan with cold water and boil the bacon for the required time. Cooking time for boiling bacon is 20 minutes to the pound, plus 20 minutes over.

British cuts of Bacon
1, 2, 9 boneless forehock joints
3 prime streaky   4 thin streaky
5 middle rashers   6 middle gammon
7 corner gammon   8 forehock knuckle
10 top back   11 prime back
12 gammon knuckle 13, 14 collar joints
15 long back   16 oyster back
17 slipper gammon   18 collar rashers
19 flank   20 bacon chops
21 gammon steaks

Bacon, Baked

Served hot or cold, baked bacon accompanied by creamed or sautéed potatoes and broccoli or green beans, makes a delicious and satisfying main course for lunch or dinner. The bacon should be soaked in tepid water for 2 hours before boiling to remove excess salt.

4 SERVINGS

3 lb. bacon gammon, collar or hock
5 fl. oz. [⅝ cup] vinegar
1 bay leaf
6 tablespoons brown sugar
   grated rind of 1 orange
   juice of 1 orange
⅛ teaspoon mace
20 cloves
5 fl. oz. [⅝ cup] cider

After soaking the bacon, place it in a saucepan and cover with cold water. Add the vinegar, bay leaf and 1 tablespoon of sugar and bring to the boil. Remove the scum from the surface of the water and reduce heat to low.

Simmer very gently, partly covering the saucepan, for 1 hour and 10 minutes, removing the scum from the surface of the water from time to time. Remove the bacon from the water, peel off the thick skin and put the bacon in a medium-sized, ovenproof serving dish, the fat side up.

Preheat the oven to moderate 350°F (Gas Mark 4, 180°C).

In a small bowl, mix the remaining brown sugar, grated orange rind, orange juice and mace together. Push the cloves into the fat of the bacon. Pour the brown sugar-and-orange mixture over the bacon and pour the cider round it.

Place in the centre of the oven and bake for 40 minutes, basting from time to time, or until the sugar is brown and crisp. Serve the bacon hot in the dish in which it has been cooked.

Bacon, Boiled

Served hot, boiled bacon is delicious with mustard, pickled onions, new potatoes and young green beans or peas. It may also accompany roast turkey or veal. Cold boiled bacon is excellent accompanied by a mixed salad and boiled new potatoes.

4 SERVINGS

3 lb. bacon gammon, collar
   or hock
5 fl. oz. [⅝ cup] vinegar
6 cloves
1 bay leaf
1 tablespoon brown sugar

Soak the bacon in tepid water for 2 hours. Place the soaked bacon in a saucepan and cover with cold water. Add the vinegar, cloves, bay leaf and sugar and bring to a boil. Remove the scum from the surface of the water and reduce heat to low.

Simmer very gently, partly covering the saucepan, for 1 hour and 30 minutes, or until the bacon is very tender. Remove the scum from the surface of the water from time to time. Drain, peel off the skin and place the bacon on a warmed serving dish, if the bacon is to be served hot. If it is to be served cold, allow the bacon to cool in the water in which it has been cooked. This ensures that the meat remains moist. Drain well before serving.

Bacon Dumplings

These Austrian Bacon dumplings may be served in chicken soup or cooked in boiling salted water, and served with beef instead of potatoes.

16 DUMPLINGS

1 egg
4 tablespoons milk
6 slices white bread, trimmed
4 slices lean bacon, diced
2 small onions, finely chopped
2 oz. [½ cup] flour
½ teaspoon salt
2 tablespoons finely chopped
   parsley
½ teaspoon dried thyme
½ teaspoon finely grated lemon rind

In a small mixing bowl, lightly beat the egg and milk together.

Put the bread in a medium-sized mixing bowl and pour the egg-milk mixture over it. Set aside.

In a small frying pan, over moderate heat, fry the bacon dice for 4 or 5 minutes, or until they are crisp and golden. Using a slotted spoon, remove the bacon and set aside to drain on kitchen paper towels.

Add the onions to the pan and fry them gently for 5 minutes, or until they are golden brown. Add the onion and the bacon to the bread in the mixing bowl.

Add the flour, salt, parsley, thyme and lemon rind. Mix well with a spoon. If the mixture is too dry add a little more milk; if it is too wet add a little more flour.

Using your hands mix all the ingredients well together. Taste the mixture and add more salt if necessary. With floured hands shape the mixture into balls the size of walnuts.

Half fill a large saucepan with salted water or soup and bring it to the boil over high heat. Ease the dumplings in, lower the heat and simmer uncovered for 8 to 10 minutes, or until they are cooked.

With a slotted spoon, remove the dumplings from the pan. Serve immediately.

Bacon and Egg Pie

Delicious eaten hot or cold, this is an easily-made pie. It is a good dish for light lunches, suppers, or for a family picnic.

4 SERVINGS

PASTRY
6 oz. [1½ cups] flour
¼ teaspoon salt
1½ oz. [¼ cup] butter,
   chilled
1½ oz. [¼ cup] vegetable fat
2 tablespoons iced water
FILLING
1 teaspoon butter
8 oz. streaky bacon
4 eggs
½ teaspoon black pepper
a little beaten egg

Preheat the oven to fairly hot 400°F (Gas Mark 6, 200°C).

To make the pastry, sift the flour and salt into a medium-sized mixing bowl. Add the butter and the vegetable fat and cut into small pieces with a table knife. With your fingers, rub the fat into the flour until the mixture looks like fine breadcrumbs. Add 1 tablespoon of the iced water and mix it in with the knife. Using your hands, mix and knead lightly until the dough is smooth. If the dough is too dry, add the remaining iced water. Pat the dough into a ball, cover and put in the refrigerator for 30 minutes.

Grease an 8 inch diameter tin with 1 teaspoon of butter.

Break off two thirds of the pastry and set aside the smaller piece. On a floured board, roll out the larger piece into a round 2 inches larger than the sandwich tin. Line the tin with the pastry and trim the edges.

Trim the bacon rinds and chop the bacon into small pieces. Arrange the bacon pieces in the pastry shell, leaving 4 wells for the eggs. Break an egg into each well. Sprinkle with pepper. Brush the edge of the pastry with a little beaten egg. Roll out the remaining pastry into a circle and cover the pie. Trim the edges and pinch them together to seal them and make a decorative pattern. Brush the top of the pie with the beaten egg and decorate with pastry shapes. Make a slit, with a knife, in the centre of the pie to allow the steam to escape.

Place the pie in the centre of the oven

and bake for 40 minutes. When the top of the pie becomes sufficiently brown, cover with aluminium foil and continue baking. Serve hot or cold.

Bacon and Liver Rolls

Tasty and inexpensive appetizers or hors d'oeuvre, these may also be served as a accompaniment to an entrée of roast chicken.

20 ROLLS

10 fl. oz. [1¼ cups] water
½ teaspoon salt
8 oz. chicken livers
2 hard-boiled eggs
2 tablespoons chopped onion
2 teaspoons chopped parsley
¼ teaspoon salt
    freshly ground black pepper
2 tablespoons butter, softened
½ teaspoon lemon juice
1 teaspoon brandy
10 bacon slices, cut in halves

In a medium-sized saucepan, bring the water to the boil. Add the salt and the chicken livers. Boil them for 7 minutes

Rolls of bacon filled with a rich liver mixture, Bacon and Liver Rolls make a tasty hors d'oeuvre.

or until they are just cooked. Drain the livers.

Using the back of a spoon, rub the hard-boiled eggs and the chicken livers through a fine sieve into a bowl. Add the onions, parsley, salt, 4 grindings of pepper, butter, lemon juice and brandy. Stir the mixture well and chill it in the refrigerator for 30 minutes.

Spread the chicken liver mixture on the strips of bacon. Roll up the bacon strips and put a wooden cocktail stick through the centre of each one. Place the rolls under a fairly hot grill and, turning them occasionally, cook them for 10 minutes, or until the bacon is crisp. Serve hot.

Bacon Whole-Wheat Scones

These bacon-flavoured scones may be served hot with a hearty soup for a light family lunch or supper. The dough can

be prepared well in advance and baked just before serving.

16 SCONES

5 oz. [1¼ cups] wholewheat flour
5 oz. [1¼ cups] plain flour
1 tablespoon baking powder
¼ teaspoon salt
3 oz. [⅔ cup] white vegetable fat [shortening]
8 oz. [½ lb.] streaky bacon, crisply fried
5 fl. oz. [⅝ cup] milk

Preheat the oven to very hot 450°F (Gas Mark 8, 230°C).

Sift the flours, baking powder and salt into a bowl. Rub in the fat until the mixture resembles breadcrumbs. Crumble the bacon and add to the flour mixture.

Gradually stir in sufficient milk to give a soft dough. Turn on to a lightly floured surface and knead lightly. Carefully roll the dough to ½ inch thick and cut into individual scones.

Place on a baking sheet, bake for about 15 minutes and serve hot.

The dry mixture can be prepared in advance. Then add the liquid, knead, cut out and bake when needed – a good idea for a brunch snack.

For a richer tasting scone, substitute butter for the white vegetable fat [shortening].

Badami Gosht

LAMB COOKED WITH ALMONDS

An adaptation of an Indian recipe, Badami Gosht (ba-DAH-mee gohsht) is fragrant and spicy lamb cooked with almonds. It makes a good lunch or dinner dish and may be served with chapatis, or bread, and with vegetables, such as aubergines or spinach. The usual cooking medium for this dish is clarified butter, which is called ghee in India.

If ghee is not available, cooking oil may be substituted

If creamed coconut is not available, soak 4 tablespoons desiccated [shredded] coconut in 12 tablespoons of water for 1 hour or until the coconut is moist and has absorbed all the water.

4 SERVINGS

- 5 tablespoons clarified butter or vegetable oil
- 2 cinnamon sticks
- 6 cloves
  seeds of 6 cardamoms
- 1 large onion, finely chopped
- 2 garlic cloves, crushed
- 1½ inch piece root ginger, peeled and finely minced
- 1½ lb. boned leg of lamb, cut into 1-inch cubes
- 10 fl. oz. [1¼ cups] yogurt
- 1 teaspoon saffron threads soaked in 2 tablespoons of boiling water
- ½ teaspoon chilli powder
- 3 oz. [½ cup] ground almonds
- 1 teaspoon salt
- 1-inch slice creamed coconut dissolved in 10 fl. oz. [1¼ cup] hot water
- 2 whole dried red chillis

In a medium-sized saucepan heat the oil over moderate heat. Add the cinnamon, cloves and cardamom seeds and cook for 1 minute.

Add the onion and, stirring continuously, fry for 7 minutes until the onion is soft. Add the garlic and ginger and continue frying and stirring until the onions are golden brown.

Add the lamb cubes, a few at a time, and fry well, stirring frequently, until they are well browned.

Put the yogurt into a small bowl. Pour in the saffron, the soaking water and the chilli powder and beat well.

In another small bowl mix the almonds with enough water to make a paste.

Pour the yogurt mixture over the lamb cubes in the pan and stir to mix. Cook for a minute and stir in the almond paste and salt. Simmer for 15 minutes.

Add the dissolved coconut cream and

Badami Gosht, a fragrant Indian lamb dish, is coloured with saffron and flavoured with almonds and coconut.

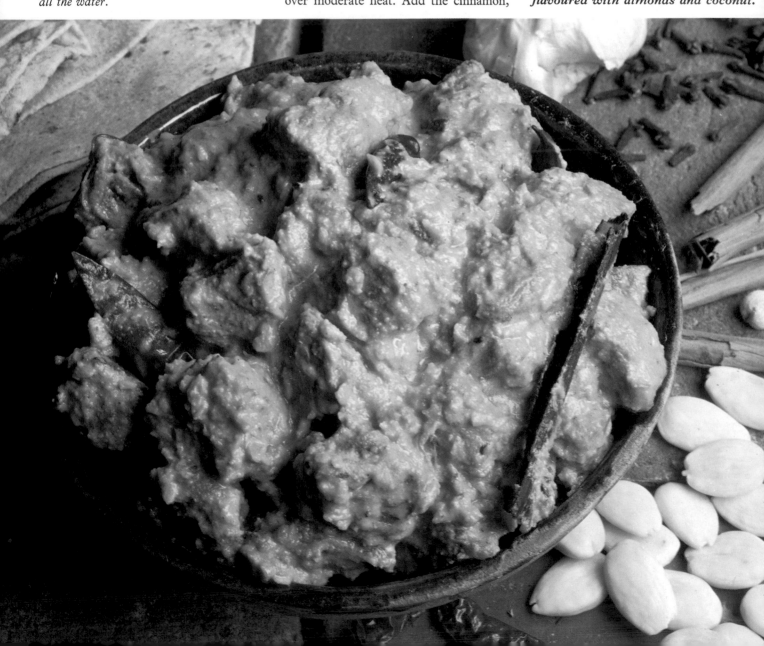

the whole red chillis. Lower the heat and simmer, uncovered, for 30 to 40 minutes or until the lamb is tender.

Cover the pan for the last 10 minutes of cooking. Serve hot.

Badminton Cup

This is a refreshing, cold, summer drink.

1¾ PINTS

½ medium-sized cucumber, peeled and sliced
4 oz. icing [1 cup confectioners'] sugar
juice of 1 lemon
⅛ teaspoon grated nutmeg
2 fl. oz. [¼ cup] Curaçao
1 bottle claret
6 fl. oz. [¾ cup] soda-water
2 borage sprigs, if available

Put the cucumber, sugar, lemon juice, nutmeg, Curaçao and claret into a large bowl. Stir to dissolve the sugar. Pour in the soda-water and some ice. Add the borage, if it is available.

Baghali Polo

LAMB WITH RICE AND DILL

Dill is traditionally used in Iranian cooking and it gives this lamb and rice dish a delicious aroma. Baghali Polo may be served as a main dish for lunch or dinner and is usually accompanied by a large bowl of chilled yogurt. You may also serve a tomato, cucumber and onion salad, made with a sharp dressing.

6 SERVINGS

4 tablespoons vegetable oil
2 lb. lean, boned lamb, cut into 1-inch cubes
2 onions, sliced
12 fl. oz. [1½ cups] water
1 teaspoon salt
¼ teaspoon ground cinnamon
½ teaspoon black pepper
1 lb. [2½ cups] long-grain rice, washed, soaked in water for 30 minutes and drained
1 lb. fresh or frozen Lima or broad beans
3 tablespoons chopped fresh dill or 2 teaspoons dried dill

Low Cal

In a large flameproof casserole, heat the oil over moderate heat. Add the lamb cubes, a few at a time, As they brown, transfer them with a slotted spoon to a plate.

Add the onions to the casserole and fry them for 10 minutes, stirring occasionally, until they are brown.

Return the lamb to the casserole and mix in ½ teaspoon salt, the cinnamon,

pepper and water. Reduce the heat to low, cover the pan and simmer for 35 minutes, or until the lamb is tender.

Put the lamb, onion and cooking liquid into a bowl and set aside.

Preheat the oven to moderate 350°F (Gas Mark 4, 180°C).

Half fill a large saucepan with water and bring to the boil over high heat. Add the rice and remaining salt, parboil for 1½ minutes and drain. In the same pan parboil the beans for 10 to 15 minutes or 1 minute if the beans are frozen.

Put half the rice into the casserole and spoon the beans and dill on top. With a slotted spoon, transfer the lamb and onions to the casserole. Spread the remaining beans, dill and rice on top of the meat and pour over the liquid in which the lamb was cooked.

Put the casserole over high heat and bring to the boil.

Remove the casserole, cover it and put it in the oven for 30 minutes, or until the rice is cooked and all the liquid absorbed. Serve immediately.

Bagna Cauda

ANCHOVY AND GARLIC DIP

An Italian dish, Bagna Cauda (BAHN yah KOW-dah) is served hot as a dip for cold raw vegetables. It is ideal for a summer party or as a first course for a dinner party. An assortment of such vegetables as cucumbers, carrots, peppers, celery, French beans, cauliflower and broccoli are suitable for dipping. Wash and peel where necessary and cut into strips the right size for dipping. Break the cauliflower and broccoli into flowerets. Wrap the vegetables in a clean, damp cloth and chill in the refrigerator. Arrange on a serving plate and serve with Italian breadsticks.

12 FLUID OUNCES

4 oz. [½ cup] butter
2 tablespoons olive oil
3 garlic cloves, finely chopped
6 anchovy fillets, finely chopped
5 fl. oz. single [⅝ cup light] cream
1 small truffle, finely chopped, optional

In a small saucepan, heat the butter and the oil. Add the anchovies and the garlic and cook over low heat, stirring and mashing with a wooden spoon.

When the anchovies have become very soft, or almost a paste, add the cream and the truffle. Heat thoroughly but do not let the sauce boil.

Serve in a bowl placed over a plate warmer or in a small, heat-proof dish over a spirit lamp.

Bain-Marie

A bain-marie (ban mah-ree) is a large, shallow pan half-filled with hot water in which smaller pans containing sauces, custards and other dishes which cannot be re-heated on direct heat are put to keep hot until required.

The bain-marie is placed on the top of the stove on a very low heat or in a warm oven.

The bain-marie resembles a double boiler, but is superior when all-round heat is required for cooking, as in the case of custards, some mousses and fish or meat loaves.

Bake Blind

The term bake blind applies to the method of baking pastry shells without their fillings.

After the pie dish or flan ring is lined with pastry, it should be chilled in the refrigerator for about 30 minutes so that the dough is well set.

The base of the shell is then pricked all over with a fork. It is then lined with crumpled aluminium foil, or greaseproof paper, and filled with dried beans or uncooked rice, kept specially for this purpose.

About 5 minutes before the shell has finished cooking, the foil, or paper, and beans are removed and the baking continued so that the pastry can colour.

Baked Alaska

An impressive dessert, Baked Alaska is sponge cake topped with ice-cream and covered with meringue. It is not difficult to prepare but it does need very speedy, last-minute preparation before serving. This famous dessert was probably invented by the 18th-century scientist Count Rumford, in Europe. It did not get its present name until 1867, when it was included in menus to celebrate the purchase of the new state. In France it is called Omelette Norvege, after Norway, another country with a very cold climate.

8 SERVINGS

4 oz. [1 cup] self-raising flour
¼ teaspoon salt
1 teaspoon baking powder
4 oz. [½ cup] butter, at room temperature
4 oz. castor [½ cup superfine] sugar
2 eggs
½ teaspoon vanilla essence [extract]
1 pint [2½ cups] vanilla ice cream, or your favourite flavour
4 tablespoons raspberry jam, or your favourite flavour

½ lb. fresh or thawed raspberries
(optional)
MERINGUE
4 egg whites
9 oz. castor [1⅛ cups superfine] sugar

Preheat the oven to warm 325°F (Gas Mark 3, 170°C). Grease and line the base of an 8-inch sandwich tin.

To prepare the sponge base, sift the flour, salt and baking powder into a large mixing bowl. Add the butter, castor sugar, eggs and vanilla and beat by hand or in a food processor until the ingredients are thoroughly blended.

Put the mixture into the prepared tin and smooth the top. Bake for 30-35 minutes, until the cake feels firm to the touch. Turn out on to a wire rack and leave until cold. Wash and dry the cake tin.

Meanwhile, soften the ice cream. Pack it firmly into the clean cake tin and return to the freezer while the sponge cake base is cooling.

When the cake is cold, split in half horizontally and place on a baking sheet. Sandwich the two halves together with raspberry jam.

If you are using raspberries arrange them carefully in a single layer on top of the cake. Make sure thawed raspberries, if using, are well drained.

Remove the ice cream from the freezer and let stand for 5 minutes. Quickly unmould the ice cream on top of the cake. Return the ice cream and cake to the freezer and freeze for 30 minutes.

Preheat the oven to very hot 450°F (Gas Mark 8, 230°C). To make meringue, put the egg whites in a large clean bowl and whisk until stiff. Whisk in the sugar a little at a time until the meringue

An impressive-looking dessert, Baked Alaska is a sponge cake topped with ice-cream and meringue.

is stiff and glossy.

Remove the cake from the freezer and quickly cover the entire surface with meringue, making sure there is no cake or ice cream showing. Fluff up the surface decoratively. Place the blade of a flat-bladed knife against the meringue and pull it away with a sharp movement to produce a little peak. Repeat over the entire surface.

Bake for 3 minutes or until the meringue turns brown on the tips. Serve at once.

Vary the combinations of jam and fruit. Using either canned or fresh fruit. Sprinkle the meringue with toasted chopped almonds, chopped walnuts or finely chopped hazelnuts before baking.

Do not freeze the assembled cake for longer than 30 minutes because if you use fruit it will freeze and be unpleasant to eat. The fruit can be omitted if you wish, instead dribble 4 tablespoons liqueur over the cake.

Bakewell Tart

This is a traditional English dessert from the 'Rutland Arms' pub in a small Derbyshire market town.

6 TO 8 SERVINGS

6 oz. [1½ cups] flour
¼ teaspoon salt
3 oz. [6 tablespoons] butter, cut into small pieces
1 tablespoon cold water
2 tablespoons raspberry or strawberry jam
FILLING
2 oz. [¼ cup] butter
2 oz. [¼ cup] castor sugar
1 egg, beaten
¼ teaspoon almond essence
4 tablespoons breadcrumbs
2 oz. [½ cup] ground almonds
icing [confectioners'] sugar, to decorate

Preheat the oven to 375°F (Gas Mark 5, 190°C). Grease an 8-inch loose-bottomed flan tin with butter.

Sift the flour and salt into a bowl, add the butter and rub in until the mixture resembles fine breadcrumbs.

Sprinkle with cold water and mix in with a knife. Using your hands, mix and knead the pastry until smooth. If it is too dry, add more cold water. Roll into a ball, wrap in foil and chill for 15 minutes.

On a lightly floured board, roll out the pastry, lift it on the rolling pin and ease it into the tin. Trim the edges, spread the jam over the base and chill.

To make the filling, cream the butter and sugar together until light and fluffy. Gradually beat in the egg, a little at a time, beating well after each addition.

Add the almond essence, crumbs and ground almonds and mix to a soft consistency, adding a little water if necessary. Fill the lined flan tin and level the surface with the back of a spoon.

Bake for 30-40 minutes or until the filling is set. Cool slightly, then sprinkle with icing sugar to decorate. Serve with custard or whipped cream, if wished.

Baking

Baking is a method of cooking food in an oven by dry heat. Bread, biscuits, pies, cakes and tarts are all baked. Meat is also baked, although the term roasting is more generally used to describe the cooking of meat in an oven.

Baking Powder

Baking powder is the name given to a number of mixtures which are used as leavening agents for bread, cakes and pastries. They all contain a proportion of bicarbonate of soda, commonly called baking soda, and an acid such as tartrate, phosphate or alum. When this mixture is moistened and heated, a chemical reaction takes place which produces carbon dioxide, causing the dough to rise.

Baking Powder Biscuits

An American recipe, Baking Powder Biscuits are like English scones. They may be served hot with butter for lunch or supper, or with jam for tea.

8 BISCUITS

7 oz. [1¾ cups] flour, plus extra for dusting
2 teaspoons baking powder
1 teaspoon salt
1 oz. [2 tablespoons] butter, chilled
1 oz. [2 tablespoons] hard margarine
5 fl. oz. [⅝ cup] milk

Preheat the oven to fairly hot 400°F (Gas Mark 6, 200°C); place a shelf above centre.

Sift the flour, baking powder and salt into a mixing bowl. Add the butter and margarine and cut them into the flour. Lightly rub the fat into the flour until the mixture resembles breadcrumbs.

Stir in enough milk to make a soft, light

An unusual type of scone, American Baking Powder Biscuits are delicious served hot with butter and jam.

dough. Add more milk if the dough is too dry, or more flour if it is too sticky.

Turn the dough on to a floured surface and knead it well until it is smooth.

Roll out the dough to ¾ inch thick. Using a floured cutter, stamp out 8 rounds, rerolling the dough as necessary.

Place the biscuits on an ungreased baking sheet, prick with a fork and bake for 10-12 minutes.

Baking Soda

Baking soda is the common name for BICARBONATE OF SODA.

Baklava

A rich cake made of thin layers of crisp pastry, filled with chopped almonds or walnuts and steeped in syrup or honey, baklava is made throughout the Middle East and Greece.

Baklava varies in detail from country to country, town to town and even from one household to the next. But in one respect it must always be the same. The pastry must be paper thin, for that is the secret of good baklava.

Balkan Champagne Cup

This is an icy party punch, easy to make but expensive.

20 SERVINGS

1 piece lemon rind
   juice of 2 lemons
2 tablespoons icing [confectioners'] sugar
1 piece cucumber peel
12 fl. oz. [1½ cups] cold soda-water
2 bottles dry red wine
1 bottle champagne

Mix the lemon rind and lemon juice with the icing sugar and cucumber peel in a large punch bowl. Add the soda-water, wine and champagne.

Immediately before serving, add a block of ice.

Balkan Chicken Pilaff

This pilaff depends on a strong chicken stock for its flavour. For convenience, cook the chicken and make the stock the day before. Serve the pilaff with a ratatouille and a salad of yogurt with chopped cucumber and mint leaves.

6 SERVINGS

STOCK
1 small chicken
1 teaspoon salt
1 onion, cut in half
2 whole carrots
4 peppercorns
PILAFF
1 lb. [2½ cups] rice, washed, soaked in water for 30 minutes and drained
3 oz. [⅜ cup] butter
1 onion, finely chopped
2 tomatoes, peeled and chopped
1 teaspoon salt
   freshly ground black pepper
1 teaspoon dried basil
2 oz. [¼ cup] walnuts, chopped

First make the stock. Put the chicken in a pot large enough to hold it comfortably. Pour in enough water to half cover it. Add the salt, onion, carrots and peppercorns and bring to the boil. Lower the heat and simmer the chicken for 40 minutes or until it is tender. Let the chicken cool in the stock.

When the chicken is cool enough to handle, remove it from the stock. Put it on a board and cut off all the meat. Put the meat in a covered bowl and refrigerate.

Return the chicken bones to the pan, adding more water if necessary to cover, and simmer for 1½ hours. Strain the stock into a bowl, cool, cover and refrigerate. When the fat hardens on the top of the stock, skim it off with a spoon.

To make the pilaff, heat 1½ pints of the stock until it boils. Cut the meat of the chicken into strips.

Melt the butter in a large flameproof casserole over moderate heat. Add the chopped onion and fry until it is golden. Add the chicken strips, stir and cook for 2 minutes. Add the tomatoes, salt, 6 grindings of pepper, basil and walnuts and cook for 1 minute. Add the rice and cook for 2 minutes, stirring continuously. Pour in the hot stock, raise the heat and bring the rice to the boil. When it is bubbling briskly, cover with a tight-fitting lid, lower the heat to very low and simmer for 25 minutes, or until all the liquid is absorbed and the rice is cooked. Serve straight from the casserole.

Balloon Whisk

Also called a wire wisk, a balloon whisk is particularly useful for beating egg whites, cream, sauces, batters and soups, as it incorporates more air and increases the volume. Balloon whisks are widely available in several sizes and are curved to fit round bowls.

Ballotine

The term ballotine (bah-loh-teen) should, correctly, only be applied to meat which has been boned, stuffed and rolled. It is, however, often used to describe a certain kind of GALANTINE which is usually served hot, but can also be served cold.

Balm

Balm is the name given to several plants of the mint family. The one most commonly used for flavouring food is LEMON BALM.

Bamboo Shoots

A popular vegetable in the Far East, bamboo shoots are a common ingredient in Chinese cookery. The ivory-coloured, conical-shaped shoots of tropical bamboo are usually about three-inches wide and four-inches long.

In the Far East, bamboo shoots are usually eaten fresh, cooked like asparagus. They are canned and exported and are available in Oriental provisions stores. The best ones are the large wedges which have been packed in water. Canned bamboo shoots require very little cooking.

Once the can is opened, the shoots should be drained and kept in the refrigerator in fresh water in a covered jar. If the water is changed every day the bamboo shoots can be stored for about 10 days.

Bamboo Shoots with Mushrooms

This Chinese recipe for Bamboo Shoots with Mushrooms is easy to make. It may be

---

Served with rice or egg noodles, Bamboo Shoots with Pork is an interesting Chinese dish.

served as part of a Chinese meal and it also makes an unusual vegetable accompaniment to grilled or roasted meat.

4 SERVINGS

12 oz. canned bamboo shoots, drained
12 dried mushrooms
4 tablespoons groundnut oil
2 tablespoons sherry
4 tablespoons soy sauce
1 tablespoon sugar
¼ teaspoon monosodium glutamate (optional)
3 fl. oz. [⅜ cup] water

Cut the bamboo shoots into thin slivers. Soak the mushrooms in hot water for 5 minutes. Drain them well. Remove the stalks, and, if the mushrooms are large, cut them in half.

Heat a heavy frying-pan over high heat for 30 seconds. Add the oil and swirl it around the pan. Add the bamboo shoots and mushrooms and fry, stirring frequently, for 5 minutes.

Add the sherry, soy sauce, sugar, monosodium glutamate and water. Cover the pan and simmer, over low heat, for 20 minutes.

Serve hot.

Bamboo Shoots with Pork

A Chinese dish, Bamboo Shoots with Pork is delicious served with other Chinese dishes and boiled rice or fine egg noodles. As is the case in many Chinese recipes, the pork, leek and bamboo shoots must be shredded. This means that they must be cut into fine, thread-like strips.

4 SERVINGS

1½ lb. lean pork, shredded
6 tablespoons soy sauce
1 tablespoon sherry
2 teaspoons cornflour [cornstarch]
1 leek, shredded
1 lb. canned bamboo shoots, shredded
5 fl. oz. [⅝ cup] groundnut oil
2 teaspoons sugar

Combine 2 tablespoons of soy sauce, the sherry and cornflour. Add the shredded pork and mix well.

Heat a large, heavy frying-pan over high heat for 30 seconds. Add the oil and swirl it around the pan.

Add the pork and the leek and, stirring frequently, fry for 5 minutes, or until the pork is well browned. Stir in the bamboo shoots.

Stir in the remaining soy sauce and sugar. Lower the heat and simmer for 10 minutes, stirring frequently.

Serve immediately.

Baked Bananas, easy and inexpensive to make, go well with roast or fried chicken, roast pork or baked fish.

Banana

The edible fruit of the banana tree, the banana is one of the most popular fruits in tropical countries where it is prized for its flavour, nutrition and cheapness.

The banana tree was known in antiquity. It is said that the serpent which tempted Eve in the Garden of Eden hid in a bunch of bananas and, therefore, one of its botanical names is *Musa paradisiaca*. The banana tree is also called *Musa sapientum* because the sages of ancient India rested in its shade and ate its fruit. The banana was known to the Greeks and Romans and Pliny, the Roman historian, recorded that the Greeks who accompanied Alexander on his expedition to India saw it there.

Native to Southeast Asia, the banana spread to the West coast of Africa, the Canary Islands and to the Americas.

Today there are more than 300 varieties of banana, all growing in hot, damp, tropical regions. The chief sources of commercial banana production are in Central America, although the best tasting bananas still come from South Asia.

Bananas are exported while they are still green and the fruit is ripened in heated warehouses. Bananas which are green at the tip are slightly under-ripe.

They should be kept in a warm place and not eaten until the skins are completely yellow or even slightly dotted with brown.

Bananas contain Vitamin C as well as a small amount of other vitamins. They have a high proportion of starch, which turns to sugar as the fruit ripens.

Bananas may be used as a vegetable or a fruit. They are delicious sliced and served with cream. They are used in many ways in cold desserts and salads and can also be baked or fried.

Bananas, Baked

Bananas baked in their skins make an unusual and delicious accompaniment to roast or fried chicken, roast pork or baked fish.

6 SERVINGS

6 large bananas, unpeeled
1 tablespoon vegetable oil

Preheat the oven to warm 325°F (Gas Mark 3, 170°C).

Rub the banana skins lightly all over with a little oil. Brush the bottom of an ovenproof dish with the remaining oil. Lay the bananas in the dish and place it in the centre of the oven.

Bake the bananas for 30 to 40 minutes or until they are soft and their skins turn black.

Serve hot with one strip of peel rolled back.

Bananas Baked with Custard

Bananas baked with bread and custard is a simple dessert that children will love.

6 SERVINGS

1 teaspoon butter
4 bananas
6 thin slices buttered bread
2 oz. [⅓ cup] raisins
1 pint [2½ cups] milk
2 whole eggs plus 2 yolks
2 tablespoons soft brown sugar
½ teaspoon grated nutmeg

Grease a medium-sized baking dish with the butter. Peel the bananas and slice into rounds. Halve the bread slices. Put the layers of the bread, bananas and raisins in the baking dish, ending with a layer of bread.

In a small pan heat the milk over moderate heat. In a medium-sized mixing bowl, beat the eggs, egg yolks and sugar together. Slowly pour in the milk, stirring continuously. Pour the milk-egg mixture into the baking dish and leave to stand for 30 minutes.

Preheat the oven to fairly hot 375°F (Gas Mark 5, 190°C).

Dust the top of the pudding with the nutmeg and bake in the oven for 30 minutes. Serve hot or cold.

Bananas Baked in Orange Juice

This dessert of bananas baked in orange juice is delicious served with vanilla ice-cream. Ripe but firm bananas and, if possible, freshly shredded coconut should be used for this dish.

4 SERVINGS

1 tablespoon plus 1 teaspoon butter
6 bananas
2 teaspoons cornflour [cornstarch]
3 tablespoons Curaçao
4 fl. oz. [½ cup] fresh orange juice
grated rind of 1 orange
2 oz. [½ cup] shredded fresh or desiccated coconut
2 tablespoons soft brown sugar

Preheat the oven to fairly hot 375°F (Gas Mark 5, 190°C).

Grease a medium-sized baking dish with 1 teaspoon butter. Peel the bananas, cut them in half lengthways and then cut them across into quarters. Place them in the baking dish.

Dissolve the cornflour in the orange juice. Mix in the Curaçao and pour over the bananas. Sprinkle with the orange rind, coconut and brown sugar.

Dot with the butter and bake in the oven for 30 minutes or until the bananas are tender and the sauce thick.

Serve hot.

Bananas Beauharnais

BANANAS BAKED IN RUM AND CREAM

A rich dessert, Bananas Beauharnais (bow-ahr-nay) is excellent for a lunch or dinner party. It is usually served hot, but it is equally good cold.

4 SERVINGS

6 bananas
1 tablespoon castor sugar
6 tablespoons white rum
4 oz. [½ cup] crushed macaroons
1 tablespoon melted butter
10 fl. oz. double cream [1¼ cups heavy cream]

Preheat the oven to moderate 350°F (Gas Mark 4, 180°C). Grease a medium-sized baking dish with a little butter.

Peel the bananas and put them in the baking dish. Sprinkle them with the sugar and the rum. Bake for 15 minutes.

Remove the dish from the oven and allow to cool for 10 minutes.

Reset the oven to warm 325°F (Gas Mark 3, 170°C).

Mix the crushed macaroons with the melted butter. Pour the cream over the bananas. Sprinkle the macaroon mixture on top of the cream. Return the dish to the oven and bake for another 20 minutes. Serve hot in the baking dish.

Bananas Caribbean

This spicy banana dessert is unusual and easy to make. Serve it with a creamy custard sauce or thick cream.

4 SERVINGS

2 tablespoons plus 1 teaspoon butter
6 bananas
2 oz. [¼ cup] soft brown sugar
4 fl. oz. fresh orange juice
grated rind of 1 orange
½ teaspoon powdered cinnamon
4 tablespoons Curaçao
6 tablespoons rum

Preheat the oven to very hot 450°F (Gas Mark 8, 230°C). Grease a medium-sized baking dish with 1 teaspoon of butter.

Peel the bananas. Cut them in half lengthways. Place the bananas in the baking dish cut side up.

In a small bowl, mix together the sugar, orange juice and rind, cinnamon and Curaçao. Pour the mixture over the

bananas. Dot with the remaining butter and bake, basting once, for 15 minutes or until the bananas are tender. Sprinkle the bananas with the rum and serve immediately.

Banana Cream Pie

This American banana pie is made with short crust pastry and topped with meringue. It is inexpensive and easy to make and it looks and tastes good.

6 SERVINGS

PASTRY

6 oz. [1½ cups] flour
¼ teaspoon salt
3¼ oz. [½ cup] vegetable fat or lard
2 tablespoons iced water

FILLING

2 ripe bananas, peeled and cut into slices
3 egg yolks
3 oz. [⅜ cup] castor sugar
¼ teaspoon salt
2 tablespoons cornflour [cornstarch]
1 tablespoon butter
16 fl. oz. [2 cups] milk
1 teaspoon vanilla essence or ¼ teaspoon grated nutmeg

TOPPING

3 egg whites
6 oz. [¾ cup] castor sugar
2 tablespoons shredded almonds

Sift the flour and salt into a medium-sized mixing bowl. Add the vegetable fat and with your fingertips rub it into the flour until it resembles coarse bread-crumbs. Add a tablespoon of iced water and mix and knead the dough until it is smooth. Add more water if the dough is too dry. Roll the dough into a ball, cover it and chill it in the refrigerator for 30 minutes.

Preheat the oven to fairly hot 400°F (Gas Mark 6, 200°C).

On a floured board, roll the pastry out and line a 9-inch pie tin. Put the lined pie tin in the refrigerator for 10 minutes.

When you remove the pie-tin from the refrigerator, prick the bottom and sides of the pastry with a fork, line it with greaseproof paper and weigh it down with dried beans or peas. Bake the shell for 10 minutes.

Remove the greaseproof paper and bake for 5 minutes more, or until the shell is golden.

Reset the oven to cool 300°F (Gas

Bananas, coconut and orange combine to make Bananas Baked in Orange Juice a delicious dessert.

Banana Cream Pie, made with short-crust pastry and topped with meringue, is a tempting dessert.

Mark 2, 150°C).

To prepare the filling, beat the egg yolks in a medium-sized mixing bowl with a whisk or wooden spoon. Gradually beat in all of the sugar, salt, cornflour and butter.

Put the milk in a small saucepan and, over moderate heat, bring it almost to the boiling point. Pour the hot milk slowly into the egg mixture, stirring continuously. Place the bowl in a pan of boiling water and cook and stir the custard until it thickens. Cool the custard and then add the vanilla essence or nutmeg. Arrange the banana slices in the baked pie shell. Pour the custard over them.

Beat the egg whites in a small bowl with a rotary beater until they are stiff. Beat in one tablespoon of sugar and then fold in the remaining sugar. Pile the meringue on top of the custard and spread to cover the top completely. Sprinkle with the shredded almonds and bake for 15 to 20 minutes. or until the meringue is lightly browned.

Serve cold.

Bananas Creole

This cold dessert is a mould lined with slices of fresh pineapple and filled with a mousse flavoured with rum. It takes some time to prepare, but can be made well in advance and is an unusual and delicious dessert for a lunch or dinner party.

4 TO 6 SERVINGS

1 medium-sized pineapple
1 pint [2½ cups] water
8 oz. [1 cup] sugar
2 tablespoons light rum
4 bananas
MOUSSE
2 whole eggs plus 2 yolks
2 oz. [¼ cup] sugar
½ oz. gelatine
2 tablespoons hot orange juice
2 tablespoons light rum
5 fl. oz. double [heavy] cream, whipped

Peel the pineapple and cut into thin slices. Put the water and sugar in a medium-sized pan and, stirring continuously, dissolve the sugar over low heat. When the sugar is completely dissolved, raise the heat and bring the syrup to the boil. Boil for 5 minutes. Place the pineapple

slices gently in the syrup, add the rum, lower the heat and simmer for 15 minutes, or until the pineapple is tender. Remove the pineapple slices carefully, drain and set aside to cool.

Peel the bananas, cut them in half lengthways and lay them in a heatproof dish.

Bring the syrup to the boil and pour it over the bananas. Leave for 15 minutes, then drain the bananas and set them aside. Discard the syrup.

Line a plain mould with the pineapple slices and set aside.

Whisk the whole eggs, yolks and sugar in a medium-sized bowl. Place the bowl in a pan of simmering water, over low heat, and whisk until the egg-and-sugar mixture is thick.

Remove from the heat, place the bowl over crushed ice or cold water, and continue whisking until the mixture is cold.

Dissolve the gelatine in the orange juice and stir into the egg mixture with the rum. Fold in the whipped cream. Place the bowl on ice and stir. When the mousse is on the point of setting, pour it into the mould. Chill in the refrigerator until completely set. Unmould on to a serving dish, surround with the bananas and serve.

Bananas, Fried

A delicious garnish for chicken or meat, the bananas and the batter may be prepared in advance, but the bananas must be fried at the last minute.

4 SERVINGS

4 bananas
3 tablespoons olive oil
1½ tablespoons lemon juice
½ teaspoon salt
⅛ teaspoon paprika
BATTER
2 oz. [½ cup] flour
⅛ teaspoon salt
¼ teaspoon white pepper
4½ tablespoons vegetable oil
3 fl. oz. [⅜ cup] warm water

Peel the bananas and cut them in half lengthways. Place them in a dish. In a small bowl mix the olive oil, lemon juice, salt and paprika and pour it over the bananas. Leave the bananas to marinate for 20 minutes.

Meanwhile, prepare the batter. Sift the flour, salt and pepper into a small mixing bowl. With a wooden spoon, mix in ½ tablespoon of the oil and the water slowly. When the mixture is smooth, beat well. Leave the batter to stand for 30 minutes.

In a medium-sized frying-pan heat the remaining oil over moderate heat.

Drain the bananas and dip them in the batter. Fry them until they are golden on both sides. Drain on kitchen paper towels and serve immediately.

Banana Fritters

Banana Fritters flavoured with brandy make an unusual dessert. Use only firm bananas, otherwise the bananas will disintegrate if they are too soft.

4 SERVINGS

6 bananas
4 fl. oz. [½ cup] brandy
1 tablespoon brown sugar
BATTER
4 oz. [1 cup] flour
1 teaspoon salt
2 egg yolks plus 1 egg white
1 tablespoon olive oil
5 fl. oz. [⅝ cup] milk
4 tablespoons vegetable oil
2 tablespoons sugar

Peel the bananas, cut them in half lengthways and place in a dish. In a small bowl mix brandy with brown sugar. Pour over the bananas and leave to marinate for 20 minutes.

Sift the flour and salt into a medium-sized mixing bowl. Make a well in the centre of the flour and drop in the egg yolks and olive oil. Add the milk a little at a time and, beating continuously, gradually incorporate the liquid into the flour. Mix to a smooth batter. Cover the bowl and leave the batter to stand for 30 minutes.

Just before frying, beat the egg white with a wire whisk until it is stiff and fold it into the batter.

In a medium-sized frying-pan, heat the oil over moderate heat. Remove the banana halves from the marinade and dip them into the batter. Fry them in the hot fat until they are golden on both sides. Drain on kitchen paper towels, sprinkle with sugar and serve immediately.

Bananas with Orange

Easy to make, Bananas with Orange is a delicious dessert which should be served very hot with chilled orange butter and sponge fingers, shortbread or other plain, sweet biscuits [cookies].

4 SERVINGS

4 oz. [½ cup] butter
4 oz. [½ cup] plus 4 tablespoons soft, brown sugar
grated rind of 1 orange
3 fl. oz. [⅜ cup] Cointreau
8 bananas
5 oranges

Preheat the oven to moderate 350°F (Gas Mark 4, 180°C).

Make the orange butter first. In a medium-sized mixing bowl, cream the butter thoroughly with a wooden spoon. Slowly add 4 ounces [½ cup] sugar and the grated orange rind and beat well. Add 2 fluid ounces of Cointreau, beating until the mixture is smooth and all the liqueur is absorbed. Cover and refrigerate.

Peel the bananas and cut them into slices. Peel the oranges, remove all the pith and cut them into thin slices.

In an ovenproof dish, arrange the banana and orange slices in layers, sprinkling each layer with the remaining sugar. Add the remaining Cointreau. Bake in the oven for 25 minutes. Serve immediately with the orange butter.

Banana Pudding

This light and fluffy Banana Pudding is very quick to make and it requires no cooking. It should be served very cold.

6 SERVINGS

2 lb. ricotta cheese
6 bananas, mashed
2 teaspoons lemon juice
4 oz. icing [1 cup confectioners'] sugar
2 tablespoons sweet white wine
½ teaspoon almond essence
1 oz. [¼ cup] flaked almonds
6 sponge fingers, crushed

Press the ricotta cheese through a fine strainer into a medium-sized bowl. Add the bananas, lemon juice, sugar, wine and

Bananas deep-fried in batter are a tempting and unusual garnish for almost any meat dish.

almond essence. Beat until the mixture is fluffy. Mix in the almonds.

Pour the mixture into a serving dish and sprinkle the sponge finger crumbs over the top. Cover and place in the refrigerator for 2-3 hours before serving.

Banana and Raspberry Cream

A simple, uncooked dessert with a fine balance of flavours, this may be served at a lunch or dinner party.

4 SERVINGS

    6 bananas
    1 lb. raspberries
    10 fl. oz. double cream [1¼ cups heavy
      cream]
    4 tablespoons castor sugar

Peel the bananas and cut them into rounds. Arrange the slices in a dish.

Mix the raspberries with the cream and push the mixture through a sieve. Mix in half the sugar. Taste to check the sweetness and add the rest of the sugar if necessary. Pour the cream mixture over the bananas. Chill well before serving.

Bananas in Sherry

A simple banana dessert, flavoured with honey and sherry, this is very easy to prepare.

4 SERVINGS

    4 tablespoons melted butter
    6 bananas
      juice of 1 lemon
    3 tablespoons clear honey
    3 fl. oz. [⅜ cup] sherry

Preheat the oven to fairly hot 400°F (Gas Mark 6, 200°C). Grease a baking dish with 1 tablespoon butter.

Peel the bananas and cut them in half lengthways. Place them in the baking dish and pour the lemon juice over the top.

Mix the honey and sherry and remaining butter together and pour over the bananas. Bake for 20 minutes, or until the bananas are heated through. Baste twice during cooking. Serve hot.

More a cake than a bread, this Banana Walnut Bread is quick, easy and inexpensive to make.

Banana Walnut Loaf

A moist bread, Banana Walnut Loaf is very easy to make and good to serve at tea-time or with coffee.

ONE 9-INCH LOAF

    5 oz. [⅝ cup] sugar
    2 oz. [¼ cup] plus 1 teaspoon
      vegetable fat
    3 eggs
    4 bananas, mashed
    8 oz. [2 cups] flour
    1 teaspoon baking powder
    ½ teaspoon salt
    ¼ teaspoon bicarbonate of soda
      [baking soda]
    6 oz. [1 cup] walnuts, chopped

Preheat the oven to moderate 350°F (Gas Mark 4, 180°C). Grease a 9-inch loaf tin with 1 teaspoon fat.

In a medium-sized mixing bowl, beat the sugar, vegetable fat and eggs together with a wooden spoon. Beat until it is light. Beat in the bananas.

Sift the flour, baking powder, salt and soda into the banana mixture and beat well. Stir in the walnuts.

Pour the mixture into the loaf tin and

bake for 1 hour, or until the loaf is done. Test by inserting a warm, dry skewer in the centre of the loaf. If it comes out clean, the loaf is ready. Turn the loaf out of the tin and allow to cool before slicing.

Banbury Cakes

These traditional English cakes are made of puff pastry and filled with dried fruit. They are light and crispy and may be served with tea or coffee.

MAKES 16 CAKES

PASTRY
8 oz. [2 cups] flour
¼ teaspoon salt
8 oz. [1 cup] unsalted butter
5 fl. oz. [⅝ cup] iced water
FILLING
2 oz. [¼ cup] butter
2 oz. [¼ cup] sugar
1 small egg yolk
2 oz. [⅓ cup] sultanas or raisins
2 oz. [⅓ cup] currants
1 oz. [⅓ cup] cake crumbs
1 oz. [¼ cup] candied peel, chopped
½ teaspoon ground ginger
¼ teaspoon ground nutmeg
    grated rind and juice of ½ lemon
1 egg white, lightly beaten

Sift the flour and salt into a medium-sized mixing bowl. With a table knife, cut 2 oz. [¼ cup] butter into the flour. Crumble the butter and flour with your fingers and, with the water, mix to a firm dough. Knead the dough to make it pliable. Cover with greaseproof or waxed paper and refrigerate for 15 minutes.

Put the remaining amount of butter between two pieces of greaseproof paper and beat it with the back of a spoon or a wooden mallet into a flat oblong slab about ¾-inch thick.

On a floured board, roll out the dough into a rectangular shape ¼-inch thick. Place the slab of butter in the centre of the dough and fold the dough over it to make a parcel. Refrigerate for 10 minutes.

Place the dough, with the folds downwards, on the board and roll out away from you into a rectangle. Fold the rectangle in 3, the open end facing you and roll out again. Refrigerate for 15 minutes. Repeat this twice more.

Preheat the oven to hot 425°F (Gas Mark 7, 220°C).

To prepare the filling, cream the butter and sugar in a small mixing bowl with a wooden spoon. When the mixture is well creamed, beat in the egg yolk. Mix in the sultanas, currants, cake crumbs, candied peel, ginger, nutmeg, lemon rind and lemon juice.

Puff pastry filled with a spicy, dried fruit mixture, Banbury Cakes are traditional English tea cakes.

On a floured board, roll out the dough thinly and cut it into 4-inch rounds. Dampen the edges with water and put a spoonful of mixture on to each round of pastry. Fold the pastry over the filling and turn upside down. Pat each cake into an oval shape and make 3 cuts in the tops. Place on a baking tin. Brush with beaten egg white, dust with a little sugar and bake for 20 to 25 minutes, or until the cakes are crisp and golden.

Remove the cakes and cool on a rack.

Bangra Masala

SPICED HERRINGS

This recipe for Bangra Masala (bahn-grah ma-sah-lah) is an adaptation of a recipe which comes from the west coast of India where in the winter and spring a herring-like fish called bangra *is abundant and cheap. It can be served as a main course accompanied by rice and spiced vegetables.*

4 SERVINGS
4 herrings, cleaned and gutted
2½ teaspoons salt
    juice of ½ lemon
3 tablespoons flour
1 teaspoon ground turmeric
4 to 6 tablespoons cooking oil

FILLING
3 tablespoons cooking oil
2 small onions, finely minced
1 large garlic clove, crushed
1½-inch piece fresh ginger, peeled and finely chopped
1 teaspoon ground turmeric
1 teaspoon ground coriander seeds
1 teaspoon chilli powder (optional)
1 teaspoon garam masala
6 tablespoons tomato purée
    juice of ½ lemon

Wash the herrings and wipe dry with kitchen paper towels. Sprinkle the inside of each fish with ½ teaspoon of salt and set aside.

To make the filling, heat the oil in a medium-sized frying-pan over moderate heat. Fry the onions until they are golden. Add the garlic and ginger and, stirring constantly, cook for 2 minutes. Add the turmeric, coriander, chilli powder (if you are using it) and garam masala and fry well for 8 minutes, stirring constantly. If the mixture gets too dry sprinkle with a little water and continue frying.

Add the tomato purée and lemon juice and, stirring, cook for 3 minutes. Remove from the heat and divide the filling into 4 equal portions. Spoon a portion inside each fish.

Gash the sides of the herrings with a sharp knife and rub in a little lemon juice. Mix the flour, turmeric and remaining salt on a plate. Dip the fish into the flour mixture, rubbing it well into the gashes.

In a large frying-pan, heat the oil until it is hot enough to spit when the fish is put in. Fry the fish until it is cooked and crisp, approximately 10 minutes, or place under a hot grill.

Bannocks

A variety of large, round cake, or girdle-scone, from Scotland, bannocks can be made from oatmeal, wheat, barley or pease. Of the many varieties the best known are the Selkirk bannock, which is similar to a fruit bun, and the Pitcaithly bannock, which is like shortbread.

Banyuls

Banyuls is a popular French fortified dessert wine. The vineyards of Banyuls are on the lower slopes of the French Pyrénées. They provide three sweet wines—a red, a rosé and a white.

Hot Scottish Baps, split and buttered, are traditionally eaten at breakfast.

Baps

Soft, white, Scottish breakfast rolls, baps are delicious served hot with butter. They are simple to prepare, but they cannot be made in a hurry. Though baps are best served hot from the oven, they can be kept a short while and reheated.

8 ROLLS

1 lb. [4 cups] flour
½ teaspoon salt
5 fl. oz. [⅝ cup] plus 2 tablespoons milk
5 fl. oz. [⅝ cup] water
1 teaspoon sugar
1 tablespoon dried yeast
2 oz. [¼ cup] butter

Sift the flour and salt into a large mixing bowl. Put in a warm place.

Warm the milk and water, place in a bowl and add the sugar. Sprinkle the yeast on top. Leave in a warm place for 15 minutes or until it is frothy.

Rub the butter into the warm flour-and-salt mixture. Make a well in the middle of the flour and pour in the frothy yeast mixture. With your hands, mix into a soft dough, adding 1 or 2 teaspoons more warm water if necessary.

Place the dough in a greased bowl, cover with a clean cloth and leave it to stand in a warm place for 1 hour or more until it doubles in size.

Preheat the oven to hot 425°F (Gas Mark 7, 220°C).

Grease a baking tin with a little butter and dust with flour. Remove the risen dough from the bowl and knead it on a floured surface. Divide it into 8 equal pieces. Knead each piece separately and pat it into an oval shape. Flatten each piece, place on the baking tin and leave in a warm place for 15 minutes.

Brush each bap with the remaining milk and bake in the oven for 15 to 20 minutes. Serve hot with butter.

Bara Brith

A traditional Welsh fruit cake, Bara Brith means 'speckled bread'. There are two varieties of Bara Brith. One is a rich fruit cake which is eaten at Christmas. The other is a popular bread or bun which is made with yeast.

Barbecue

Called *barbe à queue* by the French, this method of cooking was originally described as a way of roasting whole animals or fowls in the open. Spitted from beard, *barbe*, to tail, *queue*, the animal was roasted in a closed or open pit over heated stones, coals or a wood fire.

It is said that this cooking method was introduced into America by French buccaneers in the seventeenth century. It is more likely, however, that it was already being used by the American Indians.

Barbecueing is popular in the United States where, in good weather, food is cooked out-of-doors on braziers or grills over charcoal fires. Some equipment is necessary and appliances ranging from simple braziers to complicated electrically operated spits are widely available. Simple equipment, however, can be improvised.

Grilling, spit and skewer cooking, pit roasting and smoke cooking are the four main methods of barbecueing.

Grilling and spit and skewer cooking are the two methods most commonly used. Pit roasting has died out, except in New England where the clambake still remains popular and in Polynesia where the *luau* (loo-ow) is enjoyed.

Smoke cooking is a process which cooks the meat and flavours it at the same time. This is not practical for most people because a special oven, made of brick or metal, is required.

Barbecue is also a term now used to describe dishes in which meat, fish or fowl is marinated, then grilled or baked in the oven and basted or served with spicy, piquant sauces.

Barbecue Sauce

This is a good piquant sauce to serve hot with grilled meat or chicken. It can also be used for basting during grilling.

8 FLUID OUNCES

1 oz [2 tablespoons] butter
1 onion, chopped
1 garlic clove, crushed
½-inch piece fresh ginger, peeled and finely chopped
5 fl. oz. [⅝ cup] water
14 oz. canned tomatoes
1 large celery stalk, chopped
2 tablespoons lemon juice
2 tablespoons vinegar
2 tablespoons tomato purée
1½ tablespoons Worcestershire sauce
2 teaspoons brown sugar
½ teaspoon dried oregano
1 large bay leaf
1 teaspoon salt
¼ teaspoon nutmeg

Melt the butter in a small saucepan over moderate heat. Add the onion, garlic and ginger and fry until the onion is soft and translucent.

Add all the remaining ingredients, cover and cook over low heat for 40 minutes. Strain the sauce, taste, and add more salt and sugar if necessary.

Barbecued Beef, Chinese Style

Chinese Barbecued Beef is served on a bed of fried spinach. It is a dish which is delicious and pleasing to the eye.

4 SERVINGS

3 tablespoons soy sauce
3 tablespoons red wine
1-inch piece of fresh ginger, peeled and grated
2 teaspoons brown sugar
¼ teaspoon cayenne pepper
¼ teaspoon black pepper
1 lb. fillet of beef, cut into ½-inch slices
8 tablespoons vegetable oil
2 lb. spinach, washed and stalks removed
1 teaspoon salt

In a large bowl, combine the soy sauce, wine, ginger, sugar, cayenne and black pepper. Add the beef slices and leave to marinate for 2 hours, basting and turning them occasionally.

In a large, heavy frying-pan, heat 6 tablespoons of oil. Add the beef and, stirring frequently, fry over moderate heat for 5 to 10 minutes, depending upon how rare or well-done you want the meat.

In another heavy frying-pan heat the remaining oil and, stirring frequently with a wooden spoon, fry the spinach until it is tender. Roughly chop the spinach. Add the salt and mix well.

Arrange the spinach on a serving plate and spread the fried beef over it. Pour the beef juices over the spinach and beef. Serve hot.

Barbecued Chicken

Served with a green salad with vinaigrette dressing and sautéed or baked potatoes, Barbecued Chicken is an easy main course to prepare for a lunch or dinner party.

4 SERVINGS

2 small chickens
4 tablespoons vegetable oil
SAUCE
2 tablespoons olive oil
2 tablespoons Worcestershire sauce

2 tablespoons tomato purée
1 small onion, grated
3 tablespoons red wine
1 garlic clove, crushed
2 teaspoons paprika
½ teaspoon cayenne pepper
1 teaspoon salt
½ teaspoon black pepper
1 teaspoon brown sugar

Split the chickens in half. Wash them under cold, running water and dry them thoroughly.

Put the ingredients for the sauce in a large bowl and mix them together.

Preheat the grill to moderate. Put the chicken pieces in the grill pan, skin side down. Using a pastry brush, brush them with 2 tablespoons of the oil. Place under the grill and cook for 10 minutes.

Turn the chicken pieces. Brush the skin with the remaining oil and grill for 20 minutes. When they are golden brown, baste them with the sauce. Continue basting every few minutes until the chicken is completely cooked. Arrange the chicken on a warmed serving dish.

Strain the remaining sauce, with the pan juices, into a small saucepan. Heat gently, pour over the chicken and serve immediately.

Barbecued Duck

An excellent lunch or dinner dish, barbecued duck is roasted in the oven and basted with a piquant sauce. It may be served with broccoli and baked sweet potatoes.

4 SERVINGS

1 x 5 lb. duck
1 teaspoon dry mustard
¼ teaspoon cayenne pepper
½ teaspoon freshly ground black pepper
SAUCE
1 garlic clove, crushed
¼ teaspoon Tabasco sauce
2 tablespoons Worcestershire sauce
2 tablespoons tomato purée
4 tablespoons red wine
2 teaspoons paprika
grated rind and juice of 1 orange
2 tablespoons lemon juice
1 teaspoon brown sugar
¼ teaspoon black pepper
½ teaspoon salt
2 teaspoons arrowroot mixed with 1 tablespoon water

Preheat the oven to hot 425°F (Gas Mark 7, 220°C).

Rub the duck all over with the mustard, cayenne and black pepper. Prick the skin

all over with a fork, place the duck on a rack in a roasting pan and roast for 20 minutes.

Take the duck out of the oven, remove the rack and pour away the fat from the roasting pan. Put the duck back in the pan without the rack.

Mix all the ingredients for the sauce, except the arrowroot mixed with water, together in a small bowl and pour them over the duck.

Reduce the oven heat to moderate 350°F (Gas Mark 4, 180°C).

Return the duck to the oven and, basting every 15 minutes, roast it for 1 hour, or until the bird is tender.

Remove the duck from the oven, place it on a heated serving dish and keep hot.

Place the roasting pan on moderate heat. Stir in the arrowroot mixed with water and bring to the boil. Cook, stirring continuously, for 2 minutes. Pour the sauce over the duck and serve immediately.

Barbecued Fish

Grilled fish steaks served with a piquant sauce are an inexpensive lunch or dinner dish which is very quick to make. Serve the fish with peas, French beans or hot buttered broccoli and creamed potatoes.

4 SERVINGS

4 large cod or haddock steaks, about 8 oz. each
1 teaspoon salt
2 oz. [¼ cup] butter
SAUCE
8 fl. oz. [1 cup] red wine
⅛ teaspoon cayenne pepper
1 teaspoon prepared mustard
2 teaspoons chilli sauce
2 tablespoons lemon juice
1 teaspoon brown sugar
1 tablespoon capers
½ tablespoon salt

Preheat the grill to moderate. Sprinkle the fish steaks with salt and dot them with half of the butter, cut into small pieces.

Place the fish steaks on the rack of the grill pan. Place under the heat and grill the fish for about 4 minutes on each side. The fish is cooked when the flakes separate easily when tested with a fork. When the fish is cooked, remove it from the grill. Place the steaks on a serving dish and keep hot.

Left: A main dish for a dinner party, Barbecued Duck is roasted and basted with a piquant sauce.

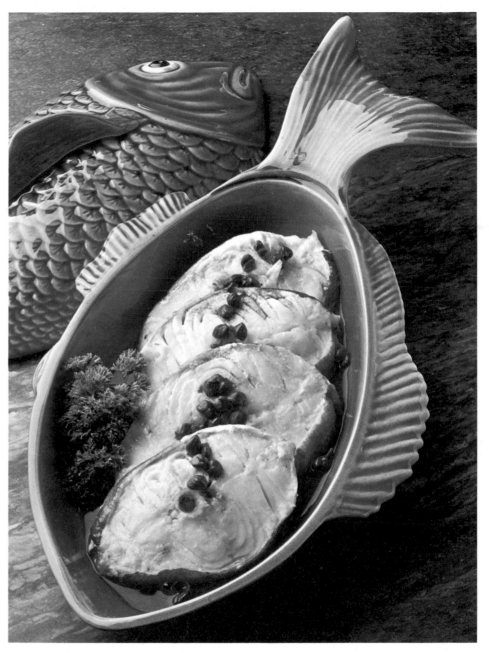

Barbecued Fish is a tempting dish of grilled fish steaks, served with a piquant caper sauce.

Pour any juice from the grilling pan into a small saucepan. Add the remaining butter and melt it over moderate heat. Add all the ingredients for the sauce. Stir to mix and bring to the boil. Reduce the heat and simmer for 10 minutes. Pour the sauce over the fish steaks and serve immediately.

Barbecued Lamb

  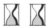

A spicy way of cooking lamb, this recipe includes commercially prepared sauces. The lamb, delicious hot or cold, may be served with new potatoes and whole new carrots.

6 SERVINGS

1 large garlic clove
1 x 3 to 4 lb. leg of lamb
2 teaspoons prepared mustard
½ teaspoon ground ginger
1 teaspoon salt
½ teaspoon freshly ground black pepper
2 tablespoons flour
SAUCE
4 tablespoons chutney
3 tablespoons Worcestershire sauce
2 tablespoons soy sauce
2 tablespoons tomato purée
2 tablespoons red wine
3 tablespoons melted butter
¼ teaspoon cayenne pepper
1 onion, finely chopped
1 teaspoon brown sugar

Preheat the oven to hot 425°F (Gas Mark 7, 220°C).

Cut the garlic clove into slices. With a sharp, pointed knife make slits in the meat and insert the slices of garlic. In a small bowl mix together the prepared mustard, the ginger, salt and pepper. Rub the mixture over the surface of the meat. Coat the meat with flour.

In another small bowl mix together all the ingredients for the sauce. Put the lamb in a roasting pan and place in the centre of the oven.

After 20 minutes lower the heat to fairly hot 375°F (Gas Mark 5, 190°C). Pour the sauce over the lamb and roast for 1 hour, or until the lamb is cooked, basting with the sauce every 15 minutes. If the basting liquid starts to dry up, add a little stock, water or wine. The sauce should be fairly thick.

To serve hot, place the meat on a warmed dish and pour the sauce over it. To serve cold, put the lamb on a cold plate, pour the sauce over it and allow it to cool before slicing.

Barbecued Pork

This is a simple dish to make for an informal dinner party. Barbecued Pork may be served with sautéed potatoes and broad, or French, beans.

6 SERVINGS

$\frac{1}{2}$ teaspoon ground ginger
$\frac{1}{4}$ teaspoon cayenne pepper
$\frac{1}{2}$ teaspoon black pepper
2 teaspoons salt
1 tablespoon brown sugar
4 lb. loin of pork, boned and rolled
2 tablespoons vegetable oil
SAUCE
2 tablespoons chilli sauce
2 tablespoons soy sauce
2 tablespoons Worcestershire sauce
2 tablespoons tomato purée
2 teaspoons prepared mustard
1 tablespoon vinegar
1 teaspoon brown sugar
1 garlic clove, crushed
1 large bay leaf

Preheat the oven to moderate 350°F (Gas Mark 4, 180°C).

Mix together the ginger, cayenne, black pepper, salt and sugar in a small bowl. Rub the mixture all over the pork.

Heat the oil in a large flameproof casserole over moderate heat. Add the pork and brown it well on all sides. Drain all the oil from the casserole.

Mix all the ingredients for the sauce together. Pour the sauce over the pork. Cover the casserole and place it in the

middle of the oven. Cook for $1\frac{1}{2}$ to $1\frac{3}{4}$ hours, basting occasionally.

To serve, carve the pork and place the slices on a heated serving dish. Bring the sauce in the casserole to the boil, skim off the fat and strain over the meat.

Barbecued Pork Chops

A tasty main dish, Barbecued Pork Chops are simple to make. Serve them with new potatoes and a green salad.

4 SERVINGS

2 tablespoons vegetable oil
$\frac{1}{2}$ oz. [1 tablespoon] butter
4 pork loin chops
5 fl. oz. [$\frac{5}{8}$ cup] tomato purée
1 onion, finely chopped
3 celery stalks, chopped
5 fl. oz. [$\frac{5}{8}$ cup] red wine
   juice of 1 lemon
1 tablespoon brown sugar
1 teaspoon prepared mustard
1 teaspoon salt
$\frac{1}{4}$ teaspoon black pepper

Preheat the oven to moderate 350°F (Gas Mark 4, 180°C).

Heat the oil and butter in a large, heavy frying-pan. Add the pork chops and brown them on both sides. Remove them with kitchen tongs and place them in a shallow, ovenproof dish.

In a small bowl combine the rest of the ingredients and pour over the chops. Cover the dish and place in the centre of the oven. Bake for 1 hour and 20 minutes, basting occasionally. After 40 minutes remove the cover and cook uncovered for the rest of the cooking time.

Barbecued Prawns or Shrimps

   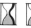

Ideal to serve for a buffet or as an hors d'oeuvre, Barbecued Prawns are easy to prepare. The prawns are eaten by holding them by their tails and dipping them in the sauce.

4 SERVINGS

2 lb. large frozen prawns or shrimps, shelled
4 tablespoons white wine
4 tablespoons olive oil
2 tablespoons tomato purée
2 teaspoons marjoram
1 garlic clove, crushed
1 tablespoon finely chopped chives
1 teaspoon salt
$\frac{1}{4}$ teaspoon black pepper

(Low Cal)

Place the prawns in a large shallow dish and leave to thaw for 1 to 2 hours at room

temperature. Drain the prawns and dry them with kitchen paper towels.

Mix the remaining ingredients for the sauce in a large bowl. Add the prawns to the sauce and stir them gently to coat them with the liquid. Leave the prawns to marinate for 4 hours.

Preheat the grill [broiler] to very hot.

Pour the prawns and the sauce into a shallow baking tin which will fit under the grill. Spread the prawns out evenly in the baking tin.

Put the baking tin under the grill.

Baked in a sweet and sour sauce, Barbecued Spareribs is an unusual, tasty and inexpensive dish which is easy to make.

Cook the prawns for about 3 minutes and baste frequently with the sauce. With a spoon, turn the prawns over, baste again and cook for a further 5 minutes or until they are lightly brown.

Using a slotted spoon, remove the prawns and arrange them on a heated serving dish. Spoon a little of the sauce over the top. Strain the remaining sauce into a sauceboat.

Barbecued Spareribs

Spareribs baked in a sweet and sour sauce make an easy and inexpensive main dish for lunch or dinner. Serve them on their own followed by a fresh mixed salad.

4 SERVINGS
2 tablespoons vegetable oil
1 garlic clove, crushed
1 large onion, finely chopped
5 fl. oz. [⅝ cup] tomato purée
3 tablespoons lemon juice
½ teaspoon salt
¼ teaspoon black pepper
½ teaspoon dried sage
4 tablespoons light brown sugar
4 fl. oz. [½ cup] beef stock
4 tablespoons Worcestershire sauce
2 teaspoons dry mustard
3 lb. sparcribs of pork, cut into serving pieces

Preheat the oven to fairly hot 400°F (Gas Mark 6, 200°C).

Heat the oil in a large frying-pan over moderate heat. When the oil is hot, add the garlic and onion and cook for 3 minutes, stirring frequently until the onion is translucent and soft but not brown.

Add the tomato purée, lemon juice, salt, pepper, sage, sugar, beef stock, Worcestershire sauce and mustard to the mixture in the frying-pan and stir well. Simmer over low heat for 10 minutes, stirring frequently. Remove the frying-pan from the heat.

Put the spareribs on a rack in a large roasting tin. Pour the sauce evenly over the spareribs. Bake in the middle of the oven for 1 hour, or until the spareribs are brown and crisp, basting the ribs with the barbecue sauce every 15 minutes.

Serve hot.

Barbecued Veal Chops

This is an extremely easy and, at the same time, a very tasty way of preparing veal chops. For average size chops 20 minutes grilling is just right, but adjust the timing for very thick chops. Serve with a green vegetable.

4 SERVINGS

4 veal chops
1 onion, chopped
1 garlic clove, crushed
½ teaspoon ground coriander
½ teaspoon dried mixed herbs
¼ teaspoon chilli powder
1 tablespoon chopped parsley
1 teaspoon salt
¼ teaspoon black pepper
3 tablespoons olive oil
2 tablespoons vinegar
1 tablespoon tomato purée

Put the veal chops in a shallow dish. Mix all the remaining ingredients in a small mixing bowl and pour over the chops. Leave the meat to marinate for 3 hours at room temperature.

Heat the grill to hot. Remove the chops from the marinade and place them under the grill for 2 minutes. Lower the heat to moderate and cook for 8 minutes, marinating whenever the meat looks dry.

Turn the chops over and spread with the remaining marinade. Raise the heat to high again and grill them for 2 minutes. Lower the heat and continue grilling for 8 minutes more. Serve immediately.

Barbel

A river fish belonging to the carp family, barbel is so named because of the fleshy filaments, or barbels, hanging from its mouth or from the corners of its jaw.

The species of barbel found in European rivers rarely exceeds 16 pounds. The barbel of the Nile, however, weighs as much as 70 pounds. Gastronomically, barbel is a poor fish. Its insipid-tasting flesh is coarse and woolly and it has too many bones to make pleasant eating.

The most edible barbel is found in the Loire in France. The larger ones are most suited to poaching, braising or baking. The smaller-sized fish, known in France as *barbillons*, are usually grilled or fried.

Barberry

The berry of a plant called berberis, barberry grows in the temperate regions of the world. There are over 200 species of barberry, many of them prickly, ornamental evergreens.

The common barberry was introduced into the United States and Great Britain from temperate Europe and Asia, but, because the plant acts as host to a destructive wheat rust, its cultivation is forbidden in many places and a rust-resistant variety is grown instead.

Barberries are used in sauces, tarts and pies, and are also preserved in sugar. In Scandinavia the berries are a popular flavouring for drinks, sorbets and syrups.

In India, the Nepal and Asiatic barberries are dried in the sun and eaten like raisins. The Darwin barberry, from Chile, is widely grown in England as an ornamental shrub and bears quantities of edible little berries.

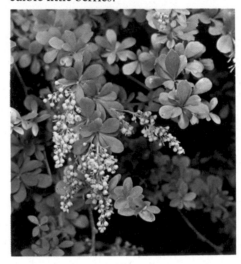

Bard

A culinary term, to bard is to cover the breast of a fowl or a piece of meat with slices of fatty bacon or pork to keep the meat moist and to protect it during cooking. The barding fat is removed before serving, except in the case of roast game.

Barley

A cultivated cereal as old as the earliest beginning of agriculture, barley is grown over a wider range of climate than any other grain. One of the five staple grains used for human consumption and malting, barley is most important as a livestock feed.

Barley is believed to have been used by prehistoric man for making beer. Today, more than 10 per cent of the world crop is used for this purpose.

When the husk is removed barley is called pot barley, scotch barley or hulled barley and is used in the preparation of stews, soups and haggis. Husked barley, steamed, rounded and polished in a mill, is known as pearl barley and is used to thicken soups and stews. Pearl barley ground into a fine flour, is called patent barley.

When barley is ground coarsely to make a wholemeal flour it is called barley meal and is used to make porridge and gruel. It is also used in the preparation of some kinds of bread. Pressed and flattened barley grains are called barley flakes and are used in making milk puddings and gruel.

Barley Bread

Barley Bread, which has a subtle, delicate flavour, is close-textured and retains its freshness for a number of days. Dried yeast is used in this recipe, but fresh yeast may be used instead if it is easily available (use double the quantity for fresh yeast).

ONE 3lb. LOAF
OR TWO 1½lb. LOAVES

1 large potato, quartered
1½ lb. [6 cups] strong white flour
½ teaspoon ground ginger
1 tablespoon salt
1 sachet easy-blend dried yeast
3 oz. [1 cup] barley flakes
12 fl. oz. [1½ cups] milk
4 teaspoons light soft brown sugar
¾ oz. [1½ tablespoons] butter, plus extra for greasing

Cook the potato in a little water until very soft. Drain, reserving the cooking liquor, and mash the potato with 5 fl. oz. [⅝ cup] of the liquid.

Sift the flour, ginger and salt into a bowl. Stir in the yeast and barley flakes.

Warm the milk, sugar and butter to blood heat, then stir into the potato to make a smooth paste. Pour the paste on to the flour and mix well to a smooth and elastic dough.

Turn on to a well floured surface and knead for about 10 minutes, adding up to 6 tablespoons more flour to the mixture as the dough becomes sticky.

Form into 1 large or 2 small loaf shapes. Put into 4½ pint greased loaf tin or 2 × 2¼ pint greased loaf tins. Cover with oiled cling film and leave in a warm place for 3-4 hours until it has doubled.

Preheat the oven to hot 425°F (Gas Mark 7, 220°C).

Uncover the loaf and bake for 10 minutes, then reduce the heat to fairly hot 400°F (Gas Mark 6, 200°C) and bake for 35 minutes or until the bread sounds hollow when tapped underneath. Turn out on to a wire rack and leave to cool completely.

If you want to freeze one of the loaves, wrap it in heavy-duty film. It will keep for 4 weeks. To thaw, loosen the wrapping. Leave at room temperature for 4 hours, or overnight in the refrigerator.

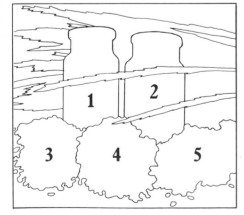

BARLEY

	1 Patent barley
2 Barley meal	3 Pearl barley
4 Flaked barley	5 Pot barley

Barley Country Soup

This delicious soup with vegetables and barley is nourishing and filling so it makes a meal on its own. Serve it with crisp bread or toast. Other vegetables may be used if preferred and, if chicken livers are not available the soup is equally good if minced [ground] beef is added instead. The yoghurt stirred into the soup before serving gives it an extra special flavour.

6 TO 8 SERVINGS

2 oz. mushrooms, chopped
4 oz. chicken livers, chopped
2 large carrots, scraped and thinly sliced
2 parsnips, peeled and diced
1 small cauliflower, separated into flowerets and washed
1 large celery stalk, chopped
1 teaspoon oregano
$\frac{1}{4}$ teaspoon nutmeg
1 bay leaf
1 teaspoon salt
$\frac{1}{4}$ teaspoon black pepper
$2\frac{1}{2}$ pints [$6\frac{1}{4}$ cups] cold water
1 pint [$2\frac{1}{2}$ cups] chicken stock
$1\frac{1}{2}$ oz. [3 tablespoons] butter
2 oz. [$\frac{1}{4}$ cup] pearl barley
2 large potatoes, peeled, sliced and diced into $\frac{1}{2}$-inch cubes
5 fl. oz. [$\frac{5}{8}$ cup] yoghurt
1 tablespoon chopped parsley

Put the mushrooms, chicken livers, carrots, parsnips, cauliflower, celery, oregano, nutmeg, bay leaf, salt and pepper

Low Cal

123

in a large heavy saucepan. Pour in the water and chicken stock. Place the pan over high heat and bring to the boil. Reduce the heat to low. Cover the pan and simmer for 30 minutes, or until the vegetables are cooked.

Remove the pan from the heat and strain the vegetables and livers into a medium-sized bowl. Return the liquid to the saucepan. Set the livers and vegetables aside.

In a small saucepan, melt the butter over moderate heat. Remove the pan from the heat and stir in the barley to coat it with the butter.

Add the barley to the stock in the saucepan and stir well. Place the pan over high heat and bring to the boil.

Reduce the heat to low. Cover the pan and simmer for 15 minutes, stirring occasionally.

Add the potatoes to the pan and simmer, covered, for a further 15 minutes, or until the potatoes are tender when pierced with a knife.

Return the reserved livers and vegetables to the pan and stir well to combine with the barley. Simmer for 10 minutes.

Remove the pan from the heat and pour the soup into a warmed soup tureen. With a metal spoon, lightly mix the yoghurt into the soup. Sprinkle with the parsley and serve immediately.

Barley and Mushroom Casserole

Cooked in this way, barley makes a delicious alternative to potatoes. It may be served with lamb, beef or poultry. Chopped fresh parsley or thyme may be added. For the best results, use fine or medium-sized pearl barley.

4 SERVINGS

2 oz. [¼ cup] butter
2 medium-sized onions, chopped
10 oz. mushrooms, wiped and sliced
7 oz. [1 cup] pearl barley
¾ teaspoon salt
¾ teaspoon black pepper
10 fl. oz. [1¼ cups] chicken stock

Preheat the oven to warm 325°F (Gas Mark 3, 170°C).

Melt the butter in a frying-pan over low heat. Add the onions and cook, stirring occasionally, for about 5 minutes, or until they are golden. Add the mushrooms and cook for 3 minutes.

Barley is an interesting change from potatoes or pasta. Try this savoury Barley and Mushroom Casserole.

Transfer the onions and mushrooms to an ovenproof casserole. Add the barley, salt, pepper. Pour in the stock and stir to mix the ingredients.

Cover the casserole and place in the oven. Cook for 40 minutes or until the barley is tender and all the liquid is absorbed.

Barley Sugar

A brittle toffee, barley sugar is made from sugar which is boiled with water and flavoured with lemon. Originally, barley sugar was made with barley water and sugar and was more acid in flavour than the modern sweet.

Barley Water

A drink made from blanched pearl barley simmered with water and flavoured with lemon and, sometimes, a little sugar, barley water is an easily digestible and nutritious beverage which is often given to invalids.

Barley Wine

This is the name given by some brewers to their best brew of beer. In Britain, barley wine is the name of a strong, sweet, bottled beer. In the United States, barley wine is known as malt liquor.

Barm Brack
IRISH FRUIT LOAF

A traditional Irish fruit loaf, Barm Brack is made with yeast. It is eaten all the year round in Ireland, but especially at Hallowe'en when, traditionally, a gold ring is baked in it. Whoever finds the ring is supposed to be married within the year.

2 SMALL LOAVES

4 tablespoons plus 1 teaspoon sugar
10 fl. oz. [1¼ cups] tepid milk
½ oz. fresh yeast
1 lb. [4 cups] flour
½ teaspoon ground cinnamon
¼ teaspoon mixed spice
¼ teaspoon salt
1 oz. [2 tablespoons] butter
2 eggs, lightly beaten
6 oz. [1 cup] raisins
2 oz. [⅓ cup] currants
3 oz. [½ cup] candied peel
1 tablespoon caraway seeds
GLAZE
2 tablespoons sugar
3 tablespoons boiling water

In a small mixing bowl dissolve 1 teaspoon of sugar in the warm milk.

Crumble the yeast on top and mix with a spoon. Leave in a warm place for 20 minutes or until frothy.

Sift the flour with the remaining sugar, cinnamon, spice and salt into a large, warm mixing bowl. With your fingertips, rub in the butter. Make a well in the centre of the flour mixture. Pour in the frothing yeast and milk, and the beaten eggs. Mix well with a wooden spoon. Then, using your fingers, mix the dough into a ball.

Place the dough on a floured surface and knead well until it is smooth and elastic. Sprinkle the raisins, currants, candied peel and caraway seeds on to the dough and knead them in. Place the dough in a greased bowl, cover with a clean cloth or a polythene bag and leave in a warm place for 1 hour, or until the dough doubles in size.

Preheat the oven to fairly hot 400°F (Gas Mark 6, 200°C). Lightly grease two 1-pound bread tins.

Turn the risen dough on to a floured surface. Divide it into two portions. Lightly knead each portion, shape into rounds and put into the bread tins. Cover and leave in a warm place for 30 minutes.

Place the bread tins in the oven and bake for 1 hour.

To make the glaze, dissolve the sugar in the boiling water. Remove the loaves from the oven and brush the tops with the sugar-and-water syrup. Return the loaves to the oven for 3 minutes.

Turn the loaves on to a wire rack and leave to cool.

Baron of Beef

The cut of beef which consists of both sides of the back or two sirloins which is left uncut at the bone and roasted, a baron of beef can weigh from 50 to 100 pounds, depending on the size of the animal.

Today, a baron of beef is rarely served, except at banquets or at large restaurants. The term 'baron' is also applied to a large cut of mutton or lamb comprising the saddle and the two legs.

Barquettes

A French culinary term, *barquettes* are small oval or boat-shaped pastry shells. The shells may be filled with either sweet or savoury fillings and then baked in the oven. They may also be BAKED BLIND and then filled with crushed and sweetened fresh fruit such as strawberries, raspberries or gooseberries. Filled with prawns, shrimps, crayfish or mussels and topped with mayonnaise they make delicious hors d'oeuvre.

Barquettes aux Abricots

APRICOT TARTS

  ①

Attractive with a slightly tart, fresh taste, Barquettes aux Abricots (bahr-ket oh-zah-bree-koh), may be served with afternoon tea, or with coffee after dinner. Canned apricot halves may be substituted for fresh apricots, but they must be thoroughly drained and dried on kitchen paper towels before using. To make these tarts you will need a fluted, oval-shaped pastry cutter and 10 to 12 boat-shaped barquette moulds. The moulds are either deep with fluted edges or plain-edged and slightly shallower. The ones recommended for use in this recipe are about 2-inches long. It is possible, however, to get larger ones that are 3½-inches long. It is also possible to buy a cutter to match the size of the mould, which helps save time when lining the mould.

10 TO 12 SERVINGS

PASTRY
 4 oz. [1 cup] flour
 1 oz. icing [¼ cup confectioners']
   sugar
 2½ oz. [5 tablespoons] butter, cut into
   small pieces
 2 egg yolks
FILLING
 3 tablespoons finely ground
   almonds
 5-6 fresh apricots, stoned and
   quartered
   small bunch of ripe seedless
   grapes
 6 tablespoons apricot jam
 1 tablespoon brandy

Apricots in light, boat-shaped pastry, Barquettes aux Abricots are delicious with tea or coffee.

To make the pastry for the barquettes, sift the flour and sugar into a mixing bowl and make a well in the centre.

Add the butter and egg yolks. Using your fingertips, gradually blend into the flour, then knead until smooth. Wrap in cling film and chill for 30 minutes.

Roll out the pastry to ⅛ inch and use to line the barquette moulds. Prick the pastry and chill in the refrigerator for 10 minutes.

Preheat the oven to hot 400°F (Gas Mark 6, 200°C). Place the oven shelf above the centre.

Divide the ground almonds between the barquettes and arrange 2 apricot quarters, cut side down and a few grapes in each one.

Bake for 20 minutes. Leave the barquettes to cool in the moulds for 10 minutes, then remove the pastry from the moulds and cool on a wire rack.

Put the apricot jam and brandy in a small pan over a low heat until dissolved. Rub through a sieve, then spoon a little glaze over each barquette. Allow to set, completely.

Try various fruit to fill the barquettes such as plums, redcurrants, raspberries and grapes.

Barracouta

A large, rough-scaled, salt-water fish common in Australia and New Zealand waters, the barracouta is also caught off the South African coast where it is known as *snoek*. The flesh of the barracouta resembles that of tuna fish. It is eaten fresh, and is also smoked and canned.

Barracuda

Predatory, pike-like fish, barracuda inhabit tropical and semi-tropical seas. They range in size from 3 to 10 feet and have long, pointed jaws filled with razor-sharp teeth. The giant pike and the great barracuda, found in the South Pacific, are reputed to be the most vicious and their attacks on swimmers are often mistakenly attributed to sharks.

The barracuda is an excellent big-game fish because of its stamina and fighting spirit. It is also fished commercially and its meat sold both fresh and canned.

Barsac

Barsac is a sub-area within the SAUTERNES wine district in BORDEAUX which gives its name to a sweet, white wine. Barsac goes by the generic name of SAUTERNES.

Basil

There are over 50 varieties of basil, each differing in some way from the others, either in the shape or colour of the leaves or in the size of the plant. A native of tropical Asia, and known in India as *tulsi*, basil is regarded as a sacred plant and is used in religious ceremonies as well as medicinally.

Sweet basil is the variety of this herb which is most used in cooking. The leaves have a spicy, clove-like flavour when they are fresh, but the taste alters when they are dried. Basil is traditionally used to flavour turtle soup and is also one of the main ingredients, with garlic, for flavouring Pistou, a popular soup in Provence. Basil has a particular affinity with tomatoes and makes an excellent ingredient in most tomato dishes.

Basil Baked Tomatoes

Tomatoes and onions baked with basil make a fragrant and tasty accompaniment to roast pork, lamb or chicken.

4 SERVINGS

3 oz. [⅜ cup] butter
2 large onions, thinly sliced and
    separated into rings
10 large tomatoes, thinly sliced
2 tablespoons chopped fresh basil,
    or 2 teaspoons dried basil
6 grindings black pepper
1 teaspoon salt
1 teaspoon sugar
3 oz. [1 cup] fresh breadcrumbs

Preheat the oven to fairly hot 400°F (Gas Mark 6, 200°C). Lightly grease an ovenproof dish with 1 tablespoon butter.

Melt 2 tablespoons butter in a large

Basil Baked Tomatoes is an unusual and fragrant accompaniment to pork, lamb or chicken.

---

frying-pan over low heat. Put in the onion rings and fry them for 10 minutes, or until they are tender but not brown. Remove the frying-pan from the heat.

Put a layer of onion rings on the bottom of the ovenproof dish, sprinkle with a little basil and cover with a layer of tomato slices. Add a little pepper, salt and a sprinkling of sugar. Dot with 1 tablespoon butter, cut into small pieces. Repeat the layers until all the ingredients have been used.

Cover the top with breadcrumbs and dot with the remaining butter. Place the dish in the oven and bake for 30 minutes. Serve hot.

Basil and Tomato Aspic

This smooth, fresh-tasting tomato aspic may be served with various cold meats together with other salads. An attractive dish to serve at a cold buffet lunch or dinner, it can be made two or three days in advance and kept in the refrigerator.

4 SERVINGS

1 pint [2½ cups] canned or bottled
    tomato juice
¾ oz. [3 tablespoons] gelatine
5 spring onions [scallions], chopped
1 tablespoon chopped fresh basil
    or 1 teaspoon dried basil
1 tablespoon brown sugar
    juice of ½ lemon
½ teaspoon salt
4 grindings black pepper
5 fl. oz. [⅝ cup] mayonnaise
6 radishes, sliced
½ cucumber, diced
1 apple, peeled, cored and diced
5 black olives, stoned and chopped

Warm 5 fluid ounces of the tomato juice in a small pan and pour it into a small bowl. Add the gelatine and stir to dissolve. Put the bowl over hot water and set aside.

Pour the remaining tomato juice into a small saucepan and bring it to the boil over moderate heat. Add the spring onions, basil, sugar, lemon juice, salt and black pepper, and simmer for 5 minutes.

Remove the pan from the heat and mix in the dissolved gelatine. Set aside to cool.

When the tomato mixture is cool, mix in the mayonnaise, radishes, cucumber, apple and olives.

Pour the mixture into a wet 1½-pint mould. Chill in the refrigerator for at least 2 hours before serving. To un-mould, run a knife around the edge of the mould and then dip the mould quickly into hot water. Place the serving plate on top of the mould and turn upside-down.

Basquaise, à la

A garnish for large cuts of meat, *à la Basquaise* (ah lah bahs-kayz) is composed of fried button mushrooms, moulded Anna potatoes and chopped ham.

Bass

The name of several voracious, spiny-finned sea and river fish, the bass best known in Europe is the sea bass. Also known as the sea wolf and sea perch and, in France, as the *bar*, it is caught in the Mediterranean and along the Atlantic coast of Europe. Because it has a super-ficial likeness to the salmon in shape and colouring, in England bass is some-times called sea salmon or white salmon.

Many varieties of bass live in the coastal waters, rivers and lakes of America. The striped bass, the large and small-mouthed black bass, and the calico bass make good eating and are considered excellent game by anglers. Gastrono-mically, the sea bass is the best of the species, with firm, lean, fine-textured flesh and a delicate flavour.

Large bass are poached and served hot with melted butter or a HOLLANDAISE SAUCE or cold with a SAUCE VERTE. Smaller bass can be grilled, baked or braised. Heavily spiced sauces should not be used because they will spoil the fish's delicate flavour. Nearly all ways of cook-ing salmon can be used for preparing bass.

Bass Baked in Lemon and Mushroom Sauce

Covered with a lemon and mushroom sauce and baked in the oven, sea bass is easy to prepare. Served with sautéed potatoes and petits pois *it makes a delicious main course for lunch or a dinner party. It may be accompanied by a full-bodied dry white wine.*

4 SERVINGS

8 bass fillets
2 oz. [¼ cup] butter
1 oz. [4 tablespoons] flour
1 teaspoon salt
¼ teaspoon white pepper
1½ pints [3¾ cups] tepid milk
1 bouquet garni consisting of 4

parsley sprigs, 1 thyme spray and 1 bay leaf tied together
4 tablespoons lemon juice
8 oz. mushrooms, wiped and sliced
1 lemon, quartered

Preheat the oven to moderate 350°F (Gas Mark 4, 180°C).

Wipe the fish with kitchen paper towels and place in a large, shallow oven-proof dish.

Melt the butter in a small saucepan over low heat. With a wooden spoon, stir in the flour, salt and pepper and cook for 1 minute. Gradually pour in the milk, stirring constantly. Bring to the boil. Add the bouquet garni, lemon juice and mush-rooms, and stir well. Simmer for 5 minutes.

Remove and discard the bouquet garni. Cover the fish with the sauce. Cover the dish and bake for 30 minutes. Garnish with lemon quarters.

Baste

A culinary term, to baste is to moisten food by spooning hot fat or liquid over it while it is cooking, usually in the oven. This improves its flavour and appearance. Long-handled spoons or basting syringes are available for this purpose.

Batatas à Portuguêsa

PORTUGUESE FRIED POTATOES

Fried in a mixture of butter and olive oil, Batatas à Portuguêsa (bah-tah-tah ah por-too-GAY-zah) make a pleasant accom-paniment to most meat dishes. In Portugal, these potatoes are traditionally arranged in a ring around the meat on the serving plate.

4 SERVINGS

3 oz. [⅜ cup] butter
4 tablespoons olive oil
2 lb. potatoes, peeled and sliced
1 small onion, thinly sliced
1 teaspoon salt
¼ teaspoon black pepper
1 tablespoon finely chopped chives

Put the butter and olive oil in a large, heavy frying-pan over moderate heat. When the butter melts add the sliced potatoes and onion.

Fry the potatoes and onion turning them frequently with a spatula for about 25 minutes, or until they are cooked and are crisp and a golden brown colour.

Remove the potatoes from the frying-pan. Pour off any excess fat. Place the potatoes and onion in a warmed serving dish. Sprinkle with the salt, pepper and chives, and serve immediately.

Bath Buns

These traditional buns, first made in the English spa of Bath at the beginning of the 18th century, have a craggy uneven shape and sugar lump topping.

12 BUNS

14 oz. [3½ cups] strong white flour
1 sachet easy-blend dried yeast
1 teaspoon castor sugar
6 fl. oz. [¾ cup] warm milk
½ teaspoon salt
2 oz. [4 tablespoons] butter, diced
3 oz. [⅜ cup] sugar
4 oz. [⅔ cup] currants
2 tablespoons chopped mixed peel
3 eggs
coarsely crushed sugar lumps
oil for greasing

Sift 4 oz. [1 cup] flour into a large bowl, then stir in the yeast and castor sugar. Pour in the milk and mix to a smooth bat-ter. Cover with greased plastic and leave to rise for about 20 minutes until frothy.

Sift the remaining flour with the salt, then rub in the butter. Stir in the sugar, currants and peel.

Lightly beat 2 eggs and add to the yeast batter with the flour and fruit mixture. Mix well with a wooden spoon to make a soft sticky dough. Beat for 10 minutes with the spoon or with the dough hook of a table-top mixer for 2 minutes.

Cover with greased cling film and leave to rise in a warm place for 1-1½ hours. Grease a large baking sheet with the vegetable oil.

Beat the risen dough with a wooden spoon for 2 minutes, then spoon on to the prepared baking sheet. Make 12 equal heaps and space them well apart to allow for expansion. Cover with greased cling film and leave to rise in a warm place for about 20 minutes, or until well risen.

Meanwhile, preheat the oven to fairly hot 375°F (Gas Mark 5, 190°C). Position the shelf above the centre.

Uncover the buns. Beat the remaining egg with a few drops of water and brush over the tops of the buns. Sprinkle with crushed sugar lumps. Bake the buns for about 20-25 minutes, until risen, golden brown and the undersides sound hollow when tapped with your knuckles. Return to the oven for 3-5 minutes if not done.

Transfer the buns to a wire rack and leave to cool. Serve buttered, if wished.

Bath Chap

The lower half of a pig's cheek, a bath chap is cured in the same way as bacon and is usually eaten cold. When it is not too fatty, a boiled bath chap, served cold,

Amandes (bah-toh-nay oh-zah-mond) *are little fancy cakes in the shape of sticks. They may be served with after-dinner coffee or with an ice-cream dessert.*

MAKES ABOUT 80 STICKS

8 oz. [1¼ cups] blanched almonds
8 oz. [1 cup] castor sugar
1 egg white
2 fl. oz. [¼ cup] rum
ICING
1 egg white
4 tablespoons granulated sugar

Preheat the oven to moderate 350°F (Gas Mark 4, 180°C).

Lightly grease a large baking sheet and dust it with flour.

With a pestle and mortar, pound the almonds and sugar together. Add the egg white, and mix in with enough rum to make a stiff paste. Alternatively, if you have an electric blender, put in the almonds, sugar, egg white and rum and blend into a smooth paste.

Lightly dust a marble slab or working surface with flour. Place the almond paste on it and roll out with a rolling pin into a rectangle ⅛-inch thick. Cut the paste into strips ½-inch wide and 3-inches long.

Lightly beat the egg white in a saucer. Put the granulated sugar on a plate, dip the almond sticks into the beaten egg white and then into the granulated sugar. Place the almond sticks on the baking sheet and bake in the oven for 8 minutes.

Battenberg Cake

An attractive sponge cake in a two-coloured, chequer-board design, Battenberg Cake is usually iced with almond paste. Make the cake two days before you need it because it has to stand for at least 48 hours before it is cut.

6 SERVINGS

8 oz. [1 cup] butter
8 oz. [1 cup] castor sugar
4 eggs
8 oz. [2 cups] self-raising flour
½ teaspoon vanilla essence
2 to 4 tablespoons milk
2 tablespoons cocoa
2 tablespoons apricot jam
ALMOND PASTE
4 oz. icing [1 cup confectioners'] sugar
4 oz. [½ cup] castor sugar
8 oz. [1⅓ cups] ground almonds
1 teaspoon lemon juice
a few drops almond essence
1 egg, lightly beaten

Preheat the oven to fairly hot 375°F (Gas Mark 5, 190°C).

Bath Buns, rich with currants and candied peel, are traditional English tea-time favourites.

is delicious and superior to pickled pork.

Although it is usually sold ready-cooked, cooking a bath chap at home is not complicated. A bath chap fresh from the pickle should be washed under cold, running water for 5 minutes. If it has been long-cured, however, it should be soaked in tepid water for at least 6 hours before boiling.

To cook a bath chap, place it in a large saucepan of cold water and bring the water to a boil. When the water is boiling, reduce the heat and simmer gently for 2½ hours.

Take the chap out of the saucepan and remove the skin. Sprinkle the fat side with browned breadcrumbs and bake in a

fairly hot oven 400°F (Gas Mark 6, 200°C) for about 30 minutes. Cooked in this way, a bath chap may be served hot or cold.

Bath Oliver

Large, thin, pale-coloured water biscuits, Bath Olivers are usually eaten with strong cheese. They were invented by a Dr. William Oliver of Bath in the eighteenth century for the benefit of his dyspeptic patients. The biscuits, now made commercially, are still stamped with an outline of Dr. Oliver's head.

Bâtonnets Aux Amandes

ALMOND CAKES

A type of petits fours, Bâtonnets aux

Bat

Prepare a 9-inch by 6-inch cake tin by cutting a piece of aluminium foil the exact length of the base, but 6 inches wider than the width. Fold a pleat in the middle so that the foil lies quite flat on the bottom of the tin and the pleat stands up, forming a wall which divides the tin into two oblongs of equal size.

With a wooden spoon, beat the butter and sugar in a medium-sized mixing bowl, until the mixture is light and creamy. Add the eggs, one at a time, along with 1 tablespoon of flour. Stir well to mix.

Fold in the remaining flour and the vanilla essence. Mix in a little milk, if it is necessary, to make the batter of a consistency that will drop easily off the spoon. Pour half the cake batter into one half of the prepared cake tin.

Mix the cocoa into the rest of the batter, add a spoonful of milk, if necessary, and pour it into the other half of the tin. Bake in the oven for 45 minutes. When the cake is cooked set it aside to cool.

While the cake is baking make the almond paste. Sift the icing sugar and the castor sugar together into a medium-sized mixing bowl. Mix in the ground almonds. Add the lemon juice, almond

For a Battenberg cake, divide the cake tin in half by pleating the foil lining down the middle.

Pour the white cake batter into one-half of the tin, and the cocoa-flavoured batter into the other.

Combine the almond paste ingredients and knead the mixture on a work surface dusted with icing sugar.

Remove the cake from the tin and carefully cut both pieces in half lengthways.

Join the brown and white halves of the cake together with the apricot jam and glaze the top of both halves.

Place the other two halves of the cake on top of the first two to make a chequer-board pattern.

Coat the cake with apricot jam and wrap the rolled-out almond paste around it.

The finished Battenberg cake should be kept in an air tight tin for two days before serving.

essence and enough beaten egg to bind all the ingredients into a paste.

Sprinkle your working surface with a little icing sugar and put the paste on it. Knead the almond paste until it is smooth. Be careful not to over-knead as the paste will become oily.

Remove the cake from the tin. Trim the two halves to equal size and cut each in half lengthways. Spread the side of one piece of white cake with the apricot jam and place a brown piece next to it. Spread jam on top of the two halves. Repeat with the other two halves of the cake, alternating the white and brown, and place on top of the jam covered layer to form a chequer-board pattern. Press gently together. Spread the remaining jam over the top and the sides of the cake.

On a lightly sugared board roll the almond paste into an oblong large enough to encase the cake. Wrap it round the cake, trimming the edges to leave the ends of the cake uncovered. Crimp the top edges to make a border and, with a knife, score a criss-cross pattern on the top. Keep the cake in a tin with a tight-fitting lid for two days before serving.

Batter

Consisting essentially of flour, milk and eggs, batter is a thick liquid mixture of a consistency that can be stirred, beaten or 'battered'. Batter forms a basis for pancakes, waffles, cakes and Yorkshire puddings. It is also used for coating fish or meat for frying or for making fritters.

When making batter, the proportion of liquid and oil or butter varies from recipe to recipe depending on how thick or thin the batter is required to be. The method, however, remains the same.

The flour, salt and sugar (if a sweet batter is being made) are sifted into a bowl. A well is made in the flour, exposing the bottom of the bowl. The eggs are then broken into the well and half the milk is poured in.

A wooden spoon or wire whisk are considered best for stirring. Only the eggs and milk are stirred at first and the flour is slowly incorporated, a little at a time. More milk is gradually added and the stirring is continued until the batter has a thick and creamy consistency.

When the batter has reached this stage, the mixture should be thoroughly beaten with a whisk. Oil, or cooled melted butter, and any remaining ingredients required by the recipe may then be added. The batter should be beaten for a few more minutes and then left to rest.

Batter should always be allowed to rest,

To prepare batter, sift the flour and salt into a bowl. Make a well in the flour and break the eggs into it.

Pour half the quantity of milk on to the eggs in the well of flour in the mixing bowl.

With a wooden spoon, or wire whisk, stir the eggs and milk and slowly incorporate the flour.

Gradually add more milk and continue stirring the batter until it is smooth and creamy.

preferably in a refrigerator, for at least one hour before use. If the recipe calls for a stiffly beaten egg white, this is folded into the batter just before it is used.

Batter for puddings and thick pancakes requires less liquid than batter for crêpes or light pancakes. Thicker batters are usually required for coating fish or meat for frying.

Pancake batters are best when cooled, melted butter is used, although oil may be substituted for savoury pancakes. For a lighter batter, water may sometimes replace a proportion of the milk. Stiffly beaten egg whites, added at the last moment, give pancakes a light and fluffy texture.

If a dry pancake is required the butter or oil may be omitted from the batter, but in this case the pan should be well greased. If the batter does contain oil or butter, the pan will require a little greasing.

Batter Pudding

This is a filling, hot dessert for a winter lunch or supper. Serve it with a hot jam or marmalade sauce, or sprinkled with brown sugar and dotted with butter.

4 SERVINGS

5 oz. [1¼ cups] flour
⅛ teaspoon salt
2 tablespoons sugar
½ teaspoon grated orange rind
2 egg yolks
5 fl. oz. [⅝ cup] milk
2 egg whites
1 tablespoon butter, softened

Sift the flour and salt into a medium-sized mixing bowl. Mix in the sugar and orange rind and make a deep well in the flour down to the bottom of the bowl.

Put the egg yolks into the well and add half the milk. Stir the mixture with a wooden spoon for 5 minutes, or until it has a creamy consistency. Add the rest of the milk and beat with a rotary beater for 5 more minutes.

Leave the batter to stand for 1 hour in a cool place.

In another medium-sized mixing bowl, using a wire whisk, beat the egg whites until they are stiff. With a spatula fold the whites into the batter.

Grease a medium-sized pudding basin with the butter and pour the batter into it. Cover the top with greaseproof or waxed paper and tie with string.

Place the pudding in a steamer or in a large pan filled with enough water to come half-way up the sides of the basin. Over moderate heat, bring the water to the boil.

Lower the heat, cover the pan and steam the pudding for 1½ hours, replenishing the water as it evaporates.

Remove the pudding basin from the steamer. Take off the greaseproof paper. Leave the pudding to stand for 1 minute before turning it out on to a warmed serving dish. Serve immediately.

Batuto

Finely chopped vegetables and herbs which are fried and mixed with diced pork or ham are the base of many Italian stews and soups, particularly in Roman cooking. This base when uncooked is called *batuto* (baht-too-toh). When it is cooked it is called *soffritto* (sohf-FREET-toh).

Bauernsuppe

GERMAN PEASANT SOUP

A country-style German soup, Bauernsuppe (bowrn-zoo-per) may be served either as a first or as a main course. The quantity given in this recipe will be sufficient for 4 people as a main course. Serve this hearty soup with crusty French bread.

6 SERVINGS

2 oz. [¼ cup] butter
2 lb. stewing steak, cut into small cubes
2 onions, chopped
1 bouquet garni, consisting of 4 parsley sprigs, 1 thyme spray and 1 bay leaf tied together
1 garlic clove, crushed
1 teaspoon paprika
1 teaspoon salt
1 oz. [4 tablespoons] flour
4½ pints [5½ pints] beef stock
2 large potatoes, peeled and diced
½ tablespoon finely chopped fresh dill
2 oz. [½ cup] grated Parmesan cheese

Melt the butter in a large, heavy pan over moderate heat. Add the meat cubes and fry them, turning occasionally with a spoon, until they are browned.

Add the onions, and fry for 8 minutes, or until they are soft and transparent. Add the bouquet garni, garlic, paprika and salt and stir well.

Mix in the flour, lower the heat and cook, stirring, for 5 minutes. Gradually stir in the stock. Bring to the boil. Cover the pan and simmer for 1 hour, stirring occasionally. Add the potatoes, cover and

---

A filling, meaty German soup, Bauernsuppe is served either as a soup or as a main course.

simmer for a further 45 minutes.

Ladle the soup into individual soup bowls. Sprinkle the top with the dill and grated cheese. Serve very hot.

Bavarian Strudel

PASTRY FILLED WITH APPLES

An inexpensive, apple-pastry dessert, Bavarian Strudel is quick and easy to make. Serve it hot with thick, cold cream or cold by itself.

4 SERVINGS

8 oz. [2 cups] sifted flour
2 tablespoons sugar
⅓ teaspoon salt
3 oz. [⅜ cup] butter, chilled
2 tablespoons vegetable fat
4 tablespoons milk
FILLING
2 lb. cooking apples, cored, peeled, and thinly sliced
2 oz. [⅓ cup] sultanas or raisins grated rind of 1 lemon
½ teaspoon mixed spice
4 oz. [½ cup] sugar
2 tablespoons fresh breadcrumbs
2 tablespoons milk for glazing icing [confectioners'] sugar

Preheat the oven to fairly hot 400°F (Gas Mark 6, 200°C).

Sift the flour, sugar and salt into a medium-sized mixing bowl. Rub the butter and vegetable fat into the flour with your fingertips until the mixture resembles fine breadcrumbs.

Pour in the milk and mix it in to make a dough. Knead and pat lightly until smooth. Wrap it in greaseproof or waxed paper and refrigerate for 20 minutes.

Mix the sliced apples, sultanas, lemon rind, mixed spice, sugar and breadcrumbs in a bowl.

On a floured surface, roll out the pastry into a long oblong shape about 5-inches wide. Place the pastry on a baking sheet. Spread the apple filling down the centre, lengthways. Fold the pastry over the filling, leaving the ends open so the filling can be seen.

Brush with milk and bake for 20 to 30 minutes, or until the pastry is golden.

Sprinkle the top of the strudel with icing sugar and cut into thick slices.

Bavarois

Bavarois (bah-vahr-wah) is a classic dessert. It is a rich egg custard blended with thick cream and lightly set gelatine and usually moulded. Bavarois can be flavoured with vanilla, coffee, orange, lemon, almond, pistachio, chocolate,

rum, liqueurs or fresh fruit purées. Chopped glacé fruits, chestnuts or fresh fruits can also be added. For a spectacular dinner party dessert, it is possible to make a combination of flavours and colours in a single mould and serve it with a fruit sauce.

This luscious dessert can be made in any metal mould with a sharply defined attractive shape. Oil the mould with a flavourless oil that will not affect the delicate taste of the bavarois. Almond oil (available from the chemist) is ideal. To unmould the bavarois, gently loosen the top edge with the tip of a sharp knife. Dip the mould, up to the rim, in very hot water for a second, then quickly turn out on to a *chilled* flat serving dish.

The decoration can be simple or elaborate, depending on the occasion, using whipped cream, fruits, nuts or chocolate. Flowers, such as marigolds and nasturtiums, add a touch of elegance.

Bavarois

BAVARIAN CREAM

A classic, moulded dessert, Bavarois (bah-vahr-wah), or Bavarian Cream, is a soft egg custard mixed with gelatine, whipped cream and flavouring. Properly prepared it has a smooth velvety quality and is regarded as one of the best moulded desserts.

4 TO 6 SERVINGS

1 teaspoon vegetable oil
1¼ pints [3 cups] milk
1 vanilla pod
5 tablespoons sugar
5 egg yolks
½ oz. [2 tablespoons] gelatine
3 tablespoons water
5 fl. oz. double [⅝ cup heavy] cream

Using a pastry brush, grease the inside of a 2-pint mould with the vegetable oil. Place the mould upside-down on kitchen paper towels to drain off the excess oil.

Put the milk and the vanilla pod into a medium-sized saucepan over moderate heat. When the milk is hot, but not boiling, remove it from the heat.

Put the sugar in a medium-sized mixing bowl. Make a well in the centre of the sugar. Drop the egg yolks, one at a time, into the well and, with a wooden spoon or spatula, beat the yolks, slowly incorporating the sugar. Continue this process until all the egg yolks and sugar are well mixed and beaten.

Remove the vanilla pod and, beating all the time, pour the milk in a thin stream on to the egg-and-sugar mixture.

Place a large pan, one-third full of water, on high heat. When the water is just about to boil, turn the heat to very low. The water must be hot but not simmering. Place the bowl with the egg-and-milk mixture in the water and, stirring slowly, cook until the custard is thick enough to coat the spoon. Be careful not to overheat the custard as it will curdle.

In a small saucepan over low heat dissolve the gelatine in the water. When the gelatine is completely dissolved, stir it into the custard.

Strain the custard through a sieve into a bowl. Place the bowl over ice in a bowl. Stir continuously until the custard thickens.

Whip the cream in a small bowl with a wire whisk until it is thick but not stiff. Lightly fold the cream into the

thickening custard and pour the mixture into the mould.

Cover the mould with aluminium foil or waxed paper and refrigerate for 6 hours or until the Bavarian Cream is completely set.

To serve, dip the bottom of the mould into hot water for 1 second. Run a knife around the edge of the cream and turn it out on to a chilled serving dish.

Bavarois au Chocolat
CHOCOLATE BAVARIAN CREAM

  ①

Flavoured with dark chocolate and rum, Bavarois au Chocolat (bah-vahr-wah oh SHOH-koh-lah) *is a rich, cold dessert. Serve it in a serving dish and decorate with whipped cream and dark chocolate curls.*

An impressive dessert, Bavarois au Chocolat is richly flavoured with chocolate, coffee and rum.

4 TO 6 SERVINGS

vegetable oil
1¼ pints [3 cups] milk
4 oz. plain [semi-sweet] chocolate, grated
3 oz. [⅜ cup] castor sugar
4 egg yolks
½ oz. [2 tablespoons] gelatine
4 fl. oz. strong black coffee
1 teaspoon vanilla essence
5 fl. oz. double [⅝ cup heavy] cream
2 tablespoons rum

Using a pastry brush, grease the inside of a 2-pint mould with a little vegetable oil. Place the mould upside-down on

134

kitchen paper towels to drain off the excess oil.

In a medium-sized pan heat the milk and chocolate over moderate heat. Stir to dissolve the chocolate. Take the pan off the heat and set aside.

Put the sugar in a medium-sized mixing bowl. Make a well in the centre of the sugar. Drop the egg yolks, one at a time, into the well and, with a wooden spoon or spatula, beat the yolks, slowly incorporating the sugar. Continue this process until all the egg yolks and sugar are well mixed and beaten.

Pour the warm milk and chocolate mixture in a thin stream on to the egg-and-sugar mixture, beating all the time.

Place a large pan, one-third full of water, on high heat. When the water is just about to boil, turn the heat to very low. The water must be hot but not simmering. Place the bowl with the egg-and-milk mixture in the water and, stirring slowly, cook until the custard is thick enough to coat the spoon. Be careful not to overheat the custard as it will curdle.

Remove the custard from the heat and set aside.

In a small saucepan over low heat dissolve the gelatine in the coffee. Add the vanilla and stir to mix. When the gelatine is completely dissolved, stir it into the custard.

Strain the custard through a sieve into a bowl. Place the bowl over ice in a bowl. Stir continuously until the custard thickens.

Whip the cream in a small bowl with a wire whisk until it is thick but not stiff. Lightly fold the cream and the rum into the thickening custard and pour the mixture into the mould.

Cover the mould with aluminium foil or waxed paper and refrigerate for 6 hours or until the Bavarian Cream is completely set.

To serve, dip the bottom of the mould into hot water for 1 second, run a knife around the edge of the cream and turn it out on to a chilled serving dish.

Bavarois Clermont
BAVARIAN CREAM WITH MARRONS GLACÉS

Bavarois Clermont (bah-vahr-wah CLAIR-mohn), *which is flavoured with* marrons glacés, *preserved chestnuts, is a very elegant dessert for a dinner party.*

8 SERVINGS

1 teaspoon vegetable oil
1¼ pints [3 cups] milk
1 vanilla pod
4 oz. [½ cup] sugar

4 egg yolks
½ oz. [2 tablespoons] gelatine
4 tablespoons water
10 fl. oz. double cream [1¼ cups heavy cream], chilled
8 oz. marrons glacés, finely chopped

Using a pastry brush, grease the inside of a 3-pint mould with the vegetable oil. Place the mould upside down on a double layer of kitchen paper towels to drain off the oil.

Put the milk and the vanilla pod into a medium-sized saucepan over moderate heat. When the milk is hot, but not boiling, take the saucepan off the heat and set aside to cool.

Put the sugar in a medium-sized mixing bowl. Make a well in the centre of the sugar. Drop the egg yolks, one at a time, into the well and, with a wooden spoon or spatula, beat the yolks and sugar until the mixture is light and fluffy.

Remove the vanilla pod and slowly pour the milk on to the egg and sugar mixture, beating all the time.

In a small saucepan set over low heat, dissolve the gelatine in the water, stirring constantly. Remove the pan from the heat and set aside.

Place a large saucepan, one third full of water, on high heat. When the water is just about to boil, turn the heat to very low. The water must be hot but not simmering. Place the bowl with the egg and milk mixture in the water and, stirring slowly, cook until the custard is thick enough to coat the spoon. Be careful not to overheat the mixture or it will curdle.

Stir in the gelatine. Cook, stirring, for a further 2 to 3 minutes or until the mixture is smooth.

Strain the custard through a sieve into a medium-sized bowl. Place the bowl over ice in a bowl. With a wooden spoon, stir continuously until the custard begins to thicken.

With a wire whisk whip the cream in a medium-sized bowl until it is thick but not stiff. With a rubber spatula lightly fold the cream and the chopped marrons glacés into the thickened custard and pour the mixture into the mould.

Cover the mould with aluminium foil or waxed paper and refrigerate for 8 hours or overnight, until the Bavarian Cream is completely set.

To serve, dip the bottom of the mould into hot water for 1 second, run a knife around the edge of the cream and turn it out on to a chilled serving dish. Decorate the Bavarian Cream with additional stiffly whipped cream.

For a really spectacular decoration place whole marrons glacés around the bottom.

Bavarois à L'Orange
ORANGE BAVARIAN CREAM

This recipe for Bavarois à L'Orange (bah-vahr-wah ah lor-ronj) *differs from other Bavarian Cream recipes because it incorporates the stiffly beaten egg whites into the custard. This gives a lighter texture to the finished cream. Fresh orange segments, soaked in syrup and orange liqueur, may be used as a garnish.*

4 SERVINGS

1 large fresh orange
½ tablespoon gelatine
10 fl. oz. [1¼ cups] creamy milk
3 oz. [⅜ cup] castor sugar
4 egg yolks
5 fl. oz. [⅝ cup] thick cream
3 tablespoons Cointreau or Grand Marnier
oil for greasing

Very lightly oil a 1-pint mould. Prepare a double boiler with 1-inch boiling water.

Wash and dry the orange, then grate the rind from it with a fine grater. Squeeze the juice from the orange into a small bowl and sprinkle over the gelatine; leave to soften. Gently warm the milk.

Put the sugar and orange rind in a mixing bowl and make a well in the centre. Drop in the egg yolks, one at a time, and beat with a wooden spoon, slowly incorporating the sugar.

Pour warm milk in a thin stream on to the egg yolks, beating constantly. Place the bowl on top of the hot but not boiling water. Stirring slowly, cook the custard until it is thick enough to coat the back of the spoon. Do not overheat or the custard will curdle.

Immediately remove the thickened custard from the heat and stir in the softened gelatine, stirring until dissolved. Put some ice in a large bowl and stand the mixture in it to cool for about 15 minutes.

Meanwhile, whip the cream until it thickens slightly. Lightly fold the cream and orange liqueur into the thickening custard. Pour the mixture into the mould.

Cover with cling film and chill until set. Allow 5-6 hours or overnight.

Decorate the Orange Bavarois with mandarin orange segments well soaked in orange liqueur. Pipe a shell or star border in whipped cream round the base.

Bavarois Praline
BAVARIAN CREAM WITH CARAMELIZED ALMONDS

Served with whipped cream, Bavarois Praline (bah-vahr-wah prah-leen) *is a*

delicious dessert for a lunch or dinner party. Hazel nuts, or a mixture of hazel nuts and almonds, toasted and coated in caramel may be substituted for almonds. Praline may be stored for several weeks in a tightly covered jar.

A Strawberry Bavarian Cream may be made with this recipe by substituting strawberries for the praline and omitting the almond essence. Use 5 egg yolks instead of 7, because the strawberry pureé will bind the Bavarian Cream. Dissolve the gelatine in 4 fluid ounces of orange juice. Force ½ pound of fresh strawberries through a fine sieve and fold 8 fluid ounces of the strawberry purée into the custard with the whipped cream.

6 TO 8 SERVINGS

PRALINE
2 teaspoons vegetable oil
3 oz. [⅜ cup] sugar
2 tablespoons water
3 oz. [½ cup] roasted almonds, shredded or ground

BAVARIAN CREAM
1 teaspoon vegetable oil
4 fl. oz. [½ cup] strong black coffee
½ oz. [2 tablespoons] gelatine
6 oz. [¾ cup] plus 1 tablespoon sugar
6 egg yolks
2 teaspoons cornflour [cornstarch]
12 fl. oz. [1½ cups] hot milk
5 egg whites
⅛ teaspoon salt
5 fl. oz. double [⅝ cup heavy] cream, chilled
1 tablespoon vanilla essence
¼ teaspoon almond essence

First make the praline. Grease a large baking sheet with the vegetable oil. Place the sugar and water in a small saucepan and, over moderate heat, cook for 4 minutes, or until the syrup turns light brown. Shake the pan occasionally. As soon as the syrup reaches the desired colour, remove the pan from the heat. Do not let the syrup darken too much or it will have a bitter taste.

Stir in the almonds and replace the pan on the heat. Bring the mixture to the boil and pour the syrup on to the baking sheet. Leave it to cool for 15 minutes. When it has cooled and hardened, break into pieces. Crush it to a fine powder with a pestle and mortar and set aside.

Using a pastry brush, grease the inside of a 2-pint mould with a little vegetable oil. Place the mould upside-down on kitchen paper towels to drain off the oil.

Pour the coffee into a bowl and sprinkle in the gelatine. Stir it well and place to one side to allow the gelatine to dissolve.

Put 6 ounces [¾ cup] of the sugar in a large mixing bowl. Make a well in the centre. Drop in the egg yolks, one at a time, into the well and, with a wooden spoon or spatula, beat the yolks, slowly incorporating the sugar. Continue this process until all the egg yolks and sugar are well mixed and beaten and add the cornflour [cornstarch]. Pour the hot milk in a thin stream on to the egg-and-sugar mixture, beating all the time.

Place a large pan, one-third full of water, on high heat. When the water is just about to boil, turn the heat to very low. The water must be hot but not simmering. Place the bowl with the egg-and-milk mixture in the water and, stirring slowly, cook until the custard is thick enough to coat the spoon. Be careful not to overheat the custard as it will curdle.

Remove the custard from the heat and stir in the gelatine. Reserve 2 tablespoons of the crushed praline and stir the rest into the hot custard. Place the bowl in a larger bowl of ice cubes. Continue stirring until the custard is thick and almost set.

Put the egg whites in a medium-sized bowl with the salt. Beat them with a wire whisk, or rotary beater, until the whites stand up in soft peaks. Sprinkle the remaining tablespoon of sugar on to the egg whites and continue beating until the mixture is stiff. Fold the egg whites into the custard.

Whip the cream in a small bowl with a wire whisk until it is thick but not stiff. Lightly fold the thickened cream and the vanilla and the almond essence into the thickening custard and pour the mixture into the mould.

Cover the mould with aluminium foil or waxed paper and place in the refrigerator for 6 hours or until the Bavarian Cream is completely set.

To serve, dip the bottom of the mould in hot water for 1 second, run a knife around the edge of the cream and turn it out on to a chilled serving dish. Sprinkle the top with the reserved 2 tablespoons of crushed praline.

Bay Leaves
The dark green, fragrant leaves of the bay tree or sweet laurel (*Lauris Nobilis*), bay leaves are one of the most commonly used culinary herbs. The tree is native to Italy, Greece and North Africa. It was introduced into Britain over 400 years ago and was taken to North America by the early settlers.

The sweet laurel was believed by the ancient Greeks to be the nymph Daphne and the tree was sacred to the god Apollo. The victors of the Pythian games were crowned with laurel leaves and laurel became the symbol of triumph in Greece and later in Rome.

The bay leaf is used as a flavouring for puddings, pies, stews, soups and court bouillons, and a leaf is always included in a bouquet garni.

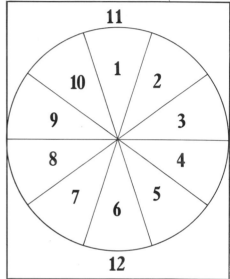

Beans
1 Oea Beans	*2 Flageolet*
3 Black Beans	*4 Broad Beans*
5 Haricot	*6 Pinto Beans*
7 Lima Beans	*8 Butter Beans*
9 Soya Beans	*10 Red Kidney Beans*
11 French Beans	*12 Runner Beans*

Bean
The seeds and pods of a wide variety of leguminous plants, beans are usually served as a vegetable. The seeds are a very good source of protein and of vitamin B and, when fresh, beans also contain vitamins A and C. In Europe until the sixteenth century, the only vegetable known as a bean was the broad bean. Today, however, the name applies to a large variety of this type of vegetable.

Among the various types of available beans are broad beans or Windsor beans, which are known as fava beans in the United States. Butter beans, large, flat and white, were originally found in South America. Flageolet, which are the pale green seeds of a choice variety of haricot or French beans, are usually sold dried in Britain. French beans are a smaller, more delicate bean than runner beans, but

they are of the same family and the pods as well as the seeds are eaten.

Haricot is the name given to a wide variety of bean plants, the best known being the French and kidney bean. In Britain this name is applied more particularly to the dried white seeds of dwarf or climbing haricot plants. In the United States these are known as navy beans.

Haricots vary considerably in size and can be green, brown, purple or red. Kidney beans are large, dark red, kidney-shaped beans which are often used for baked beans. Lima beans, originally from South America, are a delicate green or white colour and are of the haricot variety. The seeds may be eaten fresh or dried.

Oea beans, also known as black-eye peas or cow beans, are small, white peas with a black spot. They are used in cooking in the United States, particularly in the south. Pinto beans, which are

dappled pink in colour, and black beans are primarily eaten in Mexico where they are called *frijoles*. Runner beans, also called scarlet runners and string beans, are larger and longer than French beans. Soya beans, which are Chinese in origin, are rich in vegetable protein with a fairly high fat but low starch content.

Bean and Bacon Soup

This filling and tasty soup may be served at an informal lunch or dinner. It also makes a good main course, served with French bread, for a family lunch.

6 SERVINGS

12 oz. [1½ cups] dried butter [lima] beans
2 lb. bacon hock with bone
1 large onion, cut in quarters

1 large garlic clove, crushed
3½ pints [8¾ cups] water
1 bouquet garni, consisting of 4 parsley sprigs, 1 thyme spray, and 1 bay leaf tied together
½ teaspoon white pepper
20 large black olives, cut in half
3 tablespoons chopped parsley

Put the beans in a bowl and cover with water. Leave them to soak overnight.

Drain the beans and put them in a large saucepan with the bacon, onion and garlic. Cover with the water, place the pan on high heat and bring to the boil.

Add the bouquet garni and pepper to the pan and stir well. Lower the heat and simmer the soup for 1½ to 2 hours, or until the beans and bacon are cooked.

Remove the bacon hock and cut the meat into pieces. Remove the bouquet garni and discard. Purée some of the

Bacon, beans and olives combine to make this tasty Bean and Bacon Soup that may be served as a one-dish meal.

beans, using a fork or an electric blender and add to the soup to thicken it. Stir in the bacon pieces and olives. Taste and add salt and more pepper, if necessary.

Pour the soup into individual bowls, sprinkle with the parsley and serve hot.

Bean Curd

Square, custard-like cakes of cooked, puréed and pressed soya beans, bean curd is sold in Oriental provision stores.

The cakes, which are about ½-inch thick and 3-inches square, should be drained and stored in fresh water in a covered jar in the refrigerator. They will keep for up to two weeks if the water is changed every day. There is no substitute for fresh bean curd in Chinese cooking.

Bean Curd and Crabmeat

A Chinese recipe, Bean Curd and Crabmeat will serve 4 people as a main course, or 6 to 8 people as part of a Chinese meal. This dish must be quickly cooked, so before you begin to cook be sure you have all the ingredients prepared and within easy reach.

4 SERVINGS

½ lb. fresh or canned crabmeat
4 cakes of fresh bean curd, about 3-inches square and ½-inch thick
3 tablespoons groundnut oil
1 spring onion [scallion], chopped
1 teaspoon peeled and finely chopped fresh ginger
1½ teaspoons salt
3 tablespoons chicken stock
⅛ teaspoon freshly ground black pepper
½ teaspoon cornflour [cornstarch]
5 teaspoons cold water
5 watercress sprigs

Pick over the crabmeat and discard all bits of cartilage and shell.

Slice each square of bean curd into ¼-inch slices. Cut each slice in half.

Put a heavy, 12-inch frying-pan over high heat for 30 seconds. Add the oil, swirl it about in the pan and heat it for 30 seconds. Turn the heat down to moderate when the oil is hot.

Stir in the chopped spring onion and the ginger. Add the bean curd, salt and chicken stock. Bring to the boil, cover the pan and cook over moderate heat for 3 minutes.

Stir in the crabmeat and black pepper and cook for 1 minute.

Mix the cornflour with the water and add it to the crabmeat. Stirring constantly, cook for 1 minute, or until the crabmeat and bean curd are coated with a clear, light glaze.

Put into a warmed serving dish, garnish with sprigs of watercress and serve at once.

Bean-Curd Skin

Large or small, thin, stiff sheets of dried bean curd, bean-curd skin is available in Chinese provision stores. It requires no refrigeration and will keep indefinitely. There is no substitute for bean-curd skin in Chinese recipes.

Bean Salad

A favourite dish in the southwestern part of the United States, Bean Salad goes well with cold meat or a grilled steak.

4 TO 6 SERVINGS

8 oz. [1 cup] red kidney beans
6 oz. [¾ cup] white beans, such as haricot or butter [dried lima] beans
4 oz. [½ cup] chick-peas
1 red pepper, the white pith removed, seeded and coarsely chopped
1 small onion, finely chopped, or 3 spring onions [scallions], chopped
1 garlic clove, crushed
2 tablespoons chopped fresh chives
2 tablespoons white wine vinegar
6 tablespoons olive oil
1 tablespoon lemon juice

½ teaspoon salt
¼ teaspoon black pepper

Soak the beans and peas in water overnight. Put them in a large saucepan, cover with water and bring to the boil over high heat. Cover the pan, lower the heat and simmer for 40 minutes or until tender. Drain and cool.

In a large salad bowl, combine the beans, peas, red pepper, onion, crushed garlic and chives.

In a small bowl, combine the vinegar, lemon juice, oil, salt and pepper. Mix, add to the bean mixture and toss well.

Refrigerate for about 30 minutes and before serving, leave at room temperature for 10 minutes.

Bean Sprouts

Rich in vitamin C, young sprouts of the mung or soya bean, which are about two-inches long, are a common ingredient in Chinese dishes. Sold fresh and in cans, they are becoming increasingly popular as a vegetable and a salad ingredient in Western cooking.

Canned bean sprouts should be thoroughly drained before using. The heads and tails of fresh bean sprouts can be removed before use, but it is not necessary. The fresh sprouts will keep for up to two weeks if they are stored in water in a covered jar in the refrigerator.

Bean sprouts must be cooked very quickly so they do not lose their crispness.

Bean curd—cakes of puréed soya beans—and bean-curd skin—strips of dried curd—are used in many Chinese dishes.

Bean Sprouts with Ginger

A deliciously crisp, quickly made vegetable dish, Bean Sprouts with Ginger must be cooked just before serving.

4 SERVINGS

3 tablespoons cooking oil
1 large onion, finely sliced
1-inch piece of fresh ginger, peeled, finely sliced and cut into thin strips
1 teaspoon salt
1 lb. fresh bean sprouts

Heat the oil in a large frying-pan over high heat. Add the onion, lower the heat to moderate and fry for 6 minutes, stirring occasionally with a wooden spoon. Add the ginger and continue frying for another 4 minutes.

Add the salt, stir to mix and add the bean sprouts. Raise the heat and, turning and tossing the bean sprouts, fry them for only 2 to 3 minutes.

This crunchy Bean Sprout Salad is unusual and attractive.

Bean Sprouts with Green Peppers

A Chinese dish, Bean Sprouts with Green Peppers can be served as part of a Chinese meal or as an unusual vegetable accompaniment to roast chicken or grilled fish. Cook it at the last minute.

6 SERVINGS

2 lb. fresh bean sprouts
2 large green peppers
4 tablespoons vegetable oil
3 tablespoons white wine
2 teaspoons salt
¼ teaspoon monosodium glutamate

Soak the bean sprouts in cold water for 15 minutes. Drain well. Wash the green peppers. Remove the seeds and white pith and cut the peppers into fine, almost threadlike strips.

Heat the oil in a heavy frying-pan over high heat. Add the bean sprouts and shredded green peppers and, stirring constantly, cook for 3 minutes.

Add the wine, salt and monosodium glutamate and, still stirring, cook for 2 more minutes. Serve hot.

Bean Sprout Salad

This fresh, crunchy salad is ideal to serve with or after grilled fish or chicken, or with other vegetarian salads.

4 SERVINGS

1 lb. fresh or canned bean sprouts
2 oz. canned pimiento, chopped
1 pickled cucumber, chopped
1 tablespoon chopped chives
DRESSING
2 tablespoons olive oil
1 tablespoon wine vinegar
½ teaspoon prepared mustard
2 teaspoons soy sauce
½ teaspoon sugar
½ teaspoon salt

Put the bean sprouts in a salad bowl with the pimiento, pickled cucumber and chives.

Mix all the ingredients for the dressing together, making sure the salt and sugar are dissolved. Pour the dressing over the salad. Toss the salad well and put in a refrigerator or a cool place for 1 hour before serving.